THE I

D1629610

11724404

# FOUR YEARS OLD
# IN AN
# URBAN COMMUNITY

## JOHN AND ELIZABETH NEWSON

*Child Development Research Unit*
*University of Nottingham*

*London*

## GEORGE ALLEN AND UNWIN LTD

RUSKIN HOUSE · MUSEUM STREET

FIRST PUBLISHED IN GREAT BRITAIN IN 1968
SECOND IMPRESSION 1969

SBN 04 618010 9

PRINTED IN GREAT BRITAIN
in 11 on 12 pt Times Roman type
BY UNWIN BROTHERS LTD
WOKING AND LONDON

# ACKNOWLEDGMENTS

The research study which this book reports was financed by the Nuffield Foundation. It could not have been carried out without the Foundation's generous support, and we should like especially to offer our grateful thanks to Mr Brian Young and Dr J. W. McAnuff for their continued help and encouragement.

We must again acknowledge with gratitude the assistance of the City of Nottingham Health Department, and in particular the Medical Officer of Health, Dr William Dodd, and his staff, who once more gave us full co-operation in the compilation of our sample. We are also indebted to the City of Nottingham Education Committee; especially to the Director of Education, Mr W. G. Jackson, to the Superintendent of the School Welfare Department, Mr M. G. Taylor, and to the School Welfare Officers, who have shown us the utmost kindness in checking and tracing the addresses of the children as we follow them up. We count ourselves fortunate indeed to be able to work with research-minded authorities such as these.

A study of this sort is absolutely dependent upon the quality of its interviewers. We are very conscious of the debt we owe to ours, who do not restrict their skill to the interview itself, but offer us their interest, their perspicacity and their understanding at every stage of our work. We are often asked what qualities we look for in a good interviewer: our answer is *intelligence; flexibility;* but, above all, *niceness:* and these qualities we have found. Our especial thanks to Joan Burgess, Jean Crossland, Jean Jacobs, Clare Jones, Dady Key and Erica Mattingly.

One of the pleasures that arise out of publishing a book on a research project, not anticipated by us but nonetheless welcome, is the correspondence and visits it brings from others of similar interests or working in allied fields. Obviously we cannot mention all these friends and colleagues individually; but we should like them to know how much we value these interchanges of views and the new insights which we have gained from them.

Our own children continue to be the most educative element in our lives, as well as the most entertaining and engrossing: to Roger, Carey and Joanna, our gratitude and our love.

*Finally, to the 700 mothers who have welcomed us into their homes and found time in their busy lives to talk to us, we can never adequately express our thanks. They are the co-authors of this volume. Once again, our book is dedicated to them, and to the children in whose growing-up they so generously allow us to share.*

# CONTENTS

A*

# LIST OF TABLES

The reader will find it advisable to consult Appendix II for the statistical procedures upon which these tables are based.

# CHAPTER 1

# BACKGROUND AND INTRODUCTION

This book is about a group of seven hundred children as they reach their fourth birthdays in the English Midland city of Nottingham. It is about the social and material context of their lives: the streets and street-friendships, backyards and neighbours, homes and families, which make up the kaleidoscope of their everyday environment. It is about the emotional tie which forms the core of each child's experience—his relationship with his parents; and in particular, since he is only four years old, it is about the behaviours and emotions which are generated between the child and that person with whom he spends the greater part of his waking life—his mother.

Our study of four-year-old children is the second phase in a long-term project designed to investigate parent/child relationships in developmental sequence. Our aims are threefold. Firstly, we hope to achieve a very detailed picture of the child himself at successive stages of his development from babyhood to late adolescence, a picture built up from his behaviour not in a clinic or nursery school setting, but in his more natural habitat, the home and its immediate surroundings. Secondly, we want an equally clear picture of the mother's behaviour in relation to her child, and to see how this alters and develops, both in accordance with the child's objective age, and in response to his idiosyncratic needs and demands; and we are interested not only in her actual observable behaviour, but in her own attitudes, emotional and intellectual, towards her behaviour. Thirdly, we look for the emergence of patterns in the data which we collect, and these may be of two kinds: they may be cross-sectional patterns, leading us to draw conclusions which have validity within a particular age-phase; or they may be longitudinal patterns, much slower to emerge, from which *eventually* we may learn something about cause and sequence in child-rearing and personality growth.

The first stage in this research project was described in our study of mothers and their year-old babies.[1] Integral in itself, we nevertheless planned, with more hope than confidence, that this should be dovetailed into a much more ambitious investigation which should follow children through their childhood and adolescence, and indeed into early adulthood, if this proved practicable.[2] We have been fortunate enough to obtain the financial support necessary for the continuance of this work, and we are committed, gladly, to its completion. The chief value of a follow-up study of this sort is, of course, the long perspective which we shall finally achieve of the upbringing of any individual: a perspective in which the details are not the inevitably distorted reconstructions of parents' memories, but rather a related series of portraits from life, each one true to the child and to the mother at a specific moment of time. It is such an accumulation of contemporary rather than retrospective data which is needed if the more complex questions of socialization are to be answered; and, while at any given age we are interested in *all* the problems and pleasures characteristic of that phase of development, in the long term it will be the recurrent theme of socialization, sometimes hidden, sometimes very explicit, but always relevant to every situation involving children and parents, which runs like a master thread through any sequential study of child rearing. For this reason, we are continually alert to the *moral atmosphere* in the home: by which we mean simply the extent to which, and the means by which, behaviours and attitudes are presented to the child in evaluative terms as good or bad, right or wrong, acceptable or unacceptable.

Basically, then, we are trying to understand the process of child-rearing *as it happens* in a fairly typical English urban community. It must be understood that it is not our role to make recommendations: we are not interested in what *ought* to happen, except in so far as the mother is affected, both in what she does and in her appraisal of what she does, by an awareness of

[1] Newson, John and Elizabeth: *Infant Care in an Urban Community;* Allen and Unwin, London, 1963; reprinted by Penguin Books, Ltd., 1965, under the title *Patterns of Infant Care in an Urban Community*. Where page references to this book are made here, they will refer to the earlier edition.

[2] A total follow-up between one year and four years was not attempted, for various reasons. 275 children out of the present sample were also seen at 1 year. The remaining 425 comprised a newly drawn sample whose mothers were interviewed for the first time at age 4. In successive research stages from this age onward, 100% follow-ups are being attempted.

'ought' attitudes existing in her community. We make at the outset certain assumptions, which need to be stated even though we believe them to be generally agreed:

1. The family is the fundamental social group to which humans give allegiance. Cultures vary as to how far they extend family ties and how rigidly such ties operate, but the family remains the basic unit.

2. Throughout the world it is normal for the process of socialization to be initiated by the parents: it is from their behaviour towards him that the child first learns to label his own actions as 'good' or 'bad'. The network of social relationships through which the process continues is gradually extended, earlier or later in the child's life according to the family and community structures of the individual culture; in our own society, the nuclear family excludes outsiders for a relatively long period, so that, for English children, the process of socialization will tend to be mediated through social interaction of a most intense and intimate kind within the family right up to school age.

3. However long the child is restrained from full interaction with people outside his own kin, the family itself is always a part of some wider community with which it is functionally related. This is still true where the family deliberately rejects, or is rejected by, the community, and where the relationship is thus one of withdrawal: the family may choose to spurn the community, but it cannot choose to deny its existence. This like-it-or-not involvement means that child-rearing does not and cannot take place in a social vacuum. Within any society, the range of available occupations, work-roles and work-habits, income and demands upon income, standards of nutrition and housing, educational possibilities, and the geographical environment all interact in more or less subtle ways to evolve the customs and beliefs, attitudes and fashions, which make up what has aptly been called the web of culture; and the individual family's place in these systems, whether objectively or subjectively assessed, can be ignored neither by the members of that family nor by anyone who tries to understand its internal relationships.

*Some notes on method*[1]

Numerous attempts have been made in the past to show that specific practices in child upbringing are responsible for specific

[1] This chapter is concerned chiefly with the principles upon which our research methods are based. Details of sampling, statistical procedures, etc. will be found in Appendix II.

consequences in the adult personality, either individual or col-
lective. Workers in the anthropological and psychoanalytic fields
in particular have demonstrated to their own satisfaction the
operation of such a process.[1] However, while these studies have
often provided us with valuable new insights, more rigorous
research has on the whole been disappointing. Nevertheless, no-
one seriously doubts that the way in which parents behave towards their children has some effect upon the kind of people
those children become; why, then, is it so difficult to pinpoint
cause and effect?

The answer is, we suggest, that specific practices in child care
—breast- versus bottle-feeding, early versus late toilet training,
and so on—are a good deal less important in the long term than
the spirit in which they are carried out. Parental attitudes and
values—their whole philosophy of child-rearing—must have a
pervasive and profound effect upon the developing child: indeed, parents themselves intend this to be so; and if research
results fail to demonstrate such an effect, we can only conclude
that the research methods were inappropriate. To an extent
psychologists must accept the blame for this, in that, by con-
centrating so emphatically upon specific child-rearing practices
and their supposed effects, they have been led to spend over-
much time upon attempts to verify these hypotheses and so have
diverted attention from the total climate of the child's upbringing. Even where a more inclusive approach has been
attempted, it has tended to confine itself to personality variables of the parents and to stop short of the community pressures impinging upon the family from outside. While dimensions
of personality and attitude such as accepting/rejecting, per-
missive/restrictive, authoritarian/democratic, etc., are clearly of
great significance in a description of parental behaviour, we do
not believe that they are in themselves adequate measures of the
whole parent/child situation, especially after the first year of life.

Our basic tool of investigation has been and remains the interview: primarily because it seems to give exceptionally good
value in terms of detailed data on both behaviour and the attitudes underlying behaviour. In any human activity, the factual
event and its associated feeling are of equal importance for our
understanding. For instance, it may be a fact that a mother regu-

[1] See Sprott, W. J. H.: *Social Psychology*, Methuen, London, 1952, for a
useful review of some representative studies of this sort.

larly smacks her child in certain situations, and it may also be true that this mother feels guilty whenever she thinks about smacking her child: it is the *conjunction* of these two things which is important. In the assessment of the socialization process, it may be very misleading to rely on either behaviour or attitude taken in isolation: even a four-year-old child is aware that slaps of the same objective force have totally different meanings according to the feelings and intentions which lie behind them.

It is the normal function of conversation to probe such subtleties if one really wishes to know about the opinions and motives of those with whom one converses. Once talk is flowing freely, in fact, it will be very difficult indeed for the participants to discuss their own behaviour *without* expressing any attitude towards it: and it is from such expressions of feeling, as much as from a knowledge of events, that the hearer is enabled to predict behaviour in future situations. Thus, if we want to predict how A will behave when next he meets B, the most obvious thing to do is to talk to A about B. From this conversation, *provided that we are not personally involved in the A/B relationship*, we may expect to gain a very fair idea both of what happened in previous encounters and of how A feels about B. Conversation is by far the most economical means, in terms of time and effort, of arriving at a valid assessment of a situation.

There has been a fashion in psychology, probably arising out of the discipline's persistent insecurity feelings about its scientific status, to devise tortuous tests for the investigation of human feelings and attitudes, and, in the pursuit of objectivity for its own sake, to use such roundabout methods even where the most common-sense course of simply discussing his feelings with the individual would be more appropriate. Often the status of the individual as a thinking person, with the possibility both of making his own insights and of voluntarily supplying material which will allow others to make insights, seems to be mislaid on the way. The projective test, for instance, is useful in direct proportion to the subject's failure to detect its purpose. To a lesser extent this is also true of the attitude test, which has the additional disadvantage that it fails to capitalize on the subject's ability to examine his own attitudes, and thus both wastes available information and produces frustration by forcing him to prune every answer to fit arbitrary agree/disagree categories.

Both of these types of test have a useful role to play in psychological research; but it is our thesis that the use of an 'objective' test does not *ipso facto* produce meaningful data, and that, conversely, the introduction of the explicit social relationship of direct personal conversation can, given adequate safeguards, produce material which is equally reliable, and which illumines with much greater clarity and in far more detail the real-life situations which it is our aim to understand.

If conversation is to be used as a scientific tool, it is of primary importance to ensure that the subject feels free to say anything he or she wishes. In our own research, this is done in two ways.

Firstly, there is no question of the parents' methods of child-rearing being judged in any way. We have in any case no desire to do this, believing as we do that judgments are often made all too glibly by people who are professionally concerned with parents and children, frequently without either understanding or supporting evidence; if we felt qualified to judge, however, to do so even by implication would at once frustrate our purpose of providing an atmosphere in which it is understood that *whatever* may be said will be acceptable. To this end, we start by deliberately underplaying any status which we might seem to have as experts; in the letter which arranges our appointment, we write under no psychological or medical label—which, for good or ill, would present us in a certain image—but merely from the Child Development Research Unit at the University, which has no defined image for the majority of the mothers we see. Readers of our earlier study may remember that the greater part of the interviewing was then carried out by health visitors, and that the answers which they received were in some areas significantly distorted in the direction of the views which mothers associated with the health visitor label. We pointed out then that this was no reflection on the skill of the health visitors as interviewers, but the inevitable result of the fact that they were identifiable with a group whose views were known. The major benefit which financial support has brought to this research, however, has been the possibility of training our own interviewers specifically for the work they have to do, and of keeping them under continual supervision by means of the tape recordings which they return. All our interviewers are married women with young children of their own, and the mothers are aware of this. We believe this provision to be important in achieving a satisfactory relationship with the mother, since she knows that the person talking to her has herself faced the practical demands of parenthood: a criticism often made of health visitors (frequently unjustified, but part of the image) is that 'they tell you what to do, but they don't *really* know what it's like'.

The second way in which freedom of speech is encouraged is by using a deliberately open-ended technique. The core of the interview is a schedule of carefully-phrased questions,[1] and these are to be asked verbatim; but the interviewer is free to ask additional questions if she thinks it useful to do so, either to probe further into a topic which has been introduced by the scheduled questions,[2] or to explore any other topic which the mother may have touched upon, but which is not covered by the interview because of its specificity to this particular child.[3] The conversation is thus allowed to follow its own natural lines of development. While the nature and form of the scheduled questions are very carefully determined, the mother is not forced into a limited set of responses.[4] She can answer at length; she can state any qualifications and reservations she may wish to make, and indeed she is encouraged by the interviewer to do this. Just as we make no evaluations as to the rights and wrongs of her child-rearing methods, so we do not try to judge the information she offers as trivial or important: if she thinks it important then it is accepted as such. The function of our questions is both to trigger off the mother's own discussion of the topics in which

[1] See Appendix I.

[2] Typical examples of the way in which spontaneous probe questions are used to fill out a picture will be found on pages 215-6, 219, 225-6, 290, 327. Where non-scheduled probes are quoted, they are given in full as spoken; the use of multiple dots ('Would you leave it at that, or . . .?') denotes not omission but a deliberate tailing-off technique.

[3] For instance, if the child has come in contact with death, or has suffered the father's desertion, extra questions will be asked about his reaction to such experiences if this can be done without distressing the mother unduly; or if the child is in any way physically handicapped, we would want to know whether and in what way this affects his upbringing.

[4] There is one exception to this rule: Question 105 deliberately asks the mother to rate herself, in comparison with others, as 'very strict', 'rather strict', 'rather easy-going' or 'very easy-going'; if she replies 'about average', it is pointed out that this formal rating scale is designed to prevent such an answer, and she is asked which side of 'average' she leans towards. While the very novelty of this approach in the interview context is stimulating of discussion, many mothers find the task difficult and restrictive, and we would be chary of using it more than once.

we are interested and also to allow her to introduce any topic which *she* may consider of interest. It is only at a later stage, and on the basis of these *total* answers (which the tape recorder stores for us in full) that we attempt to classify for the purpose of statistical analysis the sorts of things which mothers typically do or say. That they are not during the interview forced into predetermined response categories is, we believe, of some importance, since this is a major irritant of the conventional survey interview, which often leaves respondents with the feeling of having been pigeon-holed and classified within a tight frame of reference that gave no scope for what they really wanted to say. This we do our best to avoid.

The unbreakable rule that interviewers must never give any impression of making value judgments has implications which extend beyond mere interviewing technique. The methods which we use are open-ended, not only in the sense that any kind of answer is acceptable, but also in the sense that we are at this stage more concerned with detailed and precise description than with the testing of theoretically derived hypotheses about the presumed consequences of specific practices. Although eventually we expect to be in a position to build useful evaluations on the basis of objective evidence amassed over the full childhood span of our individual subjects, the making of value judgments about other people's child-rearing methods, which all parents (perhaps all human beings) regard as their inalienable and rather pleasurable right, seems to us a luxury which is necessarily separable from sociological interpretation, and against which the research worker must accept a self-denying ordinance, at least for as long as his fieldwork remains incomplete. This point needs to be emphasized because, wherever child upbringing is discussed, value judgments almost invariably crowd out objective evidence. Nearly everyone has strong opinions about how children should be brought up, which probably derive basically from the fact that each one of us has been subjected to this process; in addition, those of us who are parents continually take practical decisions with our own children which are in effect irreversible, and we therefore have a vested interest in championing our own beliefs and methods against those contrary opinions which we perceive as threatening to our self-esteem as parents, and are all too ready to resort to irrational ways of thinking in order retrospectively to justify ourselves to ourselves. Let us reiterate: this book is descriptive rather than evaluative. The reader need not expect to find in it a final chapter full of cure-all recommendations.

We do not start with pre-conceived hypotheses; rather, we look for meaningful patterns in the material as it emerges. This means in effect that, rather than force our data into a theoretical framework prepared in advance of fieldwork, we try to split it along natural lines of cleavage and deliberately restrain ourselves, at least during these early stages, from predicting where these lines of cleavage will appear. Thus we did not originally set out to make a study of the influence of social class upon child upbringing: our intention was to investigate child upbringing in *all* its aspects, and to see which influences were of particular significance. We might have found that the child's sex or his family position, was the major element by which different patterns of child-rearing were distinguished; in fact we found that, during early childhood at least, these were of far less importance than the class-affiliated attitudes which entered into almost every area of parent/infant behaviour.[1] In the second phase of the research, reported in this book, we should have been prepared to abandon the factor of social class if we had found that it was no longer significantly operative at this age, and we have looked for other lines of cleavage which might have been gaining in importance; but the reality is that class affiliations remain pervasively powerful even in the minutiae of the four-year-old's daily life, and we can only report what we find. We occasionally encounter (among middle-class people) a sentimental attitude that talking about class, especially where children are involved, is somehow not quite nice. The research worker in this field, middle-class himself by definition, is very vulnerable to accusations of snobbery and poor taste when he calls attention to class differences, especially where he is not primarily concerned with setting right social injustices. Ourselves second-generation middle-class, we sometimes envy those of our colleagues in this field of study whose background is impeccably working-class, and who therefore enjoy a privileged position as social commentators. Our own view is, however, that the coming of the classless society will not be helped by a refusal to acknowledge that very deeply rooted differences in attitude

---

[1] These are summarized in Newson, John and Elizabeth, 1963, *op. cit.*: Table XXXI, page 215.

continue to exist, and need to be understood and accepted before any rapprochement is possible.

The reader will find that evidence in this book is presented in two forms, which are in fact complementary to each other: numerical data is given in tables of statistics, which are interpreted, amplified and elaborated by means of verbatim quotations from our recorded transcripts. This constant interplay between impersonal statistics and highly personal testimony is an essential part of our research method. Numerical data on its own can offer only an assessment of the facts as they exist; it cannot tell us *why* they exist, what are the feelings and the pressures which lie behind behaviour: for insights of this sort, we must look to what was actually said by the mother, to the subtleties and shades of meaning which were conveyed by the words she used. Conversely, to rely on quotation alone would be highly dangerous; since we cannot present 700 unabridged transcripts (Heaven and our publishers forbid!), selection must inevitably be made, and this could be a very potent source of distortion, were it not for the discipline which the core of statistical evidence from which we work imposes. Every discussion in this book thus proceeds from an initial statistical analysis, followed by total immersion in several hundred quotations, from which we hope to emerge with some understanding of the problem, and which usually results in further statistical analysis in order to confirm or reject the hypotheses which suggest themselves.

It should be added here that we also consider it vitally important that at least one member of the directing team in research of this kind should be personally involved in the face-to-face experience of interviewing: interviewers cannot be adequately trained, *nor can material be realistically interpreted*, if this direct participation is missing. Reciprocally, the interviewers themselves, if they are (as they must be in this work) genuinely interested in the research problem, acquire insights which can make a valuable contribution to the planning of further stages, and which we gratefully make use of.

A word needs to be said about the way in which quotations are given. They are attributed in terms of the father's occupation mainly in order to give depth and identity to what is said; occasionally this has been omitted for the sake of brevity if the quotation occurs in the body of the text and the occupation has no relevance to the content. All forenames and surnames have been altered where they occur, and we have made some attempt at verisimilitude: that is, Nottingham names have been replaced by Nottingham pseudonyms, Irish by Irish, etc.—and we have also tried to choose pseudonyms which we thought the mother would like! Both forenames and surnames have been used consistently: if a name occurs more than once, it is the same child who is referred to, and this consistency holds good between as well as within books. It need hardly be said that nothing has been written into the quotations; where cutting has been necessary, it has been done with careful regard for both feeling and sense of the passage, and has been avoided where it involved the distortion of either. Finally, we cannot do better than borrow a felicitous sentence from Jackson and Marsden: 'We have tried to put down the actual language used by men and women, even when deviant from the Queen's English, because to retranslate it without losing shades and weightings of meaning would have been beyond our powers, and to "correct" it, beyond our desires'.[1]

A question which we are sometimes asked is 'How do you know that the mother is telling you the truth?' The short answer is that we *don't* know; but we may ask in return, 'Why should she not?' Given a situation in which she knows that her anonymity will be respected; given that she has no means of knowing the interviewer's opinion; given, too, that we are committed neither to judge her ourselves nor to divulge information to any person or authority which might judge her; given, in short, that no strings are attached to her allowing the interview to take place at all: there is no reason why the mother should not respond with frankness, and this we believe she almost invariably does. It must be remembered also that the interview itself is rather long—at the four-year-old stage it normally took over an hour and frequently considerably longer—and it simply is not practicable for a person consistently to dissemble for that length of time. Perhaps more important than any of these points, however, is the fact that the interview deliberately approaches every area of parent/child interaction from a number of different angles. The single, bald question is avoided. It is perfectly true that a mother may return only a conventionally acceptable answer where a topic is merely raised and then dropped immedi-

1 Jackson, Brian, and Marsden, Dennis: *Education and the Working Class;* Routledge and Kegan Paul, London, 1962.

ately; but if her questioner continues to explore her attitudes through a series of related enquiries, and if she sees that more than a polite interest is taken in her feelings and opinions, she is likely to reply with honesty and in some detail.[1] The multiple approach not only gives the interviewer an opportunity to assess her data's internal consistency, but also, equally valuable, gives the mother a chance to qualify, moderate, emphasize, illustrate, expand, and, if she wishes, go back on her statements: 'When I said just now ... what I really meant was ... '; 'Oh, another thing I should have mentioned'; 'Yes, and here's *another* reason why I think ...', and so on. Similarly, the interviewer herself is enabled to check and amplify what has been said: 'Earlier on you said ... how does that fit in with this?' This flexibility in itself makes for a readiness in the mother to be as helpful as she can. In general, it may be said that, once the mother joins in the conversation, she is likely to tell the truth: the few interview schedules which came back marked 'did not feel she was being frank' almost without exception involved monosyllabic mothers whose main concern was to get the interview over quickly.

Fundamentally our principle is that the mother is the expert on her own child. She knows more about him than anyone else; she knows about him *in more situations* than anyone else. Much of her knowledge is available from no other source. Her expertise is not necessarily systematic, or even conscious: she might be completely at a loss if she were asked to produce a case-history of her child, and often she is astonished at the very extent of the information which she finds herself able to give us. She will also be the first to admit that her detailed knowledge of the child is not always matched either by an understanding of him or by an ability to cope successfully to her own or anybody else's satisfaction: 'I don't know Roger *at all*', cried one mother des-

---

[1] A good example of the initial answer which is merely 'conventional', and which needs to be followed up if anything of value is to be learned, is elicited by the question in our study of babies: 'Did you have any special reason for not breast-feeding/stopping when you did?' Answers are highly stereotyped variations on the physical reasons of unsuitability or shortage of milk. It is only when extra questions are asked—'Did you enjoy feeding the baby? Do you think you'd have stopped anyway, even if you'd had enough milk?'—that the operant reasons of inconvenience, distaste and embarrassment begin to emerge. 72% of the sample gave initial 'physical' answers; 55% later said that they had not wanted to breast feed and would not have gone on anyway. Newson, John and Elizabeth, 1963, *op. cit.*, pp. 46–50.

pairingly, 'I just *do not understand* him, I don't know where to *begin*'—nevertheless, she was able to give us a picture of her highly complex little boy which was outstanding both in detail and in depth of insight. It is also true that a mother who is not aware of her failure to understand can at the same time furnish us with the material to perceive the pattern of relationships which thus far has been hidden from her own perception. The function of this research, then, is simply to tap a rich source of information which already exists but which too often is ignored: the ordinary mother's ability to examine her own behaviour and her own feelings, and, if we only give her the opportunity, to share them with us.

# CHAPTER 2

# THE CHILD IN HIS CONTEXT

It is a truism that dealing with small children is not just a matter of deciding what is the best thing to do and then doing it. Nor are the compromises merely between the parents' principles and the child's personality. Anyone who talks to large numbers of parents must be struck by the recurrent theme: 'Of course, I should like to behave differently over this, but with things as they are . . . .' Probably the majority of parents must at some time be faced with circumstances, temporary or permanent, which are not in harmony with their aims and intentions in bringing up their children, and which may be directly erosive of their principles. It is clear that one cannot hope to understand the demands which parents make upon their children, nor the restrictions which they try to enforce, without taking account of the total social context within which any particular family is embedded.

The degree of conflict between a mother's ideals of behaviour and her environment will of course vary from situation to situation, and from one woman to another. She may never be fully aware of the extent to which her treatment of the child is conditional upon her social and material circumstances: thus the owner of an automatic washing-machine may pride herself on her ability to take toilet-training 'relaxedly', without pausing to probe what would be her reactions to a perpetually damp toddler if she were reduced to a sink with cold running water only; and the mother who can answer our question 'What do you do if there's a disagreement or a quarrel?' with a blithe 'I yell for Nanny' may or may not be conscious of her dependence on Nanny as a buffer between herself and the less pleasant aspects of her children. At the other end of the scale, this sort of conflict may be so great as to take on almost obsessional proportions for the mother. '*If only* we could get a place of our own'—away from grandma, who nags the children and sets the whole family at loggerheads; '*if only* we could get away from this district'—where the traffic roars non-stop, and the neighbours are 'not very particular', and the neighbours' children swear infectiously; '*if only* the woman next door would understand that kids have got to make a bit of noise sometimes—it's bang, bang, on the wall all day, and shouting at them as soon as they go out in the yard, and she's got them that nervous!' So the mother is forced to shush the child against her will, or to restrict him, as she believes, unnecessarily; with a corresponding increase in her own emotional tension. In more subtle ways, too, and in many different areas of the child's life, the mother's behaviour towards him is modified by material situation and social climate: by the physical difficulties of living in over-crowded and perhaps squalid surroundings, or by the no less compelling, if less tangible, pressures of family and neighbourhood behaviour patterns. Individual problems such as illness, unemployment or marital disturbances may bring additional changes to the mother-child relationship.

For those of us who try to understand the complexities of child-rearing—and particularly for those who professionally criticize the way other people bring up their children—it is essential to bear in mind that parents do not have unlimited scope for manoeuvre in deciding how they will and how they will not behave. Most parents have some basic philosophy of child-rearing, and most hold certain principles and values which they consider important and which they hope to implant in their children; but it is also clear that their actual handling of practical day-to-day issues is often tempered by expediency and by the necessity of coping somehow with an environment or situation not chosen by themselves. These factors are relevant before we even begin to consider the ways in which rational intentions on the part of mother or father can be undermined by the emotional currents of close personal relationships. In this chapter we shall discuss some aspects of the background of our four-year-olds' lives; but so fundamental a theme could hardly be confined within a chapter, and it will recur in this book as it recurs in the children's daily experience.

## Housing

What sort of a place is home, where the ordinary four-year-old spends almost the whole of his time? What does he see of his neighbourhood as he trots with his mother to the grocer's? In what surroundings does he watch television or tinker with his toy lorry? What does Nottingham mean to a Nottingham child?

The housing areas in Nottingham can be divided rather arbitrarily into three categories: central, council estate and suburban. The central area, bounded by Nottingham Road and Sycamore Road to the north, Triumph Road and Sneinton Elements to the west and east and the Trent itself in the south, is distinguished by its density of bricks and mortar: on the map it stands out as a darker patch, on closer view made up of narrow streets, tightly packed in, edged almost without a break by terrace houses. In the main central dwelling areas—Radford, The Meadows, Sneinton, New Basford and Hyson Green—the terraces are made up of very small two-storey houses; but the area also includes streets of much larger Victorian and Edwardian villas and terraces, built with servants in mind, which have known better days. These are rarely occupied by single families, and are often let off entirely in single rooms; the coloured population of Nottingham is mostly to be found in 'flats' of this kind, and the four-year-olds we see in these houses usually belong to Irish families. In general, it can be said that the more firmly rooted young working-class families tend to make their homes either in the more permanent communities of the small terraces or else (by very virtue of their roots) in the council house districts.

In terms of everyday experience and neighbourhood pressures, living in a council house will mean different things according to its situation. Nottingham has three really large council estates: Clifton, which is south of the River Trent, outside the city proper but within its jurisdiction; the Aspley/Bilborough/Broxtowe complex, oldest of the three[1] and beginning to show its age, on the west side of the city; and, to the hilly north, spreading towards Sherwood Forest and the coal fields, the still-growing Bestwood and Bestwood Park Estate. These three monsters between them accounted (at the end of 1964)[2] for 57% of the total provision of council houses; and it is only the families living in these extensive council areas whom we have included in

[1] Aspley was originally started in 1930, Bilborough in 1936 and Broxtowe in 1937; all three were added to in 1947–1952.
[2] At this date there was a total of 34,796 council houses in the city, of which 19,956 were on the large estates.

our 'estate' category. Typically, shopping facilities, libraries, schools and pubs (though not cinemas) are provided within the boundaries of these estates, so that it is not necessary for the housewife to leave the estate at all except for major shopping expeditions.

There are other, much smaller, agglomerations of council houses; some of these (at Lenton Abbey and Sneinton Dale, for example) are sometimes known as estates, although consisting of only twenty or so streets; some are isolated single streets of council property; one (Wollaton Park)[1] is very exceptional in that, originally planned in 1926 as a council estate mainly for white-collar workers, about 50% of its well-designed bungalow dwellings are now privately owned and the estate houses a range of occupational groups from Class I to Class IV, though perhaps no unskilled workers. All these smaller council-owned areas have in common the fact that, in contrast with the Big Three, they are very far from being self-contained, and few can provide for more than immediate household needs; those who live here are forced to have continual commerce with the world outside the estate. Housing of this sort we have therefore included in the suburban category, as it tends to be outside the central area; where, as occasionally happens, two or three council houses have sprung up on a vacant plot within a densely populated central district, these have been classified as belonging to the area by which they are hemmed in.

It should be remarked that Nottingham's more overcrowded quarters are undergoing a fairly rapid change. Much of the eastern end of Radford, for instance, has been pulled down, and Nottingham's first blocks of high council flats have been built here. The occupants of these flats, however, still look out over the cobbled back streets, communal yards and outside privies of a Radford not very much altered basically from the pre-war and immediately post-war portraits drawn by Alan Sillitoe[2]. None of the children in our study lives in a council flat.

Our final category, that of suburbia, is thus a frankly miscellaneous grouping, including all housing which belongs neither to the tight grids of streets in the centre of the city, nor to the loose-knit crescents and curlicues of the sprawling estates. As

[1] See Stanley Gale: *Modern Housing Estates*, Batsford, London, 1949.
[2] Alan Sillitoe: *Saturday Night and Sunday Morning* and *Key to the Door*, W. H. Allen, London, 1958 and 1961.

well as the smaller council-house groups, it takes in all varieties
of private ownership, from small 100%-mortgage semi-detached
villas to large detached houses in spacious gardens, worth
£10,000 and more by 1964 values; not that very many of our
young families live in those. Along with these go small terraces
of houses, owned or rented, which still survive on the outskirts
of the city; in style of building they are often indistinguishable
from their sootier counterparts in the city centre, but here in the
suburbs they at least have more elbow room, the air is percepti-
bly fresher and, in their occasional long narrow strips of front
garden, they may even retain some of their character as the former cottage dwellings of a rural working class.

We devised this classification of housing on an *ad hoc* basis,
conscious that, while it was logical enough, other systems could
be equally logical: one might well classify according to private
rental, public rental and private ownership, for instance, or
according to the rateable value of property; and even within our
own framework there are clearly many possible and useful sub-
categories. The three headings we used, however, had a double
advantage: they were simple to apply, and they corresponded to
geographical areas with a noticeably different 'feel' to them.
Having chosen our classification without regard to relative popu-
lations, we were moderately surprised to find that a random
sample of the families of four-year-olds does in fact divide
according to this system into three almost equal groups. Class
differences will, of course, be expected, and they are set out in
detail in Table I.

Middle-class (white-collar, managerial and professional) fami-

TABLE I

*Types of residential background of four-year-olds:*
*by occupational class*

|  | I & II[1] | IIIwc | IIIman | IV | V | ALL |
|---|---|---|---|---|---|---|
|  | % | % | % | % | % | % |
| Central area | 6 | 16 | 43 | 41 | 45 | 34 |
| Major council estates | 14 | 34 | 34 | 35 | 38 | 32 |
| Suburban | 80 | 50 | 23 | 24 | 17 | 34 |

[1] Registrar General's classification is used, with slight modification. See
Appendix II.

lies in general are less likely to be found in the central area; but the shop and clerical workers (IIIwc) take their full share of council houses on the larger estates, and here only the professional and managerial classes are under-represented. Those in Class I and II tend to be doing work of service to the estate, rather than commuting from it; thus these fathers are likely to be clergymen, doctors, teachers, police officers and shop owners, and, in the case of the first two at least, their houses are likely to be specially planned for their profession, and rather grander than the normal run of council houses.

A quick look at some typical houses may help to illuminate the background against which Nottingham children grow up. The smaller terrace house is built of red brick in blocks of about six or eight dwellings. Each block is separated from the next one along the street by a narrow snicket or alley-way, which leads to the back yards. These may be divided from each other by low fences, each yard opening on to a back alley running parallel to the terrace; or there may be only one long communal yard, often ungated, criss-crossed by washing-lines, noisy with children, and backed by the usual line of brick privies. The front doors of these houses normally open straight from the front parlour on to the street; but there is also another type of plan in which the blocks of eight are each laid at right angles to the street in small double terraces of twelve or sixteen houses: here the front doors of one block face the front doors of the next across a traffic-free paved front yard, while the communal back yard is separated by the privies and a wall from the back yard of the next block along the street. This arrangement has the virtue of allowing the children twice as much traffic-free space in which to play; on the other hand, the front yards are almost never fenced off from the street, and display the usual disadvantages of communal use.[1]

The front room is still, in most cases, the 'best' room, and therefore kept for special occasions. In the better-off houses it may be rather grand and chilly, with three-piece suite or 'studio couch', carpet, china cabinet, and coloured photographs, professionally taken, of wedding groups and babies lying pinkly on rugs. Some families do use their front rooms for evening leisure, and in these houses the room will often be extremely comfortable and well looked after; but in some of the poorer homes the

---

[1] Discussed later, pp. 130–3; see also pp. 37–8.

B

front room may be no more than a store room and passage-way: left unfurnished, unheated and often uncleaned, it becomes a depository for pram and pushchair, bicycles, handcart, and the discarded junk of the whole family.

The back kitchen is the heart of the terrace house. Here the family lives its life. Here meals are eaten, first steps taken, quarrels fought out, decisions made. The baby watches his world from the pram in the corner; the toddler pursues his own schemes under the table, or enjoys his 'five minutes' love' on his mother's lap in the easy chair; this is the base for the child's early forays into the world outside, the first goal of children breathless from school; here 'missus next door' drops in for 'a bit of a natter'; here father stumps in heavy-footed from work, and relaxes at the cloth-spread table-end over his tea and the *Evening Post*. Here, too, is the television set, always a good indication of the family's true living room. The mother who is not at work must spend more than half her waking life in this room, or in and out to the tiny lean-to scullery beyond it; if she is doing 'homework'—machining or lace-work, perhaps—she will probably find space for this too in the cheerful clutter of the kitchen.

To the middle-class southerner, the most noticeable thing about a terrace-house is its enormous fire. However dilapidated the furniture, however grubby the walls, the fire is banked high and blazing from early autumn onward, a striking contrast to the single bar of an electric fire which is the welcome one tends to find in middle-class houses. As Hoggart says, 'Warmth, to be "as snug as a bug in a rug", is of the first importance . . . . A good housewife knows that she must "keep a good fire" . . . a fire is shared and seen'.[1] A second characteristic, true for the majority of these kitchens, is the good condition of their decorations. The walls may be bumpy or damp, the plaster crumbling, but the poor fabric of the house is covered up with brightly patterned wallpaper, the woodwork glossily painted. Many of these families reckon to renew paint and paper every two years or so (which may well be necessary where the damp continually seeps through); and while the result, in its popular-contemporary styling, is a long way from the romantic white-washed cottage kitchen, it could hardly be denied that this outcome of the commercial 'do-it-yourself' campaign is wholly beneficial.

[1] R. Hoggart: *The Uses of Literacy*, Chatto and Windus, London, 1957.

Lino with a hearthrug (and sometimes an extra carpet square between them), a fairly solid table and chairs, a couple of easy chairs and a sideboard make up the furniture in the small room which is almost always so crowded that free movement about the room is impossible. Washing and cooking go on in the scullery, but the ironing is done companionably with the family, and the sideboard often reveals its kitchen status by the clean unironed clothes spilling from its cupboard doors. Pictures are not very common apart from family photographs; decoration is more often provided by coloured plaster plaques and brass or glass ornaments. Plastic flowers are much used; but it must be remembered that there has been something of a technological revolution in the plastic flower industry (one can now buy a highly deceptive potted geranium entirely in polythene, not to mention the ivies and rubber plants beloved of *House and Garden*), and plastic flowers have become noticeably better-class during the fifties and sixties;[1] their rise in status has been obvious even within the two years of interviewing for this study.

Warmth, comfort and colour are the norm in terrace-house kitchens; but there are, of course, a minority which provide no more than a (still warm) shelter. Inadequacy of income may be the sole reason. Mrs W.'s family of four children is on National Assistance, her husband disabled and in bed for long periods, and her kitchen is bleak despite the fire, with thin scrubbed lino, clean but peeling walls, no easy chairs or ornaments and no source of hot water but the kettle; mother and children wear, in January, cheap cotton frocks and spotless shrunk cardigans. Often, however, lack of money is complemented by other inadequacies, whether as cause or effect we need not attempt to judge here; the result is seen in walls which would be bare if it were not for the dirt, floors with nameless substances trodden into them, chairs with a sticky patina thick enough to scrape, children whose grime is clearly several days old, and a pervasive sour smell. Dirt is not confined to the very poor, however, nor to the terrace houses (though the disadvantages of lack of plumbing and decaying fabric with which they start off make it inevitable that a woman here will be more quickly defeated by

[1] Dennis Chapman points out that there are now companies which specialize in providing bouquets and arrangements of plastic flowers, changed regularly, for office and hotel foyers (private communication). They are also featured both by Woolworth's and in the gift and garden departments of such 'high-class' shops as those belonging to the John Lewis group.

it); a fair number of families live in relatively well-furnished houses with a comfortable disregard for the ingrained grime of the walls, floor and soft furnishings. Often the father of the family works at a dirty job without washing facilities, and the wife becomes inured to the daily additional layer of 'swarf' on his return home. In such a household, while there may be a conventional protest from the mother as wet trickles down the baby's drip-marked legs or the toddler spills his sugary tea, no attempt is made to mop up the mess, which joins other homely elements in the sodden-looking carpet. But at least there *is* a carpet!—and the fierce heat in the room will soon dry up these haphazard deposits.

We wanted some easy practical index of the cleanliness or otherwise of the house, and our housewife interviewers made a quick two-way assessment of this by asking themselves the question 'Could this be cleaned up in one day's work?' If the answer was no—that is, if the dirt was so ingrained as to demand redecorating and furnishing rather than cleaning—the house was rated as 'dirty'. Untidiness was not taken into account, nor was the cleanliness or otherwise of clothes or bodies. On this criterion, less than 7% of all houses in a random sample were dirty; this proportion, for many very obvious reasons, increases as one goes down the social scale, reaching a proportion of about one in four in the homes of the unskilled manual group. It must be remembered that all the houses in the sample contain small children, and that both the absolute number of children and the person-to-room ratio increase rapidly from Class I and II to Class V.

TABLE II

*Proportions of houses rated as 'dirty': by social class*

| I and II | IIIwc | IIIman | IV | V | All (random) |
|---|---|---|---|---|---|
| % | % | % | % | % | % |
| 1 | 0 | 6 | 9 | 25 | 6·6 |

The do-it-yourself enthusiasts on the big council estates are not so hampered by dirt and decay. At the same time, the houses are small enough to be easily and fairly cheaply papered and

painted by the amateur. The result is a standard of decoration
and redecoration which puts many of the larger privately owned
houses to shame. Two patterns of wallpaper for the walls of a
room, and often a third for the ceiling, is normal; paint is in
bright assertive colours, furniture is mass-production 'contemporary' (far more so than in the terrace houses), and curtains
run to frills and flounces in terylene and flocked nylon. Ornaments are abundant, with an especial fondness for brass and
imitation wrought iron, for decorated pottery and for comic
animals in wire and plastic with some vague function such as
holding matchboxes or letters. There are more pictures in these
houses (there is more room on the walls), and the coloured
photographs are joined by flower prints or one of the pseudo-
'artistic' best-selling reproductions. Royalty on the wall is not
so popular as formerly, except on the occasional calendar; far
more common is the current pop-singing group, though these
pictures betray the evanescence of their popularity by being
propped on mantelpiece or sideboard rather than given the
permanence of a nail in the wall. Occasionally there is a small
bookcase, often a coffee-table.

For the woman moving from a central terrace house to a
council house on one of the big estates, there are enormous
practical changes in her daily life. To the mother with small
children, probably the most important of these is the plumbing.
She now has both bathroom and lavatory upstairs, where before
she washed the children in the kitchen sink and took them across
the yard in the daytime, using a bucket at night. Hot water is
now on tap in the kitchen as well as upstairs: no more reliance
on kettles, gas-boilers or the hire-purchase of a separate water-
heater. The second big difference is the garden—big enough for
flowers, a few vegetables, lawn and a swing for the children, a
place where toddlers can play in the open air but away from
traffic, with a gate you can shut. In town, small children often
have to be kept in the house for fear of their wandering from the
open yards, and protection from bullying children and frightening dogs who share the communal yard may also be a problem;
in a council house, as in any private house with a garden, the
mother can secure the gate and leave the child to wander in and
out of the back door as it pleases. The peace of mind this allows
can be judged by contrast with the worries of two central-area
mothers. Mrs Robinson, living in condemned property twenty

yards from Radford's busiest street, kept returning to this theme:

> But it's a pity we've got no garden and nowhere to play—I think somewhere to play is essential where children are concerned —there's no scope for them here, unless they go on to the recreation ground, the park. I mean, children have got to know they can play safely, they can play without you being worried, because around here you daren't let them out of your sight because of the traffic. And I think that at their age it's *essential* that they should play, because everything is learned in play—to play nice together, and not fighting. (Later) But if I had a garden, it'd be different. I mean, here they're under your feet all day, and it gets on *their* nerves as well as getting on mine.

Mrs Brennan's Theresa had been run over and suffered a broken leg six months earlier:

> But I mean, I've been so very fearful with her—I've never let her off the yard. Of course, we've got no gate in the terrace, and we've put up an old crib or something like that, to keep them in, or somebody'll go out with them. But I had to leave it off one day—the coalman—and of course she was out and running across the road, and a car . . . whether it ran into her or she ran into it, we don't know. There wasn't anybody about. I'd only just *been* out that minute to see where she was, and I—I couldn't *believe* it. I wouldn't have minded if I just didn't bother and let her roam the streets. But to be out all the time to her, watching how she is, and then this happens . . . . It's frightened her, but I don't think it's frightened her so that she won't go out. I mean, if I let her on the yard and she saw other children going out, I think she'd be after them if she got the chance.

Inside the council house, especially on the two newer estates, there is again more space for play. Instead of parlour, kitchen/living-room and tiny scullery, the usual arrangement is a small kitchen off one large living-room, often a through room with windows looking on to the front and french windows giving access to the back garden. The kitchen, usually equipped with light modern furniture and gadgets, may be used for breakfast and for members of the family eating on their own, but is too small for the whole family; when they are in together, they will eat at the dining table at the end of the living room. This room is otherwise used for the less arduous household tasks, for leisure and for the children's play, and is truly a *living* room—in the council house there is no wasted 'best' room. Together with better-planned space and more amenities, the estate families also enjoy cleaner air: they are away from the dirty centre of the city, they may only burn smokeless fuel (though this evokes some grumbles), and the freshness of their curtains and furnishings generally bears witness to this additional lightening of the housewife's labour. From the edges of the northern and southern estates, the view is completely rural, and likely to remain unspoilt. It must be added, however, that many women complain of loneliness on the big estates and seem to find it difficult to make new friends there, despite the enormous choice which the estates offer of neighbours of similar age and situation. Others find the size of these housing areas daunting—'soulless' and 'like a concentration camp' are two descriptions of Clifton —possibly partly because the estates do not so readily break down into compact neighbourhood units as do the back streets of Radford and the Meadows.

The suburban group of housing is, of course, the least homogenous. The council houses among them will mostly resemble those of the estates in amenities and floor space, although the quality of their finish varies somewhat. The private houses, almost without exception, have their own gardens. Most of the private houses are three-bedroomed, with two medium-sized living rooms, and probably the majority have no better facilities than the council houses; many of them are certainly shabbier than the better-kept of the houses on the Clifton and Bestwood estates.

In furnishing, the range of both taste and quality is very wide in the privately-owned houses. Antique, reproduction, good modern, tawdry modern, cheerful mixture and nothing-in-particular—all are represented. Incomes vary from about £600 to about £10,000-with-expense-account, and naturally the contents of the house, as well as the houses themselves, vary accordingly. It is still rather rare to see more books than a very small bookcase will hold; but pictures are coming into their own, as the family photographs retreat from the living-room: Van Gogh, Redouté roses, and occasionally a really fine print or even an original, if only a pale and amateur water-colour. As the houses increase in value, the space behind the front door gets larger and larger: from nothing at all in the terrace houses, through just-room-to-turn-round in the council house, to what can decently be described as a hall: this again provides room for pictures, as well as hall-furniture (necessarily a middle- and upper-class phenomenon) and a telephone.

The change to a slightly larger house can mark a new stage for a mother in her dealings with her children. Protection from traffic is the first need; a place of their own to play in is the second. The separate day nursery and night nursery of one of our children is very much an exception; but many middle-class parents, particularly in the professional group, make great efforts to provide at least a corner which the child may regard as his own. This is not necessarily a matter of having more rooms to allocate; often the playroom will double as a children's bed-room. The difference is that the room is thought of as a place to be during the daytime, equipped for the purpose, and heated so as to make it habitable throughout the year. Clearly, one needs extra money to heat two rooms; but professional people are per-haps more likely to regard the playroom as an educational need, and this attitude will often be reinforced by the father's wish to work at home in peace and quiet. We have already quoted Mrs Robinson on the strain imposed upon both mother and child by a lack of garden—'they're under your feet all day, and it gets on *their* nerves as well as getting on mine': the respite from con-tinual togetherness afforded by a garden is more than doubled by the acquisition of a playroom. 'I simply dote on my children when I can watch them playing at the other end of the garden with fifty yards between us', said one middle-class mother, not altogether jokingly, who had recently moved in order to have more space, 'and their voices *from the next room* are really rather attractive!' An advertising manager's wife mentioned the playroom as conducive to family harmony, and also thought that it encouraged the child to have a life of his own; commen-ting on her little boy's independence and ability to do without her company, she said:

> I'd say he was slightly unusual in that way, from what I've seen of other people's children. But then, other people's children don't have playrooms, you know what I mean? We've done without a dining-room, you see, so that they can have a room.

—and later, remarking that she and the child rarely got on each other's nerves, she added

> Again, I think the playroom has a lot to do with this, because we're not under one another's feet. You know what I mean—I don't have to clear him out of here when I want to clean up in here. As I say, the playroom has made things a lot easier all round. They don't tend to get in my hair, sort of thing.

This mother has two children; obviously, the greater the number of children, the more likely they are to get 'in the mother's hair' or 'under her feet'; and the size of family would certainly have to be taken into account in assessing the pressure on individual mothers or on class groups. Table III shows the numbers of children in our families at the time of interviewing, broken down by social class and with the totals corrected to random sample proportions.[1] It must be remembered that many of these families are by no means completed, and that we have no means of knowing whether they are or not.

TABLE III

*Number of children in family: percentage of social classes*

|  | I & II | IIIwc | IIIman | IV | V | All classes random sample |
|---|---|---|---|---|---|---|
|  | % | % | % | % | % | % |
| Only children | 17 | 19 | 10 | 9 | 1 | 11 |
| 2 children | 49 | 44 | 31 | 33 | 22 | 35 |
| 3 children | 19 | 25 | 26 | 25 | 20 | 24 |
| 4 children | 9 | 7 | 11 | 13 | 19 | 12 |
| 5 or more children | 6 | 5 | 22 | 20 | 38 | 18 |

It can be seen that families with only one or two children are more likely to be found in the middle classes. Families with four or more children are more likely to be working-class, while those with five and over occur six times as often in Class V as in the middle-class group. The majority of middle-class families (64·5%) have two children or less: the majority of Class V families (57%) have four children or more. This factor of family

[1] See Appendix II.

B*

size needs to be borne in mind, together with other background differences, when class comparisons of behaviour are made.

Despite the differences in family size, the average age of the mothers at the time of the interview varied by less than two years across the classes, and then in the direction of younger working-class mothers. The range of ages is about as wide as possible, given that all the children were born legitimate: the youngest mother was twenty, the oldest fifty-three. The pattern of ages across this range does show a greater class variation: there is a heavy concentration of middle-class mothers in the early thirties, whereas the working class-concentration is lighter, and comes about two years earlier, the spread of ages being greater in both directions. It must be remembered that, as well as having larger families, working-class mothers also have their first babies at an earlier age;[1] and their pregnancies tend to be less widely spaced than those of middle-class women.

TABLE IV

*Social class and average age of mother at time of interview*

| Years | I & II | IIIwc | IIIman | IV | V | All (random) |
|---|---|---|---|---|---|---|
| | % | % | % | % | % | % |
| 27 and under | 9 | 13 | 32 | 21 | 27 | 24 |
| 28–31 | 27 | 42 | 24 | 32 | 27 | 28 |
| 32–35 | 37 | 18 | 22 | 18 | 23 | 23 |
| 36 and over | 27 | 27 | 22 | 29 | 23 | 25 |
| Average ages in years: | 33·9 | 32·7 | 31·6 | 32·8 | 32·1 | 32·3 |

From the child's point of view, then, the working-class four-year-old, compared with his middle-class counterpart, will be less likely to have play-space of his own inside the house, and such space as there is will tend to be overcrowded; he is more likely to have siblings of an age to play with him, more likely to have much older ones as well, of an age to mother him or boss him around, and more likely also to have to share his mother's attention with other pre-school children and babies.

The other main factor which decides the amount of attention which a child can expect to receive from his mother is her own

1 Newson, John and Elizabeth, *op. cit.*, pp. 151–2, 155–6.

working life outside the family. Much interest has been focused during the sixties on the problems of married women at work and on those of the children whom they leave behind them.[1] Nottingham is traditionally a city affording high employment for women, and in 1964 the eagerness of young mothers to return to the factories was still being offered by a local paediatrician at a medical conference as a major reason for the decline in breast feeding. We found in our survey of one-year-olds, however, that the number of their mothers then in full-time work was negligible: less than 2%. For the great majority of legitimate four-year-olds at least, the absent mother is still no problem: only 5% of our sample of mothers were in full-time work, and a fifth of these were working at home, either creatively, secretarially or in shops attached to the living quarters of the family. As might be expected, part-time work showed a greater increase: from 8% of mothers of year-old babies, to 23% of mothers of four-year-olds. Many of these women worked less than eight hours a week; three or four hours' domestic work or an afternoon's teaching in a school or adult class were common part-time occupations, and more than a sixth of the part-timers worked only at home.

One further aspect of the child's immediate background which cannot be neglected is the possible presence of other adults apart from his parents, living within the home. The numbers involved here are not very great, and a detailed discussion of the effects upon upbringing or upon the child himself is outside the scope of this study; nevertheless, the sidelights which we have on this situation point to an interesting line of investigation. Inevitably, the child's social environment is radically altered by the introduction of another person into the household, even if this new member is merely a lodger, without close familial claims upon the child; where there are direct and perhaps authoritarian kinship bonds, the child may become the pawn of conflicting interests, or possibly learn to manipulate those in-

[1] See especially the following studies: Jephcott, P., Seear, N. and Smith. J. H.: *Married Women Working*, Allen and Unwin, London, 1962; Yudkin, S. and Holme, A.: *Working Mothers and their Children*, Michael Joseph, London, 1963; Klein, Viola: *Britain's Married Women Workers*, Routledge and Kegan Paul, London, 1965; British Federation of University Women (ed. Constance Arregger): *Graduate Women at Work*, Oriel Press, Newcastle-upon-Tyne, 1966; *and also* Hannah Gavron: *The Captive Wife*, Routledge and Kegan Paul, London, 1966.

terests for his own ends. 'The coming of another adult into the family of procreation', writes Bossard, 'changes the structural form of the family in that it enlarges the series of continuing relationships which comprise it, as well as alters the whole form of the structure . . . . Perhaps the basic fact about the presence of "other persons" in the home is that they are not acceptable equally to all members of the family . . . . A good many domestic situations might be summarized in the statement that the presence of a younger adult in the family means a potential competitor for the affection of the child; and the presence of an older person, a potential competitor for his control.'[1] Where the additional member is a grandmother or aunt, this may also considerably affect the degree to which the father is expected, or indeed permitted, to participate in the child's care.

Even before one begins to probe the complexities of social relationship which an extra person involves, the modification of the outward show of behaviour can already pose problems for the whole family. There are many forms of behaviour which a mother, while she is prepared to admit them and discuss them, is not prepared to demonstrate to an outsider. Shouting at the children, for example, tends to be something which, accepted and understood within the intimate family group, is not felt to be acceptable in the presence of other people, at least for most middle-class mothers; in the same way, cuddling of children past the toddler stage may be felt, both by mother and child, as a form of 'sloppiness' to be indulged in only privately. Thus both these normal expressions of feeling may be watered down into more formal shows of displeasure or affection. 'It's a tremendous relief, I feel I can be natural with them again', said a professional-class mother after the departure of her (perfectly satisfactory) *au pair* girl; and a foreman's wife groped for words to express her difficulty in being consistently firm with her children when the expedient thing was to let matters slide rather than disturb the lodger.

> I *tend* to be strict, but I'm *not*, sort of thing . . . I'm afraid I'm not very good at forcing a child—I'm not very good at putting my foot down. As I say, I think a lot of it is with having my husband's friend here . . . .

1 James Bossard and Eleanor Boll: *The Sociology of Child Development*, 3rd ed., p. 36; Harper Bros., New York, 1960.

At the same time, the presence of a witness can be an extremely potent factor in putting the mother on her mettle in her dealings with the child, for it makes public any significance which the situation may already have as a trial of strength. The witness as an exacerbator of tension is a phenomenon which continually recurs in an independent investigation which we have been making into conflict situations between mothers and children;[1] and we shall want to return to this theme later on in the present study.[2]

If the passive observer has a disturbing influence on parent-child relationships, how much more so the relative who exercises a right to interfere—either by treating the child in a way wh'ch challenges the mother's principles, or by directly criticizing her.

He is rather spoilt, unfortunately, not through us, but my parents. . . . I've been fighting a losing battle ever since the day he was born.

Well, I try to chastise her, you know, as *I* think; but you see it's undermining it all the time with those two being here (grandparents), because I'm told I'm doing wrong, but I don't think so . . . . She can do what she likes with those two, sometimes she does talk to them something awful and they don't say anything back to her—well, that annoys me.

Mrs Stoneham had been enlarging on the differences between her mother's ideas and her own—'Always nag, nag, nag. I've sort of stood on my head to give David all the latitude that I didn't have'—and the interviewer asked whether David's granny, who lived with the family, interfered at all with him.

She would, if I didn't, sort of, keep a very firm . . . . I think she thinks I'm far too lax sometimes. But the odd thing is, she nags and he doesn't take any notice of her. And if I say anything, he says "Mummy says so". Yet I'm really the lax one, and he takes far more notice of me and my husband.

To a lesser extent, grandparents living close by can also exert a good deal of authority in their children's families. Working-class mothers in particular, whose own parents are far more likely to live within dropping-in distance, often mention com-

[1] To be published in due course.          [2] Pp. 230–2 and 452–3.

ments from the older generation; one's impression is that working-class grandparents are less inhibited in their criticisms than those of the middle class, who also criticize but usually seem to make some effort at subtlety. Probably this is partly a reflection of the greater acceptance of matriarchal authority which other investigators have found in working-class young women.[1]

Painter's wife:

> When I first had mine, I used to ask my mother, you see, and I did as she said; so really I'm bringing mine up the way she brought us up. But there's one thing: my mother don't like me hitting them, she shouts at me for that; and yet *we* were hit, she used to hit us, not a lot, but if we really needed it; but she won't let me. Sometimes she'll come down here, and our Lorraine'll say "Me Mam hit me today", and then my mother'll turn on me and say "What did you want to do that for, then?" She doesn't approve of hitting at all now; and my dad's worse still. If I hit them when *he's* there, I soon know it—I get one myself! Oh, I've done that; I smacked June one day in front of him, and he turned round and clipped me one. He says "You're not too old for a good hiding, you know, even though you *are* married".

If these mothers' comments about outside members of the household tend to be critical, this is no doubt partly to do with the context in which they were speaking. Some grandparents certainly play a useful and valued part in the life of the family, but we did not ask about the child's contact with relatives outside the nuclear family circle. It is probable that such contact would be much more important for children in abnormal circumstances of various sorts: in particular, perhaps, children of unmarried mothers, and those who had lost one parent either by separation or by death.

Clearly, both from the child's point of view and for the rest of the family, the experience of having another adult in the house will vary considerably according to whether that adult is a grandparent, an *au pair* girl or nanny, an aunt or uncle, or a lodger. These children cannot therefore usefully be grouped together, except inasmuch as they all have to maintain an extra

---

[1] Young, M., and Willmott, P.: *Family and Kinship in East London*, Routledge and Kegan Paul, London, 1957. Kerr, Madeline: *The People of Ship Street*, Routledge and Kegan Paul, London, 1958.

not-quite-family relationship and also cope with a more complex web of social interaction and perhaps social strain. Once separate groups are distinguished, however, the numbers become too small for useful comparisons to be made.

The total of households which include additional adults is 10%, and in this there are no significant class differences. Nearly all these people are relatives; lodgers and others account for less than 2%. Even in the professional group, *au pair* girls are statistically very infrequent (less than 3% of that group), and we have no nannies at all in our sample: the one nanny we ever found was in our pilot sample. Female relatives occur more than twice as often as male relatives; one might expect this, if only because of the greater life span of women. What is more interesting is that the wife's relatives occur twice as often as those of the husband, so that in the total sample of 700 cases we found twenty-two maternal grandmothers living in the house, but only nine paternal grandmothers. The only class difference of any interest is that the unskilled labourers' wives seem less inclined to have their parents or parents-in-law living with them, but more inclined than other classes to give a home to sisters or other relatives; there may, however, be an Irish influence here.

In the course of this chapter, we have attempted to set the child in his social and material context; to show some of the more systematic ways in which this context may vary, particularly according to the socio-economic group in which the child finds himself; and to indicate too some of the more haphazard variations of environment. At an earlier stage we saw that social context was already having its influence upon the baby's experience before he was four weeks old; by four years, he is beginning to know his way about his own restricted world of relationships, sanctions and norms, and he has a fair idea of its accepted behaviour patterns and of its ways of dealing with deviance. It is to this centre of our stage—the four-year-old himself—that we now shift our focus.

# CHAPTER 3

## FOCUS ON FOUR-YEAR-OLDS

Because our questions are addressed to the mother of a four-year-old child, and are mainly directed towards exploring her interactions with that specific child, it will be important throughout the course of this book constantly to bear in mind what a four-year-old is like. The present chapter will be largely devoted to establishing some sort of composite mental image of such a child as he comes under our scrutiny during this brief period of the eight weeks around his fourth birthday.

To pinpoint in imagination any particular stage of development can be difficult, even for an experienced parent with reference to one of his or her own family: children, after all, pass rather quickly and imperceptibly from one stage to the next, and on looking back it is easy to telescope together widely separated periods, and even to confuse one child with his siblings. It is also fair to say that our own concentration upon one short period of time, while it is convenient as a point of reference and valuable in allowing us to establish ranges of comparable behaviour, is artificial to the extent that it is more normal for the child to be viewed within a continuous developmental progression.

Pinpointing behaviour with reference to an age-scale is, of course, exactly what is done when a child is tested against developmental or intellectual norms; but for our purpose in this chapter it will not be enough merely to draw attention to what the average four-year-old can accomplish in standardized test situations, or to quote behavioural norms. Descriptions based on this kind of information[1] are quite clearly valuable in an educational or child guidance setting; but from our point of

[1] For example: Terman, L. M., and Merrill, M. A.: *Stanford-Binet Intelligence Scale, 3rd revision*, Harrap, London, 1961; Gesell, A.: *The First Five Years of Life*, Methuen, London, 1954 edn.; Doll, E. A.: *The Measurement of Social Competence*, Educational Test Bureau, Minneapolis, 1953; Stott, D. H.: *Bristol Social Adjustment Guide*, University of London Press, 1958.

view they suffer from one disadvantage. The search for universal norms inevitably selects items of *typical* child behaviour (such as self-feeding or dressing) which almost all children will manifest sooner or later, despite rather extensive differences in their social and cultural background. In a sense, they are the result of the pursuit of a lowest common denominator in child behaviour. In practice they also have the effect of minimizing the significance of individual temperamental differences between children, and, in particular, of underemphasizing many of the important variations which result from dissimilarities in children's social and material experience and in the opportunities they have for learning: indeed, this is often their expressed intention.

From the present standpoint, then, it is not of primary importance to know what four-year-olds as such are capable of doing. Given the necessity, given a certain climate of expectation, four-year-olds *can* behave in ways which, for the ordinary Nottingham pre-school child of the nineteen-sixties, are outside the bounds of credibility. A beggar-child in Calcutta *can* if necessary support himself by his own scavenging; a child brought up under eighteenth century evangelism was *capable* of subjecting his own soul to a painful and pessimistic scrutiny;[1] and in Nottingham itself, little more than a hundred years ago, many four-year-olds were already caught up in the expectation that children of the labouring classes should lose no time in taking their share of the labouring.[2] All these things are possible to four-year-olds: none of them belongs to the world of our own seven hundred. So we must ask, not what these children might do, but what they do in fact do in the circumstances in which they variously find themselves: circumstances which incidentally include all the pressures and restrictions, both manifest and latent, which ordinary Nottingham parents bring to bear.

The average four-year-old in England today is healthy and well-nourished; in consequence, he has an abundance of physical energy, a fact which becomes painfully obvious to parents whenever it is directed into socially unacceptable channels. Sometimes the mother will complain that she cannot keep pace with the child's capacity for activity; and the running-out of his

---

[1] Paul Sangster: *Pity My Simplicity*, Epworth Press, London, 1963.

[2] This point is taken up again in our discussion of pressures for independence, pp. 67-8.

energy seems typically to show itself in a sudden state of exhaustion rather than a gradual slowing-down through the day. Although most of these children enjoy a quick 'five minutes' love' on mother's lap after dinner, almost none of them has a proper afternoon nap; the length of a short television programme is, for most, the limit to sitting still. Indeed, some mothers make the child sit quietly on the settee as an effective punishment for quarrelling or rowdiness.

Most normal four-year-olds have already developed all the basic skills of locomotion; they can walk, run, jump and balance with proficiency and grace. However, many of these motor abilities have only recently been mastered, or are still in the process of being elaborated and perfected, and they continue to afford satisfaction for their own sake, without need for the reinforcement of competition and rule-structure. For this reason, children of four usually respond enthusiastically to the challenge of a new locomotor experience: climbing, sliding, somersaulting, skipping, see-sawing, swinging and so on. 'It's the only time she ever sits still', said one mother, rather oddly, of her daughter's passion for the garden swing. The child will be fascinated at the sight of other children performing this sort of activity; and, his interest once aroused, he will often practise with absorption and concentration until he too can say 'Look at me'. With special instruction, children of this age may already have developed a high degree of skill in much more complex motor performances such as ice-skating, ski-ing, swimming or riding a pony; though it is, of course, very exceptional for an English child to be given the opportunity to practise any of these arts at this age. That children as young as this can achieve such accomplishments, however, does suggest that, for the ordinary child, the degree to which he learns to direct his own body and co-ordinate his movements is partly dependent upon the kinds of stimulation which his environment provides. Most English children nowadays, for instance, do have access to at least one large wheeled toy such as a tricycle, a pedal car, a scooter, or perhaps just a set of old pram wheels; and with these they rapidly develop a surprising degree of control. The harrowed adult, watching a three- or four-year-old pedalling full tilt at a brick wall, and knowing that his hand span is too small for him to use the brake, is reproved for his anxiety by the graceful last-minute turn with which the child saves himself and brings the tricycle to a stop.

Makeshift skills of this sort are indeed necessary where a child must both avoid obstacles and keep his balance within the confines of a busy pavement.

For the urban child, experience of these activities is somewhat limited by his immediate environment. At four he will rarely be allowed to wander unaccompanied more than a hundred yards or so from his own door, for fear of accident. If there is a back yard or a traffic-free 'front', he may be told to keep within it, or to go no further than the few feet of pavement immediately outside. Children with gardens will be similarly restricted; but they at least have more room to dispose their belongings, and often a patch which is recognised as theirs for digging or other projects. They may even, though rather more rarely, have unlimited rights over the whole garden: 'It's never been dug for years, and they can do just what the heck they please with it, and they just do', said an office manager's wife. In gardens, swings are fairly common; in back yards very rare. In either, though rather exceptionally, there may be a sandpit; but plastic paddling pools wear out too quickly and make too much mess in a concrete yard, and, though increasingly popular, are restricted mainly to families who can boast a patch of grass.

For the ordinary family in normal circumstances, father is out at work and any older brothers and sisters are at school or themselves at work; thus the responsibility for looking after the four-year-old during the day, for keeping him happy and for keeping him safe, falls almost exclusively upon his mother. Most children of this age have considerable resources within themselves for being busy and occupied, and also for self-protection. They are endlessly interested in their world, and they are sensible enough to understand the main prohibitions by which their mothers guard them. On the other hand, they may need a certain amount of help in starting off an occupation such as pastry-making or painting, together with intermittent assistance with difficulties as they arise—tying things, moving heavy objects, or performing the more intricate manoeuvres; they are also still creatures of impulse, responsible while they are actually thinking about traffic or fire risks, but not altogether to be trusted to remember the dangerous aspect of such situations, nor to make quick judgments in moments of emergency. Most mothers will therefore take care to be in more or less constant touch with their four-year-old: they like to be certain where he is at any time; they listen with half an ear for any alteration in the familiar sound-pattern of his play, ready to investigate the deviation which suggests mischief; and if the child is quiet on its own for more than half an hour or so, the mother will usually go and check that everything is well.

In practice, however, such checks will not often be necessary, since the child himself takes the initiative in keeping tabs on his mother. He too likes to know where she is and what she is doing; he too is alerted by a change in the background noise pattern of her work, and will come running to investigate anything which might be of interest. Problems and complaints are naturally brought to the mother; she is expected to arbitrate in quarrels, to reassure him in fear, and to minister to his hunger, thirst, cold or pain. Many children make a constant companion of their mother, following her round the house as she cleans and tidies, helping her in her housework or using her continually as an adjunct to their own play.

Factory manager's wife:

> I play with her a lot as I'm going round the house. I'm the little girl, and she's the Mummy. We get through a good morning like that.

Sales manager's wife:

> Well, this morning she had her cookery set out and a box of chocolate beans, and she was making cakes and we all had a party, with paper hats and all that, and I was doing the ironing but I sort of joined in and that.

Miner's wife:

> He's very good. I enjoy him playing with me, and he helps me a lot; he helps to make the beds and he helps me to dust.

Cycle worker's wife:

> Just before you came, she was you. She went out and knocked on the door, and she says "I'm the lady with the tape-recorder". So I says "What can I talk to you about?"

Perhaps the major demand made by the four-year-old upon his mother is indeed that she should talk to him. The year between the third and fourth birthdays is characterized by rapid progress in language development, closely allied with a steady

broadening of the child's conceptual range. This is the period of
'Why?' and 'How?' The child's clearer understanding of basic
concepts brings him to an awareness of what questions need to
be asked; his surer command of words and syntax enables him
to ask them. It is no longer enough that mechanisms work and
events happen: he wants to know *how* things work, *why* they
happen. And the fact that he is also becoming more adept at
putting a string of connected thoughts into words has the effect
of directing the adult's attention away from his earlier endearing
idiosyncrasies and verbal mannerisms, and towards the *content*
of the ideas which he is trying to communicate. This in turn
stimulates the child to express himself more adequately in whole
sentences or series of sentences, which often now have an
extremely complex grammatical structure. In short, real conversation becomes possible with a child of four, and it is probably this more than any other development which makes him
seem so much more of a personality. Most mothers welcome
their child's conversation, and find in it a source of deep pleasure
to themselves; at the same time, many also find themselves
flagging sometimes under the tirelessness of a child's continual
chatter.

Insurance agent's wife:

> I like her to take an interest in everything and anything. Yesterday
> she asked Daddy "How does the sky get up there?" I think it's
> marvellous when they start to ask questions like that. She queries
> things. Like why does smoke go up the chimney or little things,
> and I think it's marvellous when they start to take an interest.

Clerk's wife:

> I like talking to her, you know. I tend to talk a bit too grown-up
> to her at times. I forget she's only four, and I go rambling on,
> you know, as if she's a grown up sometimes. She's very quick
> when you're talking to her, to understand.

Mrs Munn, an estimator's wife, mentioned 'her conversation'
as something she especially enjoyed about Nicola; but when she
was asked 'What sort of things make you get on each other's
nerves?' she said:

> Well, I think really when she keeps asking questions, and, I
> mean, I don't mind *sensible* questions. But sometimes it's "Where

does so-and-so come from?" and then it goes on from there, until it gets ridiculous, and I just can't . . . you know . . . Well, she wants to know "Where does the bath water go?" Well, I can get it to the sea, then she wants to know where it goes from *there*! She'll start getting a bit ridiculous with it, and that *is* where we disagree.

The same question brought a similar answer from a postman's wife:

Well, she *chatters*; and if you wasn't here now, this'd be just about the time she'd have *got* on my nerves! She starts off first thing in the morning, and by about half past eleven she does *really* get you down. It's usually make-believe; but she makes me *answer* her all the time, that's the trouble.

An office manager's wife, however, found her little boy's conversation a challenge to her own mental alertness:

I enjoy his questions, quite honestly; since he's been asking questions, I've really started thinking again, more or less! (He's got an enquiring mind, has he?) Yes, he has. He's started just recently. AND he won't be put off, even with my answers—if they aren't right, you know, he wants to go further.

It is, of course, easy to over-estimate children's understanding at this age, and their very fluency as conversationalists, combined sometimes with an ability to assume the social mannerisms of their elders, often contrasts rather strikingly with a failure of comprehension which can be simultaneously bizarre and charming. At the same time, the mad logic of the four-year-old mind has a basis of practicality, so that his wildest conclusions can sound disconcertingly like common-sense; the mother who carries on a conversation of this sort with only half her mind on it can be brought back with a shock to find herself agreeing with the most outrageous propositions. There is often a Lewis Carroll quality about talk with a normal intelligent four-year-old: a child of this age, though he may enjoy the story of 'Alice', is not usually *amused* by its dialogue because it matches so well his own thought sequences.[1] Conversation with four-year-olds can

[1] Perhaps no modern writer has a better ear for small children's dialogue than Shirley Jackson; her portrayal of her young family in *Life Among the Savages* and its sequel *Raising Demons* is recommended to all students of childhood (Michael Joseph, London, 1954 and 1957).

well range freely from the sublime to the totally absurd; but in
the process the adult may sometimes be made aware of how
exciting the world can seem, if only one can borrow some of the
child's curiosity.

Interior designer's wife:
> Oh, well, I enjoy seeing things through his eyes. He sees much
> more than we do now, you know, obviously because everything's
> so much more new to him, and things we take for granted so
> much. We enjoy going out in the park, and looking at the horses
> when we see them, and we go to the Castle and the shops together.

Actor's wife:
> She can't bear the thought of never having been here. When
> I talk about what I did as a child, or things like that, she says
> "Was I in your tummy?" And so, to settle it, I said "Yes, you
> were always in my tummy", you see, and then she said the other
> day, "Were you in *your* mummy's tummy before you were born?"
> and I said "Yes", and she said "Oh, there must have been loads
> and loads of us in there!" She can't *think* that she was never
> here, you know.

As an intellectual stimulus, the importance of conversation
to an average four-year-old can hardly be too much emphasized;
and, even where there are other children in the family, it will be
the mother who supplies most of it. She is also the one to sing
songs with him and to explain the words, to draw his attention to
new experiences, to count and to name colours, and to repeat
bedtime prayers; she may even be important in passing on to
him the traditional skills of her own childhood: skipping, top-
whipping and ball-bouncing, and the incantations which go
with them.

Builder's labourer's wife:
> If she's playing at ball, I say "Let's have a go, duck", and she'll
> chuck it to me and I'll chuck it back. Or if she's trying to skip,
> I try and learn her to skip. (And do you skip too?) Oh, yes!
> (Are you playing like a mother or teacher, or are you playing like
> a child when you're playing ball?) Well, I throw it up, and I try
> and learn her to play, and to say what you *do* say. She's got a lot
> of little tennis balls, you see, and I say, "Now, you throw that
> one, and I'll throw this one, and let's see if we can chuck it—you

know—and you say what *I* say", you see, and then she tries to say the words what I'm saying, you see.

Usually, then, for any four-year-old his mother is his most constant source of social interaction, and it is clear that it is not only the child whose needs are satisfied by this. It was often stressed by our informants that from this particular child, grown out of babyhood and as yet undistracted by school, they derived real companionship; to have a child of this age may indeed do much to mitigate a housebound mother's sense of isolation. The point was well made by one young woman who had recently been deserted by her lorry-driver husband:

Well, really, we're more like sisters, you know, than mother and daughter. We've been together all the time. You see, she talks to me like a grown-up, and of course I talk back to her. I never talk to her baby talk. I've always spoken to her as a grown-up, and, well she likes nearly everything I like, you see, and she goes everywhere I go.

These two are entirely dependent upon each other; Mrs Adam's isolation is that of the mother of nine, the rest of whose family is out all day:

Oh, we get a lot of laughs—the things and that, that she does! At the moment she's got the twist craze, she does the twist (dance). And, you know, some of the things she says—she says some funny things. She talks to you a lot, you know, if she's been anywhere or anything. She'll tell you about it, you know. She goes to the Salvation Army, and she really enjoys it, and she'll come home and sing and tell you all about it and that. You couldn't feel lonely, you know, because she talks to you quite a lot.

A garage manager's wife, although she had another child eighteen months younger, added, 'I don't want him to go to school really. I think I shall miss him a lot.'

Where there is no baby to limit their scope, mother and child are able to indulge in little outings together—to the shops, to the park, or on more ambitious expeditions to a cinema or into town—and it is difficult to say which of the two derives most pleasure from these trips, which sometimes seem to have an almost conspiratorial quality of enjoyment.

Long-distance lorry driver's wife:

> Last week we made haste with the housework, and the older one was stopping to dinner at school, you see, so we went off in the bus to town. We had a look round Marks and Spencer's, only we didn't buy anything, and then we went and had us dinner in Woolworth's, she loves doing that, you see. And then we went and saw that Cliff Richard film, what is it, 'Summer Holiday', and she thought that was smashing, so after that we came home and she was dancing round all teatime, showing her Dad how they went on in the film and that.

University lecturer's wife:

> One thing *I* get tremendous pleasure out of, is *her* capacity for enjoying little treats. And not necessarily treats for her—for instance, if I take her out shopping and we go to buy some clothes. It doesn't matter whether it's something for her or for me, and it doesn't matter whether it's a new dress or just a vest or a pair of socks, she gets a thrill out of choosing and discussing and deciding. Shopping is a thing I enjoy myself, however dull the things are that I'm buying, so this is really something we get a *lot* of fun out of together. I think she's got a natural dress sense, she's *interested* in what things look good on her and what doesn't; so we have a lot of fun and we come home very pleased with ourselves.

The child's increased intellectual and communicative ability has two major effects upon his mother's attempts to control his behaviour: on the positive side, it is now possible to reason with him; on the negative, he can now oppose his reason to hers, often only too convincingly. Along with his questioning of the whys and wherefores of the world may go an argumentative, negativistic attitude towards his mother's wishes, which sometimes seems to be founded more in a desire to show independence through a purely verbal opposition than in any real intention to disobey.

Milkman's wife:

> He makes excuses—he's always got an answer! Although he does *do* the things; but he's always got to have his little word *first*, and that makes me real cross. I know he's going to do it, but as I say, he always has to have this little argument, he'll say "I don't want to do it" or "I'm just doing so-and-so".

'Answering back', 'rudeness', 'cheekiness'—these symptoms of the child's greater linguistic fluency in communication begin to assume great importance to the mother in her dealing with him, and many children quickly discover just how powerful is this verbal weapon in upsetting their mother's equilibrium. Not many mothers find themselves able to take the positive attitude of Mrs Trease, a research chemist's wife: 'I don't mind cheek when it's experimenting with words, because that's really quite creative!' Although some find 'funny cheek' amusing and permissible, though not exactly to be encouraged, 'defiant cheek' is almost always reacted to as threatening, particularly if it is witnessed by outsiders.

Works manager's wife:

I hate children to be cheeky at all. One thing I really do hate, and he does it occasionally, is, you know, mocking you and saying exactly what you've said. If I happen to be correcting him about anything, it really annoys me when he starts to mock you, everything you say, especially when I'm angry. Of course, normal conversations when he does that, I don't mind, I don't consider that as cheeky; but it's if you happen to be correcting him in any way. It really gets me, that does.

Foreman's wife:

I can't stand cheeky children. No real cheekiness, by any means. I mean, all children are a bit inclined to ... mind you, *we* weren't as children, I don't know what's different about us to our parents, but I would never dare to answer my mother back. I don't mean they were cruel to me, but it just wasn't in us to ... well, we just *didn't* answer back in those days, did we, even the teachers were different at school, you were frightened to say ... but now, I mean, they talk to their teachers as if they're talking to another child, sort of thing, don't they? I would never stand for any *real* cheekiness, and I would *never* stand for a child showing me up outside. Well, if they show me up inside, then I would talk to them and explain to them, talk to them the best way I could, but if they showed me up outside, then I would smack them most definitely.

We shall be returning later on to this whole question, which basically involves a loss-of-face confrontation; from the developmental point of view, the advent of 'cheek' is interesting because

it marks a new stage in the child's ability to manipulate inter-
personal situations. Many children of four are socially very
mature; certainly children of this age are capable of responding
to other people in ways which are both subtle and sophisticated.
In fact, their ability to show such complex 'adult' emotions as
indignation, disdain, shame, embarrassment and wounded pride
often seems to contrast quite strikingly with their much more
limited ability to understand relatively simple logical explanations. Sometimes they display, and use, an insight into personal
relationships which is disconcerting.

Social worker's wife:

> I think probably James is very cunning at a kind of exploitation
> of situations. He's terribly good at it for one so young! He has a
> marvellous technique of rubbing my husband and myself up the
> wrong way so that we end up fighting with *one another*, and this
> really reduces me to a state of impotent fury. This sort of thing
> he is very good at, he's a great judge of situations.

Where there is already some lack of harmony, the child can be
wilfully disruptive.

Railwayman's wife:

> Answering back? I never heard anything like it! (Do you mind?)
> Well, I do, but I don't know what to do about it. I mean, like—I
> don't smack her hard, but she's got a will of her own, Vicky has.
> (What sort of thing . . .?) She keeps repeating she's going to tell
> her Dad. Not that it's anything wrong. But it annoys me to
> think that children can repeat to their Dad and cause trouble,
> sort of thing. But he believes her. I mean, if there's anyone he
> dislikes—I said to her "We'll go to Aunt Edie's this afternoon",
> I said, "but don't tell your Dad". He'd only been in half a minute—
> first thing she comes out with, "Daddy, we've been to Aunt
> Edie's this afternoon, but I haven't got to tell you"!

Cycle worker's wife:

> He does come in sometimes and say his Dad's hit him, because
> he knows I don't agree with it, and all the time his Dad *hasn't*
> hit him. And his Dad says "I *will* give you a good hiding for
> saying that", you know.

Cutter's wife:

> This morning I had to smack her, and she stood there and said
> "I want my Daddy, I want my Daddy", because if he's in he

shouts at me for hitting her. He doesn't agree with me hitting
her. He doesn't chastise them—not in the way I do. He just tells
them. Of course Mitzie answers back occasionally—well, more
often than not—and he laughs at her, and I don't like that. And
that's why she tries to do what she can to me, you see. If I smack
her—same as this morning, she said "Don't you smack me. I'm
telling my Dad of you when he comes home. My Dad says you
haven't got to hit me". You see—then she gets another one.
I say "I couldn't care less. If you go tell your Daddy, you'll get
another one". And that's it.

Also sometimes interpreted as 'cheek' or 'getting a bit above
himself' is the adoption of adult social postures, often with a
deadly accuracy quite discomposing to the mother who recognizes in them her own behaviour. Little girls particularly tend
to be adept at reproducing the conventions of polite adult dialogue in their play, and, with especial skill, caricaturing their
parents' righteous tones over the misdemeanours of dolls,
siblings, or even their own mothers. Most mothers enjoy the
comic aspect of their own mannerisms exaggerated into pom-
posity in so small a child, and the common attitude is a rueful
acceptance—it is hardly fair to scold a child for imitating its own
mother!

Bleacher's wife:
Well, to be quite honest with you, I enjoy the part that I really
ought to smack her for—well, not smack her, shout at her.
Stuart (older brother) wouldn't defy you, and he'd very rarely
answer you back. Now Edwina's the type who'll have the last
of anything if it kills her!—and sometimes I say "Now, Edwina,
I won't tell you again", and she'll talk back, you know—"Always
*bellowing*"—and she'll sit like this, you know, and *mesmerize* you,
her head nodding away, and I say, "And don't you talk to me like
that!"—"Well, you made me do it, I *told* you not to go on at me".
And she's ever so serious about it, and I have to turn my head
away to smile. Then I tell her, "Now you go and do so-and-so,
I won't tell you again", and she says "Oh, all *right*", and she
really gets hold of this door, you know, and walks out and gives a
final exit! I sit there and kill myself laughing, more at the expressions
than anything. And if I tell Stuart to do something, she says
"You do as Mummy tells you". She's an awful little madam. I
really ought to say, "You just have a bit less, Edwina, I'll do the
chastising, not you". But she's so funny that even Stuart turns

to me, and we look at one another and laugh. She's so very serious, and as I say, I really ought to let her know what her place is. But she's comic with it, and we let her get away with it.

**Publisher's wife:**

Very often he'll say something and it's something I've said myself to him, and it can be quite disconcerting. Well, he's said to me, "That's the sort of thing you get your bottom smacked for!"—but, I mean, you can't grumble at it, because it's what you've said to him.

The four-year-old's satisfaction in the rehearsal of adult roles is necessarily accompanied by an interest in observing and communicating with adults both inside and outside the family. Here again, his new-found linguistic facility is directly contributive to the widening of his social horizons; the child whose vocabulary is small and whose pronunciation is idiosyncratic finds it difficult to make himself understood by strangers, but most four-year-olds can successfully ask for an extra pint from the milkman, pass the time of day with the baker's boy, and even run down to the corner shop for a couple of things their mother wants in a hurry. Tradesmen calling at the door, local authority maintenance men, bus conductors and shop assistants all seem to enjoy chatting to young children—at least, in Nottingham they usually take the initiative in doing so— and the child who is ready and willing to talk back will quickly build himself a growing circle of adult friends and acquaintances, each of whom has a function in opening up for him new avenues of interest. Some of them will open his eyes to work roles quite different from that of his own father; some, in shops particularly, will actively help him to learn such social lessons as waiting one's turn, making requests in an acceptable manner and paying one's way. Some, by mischance or by some thoughtless action, become figures of terror and horror; others, all unknowing, are endowed by the child with a heroic glamour. Men down holes and up ladders are usually prepared to pass on a little specialized knowledge to the inquisitive onlooker; neighbouring children's parents introduce the child, directly or indirectly, to the notions of different expectations, different standards, different values—and different maternal attitudes: 'Philippa's mother', one of our daughters informed us darkly, 'is *not as nice as you might think*'.

For any pre-school child, whether his friends and playmates are congenial, or indeed whether he has anyone to play with at all, is very much a matter of luck. His physical restriction to the area immediately surrounding his own house means that he is limited almost entirely to children living close at hand; he cannot go farther afield in order to widen his choice. For some children, this will mean no peer-group company at all; they are completely dependent upon being taken to other children's homes, or having other children brought on visits to them.

Miner's wife:

> He plays with other children when he has the chance, yes. You see, there are a lot of children round here, but they're all over that big road (a very dangerous narrow hill with constant heavy traffic)—there's quite a large family of children, seven of them, over the road, and some of the children he could play with, but the trouble is, you see, he has to get to them. Now it's all right, I could take him across, but he's liable to run back again. You see, they might say "Oh, go and ask your Mum for something", and he'll come running over the road. Well, although he's pretty good at crossing roads, he isn't old enough to realize that those buses can start off at any time, so I don't let him go across, and there isn't really any children this side, his age, that he can play with.

For others, their lack of mobility may result in their being plagued by the inescapable presence of some child who frightens or hurts them.

Administrative assistant's wife:

> It was very difficult, the boy next door used to beat the living daylights out of him; he used to hate this. It was very mixed: he wanted to play on his own to get peace and quiet, but he wanted to play with other children as well. It was a bit difficult to draw a happy medium.

Most of these children, however, do apparently succeed in finding at least one reasonably pleasant playmate of similar age, and do in fact spend a fair amount of time playing with them. Four-year-olds enjoy the company of their peers, although, as we shall see presently, these paths of friendship are by no means thornless. For those who can find no other children with whom

to play and squabble and play once more, there are the moderately satisfying alternatives of playing with mother and finding
companions in fantasy; and perhaps the physical circumscrip-
tion of these children's lives has much to do with the fact that
this is a peak age both for fantasy playmates and for fantasy
events. These topics, too, we shall be examining more closely.

One means of providing both adult and child companionship
is, of course, the nursery school, play group or day nursery.
This is easier said than done, however: in Nottingham, as in
most of Britain, it is not easy to find a place in an education
authority nursery school (registration on the waiting list as
soon as possible after birth is advised, and some eager parents
register their children before birth); and other nursery education is not cheap, even if a vacancy can be found. For some
children, the shortage of nursery schools causes real frustration, not just because they are ready for a companionship which
does not exist within their geographical range, but because
intellectually they are reaching out for new experience with an
impatience which their parents are quite unable to satisfy.
Accommodation difficulties, shortage of money, or personal
inadequacies in the mother herself (of which she may be fully
aware): these can make it impossible for her to provide the
opportunities for physical, conceptual and social adventure and
experiment which the intelligent four-year-old so badly needs,
and which the good nursery school or play-group is so well
equipped to supply. Only 11% of our sample attends any sort
of nursery group; and this includes a range of attendance from
the long hours of the day nursery, through full-time and half-
time nursery schools and classes, to the play-groups, run in the
main by enthusiastic amateurs and taking some children for
only a few hours a week.[1]

No discussion of the intellectual and social world of the four-
year-old can afford to neglect the influence of television, now
almost universally an important element of his daily life. The
child of three, with his more limited comprehension, will not
have the patience to sit still for long in front of the screen, but
by the age of four most children are capable of following at
least some programmes with rapt attention. If they have older

[1] A discussion of the different types of nursery groups contemporaneously
available in Great Britain will be found in Elizabeth Newson: 'Provision for
the Pre-School Child'; in British Federation of University Women, 1966, op. cit.

siblings, this in itself will provide a social context in which it is companionable to watch television at certain times of the day. Indeed, for some children the pattern of family life in the early evening seems to be geared more closely to the television schedule than to the clock. A miner's wife, discussing her little boy's bedtime, said:

> Well, it's half past six Mondays; seven o'clock on Tuesdays; 6.30 Wednesdays; 6.30 Thursdays and seven o'clock on Friday; and in the weekends it's 6.30. It's all to fit the television, you see.

Our interview was not specifically designed to throw light upon the influence of television on children in the pre-school age group, and we are therefore in no position to comment on the emotional involvement of children when watching programmes which might be considered unsuitable for them. It is, however, quite clear from mothers' spontaneous comments (especially in connection with our questions about fears, fantasies, bedtime and telling children the 'facts of life') that they do watch a very wide variety of programmes which must inevitably serve to widen their experience, in the sense that even very young children today have a window through which to view a whole world of people, phenomena, artefacts and events of which an earlier generation of children could never have become aware until a much later age. And this in itself stimulates them to ask questions and to follow up trains of thought—sometimes to the embarrassment of their parents. Both the following quotations are in answer to the question 'Does he know where babies come from?'

Dry cleaner's wife:

> I hope he won't ask me yet. But he watches the TV, you know, and he sees these schools programmes—there was one about fishes the other day—and I don't know if he works on them in his little mind and puts two and two together, but he hasn't said anything about it *yet*.

Tobacco packer's wife:

> Oh yes, she knows! She saw a cow being born on television the other day!

Quite aside from television's influence upon the child's range of knowledge, of course, it is likely to play some part in his appraisal of social relationships. If observation of the ways of other children's families and other children's mothers is important to the child's social development, one cannot help speculating upon the effect of the endless succession of sweetly idealized television 'mummies' who so devotedly minister to their children's needs during every commercial break. But no doubt the depth psychologists of the advertising agencies have this particular factor well under control.

In this chapter we have tried to show that the distinctive characteristic of the child at this age is a strongly marked personality with a new interest in social relationships and a new ability to manipulate them. No-one with a four-year-old in the house can avoid being conscious of him as a very individual person with very definite needs and opinions. In his interactions with his mother or with anyone else, he is not simply passive and responsive: he initiates actions, he makes requests and demands, suggestions and counter-suggestions. Already he shows clear personality traits: he may be adventurous or timid, cheeky or bashful, placid and equable or 'difficult' and 'highly strung'. He may tensely anticipate each new ordeal, or sit back and wait for things to happen; he may be quiet and thoughtful, or rumbustious and devil-may-care.

Publisher's wife:

> (What sort of things do you specially enjoy in him?) Well, I think it's a sort of mixed relationship. He's full of fun, he's a *lively* little boy, and he's also a very self-willed one. I enjoy the fact that he *is* lively, and that I can play with him and do things *with* him. The older boy is more a dreamer and a thinker, and you could hold much more of an intelligent conversation with him at four than you can with Neill; but I can *romp* with Neill far more than Martin wanted to romp. I do enjoy the fact that he is lively and boisterous.

No two children are quite alike, and different children call forth a different kind of response from their parents. In the last chapter we emphasized that the family circumstances place obvious limits on the ability of parents to behave as they might ideally wish to behave towards their children. As one talks to them, it soon becomes equally clear that their methods of child-rearing tend to be influenced and altered according to the

C

personality of the individual child, either because it is found that their preferred method simply does not work, is not expedient, with this child, or because it brings about such conflict with the child that neither side can tolerate it any longer. It was often said to us, 'Of course, I should have answered that one differently if it had been Tommy we were talking about'; 'You should have come to see me about Susan, she's a lot more difficult/straight-forward/interesting/typical of my children'. Throughout our discussions of specific areas of child-rearing, we shall find examples of parental behaviour modified and controlled by the force of the child's own personality; at the same time, we shall also find other forces, of class and environment in particular, which help to decide to what degree and in what direction modi-fication shall take place.

# CHAPTER 4

# PRESSURES FOR INDEPENDENCE

We suggested in the last chapter that the four-year-old's capacity for behaving in any particular manner is in practice of lesser importance than his mother's expectations about such behaviour. The degree to which a child is expected to look after his own immediate needs or to contribute in any way to the work of the household is a case in point. It is one characteristic of this particular culture pattern at this particular time that children of pre-school age are required to do hardly anything which could be called work, or which is either necessary or even useful to family or community. In fact, the idea that four-year-olds normally spend all their time playing is accepted so completely that it comes as a shock to remember the position of working-class children not much more than a hundred years ago, and to realise that the productive employment of children was not confined to the over-sixes who were exploited in mines and factories, but extended into the cottage sweat shops to include the youngest members of the labouring family. 'The age at which children began to work at domestic industries', says Pinchbeck, 'was in many instances younger than that of factory children. In pillow lace, children were taught to handle the bobbins as mere infants of three and four years old, and were often working regular hours in a lace school at five. In straw plaiting, children were sorting straws at four, plaiting at five and earning a regular wage at six . . . . In the machine lace trade, the Report of 1843[1] states: "It is common in this district (Notts, Derby and Leicester) for children to commence work at four, five and six; the evidence renders this fact indubitable". In one extreme instance personally investigated by the Commissioner, a child of four years had been drawing lace for two years, and was then working twelve hours a day with only a quarter of an

[1] Report from the Commissioners on the Employment of Women and Children in Agriculture, 1843, XII.

hour interval for breakfast, dinner and tea, and never going out to play'.[1]

The Industrial Revolution intensified and organized the use of child labour, and so finally brought about a revulsion in the public conscience; but the underlying expectation that the country's labouring force should include small children had a very long history, and was by no means itself a product of industrialization, as O. J. Dunlop points out: '. . . . it was more natural than not that children should work. There was no compulsory school attendance to prevent their doing so; there was no feeling that work was bad for them; the labour and poor laws of Elizabeth's time are imbued with the idea that children could and should work, while philanthropists of the late eighteenth century regarded it as a matter for congratulation when the inmates of a charitable home or school could maintain themselves as soon as they could crawl'.[2] And it is worth noting that the efforts of the earlier reformers were directed, not against the principle that children should work, but merely against the conditions in which they were allowed to do so.

Among our own four-year-olds, by contrast, very few children indeed are given even the simplest of household tasks to perform as a regular duty. A few mothers mentioned that a child might be *allowed* to wash up (it is significant that this would arise in answer to our question about water play); some said that they occasionally helped with dusting and polishing, or that they sometimes laid the table. Only very rarely, however, were children positively requested to do such things, and these activities might more properly be regarded as an extension of the child's play, a role rehearsal undertaken on his own initiative, and usually involving as an important incentive the mother's own presence and companionship.

Window cleaner's wife:

> If she got fed up, she'd come and help me with mopping the floor or dusting or something.

[1] I. Pinchbeck: *Women Workers and the Industrial Revolution, 1750–1850*, Routledge, London, 1930.

[2] O. J. Dunlop: *English Apprenticeship and Child Labour*, Macmillan Co., New York, 1912.

Driver's wife:

> I think she does as much as she could at her age. Often when I'm washing up, she'll say "Can I wipe a spoon, Mummy?" and I let her do it, because I think it's not . . . it's kind of a game we play, "Oh, I'm helping Mummy". She likes to do it. But I wouldn't —I mean, she's a child, a baby really, you could say—I don't believe in *making* her.

There are two exceptions to the child's general exemption from household chores, and both of them are outside the ordinary run of housework. One is tidying up; the other is the running of errands. Tidying at this age involves only the clearing up of the child's own playthings, and we shall look at this presently, together with other forms of self-help; running errands is certainly a way in which the child may contribute to the general work of the household, and is much less clearly related to his own needs.

Most four-year-olds speak plainly enough to make themselves understood by a neighbour or shopkeeper, and most are responsible enough to keep instructions in mind for ten minutes or so. Normally, the four-year-old is also the oldest child in the family who is readily available at any time of the day. Thus, in working-class districts especially, mothers do expect their children to interrupt their play occasionally in order to take a message to a neighbour or to fetch something from the shop. Simple messages and shopping errands need to be separated here, however. The first involves only the reasonably accurate repetition of what the mother has told the child to say: 'Mam's going to town, do you want any errands doing?'; 'Mummy says thank you for lending her the onion, and here's one back'. Shopping involves not only remembering the requirements but waiting one's turn and taking it when it arrives, dealing with money and change, and perhaps making decisions as to alternatives. But this difference in difficulty is offset by a difference in practical usefulness, in that shopping is something which in fact happens far more often than the need to send messages to a neighbour; it is also a skill which many mothers feel the child should be taught, whereas they tend to assume that he could communicate with a neighbour if it were necessary, and do not consciously give him practice in this. A fairly frequent response to our question 'Does he ever take messages for you?' was 'Well, he could, but it doesn't really arise'. 62% of the randomized sample do in fact take messages; a very few can even cope with the telephone, although of course most children do not have the opportunity for this.

Grocer's wife:

> Oh yes, she's very good. She answered the 'phone a *year* ago. She came back and said my friend was on the 'phone, and I didn't believe her, because she'd never answered the 'phone before, and she went back and said "I'm very sorry, Aunty, but Mummy won't come. She doesn't want to talk to you". So my friend guessed what had happened. So she sent her back again with another message. So I thought I'd better investigate, and she'd had the sense to leave the 'phone dangling at the side.

Inevitably, at this age, there are also some children whose self-possession is not yet secure enough outside the family circle for them to manage a social task of this sort.

Display artist's wife:

> She *would* do; but I don't think I could tell her anything to tell them, she'd be too shy to say it, to get it out, you know; I'd p'raps have to write it down or something.

But a few have the maturity to manufacture social situations on their own initiative.

Factory manager's wife:

> Yes, she does take messages, but she makes them up as she goes along. It's her own method. We once had a tea-party because of that. She said "Are you fed up, Mummy?" I said "Yes"; and a few minutes later I'd got two neighbours knocking on the door to see if I was all right. She'd fetched them in. She said "Well, I thought you'd like to make them a cup of tea". That is something I very rarely do, so they thought something *was* the matter!

The question we asked about shopping was: 'Does he ever go into a shop or to an ice-cream van on his own?' If the mother replied that the shop was too far away or the road too dangerous, we asked 'But does he ever go into a shop on his own while you wait outside?', in the expectation that there would be a number of mothers who would be unwilling to send their children out alone, but who at the same time would want them to acquire this particular social skill. This in fact turned out to be so. The overall proportion of children who make their own purchases, one way or another, is 79%.

There are thus several factors to be discerned in the question of whether a child shops on his own, and we will try to illustrate these. The first, and the decisive one if it is in the negative, is the child's capacity in terms of either social or linguistic maturity. We have no reason for thinking that this, for shopping purposes at least, is class-loaded in any way:[1] the following examples were chosen without regard for their occupational class.

Joiner's wife:
> She just won't. I'm afraid she's rather a shy child, Sally is.

Office manager's wife:
> No, he *never* does, because he's a mother's clinging boy.

Labourer's wife:
> I wait at the door, because there are some words he can't say properly.

Teacher's wife:
> She's not very confident—she tends to offer the money and then expect it back, things like that!

Machine operator's wife:
> When we're up at the top of the road, shopping, I'll say to her "Just go in there"—if I just want one thing—"and get me a tin of meat for the dog". And, you know, she'll just stand there in the shop, and then she'll shout and ask *me* to tell the man what she wants, you see! And she'll refuse to give him the money— she thinks it's hers! They have to come round the corner and take it off her.

The second factor is a geographical one: how possible is it for the child to reach a shop without crossing a busy main road?

[1] This is not to disagree with Bernstein and his associates. Clearly, linguistic facility, particularly the expression of abstractions, is associated with social class. On the other hand, in this particular situation, familiarity with rather inflexible linguistic patterns may well be an advantage, since confidence to get through the transaction acceptably is what is required.

Here there is a very definite class difference in favour of the working-class child living in a central area; most of the terraced streets have their small grocery and sweet shop, and it is rare indeed for a child in such a district to have to cross anything busier than a narrow back street in order to reach it from his home. The shops which serve council estates and middle-class residential areas, on the other hand, tend to be grouped together in busy roads; and their average distance from the child's home will naturally be greater: a trip to the nearest shop and back may well take him a good half-hour, too much for most mothers' peace of mind at this age.

Publican's wife:

> We are in a difficult position here, being on a busy street, but even if I was in a private house I wouldn't like her to go out alone at this age. I should be on edge all the time, wondering what was happening.

Another aspect of the geographical factor is that patrolling ice-cream vans are far more numerous in working-class areas, to such an extent as to be a considerable nuisance to the mother who has to face the demands of her children several times a day.

A third factor, which can counteract the geographical consideration, is the mother's consciousness that shopping is a useful skill, to be purposively encouraged and fostered, often in the face of the child's own shyness. This feeling is expressed by mothers of all classes, although possibly for different reasons. The next informant has come to a compromise with her little girl: she insists that the child should go into the shop on her own, but she is ready to support her if need be. This also illustrates rather well the way a very small hitch can baffle a child at this social stage.

Salesman's wife:

> She goes in on her own, but she always insists that I stand at the door; and I think that's because once she had an orange sucker, and she liked it, but next time she went they gave her a pink one, and she turned to me because she only likes the orange ones; and I think that's why she wants me at the door, to say she only likes the orange ones—I think it was a little bit of confidence she lacked, to *tell* them she only liked the orange ones.

Mrs Ripton, a shop assistant's wife, is both worried and irritated by Beverley's dependence, which she blames on the indulgence of the child's father who has 'ruined her completely'.

> The other week I gave her threepence and told her to go and buy herself a lollipop. But she said "No, *you* come, Mummy". She was a little bit nervous and shy. And I *made* her go. I said "All right, Beverley, we won't *have* an ice-cream", and walked away, and she *did* get it on her own.

One further factor is the extent to which this skill is of immediate practical value to the mother, and for various reasons this again favours the working-class child. There are few telephones in working-class areas; child messengers form a useful part of the communications network, and are frequently rewarded for their efforts by payment of a few coppers. The use of children fits in well with working-class shopping habits: working-class wives in the older districts do not expect to keep well-filled store-cupboards, nor to have a weekly order delivered, but rather to 'pop down to the shop' as and when provisions are needed and money is available. One mother sent four-year-old Raymond to the same shop on three separate errands during the interview, first for a packet of tea, then for potatoes, then (when the gas-man had called and given her a rebate of seven shillings) for some cigarettes; for each of these expeditions, Raymond received a penny, the immediate spending of which involved him in three further visits to the shop. It is clear that many working-class mothers do in fact rely on their children to help them in this way, and that, for these children, running errands is their first experience of a household job which is recognised as theirs. Raymond had done errands willingly in our presence; but his willingness was not an important consideration, as his mother made plain when we asked her later what happened when he didn't want to do as he was told:

> Just have to make him. I mean, if I want him to go to the shop, I make him go. (How?) Take him to the front door; even if I've got to march up the road with him, I'd do it.

Raymond is an unusually independent and resourceful little boy, and perhaps his mother's demands have been stepped up to

c*

match his temperament; but the expectation of this sort of help is common in central areas, though most mothers are more appreciative while the child is so young. Patrick is the latest in a line of ten helpful children, with three more to follow him; his father is an Irish labourer.

> Yes, he can do it perfectly, like. He's the only lad I have here now to do anything for me. During the holidays which are now over, I've taught Patrick to put the little message-bag on his shoulder, like, and a little note into it for the shopkeeper, and he knows where to go—gives his note and then comes back home with it. Eventually, then, every morning I gave him sixpence then, to go into the next shop, which is a bit up further, and I always get him six penn'orth of some kind of sweets or something—I don't say I'm paying him for doing a message, but it cheers him up afterwards. It's kind of encouragement, but I don't really let him know *why* I'm giving him the sixpence.

The combined effects of greater opportunity and greater pressure for working-class children to do shopping is reflected in the figures, which show a significant difference between non-manual and manual workers' children. 81% of working-class children show this form of independence, compared with 72% of middle-class children. What is interesting about the middle-class figure, however, is that, despite the geographical difficulties involved, it is so high. Shopping for oneself is clearly regarded as an important stage in growing up, and one which most children are expected to have mastered before they reach school age.

*'They're still babies until they go to school'*
*'I think they should be made to do everything'*
For the great majority of children, then, there is little pressure to undertake useful tasks for the benefit of others; even shopping errands will normally be a pleasure rather than a chore, the shopping list so often including sweets or ice-cream for the shopper. However, there are other ways in which a four-year-old can be helpful to his mother: simply by helping himself and by becoming more or less independent in such things as dressing, undressing and going to the lavatory, he does in fact relieve her of a time-consuming and often burdensome task. In these very basic activities, the child's co-operation is in any case necessary;

and he will also tend to become involved in related personal jobs—folding up such clothes as are to be worn again next day and tidying toys away. These are all things that ordinary children of this age can do independently if they want to; we were interested to find out whether they did in fact do these things in practice, and to gauge how much pressure towards self-help was exerted by their mothers.

Our questions on *what actually happens* appear in Table V, together with a breakdown of the answers given. In general, 'helps a lot' means that the mother is very much in charge of the operation and that it will take her some time; she puts clothes on and takes them off, does most of the tidying and accompanies the child to the lavatory, or at least pulls up pants for him. This category demands only token help from the child, who is for the most part a rather passive participant. 'Some help' denotes mainly supervisory but not very time-consuming assistance— the mother copes with buttons, tight jerseys and tucking in, she picks up a few toys as encouragement, she wipes the child clean after a bowel movement—in general, this is the *child's* activity, in which the mother lends a hand where things get too difficult. The category 'no help' means what it says, except that doing up shoe-laces and back buttons seemed so rarely possible for four-year-olds that we did not rate this as 'help'.

With the exception of the more awkward fastenings, most children of four can be assumed to have the skill necessary to

TABLE V

*Self-help*

| Question asked | M. helps a lot | M. gives some help | No help given |
|---|---|---|---|
| | % | % | % |
| Does he usually dress himself in the morning? | 28 | 55 | 17 |
| Does he undress himself at night? | 17 | 44 | 39 |
| Does he tidy up his clothes when he's taken them off? | 49 | 25 | 26 |
| When he goes to the toilet, does he look after himself? (Wipe himself?) | 9 | 32 | 59 |
| What about clearing up things he's been playing with? | 23 | 43 | 34 |

dress themselves; but in practice, it seems, the majority receive a good deal of help—for various reasons, as we shall see. The more slapdash activity of undressing requires far less precision and concentration; as one might expect, a considerably greater proportion of children manage this independently, but only about one in four carry it through to the point of making a neat pile of their clothes—the rest leave them wherever they happen to drop. For each of these first three items, incidentally—all connected with clothes—girls are significantly more self-reliant than boys.

At four the child is definitely expected to take himself to the lavatory, and more than half manage this entirely alone; but almost a third are helped at least to the extent of wiping or tucking in, and 9% normally are accompanied to the lavatory: this category includes a number of children who have problems in that they soil or are afraid of the lavatory or suffer from separation anxiety. In about one case in three, the mother seems to have trained the child to put away his toys without help, though not necessarily without nagging.

We combined the replies to these five questions on the child's actual self-help into a rating of independence in this area for each child. It must be remembered that what is being assessed here is what the child *in fact* does for himself, which will be a product of his own temperament, inclination and ability, and his mother's demands—demands which are themselves determined by her temperament, her circumstances and her awareness of the child's own needs. The proportions given in Table VI are again for a randomized sample.

TABLE VI

*General independence in self-help*

| Highly independent (3 or more 'no help') | Moderately independent | Not very independent | Dependent (4–5 'helps a lot') |
|---|---|---|---|
| % | % | % | % |
| 28 | 37 | 29 | 6 |

An analysis of class differences in self-help is not very productive; there is some indication that middle-class children are given more assistance in these things than working-class children, but this difference only reaches a significant level in the matter of coping with the lavatory. Only 49% of middle-class children are completely independent here, compared with 62% of working-class children. That significance is reached in this case alone probably merely reflects a greater concern for clean bottoms and tidily arranged clothing among middle-class mothers. A further test to compare these more personal tasks with the social tasks of taking messages and shopping does show a correlation, in that children who have less help in the former are a good deal more likely to be managing these social skills also.[1]

As a general conclusion on four-year-olds' functional independence, it appears that children of this age are not for the most part called upon to do as much as they are known to be capable of, even in helping themselves, and that often they would be reasonably willing to do more than is in fact asked of them. To understand why the pressures for independence are so restrained, we must turn again to the mothers' own feelings. We asked them: 'What do you feel about making a child do things for himself at this age? Do you think he should be made to do things for himself, even if he doesn't want to?' These questions were followed by others, designed to assess the mother's concern that her child should be able to cope with his own personal needs, and her satisfaction or otherwise with his achievement so far in this respect.[2] The resulting discussion raised a number of interesting points.

Simple habit is one factor which must operate to a greater or lesser extent in a majority of cases. For every child, there has been a time when it was *necessary* to do everything for him. This period lasts for at least a year, but usually a good deal longer; and during this time the mother works herself into a routine of caring for the child. In the normal way, the child gradually takes over for himself the easier jobs, such as undressing, while still continuing to receive help with tasks in which he is as yet incapable or inefficient. In most children's progress towards independence, their mothers will also have the added motivation of having their hands full, literally, as younger siblings arrive, truly helpless in their turn. But if the four-year-old is the youngest or only child, then the habit of doing things for him may well die hard, even against the mother's better judgment.

[1] See Appendix II.                    [2] See interview schedule, Appendix I.

Publican's wife:

> I think she should be doing more than she is. She's always relied on me a little bit too much, I think. I've noticed it more since I've had the baby; I didn't realize I was doing so much for her.

Civil servant's wife:

> I sort of go along in a trance, and then I suddenly realize, and say "Why should *I* do all this, when *you're* old enough to do this? Now come along, let's *all* help . . . ."

There does seem to be a general consensus of opinion that children at four are old enough to make some contribution towards looking after themselves; the attitude that 'they're still babies till they go to school', echoed in the next quotation, is not at all typical.

Twist hand's wife:

> No, I don't think they should really—I think it's wrong. I think while children are under school age, the parents should more or less do everything for them.

Most parents feel that it is not enough for the child merely to stand passively to have his clothes put on and taken off; nor should he demand his mother's presence with him in the lavatory. At the same time, there is a general realization that children are often reluctant to do these things to order, and that it requires patience and tact, and above all, time, to overcome this. In other words, most mothers recognize—sometimes from personal experience with a previous child—that satisfactory results are not best achieved by forcing the pace, and that it is particularly futile to get the child into an emotional and negativistic state over independence. Nor is it pleasant for the mother herself. The most frequent response to these questions, therefore, was in some form an objection to the phrase 'Do you think he should be *made* to do things . . . ?'

Administrator's wife:

> Well, *encouraged*, I think perhaps, instead of *made*. I mean, I don't hold myself up as an example, but I'm afraid I don't actually *make* David do anything, and I've found him most co-operative. But we do it rather by, well, discussing *why* he doesn't want to

do a thing. I never actually force him to do anything. But I find that he's very reasonable, and I think it's because I've been fairly —I treat him as an adult, you see, as far as possible.

## Labourer's wife:

I don't say *make* them do. You know, I try to *get* them to do more for themselves. But I wouldn't really *force* them to do it—I mean, that'd be idle-itis on my part, sort of thing. But I like to tell them that they must learn to do things for themselves.

## Miner's wife:

I've been rather worried about him being slow at doing things himself. But I shouldn't force anything on them, no. 'Cause I think you set up a barrier, sort of thing. You've sort of got to humour them, and, er, encourage them, haven't you, to do these things.

## Stone caster's wife:

Yes, he's quite good about tidying—better than the other one was! (Do you think he should be made . . .?) No, I don't—not going by the other one; I used to demand that he cleared them up, and I found I didn't get anywhere. So I left this one to do as he pleased, and I suddenly find him clearing everything up himself. . . I look round and find he's put it all away in the box. (So you haven't taken a lot of trouble to . . .?) No, I just left him to find his own way. You can *suggest* that they pick things up, but if you *demand* it you get nowhere—at least, that's what I find.

Tidying is, in fact, a job which is much objected to by many children, and our question on this was often greeted with a rueful laugh. It is already clear that mothers are not usually happy about 'forcing' their children to do these jobs at this age; at the same time, it is fairly generally agreed that children cannot for ever expect others to pick up all their toys after them, and that a start must be made in getting this across to the child. Some mothers have indeed succeeded in making tidying-up a routine from the beginning, sometimes to such a degree that one toy is replaced before another is taken out. Mrs Ellis is a thoughtful and lively young woman, wife of an administrative assistant; her upbringing of Jeffrey, her only child, has shown a consistent firmness from his earliest months:

The earlier the better, well there's ways of getting round a child, they're very susceptible at this age. You can do things with them by persuasion, which you lose the advantage of when they're a bit older, I should imagine, and then I presume it's nag, nag, nag—you say "do this", whereas if you form a habit at this age, I think you sow the seeds for life. With Jeffrey, clearing away things was a matter of persuasion for a little while. He used to get hold of his big toy-box and tip it up, and it was strewn as far as you could see, and the prospect at bedtime to start clearing it away was just too much. To begin with I did help him a little, of course—he was only two, as I said—but after a bit it would be Jeffrey who'd frequently clear things up at bedtime, and he used just to get on and do it. He's learning now that if he gets them out he's got to put them away, and therefore he just gets out what he wants.

A good deal of patience may be needed before the child accepts the principle of tidying up his own mess to the extent that he actually does it without any help at all; but the majority of mothers do feel that the foundations for this should be laid during the pre-school year, both for tidying and for other forms of self-help; for many of them, school is very much in mind as a deadline for basic independence.

Publisher's wife:

I don't think you can insist on everything; because on some days, when they feel a little bit off or don't want to do it, I think you can go too far and put them off doing it completely; on the other hand, I do think that if you don't do it now, I've seen from experience that they're not going to do it at all until very late. Apart from that, it's part of the framework he's got to fit in with, isn't it?[1]

Electrician's wife:

Well *now*, because it's the year before school, I want him to start. I want him to start to be able to dress himself and put his coat on and things. You know, with Jimmy I used to do it right up until he went to school; and it wasn't until the day before he went to school that I realized that he'd never put his coat on himself, and I mean, I was in a ghastly dilemma. So with him, you see, I realize that he's *got* to learn to do it now.

[1] See this same mother's statement on page 373.

Shop assistant's wife:

> Well, in a certain aspect I do think they should be made to, because they've got to learn to defend themselves, I mean she's only got another year before she goes to school. She's got to learn to more or less do things for herself there, because the teacher won't. I mean, I keep saying to her—she gets lazy and won't pull her pants up after she's been to the toilet sometimes—and I say to her, "You know, the teacher won't do it for you when you get to school. You've *got* to do it yourself". And I leave her there with her pants round her legs until she *does* do it herself.

Looking further ahead than school, early training in keeping tidy may be seen as setting a standard for tidiness in adult life as well; as usual, however, someone is ready to take the opposite point of view.

Publican's wife:

> You must make them. If a child gets used to *not* putting things away, later on they are just untidy. I was never allowed to do things or told to do things, and now I am very untidy myself.

Insurance agent's wife:

> I don't agree with it at all, not *making* them do it. Helping Mother, yes, but not . . . . I think it's with me never doing it, you know. I never had to do anything at home, and it was so nice, and now of course I help my mother, and Jill helps me if she wants to.

The question is, how to achieve independence painlessly?— for few are prepared for it to be painful. Mrs Flanagan, a labourer's wife who says 'I tell them they'll get smacked if they don't get cracking and do it', is in a very small minority. The favoured method is to make the job as pleasant as possible, usually by participating in it and by encouraging the child to look upon independence as a source of prestige.

Scientific research worker's wife:

> I wouldn't force it—for example, if I say to him "Pick up your toys", and he says "No, I'm not going to"—the more I insist, the more stubborn he'll get. Eventually I can't back out, so I would eventually use force, and I don't like doing that. I'd rather

get down on my knees and pick up a few myself, and then he'll start and do it quite willingly.

Teacher's wife:

I think they should be *encouraged* to do them, and I think if they're encouraged they enjoy doing them. (Have you taken a lot of trouble . . .?) No. She has enjoyed doing things. She has found that people remark on it—she enjoys being flattered.

As a principle, this seems to work reasonably well, provided the mother is prepared to give and take, and on this question most mothers are: pressure in general is not very great. In some individual cases, of course, the mother does a good deal more giving than taking: the child is more than usually dependent or temperamental, and the mother is willing to make allowances for this. One has the impression that dependence is not something which gets under the mother's skin, in the way that, for instance, food-finickiness or failure of toilet training do.

Salesman's wife:

He does as much as he's capable of. Probably I'd like him to be a bit more capable; but he just isn't. He tries—he does his best, and I'm satisfied there. I know some children could do more.

Newsagent's wife:

It is the usual bone of contention. He should, but he doesn't. When I get really cross about it, he says "Will you help?"—and help means do about 96%, but he will show willing then. (Do you think he should be made to . . .?) Not particularly. Whoever heard of a child of ten that can't dress himself? I think eventually if you leave them alone it just comes naturally. I think social pressures make them do these things eventually.

University lecturer's wife:

(Dressing himself) He used to. But now he's stopped. He *can*, it's a matter of how he takes it. I mean, some mornings he'll do it *all*. Other mornings he won't do any. He's perfectly able to do the lot; but when he wakes up that way—he's just playful and he doesn't do it. (Undress?) Again, it varies. If it's *his* idea to have his bath, he does. If it's our idea, he doesn't. Again, he's able, but not always willing. (Toilet?) It varies. If I'm at home, I wipe him; if it's anybody else, he does it all . . . (Do you think he should be made to . . .?) I think he ought to be *able* to do things. I would train him in the skills. But I think there are occasions when, either through playfulness or tiredness, the child won't do it, and on those occasions I wouldn't make a big issue over it; and also, sometimes, I think you're bound to do it, in your own interest, for quickness.

Business-owner's wife:

I think he would quite willingly let me take him to the toilet and look after him and clean his teeth and wash him, you know. He would quite willingly let me do all that. But I think they should start. (Do you think you ought to be stricter . . .?) Well, I think I *should*, but I haven't the time—it's the old cry, isn't it! It takes so much longer to wait for him.

The point these last two mothers make, that one hasn't time to wait for a slow child to do things, is echoed again and again. It far outnumbers the opposite view, that one hasn't time to do the job oneself. Of course, the time factor is augmented by an irritation factor: on the question of tidying in particular, many mothers feel that getting the job done by an unwilling child is hardly worth the effort and emotion of enforcement, and they get on with it themselves, hoping that the child will come to it in his own good time without much pressure on their part.

Depot manager's wife:

(Dressing and undressing) I suppose he's never been taught to. There's usually one or two of them going to bed together; so it's quicker for me to do it and get it out of the way. And this one has got rather a temper, I'm afraid. So it's easier for me to do it myself.

Lorry driver's wife:

Oh, you just pick them up yourself as you go along, don't you? You don't worry them, do you? You can't be nattering at them all the time, can you? They're only young, aren't they?

A few who began by feeling like this are unable to take such a light-hearted attitude now that the child is nearing school age; having neglected training for the sake of speed, they fear that they have already left it too late.

### Shop assistant's wife:

Well, compared to other children, which you *shouldn't* compare your own children with others, but I've found there are children who will dress themselves before they're four years of age, and they do try to undress themselves. But I've done it for quickness, I think, and sometimes I haven't got time to wait while she dresses herself. I'm one who's always in a hurry, I've always got to do things in a hurry—I've got to do that, and it's *got* to be done *that day*, you know what I mean, And I think I've done wrong by helping her. . . .

### Clerk's wife:

I think she *should* be made to do things herself, but it takes such a long time that I just do it—you know, I get fed up with waiting. She *can* do it; it's my fault that she doesn't do it, you know. It's that she's so slow. I suppose I give in, I really think I should perhaps be stricter, really.

These mothers equally reject real coercion, so that they tend to feel a certain amount of guilt, together with a strong sense of dilemma.

Some mothers, again, take the line that the child *ought* to help, and they attempt to make him: but faced with an obdurate child, they lose every time. The trouble here seems to be that although they no longer expect to win, they cannot make up their mind to come to a compromise with their earlier expectations; the pattern becomes one of a nagging mother repeatedly worn down by the child's obstinacy, and by time being against her, while the child itself becomes habituated to refusal. Neither of the next two informants is happy about this situation: Mrs Williamson, who speaks first, worries about it; Mrs Lievesley has had similar trouble with her four older children, and is moderately resigned.

### Miner's wife:

Susan's been, kind of, ruined, you know. She's been that spoiled, you can't make her understand things; unless you really smack her, you know, and make her do it. I realize I just let it slip, you know. But I mean, dressing and undressing, she should be doing that by now. (Do you think you ought to be stricter . . .?) Yes, I do. If I persevered a bit more, she would do, you know. But she cries. She's that mardy,[1] and she starts crying and it goes through me so, I just let it slip by, kind of thing.

Railwayman's wife:

Yes, I think she *should* be made to do it herself. Same as I said to her, "Get these paints up, Vicky"—ready for you to come, sort of thing—and she says "No, do it yourself". She did! (So what happened?) I had to do it myself. I mean, say I smack her and make her cry; I don't think that's worth it—I can't stand the noise at my age (43). I'd sooner do it myself.

These last two quotations raise another aspect of independence: that, once the mother demands certain behaviour on the part of the child, she will suffer a loss of face if he refuses. This, of course, is a basic reason why mothers of obstinately dependent children reach a compromise early: if their demands are persisted in for these tasks to be done by the child, the recurrent nature of the tasks is likely to involve them in a series of battles which cannot be won. They therefore accept that discretion is the better part of valour, and postpone or modify their demands. Loss of face, as we shall see later on, is a powerful consideration in the interchanges between mother and child. Mrs Williamson and Mrs Lievesley are already embroiled in relationships with their children in which they repeatedly lose face, and they are not the only mothers to see this as a major predicament, to which they return several times during the interview, and to which we shall return ourselves in Chapter 13.

The alternative to losing face, once a demand has been made and refused, is 'showing who's gaffer'.[2] For most mothers, although it is a theme which constantly recurs elsewhere, this does not seem to arise so often in the situation of self-help. The next quotation illustrates the possibility, however.

Foreman's wife:

I think it all depends at the time, doesn't it? It all depends on the *attitude* that they don't want to do it. If he turns round and

[1] Spoilt and grizzly. For discussion of this dialect word, see *Infant Care in an Urban Community, op. cit.*, pp. 85–6. A map showing the geographical area of 'mardy' is given in Iona and Peter Opie's *Lore and Language of Schoolchildren*, Oxford University Press, 1959, p. 177.

[2] *Gaffer* = *boss*. Often used in the sense quoted here, it is also used to mean the head of the household, the boss or manager of a business or the foreman of a work-gang.

tells me he's not going to do it, well, then that gets my back up, because if I've said he's going to do, well, somebody's got to be gaffer. Well, that's the situation, isn't it? But if he's playing or doing something else, I don't, 'cause really I think sometimes you could do it quicker yourself while you're shouting at them. No, I don't mind if it doesn't come to a battle, it's all depending what attitude.

But we did also find a few mothers seeing independence training as a basis, not merely for a well-regulated childhood, but for the whole system of values through which the child was to be integrated into a society which demands a degree of conformity and obedience. The quotations below come from two very different mothers who have reached similar conclusions from totally dissimilar economic backgrounds; what they do have in common, which is probably the significant factor, is a Catholic upbringing.

Teacher's wife:

> This is probably the wrong idea. But I *genuinely* believe that life is—one has to accept *so* much discipline, that the sooner it's instilled into one that one should be amenable to it, the better.

Labourer's wife:

> (Do you think he should . . .?) Well, I wouldn't like to use the word '*should*' in a rough way. If you say it in a more gentle way to him—yes, let him understand that it's got to be done—they'll actually take over from there. But I wouldn't like to *demand* them to do the thing—not in a harsh tone of voice, like. . . . It'll take a bit, probably, they won't do it immediately. Of course, the child has an idea in their own head, I suppose, that they want to be master if they can at all, not only over toys now, but other problems; but if you keep on, and it comes to you being a bit strict, and you *do* be a bit strict, well, naturally that child will understand that it's got to obey you, the parent or the Mother Superior or whoever it may be, and you don't have to go to extreme nastiness or hurtfulness or anything like that, because eventually you'll get it done if you use the right method, like.

Both these mothers are inclined to enlarge upon statements of what they do with some exploration of the pattern of principles and values which govern their behaviour. It is worth noting in passing that, while this is common among professional men's wives, but uncommon among the wives of labourers, it happens with relative frequency among Irishwomen, of whatever class, together with an undeniable verbal facility. Their religion may well lie behind this consciousness of basic principles; we can offer no cultural explanation for a national gift of the gab, and do not claim to be the first to have noticed this!

Briefly to sum up: the main factors which operate to decide the pressure which is put upon the child to look after himself at this age are the mother's desire to be free from these chores herself, and her feeling that self-help must eventually be trained into the child, countered by her reluctance to force independence upon him if he is unready or very unwilling. As in most areas of child care from babyhood onward, the individual child himself exerts considerable influence upon the final result: most mothers are prepared to modify their demands to suit his personality—or perhaps it would be more correct to say that they *do in the end* modify their demands, for a number are very ill-prepared for this necessity, and reach a compromise only after battles and heart-searchings, often borne mainly by the eldest child. As one middle-class mother put it, 'I think that with a second child you get a different outlook towards it. With an only child, or a first one, I've found, you want perfection; and I look back on it, and the child can have hours of torment while you're trying to perfect it'. It is true, of course, that most children enjoy doing things for themselves *when they feel like it*; and indeed, conflict in this respect at the age of two or three years would probably centre upon the child's determination to do things for himself which his mother knows she will have to do in the end—the time and irritation factor at its peak. But the fact remains that, by four, most children object at least sometimes to at least some of these activities, and many are as bored by them as their mothers are; so that discrepancy between expectations and reality is almost inevitable.

### 'She gives me no peace whatsoever ... '

A rather different form of independence or self-reliance is manifested in the child's ability to amuse himself, rather than demanding constant attention from his mother. At this age, of course, self-sufficiency of this sort is only a relative matter. Most four-year-olds will react strongly against the possibility of being cut off from familiar people. They like to know that their mother, in particular, is accessible if they want her, and they are not content to be left entirely alone for very long. More positively, studies of nursery school children[1] show that by the age of four they are already turning outward from companionable but basically solitary play towards group activities of a more truly social nature.[2] Undoubtedly four-year-olds get a great deal of pleasure from the company of other children and, despite minor squabbles, are generally a good deal more contented and less demanding of adults when suitable playmates are available.

Restricted to their own home, however, and particularly when weather and traffic conditions make it impossible for them to play outside, it can require some skill and patience to keep children happy. Children certainly vary in their ability to keep themselves busy and amused[3]—the more intelligent and the more imaginative[4] have a head start—and environments also differ in the stimulation which they offer to the child to play on his own. Nevertheless, the problem of coping with the needs of children while getting through the housework was a familiar one to almost every mother we talked to: our question 'If he keeps wanting you to do things for him when you're busy, what do you do?' was another signal for the rueful grin in recognition of a predicament to which they were all too well accustomed. An additional question, 'Do you think a child of this age should be able to amuse himself most of the time, or would you expect to have to spend a lot of time on keeping him happy?' took the topic a little further.

Clearly, there are several types of response possible towards

[1] For instance: Christianson, H. M., Rogers, M. M., and Ludlum, B. A.: *The Nursery School: adventure in living and learning*; Houghton Mifflin Co., Boston, 1961.

[2] 36% of these children still like to play on their own most of the time; 45% like it 'sometimes'; and 19% do not like playing on their own at all. There is a significant class divergence here, however: 23% of working-class four-year-olds prefer never to play on their own, compared with only 7% of middle-class children. Middle-class children are, of course, more likely to *have* to play alone, since their families are smaller.

[3] 48% of these children are said to be capable of playing on their own, without needing the mother's attention, for more than an hour; 24% could be expected to do this for between 31 and 60 minutes; but 28% never play on their own for more than half an hour at a time. Class differences are negligible here.

[4] What makes a child more imaginative is another question; we have no ready answer, but will touch on this in Chapter 7.

the child's demands, ranging from ignoring him, through delayed responses with or without a bad grace, to an invariable and willing responsiveness. In a further category is the mother who comes to an agreement with her child that a certain period of her day belongs to him, on the understanding that he must amuse himself while she is busy: this apparently satisfactory solution seems to be characteristic of the mother who is both child-centred and fairly well organized.

Technician's wife:

> I don't see there's any reason why they shouldn't be able to amuse themselves as long as the mother is prepared to give up part of her afternoon. You see I make a point of taking them out in the afternoon and I get my work done in the morning, so that what doesn't get done today gets done tomorrow, and they've got used to that routine of knowing that they've to play on their own till after dinner, and I'm quite prepared to down tools and take them out then, you see. I mean, you can't do any more with a house to run, can you?

Publisher's wife:

> I don't expect him to amuse himself *most* of the time; what I *do* do is, when I'm busy in the mornings I expect him to, but then of course he's done that from being a baby, he hasn't had a lot of attention in the mornings; but especially from half-past-three onwards with Martin (brother aged 6) coming home from school, I do usually try to spend that time with them; I've nothing to do, I can read to them or play with them; or in the morning, if he is obviously getting bored with, say, not being able to get out for several days, well I'll leave it and play with him for half an hour then. But on the whole I think they should have *some* resources; but as I say, at four you can't expect them to do *everything* alone.

Bank clerk's wife:

> Well I think he should at this age, though it is a boring age, just before school time. He used to play better a year ago than he does now. He didn't used to get so bored. I take him out in the afternoons to relieve his boredom, otherwise he just rolls about.

A somewhat similar attitude of give-and-take is expressed by two mothers in full-time employment: the first works at the cycle factory all day and the second does research work partly out and partly at home. Both children are at part-time nursery school, and the first is also in the care of a neighbour for part of the day.

Textile packer's wife:

> I stop and do it, because I don't see much of him now, so I give him all my attention when I am home. He *can* amuse himself, but then I'd rather him have a bit of company. I wouldn't want him to, sort of, play all the while by himself.

University lecturer's wife:

> I do try and attend to her when she wants it—mainly because she has to put up with quite a lot of my being absorbed in something else, and therefore I try to show willing at *any* time. But sometimes she might have to ask three times, simply because I'm thinking hard and don't hear her, and I think she understands that, because it happens the other way round, too, as I've pointed out to her; or I might say "Wait just a minute till I write this down". I don't cut myself off from her, she's in and out all the time.

Almost inevitably, concessions have to be made on both sides; very few mothers feel able to drop everything at any time, at the child's pleasure. Mrs Fields is one of these exceptional mothers: she has always been totally absorbed in her two children, one of whom is very slightly handicapped.

Tailor's presser's wife:

> I do it for him at once, believe it or not. I mean, *you* may think it's nothing much and he can wait, but in a kiddy's mind it's important, just as much as your things are to you.

A much more frequent response distinguishes between necessary and unnecessary demands, those which the mother wishes to fulfil and those which she does not; or, in particular, demands which serve a useful purpose *for her* in buying a new period of peace, and those which do not.

University lecturer's wife:

> Well, I suppose if it's reasonable I do it; if it's something that will contribute to his activity. I mean, for instance, if he says "Will you get my long trousers, I want to play outside", and I

say "Look, I'm washing up—can't you go and get them yourself?"
and he says "No, they're in the airing cupboard, I can't reach"—
then I will go and do it, because it seems to me that he needs
that and then he won't come back any more. If he says "I want
to paint" and I don't want him to paint because it will make a
mess and I just can't stand it, I say "No, sorry, I can't", and he
stops—he's that sort of child.

Metal polisher's wife:

If he's being good and he asks me to do things, I'll probably
do them. But if I know he's playing me up and just wants me for
the *sake* of wanting me, I say to him "Well, you're a big boy now,
and you've got to do them yourself". (How do you tell the
difference?) Well, knowing Derek and what he gets up to, I just
read him like a book. Some mornings he'll drive me round the
bend. I always know when he's got it on him, because he'll wake
up with the niggles—he'll start crying and that, and that's a sure
sign. . . . (But if he's been good you'll do what he wants, when he
wants?) That's it. Then he deserves it, you see.

Miner's wife:

Well, I do it if it's something—er—well, say she wants me to
fasten something on her dolly, well I'll do that, because when it's
done it's done, you see. I do it because she's a good girl after
that. If I *don't* do it, she's saying "Mummy, will you do it?
Mummy, will you do it?"—all the time like that, you see. Well,
once it's done, it's done, so I like to do it straight away, you see.

Few mothers are able to stand out against attention demands of
this sort, and most give in sooner or later and attend to the child,
perhaps grudgingly, if only because they are worn down; it
must be remembered that most four-year-olds have a rather
poor capacity to wait for what they want, combined with a useful flair for reiteration.

Export packer's wife:

If I haven't got time, he'll have to wait a minute. It's all the
while "wait a minute"! But eventually I have to do something,
because he never gives up. He never gets fed up of asking.

Clerk's wife:

I tell her to do it herself. (Laughed) I tell her so many times,
that in the end I do it anyway, but . . . I do get a bit mad with her.

Miner's wife:

> (About how long will she play on her own without wanting
> your attention?) Oh, dear me, not two minutes! Not *two minutes*!
> Susan wants my attention *all* the time. She gives me no peace
> whatsoever, she doesn't. I say "Wait a minute. Wait a minute
> till I've done this". But in the end she wins, you know, she gets
> on my nerves that much, I just put my things down and smack
> her one, and still do it for her, you know. Mostly I do it for her,
> even if I'm cleaning the floor. No matter what I'm doing, she
> gets it done!

The following three mothers profess themselves a good deal
more hard-hearted than the norm:

Labourer's wife:

> I turn a deaf ear. If you took notice of kids, you'd be running
> every five minutes—well, you would, wouldn't you?

Baker's wife:

> I just tell him to wait. I can't bear to be interrupted when I'm
> working, and I think he understands that now.

Labourer's wife:

> I usually put the wireless on full blast so that I can't hear them.

That the situation itself is almost universal is clear enough,
whether it gives rise to mere irritation and frustration or a real
dilemma. The ideal of the 'good mother' is that she serenely
copes with children and housework, turning from one to the
other with a willing smile as the need arises, or combining the
two without difficulty. Mrs Farrell, a bricklayer's wife, has a
noticeably happy relationship with her two little boys: when they
were babies she used to do her housework in the evening so as
to devote the day to them; now they are four and just five, she
still gives them a good deal of time, but manages in other ways
as well:

> Well, he'll want me to praise him; you know, he'll be playing
> with his fort here, and if the soldiers fall down when he's shooting
> them with his cannon, well he'll want me to look at them and
> praise him; and you know, if I'm busy, if I'm doing the ironing
> or anything, I'll keep saying "Oh, you *are* a good lad, I'm going

to tell your Daddy tonight"—you see, they like encouragement, you know.

But Mrs Farrell has no older children, nor does her husband come home at midday. For many mothers, the need to get things done to a particular time and the competition for their attention from other members of the family present a real problem in responding to what they accept as the quite justified needs of the child.

Social worker's wife:
> In *principle* I try and do as much as I can, but probably there comes a point—a deadline in time, for some reason or another; then I just have to say oh, I'll try later on, but this doesn't meet with much approval!

Nylon knitter's wife:
> That's the only thing I've got against having big families young, you know, all together. You sort of can't give them the attention you'd like to. Teatime is one mad rush. I'm trying to get the dinner ready, one's crying for a feed, the other one's getting tired and probably the other one wants something, and there they are all between them. And then Harry (brother, 7½), he's trying to concentrate. He's very strong on studying at the moment. He's at that age, you know, school's very appealing, and learning to write and arithmetic, and he'll say "How do you spell this, Mummy?" and I say "I haven't got time, Harry—you'll just have to leave it". *That's* what I'm trying to get at, about giving them time and amusing them. I haven't got, always, the time that is necessary, that's why I'm sorry that they're all so young together. If they were that little bit . . . it pays in one way and not in the other. Then at night-time, when I *have* got an hour to spare, I think "Oh dear, I wish I'd helped them". But I can't realize that, at the time—I just couldn't, you see. They're demanding so much from me, especially at that hour when they come home from school. He cries when I fetch him out the nursery— he doesn't cry when I leave him—and they say it's because he realizes he's been away from me all day. And I think they're all the same. That hour that they come out of school, they start.

A great many mothers also put forward the view that, although four-year-olds are able to be a good deal more independent and resourceful in amusing themselves than are three-year-olds, their very maturity means that they need more attention rather than less. Part-time nursery school education is the obvious answer for such children, but is only available to a few. The social worker's wife quoted above (herself a trained social worker) added:

> Oh, I would expect to have to spend a lot of time on him. I find children of this age are terribly curious. They want to ask questions all the time. They like doing things, but they're not always quite sure how to set about it, and you have to be continually showing and explaining.

—and a clerk's wife echoed the mother whose child 'just rolls about' with boredom:

> I think they need you to spend a lot of time on keeping them happy, because I think they get really bored at this age, you know. They're ready for school, I think—well, *she's* ready for school, and I think a lot of four-year-olds are. There's no nursery round here—well, there's a nursery on Haydn Road, but you can't get them in there, not unless you're out at work.

We may now present two tables of findings which, together with the previous two on the amount of self-help shown by four-year-olds, complete the picture of how much these children do for themselves, how much pressure is exerted by their mothers to this end, and how far dependent behaviour is responded to. Table VII gives an evaluation of mothers' attempts to make the child do things for himself. Each mother was assessed on a four-point scale as being 'highly protective', or exerting 'little pressure', 'moderate pressure' or 'high pressure'. This assessment was made on the basis of her answers to questions 7, 8, 9 and 16,[1] all of which ask for the mother's attitudes; so that the rating scale is independent of the child's actual behaviour (except in so far as the mother's attitudes themselves, as we have seen, are likely to have been modified by the actual behaviour of the child and his siblings). Thus a child may be extremely self-reliant despite the fact that his mother has no expectations that he should be so; conversely, a mother's continued efforts to make him help himself may be thwarted by her child's deter-

[1] See interview schedule, Appendix I.

mination or indifference. We have used the term 'highly protective' to describe a small group of mothers who positively
prefer the child to be dependent at this age: to qualify for this
category, the mother had indeed to show some pressure upon
the child *not* to be self-reliant, and evidence from other parts of
the interview might be taken into account if we were in doubt
about this placing. 'Highly protective' (and possibly 'little
pressure' also) may or may not correspond to what others would
call 'over-protective'; we are not willing to make this value judgment on the evidence that exists. There is no suggestion of any
class difference in these pressures.

### TABLE VII

*Mothers' pressure for independence*

| Highly protective | Little pressure | Moderate pressure | High pressure |
|---|---|---|---|
| % | % | % | % |
| 3 | 58 | 36 | 3 |

It seems pertinent here to compare mothers' pressure for
independence with the actual results in their children. If one
combines the data on general self-help with that on whether
children go shopping or take messages, making a straight
dichotomy between the more and the less independent on these
criteria, it can be said that 59% of a random sample of children
are 'independent'. Dividing the table above into two groups of
61% and 39% and cross-correlating, it then appears that, of
those who exert more pressure, 80% have 'independent' children; of those who exert less pressure, only 46% have independent
children. Clearly, pressure for independence does have some
results. On the other hand, it would be a mistake to assume that
this correlation necessarily indicates a causal relation in every
case between pressure and resulting independence; as we have
seen, the child's willingness to be independent is itself a potent
factor in determining how much pressure the mother expects
to exert.

In Table VIII, an assessment is made of mothers' responsiveness to their children's demands. Again a four-point scale of
behaviour is used, based on the mother's answers to questions
13, 14, 15 and 16 in the schedule; it will be seen that her answer

to question 16, 'Do you think a child of this age should be able to amuse himself most of the time or would you expect to have to spend a lot of time on keeping him happy?', does in fact contribute to two different evaluations, of responsiveness and of pressure for independence. Questions 14 and 15 refer to the mother's response to specific demands on the child's part for affection and cuddling; since they contribute to the rating of the mother's general responsiveness, it is convenient to present their results at this point, but the questions themselves will be discussed in the final section of this chapter.

Examples of the different categories of responsiveness have already been given, and the headings we have used are, we hope, reasonably self-explanatory. It may be useful to point out that the two middle classifications are distinguishable chiefly by the intention behind the behaviour: the mother who is 'mostly responsive' *basically intends* to respond to the child, but may be prevented by pressure of other demands, whereas the mother who is responsive 'if pushed' *basically intends* to ignore the child and get on with other things, but may be prevented in this intention by the pressure of the child's own demands. At the two ends of the scale are those women for whom one source of demands so clearly takes precedence that the other can calmly be dismissed. Again, class differences are not significant.

TABLE VIII

*Mothers' response to the child's demands for attention or affection*

| Invariably responsive | Mostly responsive | Responsive if pushed | Normally unresponsive |
|---|---|---|---|
| % | % | % | % |
| 6 | 66 | 25 | 3 |

The main finding of interest which emerges from all these tables is the predominance of the permissive and responsive attitude towards children in this as in most other areas of upbringing. Mothers may want their children to do things for themselves: they are seldom prepared to enforce this against the child's will. They may hope to be undisturbed in their work; only 3% pursue this to the point of an adamant refusal. The recurrent theme of so many conversations with mothers—a truth which most parents come to realise, but of which they are too seldom warned by manuals of child care—is the child's own power to attain his ends, either by active or by passive resistance which is more than a match for his mother's determination unless she is prepared to be really hard—which she is not. The group of interest in Table VIII is not the firmly unresponsive 3%, so much as the *intendingly* unresponsive 25% who fail to hold out against the firmness of the child.

*'He thinks "Well, she's got naught to do, she can cuddle me"'*
It is not easy, at this age, to draw a very sharp dividing line between the attention demands of the child and his need for love and reassurance through physical contact of a more direct kind. It seemed important, therefore, for us to know to what extent four-year-olds are still picked up and cuddled, and how mothers feel about this. The topic was directly explored twice during the interview: firstly from the angle of the mother's attitude to clinging, 'babyish' behaviour, and later on the more general question of whether the warm display of her affection in kissing and lap-nursing was appropriate, in her opinion, with a child of this age. The subject also came up indirectly in many interviews, notably during discussions on jealousy, bedtime and the aftermath of battles between mother and child. We shall confine ourselves now to considering children's demands for mothering and their mothers' response; the larger question of maternal warmth and its expression or inhibition will be investigated in Chapter 15.

Like other sorts of dependent behaviour, a child's desire to cling to his mother is considered normal and right during babyhood, but is expected gradually to disappear and be replaced by more independent behaviour during the next few years; and, as with other slowly progressive changes in the child, mothers vary as to what they feel to be an acceptable rate of growing up. They also differ in their tolerance of temporary set-backs in the process: some expect children's development to proceed on a two-steps-forward-and-one-step-back principle, and accept babyish behaviour with serene indulgence; some immediately regard such behaviour as a symptom that something is amiss; others see it as an attempt by the child to 'play up' or 'try it on', and react as they would to other 'naughtiness'. Children, too,

D

of course, also vary in temperament, from those who need continually renewed physical contact, through those who demand
this sort of reassurance only intermittently or in response to
situations of insecurity, to those who seem already to have passed
through an emotional weaning and who either are comparatively self-contained or put up a good imitation of being so.
Naturally, also, the attitude of a mother towards this question
is likely to be influenced by the extent to which her own child is
currently making affection demands, and the child's behaviour
will in turn be influenced by the mother's underlying attitude,
so that, as usual, there is a very complex interplay of forces here.

We asked: 'Does he ever come clinging round your skirts and
wanting to be babied a bit? What do you do? (or What would
you do if he did that at this age?)' 16% of these four-year-olds
were said to do this often and 47% sometimes, a total of 63%
for whom this behaviour was not unusual. The remaining 37%
were said never to do this sort of thing, and many of their
mothers would have regarded it as so abnormal, for this child
at least, as to need investigation and explanation; the influence
of the mother's own attitude, however, is usually quite clear.

Bleacher's wife:

> Ooh—I'd take her to the doctor to find out why. Oh no, I wouldn't
> expect that at four years old, oh no.

Factory manager's wife:

> Oh no, never—I hate that! I should know there was something
> the matter with her, she was ill. If she did that, I'd give her an
> aspirin.

Insurance inspector's wife:

> Oh *no*, he's a proper boy! Oh *no*! Oh, I don't know *what* I should
> do! Let me see—well, I think I should be cross, really, I just
> wouldn't expect him to do that at this age, I think he should
> be out of that by now.

A few children were clinging despite their mothers' disapproval.

Labourer's wife:

> If she wasn't poorly and was just being mardy, I'd say "Oh,
> don't be silly". You know—I don't like it—I don't like her to do

anything like that unless there's a reason for it, you see. I think it's mardiness with them at this age.

It is clear, however, that only a small minority of mothers would refuse to respond with a cuddle if the child seemed to need it.[1] Some, indeed, expressed a wistful regret that their children no longer spontaneously demanded a hug and a kiss.

Advertising manager's wife:
I'd be glad, in a way. They've both been very independent boys who never wanted cuddles. My mother was very disappointed when she came to see them at first. They've both been like that—not wanting affection and that. They like to *know* that my husband and I love them, sort of thing. They don't want it *shown*, if you know what I mean.

Machine operator's wife:
No, not now—not at all. She'll often say "Do you love me, Mummy?" But not cling, no. (What would you do if she did that at this age?) Well, I should like it. (You wish she did, do you?) Yes (laughed), I should like it. Now a friend of mine, her little girl *does*, you know, and it irritates her—she can't abide being slopped over. But I'd like Carolyn to.

It was often pointed out that clinging behaviour is particularly likely to occur in certain situations; for instance, even mothers who felt that they should discourage babyishness or 'slop' would still expect to nurse a child who was unwell. Jealousy of a younger sibling was also a frequent cause for the child's clinging to his mother or asking to be picked up, and was normally responded to; the last of the following quotations shows an inflexible attitude towards roles which is unusual.

Railwayman's wife:
Well, I don't believe in petting them up a lot—I mean, if they're ill I will, but I don't believe in a lot of cuddling, not when they're growing up.

Technician's wife:
Oh, well, I believe in giving a fair share of love, you see; with having the little baby it makes a difference, you see, they're bound to take that little bit extra attention, because they're so

[1] 5% deliberately discourage shows of affection (see pp. 483-4).

little, you see. I don't believe in them not having their share of love. If he's sleepy sometimes and he wants a story, or even if he's not, I take him on my knee; or when she's gone to bed I let him have half an hour on my knee, because I think it gives them a bit of security. I mean, otherwise they feel a little bit pushed out.

### Engineering worker's wife:

I don't know, I think I'd tell her to stop being mardy. She won't do it, for the simple reason that we've got baby (10 weeks), and she knows he's the baby and she's not.

In a number of cases, clinging behaviour was an obvious reaction on the part of the child to some special fear or worry. The quotations that follow all describe children under some sort of stress, whether momentary or relatively permanent. The first child is a 'textbook' example of separation anxiety; the second is reacting to being deserted by her father three months previously; the third has a deep-seated horror of physical defect; the fourth is merely shy. The last child is just one example of a characteristic anxiety reaction to the mother's anger; it is especially common where anger has taken the form of verbal threats of withdrawal by the mother, either of her love or of herself from the child, and we shall return to this in Chapter 14.

### Miner's wife:

Ever since I left her that time I had to go into hospital (two periods, 17 days each, child aged 2 years), she doesn't trust me any more. I can't go anywhere—over to the neighbours or to the shops— I've always got to take her. She wouldn't leave me. She went down to the school gates at dinner time today. She ran like mad home. She said, "Oh, Mam, I thought you was gone!" She can't forget it. She's still round me all the time. I just sit down and put her on my knee and love her. Definitely. If I don't do it, she says "Mam, you don't love me any more"; I've *got* to sit down.

### Lorry-driver's wife:

Yes, all the time just lately—only since he left. (What do you do?) Well, if I'm not busy I sit down and nurse her, because—you know—she's continually clinging round me, she keeps saying, "Do *you* love me? *You* won't leave me, Mummy, will you?"— and so I sit down and try and talk to her about it, you know; but

rally to the child. To begin with, in fact, they are often strenuously resisted. But, however much he may object to the process, every child must eventually learn to establish some sort of *modus vivendum* with his peers if he is ever to lead a normally sociable life; and, if parents are not yet tuned to this need, they cannot escape awareness of their responsibilities once their child makes any sort of contact with children from other families.

It is not very surprising, then, that by the time children are four years old most mothers feel that it is desirable for them to mix with others of their own age, even if this precipitates a certain degree of conflict. It seems to be generally accepted by them that there will be a stage of vigorous social interaction of the less civilized kind, that this is often necessary in order to grind down the rough edges of childish egotism, and that at this age, while he can still advance or retreat more or less at will, it is important for the child to begin to learn something about the give and take of social life beyond the nucleus of his immediate family. In particular, the potential battleground of school looms ahead in the mother's mind, in this as in the area of self-help: the knowledge that there the child will have to cope with many different social approaches, without possibility of retreat, confirms most mothers in their belief that now is the time to get into practice.

In fact, however, despite the crowded conditions of modern urban living, it is clear that many four-year-olds do not have great opportunity for playing regularly with others of similar age; and, where other children are available, play comparatively rarely takes place under the kind of adult supervision which encourages more civilized behaviour and promotes social learning of the more constructive sort. We have already mentioned that the provision of nursery schools and classes by the community is totally inadequate to meet the demand; the recent formation of a number of privately sponsored play groups, run by the mothers themselves, can be taken as symptomatic of a widespread need, of which middle-class mothers are particularly aware. The total proportion of children in our sample attending any form of nursery class, play centre or informal play group, including both those at fulltime nurseries and those going to a playgroup as infrequently as one afternoon a week, is 11 %. In the absence of provision of this sort, opportunities for play occur mainly informally, and not always satisfactorily, with the

D*

children of friends and neighbours; apart from this, the child is dependent upon having siblings of suitable age. We asked how often in practice children played with brothers and sisters and with children outside the family:

TABLE IX

*Frequency of playing with siblings and with other children*

|  | Often (*most days*) | Sometimes | Never |
|---|---|---|---|
|  | % | % | % |
| Siblings | 57 | 24 | 19 |
| Other children | 56 | 37 | 7 |

It is perhaps of interest that these proportions do not vary significantly with respect either to social class or to the different residential districts (central, estate and other). The extent to which children play regularly with others seems instead to depend upon a number of more accidental factors, such as whether there happen to be suitable playmates within safe 'running round' distance, or whether the mother herself has friends with young children living nearby. In a number of cases, a major difficulty is the traffic hazard; there are no children close enough to visit and be visited without supervision across roads, and consequently the child's social life is limited to occasions when children can be brought to play with him or when he can be taken to play with them. Since this immediately becomes a more formal situation altogether, involving adults giving time and effort to the project, and perhaps the provision of a meal for the visitors, in practice it tends to happen rather rarely and intermittently, and the child's social environment becomes very narrowly circumscribed. Among the 7% who never play with other children outside the family are some who are completely housebound because of the traffic danger. One such example is given on page 62; and a laboratory technician's wife, living a hundred yards from an estate road much used by heavy lorries, says 'No, he *never* goes out to mix with other children, because I mean you've got to be so careful with it being a main road'. Glenda, one of the fortunate few who do go to nursery school in the mornings, would otherwise be completely deprived of play with children of her own age; her mother, a commercial traveller's wife, says:

Yes, she has that swing over the door; when I bring her back from the nursery, I put her in there so that I'll know where she is; because we haven't got a back yard, and she automatically comes out on the front again from the back of the house.

Perhaps at this age the ideal arrangement is for the child to have just one 'special' friend living close by; it is then possible for them both to move freely from one house to the other and back again, each benefiting from a comparatively stable friendship, from the experience of coming into the orbit of a different maternal authority, and from extra play space and play material. An important factor in the success of such a relationship is that one friend can easily be absorbed into the family life; in particular, it is not too disruptive to have the child and a single friend playing together indoors as well as outside, whereas a group would cause a degree of upheaval which many mothers will not tolerate. A paired friendship also works well from the mother's point of view, since it means, at this age, that she always knows exactly where her own child is, and can make happy reciprocal arrangements with the other child's mother, so that one keeps a responsible eye upon both while the other is freed for a while. Often mothers come to know each other well through the friendship of their children, and may then even be willing to concede to each other the right to discipline both children, should the need arise.

When more than two children habitually play together, however, the position becomes more complicated. In the first place, by no means all mothers are prepared to keep open house, or even open garden, for a whole crowd of young children. Even if they start out with hospitable intentions, the situation rapidly turns sour on them when, as so often happens, the other mothers are not so welcoming or the children themselves choose always to play in the same child's garden. This leads to many wry remarks on the part of the 'favoured' mother, and sometimes to an irritable snubbing of the too-constant visitors which she would not originally have intended at all. In the second place, with more than two children there is an increased likelihood of ganging-up and general conflict; keeping the peace can become a bigger proposition than the mother can cope with. The wife of a dancing instructor was critical of what she regarded as a failure on her part:

I think I'd be all right with Tim on his own. But all the children in the street come and play in *this* yard, you see, and sometimes there are eight of them. Well, it's sort of *force of numbers* that gets me down a bit, you know. Sometimes I can't face eight of them and give them discipline. So I just let it ride.

If the children do remain peaceful, not many mothers are prepared to put up with the noise and untidiness which a gang of children indoors inevitably involves. When you live in a small terrace house, two up and two down, you do not have to be exceptionally houseproud to appreciate the clear distinction between indoor and outdoor play—and to make sure that the gang gets no further than the kitchen door with its enquiry, 'Is Jimmy coming out to play?' Thus the larger groups tend to be forced into being fine-weather friends only, and Jimmy's social life may in fact be directly dependent upon the time of year:

> Well, he plays mostly on his own, because if you have children in they make such a wreck of your furniture; but now the weather's getting nice, I shall let him go out now.

Even when a number of young children live close together in the same neighbourhood, then, this does not necessarily ensure that they will all be allowed adequate opportunity for group play; and if they do play together, their experience will not always be of the kind encouraged by the specialist in nursery education as a valuable medium of constructive social learning. Left to themselves, a group of pre-school children do not have an invariably civilizing influence upon each other, though they may provide a useful foretaste of the hierarchies of a competitive society. This last is indeed seen as the primary function of 'playing out' by many mothers, especially, though not exclusively, by manual workers' wives; here are two who are consciously preparing their children for a competitive world, and a third who expects her daughter to find some sort of rough justice without her help.

Miner's wife:

> I'd say "go and hit him back, then—go and fight your own battles". Because I mean they've got to learn to stand on their own feet—it's no good really molly-coddling them, is it?

Salesman's wife:

> Well, I *have* told him to hit back, yes, because I'm afraid he doesn't hit at all. He's not that type. If he's got something he's quietly playing with, the other children will come and take it out of his hands—"*We* want it"—and they've got more strength than him, and by brute force they'll get it off him, and then I'm afraid I will say "Go on, get it back yourself—take it off him". I tell him to stick up for himself; I do because he's that type of child. I do try to make him a bit more aggressive than he is— I'm afraid you've got to be in this world.

Lorry driver's wife:

> If there's a couple of littl'uns fighting, and she got the best of them, well, that's the best of British luck, let the other one have a good go another time.

But there are others who feel that four is too young for such a harsh initiation, and that the value of social play is directly dependent upon the desirability of the other child's behaviour and (therefore) the amount and quality of adult supervision available. These mothers, mainly in the professional class, are the ones who organize play-groups and tea-parties, pay for private nursery school education (but not for day nurseries), keep a close watch on their children's play, and in general expect to *provide* suitable company, just as they provide food, clothing and education: the child is not expected to find his own friends or else do without. For these mothers, the principles which they are trying to lay down at this age are not those of survival through aggressive competition, but of peaceful co-existence, with the accent on peace.

Scientific research worker's wife:

> I try to make both of them understand that if somebody comes here to play with them, then somehow they are their guests, and you are nice to your guests, you let your guests play with your toys, and not as soon as he picks up your favourite toy go and snatch it away from them, "It's mine!"

Teacher's wife:

> I want her to go to kindergarten . . . she so loves the company of other children of her own age, and I feel it would be happier for *her* to have something more interesting to do. . . . I think she'd thoroughly enjoy it, and this is my intention . . . not to *learn*, but to be *organized*. She must be *organized*, quite frankly.

Teacher's wife:

> I tell them that the first one to stop hitting is the most sensible, because it just breeds more hitting.

The control of aggression is in fact for most mothers the central problem of children's social play, whatever the attitude they take. Children of this age are not particularly inhibited when they want their own way; as a social worker's wife said, 'they tend to be so ferocious if they are frustrated by another child'; and a sales representative's wife added: 'I don't think they should be fighting. But still they do. They've just got that *bitterness* in them—haven't you, Debbie?' Children do, of course, vary in their own taste or capacity for initiating or provoking aggression, and they differ markedly in their response to aggressive behaviour on the part of others. But it is noticeable that, while especially pacific or pugnacious children exacerbate the mother's problem, they do not in themselves create it: it is almost inevitable where two or more children play together, and it was rare in our sample to find a mother who had not as yet had to reach some decision on coping with quarrelling. Obviously, real difficulties can arise where a neighbouring child is exceptionally aggressive, or where there is ganging-up against one child; mothers worry especially when their own child seems by nature less well equipped to compete successfully in the rough and tumble of inadequately supervised play. We saw one example of this on page 62, where the child was temperamentally at a disadvantage; Ian, on the contrary, is not a passive child (all his family are inclined to be violent, and his mother elsewhere calls him 'a real terror when he starts'), but he is under-sized, and his back door leads on to a communal yard shared by a rowdy gang of children from six different families:

Packer's wife:

> He's a bit smaller than the others, and they seem to tend to get him out of my sight, and then they're thumping him and smacking him, because they know he's going to cry, and if he tries to retaliate he just can't, because he can't win, he's too small. He'll have a go. But they always come back with a bit harder than he just give out. He's at a disadvantage. I don't want to let him mix, for that *reason*. . . . If they're round the corner and you hear a yell, you know they're doing *something*. Then they'll all run like mad

when they see me. If he could *grow* a bit, put a bit more *weight* behind him . . .

'The little girl next door is a demon, and swipes Mandy across the head', said an engineering worker's wife; and a miner's wife lamented her daughter's pacifism:

> She is the softest kid. She don't like to hurt anyone. She just stands there and cries and cries. I shout at her she *should* defend herself—she's big enough. Naturally she has not just got to stand there. I've got to learn her to defend herself.

Not unnaturally, the story was most often of other people's rough children picking on or attacking the child under discussion; aside from parents' reticence about their own children's faults, the four-year-old must expect to meet outside a group of children who are in the main older and larger than himself. Nevertheless, a fair number of mothers were prepared to acknowledge their own four-year-olds as the local troublemakers; it is perhaps a commentary on our competitive society that over-aggressiveness seemed much less worrying than under-aggressiveness.

Unemployed labourer's wife:
> He hits everybody he plays with. They are all frightened to death of him.

Miner's wife:
> Mostly it's always mine that's to blame—because when she's playing out, she's a bit of a bully, you know—oh yes. She's really got it in for them down at the bottom, that woman's got two a bit older than mine, and you know Karen just doesn't like them, that's all, They're always having rows.

Storekeeper's wife:
> Well, if it got too far I'd interfere—when it comes to tapping[1] and doing—but Lorrae's a devil for tapping *first*—she always taps them and then runs away.

'*She's* your *friend, Gwen, go back and hit her*'
Against this background of an almost universal maternal experience of dealing with children's quarrelling, whatever the child's

---

[1] In Nottingham, it must be remembered, *tapping* = *hitting*.

personality or the mother's views on the necessity for aggression, we can look directly at the questions we asked and the attitudes and behaviour which they disclosed. Our basic questions were intentionally open-ended, and to begin with no attempt was made to code the separate answers individually. After establishing whether the child played with others at all, the questions in order ran as follows:

18. What do you do if there's a disagreement or a quarrel?
19. In general, do you think that children should be left to settle their own differences at this age, or would you interfere?
20. Suppose N comes running to you complaining of another child? What do you do?
21. Do you ever tell N to hit another child back?
    if YES: Can you give me an example of when you might do that?
    if NO: Is there any situation in which you might do that?
22. There seem to be two sorts of quarrelling he might get into—quarrelling with his brother/sister, and quarrelling with other children. Do you find you act differently in those two situations?

On reviewing the verbatim responses to this series of questions, it seemed feasible to make an overall assessment of mothers' responses to children's quarrels (leaving aside for the moment the question of hitting back) in terms of three degrees of their willingness to intervene. This three-point scale can best be explained in the form of a table (see Table X).

In using this scale, it must be borne in mind that any mother of a four-year-old will eventually feel bound to interfere if the quarrel becomes sufficiently serious: that is to say, any normal mother will take action in an obvious case of bullying by an older child, or where there is a likelihood of some real physical injury being done to one of the children. Mrs Garnett, for instance, the publisher's wife whom we have quoted elsewhere, will *in the end* interfere; but her answer clearly falls into Category C, in that she waits until the moment when weapons are drawn, and sometimes a little longer.

Well, I try to ignore it unless it's obviously getting to blows, when of course I try to be impartial and sort of separate them; I try not to interfere in baby squabbles, because after all you're always convinced that it's your own that's being put on, and very often he's the one that started it. But if they come to blows—I mean, one day they were playing, the three of them (Neill, brother aged 6, friend aged 4), with spades, and then they started raining blows on each other, and Neill got the cut eye. But there again: wait until obviously you've *got* to separate them, and then give them all a lecture; but I try not to interfere. (If it wasn't spades, but just hands or fists . . .?) Well, they can't do a great deal of harm with their hands. I tell them they mustn't fight, but on the other hand, if someone hits him I wouldn't stop him defending himself.

TABLE X

*Classification of maternal attitudes towards intervention in children's quarrels*

| Categories | Illustrative comments |
|---|---|
| A. *Mother accepts role as arbitrator*<br>She emphasizes that she does interfere in order to ensure that justice prevails. She is therefore prepared to hear both sides of any dispute, and attempts to discover the rights and wrongs of the case before giving judgment and/or taking action. | 'I try to be very fair'<br>'I try to see both sides'<br>'Find out who is in the wrong'<br>'Help them to see reason'<br>'Talk it over between them'<br>'Go into it and work out what it was all about' |
| B. *'Half and half'*<br>Attitude evenly balanced between A and C; prefers one attitude but finds it impracticable; insufficient information to categorize. | 'Tell them both to shut up or they'll go to bed'<br>'I'd rather leave them to it, but they'd go on for ever'<br>'Depends on the mood I'm in' |
| C. *Mother prefers to let the children settle their own differences*<br>She believes that children must learn to fight their own battles without adult assistance. For this reason, she does not usually listen sympathetically to complaints, and tells her children not to come telling tales. Generally speaking, she will try to leave them to it, rather than become involved herself. | 'I usually turn a deaf ear'<br>'Say "Now don't come tittle-tattling" '<br>'Take no notice'<br>'Let them carry on'<br>'Say "It's no use running to me"'<br>'Wait till the blood comes running under the door!' |

Some mothers also qualified their answers in a number of other ways, so that our classification really provides no more than a rather crude bipolar assessment of attitudes: and even this was not always possible, as is indicated by the fact that nearly half of our cases were eventually assigned to the indefinite middle category. This cautiousness on our part does mean, however, that the cases which appear in the two outside categories are those in which the attitudes are fairly unmistakable. Analysis of the scale by occupational class shows a very clear class trend.

TABLE XI

*Mothers' attitudes towards intervention in children's quarrels, as a function of social class*

| Coding category | | | Social class | | | |
| --- | --- | --- | --- | --- | --- | --- |
| | I and II | IIIwc | IIIman | IV | V | All |
| | % | % | % | % | % | % |
| A. Mother accepts role as arbitrator | 37 | 25 | 21 | 18 | 20 | 23 |
| B. 'Half and half' | 44 | 50 | 46 | 44 | 37 | 45 |
| C. Mother lets children settle own differences | 19 | 25 | 33 | 38 | 43 | 32 |

The overall difference between the various social class groups is highly significant. Middle-class mothers, and especially those in the professional and managerial class, more often stress their role as arbitrators in dealing with their children's quarrels (as we suggested earlier, they are more inclined towards close supervision of the children's activities generally); however, as we move down the social scale, more and more mothers emphasize the importance of children learning to 'stand on their own two feet' and settle arguments for themselves without the help of adult intervention. The middle-class group might put it another way, and say that working-class mothers cannot be bothered to give the time and patience to arbitration; to which the working-class woman might retort that middle-class mothers are too possessive and too fond of organizing their children to allow them to settle things independently in their own way. Perhaps the details of the picture can be filled out a little by the individual mothers themselves. The occupations given reflect the statistical findings, that, while there is a clear class trend, this is an area in which divisions are not inflexible. Of the group below, the mother whose statement is most atypical of her occupational class is Mrs Cullinan, the Irish labourer's wife whom we have quoted before (pp. 74 and 86) and shall quote again; we have a weakness for her almost Biblical prose.

Clergyman's wife:

The first thing I do is separate them—if it's a bad quarrel; I mean, if it's just, you know, 'yes you did', 'no you didn't', I leave it to work itself out, providing no one gets hurt; but if it's a *bad* squabble in which people are fighting and shouting, then I separate them, and they have one corner each until everyone's quietened down; and when we've said we're sorry, we go into it and work out what it was all about: and then we try and put it right.

Sales representative's wife:

Well, if my child is definitely in the wrong, I tell the other little boy to go away and play a bit, and that he'll come out and play again later; and bring him in and talk to him and tell him that probably he's done something wrong. But if it's just a little bit of where they've been playing together too *long*, perhaps, I just try and change the game they're playing: if they're playing with guns, get the swing out and try and alter the game a bit.

Miner's wife:

I think you need to help them to understand. They don't know what is right and wrong, really. I help them sort it out, or they would be crying there all day. They don't understand what they are arguing about.

Labourer's wife:

Well, sometimes I do have to stand and think if it's a big dis-agreement, so I have to find a way to level that thing out and make it even, so that no child would feel offended or think that I'm taking one part more than the other; so I come to a conclusion in my own mind without the child knowing it, and I manage to settle that affair between the two as best I can, and make the older child the more satisfied—the more understanding about the problem, whatever it would be, like. I wouldn't leave them on their own completely. I would for a few minutes, like, to see what way it was going, but then natually I would. . . . I would either have some little thing to say or try to square up the deal some way or another, when I find them not being able to do it themselves.

## Social worker's wife:

You have to try and reach some sort of compromise—say "You have it, and in a little while you can change over", that sort of thing. Try and act as mediator. . . . I try not to come *running* to interfere. I generally make a suggestion first, or I say, "Well, go back and ask—say please, and then perhaps you'll get it!" But then perhaps he'll come back again and again, and if it goes on *too* long I'll probably then come, but certainly not in the very beginning.

## Coal merchant's wife:

I don't like to interfere too much—it depends what they're doing to each other. You see Peter's got a mark there—*somebody* (looked at his sister) bit him. That's where I'd interfere—when it gets violent. But you see I think really people who've got children only a year apart *have* to interfere a bit more—they won't give in to each other, you know. Mine don't. I mean, if there was five years' difference, the older one would p'raps give in to the little one—like next door, you see, that's how hers are. But these won't give in at all—*never*.[1]

## Driver's wife:

I think they're better left, really. They get out of it quicker if you're *not* there—you know, if they're playing out on the front. I can be upstairs and I can hear them. They don't know that you're listening, and it'll be all over in less time than if I was there. I think you interfere, probably, more than you should. You know, it's nature really.

## Foreman's wife:

It's just a waste of time to interfere, I think. It's only a childish argument when all's said and done—"Jane's got my dolly" or "Linda's got my—something else". "Oh, go and sort it out for yourselves", I say.

[1] A wider age-gap brings its own problems, however; see the depot manager's wife on page 125.

Knitter's wife:

> Well, if he says "So-and-so hit me", then I ask what *he* did first, or, you know, tell him not to be mardy, because I think if you do that once they'll be running all the while—they'll *keep* coming in.

Machine operator's wife:

> Well, I just leave them to get on with it, because Carolyn's mardy, you know. They get the idea that you're going to be there all the time, you know—and when they get to school, well, you *won't* be there, to sort them out of the argument. If she comes running in, say, from a neighbour's, then I just take no notice, because I know what Carolyn is for tapping. (Is it usually her that hits first?) Well, usually, yes. But Michael, he's with her now, he'll often land out at her, you know; and then Carolyn'll cry, whether it's hurt her or not, and come running in; and then it's just mardying her to interfere. So I tell her then that I shall hit her if she ever does it again—which she does. I mean, she *always* comes in crying. (And do you hit her for it, in fact?) Well, I have just lately, because I mean it gets you down when they keep running in. ( (following up an earlier statement) So you would rather she just hit back. . . .?) Oh, yes—I would—well, I think they have to, these days.

'Hitting back' forms, of course, a corollary to the notion of leaving children to settle their own differences: the child who runs in complaining is doing so *instead* of hitting back, or because his retaliation has not been effective enough. If the mother then tells the child to hit back, it is in the hope that thereby he will settle his argument without her further involvement. If, on the other hand, she reacts by coming to intervene, this will normally preclude hitting back on this occasion. It is extremely rare for arbitration *on the spot* (as opposed to advice given from a distance) to take the form of making the child hit back; where this does happen, there always seem to be special circumstances, as when a mother makes a much larger sibling present a sitting target for retaliation. The only situation in which supervised retaliation is common occurs where the original injury was a less orthodox one than mere hitting: hair-pulling and, especially, biting are typical examples. Formalized retaliation of this sort can only happen with the assent of both children's mothers, of course, and for this reason it occurs mainly between siblings; but it can happen between mere friends, given sufficient agreement between their mothers.

Salesman's wife:

> We had one episode where one of these little girls he plays with bit a lump off his thumb. It was right the very top, and she bit right through it, and for a time it was very bad indeed. And her mother brought him back down here and told him to bite her. She said, "Bite her, and bite her hard"; but we couldn't get him to touch her. He wouldn't touch her. He said "Mummy says you mustn't bite", he says, "it's naughty to bite". And so we said, "Bite Annette, and then she won't bite you again". "No"—and he wouldn't touch her. But he often says to her, "You bit the top off my thumb!" But he never would retaliate. No, he wouldn't sort of have any truck with it, even though she had a good bite at him.

In asking the questions about whether children should be advised to hit back, we sometimes felt, with the middle-class mother in particular, that at this point we were pinning her down, as it were: forcing her to come to terms with the harsh reality of children's quarrelling; for, in essence, this question presents the mother with the final practical dilemma: do I, or do I not, encourage violence in my small child, even in self-defence? The question of whether children should settle their own differences need not involve a direct decision on aggression; one can 'prefer them to work things out for themselves', and close one's eyes to how this is done—as one woman said, 'I tell him to stand up for himself, and he can take that how he likes'. Partly, the difficulty arises from the difference between setting the child general theoretical principles ('Play nicely; be friendly') and telling him how to handle the unfortunate actuality ('He keeps on hitting me, what shall I *do*?) For the verbalizing middle-class mother, it is heightened by her squeamishness about putting unpleasant expedients into cold words, which seem to finalize behaviour about which she is uncertain; it would be easier to shelter behind vaguer injunctions 'not to let other children have it all their own way', and hope not to have to face their practical implications. The dilemma is exactly stated by this mother, herself an exceptionally articulate and word-conscious person who has since taken a degree in psychology and philosophy:

I don't know if you can draw a distinction here between telling a child to stand his ground over something, and hitting back. I dislike this idea of telling a child to hit, you know, because I don't believe in hitting, in theory, anyway. I think it would be a wrong thing to tell a child to hit another child; but on the other hand one might feel that a child perhaps was playing with much stronger children who were trying to take something from him. I think I might say "Well, you hang on to it if it's yours and you want it, don't let him get it all the time". Encourage him to stand up for himself, but not *use the word* 'hit'.

Possibly this verbal squeamishness—which in fact reflects a care for what is actually said to the child, very typical of professional-class mothers and to be discussed later on[1]—contributes to the striking difference between Class I and II mothers and the rest in their willingness to tell children to hit back. Table XII shows the three broad categories into which we classified parents' responses; Table XIII presents an analysis of the proportions of mothers giving these different kinds of

TABLE XII

*Classification of maternal attitudes towards telling children to hit back*

| *Categories* | *Illustrative comments* |
|---|---|
| A. No; never (usually on principle). | 'No, I wouldn't, because I don't think that teaches the other child anything, or her. In fact, I think it teaches a child to be spiteful, whereas I've never taught my children to be that way, because I *do* think it makes them spiteful.' |
| B. Yes, qualified: only in certain defined circumstances, and then with reluctance. | 'I don't like telling him; but if there was another child who was on to him *all the time*, I'd tell him to stick up for himself then.' |
| C. Yes: unambiguous and essentially unqualified (e.g. 'only smacking *back*' does not count as qualification, since it repeats the terms of the question). | 'Well, I usually say to her "Have you hit them back?" and if she says "Yes", I say to her "Well, that's all right, then", and I don't bother.' |

[1] See Chapter 14.

response, as a function of social class. While a clear majority—
61%—of the total (randomized) sample subscribes without
qualification to the principle of tit-for-tat, a clear majority of
Class I and II mothers—64%—has reservations about this, and
more than one in three of this class object on principle to the
encouragement of retaliatory aggression.

TABLE XIII

*Responses to the question 'Do you ever tell N to hit
another child back?'—analysed by social class*

| Coding category | Social class | | | | | |
| | I and II | IIIwc | IIIman | IV | V | All classes |
| | % | % | % | % | % | % |
| A. No, never | 35 | 16 | 16 | 10 | 17 | 18 |
| B. Yes, qualified | 29 | 20 | 18 | 28 | 18 | 21 |
| C. Yes, unambiguous | 36 | 64 | 66 | 62 | 65 | 61 |

Again, we can let the mothers themselves fill in the details.
The first quoted is a teacher of secretarial skills, and her little
boy was at this time an only child; she is one of the very few
for whom fighting has not yet arisen.

*Do you ever tell N to hit another child back?*

Oh, *never*! Oh no, *no*! I've heard a mother telling her child, "If
he hits you, you thump him"; and I thought this was terrible;
but I don't... I've never had this, you see, this has never cropped
up. I'd *hate* him to hit another child, I really would, I'd be very
cross with him. I suppose he's got to look after himself; I suppose
if he really was *attacked* by another child, he really would have
to stick up for himself then, but not under normal circumstances,
no. (But you can't imagine yourself actually telling him to?) I
can't, no. I usually tell him "You shouldn't", I always tell him
not to.

Clergyman's wife:

No—no. (Is there any situation in which you might do that?)
No, I don't *think* so—er—I think I would say, "Well, keep out
of his way"; it happened only recently, I said it would be better
if she'd keep out of this child's way; or "you'd better call for

Mummy". I think the general advice I've given to them all is "Tickle him".

Publisher's wife:

Quite honestly, I don't want him to fight at all. I do feel that he must if necessary defend himself, I mean I wouldn't *stop* him hitting back if I saw him through the window; but I'm not in agreement with fighting, I know that it has to happen, but I wouldn't deliberately say to him "You put up your fists and fight anyway".

Labourer's wife (Mrs Cullinan again!):

As a matter of fact, they're useless for hitting back—they'll often get the blow themselves, because they're afraid to hit back—they don't like hitting other children. (Is there any situation in which you might do that?) No, there isn't. I wouldn't like to. Now if he was bigger, and it would come that he would have to take his own part when he'd be out in the school playground and places that I wouldn't be, well, I'd like to know they were manly enough to stand up for themselves at least, but I wouldn't prompt Patrick now, at his age, to encourage him to hit back, because that might turn into more of a *boldness* than taking his own part. He might get too frequently using his hands then.

A common difficulty is that of the mother who is forced by the sub-culture-pattern to reverse her stated principles. The first mother of this group lives on one of the very large council estates; her husband has been downgraded because of illness from managerial to semi-skilled status, but the family, as seems usual in such circumstances, retains its middle-class outlook. The only working-class mother in this group lives in a very 'rough' area, and deplores it.

Well, we've told him now—he's come in so many times crying— because he's never been one for fighting: I've always said to him, "Now you *mustn't* fight, you *mustn't* hit". But now—he's had it so much done to him, one little girl dragged him down the steps by his hair, and they push him and hit him with sticks and that sort of thing—and now we just say to him "Well, you *must* go and stand up for yourself, you must go and do the same to them". (And does he do that now?) Well, now when he comes in, I'll say to him "Well, have you done it back to them?"—and he'll say, "No, I don't like to because it hurts them". He doesn't like to hurt anyone, you see, he's not that natured at all, not aggressive. But I say "Well, you *must* do it, because they do it to you and they're just as naughty". And we sort of *make* him go out; but whether he does wallop them I don't know. But, as I say, I *don't* like it, but he just must learn to stand up for himself.

### Clerk's wife:

Well, I *have* said that on odd occasions; I'm not happy about that, really. At one time I used to say "It doesn't matter what anybody else does, you mustn't hit them back"; but the trouble is, they've got knocked about so much that I've felt, well, it isn't fair. So on odd occasions I *have* said "Well, if somebody's always hitting you or doing something like taking your bike away, well, you must hit them back". I'm not happy that that's the right thing to do, but I can't think of any solution at the moment.

### Chrome polisher's wife:

Yes, I do—if another child hits her of her age, like. I have always stopped my children from kicking or biting or scratching or anything; but I have got so fed up with the children here, I have told them that they have to go out and they have got to kick, and bite, and—do all the other things these children do.

### Laboratory technician's wife:

Well, I *used* to say never hit them at all, you mustn't hit another child. But then they got on to him all the while, they were always hitting him, so that you see I was forced to tell him to stick up for himself. So now I tell him, "Well, you can hit them if they hit you first, but whatever you do, you must never hit them with something in your hand; if you've got something in your hand, you must put it down first".

It may be apposite here to add a child's eye view of this situation, written by a ten-year-old boy who had been learning to fight the hard way:

Children shouldn't be brought up too peaceful. They shouldn't be brought up thinking *bombs* are good, because in dropping bombs you don't know who you're killing; but you should let them hit back. My parents made me too peaceful, and one major reason why the other boys at school leave me out is that I was *very* peaceful not very long ago, and all the rest were already quite warlike, like most boys *are*. My parents seemed to think that it was more important not to like bombs and guns than to fit in.

The majority of mothers, whatever their general attitude, emphasize that hitting is only permissible if it is in fact retaliatory, and that a weapon must not be used; some also exclude younger children as legitimate opponents, even if they hit first. There might be some argument as to the attitude of the garage proprietor's wife who said 'If they start smacking each other, I say "Mummy does the smacking in this house, thank you, not you!" ' But there is no doubt about these mothers' views:

Shop assistant's wife:

> I make her go and hit Susan back. I say "Go and hit Susan back, else Mummy'll smack you", and she knows. I do try to make her hit back, yes. I don't want to make her a bully. But I do try to make her defend herself.

Decorator's wife:

> Well, she has been playing with boys at school, and they have been knocking her down, and I told her then to knock *them* down, because she's got to stand up for herself; she did start telling tales to the teacher and that, and I said, you know, she's got to hit them back and fight her own battles.

Bricklayer's wife:

> Tell him to hit them back, I've always done that, tell them to hit back; but then Roy will say "Well, he's bigger than me", and I'll say "Well, just you tell him", and then he'll say "Well, he'll tell me I'm mardy", so I say "Well, just you tell him he's mardy back".

Labourer's wife:

> If Peter thumps him, he'll come in crying. And I'll say "Have you hit him back?" and he'll say "No", and I say "Well, go and hit him back and don't come crying".

And there was no doubt in some mothers' minds as to their children's readiness to retaliate:

*Do you ever tell N to hit another child back?*
Lorry driver's wife:

> Oh, I don't have to, not Elaine!

**Packer's wife:**

I wouldn't have to tell Don—he'd naturally hit him back.

**Army sergeant's wife:**

Not actually *hit* them, because if I know Suzanne she'd probably use a stick. She's that kind of kid.

**Labourer's wife:**

I might; but of course *this* boy might pick up a brush, or anything like that, to hit him back, and of course I have to go after him and take it off him. He'd pick anything up and hit them back with it, sooner than use his hands, you see, though of course I've never brought him up to use anything other than his fists, you know. Probably he comes from a fighting family. Of course, they're different, the Irish. I mean, if they take after me, they won't *be* anything in the fighting. But of course my husband's Irish—you know how they are.

In general, the *principles* followed for dealing with quarrels between siblings and quarrels with children outside the family are the same; where there are differences, they are practical ones, arising either out of individual circumstances or from the inevitable modification of any social behaviour, the necessity to be a little more discreet, outside the intimate family circle.

Circumstances may well be quite dissimilar for quarrels between siblings and between peers. Obviously, if the child quarrels with siblings who are several years older, or even two years younger, than himself, the mother will not treat such a situation in the same way as she would a quarrel between equals. Again, although she is likely to have a *private* bias in judging any quarrel between her own child and another, in practice she is likely to be much more careful to arbitrate each case on its merits where an outside child is involved; inside the family, she knows too much about the children and their past record, so to speak, and, for good or ill, she will often tend to make special allowances or jump to conclusions, to the disadvantage of one or the other. Often the mother finds herself continually blaming the older sibling, until the 'spoilt' behaviour of the younger catches her up short and she is forced to make a conscious effort to change a habit of thinking which is unfair to both children.

Foreman's wife:

She's got a tormenting nature—especially with her brother (13)
—when those two are together it's a bit chaotic. It's six of one
and half-a-dozen of the other, you know; she thinks the world
*of* him, oh, he's wonderful, Terry is; but of course he's studying
at the moment, he's at grammar school, and he can't devote a
lot of time to her, and if he's doing his books she likes to torment
him. She threw them all over the floor the other night when he
was too busy to attend to her. He got his own back, he turned
her push-chair upside down—which I think is right, I mean I
wouldn't stop him, because she's got to learn that she can't have
her own way on that sort of thing. Up to lately, I've been telling
Terry that he ought to know better; but recently I've changed
my tactics, because I've noticed that it's mainly her fault, so
I've been remonstrating with this one instead of the older one.

Packer's wife:

The older one won't give in to the middle one, and the middle
one won't give in to this one, and *he* wants all his own way;
and I think, being the youngest, you tend to give in to him more.
But I've got now that I *don't*. I'm more on the other side, because
I know what a devil he can be.

Depot manager's wife:

He's inclined, with his other brothers being that much older, to
go up to them and give them a big hit, you know, because I
think he feels he can show his authority a little bit that way.
He likes to show his authority, and he can't make himself be
understood, you know. He sort of shouts, you know, if he sees
anything he wants. And I think, with him being small, the others
are inclined to look after him more, and give way to him, and
he thinks they must give way *every* time—which I don't allow
them to do; and of course I do smack *him* sometimes, then,
because I don't like to see him keep on being like that.

Clerk's wife:

I should probably tell her to hit back to another child, but to
Francis (brother, 5) I don't know what I do. I sort of side up
with him. . . . I can't really remember what I do, you know. I
do it so automatically. (Is it usually her fault when she quarrels
with Francis?) Well, she's a bit awkward—she's *really* awkward,
you know, and I usually think it's her fault, you know. I am
inclined to side with him, I think. I don't know why.

A further result of the intimacy which makes circumstances different between siblings is the intense rivalry which may exist between them, or which may habitually build up in certain family situations; this may mean that the child who plays happily and generously with outsiders or with some siblings may be continually at odds with his rival over apparent trivialities, and that the mother is forced to intervene not only more often but in a quite different way.

Miner's wife:

> Well, you're bound to act differently, aren't you? With your own children—I mean, with Gary you've got to find out if there's any little jealousy, perhaps, or anything like that. You've got to find what's up.

Lorry driver's wife:

> She plays with Brendan ($2\frac{1}{2}$) *all* the time. They're very good friends, and they *don't* quarrel. She will share, there's nothing selfish about her in that respect, at least where Brendan's concerned. Now Derek, he's the next one up (5), and her, they fight like blacks, they can *never* agree over *anything*. June always wants Derek's chair and Derek always wants June's spoon. I've got a set of cutlery and they've all got different coloured handles, and of course each of them has got their own colour, knife, fork and spoon, you see. Well, as soon as Derek comes in he'll make a dive for June's colour, and then she'll want his chair, and so it goes on, you see. Yes, they're the two that fight.

### 'You can't fall out over your kids'

The discretion which must be used when other people's children are involved was a factor which continually came up in our discussions; and at this point we can look back over the complexities of parents' attitudes to childish aggression, and ask ourselves why there are these conflicting attitudes of pacification and counter-aggression, why some mothers want no part in their children's quarrels and others feel that they must intervene and arbitrate, and why, in particular, social class is a factor in these feelings.

Obviously, common politeness plays some part. We do not like to behave in ways which other people will consider discourteous—especially to their faces; and criticizing children to their parents is very definitely held to be discourteous. Although there is a long tradition, probably universally observed, of criticizing other people's children, there is also a tradition of doing this in so subtle a manner that their mother has no grounds for complaint, and can only retaliate by equally veiled references to shortcomings in the other's children. Thus, although most mothers will tell their children to hit back on occasion, they are very unlikely to do so in the actual presence of the other child's mother, since criticism of her child is implicit in this instruction; they will, however, expect her to do something herself about her own child's aggression, perhaps simply by showing that she will accept the hitting-back principle. If she does nothing, she is definitely considered to have fallen short of her duty, and the subtle way to make this clear to her, without actually 'falling out' with her, is to reprove one's own child, although he is in the right, in such a manner that the point will be taken by the other side. Here is June's mother again:

> Well, I think if there are children who aren't of the family, you're rather inclined to blame your own child more—I do, anyway, even when . . . well, now, my friend brought her two little boys, the older one's just turning five; and he's an absolute little terror. They were fighting, but I mean, you can't turn round to another person's child and say "Now, look here, you're being very naughty, just stop it", can you? So you tell your own off—I mean, I'd try to settle it *from June's end*, so to say.

Beyond the veneer of politeness, however, lies the real need for people to find some way of living in communities, often too close for comfort, and to achieve a means of preventing the open expression of disagreement so that living can in fact proceed without being threatened by inter-family explosions. The uninhibited quarrels of children are the sparks which can set off these potential explosions among the adults. And, behind the class differences which we have set out in our tables, we found another divergence: in the degree to which mothers in different class groups are conscious of the possibility that parents themselves might be drawn into active conflict.

That this possibility is a preoccupation for mothers in the manual and white-collar non-professional groups first became evident from their repeated use of a phrase so popular that it deserves the status of a traditional maxim: *You can't fall out over your kids.* The constant reiteration of this sentiment began

to bring home to us the fact that, for the working-class mother,
this is a warning which has real significance in that escalation
from childish squabble to adult quarrelling is something which
is part of the community experience: we did indeed meet
mothers who had not heeded the warning and who, having
'spoken' to a neighbour about an aggressive child, were now
'not speaking'. A cycle worker's wife had reached this point, and
was probably building up for worse to come: she had told her
neighbour that she would hit the neighbour's son if he smacked
her child again. According to the general consensus, this was
real dynamite. A builder's wife, too, was expecting trouble:

> Raymond was standing on the wall, you see, and the boy next
> door, he's eight, pushed him off the wall; and I had to go and
> tell his mother, because they're cheeky little devils, you can't say
> nothing to them, you know; so I told her about it, and she said
> "Oh, I'll see about it", and that was the last thing I heard. So
> she never seen about it, and he continued doing that for two or
> three days every morning when Raymond was on the wall waiting
> for his sister. So I said to him, "The next time he's on the wall",
> I said, "you shove him off and run home".

But this sort of trouble is too well known to working-class
women to be sought by the majority, who keep firmly in mind
that you can't fall out over your kids. Some of the variations on
the basic phrase follow.

Milkman's wife:

> I think more trouble's caused by grown-ups trying to make up
> the quarrels and then the grown-ups start quarrelling amongst
> themselves—it causes a lot of trouble. I think if you fight over
> children you'll always be fighting.

Display artist's wife:

> I just let them carry on. Because it's no use falling out—if you
> take their side, you know, well, some people are funny with
> children, aren't they?

Miner's wife:

> If the other one hits them back, it soon finishes it. I mean, if
> you go out arguing about it, they're still playing together after,
> and you can cause a row over it. I don't think there's much
> sense in fighting over them.

Commercial traveller's wife:

> If she's arguing with another child on the street and you go out shouting, and then *their* mother comes out, you sort of cause a row between you and them, you see. But there's quite a few disagreements round here, because so many families have come here, with children, you see, and there's so many children in the street they all sort of get mixed up, you know.

Labourer's wife:

> I don't argue over children, I don't believe in it. As often as not they're all right again next minute, and then where are you?

Fitter's wife:

> I leave them to sort that out themselves, because whilst you are falling out over kiddies, they are friends again, and you look fools standing there falling out.

However, it is not just a matter of looking foolish. A stoker's wife, who smacked her own children for fighting, said 'I don't smack other people's, no, it wouldn't do round here—you'd be put into court'; and she was echoed by a miner father who had been listening to his wife's opinion which we have quoted above.

> The point is, you see, that when you live in a community like you've got here (Meadows district)—a built-up area where there's plenty of children—children can cause murder between their parents; then you can go to court and you get fined more,[1] and you get bound over for two years—and the next moment the two children's playing again as happy as before! So you've got to use the better part of valour, discretion. You've got to say, "Well, she's *your* friend, Gwen, go back and hit her". And that's it. Because I've always been brought up this way: if they hit you, you hit them back and they won't be so quick in hitting you next time.

Why is it, then, that professional-class wives do not appear to worry that they may be drawn into quarrelling with neighbours over their children?—or at least it never seems to occur to them to mention it. It is certainly not that they do not care what the neighbours think; it is of great importance to them that their

---

[1] 'More', used in this sense, appears to be the exact equivalent of Runyon's 'more than somewhat'.

E

children should know how to behave in public, and, aside from their idealism, this is probably one factor in their distress when their children beat up other people's. But somehow it is just not within the social expectations of the professional-class woman to quarrel with neighbours, much less to fight with them; even 'not speaking' seems extremely rare, and is replaced by carefully polite small-talk, with civilized smiles covering up the dislike on both sides. In the same way, the children are expected eventually to control their aggressive feelings; meanwhile, since they are still too uninhibited for that, mothers do their best to contain their outbursts by arbitration, distraction, reasoning or withdrawing them from the scene of battle. They are not yet expected to manage without adult protection. So a favourite method of dealing with quarrels is to separate the fighting children for a while, tell the other child that it's time to go home, tell their own children to stay in the garden, or 'No, you can't go and play with Eleanor if you quarrel'.

How does this work out, however, in a tight-packed, over-populated district like Radford or the Meadows, such as our miner father describes? If the house has the amenity of a private fenced yard, it will be no more than a tiny patch of concrete in which no self-respecting four-year-old will allow himself to be penned for long. If the back yard is a communal one, how can one tell a neighbour's child that it is time to go home? He *is* at home. The same is true of the other playing-place, the front pavement or the terrace entry. The luxury of withdrawing one's child, or of getting rid of a troublemaker, is not for the mother whose only alternative is to bring him into the house where, together with his younger brothers and sisters, he will be literally under her feet. The mother of undersized Ian, who 'didn't want to let him mix', has no option but to let him mix; when she does try to keep the three boys in because of fighting, the noise in the tiny house becomes intolerable.

Similarly, it must be remembered that in a terrace house the woman standing at her own back door is also standing at her neighbour's. If trouble is brewing, there is not much chance for it to simmer down when the opponents are continually brought face to face with one another, and when they can never even escape from each other's voices. If the children quarrel and the mothers take sides and wives complain loudly to homecoming husbands, it only takes a casual meeting on the way across the yard to the lavatories (themselves an endless cause of strife) for angry words to develop into something more serious.

Meanwhile, as they say, the kids have made it up . . . .

The council estates, with their separate gardens and, in particular, their separate garden gates, bring to working-class wives the possibility of selecting their children's play-company, and some mothers specify this as a very real advantage; others are disappointed when, having got away from the 'rough' area, they find that some of the children who were such a bad influence on their own have also moved to the estates and are not yet used to the convention of keeping out of other people's gardens unless invited in. But the gardens are at least a safety valve—for children and adults alike. While this chapter was being written, we interviewed one of the mothers in the early part of our sample, following up her daughter who was just seven. Asked about how Elaine got on with other children, Mrs Buckle's answer was so relevant to this discussion that we include part of it here. This family lives on a large housing estate, in one of a circle of houses facing each other across a small 'close', each with its own wedge-shaped front garden.

Lorry driver's wife:

> I don't think people do fall out like they used to do. When they lived in *yards* they used to fall out, you know. But while the mums was arguing, the children was friends again! I mean, I sometimes get a bit annoyed, but I never go out and shout about it—I'm annoyed *at home*, if you know what I mean. (You think people fell out a bit more when they lived in yards?) Oh, *definitely*; 'cause, you see—now Elaine's friend lives over there, don't she? (across the close). Well, if she does anything that annoys *me*, I'm not right next door so that I *burst*—I mean, you chunter in the house and it's out of you, and you don't *say* anything then, do you? I don't know if you've noticed anybody else say that? (Well, we've been thinking this, as a matter of fact . . .) Yes, well, you see it's these *hedges* that do it. I don't think—mind you, my next-door neighbour and me, we really are friends, for years and years—but I don't think it's so friendly, you know, as we used to be when we had yards. These hedges cut everything off. But, mind you, they cut the quarrels off as well, don't they? So . . . But I try not to fall out over children—I don't think it pays you, you only get resentful, don't you? I mean, there's a *big* lad, thirteen, and he let his dog jump up at her, and I did shout

at *him*, and his mother never spoke to me no more—she was really annoyed with me, she was! But we didn't *fall out*, we just *didn't speak*. (It's easier just to stop speaking . . .) When there's hedges—yes!

It would be a mistake, however, to assume that the class difference in attitudes towards arbitration and hitting back are entirely a matter of environmental influences; the picture is a good deal more complex, and indeed the divergent trends which we have shown in this chapter, taken together with evidence from other areas of upbringing, seem to reflect fundamental and deep-seated differences in attitudes towards the general theme of controlling child behaviour which distinguish middle-class from working-class mothers.

An indication that environment is not the only factor involved is given by an analysis of attitudes towards arbitration among working-class mothers living in two types of area: the central, mainly terraced districts, and the larger estates. Since the proportion of white-collar workers living on the estates is higher than the proportion living in the central area, the comparison is restricted to manual workers' wives. Categories are as described in Table X, p.113.

TABLE XIV

*Differences in working-class mothers' attitudes towards children's quarrels, as a function of residential district*

|  | Working-class mothers in central districts (n = 194) | Working-class mothers on new estates (n = 165) | All working-class mothers (n = 463) |
|---|---|---|---|
|  | % | % | % |
| A. Mother accepts role as arbitrator | 23 | 14 | 20 |
| B. 'Half and half' | 40 | 47 | 45 |
| C. Mother lets children settle own differences | 37 | 39 | 35 |
|  | (differences not significant) |  |  |

It is clear from this analysis that working-class mothers living on the large estates are, if anything, even less disposed to arbitrate in their children's quarrels than are those left behind in the centre of the city. How can this be explained? We are not inclined to give a dogmatic answer, but we offer our own rather tentative interpretation. The adage 'You can't fall out over your kids' arises from a way of life closely related to the older urban environment—the terraces—in which most of these mothers were themselves brought up. It carries a warning which working-class mothers keep in the backs of their minds, wherever they now live. Thus working-class parents in general prefer children to settle their own differences because they believe that it is dangerous for parents to become involved. However, in the more crowded districts they often find themselves compelled to take some action—to arbitrate in some way—for exactly the same reason that involvement is dangerous: families live too close to one another. The mothers are caught in a dilemma: if I get involved, I shall fall out with my neighbours; but if I don't stop my children fighting in the yard I shall also fall out with my neighbours. On the estates, however, the fear of becoming involved remains as part of the subcultural heritage, and is still expressed verbally, but now there is the possibility of indulging it: let them settle it for themselves, they're out of earshot anyway.

In short, we would explain these results in terms of a cultural lag hypothesis: that is to say, it takes time, perhaps measured in generations, for a new physical environment to modify firmly established beliefs and values. A shift towards middle-class material standards is not automatically accompanied by a shift towards middle-class attitudes.[1]

When taken together, the findings summarized in this chapter all tend to suggest that there are significant class differences in children's early experience of the social world outside the family. At one extreme, the child is born into an environment which is likely to be described (not only by those outside it) as 'a bit rough'. There is nowhere to play except the yard or the streets, where supervision is negligible; so that once outside his own home the child encounters a social free-for-all from which he can expect only rough justice. He learns from infancy that when he is 'playing out' he must fend for himself, surviving either by

[1] The reader may be interested to compare this process of change with the decline of breast-feeding among working-class mothers once they become just prosperous enough to choose for themselves; see *Infant Care in an Urban Community, op. cit.*, Chapter 11.

his wits or by his fists, according to his natural temperament and endowment. His mother does not encourage him to complain about his peers; but he will also discover that she pays little attention to complaints from other mothers which originate from other children's 'tittle-tattling'. He thus learns that he can usually count at least upon his family's tacit support against outsiders, even when his cause is not particularly just. When things become too tough outside, he can always retreat to home base and seek the protection of Our Mam; but, if the weather is reasonably fine, he will not be encouraged to stay indoors for long, and, since there is no alternative, will soon find himself back in the rough and tumble. Outside the house, his mother's sympathy does not normally extend to active intervention on his behalf unless, as one mother said, 'they get *really* vicious'; in practice the child may find that, when the unwilling adults are finally goaded into intervening in an outside quarrel, little attempt is made to apportion blame correctly, and punishment is liable to be distributed to all the participants alike, the just no less than the unjust. Thus there are social forces which tend to make for group cohesion between children against all adults, and these may find expression in gang loyalty and hostility towards authority, even at the pre-school age.

At the other extreme, we have a professional-class child whose whole sphere of social interaction is closely supervised by a watchful adult. Whenever there is a quarrel, inside or out, Mummy is likely to intervene at an early stage, and will then want to know exactly what it is all about in order to give judgment with careful impartiality according to her findings. Telling tales will still be discouraged, particularly if spiteful motives are involved; but, despite this, the four-year-old knows that he will always get a hearing for any justified complaint, including that of other children's aggression. Mummy also reserves the right to exercise some selection in the choice of her children's playmates; thus she will discourage, and discourage successfully, a child who has the reputation for being over-aggressive, untruthful or light-fingered. In a middle-class area the children do not play out in the street as a matter of course, although they may do so; and many, at this age, will never venture outside their own garden gate unless accompanied by a responsible adult. The majority will not yet have had occasion to meet 'rough' children, or even to pass through a 'rough' district, and in some cases the chldren are so used to travelling everywhere by car that a journey on an ordinary bus becomes a special adventure.

The contrast between two such upbringings—in the area of children's play alone—is obvious; clearly, between these two extremes lies a continuum, somewhere in the centre of which middle-class and working-class values overlap and differences disappear. For the majority of children in urban areas such as Nottingham, however, the picture will be closer to the former than to the latter description.

In a society such as ours which puts some premium on aggressive competition in pursuing a career or running a business, and indeed in our very system of education, it is inevitable that children eventually come to realize that different standards and values from those of the family come into force when one is dealing with members of the community with whom one has no ties of kinship. In these circumstances, the family virtues of kindness and consideration, willingness to share and the sacrifice of one's own desires to the general good, make up an ideal set of standards against which more general moral principles can be measured. In this sense, it seems to be universally true that the child's early moral training within the family lays the foundation for all later social behaviour. For the middle-class child, supported as he is during the pre-school years by careful supervision and copious verbal explanation of the principles he must follow, this basic training is continuously reinforced by an environment in which his mother expects to exercise at least remote control at all times. For many working-class children, however, the distinction between the protected, fair-shares-for-all atmosphere of the family and the jungle of might-is-right which they find in the world outside the back door is perforce learned at a very tender age indeed; what is more, the child finds that in the outside world he is on his own, for the adults who both guide and guard him inside the house are reluctant to do either once he goes out to his peers: only in the case of real physical hurt can he count on adult intervention. For these children, the reinforcement of the more humane principles of social life will be a more intermittent affair; for in the streets and yards beyond their doorsteps, where they spend perhaps half of their waking life, it is convincingly demonstrated that here, at any rate, the weakest goes to the wall.

# CHAPTER 6

# RIGHTS AND PRIVILEGES OF PROPERTY AND PLAY

One of the more obvious signs of comparative affluence in contemporary Western society is the post-war boom in toy production. A generally more indulgent attitude towards small children combines with a natural wish to 'give these what we didn't have when we were kiddies', and fuller employment means that 'you can afford to be silly over your kids'. WHEN YOU'RE IN TOWN, TAKE HOME A TOY FOR THE CHILDREN says a local advertisement, and a high proportion of working-class mothers in particular do seem to make this a regular practice, for their smaller children at least. Many children have a six-penny toy every time their mother takes them shopping, and this may be a matter of every other day.[1]

The increasing ability of ordinary families to spare money for the children's toys has fortuitously coincided with industrial exploitation of a whole range of new materials, among which polythene and vinyl are outstanding, which are ideally suited to modern techniques of mass production. Where toys are being manufactured by the million, it becomes feasible to employ first-class designers; and improved design in the car, railway and household equipment industries will in any case be reflected in the toy replicas which make up so large a part of any toyshop's stock. For fourpence, a child can buy a perfectly modelled inch-long piglet which, short of deliberate mutilation, can be trusted to survive the hurly-burly of nursery farmyard life for several years; imaginative constructional toys, too, can be bought in small units, and are no longer stocked only by the expensive specialist shops. Of course it is still easy enough to find shoddy and poorly designed toys, at any price; but in general it can be said that durability together with really good design have never

[1] Annual expenditure on toys in Britain amounts to £7–£8 per child. *Britain: an official handbook*, H.M.S.O., London, 1967.

before been so widely available to all walks of life as they are today.

It is often suggested that the more toys children have, the less they value them. Inevitably, children who have many possessions are more discriminating and less easy to please; and it becomes increasingly difficult to give the modern affluent child the kind of present that will be treasured throughout childhood and remembered with gratitude for ever afterwards. Many of today's present-givers were brought up in an age when good toys were an expensive luxury, and are understandably disconcerted by the trends towards conspicuous consumption and planned obsolescence which are evident in the toy trade no less than in other branches of the mass consumption industries. Parents themselves often complain that children nowadays suffer from a chronic surfeit of playthings, or that they all too easily become collection-addicts, mortgaging all available moneys for weeks ahead. In fact, however, few parents seem prepared to deprive their own child of the type and quantity of toys which seem current among his peer-group; and many fathers (and mothers too) themselves become hooked by the collecting mania, poring as avidly as their children over the illustrated catalogues of super-realistic vehicles and up-to-the-minute dolls' clothes which the manufacturers so thoughtfully provide. The country's toy boxes are crammed to capacity.

The parents' wish and ability to indulge and the children's own acquisitiveness are not the only factors behind the growing accumulation of toys in nearly every home. Durability means that the average ten-year-old, unless he has actually given or thrown away his outgrown toys, has a collection of possessions dating back to when he was a toddler. Moreover, the child's attitude to his own toys must be influenced by the knowledge that few of them are unique, and that the majority are standardized factory products, identical models of which he will see in the local shop window and in the houses of his friends. If a toy does get broken or stop working for any reason, and cannot easily be mended, it can well be replaced, and the child is aware of this; parents too are becoming accustomed to the idea of replacement as an easy substitute for repeated mending, so that the child has a good chance of prolonging almost indefinitely the life of any plaything he particularly likes.

The logical assumption of the throw-away philosophy is, of

E*

course, that when broken goods are replaced by new, the broken ones are put in the dustbin; but where four-year-olds and their toys are concerned one is relieved to observe that sentimental attachment confounds logic. Having lamented the battered condition of his two-inch Massey-Harris tractor, and persuaded his fond father into buying him a gleaming new model, the unreasonable child now wants to play with both at once, and passionately resists any suggestion that the old one might now be discarded. It seems to be very typical of this developmental stage that children should be deeply attached to anything which they regard as belonging to them personally; and this attachment extends not only to favourite toys in a good state of repair, but to all sorts of broken and apparently useless bits and pieces, often of unrecognizable origin, which have come into their possession by casual gift or adoption.[1] In some cases, the child becomes an inveterate hoarder of small odds and ends, and his private caches can be found all over the house.

Foreman's wife:

She's got a place in there with all her rubbish in, and I was sorting out because—well, she collects a lot of *paper*—little bags and pictures and that sort of thing; and she saw me with them in the back kitchen, and she said "I *want* those".

Surveyor's wife:

He hoards: there's drawers in every part of the house with those tickets out of packets of tea, and old nails, and pieces of string, and bits of wood.

Builder's wife:

I tried (turning things out) the other week; and the more I was putting things on one side to throw away, Josephine was putting them back in another place. Well, in the end I had to keep them; but I decided next time I turn out, it'll be by myself! It's not only her own toys, it's other people's, I mean such as a broken pen, little things like that, you know; she just can't bear to see it thrown out. Even a broken tea-strainer the other day: "I'll throw this away", I says, "we've got a new strainer". So Josephine says, "Oh, can I have it, Mammy, it's lovely". Well, in her box it went!

[1] This possessiveness seems to be a general characteristic over and above the specific attachment of some children to 'transitional objects' such as teddies, dummies and pieces of cloth; special attachments persist in many four-year-olds, and are discussed in Chapter 10.

University lecturer's wife:

> She's got a mania for putting things away in her own secret places. The things she's got in her doll's pram!—there's hardly room for the poor doll. Little bottles, hankies, buttons, apples, toys out of cereal packets—I found five teaspoons there the other day, I'd been wondering why I'd got so few teaspoons. She's got a passion for *luggage*, of any sort—she's got an old briefcase and a couple of old handbags, and they're full to bursting; sometimes she takes one to nursery school. When we were getting ready to go away on holiday, I couldn't understand where my clean blouses had got to—she'd packed them in her own luggage, along with the doll's teaset and a tin of cat-food and a couple of wet flannels. She's put letters under the carpet, theatre tickets in the washing machine; I found a credit note for eight pounds, that I'd given up for lost, in one of her handbags. We've got a rule now when we lose anything, always go through Becky's luggage first.

In most children the magpie complex is not found in quite such an exaggerated form; but the majority of four-year-olds do seem to have a strongly developed property sense. The child's own small toys are most usually kept in one or more cardboard grocery boxes; but, as new toys are acquired and the old ones still clung to, the accumulation in a small house can become embarrassingly bulky, even if only one child is involved: 'Parkinson's Law'[1] can be restated, that small children's possessions expand to overspill the space available. At this point, the mother decides that she must have 'a good turn-out', and we arrive at another common focus of conflict.

Our central question here was: 'Suppose you were having a good turn-out, and you wanted to throw away some broken bits of toys, but he wanted to keep them: what would happen then?' Here again, this was a topic which was greeted with rueful amusement as the mother acknowledged an all too familiar situation. We had included the question partly, perhaps, because we ourselves, with our own children, were becoming conscious of a real dilemma. Starting from the basic view that a child's possessions are his own, however apparently worthless, and not to be arbitrarily disposed of by others on any pretext, we were finding that the dwindling space in the house and our children's dismay at any suggestion of 'turning·

[1] C. Northcote Parkinson: *Parkinson's Law*, John Murray, 1958.

out' presented two opposing forces which seemed irreconcilable; in these circumstances, a little judicious tidying-up by stealth was a tempting, if unprincipled, solution. We were interested to find how universally the situation was recognized as a source of conflict, both between mother and child and between principle and expediency.

It was found possible to analyse parent-child behaviour in terms of the outcome of the conflict, in three broad categories: the child wins (45%); a compromise is reached (25%); or the mother wins (30%). Since the mother always has the option of getting rid of the child's 'rubbish' if she really wants to, these results do in fact reflect her attitude reasonably accurately. Within the different categories, however, there appear certain varieties of stratagem which can be looked at a little more closely.

A very few of the mothers whose children win have not in fact reached the point of trying to clear things out, although they see the necessity looming ahead. Almost invariably, these are firstborn children who are at present spreading themselves over rooms which will later be needed for the growing family.

Miner's wife:

> We haven't come to that yet! You know upstairs, the room we don't use, it's stacked out; and that's what we *are* going to have to do, because he's going to sleep in that room. But I haven't come to it, you know, he's never thrown *anything* away, so you can imagine!

By far the greater part of this group, however, are mothers who periodically make the effort to sort out the toys, but who believe on principle that the child's own wishes must be consulted and respected, despite any inconvenience this may cause.

University lecturer's wife:

> Oh, I should keep them. I don't think it's kind to throw away their things until they're ready to part with them, though it may seem a very long time to you until that time.

Lorry driver's mate's wife:

> Well, I think I'd let him keep them, you know, if they were of sentimental value; I think they cling to things, don't they? Especially bits of broken things, more than they do a new toy.

Publisher's wife:

Well, looking back on my own childhood, I remember how bitterly grieved *I* used to be when something of mine was thrown away; something which, I realize now, was probably battered and broken, but I used to feel about it; so I try not to do that; because if *my* mother thought that, she used to just throw it away. I *don't* do that; and I find it's no use trying to sneak anything out, because they always find out; I tried it once, but I never tried it again.

Accountant's wife:

That happened last Sunday, actually. He said to his Daddy, "Can we sort the toy box out?" You can see how much rubbish there is in there; and we spent two hours with them spread all over the floor. And his Daddy was throwing a lot in the hearth to be put in the dustbin, but Graham said "Oh no, no—I want that". So I said to his Daddy, "Well, they may be unimportant to *you*"—but I know, more than his Daddy, which he treasures, you see, with being with him all day. So I said, "You'd better save those".

Lorry driver's wife:

Well, if he wanted to keep them, I should naturally *let* him keep them.

In general, this group thinks it important to secure the child's agreement to anything being thrown away, and this may be achieved by a variety of means. The mother may take pains to demonstrate that the toy cannot be mended; she may explain that it is useless and perhaps dirty or potentially dangerous; most effectively, she will try to enlist the child's active co-operation in sorting and throwing out. To be included in this category, however, the mother must abide by the child's decision, whichever way it goes.

Hosiery worker's wife:

Well, before Christmas we had a good turn-out of his toy box, and he helped me to sort them out. And there again, I let him take them in the dustbin himself, I think that makes all the difference. (And if he wanted to keep some?) Oh yes, because they often get more fun out of broken toys.

Cabinet maker's wife (herself social work trained):

> Yes, well, we had this the other day, just after Christmas; I said "Now come on, let's throw away some of this rubbish, now what can we throw away?" and I let them pick out what we *could* throw away; and in fact some of the stuff I knew he'd want afterwards, so I deliberately kept them, you see. But one or two bits he did say to me afterwards "Where is it?", so I said to him, "Well, you said it could go in the dustbin, so it's *gone* in the dustbin". So he was a bit upset about it. I had to explain to him that *he'd* said it could go, you see; so he soon got over it.

The group which reaches a compromise with the child does this essentially by giving him more time, with the reservation that eventually the clear-out will take place. Sometimes the child understands this; more often, however, the mother shirks making her intentions quite clear, and merely resolves to make her sortie to the dustbin at a later date in diplomatic privacy. To qualify for the 'compromise' category, a reasonable length of time—at least a day or two—must elapse before the broken toys are removed; the mother who allows the child to keep his things and then throws them away as soon as his back is turned is deemed not to have reached a compromise, but to have won. The quotations that follow all come from mothers in the 'compromise' group.

Milkman's wife:

> If they were broken, I should explain to him that they were broken and that they *weren't* any good and he couldn't play with them, and I should turn them out; and if he was really persistent and wanted them, then I should let him keep them until he'd forgotten about it and *then* out them. It's no good upsetting him for nothing. (Father:) His best playthings are his broken things, aren't they? He plays more with broken things than he does with the others!

Scientific research worker's wife:

> Oh, I'd just leave them and get rid of them when he's not there. (Do you mean as soon as you could?) Oh, no, let him play with them for another little while. I have tried to put things in the rubbish bin and let him watch me doing this, explain that it is broken, it's no good any more: well, it may look no good to me, but it's treasure to him, and he goes and picks it out of the bin.

Newsagent's wife:

> I should let him keep them, and then one night when he had gone to bed I should get rid of them, because he would forget them—which is probably all wrong, but it doesn't make an issue of it, and it saves an awful lot of wear and tear.

It is not difficult to detect a certain uneasiness in many of these mothers' minds as to the ethics of throwing the child's possessions away behind his back. In fact, the situation poses the dilemma so often met with by contemporary mothers: in theory they want to give the child a democratic freedom of choice, but in practice only if he choose suitably. And this, of course, is only one aspect of the broader problem: that parents today still have at the back of their minds a picture of the obedient, well-behaved product of a strictly authoritarian upbringing, without being prepared themselves to adopt a strictly authoritarian role. In the situation we are discussing, therefore, many find themselves in the position of maintaining before the child their chosen image as a democratic and permissive parent, while achieving what *would have been* the results of obedience by a subterfuge.

In our final category, then, the mothers have in common that they win; but some first pay lip service to the child's property rights by consulting him, only to follow their original intentions as soon as he is out of the way. The majority of the mothers who win, however, do not bother to go through the motions of consultation (often because they have had earlier experience of their children's obstinacy), but simply take care not to be caught between toy box and dustbin. Finally, a minority of 'winning' mothers do so by open force of authority: the protests of the children are over-ruled. These three aspects of winning are all represented in the group of quotations which follows.

Labourer's wife:

> I give her the privilege of keeping them just till she's not there, and then they go when she's not watching. Then she doesn't miss them at all, then.

Fitter's wife:

> It's surprising what one can do when they're in bed! It takes a bit of tact and that—but when they're in bed I can throw them away. However many toys they've got, they hate to see you

throwing anything away—which is automatic. But they wouldn't miss that toy—it's only because they see it there and know you're going to throw it away, that they want it. So you've got to be more or less crafty!

### Miner's wife:

Oh, I do it at night when he's in bed. I've cleared a lot of stuff out. If he knew, he'd cry; because even if they're broken he wants to keep them. He's missed things often, it's "Where's so-and-so, where's so-and-so?", but I've said "I don't know where they are" (laughed). But I have chucked quite a lot of stuff away. You can't keep everything.

### Aircraftman's wife:

I should wait until she wasn't there and then throw them away. It saves a lot of tears. I would explain that the toys were dirty and broken, I'm sure she would understand she didn't want them—if she found out!

### Shopkeeper's wife:

Well, we had this last week, didn't we? We have to be really firm. She wants to keep every other tiny bit. I think on the whole it's better to do these jobs when they're not there, because I suppose it hurts them to have their treasures taken away.

### Doctor's wife:

Well, I'm afraid I'd throw them out. I'd explain to her that they were no good, they were rubbishy, and I think she'd give in, you know. You can't give in to them all the time, you'd have the house chock-a-block.

### Railwayman's wife:

She starts crying. You can't do anything about it, can you, just throw it in the dustbin and hope for the best.

### Builder's wife:

Oh, I throw them away; if I think they're no good, there's no arguments about it, it's no good, out it's going. (Sister (7) added:) And he cries when she throws his bits away.

### Nylon winder's wife:

Oh, he usually goes to the bin and tries to get them out. He did that the other week. (And what happened then, did you let him keep them or did you say no?) No—I put the dustbin lid on and smacked his hand and took them away.

Although it is possible to distinguish these categories of behaviour, they probably do not represent very precise differences in maternal attitude along any strictly unitary dimension. The two extremes of unconditional permissiveness and undisguised authoritarianism are no doubt reliable enough; but, between these opposites, some mothers were clearly inconsistent in their behaviour, according to how strongly they were feeling the need to clear up and how passionately the child protested. It is also true that a shift in attitude may take place as the family grows, either from democratic principle to desperate expediency, or, in the opposite direction, from strict tidiness to a more relaxed view.

An analysis of mothers' attitudes by social class shows no significant class trends. There is an inclination on the part of shop and clerical workers' wives to compromise rather than let the child win, and the reverse is true of unskilled workers' wives; but these are the only differences which emerge.

For the sake of giving a complete picture, it must be added that there are a very few children who do not present this problem of possessiveness at all. Far from rejoicing at their escape, however, their mothers tend to be a little perturbed at what they correctly regard as an abnormal[1] indifference to ownership.

Army officer's wife:

I sometimes worry because he doesn't care *more*. I think he should care more—not that he doesn't care for his toys themselves, because he does, but he doesn't worry if they get broken.

Chemical worker's wife:

I don't think it would interest her. I haven't done it, but I don't think it would worry her. She doesn't value anything, she doesn't value her toys at all. If they're broken up, she'll go and put them in the dustbin herself. She likes them all got rid of. She's the only child I've got that's like that—she's really destructive, I should call her a destructive child.

Conversely, there are a few mothers who themselves are hoarders on the child's behalf: re-creating something of their own

1 In the statistical sense only.

childhood through the toys of their children, or perhaps clinging
to their last-born child's babyhood, they take the lead in finding
houseroom for a cupboardful of childish relics. Maternal sentiment is, of course, apt to be directed mainly at the more obviously lovable toys—the teddy-bear, the first rag doll, the folksy
wooden train; mothers do not have a natural fondness for the
brown-paper bags full of bottle caps or the collections of little
wheels which engage their children's affections and cause all the
conflict. Thus Mrs Squires, who said that 'you've got to be
more or less crafty' about throwing out rubbish, refers in our
next quotation to outgrown rather than outworn toys:

> He's got a terrible lot of toys. He's got some toys, plush toys,
> my mother bought him—actually they are getting a bit small for
> him. But I haven't given them away—to be honest, I can't bear
> to part with anything of his! I'm terribly sentimental where
> that's concerned, you know—I hate to give anything of his away.
> Although he probably wouldn't mind it in the least!

*'She'll take a sweet out of her mouth to give to another child'*
*'If I give anything away, there's heck to pay'*

The question which we have been discussing was in fact only
one of three basic questions through which we tried to explore
mothers' attitudes to their children's possessions, and, in particular, how far children's property rights are taken seriously.
The first question of this group, introduced by the 'scene-setter'
question 'Does N make a fuss if you give away something of his
to another child?' was simply 'Does it often happen that you do
this?'; all we wished to know from this was whether the disposal
of the child's possessions without reference to him was within
the mother's normal framework of behaviour or not. The 'good
turn-out' question followed, and was followed in turn by: 'If
you've broken something of his by accident and it can't be
mended, what do you do about it?' Throwing away cherished
odds and ends emerged as the most familiar and the most con-
flict-provoking situation, and consequently these replies were
the most revealing from the point of view of parent-child relationships in general; but the briefer responses to the other two
questions are not without interest.

Our probe on giving things away was somewhat unsatisfac-
tory: we decided later that it could have been better worded.
It was one of those occasional questions which function well

during the piloting but begin to show their faults over a wider range of interviews. In this case, misunderstanding could arise in that the mother sometimes took the question to refer to the temporary sharing of toys rather than permanent giving, and had to be corrected; in addition, further probing was too often necessary in order to ascertain whether or not the gift would still be made by the mother in the child's despite. In practice, therefore, we were less than happy about the reliability of these answers; and for this reason we do not propose to analyse them numerically on their own, though they can be allowed to contribute to a final assessment of mothers' attitudes towards children's property.

There seem to be two occasions on which a child may be pressed to give away some of his toys, and neither arises very often. Firstly, there is a fairly universal approval of generosity as a virtue in children, and many mothers feel that they should take active steps to encourage this. Some middle-class mothers remember from their own childhood choosing toys from their toy cupboards to give away at Christmas to 'the poor children', and they may attempt to repeat this traditional act of charity with their own children: not always with success, however, since grateful recipients for other people's old toys are not so easily found nowadays; perhaps, too, we are not so complacent about giving away worn toys when our own children have so much that is new. Be that as it may, the poor are still used by some mothers as a convenient peg on which to hang a lesson in charity, even though the actual handing over of the gift may be difficult to arrange.

Scientific research worker's wife:

> Usually if I clear the toy cupboard I do it when he is out of the way somewhere, and he does notice, he asks me afterwards, where is this and where is that; and I explain that I have given it to a little child who didn't have as many toys; and that usually goes down very well.

Paint sprayer's wife:

> Well, we give something away every Christmas at the Christmas service—you know, the crib; and this year—he hasn't given before—this year he said No, he wouldn't want to go. So I said then it wasn't very nice, because some children hadn't got any

toys. So in the finish he let me wash his duck and he helped me; and a little rabbit; and we wrapped them up in paper and everything was all right. But about three weeks later he said, "Sometimes, you know, Mummy, I wish I'd got my duck and my little rabbit". But he just talks about it, I don't think he *really* . . . But I wouldn't give anything away without his consent.

The other occasion for giving things away is the less formal one on which a visiting child, usually a toddler, takes a fancy to something belonging to the four-year-old, whose mother then either takes it upon herself to make the gift or else tells her child to give it away. Some children are quite happy to do this, and enjoy being in the position of benefactor: Gavin, for instance, 'likes to think that children want something he's got and that they can have it if he gives it them—if any of his cousins come up and they take to a little toy, Gavin will say to them "You can take it home", and he gets pleasure out of it'; Celia, too, will 'take a sweet out of her mouth to give to another child'. If the child does object, however, this is a situation in which he is particularly likely to be over-ruled. The mother is embarrassed by her child's apparent selfishness; she has already committed herself to the gift in front of the other child's mother, and feels she cannot go back on this now; and, while she could moderate her demands in a private conflict with the child, in public the loss of face which this would entail will be too damaging. Social pressures thus tend to ensure that the child is made to conform with his mother's suggestion, which may originally have been made quite casually and in response to an equally casual whim on the part of the visiting child.

Lathe operator's wife:

Well, I don't give anything away, not unless I have to. I don't think it's fair. I mean, if it's hers it's hers. But if a little cousin— you know, if I say "Can little Maggie have this?"—she'll say "Yes, she can". If I ask her first, you know. But if *I* give anything away, there's heck to pay!

Grocer's wife:

Sometimes her cousin will take a liking to a little thing, and I'll say he *can* have it. It's probably only a very small thing. But . . . she'll go sulking and crying: "It's mine—it's not fair—I never take anything of *his*". I make her give it up.

Salesman's wife:

> Well, she did make rather a fuss when I gave my friend's little boy a little soldier—she had some little toy soldiers, those plastic ones, and I gave him one because he rather fancied it, you see, and she did cry, and we had a bit of a storm; but nevertheless I still didn't ask him for it back—I mean, she'd got three more, good gracious!

Between formal charity and the mother's impulsive giving to visitors, there is also a combination of the two in which the mother suggests that babyish toys should be passed on, usually to relatives and often to younger siblings. This situation has neither of the pressurizing factors of the other two: it is not an occasion specifically created for testing the child's generosity to those less fortunate than himself, nor is it acted out under the critical appraisal of another parent. The mother is thus able to postpone or cancel the whole affair if the child objects, or at least has time to talk him into the frame of mind in which 'he thinks it's rather nice that a baby's going to have something that was his'. Similarly, the passing-on of clothing for which the child has developed an attachment can usually be achieved fairly painlessly by persuasion and tact, aided by the fact that, to the child himself, having grown out of his favourite jersey is a much more self-evident proposition than having 'grown out of' his woolly rabbit.

In general, however, it is clear that giving toys away is something for which most mothers feel neither the need nor the inclination, and that, on the whole, children have control over their toys for at least as long as they remain intact. It is noticeable that the deterioration of a toy into 'rubbish' often undermines the child's property rights rather effectively, in that we have 55% who will dispose of broken toys without reference to the child or who merely allow further time before doing so, compared with only 35% who might possibly give toys away;[1] similarly, a mother might vigorously defend her child's rights over his unbroken toys, but feel quite differently about his entitlement to keep 'bits and bobs'. 'I would ask him first', said

[1] From the replies given it is quite plain that 'clearing things out' is a familiar problem, whereas giving things away arises rather rarely; so that, in the latter case, we tend to be dealing with attitudes to a hypothetical situation, rather than with known behaviour.

Mrs Parr, a cold-storeman's wife, 'I don't believe in giving a child's toys away, because after all you'll have bought them *for* him, and that belongs to him, and naturally ... the same as me, if anyone gave anything of mine away'; but on the question of turning out broken things that Nicholas wanted to keep, she said: 'I put them in a separate box and leave it on the top of the stairs, and then when I've finished upstairs and I'm quite sure he's forgotten about them, I'll throw them out'.

*'Her doll got broken; I told her it had got to go to Jesus, and put it in the dustbin'*

The reaction of the mother when she breaks something belonging to the child is also variable, with the majority believing that such a situation demands some kind of compensation on their part, either in words or in action. Only 15% adopt an extra-punitive line ('tell him he shouldn't leave his things about for me to tread on'), and 6% an evasive attitude ('chuck it in the dustbin quick and hope to get away with it'). 60% of working-class and 50% of middle-class mothers put the main emphasis on material restitution:

Labourer's wife:

> Well, I do my best to replace that thing or the nearest to it if he liked it and fancied it, and I would feel really sorry that I had broken it. I'd find the nearest thing possible as *soon* as I could when I was out shopping, and when he was quiet and it had been forgotten, I'd unexpectedly give him this toy or whatever it was, and he would be ever so delighted.

Working-class mothers are rather conscious of their children's material needs—'I like to give these what *I* never had'—and they are prepared to acknowledge an obligation to replace broken things; but they are not so ready as middle-class mothers to put their own fault into words.[1] Only 18% of working-class mothers put the main emphasis upon the need to apologize in this situation, compared with 31% of middle-class women. For this group, apology is sufficient recompense: 'I just told her that it was an accident, and I couldn't help it, and I was sorry, and that was it'. The situation may also be used as a lesson in reciprocal obligations:

[1] The wider implications of this characteristic are discussed in Chapter 14.

Showroom foreman's wife:

> I try to make him understand that it's broken, it's just one of those things; if he breaks anything of his Mummy's, *I* have to understand, the same way.

—and two teachers' wives are still more explicit:

> If I've broken something of hers, I say I'm sorry, and she usually follows suit and says "I'm sorry" about things *she's* done.

> I'd discuss it with her—an example of what ought to happen the other way round, if she breaks something of mine, what should *she* do?

Extremely rarely—since children of this age seldom have monetary resources of their own—the broken toy's replacement is also used to teach reciprocity; this use of situations as model for a verbally explained principle is very characteristic of middle-class methods of upbringing.

Company director's wife:

> If it's not a big article, I promise to get him a new one. We *always* keep promises. If he breaks anything, like he broke a glass a few weeks ago—first time I've ever done it, because now I think he's getting old enough—he has a money-box, and I took the money out of it, and we went and bought a new glass.

Not everybody is so careful about keeping promises, and the child weeping over broken toys is occasionally pacified by the quick expedient of a glib assurance of replacement, with no intention of this ever being fulfilled. It is significant (as we shall see later) that this is only admitted to by working-class mothers; the middle-class mother may forget or neglect to carry out her promises, but her intentions at the time are honourable. The deliberately false promise is not a frequent response, however, and is explicitly disapproved of by the majority of working-class wives, who, as we have seen, tend to pay a good deal of attention to children's material wants; the third of the three manual workers' wives below appeases her conscience by using a *form of words* which is accurate, although its purpose is to deceive the child.[1]

[1] In view of her concern for verbal accuracy, a very middle-class trait, we were interested to find on our follow-up, three years later, that this family has now moved into Class II.

Metal polisher's wife:

> I'd probably just say that to shut him up—it's the coward's way out, I know!

Labourer's wife:

> I tell him, and he cries a bit and says "Will you buy me a new one?" and I say "Yes", just to keep him quiet. But he never gets it.

Skilled industrial worker's wife:

> Well, I always tell him about it and say I didn't do it on purpose, you know, and say I'll try and get a new one; "I'll try and see if I can see one", I say. I don't say "I'm *going* to get you one"; I always say, "If I see one in a shop, I'll get you a new one". Then if he asks, I say "I haven't seen one, I'll keep looking", and he's quite content with that.

The general conclusion which we can draw from the answers to this whole group of questions is, then, that most mothers believe that their children have certain rights of ownership which should be respected, but that well over half will over-rule the child's wishes for the sake of the considerations of space and order if the child's possessions are broken and therefore classifiable as rubbish. The answers may be combined to give a rating for each mother as to the respect which she shows *in practice* towards her child's property rights. *High respect* means that she never either gives or throws away his possessions, broken or unbroken, without permission; *moderate respect*, that she might do one of these things, but not both; *little or none*, that she apparently has no qualms about doing either, and in fact arrogates to herself all rights over her own child's possessions. It should be borne in mind that the middle category includes a high proportion who are basically sympathetic to the child's fondness for broken oddments, and who allow him to keep some of them, but who do a certain amount of surreptitious weeding-out in the admitted knowledge that the child would object if he were present. These mothers might be called faint-hearted in their unwillingness to face the child, or unethical in their flouting of his justifiable needs, according to one's authoritarian or permissive point of view: and certainly the mothers' own feelings often show a consciousness of this two-edged criticism. Apart from the minor differences which we

tic help, so that the prospect of clearing up after the children is not quite so daunting: if there is an *au pair* girl, she may be spared it altogether. While some of her furniture may be very good, and therefore to be protected from the child, she will probably also have a certain amount of especially robust furniture, chosen with the children in mind, which they are *expected* to use roughly; whereas the working-class woman, less likely to venture into the auction-rooms which are the cheapest source of really child-proof pieces, not only has less sturdy furniture but can less easily afford its replacement or repair. This is not to say that working-class children have no opportunity at all for noisy and messy play, but that, while the middle- and upper middle-class home is deliberately equipped to withstand this sort of activity, lower middle- and working-class children tend to be shooed outside and expected to keep noise and mess in the yard. Inevitably, this will mean some reduction in such play, especially during the winter; and amusements such as painting will probably be lost altogether because there are no facilities for them in the yard. Nor should we underestimate the psychological difference for the child between having his activities classified as creative and welcomed in the house, and having them relegated to the yard as a nuisance.

It is perhaps worth looking at individual types of restriction in a little more detail, since they show up some differences in attitude. Reasons for objecting to noise tended to be tied either to the personal vulnerability of the mother ('My nerves won't stand too much of it') or, as we have seen, to consideration of special circumstances of night workers or small babies in the house or close by. In general, however, it was felt that a fair amount of noise was inevitable where four-year-olds were concerned, and neighbours who made a lot of fuss about it, in the absence of special needs, tended to be resented. The general view was that noise was something to be tolerated until 'she sort of gets to the pitch where she's screaming *a lot* and I can't stand it, and then I tell her not to scream *so much*'.

Civil servant's wife:

> One rainy afternoon they both had their drums out, and I hate the noise of it. So I stuffed cotton wool in my ears and let them get on with it for about half an hour. If I think they're doing it deliberately to torment me, then I stop them.

Few, however, would be quite so positive as Mrs Harrison, a railwayman's wife:

> Yes, I believe in noise. Yes, I believe in a lot of noise, yes. I don't believe in keeping them quiet, I think it upsets the brains for the child, that he thinks "Well, why *shouldn't* we make that noise?"—they don't understand it, not the young ones. I mean— if, say, they get to about twelve or fourteen, *then* you can say, well, "Don't you think it's time you quietened down a bit?" I mean, that's all I should do in any case. But little ones, I think you should leave them to *make* the noise. Mind you, if anyone's ill, I should say then, well, quieten him a bit, then; but not in an ordinary home where there's life in it—no, just let them carry on.

On the question of using furniture for play, Mrs Harrison said 'Yes, they do all that—their home's a home'; and she was echoed in her attitude by a lorry-driver's wife, who told us: 'She has a double bed with Lena (aged 15); oh yes, she jumps on that, that won't hurt, will it? They've got to amuse theirselves, children have, haven't they? They've got to play!' Another permissive mother, a window cleaner's wife, has had serious trouble from her council-estate neighbours who 'had the Guildhall man down' because of the noise her children made playing Cowboys and Indians in the garden; on the subject of jumping on the bed, she said:

> Jump? They go mad! Oh dear, you want to hear the racket! "We're only playing", they say, "We're only playing"! I say, "Yes, and you'll come through the ceiling in a minute, with your 'only playing'!" And chairs—ooh, yes. Dianne, the one at school, says "I'm going to make a den", and she takes me clothes-horse up and coats up, pillows, and—ooh, they don't half make a mess!—everything's upside-down. They're den-mad! Aren't you, Tina?

Many mothers shut their eyes to the ravages of the children, weighing the damage against their enjoyment, and more or less willingly postponing the pleasures of house-pride until the family is older.

Miner's wife:

> I let him jump on his bed. I think it's great fun—I've done it myself! He does play with the furniture. He plays with the chairs

and the settee—they're all ripped up because he plays horses, you see he uses the arms of the settee for horses; and he puts the chairs all lined up for a train.

Cotton winder's wife:

He's train-mad! We usually have the chairs out all along here. We go to the pictures on them one day—the next day you come in here, and the chairs are in the same position, but you're in a train. You have to get in before you know what you're on!

Machine operator's wife:

I was going to go for a three-piece, you know, and we went to Baker and Plumb's, and there was a marvellous one; and my husband said "*NO*—not until they're both at *school*", you know —and I was really disappointed. And then—a few days after— Mark fetches all these cushions off—he likes to play with them on the floor, because they're Dunlop, you know; and he gets his feet fast in the wires underneath; and I thought to myself, "Well, I'm glad I *didn't* have that three-piece"—you know? I mean, I think you'd ruin *their* life for them, while they're so tiny. I mean, when you keep saying to them, "*don't* do this" and "*don't* do that"—it must sound like a record to them.

It is also perhaps true that some mothers are not naturally very houseproud, and so have no difficulty in maintaining an accepting attitude towards the children's depredations; the office-manager's wife whose children 'can do just the heck they please with the garden' added, 'I'm afraid I'm not very careful with the furniture—a constant source of displeasure to my husband'; and an interviewer commented on one visit that 'Andy was hammering nails into the cupboard and cutting notches in the table with a knife while I was there'.

It was common among working-class families in particular to allow play with chairs and tables but to forbid the use of beds for jumping on, mainly on the grounds that bedsprings were easily damaged and expensive to replace; but a comprehensive ban on using furniture for play—'It's not because I'm proud of my furniture, because I'm not, but I just don't think it's right'— was comparatively rare.

Perhaps because we had specified certain typical ingredients of messy play—water, paint, earth and flour—answers tended to centre mainly upon these materials. The chief complaint arose out of the nature of the substances—that they are amorphous and tend to spread further than was intended. A number of mothers had started with the intention of letting the child paint neatly in a painting book, or make prim sandcastles in a corner of the garden, but felt they had taken on too much as the paint smudged and ran, and earthworks appeared on lawn or path. Some mothers, as we have seen, sequestered paint-boxes; others took the heart out of the game, one could not but feel, by banning its basic component.

Cutter's wife:

> Well now, at Christmas she had a cookery set, and I let her mess about with that. But she got paste everywhere, so I didn't let her have it no more—well, I let her have it, but without any flour.

Office-worker's wife:

> I don't like her to have water—she's inclined to make herself wet through. (You said she likes to play at washing dolls' clothes?) Not with water, though—dry washing. I wouldn't let her do it with water.

As one might expect, since they need to be specifically provided by the mother, flour and paint were the least widely attainable by four-year-olds; but most had access to water (some regularly and joyfully helped with the washing-up), and very few of those who had gardens or earth yards were forbidden to dig in them, so long as they kept their excavations within limits. A few middle-class mothers had gone to some trouble to find other attractive materials—'I've got them some clay from a pottery, and they have a glorious mess'—and blackboard chalks and plasticine are very cheaply available from most newsagents' shops in Nottingham. We also found some messy activities that had not occurred to us:

Lorry driver's wife:

> Sometimes I give her some jam in a pot and some sheets of paper, and she's making sandwiches. Anything for peace!

The clearest agreement of all was reached on the subject of dirtiness. 'Does it bother you if he gets really dirty while he's playing?' was the question, and there was a firm consensus of opinion that children of this age must inevitably get dirty, and that if one *was* bothered, one would simply have to make the best of it.

Sales manager's wife:

> Well, I mean, it *bothers* me, but I try and keep it in perspective. They've got to get dirty when they're playing. I mean, I don't like to see them *looking* dirty, but I don't say "You can't play with that today because you'll get dirty".

The following responses represent only a handful of cases, and it may be significant that these children are all girls:

Labourer's wife:

> It does. I don't like to see children in dirty clothes. I try and tell her she must keep clean, and make her wear an apron.

Cycle worker's wife:

> I get mad at her if she gets her clothes too dirty, because I was such a clean child.

Metal polisher's wife:

> I try to tell her that little girls shouldn't get so dirty, but it doesn't seem to have made much impression yet.

A few mothers accepted that dirt was unavoidable, but could not bear the look of it, and therefore did a great deal of cleaning up and changing of clothes during the day; on the other hand, it must be remembered that the family wash, given modern detergents and equipment, is not the heavy toil that it once was, as a labourer's wife pointed out: 'It *used* to bother me, but since I got the washer I don't bother now'. The general feeling was that only a selfish mother would seriously curtail her child's freedom for the sake of saving herself washing.

Surveyor's wife:

> It's no *good* bothering! I've given up! That's his coat out there now on the line, *and* his trousers *and* his shirts: everything out there is his. I have to change him about twice a day; oh, he gets absolutely . . . he's always on the floor, you know, rolling and one thing and another.

F

Metal polisher's wife:

> Sometimes, yes. He'll fill his bucket and mix soil to a paste and get it on his hands and it goes straight down him, and then in the winter I can't keep up with his jumpers. This is his third outfit on today. But I mean, if he kept clean all the time, I mean, he wouldn't be healthy, would he?

It is in fact typical of the great majority to regard dirt as an indication of rude health, and many suggested that they would worry if the child did *not* get dirty. There were endless variations on the theme that the dirty child is a normal, healthy child, particularly where boys were concerned. The first of this very representative group of mothers takes enormous pleasure in the rumbustiousness of her boys, the elder of whom is very slightly handicapped physically.

Presser's wife:

> By gum, no! I like to see them dirty. I think lads look rather attractive with a bit of dirt on them.

Painter's wife:

> If he's happy and healthy, he's usually dirty. If he kept clean, I should think there was something wrong with him.

Labourer's wife:

> No—it doesn't bother me one bit—I always think she'll wash! If she didn't get dirty there would be something the matter.

Chauffeur's wife:

> No—I think while they're dirty they're not ill, are they? I mean, like he is now—he's always like that. I don't mind—they bath easily.

Window cleaner's wife:

> Ooh *no*! I *like* 'em to get dirty—definitely! Look at *him* (baby)— he was clean this morning, and now look at him, and *he's* only eight months! He's *always* dirty, aren't you, duck?

Fitter's wife:

> No—soap and water's cheaper than medicine!

The purpose of this chapter has been to make some assessment of the degree to which children of four have autonomy in their play, in the two senses of being allowed to make use of the free-play materials most commonly available and having direction and control over their own possessions. We have seen that to some extent children's property rights are eroded by the family need for space and order; but what is significant in this situation is that the mother believes herself to be in the wrong in over-riding the child's will here, and will therefore tend to act surreptitiously: the *basic principle* is one of equal rights, even though this so often breaks down in practice. Once again, authoritarianism as such is rejected by the majority; but about a third of this majority at the same time cannot quite accept the disadvantages to them of a truly democratic relationship. Also rejected is the idea of the child who is seen (neatly and cleanly dressed, of course) and not heard: only 12% of mothers demand a high degree of clean, quiet behaviour in the house, and the rest impose only moderate or very moderate restrictions. The trends at work in this whole area of the mother-child relationship are those general ones of permissiveness and child-centredness which now seem central in our society: the only significant class difference in attitudes towards autonomy is found in so far as the professional class has child-centred behaviour made easier by both education and material conditions. One difference, however, which in this chapter was merely a side-issue—the greater value placed by middle-class mothers upon verbal apology after breaking the child's possessions—may be seen later on as a significant manifestation of what we believe to be a fundamental disparity between classes in mothers' attitudes towards child upbringing.

## CHAPTER 7

# SHARED AND PRIVATE WORLDS

For almost as long as children have been considered worth studying separately from the total man, the phenomenon of play has engaged the attention of philosophers and psychologists. Its function has been variously explained. Spencer saw it chiefly as the means by which the surplus energy of childhood was discharged.[1] Groos explained it in terms of instinctive modes of action through which both animal and human young developed and improved their skills in preparation for their mature role.[2] G. S. Hall believed that the child tended to repeat in his individual history activities typical of the evolution of the race: 'The best index and guide to the stated activities of adults in past ages is found in the instinctive, untaught, and non-imitative plays of children . . . . In play every mood and movement is instinct with heredity. Thus we rehearse the activities of our ancestors, back we know not how far, and repeat their life work in summative and adumbrated ways'.[3]

Freud put forward a view more closely related to the child's individual emotional needs, seeing in play both the compulsion to repeat life experiences, in order to gain emotional mastery of them, and the rehearsal of adult roles, the attainment of which is, he says, 'a wish that dominates them the whole time';[4] and Melanie Klein and others developed this into a conception of play as the symbolic acting out of wishes and ideas almost exclusively deriving from infantile sexuality.[5] Margaret Lowen-

[1] Spencer, H.: *Principles of Psychology*, Vol. II, Chap. ix; Williams and Norgate, London, 1855.

[2] Groos, K.: *The Play of Animals* and *The Play of Man*, originally published in 1896 and 1899.

[3] Hall, G. Stanley: *Adolescence*, Vol. I, Chap. iii, Appleton, New York, 1920.

[4] Freud, S.: *Beyond the Pleasure Principle*, pt. II, Hogarth Press, London, 1950. (Strachey translation; the 1922 translation gives this as 'the dominant wish of their time of life'.)

[5] As a general reference, we may give Klein, Melanie: *Contributions to Psychoanalysis, 1921–1945*, Hogarth Press, London, 1948.

feld, while drawing much from psychoanalytic ideas, refused to be bound within so narrow a framework, and saw the child's play as his 'work, thought, art and relaxation (which) cannot be pressed into any single formula'; she continues, 'It expresses a child's relation to himself and his environment, and, without adequate opportunity for play, normal and satisfactory emotional development is not possible'.[1]

Although students of child development have differed in their conception of the precise role of play, there is, then, a fundamental agreement that here is a phenomenon deserving very close attention because it seems to serve important biological functions for the child's growth towards maturity: in particular, in that it facilitates both conceptual development and social and emotional learning. And it is clear from our conversations with mothers that the majority of them would share, whether as a reasoned or as an intuitive conclusion, this view of play as something of positive value to the child. Play for most mothers is not merely an amusement to occupy the child and keep him out of their way: those who have watched their children at play (and this includes nearly all mothers) usually seem aware of some educative element, in the broadest sense of the word, which is present perhaps more obviously at this than at any other age.

Off-licence manager's wife:

> He keeps saying, "Mummy, will you come on this bus, it's sixpence at this end". 'Course, you have to join in if you have the time. We do try to take an interest in that sort of thing, because we know that it's his mind at work all the while and he's learning all the while.

To the four-year-old, play is a serious and absorbing activity. Through it, he discovers many exciting new experiences, develops and practises a personal repertoire of new skills, and explores a fascinating world of new sensations, new materials and new situations. It is, however, especially characteristic of this age for the child to enjoy those games in which he acts a part, taking on the role of someone else: thus he may play at being the postman or a shopkeeper, a daddy or a dustman; and the little girl on page 52 is perhaps not the only child in our

1 Lowenfeld, Margaret: *Play in Childhood*, Chap. xi, Gollancz, London, 1935.

sample to add the role of interviewer to her list. Often such games will be extended to include other children or other members of the family; but even when they are played by a child on his own, it seems likely that role-playing games assist him to explore and master the intricacies of personal relationships. The exercise of his imagination through the medium of fantasy allows the child to manipulate the whole spectrum of human feeling to accommodate to his own emotional needs; in particular, by playing at being someone else he comes to break the bonds of his own ego-centricity, and to begin to comprehend and respect the needs and desires of other people. Further, he absorbs into his own structure of concepts, and by acting consolidates, ideas about the behaviour associated with the statuses in human society which he adopts in his play—'Daddies look like this'; '*Don't* call me darling, I'm the *shop*man!'—and with other children can argue out roles ranging from 'But I *must* smack you, I'm your *mummy*!' to the conversation overheard between two four-year-olds who were being 'daleks': 'Don't push me, daleks don't push people'—'Well, but they ex*term*-inate people!'[1]

Role-playing games, because they are so often essentially social, offer frequent and compelling invitations to the mother to 'let her hair down' and join in. The child needs someone to play customer to his shopkeeper, patient to his doctor or Indian to his cowboy; and, in the absence of siblings at school, the mother is often the most suitable candidate. Ball games, skipping and dancing are also better played in twos than in ones, and here again the mother may be called upon, not just to turn the rope or act as spectator, but to compete and take her turn like any other child. It is clear that there is a difference between this sort of participation, in which the mother plays *as the child's equal*, and the more consciously educative participation where the mother draws or paints with the child, 'helps him with his letters' or assists with the trickier points of Meccano or interlocking brick constructions; in these latter games there is a strong element of tuition, and the adult-child relationship is maintained. It was the mother's willingness to join in

---

[1] 'Daleks' were robot-like characters in a very popular children's television serial. Their easily-imitated droning chant of 'We-shall-ex-term-in-ate-you!' with which they advanced upon their captives, combined with an oddly attractive shape, made them quite irresistible to small children, some of whom were known to say 'I-am-a-dal-ek' as their earliest sentence.

on equal terms—to play on a childish level—which we wanted to assess at this point; and we shall refer to this willingness as 'wholehearted' participation.

The questions which we considered in the last chapter were largely concerned with situations in which the mother finds herself either opposing the will of the child or in some way curtailing his freedom to play as he wishes. In discussions of the ways in which parents exert control over their children, there is sometimes a tendency to overestimate the importance of negative sanctions and restrictions and to underestimate the means by which mothers guide the behaviour of their children by example and encouragement. We may here redress the balance, therefore, by examining how mothers exercise a positive influence by such gentle and persuasive methods as taking a special interest in certain kinds of play, encouraging the child to communicate his imaginative thoughts and fantasies, and sharing wholeheartedly in his role-playing games. It is thus of more than incidental interest to find out what proportion of mothers take their children's play seriously enough to participate on the child's own terms.

The question we asked, then, was: 'When he's playing at something, do you ever join in?' and the criterion to be met was whether the mother would enter into the spirit of the game as another child might, rather than in any sense helping or advising. If, for instance, the child were an engine-driver today, would she sit down in the imaginary train and discuss the scenery as they travelled along? or if he were an Indian, would she put on a cowboy hat and shoot at him from the shelter of the kitchen door? We found that a very high proportion—66%—do in fact actively participate in play at the child's own level: the examples that follow make it clear that for these mothers such play was both frequent and enjoyable.

Bleacher's wife:

> Oh yes; say they were playing at cowboys; well, I have to hide behind the settee, and they come riding round it, and I have to—(pantomime dying in agony)—"Oh . . . you've got me!"— all that sort of thing, you know. I act daft in *that* way.

Chauffeur's wife:

> Well, I do—if they want to play skipping, and want us to hold the rope—we turn the rope and the three of them skip, you see.

(Do you ever play as a child might play—not just *turning* the rope, but . . .?) In the yard I do, yes—if anyone saw me! I'm as bad as the kids sometimes! And shops sometimes—especially wet days—I play with them. (And what are you when it's shops?) Oh, I'm a mere customer—I can't be a shopkeeper!

## Presser's wife:

Oh yes. We get all these pillows off the settee here, and we put them in a line all along the floor here, and then we all have to get on and go for a ride. Oh, it's smashing, isn't it, Brian?

## Chemical worker's wife:

Oh, a skip, or a jump, or a little hop round; a little wrestling with *him* or dolls' games with these. (When you play a dolls' game, would you be a special person in it?) Oh, yes—I'm the patient, or the baby, or the little girl's aunt.

## Hosiery mechanic's wife:

Well, I have to. Well, just now, his father has made him a sword, like Robin Hood's, and he's got a piece of wood, and he pushes it in his belt, and then we have to fight, and I'm the Sheriff of Nottingham and he's Robin Hood.

## Miner's wife:

Sometimes, yes, we go on a rocket—he puts all the chairs out, and touches the knobs on that side, and he says "Hold on, we're going on a rocket"—and when the spin-drier's on for the noise, he says "Hold on, Mummy, we're off", so we hold on, you see.

## Builder's wife:

Oh yes, I always play house—he plays house, and he's the mummy and I'm the auntie and come to visit him.

## Cotton winder's wife:

We're usually the Shadows, you know, playing guitars. Oh, we have a jolly time!

For one or two mothers whose children were temperamentally more reserved than themselves, this sort of play was consciously seen as a means of attaining the intimate relationship which they might otherwise have missed altogether.

**Advertising manager's wife:**

> I always have enjoyed playing with them. It's always been the only way to get close to them, because they weren't cuddly children. But I always have been available, if they wanted me to play with them, you know. My husband and I play 'transports', and end up in all sorts of weird places.

Two out of three mothers, then, welcome the chance to join in the fun of playing with their children on an equal footing. It should be emphasized again, however, that the remaining 34% are by no means non-participant in their children's play; most of them would take part in play of the more dignified kind—drawing for the child or helping him with puzzles or more formal games. The distinction is that these are all activities in which it is possible to play with the child without risking being made to look foolish and without relinquishing the adult role: they are quasi-educational, and are undertaken more in the spirit of pleasing the child than to 'have a jolly time' all round.

**Sales manager's wife:**

> Well, yes—if it interests me. I help him with his train set. (Do you ever play mothers and fathers, or imaginative games of that sort?) Oh no, I never do that. I'm not very keen on imaginary things like that.

**Storeman's wife:**

> If she wants me to draw anything, I draw her a lot of circles and tell her to fill them up with faces.

**Labourer's wife:**

> I haven't got time for that sort of thing. Sometimes, if I have got time, I take them up to the common in summer and things like that. But apart from that I haven't got time.

**University lecturer's wife:**

> Well, if he's painting I will paint with him; and I will play Lego (constructional game) with him. That sort of thing. (These seem to be games in which you play as an adult—do you ever play as a child? Imaginative games, for instance?) I'd say he does that more with other children, and therefore it's the more educative play that I indulge in—not because I don't like the other, but it seems to me that's what he looks to me for, rather than coming

F*

down more to his level. I also think that, however much you'd *like* to do that sort of thing, you *are* an adult, and I think he likes it better with children.

The 34% did include a few who had found that their offers to play imaginatively were entirely unwelcome to their children, and who restricted themselves to educative play for this reason.

Grocer's wife:

> Oh yes, if I can—teaching her new words—copying them on to her blackboard, if she asks me to. Crayoning; telling her stories. (Do you ever join in as a child might?) She doesn't want me to join in so much in her games. Sometimes she'll have a shop set up with all sorts of odds and ends, and she'll put some high-heeled shoes on and be chatting away; and I'll come and buy something and she'll *freeze*—and that's the end of the game.

Stonecaster's wife:

> I think he's better amusing himself. He gets bored if I play. I'm not playing right—I'm not doing it right. He just wants to play on his own.

The number of these cases is very small, and not enough to distort the general picture of this group as on the whole preferring to maintain the adult role, in which they for the most part felt more comfortable. Some mothers felt that they were not temperamentally the best people to play childishly with their children: sometimes they would add that there were other adults available who were better suited to it than themselves, perhaps in this way expressing a feeling that such play should be provided by *somebody*.

Cashier's wife:

> I do not—I can't enjoy their games. Daddy and Granny do that.

Company director's wife:

> One afternoon a week they're with my daily help. The one afternoon, that's my afternoon off, and *she* really is very, very good—I mean, she's better than I am. I *have*, at times, let them climb over me and given them piggy-backs and horse-rides. But I mean she *devotes* fully one-and-a-half hours.

Fairground worker's wife:

> No. I think it's because I never was a child, really—with having to be grown-up so early in life. I had to do all the family washing when I was eleven . . . . I don't remember much about my childhood really—I remember all the cooking, and things like that.

Many were very definite that they felt too old for this sort of play.

Pipe inspector's wife (aged 42):

> I don't play with him. I mean, I'm old to muck about, sort of thing, and I'm not a young mother, really, am I? I mean, I had my first when I was 29, so I mean I wasn't young then, was I? As I said, I think they get on your nerves a bit when you're older—'cause I mean, I used to look after children when I was in my teens, and I mean you've got patience then, but you haven't when you're older.

However, it would not be true to suggest that the sample divides into younger mothers who play and older mothers who do not. In a random sample, approximately one mother in four is aged 36 or more; but the proportion of this age-group rated as wholeheartedly participant is still very high: 62%, against 66% for all ages combined. It is not possible to show any significant overall relationship between maternal age and degree of play participation; perhaps we really need a measure of being young in heart rather than young in years. Mrs Allingham looked surprised at our question, and answered with a laugh, 'Oh, no! I'm too old for that now!'; but Mrs Denison found the question entirely serious: 'I like to join in games with her. I want her to feel I'm interested in them. I love to play with her—I'm still a child really, when you come to think about it'. The truth is that Mrs Allingham, at 26, is in fact a year younger than Mrs Denison: the moral of which is that a mother is as young as she feels.

A factor which is related to the mother's age—the size of the family—does show a link with play participation. For families so far comprising only one or two children, the proportion of mothers rated as wholeheartedly participant was 76%, compared with 57% for mothers of larger families; these figures are based upon a randomized sample, and the difference is statistically significant. We might interpret this at its face value and assume that mothers with larger families have less time, and perhaps see less need, to involve themselves in childish games, while the mother of the only child may feel an obligation to offer this sort of attention. As a laboratory assistant's wife explained: 'Well, I feel that, with Bronwen being the only one, and with not many children round here to play with, I have to sort of take the role of playmate, as well as mother'. However, an analysis of these results by social class as well as by family size shows that such an interpretation is rather too simple.

TABLE XVII

*Mothers' play participation as a function of both social class and family size*

Percentages indicate the proportions of mothers rated as 'wholeheartedly participant'. The numerical size of the group to which each percentage relates is given in parentheses.

|  | I and II | IIIwc | IIIman | IV | V | All classes (random sample) |
|---|---|---|---|---|---|---|
|  | % | % | % | % | % | % |
| 1 or 2 children | 72 (85) | 79 (68) | 76 (92) | 84 (57) | 48 (23) | 76 |
| 3 or more children | 70 (43) | 65 (40) | 54 (134) | 66 (79) | 44 (78) | 57 |
| All families | 71 (128) | 74 (108) | 63 (226) | 74 (136) | 45 (101) | 66 |

The most striking finding is that mothers in Class V are far less likely to participate wholeheartedly in their children's play than are other mothers. It might be thought that this result could be due to the larger average family size with which Class V mothers have to cope; but the result holds regardless of the number of children, and cannot be adequately accounted for on this basis. An alternative explanation is that these mothers often have a somewhat more formal and tradition-oriented conception of the maternal role, which does not include coming down to the child's own level in play: thus Mrs Allingham, quoted above, who considered herself too old for that sort of thing at 26, was also the wife of an unskilled labourer. From the information presented in this table, it can also be shown that there is a significant difference between working-class mothers as a whole and the middle-class group—a difference which is significant despite the somewhat anomalous result found (as so often happens[1]) for mothers in Class IV. Finally, in confirmation that this trend is as closely attributable to the class factor as to that of family size, it may also be shown that a large majority of professional-class mothers are rated as wholeheartedly participant, *whether or not* they have large families. The family-size variable is thus not equally important in all social classes: it seems to be effective mainly in Classes III white collar, III manual and IV, but at the extreme ends of the class scale is overruled by another factor. One can only guess that this overriding factor must be one of educational consciousness, which can be shown in many other ways to be particularly high and low respectively in the top and bottom groups. This is probably enhanced by the high valuation set by professional-class parents upon any activity which exercises their child's general verbal facility, as this sort of play undoubtedly does.

*'There's this imaginary boy who lives with us . . . '*

From playing at being someone himself, it is not a very big step for the child to invent one or more completely imaginary characters to act parts in his play. If, for instance, he wants to play school, with himself in the romantic role of teacher, he can begin by trying to persuade some other person to join in the game. But in practice it may not always be easy for him to find someone who will both play the game of his choice and take the more prosaic part in it: his mother may be too busy to play, and other children—real children—are not always amenable to being manipulated in this way. Imaginary children, on the other hand, can be made to behave exactly as one wishes. Furthermore, imaginary characters never try to make unwelcome innovations to the game, they don't insist on having *their* turn at the most interesting point, nor do they get temperamental and threaten to walk out; in fact they can be walked out upon at the whim of their creator, without risk of reprisals, and will still be waiting for him when he wants them again. Children of this age are not very skilled at handling the complex problems of social co-operation which communal play so frequently presents; and, for this reason, solitary dramatic play on a fantasy level may

---

[1] Reasons for this were suggested in Newson, John and Elizabeth, 1963, *op. cit.*, pp. 216–7.

sometimes seem preferable to coping with a group of all too real playmates.

Whatever their motivation, most children seem to be able to extend their play by using their imagination to recruit in fantasy not only people and animals but an infinite variety of non-existent settings and materials to suit the purpose of the moment: and the more inventive child can thus provide at will all the additional props and personalities he needs to enlarge almost indefinitely the private world of his playtime life.

### Type estimator's wife:

She can make a piece of paper become lots of things. . . . At one time she used to pick things up and give them to us—pick them off the table. There was nothing there; and my husband used to say to her "You've dropped it!"—and she'd bend down and pick it up, and we never knew what it was. But she'd fetch and carry it all over the room, you know, if we gave it her.

### Clerk's wife:

The other day she said "Mind my cat! Don't tread on him, will you?" and she'd got this imaginary cat on a string, and she really thought it was there.

### Lorry driver's wife:

She'll get the table out and set it out for different people, and she'll talk to them, but there's nobody there. She's got no end of people; she *lives* on imagination. . . . She'll talk to them as if they're all there sitting down and having a good conversation with her; and yet there's only her there when you go to look.

For some children, however, there is a further stage in their fantasy at which certain of their imaginary characters begin to recur in different situations and places, and finally come to assume a semi-independent existence as personalities of some consequence in their daily life. It is not very easy to estimate accurately the proportion of children who possess persisting fantasy characters of this sort, since by their very nature they are easily hidden from the parents if the child prefers to keep them to himself. There are certainly some children who are embarrassed by an adult's interest, and others whose imaginary friends are no more than mentioned, and might be missed altogether by an unobservant mother: 'I'll say "Pardon—what did you say?" and she'll say "It's all right, Mummy—I'm only talking to Bumbler"'. One mother denied that her daughter had any fantasy creatures, but was corrected by her husband who happened to be present and knew better: 'Oh yes, she has—she's got Peter. *I'll* have to tell you something about this imaginary Peter. . . .' Sometimes, too, there may be a period during which the child refers to his fantasy but the mother fails to comprehend what he means: 'It was a dog, its name was Nimidy . . . at first, you know, I couldn't make it out. But then it dawned on me, because I'd had Mervyn, *he* used to have a bird in a box'. Clearly, we cannot hope to discover every fantasy creation by asking the mothers; nevertheless, the mother has a better chance than anyone of knowing about these things, and it seemed worthwhile at least to have a minimal estimate of their frequency. Very few studies appear to exist which make an attempt to gauge the extent of true fantasy among children: Hurlock and Burstein (working from adults' childhood memories) found that 31% of the women and 23% of the men in their sample of 700 remembered having had imaginary companions *at some time*;[1] while Margaret Svendsen, on the basis of maternal reports on 119 children from 46 'unselected' families, estimated that at least 13% of all children had such playmates.[2] It is relevant to our own assessment that in 37 out of 40 cases which she studied in detail, the fantasy creature had appeared before the fourth birthday.[3] Kanner suggests that parents, 'kept out of the cloistered privacy of the child's imaginations', are aware only rarely of these phenomena.[4] Unless previous workers have grossly underestimated, our findings contradict this: while we would emphasize that there must be fantasies that the mother knows nothing about, it will be plain from what follows that there are a great many of which she can give a very adequate description indeed. Often, in fact, the existence of the fantasy

[1] Hurlock, E. B., and Burstein, W.: 'The Imaginary Playmate', J. Genet. Psychol., 1932, 41, 380–92.

[2] Svendsen, M.: 'Children's Imaginary Companions', Arch. Neurol. and Psychiat., 1934, 32.

[3] Svendsen, too, found a difference between girls and boys: 30 of her 40 cases were girls. Our own figures show a slight female preponderance, but the difference is not quite significant. It is possible that the disparity is more apparent than real, and due mainly to girls' greater verbal fluency: the communication factor which we discuss on pp. 185–7.

[4] Kanner, L.: *Child Psychiatry*, 3rd ed., Blackwell, Oxford, 1957.

companion personally involves the mother herself, and indeed the whole family.

**Production manager's wife:**

He has Candy, a dog. When I go a walk with *my* dog, we take Candy; we have to take Candy to the edge of the pavement. I think he can really see this dog. In fact, I said to my husband, I think *I* can see this dog! His friend had a Mr Johnson when he started to play with Christopher—Christopher took over Mr Johnson, but his friend didn't like that, so Christopher went back to Candy.

**Miner's wife:**

Yes, she has Janet. It's a little girl. She came out with her—oh, more than a year ago. Everything's Janet—and yet she doesn't know anybody called Janet. But I mean—we can be watching television, and if my lad sits too close, it's "You're squashing her—get off!" And he *has* to get off, and all! I think we've all got used to Janet now.

We wanted to investigate all cases of fantasy creations, including fantasy companions, which went beyond mere *ad hoc* imaginings for the purpose of a single game. The questions we asked were:

31. Has he any imaginary people or animals or places that he brings into his play?
32. How do you react if he talks about them to you?
33. Does he sometimes tell you about some happening as if it were true, when you know it's not?
    What do you do when this happens?

Obviously certain problems of definition arise when one attempts to decide whether the child has a true fantasy or not; the borderline between fantasy and reality is often far from clear. Our problem was to make the distinction between playing *at* something—the sort of games referred to in the first part of this chapter—and the fantasies which had come to be almost as real and persisting as the rest of the child's life circumstances. We also wanted to include those activities and adventures which, although they had not occurred, the child spoke about in terms no different from his manner of speaking about real events.

Imaginary companions are, in particular, not always easy to define: most young children attribute personal feelings and distinctive personality traits to cuddly toys such as teddy bears, and it is commonplace to observe little girls especially holding long and serious conversations with their dolls. These must be counted as 'playing *at* . . .', rather than as fantasy. In general, people and animals, to be judged as fantasy creatures, had to have no material basis. Occasionally, however, it was clearly necessary to admit a character to the fantasy category because, although having a 'real' origin, so extensive a saga had been built upon this foundation that fantasy had long since outstripped reality.

University lecturer's wife:

> He has a *real* friend, a dog friend that he talks about—the dog lives in Sutton Coldfield—but this is a terrific personality, this dog, Tilly. He talks about it *a lot*. I would say it is more of a person—although it has a *basis* in reality, it's more like an imaginary thing. . . . (Do you think that if he saw her more often this would spoil his fantasy about her?) No, I don't think so—she's so well-trained and so placid that she's really like a great cushion. For instance, they're coming to stay, and we said "Maybe while they're here we'll go out in the evening"; and he said "Oh, yes. Well, if I want anything I'll call Tilly, and she'll make my cocoa".

Perhaps the best example of this is supplied by our own daughter at the same age, whose doll Susanna, rather plain and dull in appearance, was the inspiration for a complete fantasy world, fully peopled and furnished, the doings of which would be described at great length, and with total consistency from one time to another, to anybody who cared to listen. Particularly striking about these accounts were their air of forming only a part of a much larger fund of experience: which is in fact the characteristic of any brief recounting of an incident in the speaker's own life, yet this differed in referring to an entirely imaginary life. It occurred to us then that it would be possible to interview our daughter about her experiences in bringing up Susanna, in just the same way as one would interview any other mother; and this in fact we did. The result is, we imagine, a unique document—the transcript of a four-year-old's view of her supposedly four-year-old child and her opinions on its

upbringing—which is included in an abridged form in Appendix III. We should add that no concessions were made to the mother's youth: all questions were asked exactly as in a normal interview, further explanation being given only when (occasionally) it was asked for. The matter-of-fact dottiness of this transcript is very typical of small children's communications from their fantasy worlds.

We arrive, then, at a rather strict definition of fantasy, in that if it is a person, animal or place it must recur in the child's imagination from one day to another and must very considerably transcend any original factual basis. In the case of fantasy activities, it must be a reasonably frequent occurrence for the child to report these, he must talk of them seriously (i.e. not obviously joking), and he must have no motive other than the story's intrinsic interest (i.e. 'He comes and tells me his sister hit him when she didn't' is disallowed). On these criteria, we find that 28% of all children (random sample) are known to have some sort of fantasy life. It must be emphasized that all our figures refer to the children at the age of four, and that there are others who used earlier to have fantasies, but who have not mentioned them for six months or more: these are not included.

If we now separate out those children whose fantasy takes the form of imaginary companions, either human or animal, we find that these number 22%: some of these children have other fantasies as well. This figure includes 3% who have a special version of the imaginary character, in which they themselves take on another identity, and insist on being called by the name of the imaginary creature; there is a clear difference here from the child who merely plays at being, say, a shop man: a difference in the completeness of the identification, the persistence with which it is maintained and the regularity with which the child reverts to it.

Traveller's wife:

He's often Susan. We don't know who Susan is, but he'll dress up in an old dress of mine and he's Susan; and he's Susan for days and days and days. But he doesn't have another companion: it's Colin *being* Susan.

In a few cases, the child changes his identity for that of *an imaginary child with the same name*, so that the mother is faced with the tricky social situation of entertaining her own child in another identity together with another invisible child with her child's name. Carolyn's mother, a machine operator's wife, was unwilling hostess to two Carolyns and other unseen visitors as well.

> Now she's grown out of them a bit—she had loads—loads! Oh, dear!—you couldn't count them! There's Carolyn, she still has her—Carolyn's another little girl, and *she's* someone else. Carolyn's her friend, and she wants to bring Carolyn in to tea, and can Carolyn use our toilet, can Carolyn do this . . . and she'll bring her friends in, imagine they're all there and sit talking away to them.

There are certain differences to be seen in the family circumstances of children who communicate fantasies and those who do not; but before looking at these it may be helpful to illustrate the range and rich variety of these flights of fancy. We present them in the two groups we have distinguished: those which involve imaginary doings and happenings, and the perhaps more interesting, because more permanently established, imaginary creatures. In some reports, both are involved in the same story: for instance, many four-year-olds talk of an imagined school and of their adventures there, and in a few cases the teacher is no lay figure but central to the child's fantasy.

Scientific research worker's wife:

> He wants to go to school so very much; and as he can't go, he has an imaginary teacher: who presides, I guess, in his bedroom. And he often sleeps with his teacher, and he picks up bits of paper in the kitchen and says "Can I take it to school to my teacher?" and I say yes, so he goes upstairs and takes it to teacher. Oh, teacher is very much *there*. I've accepted teacher as part of the household. (Does teacher ever come to tea . . .?) Oh no—he himself meets teacher, but he is the only contact.

The 'places' which we specifically mentioned in our question mainly occurred as schools; we had had in mind a child, not in our sample, who at this age had a delightful shop called 'Nymphs and Shepherds', clearly modelled on the Nottingham store Griffin and Spalding, but with the useful advantage that money was not required; this same child also talked of an Elysian playground called 'Shining-Bright'. Elizabeth Pakenham, who includes a very interesting collection of fantasies in her *Points for Parents*, mentions a four-year-old boy who had an imaginary country named 'Double Dess', which lay 'just beyond Africa'.[1] We came across no places with actual names among these children, though some of them apparently worked in much more exciting surroundings than their fathers. Some examples of fantasy doings and happenings follow.

Insurance inspector's wife:

> He's got a fabulous imagination. He owns two garages, and he's got a chappie working for him called Johnny Raven—I don't know where he got the name from. They've got lions, and elephants, and all sorts at the place where he works.

Miner's wife:

> She'll tell you anything—you just have to sort it out, She'll tell you she's been down to the woods, and seen a big stream, and took her shoes off and paddled—and she hasn't been outside the door, you know.

Brewery worker's wife:

> Yesterday he was riding his bike back from my mother's and he was swinging one leg. So I said "What are you doing that for?" and he said "Well, the other day I cut me on my bike, and my Dad chopped my leg off, and he's glued it back on again and it's swinging". . . . I just laugh and joke about it, and say "Oh, your poor leg!"

Clerk's wife:

> Well, she came home the other week and said some other kiddy had been sick. She'd been sick all over her. "She was sick all over my face and my hair"—and she'd had to hold her over the bowl, and then the teachers had come and taken it in turns, and when they'd got tired *she'd* had to hold her again. But she was that serious over it, I really examined her. I said, "Well, you'll have to have your hair washed". I thought, well . . . I sort of *knew* the teachers *wouldn't* leave her. So I began to wonder . . . I was really puzzled. . . .

1 Pakenham, Elizabeth: *Points for Parents*, Weidenfeld and Nicolson, London, 1954. The many examples of children's behaviour with which Lady Pakenham (now Lady Longford) illustrates her 'points' are drawn from the letters of readers of a regular column on this subject which she contributed to a national newspaper. For an illuminating study of the fantasies of especially imaginative children, the reader is again referred to Shirley Jackson, 1954 and 1957, *op. cit.*

Actor's wife:

Yes, she does at the moment. I think they're sort of more outrageous things, like "We were coming home from school and
a great big wolf came out"—things that you *know* couldn't
possibly be true, more than a sort of *deviation* from the truth.

Foreman's wife:

He was sitting up in the cab of his Grandad's lorry, and he said
to his Nana, "You know, Nana, what do you think of me driving
this lorry?" She said, "You look all right, duck". He said, "*I*
used to drive one of them, when I was younger". She said "You
used to *what*?" He says, "Yes, I used to drive one of these. And
I had a big wagon before that!"

Company director's wife:

We went out for a picnic yesterday afternoon—my husband,
Louise, Giles and I—we were going along, and Giles said, "Of
course you know when Daddy was a little boy, he used to sit
in the back of the car and smoke cigarettes, and *I* used to drive
the car". Yes, he's always talking about how he used to do
things—when he was a man he used to do it; he's sort of the
wrong way round, somehow!

The mysterious time of 'when I was younger', 'when Daddy
was a little boy', 'before I was born', fascinating theme to so
many children, also exercises the imagination of the first child
in our group of those whose world is peopled by their own
creations.

Caretaker's wife:

He's always on about a horse that he had before he was born.
He's mad about horses, and he's always on about this horse.
It's ever so strange—he's always talked about it ever since he
*could* talk. It all happened before he was born, he doesn't **do**
anything with it now. But I think about it sometimes—it **makes**
you wonder.

Publisher's wife:

He's got a Mr Ghost, and a little rabbit, and a Cat—it's **Cat**
mostly. He asked me to smack Cat this morning, because it **had**
scratched him, so I smacked it. We've been through all **this**
before, I mean it's quite a normal thing, most children do it,

so I just—especially in the case of Mr Ghost, I encourage Mr Ghost. (He's a friendly character, is he?) Yes, he's friendly, they're all friendly. They're really part of the family. He'll say open the door or leave the door open for Cat to come through; usually we find Mr Ghost upstairs when we're making the beds, so we have a little talk to him then.

### Lorry driver's wife (also quoted on page 152):

She's got no end of people; she *lives* on imagination. They're always the same people. The names just appear from nowhere. I mean, she might have heard someone mention them. There's one called Mansfield—well, my husband used to say "I'm going to Mansfield this afternoon", and I think she thought it was a *person* he was going to see.

### Storekeeper's wife:

She imagines this friend at the door, Susan; you have to go and answer the door and that, you know, and then you have to say what she tells you to say. Everybody has to listen to her—her Dad does, and all. Nearly every day she'll be playing in here with her; she'd be here this afternoon if she wasn't outside. We have to say hello to Susan—she stands just *there*. (And does Susan ever come to meals?) Ooh, yes—"Can Susan come for tea?", and I say "All right", and we sit her there and we pretend. Although often she comes to tea but she doesn't actually sit down, she just stands there. You have to laugh sometimes!—but we don't laugh now, mind, because we know she really means it.

### Window dresser's wife:

She keeps pretend chickens out the garden. Oh yes, she often feeds them out the garden. We just go on about them as if they were real.

### Salesman's wife:

We have Noddy and Billa and Gunny. (Veronica: Noddy's a girl.) I don't know, when you take Noddy to Grandma's you always say "I've brought *him* again", and 'him' is for a boy, isn't it? I've always thought Noddy was a boy. (Veronica: No, it's a girl. They've got buckets on their heads. And the dog's got hair.) They've been with her about two years, I should think. When we go out and come in we have to be sure to let Noddy through the door before we close it, and sometimes we've had to go back to the gate and let him in because she insists we've left Noddy outside the gate. And he goes to Nana's with her, Noddy—he's the one that's always in her thoughts, you see. I don't think he's been on the bus with us, but he's been in the car with us. And, well, sometimes if Veronica doesn't want to love Mummy, she sometimes says "*I* don't love you, but Noddy does!" I don't seem to have them for meals—I'll probably find that later on.

Veronica's 'Noddy' is a good example of the way in which a fantasy character can come to serve a useful purpose beyond that of mere companionship; he will act as a stand-in on those days when Veronica 'doesn't want to love Mummy', thus absolving her from the guilt she might feel were she to withdraw love from her mother altogether. Fantasy personages often take the role of the child's *alter ego*, most commonly serving as scapegoat for the child's misdeeds.

Newsagent's wife:
> There's a little girl called Choany he has had since he could talk. I think she must be his naughty self, because every time anything goes wrong, Choany has done it.

Furniture polisher's wife:
> It's always Creep-Mouse. "Who's done it?"—"Oh, I haven't—Creep-Mouse has done it!"

Company director's wife:
> It's usually Michael (imaginary boy) that's done it. I say "Well, I don't know what we're going to do with Michael!" It's rather trying.

Trying, indeed—for the child who can change his identity at will is clearly at an advantage in any altercation with his mother. Mrs Piercy, however, succeeded in turning the tables on Dianne and her accomplice Jennifer.

Frame repairer's wife:
> Oh yes, she's Jennifer. She goes outside and dresses up . . . she'll go outside and talk to herself, and then she'll knock on the back door and say "I'm Jennifer, can I speak to Dianne, please?" . . . And you know, if she's a naughty girl and won't eat her dinner,

I say to her, "All right, Dianne, you just go and fetch Jennifer to me. She'll eat your dinner". And she'll go out, and come back as Jennifer, and she'll eat her dinner.

'Teddy' is an interesting, because rather typical, example of the toy around which an entire personality is elaborated:

Sales manager's wife:

> Teddy takes the place of everybody and everything; if anything's gone wrong, it's Teddy that did it. He is more or less a real person. The other dolls come out when she feels like it, but Teddy joins in everything. (Child: Teddy bought some skates with wheels!) She's full of that sort of thing.

Teddy is not only a scapegoat but also a figure of power: he can buy himself expensive toys without reference to grown-ups. Occasionally the scapegoat will be in no sense a companion, but predominantly a frightening creation: 'there are monkeys who live in the cellar, and that's why he won't go down the cellar, because they might get him; and if there's something wrong, it's always a monkey that's come up from the cellar and done it'. Even friendly creatures can sometimes get out of hand: our own daughter's 'Needy', who commuted between a shadowy corner behind an armchair and the centre of the sitting-room fire, started off with fairylike qualities which insidiously became more witchlike, to Carey's consternation; and a technical lecturer's child developed a similarly ambivalent attitude towards his imaginary playmate.

> He's got a pet dragon: it plays with him. . . . But the dragon gets in the way sometimes when Alistair's frightened. If he wants to go upstairs and it's dark, he says "The dragon might get me if I go upstairs, won't you, Dragon?"

Table XVIII presents an analysis of the incidence of fantasy communications, broken down as before by family size and social class: these two factors seemed more likely than others to exert an effect upon either fantasy or its communication (we cannot, unfortunately, separate these dependent variables), and in fact it can be seen that they do. In the first place, one might expect the ready availability of real playmates to be, to some extent, inimical to the development of an elaborate private

TABLE XVIII

*Incidence of fantasies communicated to the mother,
analysed by social class and family size*

(Numerical sizes of groups to which percentages relate are given in parentheses)

| | I and II | IIIwc | IIIman | IV | V | All classes (random) |
|---|---|---|---|---|---|---|
| | % | % | % | % | % | % |
| *Family size* | | | | | | |
| 1–2 children | 49 (85) | 28 (68) | 35 (92) | 32 (57) | 17 (23) | 35 |
| 3 or more children | 36 (44) | 33 (40) | 20 (134) | 19 (79) | 13 (78) | 22 |
| All families | 45 | 30 | 26 | 24 | 14 | 28 |

fantasy world; mothers themselves were inclined to regard such behaviour, particularly that involving imaginary companions, as a symptom of the child's social isolation, and the table shows that children with only one brother or sister, or only children, do significantly more often have known fantasies than children from larger families, even when social class is held constant. We must, of course, remember that the mother of a small family has more opportunity both to observe and to talk to any individual child in it. If one takes the singletons separately, the proportion of fantasies among them is higher still: 41% in a random sample; the figures for these children alone have not been given in full for the reason that, as we descend the social scale, the number of singletons decreases so sharply that comparisons between social classes become meaningless. Hurlock and Burstein, incidentally, believed that family size was not a factor;[1] but Margaret Svendsen found that more than half of her sample of 40 children with imaginary companions had been singletons *at the time when the fantasy was first observed*.[2] In view of the fact that the former study was based upon adult memories and the latter, like ours, upon mothers' reports, these differing results would seem to be evidence for a factor of better communication between mothers and only children, rather than for a special disposition of only children towards fantasy. The distinction between contemporary and

[1] Hurlock, E. B., and Burstein, W., *op. cit.*
[2] Svendsen, M., *op. cit.*

final family size is obviously an important one, however, for which Hurlock and Burstein do not allow.

In the second place, the evidence in this table suggests that there is a consistent and significant class influence even after allowance has been made for the confounding factor of family size: fantasies significantly increase in Class I and II and decrease in Class V. This may be interpreted in a number of ways. It is possible that Class I and II children and Class V children, having respectively above average and below average vocabularies, find this effectively facilitating, or restricting, the communication of their fantasies to their mothers: in other words, it might be that children of all classes have fantastic thoughts to an equal extent, but that they vary between classes in their ability to share these thoughts. On the other hand, it might persuasively be argued that imagination itself, even before it reaches the stage of communication, is enriched or impoverished by the child's verbal capacity or incapacity. We should need to use quite different research techniques to investigate the relative importance of these two factors, but it is probable that each of them makes some contribution. The mother's own attitude as it is affected by class may be looked at a little more closely, however, and this does seem to be relevant to how far fantasies are talked about by the child or known of by the mother. Professional-class mothers tend to be themselves verbally fluent and to respect fluency in their children: and perhaps it is simply the knowledge that he will be listened to which makes the child of this class more ready to entrust his wilder imaginings to his mother's ear. A clue to this can be found when imaginary creatures are separately analysed by social class: the differences between Class V and the rest holds good, but the divergence at the top end of the scale almost disappears. The explanation of this appears to be that imaginary characters, as is very obvious from the examples we have given, exert a more insistent claim upon the mother's attention and are less easily shrugged off than mere 'romancing' on the part of the child; at the same time they do not, perhaps, make such demands upon the child's vocabulary as do descriptions of fantasy events.

The mother who is able to enter the child's imaginative world and who is willing to accept his fantasies at face value will almost certainly act as a stimulus to the production of further fantasies, or to the elaboration of those he already has. Not all mothers are enthusiastic about these manifestations of imagination, however; and it is here that we find another subtle but definite difference between middle-class and working-class, especially lower working-class, wives. The middle-class mother typically welcomes and encourages fantasy play, taking it seriously as a normal and delightful phase of childhood, some thing to be respected and indeed treasured for as long as it lasts. She tends, too, to see it both as pleasing evidence of the child's present creativity and as a talent to be fostered as the basis for a future imaginative facility. Thus fantasy for her is not just a part of the magic of childhood, to be shared with delight, but the promise of a poetic sensitivity which might all too easily be stunted by an adult's indifference. 'I don't want her to grow up too much—I think it's very, very good, imagination, at this age', said a teacher's wife, herself a fashion designer; and a mother who had worked as an untrained teacher echoed her: 'She hasn't anyone in particular, but she talks to her toys and has very, very good imaginary games'. The middle-class mother of the little boy who owned two garages with lions and elephants in them said her reaction was just to 'string along with him. I don't prick him like a bubble, because I think it's a marvellous thing to have an imagination, and you can almost *see* the things—you can almost believe he's telling the truth!' The wife of a shop-owner said that her little boy's imagination was 'not yet' as strong as his sister's, with the implication that this was something that would eventually come with practice as they played together, and added 'I fall in with them, because to encourage their imagination like that, it's quite a big thing, isn't it?'

Almost every middle-class mother agreed with this; one of the very few with reservations was a clergyman's wife, who in this and all other areas of behaviour was particularly concerned to make her children aware of the exact import of their actions, usually in a moral frame of reference. She explained, 'Well, we have a family formula—"is this real, or is it pretend?"—and if it's pretend, well, we talk about it, but we talk about it as "your pretend" '.

In general, the majority of mothers who reported fantasies of any sort were sympathetic and encouraging in their attitudes; but it must be remembered that at least some of those whose children did not communicate fantasies had probably forestalled their occurrence by an unsympathetic attitude from the start. A mother who answers our question with 'Ooh no! I shouldn't like that!' is not very likely to 'fall in with him' or 'sit there taking it all in' when her child starts prattling about monkeys in the cellar or little girls called Choany. The fantasies which we have quoted were all received sympathetically. The mother of Choany's friend and creator, who gave house-room to two other characters as well, said: 'I just let him yatter away and talk to them, and if Choany has done something I say "That was very naughty of Choany" or "That was very clever of The Little Boy", and sort of act as if they really do exist, because they *do* exist for Mark'. Veronica's mother, hostess to Noddy, Billa and Gunny, said 'I just accept them. Sometimes I want to burst, but then I think No, it's so serious to her'. This statement of the need to respect the child's serious attitude recurs many times. A research chemist's wife, whose daughter Jessica has an imaginary friend also called Jessica, said 'I know it's not true, and I think she knows I know it's not. But we still have very serious conversations on it'; and the miner's wife whose little girl goes paddling in imaginary streams emphasized 'Oh no, I don't laugh—because if you laugh at them they seem to come down to earth, and then they get angry with you—you know?' Many mothers reiterated the difficulty of keeping a straight face, and some could not resist prompting the child to further confidences for their own amusement: 'Sometimes I do egg her on just to see how far she *does* go. I just say "Oh, did he? And *then* what happened?" and she goes on and on and on, until she's exhausted every possibility'. Another recurring theme was the necessity of allowing for the creature's presence in various ways —laying places at table, shutting doors and gates carefully and avoiding sitting on the invisible visitor; and some mothers went further still in their involvement:

Lorry driver's wife:
> Oh, she has a baby and she picks it up and puts it down, sort of thing. (And this baby isn't a doll . . .?) Oh no, it's in her mind; she wraps it up and puts it on the settee. I have to carry it about in my arms—I'm as daft as her!

It is, as we have suggested, the working-class section which produces a minority group of mothers who will tend to laugh at the child, to snub his imaginative flights, and generally to act in ways which are aimed at pricking the bubble of his illusion. In this working-class group there is often also an underlying current of anxiety. It is they who feel that there might be something disturbing about the mental health of a child who seems to this extent out of touch with reality; who distrust an imagination which, they believe, might later lead the child into plain dishonesty; or who regard the child's stories as already constituting a threat to their control of his behaviour. A few examples from this group will illustrate the disquiet which fantasy can generate.

Miner's wife:

> He's got a . . . I'll tell you what it is—it worries me sometimes—he's got a vivid imagination; and it goes on and on and on until he *lives* it; and sometimes, these imaginary people, you have to *feed* them with him, do you see what I mean? It worries me.

Fitter's wife:

> He'd make up stories like "I was at school today, and my teacher smacked me and made me go in the corner", and things like that. It got so bad that I tried to stop it, because I didn't want him to go from an imaginary story to a downright lie—because there's not much difference between the two.

Miner's wife:

> I've said to him, you know, "That's never happened, you're imagining things!" I've told him, I've said "Now, that's *wrong*—you've got a vivid imagination".

Railwayman's wife:

> Do you know, she *talks* to herself rather a lot—yes—I can't really *name* what she talks about; she talks to her dollies a lot. And she answers herself back as well, sort of thing, you know: it worried me, that did. But then I told a young woman round here, she said her child did it, so I didn't bother any more.

A number of mothers, like this last, thought their children were behaving abnormally until reassured by another's experience. One of them felt that she would have worried if it were not for her neighbour's child's example: 'the little girl next door is six months older than my little boy; and I can see him going through all the different phases six months after her'. Another mother had her mind put at rest by a chance episode in a film: 'We used to sit there stroking this (imaginary) cat, and I really thought she was going up the pole! But then I saw that film with Peter Sellers in it, and *he* had a little girl that was always imagining things; so of course I took it in. It's just one of the developments—you know, *developing*'. And the machine operator's wife quoted on page 179 was enabled to enjoy Carolyn's many friends after an acquaintance had put the typical Class I view:

> She had loads at one time, I remember telling the doctor's wife down the road about them, it worried me, because she used to carry on and on and *on* about them; and she was saying that her children never had them, and she wished they *would*.

> . . . *the sobbing in the chimney*
> *The evil in the dark closet, which they said was not there,*
> *Which they explained away, but you explained them*
> *Or at least, made me cease to be afraid of them. . . .*
> T. S. ELIOT, *The Family Reunion*

We have seen that fantasy can sometimes develop beyond the child's intentions and take on frightening aspects; and most of the fears which beset four-year-olds do in fact have some element of fantasy. If we consider the various things of which people in general tend to be afraid, we may make a distinction between those fears which stem from an appreciation of real dangers—fears of fast traffic, of fierce dogs, of war, of illness or of death—and those which are attached to objects or events which are seen as threatening but which are not in fact normally dangerous: spiders, mice, small birds in a confined space, thunder, darkness, or plumbing noises. And this latter list of things commonly feared can be sub-divided into those (such as the first three) of which the subject has an unreasoning horror, often of no known origin, and those which are terrifying because of the fantasies with which the imagination endows them: thus the darkness is feared because of the nameless evils which might be lurking unseen, the plumbing noises because they sound like groans or howls or the lurchings of some drunken burglar. It is on the whole the horrors and the fantasies which tend to dominate the four-year-old's fears, rather than the more genuine dangers of life.

To understand the reason for this, we must look at the child's intellectual and conceptual development. Fears are inevitably linked to the individual's capacity for understanding: in a very real sense, a child (or an adult, for that matter) may be too stupid to be frightened. Fear involves at least a partial comprehension of dangerous possibilities. Thus a 6-month-old baby may play happily in the bath as the water goes down the plug-hole, because as yet his concepts do not include the idea that holes are for things to go through.[1] At eighteen months, older and wiser, he screams with terror in the same situation, because he now appreciates that things go through holes, and he is afraid that he too will be sucked through; clever enough now to be afraid, he is not yet clever enough to understand the factor of size which is involved—as why should he, since the bath-water, obviously bigger than himself, disappears through the hole easily enough. It takes more time still for the child to achieve the complex understanding of the characteristics of solids, liquids and apertures which will enable him to overcome his fear.

Not many four-year-olds have either the conceptual maturity or the experience necessary for the grand-scale fears of death or war to be very real to them; four-year-olds tend to regard death (unless it affects them very closely indeed) in a rather matter-of-fact manner which can be disconcerting to the adult. In this they differ markedly from seven-year-olds, for instance, many of whom are much exercised by religious and philosophical questions, and whose fears are often bound up with these preoccupations. The fears of reality most likely to touch the four-year-old are those which both fall within his practical experience and are comprehensible in immediate terms: fears of being separated from the protecting mother, of being hurt by doctors or dentists, or of situations which they have found may both become unpleasant and move out of their control—splashing water, frisky dogs and buzzing bees, to take three common examples. Whether a child is afraid of any of these will depend largely on his previous experiences, and sufficient knowledge of these will usually show his fears to be 'reasonable' in

[1] The Psyche Cattell Infant Intelligence Test includes this concept for the first time at ten months, at which level the infant is expected merely to poke his finger into a hole in imitation of the examiner. Psyche Cattell: *The Measurement of Intelligence of Infants and Young Children* (1960 revision), Psychological Corporation, New York.

the sense that they are based upon reality, even though they may now seem exaggerated.

## University lecturer's wife:

She has a horror of mud—so much so that it's really quite a handicap. If we stop the car in the country, the first thing she looks for is mud, and if there's any at all she won't get out. Sometimes she says that she doesn't want to go for a picnic in the first place because there might be mud. It all dates back to last year, we were on a beach with rock pools, and her feet sank in the wet sand; and the children were running up the beach, and I think she suddenly felt trapped, and that they were running away and leaving her, and she had a real panic. It all started then.

## Chimney sweep's wife:

Water—she won't go near water. The boys were going fishing, and *she* wanted to go fishing. Well, she did do for quite a few weeks. Anyway—she tried to lean over something, and she fell in the Trent. She won't go near water now. We can't get her to— not even to walk by the side. I've tried coaxing her gently, you know, till she's forgotten it. But all you can get out of her is "It's dark—it's very dark under there". If she's playing with water in the sink, she'll say "It's dark". Even playing with water out in the yard, she'll say "It's dark under there, isn't it?"

## Foreman's wife:

He was frightened of the X-ray. The woman in the white coat, I could cheerfully have hit her myself, she was shouting at him because he was crying; there were five of us holding him. He screamed his head off. After that it seemed as if wherever there were white coats he'd be frightened to death. So the Clinic doctor said to me, "Bring him down, and we'll talk to him". And we used to go to the Clinic p'r'aps once or twice a week for nothing, just go in, and she'd say "Hallo, Barry, come to see us for a few minutes?" and talk a bit. And now he's quite all right with doctors.

On the whole, the four-year-old is protected from real dangers in a way which will necessarily have to change once he starts school; but from the perils which are conjured up by his imagination there is little protection, and it is to these that he is most vulnerable. He is probably now at the peak of his imaginative powers, without the firm grasp on reality which can allow an older child to subdue its fears; and, because of this, the adult's reasoned reassurances are often quite ineffective in calming a panicky four-year-old. Earlier in this chapter, we met quasi-frightening fantasy characters—monkeys, Dragon, Needy—all of which had other functions in the child's life as companion or scapegoat. Eliot's 'evil in the dark closet', however, is seen entirely as a terrifying presence, and is many times repeated.

Teacher's wife:

> She's terrified of tigers, for some reason—I think her sister has perhaps told her something about a tiger. She went through a phase of thinking there was a tiger in one of the cupboards, and I did rather squash that (mother normally encourages fantasy). I opened the cupboard and took everything out, and told her there were no tigers in England.

Office manager's wife:

> The little boys next door keep saying "There's a ghost which is going to come in your bedroom and bite your fingers", and he's got frightened of that. He has the light on all night in his bedroom.

Newsagent's wife:

> He gets a bit nervy at times. He won't go in the lounge on his own because Captain Pugwash (television cartoon character) is under the settee . . . he doesn't like to be on his own; of course, this is a very big rambling house, and if you are on the top floor you really are a very long way from the bottom. He won't stay on any one floor unless someone else is there.

Lorry driver's wife:

> She'll not go to bed without the big girl, because she's frightened of things in the dark. She'll not go alone. We have to wait till she drops asleep in here and then take her up, or she stays up till the big girl goes to bed at ten o'clock and then she goes with her.

Cableformer's wife:

> When we first moved into this house we put her in the back room to sleep, and she used to cry at night; and we asked her what it was, and she said "The butterflies are on the wall"; and we looked closely at the wallpaper, and it was a tiny loop—she

G

could see these loops and thought it was a butterfly. We had to take her out of that room and put her in another—she was all right then.

## Ashman's wife:

She's frightened at night, very frightened. (You mean of the dark?) Yes. She was *awful* at night—she's getting a little better now. But we had a terrible time. She had nursery wallpaper on the walls, and she used to wake up frightened—and it was the animals on the paper. You know, we didn't realize; there were foxes—it's ever so popular, you know!—foxes and rabbits and things like that, and she used to wake up. And mind you, when you *did* look at them—I used to go up—you could see how frightened she was. (How did you realize it was that?) Well, I didn't. It was months before I found out. She used to lay and stare at the wall, you see; and when we found out, we just had to make a sudden dash and just cover the wallpaper up in one afternoon. But *we didn't take it off the wall*—we just covered it up, you see—and I think in spasms, even now, she knows; because she once said "It's still underneath, Mummy". I don't know whether she's frightened of that now; she's p'r'aps forgotten; but even now, one night last week for instance, I went in and she was *glaring*, and she said "Look, Mummy, look!"—and it's only emulsion paint on the ceiling, but she was seeing something there, and you can't always find out, you see.

These last two mothers have had to make considerable household adjustments to soothe their children's fears, and the preceding one has had to modify her bedtime routine. In cases such as these, the child's terror is so urgent that most mothers will do whatever is in their power to alleviate it. The difficulty is, as the last mother pointed out, that 'you can't always find out'—the child may suffer miseries of fear for months or years without telling his parents what is wrong. Sometimes he is unable to find words to explain, or, as in the case of 'night terrors' (as distinguished from nightmares), he is in too distressed a state to be able to speak intelligibly and next morning remembers nothing; sometimes he will keep his fears to himself for no obvious reason, and may speak of them only years later, or perhaps never. The mother of the adult who wrote the following passage was amazed to learn of these childhood fears which she had never suspected.

Between the ages of 3 and 6, there were two things that persistently terrified me. On the wall by my bed there was a picture map of London, and in the bit that showed the Zoo there was a tiger. I found this tiger quite horrifying, and I used to lie there each morning with my face turned away, nerving myself to sit up and see him again; yet it just never occurred to me to mention it to my mother, who would immediately have got rid of it. The other fear was of two big boys who lived in the same road as my grandfather in another city. They never did anything at all to me, ever, in fact I'm sure they weren't aware of my existence. We used to go there about once a year, and though I adored my grandfather I can remember the dreadful heavy feeling in my chest when I knew we were going again and I might see them. They haunted my dreams for years, in the guise of two giants who dropped my parents into deep pits—always the same dream. None of this I ever spoke of to anyone.

Two out of three of all our children have definite and recurrent fears of which the mother is aware. Once she realises that the child is frightened, she will go through a series of remedies until she finds one that works: and that a remedy is effective is the main consideration to most mothers, even if it does upset the household, for few are unsympathetic to fear. There are no certain methods, and some fears are immune to endless ingenious expedients: the parents can only hope that the child will eventually 'grow out of it'. In general, mothers tend to favour a mixture of explanation and simple cuddling; and these usually at least have a soothing effect, even if they do not always drive the fear away. Some mothers took a great deal of trouble to give full explanations to their children, and some successfully found a way to explain in terms which a child could both understand and enjoy.

Milkman's wife:

> We've got a built-in wardrobe in the room, and she did get the idea that there was someone in there; but I put the light on and opened it and showed her there wasn't, and since then she's been quite all right. I think if a child is frightened in the night you must really get to the bottom of it, because it's no good your saying "Don't be stupid, there's nothing wrong", you've got to *make them believe* there *isn't* anything there. I remember Frank used to say "There's a tiger under my bed", but we used to get him out and let him see for himself there was nothing there.

Hospital porter's wife:

. . . My big girl started running the bath, and the tank's over his bedroom, you see, and it makes such a terrible noise, gurgling and that; and we sat here, and we suddenly heard such *screaming*. There he was at the top of the hall, screaming that this noise had frightened him. He wouldn't go back to bed, so we had to have him down till about ten o'clock to pacify him, because we couldn't get him inside the bedroom door. But I opened the tank door, and said "Look, it's the tank, and it's got lots and lots of water in it, and when you turn the tap on the water goes down the pipes and it starts to gurgle", I says, "same as when you're drinking water. It's being greedy, you see, and drinking it too fast, and that's the noise it's making". So he says "Oh, all right, Mummy, all right". So after that it never bothered him, because every time he's heard the tank he says "It's drinking, it's drinking it too quick again".

Thunder called forth some fanciful explanations in the effort to make it less menacing to the child—'I always tell her it's Jesus making the beds'—but some mothers, particularly middle-class ones, were scornful of this sort of palliative: 'I explain what it is: simply a question of clouds coming together making a big bang, none of these fallacies of coal being dropped in heaven, none of this sort of tripe'. Sometimes father would be called in to give an authoritative explanation, but one had the impression that mothers, on the whole, were more patient in dealing with fears, perhaps because they were themselves more subject to them, than fathers: some mothers had rebuked fathers who tried to laugh off the child's fears or who were cross with him for being afraid. A moulder's wife complained that her husband ridiculed their little boy for worrying about lions and tigers running up the street: 'His Daddy says he's silly. He thinks he must be mad to say things like that. I just say "Oh, I don't think they would"; but his Dad says "Don't talk stupid" and things like that'. Careful assurances that the child's fantasies cannot happen occasionally backfire, however. One mother, whose child was burdened with the certainty that he was going to meet a bull in the street, finally sat down with him and explained at length that bulls were invariably tied up or penned up, and never allowed to wander loose; whereupon the child, reassured, turned on the television set, just in time to catch the filmed news story of a bull which had broken out and was roaming the streets of a market town. It is interesting, incidentally, to see how often tigers figure in children's more far-fetched fears; devotees of Gwen Raverat's *Period Piece*, that delicious account of childhood among the younger Darwins, will remember that 'all proper grown-up beds had muslin curtains hanging from small round canopies, which were fixed to hooks in the ceilings. That was where the tigers lived. I never actually saw one myself, but that only made it the more frightening. This was one of the reasons why I never liked sleeping in my mother's room'. She adds in the caption to her child's-eye-view picture of her mother's room, complete with tiger, that 'this species is now almost extinct, owing to the progressive abandonment of the use of bed-canopies; just as the draining of marshes has diminished the number of malarial mosquitoes'.[1] Clearly fantasy tigers, like other creatures, have after all managed to adapt themselves to their changing habitat, and still thrive in the fertile jungles of the child's imagination.

Because our question on fears included examples—'the way some children are afraid of tiny insects, or the plug-hole, or things at the bottom of the bed'—it would perhaps be misleading to attempt a numerical analysis of the things children are afraid of. Nevertheless, we can look a little more closely at some of the more common types of fear. We have already discussed the category of 'things that go bump in the night'. Of the examples given in the question, the last two were in fact rare at this age, although one family of three children had each in turn slept with knees to chin in order to avoid the creatures who lived at the bottom of the bed: fears of this sort are proverbially infectious. Insects and creepy-crawly things, however, no doubt partly because of our prompting, accounted for one of the largest groups of fears. Often the mothers were conscious that their own fear or distaste was the source of the child's; sometimes older brothers, or even fathers, had indulged the male prerogative of terrifying the weaker sex by chasing with worms or spiders; occasionally a sting gave the child good reason for his fear; but, just as often, there was no clear origin for a dislike, sometimes a horror, which seemed a reaction to some characteristic of crawling things which many humans find intrinsically disturbing. It must be added that this was by no

[1] Gwen Raverat: *Period Piece: a Cambridge childhood*, Faber and Faber, London, 1952.

means true for all children, and that the little boy who reluctantly decided that he couldn't kiss his worm, because it hadn't got a cheek to kiss, would have found many to sympathize with his fraternal attitude. Even he, however, had a 'thing' about midges.

Diesel engineer's wife:

> She's terribly afraid of insects of all kinds. There's an insect, perhaps, on the floor or outside, that I can hardly see—in fact, I think it's a bit of grit—and she *insists* that it's an insect, and then I get rid of it, and it *is* an insect! She's got marvellous eyesight. But I say, "Now go outside, darling, and get a bit of fresh air", and she *won't* go out on her own. She used to; but she won't now. When I do go out and we finally get her out there, a fly or something goes by and she goes *tearing* into the house. I say, "Now look, darling. Those kind of things are *always* there, and you've got to be used to them. You shouldn't be afraid of them, because they're afraid of *you*, if anything". I explain to her that they won't harm her in any way, and that they'll always be around, so she *must* get used to it. I've always explained; I mean, I'd do anything sooner than frighten them. But so far. . . .

University lecturer's wife:

> Insects—not that he's ever had a bad experience. He's probably not very familiar with nature and insects; and, of course, flies and things in the house, one destroys; and in the garden I think he just doesn't like the thought that things are just creeping about and he can't control them.

Fears of being separated from the mother are natural and to be expected at this age wherever the child has reason to believe that this is going to happen and that the arrangements for him are not to his liking; we have discussed this to some extent in our investigation of clinging behaviour. For a few children, the possibility that the mother may leave them becomes a preoccupation which can be quite disabling: the child panics if a door happens to be shut between himself and his mother, he will not fetch a toy if it means going into another room, he may wet his pants because he cannot go to the lavatory without her, nor can he go to sleep unless she sits beside him. Most of these children's separation fears are reality-based, in that they or their mothers have been hospitalized or some other hurtful separation has already taken place. The two children described on page 100, one whose mother had twice been in hospital, the other whose father's desertion was followed by a brief but traumatic period in a day-nursery, are examples of well-grounded fears of this kind. There are others, however, who have similar fears without any such history; and others again who have suffered similar separations, including the loss of the father, without effects of this sort.

The fear of certain individual persons, or classes of person, might be said to be complementary to the fear of being separated from the mother; certainly it causes the child to cling to her for protection. Some occupations are perhaps intrinsically fearsome: dustmen have dirty faces and clanging bins, butchers wield great knives and have blood on their hands, policemen are figures of retribution and are often used as such.[1] The child needs to add little fantastic elaboration of his own to build himself a terrifying giant, fee-fo-fumming after him alone: 'A policeman passed the other day, and she came rushing in as white as a sheet—she had some tale about policemen coming for you when you're dead'. Thoughtless teasing by adults can leave its mark on the child for years.

Administrative assistant's wife:

When he was about two, we were going through the Central Market early in the morning before they'd really got going, and one of the butchers there said "Come on, let's have your head off!"—with a knife. Well, he *still* won't go through Central Market, and there's nothing I can do about it while he remembers.

Labourer's wife:

She doesn't like to be there when the coalman and the dustman come. If she sees them in the street, she'll come in and shut the doors. Every night she asks if either of them is coming in the morning.

Cycle assembler's wife:

There's a man further up the yard, he calls him Uncle Alfie; every time he sees him, he comes squealing into the house, *really* scared—he hasn't done anything to him, but he's really terrified. (Do you know why—do you know how it started?) Well, I've got a slight idea, like. He's a chap who likes a drink; and when

[1] See Chapter 14.

he's had a drink, he likes to get hold of the kiddies and lark about with them—otherwise, when he hasn't had a drink, he don't talk to the kiddies, you see; and I think he's probably frightened him, just once. And that's been enough for Philip, he runs out of his way now.

A most interesting group of fears involves things which are nearly normal but not quite: objects with some quality of the bizarre about them, things which are either blemished or exaggerated. On some children these have a highly disturbing effect. The human face is frequently involved: the child has a horror of 'funny' masks or of ventriloquists' dolls or of clowns in full make-up; it seems significant that the television programme most often mentioned as frightening this age-group is one which prides itself on the 'realism' of its puppet actors. Children are seldom worried by frankly toy-like puppets: it is the approach towards, without the attainment of, reality that unnerves them. Melvyn, who 'gets under the table and says "I don't want to watch that, Mummy" ', is joined all over Nottingham by four-year-olds behind settees and under cushions when Supercar and its sequels come on. One child, who 'isn't afraid of anything but this', illustrates the threatening quality of the bizarre very clearly.[1]

Stonecaster's wife:

> There's a club in town where we go, and occasionally we take him in. They have artistes—you know how these artistes dress up, men as women, with their painted faces? Well, he's terrified. He doesn't like that. He *shakes*—he's terrified. As soon as I see them coming, if I can get him out before he sees them, I go out.

The child described on page 101, who was deeply disturbed by physical defects, is another example from this group, and two further illustrations show how fear of *the abnormal state of normal objects* can apply to inanimate things as well as to the living or pseudo-living. The first child is also afraid of ambulances, which in fantasy she often sees taking people away; the second has many fantasy creatures, including the tiger in a cup-

---

[1] Hebb has drawn attention to a very similar phenomenon in young chimpanzees: a 'fear produced by events that combine the familiar and the unfamiliar—not by the totally unfamiliar event'. D. O. Hebb: *A Textbook of Psychology*, Chap. 8, W. B. Saunders Co., Philadelphia and London, 1958.

board which was quoted earlier, and is 'hysterically terrified' of men in overalls for no known reason.

Tobacco worker's wife:

> Houses that've been burnt—she says "Mummy, I don't want to go past that bad house". They really frighten her. There's one along the road with boards at the windows, she doesn't like it at all.

Teacher's wife:

> She's extremely afraid of broken things. Well, even if a cup is broken, she gets quite trembly; and there's a broken-down car opposite which fascinates her. She'll stand watching it and trembling and saying "*Why* is it broken?" and "When will it be mended?", and so on. I don't know why she has this fear, either. I can't even think of anything that she's broken that I've scolded her for.

What is particularly noticeable about this group is that the child is moved, not to weeping or screaming, but to an equally emphatic physical reaction: 'he hides and shuts his eyes'; 'he shakes'; 'she gets quite trembly'. The fear has in fact a quality of real horror; and this quality is found also in the final, very loose-knit group, which belong together only because they are all fears of a highly idiosyncratic nature. Fears of this kind tend to involve the sense of touch, though not necessarily so; they have in common that the child recoils and retreats from them as completely as he is able to. Four examples follow.

Miner's wife:

> Oh, she was frightened of grass when she was younger. She used to *scream* if I put her on grass. She's only got out of it . . . oh—this last three months.

Clerical officer's wife:

> Church bells—he's terrified of church bells. He won't go to bed if he hears the village bells ringing. I have to close all the windows and everything. But—he thinks every chimney over there has a church bell in it; he thinks the bells are in those chimneys. When they're ringing, he's sobbing his socks off, and we'll say "What's the matter?" and he'll say "The church bells, the church bells!" If he's outside playing and he hears them, he'll run in; he'll
> G*

not stop outside alone. He says "There's one *there*, and one
*there . . .*" and I say "No, love, they're not there (in the chimneys).
They're in the church". He knows the church, but he's afraid
to go in—he's terrified. He's really *terrified* of them. He does
cling to me then.

## Miner's wife:

Cotton wool she's *ever* so frightened of; don't know why; you
can't get her to do *that* (finger and thumb pressed together) to
cotton wool. She's not frightened of dogs—any animal—anything—
just cotton wool. It's been so ever since I can remember. I once
put some in her hand and said "Hold that, Karen", and she took
it; and she *shuddered;* and she's never touched it again.

## Joiner's wife:

I can tell you something she's absolutely scared stiff of, and
that's a feather. Don't ask me why—I don't know whether it's
the pigeons in the yard or what. But if she sees a big feather,
when it's, you know, moving in the breeze, even if it's on the
floor, she goes *hysterical*. I don't know why. But she's been
*really* frightened of them, ever since she's been old enough to
understand.

There are, of course, some children who, rather than having
one or two special fears, have a generally timid outlook on life
and approach any activity in a spirit of apprehension. The fears
of these children tend to be reality- rather than fantasy-based,
originating as they do from a too-lively appreciation of the
dangers inherent in any given situation. Typically they move
from one temporarily pervading fear to another, in each case
gradually overcoming their doubts about a situation as it
becomes more familiar to them: 'When I first had my new
vacuum cleaner, he was terrified of that, and I think it was owing
to that that he started to stutter. But he's got over the fear of the
thing now. And until about a fortnight ago he'd developed a
fear of coming downstairs frontwards—he'd come down backwards or on his bottom. But that seems to have gone'. Another
mother describes her child as 'ever so nervous altogether' and
specifies the lavatory, the big bath, and the swings in the park as
things which have worried him recently; a third child has 'gone
through phases of all sorts of things', including fire, fire-
engines and 'the men in town who call the papers'; these fears

have all been disabling in various ways, and it is fairly typical of the very timid child that while the 'phase' lasts it tends to disrupt his ordinary everyday activities. The little boy who is frightened of the top of the stairs, for instance, is considerably hampered: 'I can't get to the bottom of it. He will not come anywhere near the top once he gets upstairs. Once he's got to the top, he goes on all fours into the front bedroom and *then* he gets up; and he'll crawl all along the door frames to get to my back bedroom—and you can see he's terrified of the top; he won't even *look* at the top of the stairs. . . . He used to sit at the top of the stairs a lot, and then suddenly he got this into his mind'.

Traumatic for the child as so many of these fears are, we cannot completely disregard the play element in the state of being frightened. Sometimes, as we have seen, the fear develops out of an originally harmless fantasy; sometimes the child's own physical daring leads him into a situation which is more dangerous than he bargained for, so that what started as a pleasurable titillation of fear ends in total panic. In a similar way, children in groups or in pairs may derive a dare-devil enjoyment from scaring each other with ghost stories in darkened rooms, only to spend a sleepless night under the backlash of their own make-believe. Group fears of this sort are atypical for four-year-olds, however, except in so far as older siblings make them the unwilling sharers of their own fantasies. But in many ways it is possible to discern in four-year-old behaviour a flirtation with fear (as sometimes with other emotions) in which the child relies, not always successfully, on being able to withdraw at the critical moment. Glen's mother, with some insight, commented on her son's sudden fear of the wallpaper in his bedroom, 'I think it's a bit of a lark, really'; and Glen confirmed this diagnosis with 'Well, I thought there were lions on it, but there weren't, so I like it after all'. Craig was ambivalent about fire-engines; to his mother's mention of fire-engine sirens as his chief fear, he protested 'I *like* fire-engine sirens!' 'Well, you always run in crying when they come'; 'I *do* like them, though'. Rosemary tried to play with her mother's fears as well as her own: 'She's frightened of mice, but she's never seen any. (Are you—is that where she's got it from?) No—she thinks *I'm* frightened of cats. That's why she makes mewing noises at me— to try and make me frightened!'

In behaviour such as this, we can perhaps find a clue to another aspect of the purpose and function of play, the question with which we began this chapter. We may look upon play not simply as a way of repeating life experiences in an attempt to master their emotional implications, nor solely as a rehearsal, symbolic or direct, of roles or of desires: but as the means by which the child *tries out his emotions in a protected context*, in preparation for the time when he will be held responsible for his actions and will be expected to exercise reasonable control over his feelings. During these early years of childhood, to some extent at least he is able to throw back on to his mother the final responsibility for what he does; during this time, too, he trusts her to save him from the more extreme effects of his emotional behaviour. In play, particularly in fantasy play, his needs and desires can be acted out in the security of being able to retreat if things become too disturbing. Fear arises out of fantasy when the child goes a little too far and cuts off this line of retreat: either by becoming too deeply involved in his own imaginative process, or perhaps by allowing his behaviour to alienate the very person on whom he most depends to protect him from its excesses. Socially speaking, the achievement of flexible control over his emotions—without which he will not be accepted as a wholly sane member of our society—is the most complex and perhaps the most difficult lesson which the child has to master; and play, whether solitary, companionable, or peopled by the creatures of his imagination, provides the most sympathetic environment he is likely to find for its learning.

# CHAPTER 8

# MEALTIMES AND MANNERS

Apart from the actual bearing and suckling of children, there is probably no act which better epitomizes the maternal role than the preparation and serving of food. In performing the familiar rites of chopping and peeling, mixing and tending, and in setting before an anticipant family the pleasing results of her efforts, the mother can feel herself at one with a tradition that extends back into pre-history and that links mothers of families in every corner of the world, whether they cook in leaves, clay pots or toughened glass, by means of open fires, brick ovens or electric grills. From its very universality in time and space, the offering of food thus comes to symbolize the nurturing function of motherhood in a way which is not true of other household duties such as bed-making, dusting or washing-up; indeed, if we may accept the findings of motivational research carried out for the purpose of more effective advertising, the woman who lays upon the table a home-baked cake symbolically presents the family with a new baby.[1]

In earlier times, the skills of the ideal housewife included the preserving and storing of food for future use, the preparation of meat and fish from its newly-killed state, and the making of the family's daily bread. For the urban mother today, however, the traditional lore of kitchen and stillroom becomes less and less necessary or expected. Food is processed and packed, often even assembled into a ready-made meal, long before the housewife handles it, and comes into the shops in a form which frequently makes no greater demands upon her skill than an ability to follow the directions on the packet. Probably only a minority of young wives are prepared to tackle a Christmas cake, and fewer still have the knowledge and experience required to bake a loaf

---

[1] Packard, Vance: *The Hidden Persuaders*, Chap. 7, Longmans Green, London, 1957. The slang metaphor for pregnancy, 'to have a bun in the oven', supports this interpretation.

or draw a chicken; butchers often complain that younger women are illiterate in their understanding of butchering terms, but they themselves, by pre-packing cuts of meat in plastic film, make it unnecessary for the buyer ever to ask for her meat by name. The really good cook still earns prestige among her family and friends; but the less skilled can manage very well on an awareness of her family's tastes and an ability to match these in terms of brand preferences. In this sense at least, then, the image of 'Mother' as the person best able to provide choice dishes which uniquely satisfy the family palate remains powerful, and is indeed both exploited and perpetuated by advertising interests. For most women, therefore, the serving of acceptable meals to husband and children persists as an essential aspect of being a 'good' wife and mother; and because it is intolerable to accept that one is a 'bad' mother, that one is failing in what for the majority of women is the primary role, the child who consistently rejects the food which his mother offers him represents a potent threat to her self-esteem.

Food fads must of course be seen as part of a total social context. The child who cannot be sure whether another meal will be forthcoming today can hardly afford to be finicky over his dinner. In our study of one-year-olds, we quoted a labourer's wife comparing her own childhood with that of her children:

> I've noticed children don't eat the way we used to. I mean, they're faddy over food, they don't like this and they don't like that, whereas we—well, we'd eat what we was given, and thank God for it. That's it, I suppose—I mean, they get plenty now, they can afford to be choosy.

In short, the possibility of being choosy presupposes the existence of choice. In Nottingham there are few families living in the extremely poverty-stricken circumstances that can still be found in parts of such cities as Glasgow, Liverpool or London. Townsend and Abel-Smith have estimated that about 5% of all children in the United Kingdom live in households whose income is below the basic national assistance scale (1960 data).[1] It is possible that 35 (5%) of our families have incomes at this level—we have no data on family income—but we would guess

[1] Abel-Smith, Brian, and Townsend, Peter: *The Poor and the Poorest:* Occasional papers on Social Administration, no. 17, Bell, London, 1965.

the proportion to be nearer 3%. Nonetheless, it is certainly true to say that, while very few of our children go short of food for lack of money, those in the poorer families learn early that they need not expect much choice in what they are offered, and that if they don't like it they will have to go without, for their mother has nothing else in the cupboard. The close association of large families with low incomes introduces an additional factor here: for where six or eight or ten hungry children are clustered round the meal, he who hesitates has lost his dinner. We might expect, and we do in fact find, that in Class V significantly fewer children are said to be finicky over their food than in other social classes.

In the great majority of families, however, real hunger is a sensation hardly known to the children except by rare accident. Reared by parents some of whom have bitter memories of hungrier days, and many of whom remember the dull diet of the war years, they find themselves well placed to benefit from the general reaction towards ever more lavish, though not necessarily sensible, eating habits. Despite reports from Glasgow that rickets is once more known in that city,[1] medical officers of health all over the country are more concerned about the rising incidence of childhood obesity and dental caries.[2] Social context is relevant here, too, in that parents' emotional willingness and financial ability to indulge their children's appetites are matched by commercial pressures which continually exhort the housewife to please her family and enhance her maternal image by adding new products to her shopping list. The child who watches television advertising knows very well that choice exists, and that his breakfast Cracklesnaps can be replaced by Riceypops if he makes enough fuss. From the mother's point of view, if the husband or child shows a real dislike for a particular food, it is a comparatively simple matter to find something equally nutritious which he will accept. The child who refuses meat or

[1] City of Glasgow: *Annual Report of the Medical Officer of Health* for the year 1964, pp. 16–17.

[2] The Leicester School Health service has found it worth while to set up a special obesity clinic. Out of 12,299 children examined in Leicester schools in 1965, 303 were found to be grossly overweight; $83 \cdot 3\%$ of these obese children were from families in the lower-income group. When the clinic was first set up, in 1962, the School Medical Officer in charge commented: 'We hardly see, these days, at the School Medical Inspection, an underfed child. The number of obese children, however, is constantly increasing'. City of Leicester Education Committee: *Annual Report of the Principal School Medical Officer*, 1962 and 1965.

fish cooked in the conventional way may be quite willing to eat fish fingers or beefburgers; if he eats fresh fruit or likes black-currant or rosehip syrup, there is less need to force him to finish his cabbage; and in place of the traditional rice or tapioca pudding, mothers can afford to substitute dairy ice cream or any of a large variety of flavoured milk whips and instant blancmanges.

Amid all this plenty and diversity, it may seem odd that a considerable number of mothers expressed some concern as to whether their children were in fact eating enough: a concern which, as one might surmise, was on the whole directly related to the children's own behaviour. The child's failure to satisfy his mother's expectations seemed to arise in two ways: either he was generally uninterested in food, in the sense that he would eat only minimal amounts, whatever was provided; or his choice had narrowed to such a degree ('He'll eat nothing but sausage and mash') that his mother despaired of ever contriving a balanced diet for him. The incidence of 'finickiness' and of mothers' concern over their children's food intake is shown in Table XIX. The child's behaviour was assessed mainly on the basis of the mother's reply to the introductory Question 36, although information given at any stage of this section might modify a rating; the mother's own attitude was evaluated by the interviewer from her total response on mealtimes, but especially from her answers to questions 36 and 37:

36. We'd like to know something about N's mealtimes now. Is he a good eater, or do you have any trouble about that?
37. Do you have any rules about eating up food? (PROMPT as necessary:)
    Are there any foods that he never has, just because he dislikes them?
    Do you let him leave food on his plate?
    Do you let *him* decide how much he will have of a food that he dislikes?
    If he really refused to eat something, what would you do? (PROMPT *ALL* mothers):
    If he didn't like a meal after you'd cooked it, would you make him something else?

It must be stressed that mothers' attitudes of concern or un-concern, as we have assessed them here, are not so much a matter of *what they do* (Q.37) as of *how they feel*; the rating is made on the basis of emphasis, expression and intonation, as well as content. Thus one might find the mother of an amenable child showing no concern over mealtimes simply because her rather strict expectations are met without conflict: 'He just accepts that he eats what he's given, he knows that's the rule and he just does it as a matter of course'; on the other hand, a mother whose child is exceptionally difficult may be very concerned, not to say at her wits' end, but may have no rules at all —simply because she has moved beyond the stage of setting limits to the child's faddiness, to the point at which every mouthful taken is viewed with gratitude. It should also be noted that mothers' attitudes on table manners have no part in this assessment.

TABLE XIX

*Children's eating behaviour and mothers' anxiety about it*

|  | 'Good eater' | Varies | 'Finicky' |
|---|---|---|---|
|  | % | % | % |
| Four-year-olds' eating behaviour | 61 | 25 | 14 |

|  | Unconcerned | Mildly concerned | Very concerned |
|---|---|---|---|
|  | % | % | % |
| Mothers' reaction (4-year-olds) | 58 | 35 | 7 |
| Mothers' reaction (1-year-olds) | 90 | 9 | 1 |

*Association between child's behaviour and mother's reaction*

| 'Good eater' Mother unconcerned | 'Good eater' Mildly or very concerned | Varies or finicky Mother unconcerned | Varies or finicky Mildly or very concerned |
|---|---|---|---|
| % | % | % | % |
| 43 | 18 | 15 | 24 |

*Class differences here are not significant*

For comparison, the proportions of mothers showing concern over mealtimes when the child was a year old are included; it is quite clear that mothers, at least subjectively, experience far more difficulty at mealtimes with four-year-olds than with one-year-olds. Four-year-olds do seem to be objectively more discriminating than one-year-olds, in that they have more definite likes and dislikes and are prepared to defend them; but there is evidently also, for some children, a deliberate use of mealtimes as battlegrounds, while on the mothers' side there is probably less willingness to tolerate rejection of food at four than at one —particularly understandable when one remembers that most one-year-olds have a feeding-bottle of milk available for filling the gaps.

Let us be clear that the condition of pathological self-starvation (anorexia nervosa) is not under discussion: so far as we can judge, we have no such case in our sample. Nonetheless, the child who does not eat enough (and 'enough' is, of course, a variable term dependent upon maternal expectation and family habit) is understandably a worry to his mother, in that food refusal or poor appetite is often a first indication of impending illness. Conversely, there is a tendency to equate good appetite with good health, and to feel that growing children must eat well if they are to 'grow big and strong', a goal which is continually reiterated. However, at least where food is readily available, there appear to be considerable natural individual differences between children both in appetite and in physiological need. A study by E. M. Widdowson of the diets of over a thousand children showed large variations in their intake of calories, some children taking twice as much as others while remaining similar in size and growth rate. She concludes that 'individual requirements must differ as much as individual intakes, and that an average intake, however valuable statistically, should never be used to assess an individual's requirement';[1] and Apley and MacKeith comment that 'clearly some children are more economical and others more spendthrift in their metabolism'.[2] The child is often remarked upon by the mother as standing out from his brothers and sisters for his especially large or diminutive appetite, and the striking contrast between children at the two extremes can hardly be accounted for wholly in terms of family or maternal attitudes, though obviously these contribute.

[1] Widdowson, E. M.: *A Study of Individual Children's Diets*, Medical Research Council Special Report No. 257, H.M.S.O., London, 1947.
[2] Apley, John, and MacKeith, Ronald: *The Child and his Symptoms*, Blackwell Scientific Publications, Oxford, 1962.

David's completely indifferent to food. He hasn't any real likes or dislikes, but I've never known him be a good eater. It's been my only real worry. But he seems fit and well. But if he's got anything else to do he's just not interested in food. You see he doesn't even eat sweets between meals, or fruit, or anything like that. There's always a tin of sweets that at any time he could go to—I don't think he ever goes to it; it isn't even eating between meals that's dimmed his appetite. But that's been my biggest—my *only*—trouble with him. I often wonder how he manages to stay alive!

He's a shocking eater! He will eat if he likes things; but of course he likes so very *few* things—bread and butter, milk. He likes biscuits, preferably plain ones; a little cake. He eats *no* vegetables to speak of; a little potato, a little bit of meat and gravy. Sometimes he'll eat a milk pudding—sometimes he won't touch it. And that's about the sum total.

It's a trouble filling her—ooh, she *can* eat! In fact, I don't know where she puts it all! My husband's a good eater, 'cause he's six foot four-and-a-half, but she can match him; you know, I can put a big dinner out for her, same as my husband, and she can finish it—a really big meal, she can finish. She were born at dinner-time, and we say she's always been hungry ever since! She really enjoys her dinner. She'll have biscuits and a cup of tea and cornflakes for her breakfast, and she'll eat twelve biscuits in the morning; and then perhaps in the morning she'll come in, "Are we having a cup of coffee?" she'll say, and then she'll perhaps have a bit of cake, but it don't put her off her dinner—you have to put at least five potatoes on her dinner or else she don't think it's many at all. And she'll have meat and at least two spoonfuls of vegetables—and she'll finish it all, and *then* her pudding. And then she'll sit and eat about six slices of bread and butter and some cake for her tea. And then she's always at the milk, as well.

June is *always* hungry! She'll get up from her breakfast and say "Is it nearly dinner-time?", and after dinner it's "Well, can I have tea soon?" She's always eating. I don't *let* her eat a lot between meals, but if she could, I don't think she'd ever stop.

In most families, the pattern will be to have one, or perhaps two major meals which are intended to provide a balanced intake of food. For the majority of these children the main meal will be the midday dinner, at which meat or other protein foods, together with vegetables, will be provided, and are normally regarded by the mother as the most important daily items of the child's diet. Many children will also be offered protein foods at tea, perhaps with salad as well; and for some children, mainly in the working class, this will be the big cooked meal of the day. In addition, there will be a number of smaller meals and snacks which, taken alone, are not generally thought to provide an adequate diet, and which are not regarded as important even where the family habit is to make them rather substantial: for instance, in households where a cooked breakfast is normal, a four-year-old's reluctance to eat at this time is likely to be accepted with an equanimity that is in marked contrast to the mother's feelings about dinner-time refusals.

Snacks will mostly consist of carbohydrate foods, but may include fruit or milk. Young children are not very good at self-discipline in the sense of ignoring opportunities to take attractive snacks in order to preserve their appetites for the next main meal; and with children who are only moderate eaters there is a risk, of which their mothers are very conscious, that they may do too much 'impulse-eating' between meals and so destroy their desire for the meat, vegetables and pudding that constitute a 'proper' meal. The objection to snacks being preferred is twofold: firstly, that the child may not in fact be eating enough of the right sorts of food; secondly that, while snacks need little or no preparation, so that no loss of self-esteem is involved in their rejection, the mother who has spent time, thought and energy upon cooking what she hopes is a tempting meal naturally objects if the child turns up his nose at her efforts, or spoils a delicious plateful by distastefully stirring it into a mud-coloured sludge.

Departmental manager's wife:

Well, I must say it does make life awfully difficult; because I mean he comes in at the door: "What are we having for dinner?" and he pokes his nose in it and "Ugh! I don't like *that*!" I mean, I can only say "Well what *do* you like?" I mean, one week you get something, and it's such a joy, he *likes* it!—and of course it doesn't happen very often, but when it does, it makes your day! And so the following week you do your *utmost* to try and do it for him again, and he says "Ugh, you *know* I don't like those!"

What he does—he sits and *looks* at it, and then he sort of plays *around* with it, and then he wants a *drink*, and then he'll *talk* a bit, and then he says "Well, it's *cold*"!

It cannot be denied that among the finicky eaters there must be many whose problem has arisen out of a preference for the sweet titbits of which snacks tend to consist, and that the mother who is having difficulty over the main meals may well solve her problem if she can ensure that the child does not fill himself up with biscuits and ice-cream in between. However, in the prevailing climate of contemporary child rearing it is a good deal easier for an outsider to advocate a no-nonsense policy of this kind than for the mother to carry it through. Many factors are against her. We have mentioned that siblings often differ in appetite, and most mothers will think it unfair to allow a child who eats well to have snacks while denying them to his finicky brother; nor does it seem just to make both go without because of one child's faddiness. Fair play is again a consideration when the ice-cream man's bell jangles through the street: can one be strong-minded enough to leave one's child despondently lolly-less among his happily slurping playmates? It must also be remembered that while some 'extras' such as sweets and ice-cream are condemned on quasi-medical, quasi-moral grounds, others such as milk and fresh fruit are generally recognized as especially good for growing children. A mother may in fact pride herself on providing such acknowledged benefits in unlimited quantities—'It's a principle of mine that they can have as much as they like of milk, fruit and drawing-paper!'—even though she knows that a glass of milk with a banana is almost a meal in itself. A further difficulty is that four-year-olds are quite old enough to follow up their own impulses by finding and opening the biscuit tin, or even getting out the butter and jam;[1] to stop them, either the food cupboards must be locked up or strict rules laid down against taking food. To today's mothers this may seem harsh, since it is not usually considered naughty for a young child to want occasional snacks: Spock's 'Most young children, and plenty of older ones, too, need a snack between meals' is more acceptable advice than Mabel Liddiard's

[1] According to the Bakers' Federation, more than two-thirds of the population now chooses to buy ready-sliced white bread, so that most children will only need to take a slice from the packet Press summary issued by Ranks Hovis McDougall, Ltd., London, 1966).

'. . . allow no sweets or scraps between meals . . . a fairy story with a greedy fairy and sad results is the best illustration'.[1,2] In short, it goes against the grain for most mothers to refuse food to a child, and this is especially true for those mothers who themselves look back upon a poverty-stricken childhood.

For some kinds of poor eaters, cutting out snacks would any case appear to the mother quite inappropriate. The very few children who seem completely uninterested by food, for instance, exemplified by David on page 211, are equally indifferent to *all* foods, including sweets and biscuits. And the larger group who present serious problems because of a real antipathy to mealtimes tend to be allowed unlimited snacks simply because the mother, in desperation, sees total permissiveness as the only way of ever getting any food into the child.

### Stoker's wife:

He don't eat. If he asks me for anything, I give it him because I know he won't eat his meals when they're ready. I wouldn't restrict him—I wouldn't make him wait till mealtimes.

### Loader's wife:

I have a *lot* of trouble. I have *permanent* trouble. I very rarely get anything down Jennie. She's had not a thing to eat since she got up this morning (interviewed in afternoon)—a drink of cold water, oh, and a lump of cheese just before she went to school. I said "Will you have some milk when you come back from school?" She said yes, but. . .

### Hospital porter's wife:

He's bitting-and-bobbing in between—he don't really have a proper meal, he never has done. I always think, well, if he *is* hungry, give it him. That's what the doctor said to me, when Terry was same as him, "If he's hungry, give it him: as long as he has something to eat". 'Cause at mealtimes he just jolly well won't eat anything.

Some of the children in this category clearly use the situation to manipulate their parents for their own satisfaction. Both of Valerie's parents are subjugated to her will, in that they both

1 Spock, Benjamin: *Baby and Child Care*, Bodley Head, London, 1955, p. 226.
2 Liddiard, Mabel: *The Mothercraft Manual*, Churchill, London (both 1928 and 1954 editions).

give her their entire attention at mealtimes, to the extent of neglecting their own meal while they feed her. The power aspect of this situation is obvious to the outsider; but what the inevitably critical observer tends to ignore is that it is also obvious to Valerie's parents, whose spiralling difficulties are in no way eased by their recognition of their own ignominious role. We quote Valerie's mother at some length, because she provides a very good example of a behaviour problem that seems relatively simple from outside but nightmarishly insoluble from the point of view of those who are enmeshed in it.

Electrical engineer's wife:

We don't usually get any down her at all. (What do you do, then—how do you cope with it?) Well—she's got me fairly demented just lately with this not eating; so whenever she *has* been hungry I've just given it to her. I just don't know any other way to cope with her. Of course, my husband says she's just an idle eater; but she'll only eat it if you feed it in, and I think that's the only way to get it down her. (Well, what happens at mealtimes, can you tell me . . . ?) It's a pantomime. I sit her down, and it's "I'm not having that", "I don't want that". I put her food on a *big* plate, just a spoonful of each, so it won't look much; but by the time Valerie's messed about with it, it looks more than ever. Ooh . . . I could go mad! It's the only thing that drives me up the wall! Well, so then I start to feed her, Bill and I one at a time, one on each side of her. But some days—now, when my mother was here one day, I gave Valerie a bowl of soup and she ate it herself—that was most unusual, I mean it's an *event* when she does anything like that. But mostly we have to feed her—it's awful! But she does eat it then. But it doesn't matter *what* we get her—*I* don't know! But I always *make* her sit down at bedtime and eat her cereal; otherwise I—I think she'd die. (And how do you make her?) Just sit down and give it to her—feed her. (And does she ever make a fuss about the feeding—refuse to take it?) Oh no—she'll take it then. She has us on a string! But I mean, I've even called the doctor and told him she was starving to death; he thought I'd gone mad. He told me that a starved child has got no fat under the skin, and he showed me that she has. Of course, she drinks pints and pints of milk, and our doctor says milk is a food in itself; and I think she takes it all in, what he's saying, and that's it! (So you haven't really got any rules about eating up food because you *can't* have any rules in her case?) No, that's just it: because, same as I say to my husband, if you *make* her eat something, she's sick. I mean, I just don't know how to cope at all with mealtimes. And I think really she'd go all day and not have anything. I mean I've tried taking her out and taking her into cafés, and she'll say "Oh yes, I'll eat that"; and then you get it for her and she just leaves it. (So really she isn't eating anything but what you feed her with?) No, she isn't, apart from the odd biscuit between meals. (Do you know *why* it started?) No—of course, when they're tiny babies you do feed them, and she seemed to eat a lot then; but she never really has fed herself. Now my neighbour has a little boy, and when Valerie goes there she eats everything; and yet *I* can give her exactly the same food and she won't touch it. I mean, for instance, my neighbour says "Oh, she loves fried onions, doesn't she?"—well, I'll do fried onions and she'll not touch them. You ought to hear me going on sometimes! (Have you tried anything else—punishing or rewarding or anything?) No, I don't like that—mind you, I tell her she's done *wonderfully* if she *has* eaten anything, but I wouldn't punish her for *not* eating; because I always think that at *some* time during the day I shall get *something* into her. But mealtimes here are really a nightmare. It worries me to death, I couldn't tell anybody how much. And I mean the doctor says just leave her; but to me that's no answer. I mean, you could leave that child, and I'm sure if you left her two days she still wouldn't ask for anything. We've fetched her in and locked the door and told her that she can't go out till she's eaten it and that she can go to bed if she doesn't, but she's just the same, she'd *rather* go to bed than eat it.

The misery that is caused to the mother by chronic food refusal seems quite unique among the anxieties that normal four-year-olds initiate—probably because of its constant and regular recurrence so that the mother can never escape from it unless she is temperamentally capable of adopting a policy of *laisse-faire*. Many are not, and suffer accordingly.

Storekeeper's wife:
I should like to be strict about that, but I can't be, I'm afraid. I *try* and make him. If he won't eat it, I just give up. I've talked to him, I've bribed him, I've threatened him, I've smacked him, I've ignored him, and he's still the same. I've sat and cried.

Miner's wife:
This awkwardness over his meals—sometimes I wish I was *anywhere* except with him at mealtimes. It really gets me down.

Some finally almost succeed in turning a blind eye.

### Joiner's wife:

> I used to get very worried. I've even *cried* 'cause she wouldn't
> eat her meals. Of course, I told the doctor, and he said "It's no
> use worrying; she'll eat when she's ready to. There's nothing
> wrong with her"—looking at her, you know. So I don't bother
> so much now. But at one time we had a lot of arguments and
> tears and tantrums. I used to *demand* her to eat it, and it used to
> cause—oh, it was awful. So now, it's there, and if she doesn't
> want it, it's thrown away. That's all you *can* do. It's an awful
> thing when they're like that. Nobody knows what it's like to
> have a child that won't . . . it breaks your heart to see them refusing
> a nice dinner, it does really, when you think of all that could
> be doing them good. But you can't do nothing about it. Nobody
> can. I've found that.

Others have had the same difficulty with earlier children, and
have learned through chastening experience that the passing of
time cures faddiness less painfully and more effectively than
maternal emotion. Jennie, whose mother said she had 'permanent trouble' with her (p. 214), is pressed less than she might
be because of this source of reassurance:

> Colin is a very good eater since he went to school. I used to have
> all this trouble with Colin. That's why I'm not panicking with
> Jennie. I think she may outgrow it. Colin was *terrible* until he
> went to school; but now he eats me out of house and home!

### Driver's wife:

> I stopped (snacks) at one stage, to try and get her on to three
> meals, but it didn't make the slightest difference. I don't force
> her if she doesn't want it; and if she asks for a biscuit between
> meals—or *anything*, for that matter—I give it to her. I've learned
> by my mistakes. I tried being firm with the other two: hopeless!
> I was determined not to do it again; and it's proved to work,
> with her anyway. It's a lot better really. And it's a *lot* less worry;
> because I remember I used to cry with sheer temper over meals,
> when *they* were small. I've learned some sense since then!

We have pointed out already that the child, in rejecting the
food which his mother has prepared, may be seen as rejecting

her also, and that this in itself makes such a situation potentially highly threatening and distressing to the mother, especially when it is continually reiterated; it can hardly help her to find that the child's rejection is seconded by many of those to whom she may turn for advice. Doctors on the whole seem to try to reassure, though (as Valerie's mother found) they also tend to underestimate the extent of the mother's worry—to reassure perhaps a little too glibly; but magazine articles and books on child upbringing often present the 'training' of a healthily un-discriminating appetite as a simple matter of presenting food in the 'right' way, with the corollary, implied or explicit, that the finicky child must be the result of some failure on the mother's part. 'If *through mismanagement* the child has already learnt to have likes and dislikes in his food . . .', writes one authority accusingly,[1] sandwiching this between attributions of faddiness to '*faulty* methods of weaning' and of slowness in eating to '*mistakes* . . . made earlier on' (italics ours). Mothers who have escaped the problem with their own children frequently reflect this sort of attitude when appraising the difficulties of others, and we have been interested to find that discussion of parents' management of food-fads among non-psychologist groups de-generates more easily than any other topic into intolerant, destructive and unsympathetic criticism of the parents, even when the mother concerned is present. Few parents, unfortun-ately, will encounter the constructive approach of Apley and MacKeith, though perhaps some of the doctors for whom their book was written will successfully convey its message: 'As parents hope the child will become an adult with discriminating tastes in all fields, it seems reasonable to treat these preferences with some respect. . . . It should be made easy for the child to resume eating without "losing face". . . . The less there is of attitudes of victory and defeat (on either side) the sooner the problem of food refusal or dawdling will clear up'.[2]

The frantic trying of one strategy after another, mentioned by the storekeeper's wife on page 216 and by many others, seems one aspect of the feeling of failure. We give the example of one more 'problem eater' at some length. This mother is of special interest in that she is doubly aware of the possibility of censure:

[1] Edge, Patricia: *Child Care and Management from Birth to Adolescence*, Faber, London, 1953, Chapter 16: 'Some bad habits of early childhood'.
[2] Apley, John, and MacKeith, Ronald, 1962, *op. cit.*

herself a primary school teacher, she can view her maternal predicament through professional eyes.

## Businessman's wife:

We have *terrible* trouble over him; though he's getting better. We do have rules, in theory; but it's no use whatsoever. (So what happens?) Well, this started from, I suppose, about $2\frac{1}{2}$, and it has gone on; and *every* meal was a *battle*. He would come to a meal-table and eat *nothing*, and it wasn't that he was fed particularly in between, because he wasn't. In the end, I decided that I would *have* to feed him on what he liked. So I make sure that in the meal there is *something* that he likes and will eat, and *every* time that is what I have to do. I have to think what he *will* eat and put that . . . that is what I have to do. (Is there quite a variety of things he will eat, or . . . ?) Not a lot—um—he likes rice pudding; *we* get tired of it fast, five times a week! And he will eat certain other kinds; he won't touch fruit cooked—he'll eat it raw—and he won't eat tinned fruit at all. He's not really fond of meat. He'll eat things like fishcakes and hamburgers—things that are, what shall we say, prepared already; but he wouldn't eat a piece of meat off the joint, or a chop; and he will not have gravy on any food—if you put gravy on, he just *will not eat it*. (When you have battles, what happens?) Well, he just didn't eat it. (What methods did you use, to . . . ?) Well, we used *everything* in turn. He was forbidden ice-cream and sweets; we did have a spell when we smacked him, but we gave up, because we don't believe in smacking children if it has no results; and I think we *did* have a time when he was sent to bed. But we also gave that up pretty quickly, because obviously it had no effect, and there just wasn't a point. (So finally, more or less, he's won, for the moment?) I would not have *believed* it! Any other mother, I would have said it was her own fault—I would! (Later, in answer to Q.117, 'Do you think you've changed in your ideas about bringing up children?') I'm not half as strict as I would have been! And this business of the food—I would *never* have believed it! (It seems a little bit contradictory—I mean, you say you *don't* find yourself doing things you don't approve of; at the same time, you're criticizing yourself over that . . . ?) Oh, well, I think . . . I mean, it is a sort of generally accepted idea that it's the parents who are to blame, isn't it?—the parents are too soft with them. The *doctor* would say that to *you*. I'd have said it myself; but I defy *anyone* to get him to behave differently. I think there just *are* some children that don't run to the patternbook, you might say.

*What is the matter with Mary Jane?*
*I've promised her dolls and a daisy chain,*
*And a book about animals—all in vain—*
*What is the matter with Mary Jane?*

*What is the matter with Mary Jane?*
*She's perfectly well, and she hasn't a pain,*
*And it's lovely rice pudding for dinner again!—*
*What is the matter with Mary Jane?*

A. A. MILNE, *When We Were Very Young*

Our examples thus far have concerned children whose refusal of food is so frequent and so general as to constitute a real problem to their parents. All of these children have been classified as 'finicky', for want of a better word; and, as we have seen, the category includes a very few who are simply indifferent to food. The 'good' and 'variable' eaters, too, however, have their likes and dislikes—what Apley and MacKeith would regard as 'evidence of (the) child's having attained a normal stage of healthy development towards independence'[1]—and parents may differ as to how far these preferences should be tolerated.

We can say at the outset that A. A. Milne's classic picture of Mary Jane, the child who hated rice pudding, is no longer credible. The child today who has merely one or two real dislikes is almost never reduced to the screaming and kicking tantrum in which Mary Jane is depicted; rice pudding would have been removed from his menu long before this. The point is that the mothers who nowadays reach the stage of promising 'dolls and a daisy chain and a book about animals—all in vain' are dealing with children *who dislike almost everything* (which can hardly be true of Mary Jane, or the supposed speaker would not be so obtuse about the rice pudding!)

In general, then, the feeling is that a few individual preferences are to be respected by the mother, both by avoiding (by allowing the rejection of) disliked foods, and by providing favourite foods more often; it is where too many dislikes are expressed, or where the child tends to be capricious in his day-to-day preferences, that the mother's patience is liable to be strained, and she may begin to feel that 'the line has to be drawn somewhere'. Even so, some mothers were prepared to take a good deal of trouble to meet their children's preferences.

[1] Apley, John, and MacKeith, Ronald, 1962, *op. cit.*

Grocer's wife:

She likes the things she likes, only they're limited. She's got a baby leaning towards the Heinz dinners—she prefers Heinz baby dinners, the 'junior' sort (*purée* with soft lumps, as opposed to sieved), to ordinary dinner, even roast chicken—anything like that won't tempt her. I make her eat it sometimes, but she'll only mess it about. The only time she *will* eat a good dinner is when she has two or three tins of Heinz. I don't do just one. Once she went up to her cousin's for the day; I sent her Heinz dinners up with her.

Lathe engineer's wife:

One thing she loves, and that's pork pie. If we go out to tea anywhere, I usually have to take some pork pie in case they haven't got it, I mean *everybody* doesn't buy it. Oh dear—she takes a lot of suiting, really!

The social situation is, of course, a potent factor both for the genesis of dislikes and for their suppression: one can see this happening in the group fads and fancies of any school canteen. We have many examples of children 'catching' individual dislikes from other children or from the parents themselves.

Policeman's wife:

The other week my neighbour came in, and she happened to say her little girl didn't like cabbage: well, I can't get Della to eat cabbage now! I mean, you have to be so *careful*, you know—you really have. I mean, the other week my husband and I were talking about some steak and kidney we had; and it was my fault, it wasn't nice, and I said "Ooh, I don't like this steak and kidney" —and ever since, she won't touch it!

University teacher's wife:

He has learned a lot of finicky behaviour from his brother. If Daniel comes in and says "Why have we got this horrid stuff?", Charles says "I don't want this horrid stuff either".

When the social group acts in the opposite direction, to shift the child out of its finicky behaviour, the mother is usually in two minds whether to be pleased or sorry: pleased that the child is less faddy than she thought (and that he is behaving 'well' while away from her), she yet feels that this is in some way a duplicity which reflects upon her handling of the situation. It does in fact usually confirm her diagnosis of the problem as in part an emotional one between herself and the child, especially when (as tends to happen) the child's food refusal persists when he is with her. The social factor comes into operation both with 'variable' children and with more serious cases. Valerie (page 216), normally fed every mouthful but scoffing fried onions in the neighbour's house, is a fairly typical example; so, for the variable group, are the grocer's daughter who prefers Heinz baby dinners and a child who attends nursery school.

Grocer's wife:
> . . . Once she went up to her cousin's for the day; I sent her Heinz dinners up with her; and she *insisted* on having what they'd got, after I'd said she'd only eat Heinz's! She said "You needn't have bothered to undo those tins. I'll eat what *you* have", and she ate things that she *never* eats at home.

Shop assistant's wife:
> She never used to be a good eater until she started nursery school and stopped for her dinner. The teacher used to say she'd eat everything, you know. She felt as if she'd rather eat it than make a song and dance about it, I think. But she's still not too good at home. . .

By and large, parents' attitude to genuine food preference is a flexible one; as we saw at the beginning of this chapter, this is a comparatively easy attitude to maintain in present-day housekeeping conditions, and also fits in well with other child-rearing values. We should not leave out, however, a few families in which flexibility is carried to extremes in that every member eats as and when he pleases—total demand feeding, as it were. On the whole, where this happens we will expect to find the household geared to manual workers (who normally are fed as soon as they get home),[1] together with a contributory factor of overcrowding. This semi-skilled worker's wife, for instance, cannot seat all her family round the table; food refusal in the circumstances which she describes hardly arises.

> I can't say he's a good eater and I can't say he's a poor eater; I mean we never have it to a set time. We have it when we feel like it. If he wants it, he'll go and get some bread and that. If

[1] See Newson, John and Elizabeth, 1963, *op. cit.*, p. 208.

he's hungry, he'll come in and get a slice. He'll help himself. We
have it when we feel like it—we come back from the shops in
the morning and have cobs and meat.

Very closely linked with parents' tolerance of preferences and
fads, quite obviously, is the question of whether the child is
allowed to leave food on his plate. It is not quite the *same*
question, in that leaving bits of food, as opposed to refusing it
as it is offered, very definitely involves waste and can therefore
bring in moral considerations. 'I think it's just terrible', said a
metallurgist's wife; 'Half the world is hungry—and I know it
can't really help whether they eat theirs or not—but I feel *awful*
putting platefuls out for the birds, I mean don't you?' There is
also the factor of good manners: most mothers will have at the
back of their minds that the child who has the habit of leaving
sordid little mounds on his plate will be disapproved of if he
does so on social occasions, and might find himself in more
positive trouble once he gets to school.

On the basis of their answers to all the questions included
under Q. 37 (see page 208), the mothers' actual behaviour in
response to this situation was categorized as shown in Table XX.

A clear majority of mothers (54%) do not use sanctions of any
kind, other than mild persuasion or remonstrance, in order to
get the child to 'leave a clean plate', even though the clean plate
is much valued and praised. Mothers who both have strong
moral views about this and are prepared to enforce them are
clearly in a minority; it should, however, be noted that there
are many who have strong feelings that the wastefulness is
wrong but equally firm convictions that children should not be
forced to eat: the metallurgist's wife quoted above is among this
group. The fact that 'half the world is hungry' is probably
closer to ordinary people's consciousness nowadays than it has
ever been; at the same time, hunger as a social evil has receded
from their immediate experience, so that 'waste not, want not'
as a moral attitude no longer has quite the force that it had in the
war or pre-war years. On the whole, however, we would suppose
the results shown in Table XX to be an expression of increasingly permissive attitudes towards children's wishes rather than
of a new complacency about wastefulness. Sometimes parents'
unwillingness to compel the child to eat was reinforced by
unpleasant childhood memories.

TABLE XX

*Mothers' responses towards children leaving food on their plates*

| | Category | Illustrative quotation | Percentage in random sample |
|---|---|---|---|
| | | | % |
| Firm sanctions (9%) | 1. Unlimited pressure | 'They're not allowed to leave any unless they're ill. . . . I would finally smack her and make her . . . upstairs to bed . . .' | 2 |
| | 2. *Has* to eat amount prescribed by mother | 'Yes, I make her eat everything that's put out for her' | 7 |
| Mild sanctions (37%) | 3. Child may choose how much, but must eat that. | 'She can take as little as she likes, but once she's taken it she's got to eat it' | 1 |
| | 4. Mild pressure: may leave a little. | 'She's not particularly fond of cabbage, but I make her eat a bit at least' | 36 |
| No sanctions (54%) | 5. No pressure beyond mild persuasion | 'I don't believe in forcing them; they eat when they're ready, and that's it' | 23 |
| | 6. M's main concern is that child should eat: provides alternative (*after* refusal) | 'Well, I'd have to give her something else; I couldn't leave her, could I?' | 31 |

Class differences here are not significant

### Milkman's wife:

I'm not a great believer in forcing children to eat. My mother used to me, and I can remember feeling really sick over it, and I thought *then* that I never would with mine.

### Unemployed labourer's wife:

I do worry, but I don't do anything to force them. When I was small I was made to eat, so I know what it feels like. My father made us eat everything—big lumps of fat and all! And if we didn't, he'd say "You'll get no tea until you do", and we didn't, at teatime we got our cold dinners put in front of us again. My father was very strict—*too* strict, I think. I couldn't do that to mine.

This attitude of extreme strictness about the child finishing what is on his plate lingers on in only a very few cases: where it appears, it is fairly unmistakable, however. The first example below is to some extent hypothetical, in that final sanctions are rarely resorted to; the third mother has always had feeding difficulties with this child,[1] and has reached the stage when every lunchtime becomes a focus for intense stress in both mother and child.

Professional engineer's wife:

I would make her; I should tell her she must, or she would have no pudding. (And if she preferred to leave it and have no pudding?) Oh dear—well, I think I should threaten a smack, I think I would finally smack her and make her. Of course, it doesn't really come to that—we make little games, play that the spoon is an aeroplane and so on. But yes, if necessary I think I would smack her. (And suppose she still wouldn't eat it, even when she'd been smacked—would you leave it at that, or . . .?) Well, I don't know, I can't imagine it really happening. I suppose then she'd be sent upstairs to bed or something. (You do feel quite strongly about them eating up their food?) Yes, I do, because I think if you don't make them from the beginning it makes them very fussy by the time they're this age. If you once give in to them over it, they'd *never* eat the food they're given.

Nylon winder's wife:

I always say "If you don't clear your dinner-plate, you don't get any pudding". (And do you stick to that?) Oh yes—if they don't eat, they don't get any pudding and I warm their dinner up for their tea. And it's learned them. (And if he still refused to eat it when it was warmed up, what would you do?) I should have to persuade him—feed him. (And would he have to eat that before he had any tea?) Oh yes.

[1] As Peter reaches seven, this is still the biggest problem. Readers who see this as a serial story (as we do ourselves) may like to compare other quotations from Mrs Brown: *Infant Care in an Urban Community*, three quotations in Chapter 6, 'The Roots of Socialization'; see also pages 212 and 359, this volume.

H

Departmental manager's wife:

> I make him eat what I think he ought to have. With Peter, that's not very much. (How do you make him?) Oh, forcibly—by feeding him. Breakfast he's usually all right on—but with lunch! He starts off all right, but then he says "I don't want any more", and that's when I get cross! (And suppose he still refuses when you feed him?) Oh, well, he doesn't—well, I mean, there *have* been times when, as we've put it in, it's come out, sort of thing; but he has to have it just the same. (And what do you do?) Oh, I smack him. (And if you've gone through all the battles, and you've smacked him, and he *still* won't eat . . .?) Oh, well, we haven't really come to that; he's been sent to bed once or twice.

'No pudding' is the most common sanction used for not finishing the first course; clearly, for real food refusers (like Valerie, for instance) it is not an appropriate threat, since they create equal battles over eating the sweet course. Mothers were only allotted to category 2 if this threat was adhered to.

Clergyman's wife:

> If it is something which I *know* she doesn't like—I mean something that I've put on her plate accidentally—she could leave it. If, on the other hand, it's something which I think she's just being stupid about, she may leave it on her plate, but she gets either no pudding, or if it's at pudding-time she gets no sweet afterwards.

Cabinet maker's wife (social work trained):

> I don't know what other folks do when they don't eat; I think it would worry me—I don't know. But I don't seem to have had much trouble with mine in the eating line: whether it's because I've always insisted that they *have* eaten it, from early, like . . . (And when you say you insist, just what do you do—how far do you go *on* insisting?) Well, I say "Now come on—eat it up —you can eat this" (firm and cheerful voice) and p'r'aps I'll take the spoon and feed him—pick it up and say "Now come on, let me give it to you", and, you know, he gets it down. But I think actually I'm a little bit *too* strict in that line, I don't know. I might persuade him in this way, "If you don't want your dinner, you won't have any pudding". I don't think I'd actually smack him. I'd shout at him, but I don't think I'd smack him, no.

As we have seen, only 1% mentioned a rule that the child might choose his own amount, but that once it was taken he would have to finish it. As one might expect for a rather formal arrangement based on explicit reasoning, the mothers in this small group were almost without exception middle-class.

Teacher's wife:

> She does tend to ask for things and not eat them, which causes great annoyance and lost tempers at mealtimes. When the food is put out, they're asked—each child is asked—what they want, and if a child has asked for something, she *must* eat it. If they were just given a plateful of food and there was something on it they *really* disliked, then I would allow them to leave it.

The most popular group, with 36%, was that in which the child was allowed to leave a little; the pressure used was in the form of persuasion rather than threats or actual punishment. Especially common in this group was the mother whose 'persuasion' took the form of feeding the child. Unfortunately we have no figures on the number of children whose mothers are prepared to feed them if they are slow or reluctant, but the proportion is very considerable: at a guess, perhaps half. For most of these, the feeding will continue for only a few spoonsful, to restore the momentum, as it were. A few mothers fed the child in response to what they, probably correctly, diagnosed as a special period of need, a regressive phase brought on by stress.

Steel erector's wife:

> We've had a lot of trouble with his food. Since the baby came, I've had to feed him and he'll not feed himself. He'd sit for hours eating his dinner. He'll eat it when I feed him; he just doesn't want to feed himself. (How do you manage—do you feed the baby first?) No—she feeds herself! She doesn't want feeding—I just have to feed her in the morning because she makes such a mess with her cornflakes. No, we have ours first, then I put his out and sit and feed him. He'd start on his own, but then he starts messing about.

Lorry driver's wife:

> He doesn't like greens or anything like that, but I have said something to him like "You'll never grow into a big man like your Daddy—you'll never be able to drive a lorry", and of course now he eats most of them.

Shop assistant's wife:

> She's a lazy eater. She'll eat it if you feed her. But I won't feed her. I make her do as she's told—I'll say "You eat all that and then Mummy's got something for you". But I find that what she doesn't eat at one meal she'll make up on the next, so it doesn't bother me quite so much.

In this group also are the mothers (and fathers) who go to a good deal of trouble to get the food down by dint of games or ruses, many of which involve the parent doing the actual feeding.

Foreman's wife:

> We coax him: well, cabbage, that makes your hair curl; different things—one makes his ears waggle, and as you give him a spoonful he says "There it goes, they're waggling", and he'll eat it up.

Miner's wife:

> We'll play a game, if he's got so many potatoes I'll say "This is Mummy Potato, this is Daddy Potato", try and get him on like that, you see.

Teacher's wife:

> The weak method—it's quite ridiculous—is that I offer the food and don't look, and they'll eat it up.

Miner's wife:

> I find if I just put ever such a little bit on, and then get another plate and put the same amount on that, she'll eat it better off the both plates than what she will with just the one plate. She thinks she's ever so clever! That's all right till it's pudding-time; and with umpteen plates, one pudding doesn't go ever so far! But she always has two plates, with just that little bit on each.

Among the total of 54% who use no pressure other than the mildest of persuasion, 23% draw the line at providing an alternative once the meal has been offered and rejected. Of these, however, many would take into account the child's likes and dislikes *before* offering anything, or would actually ask the child what he would like before starting to prepare the meal, which may involve cooking a special individual dish to suit the child's preference: 'I cook what they like. I ask them first. With kiddies, you can't afford to have waste'. Some examples of mothers who apply no sanctions follow; none of these would go so far as to cook an alternative[1] once the meal had been started.

### Lorry driver's wife:

I never make a child eat what she says she don't like, because I think it puts them off other things. I say "If you don't want it, leave it", I always do that, then you find when they get bigger they'll eat it; just as long as you don't *make* them eat it.

### University teacher's wife:

He's got a natural, healthy, *limited* appetite, I should say. If I try to force him when he doesn't want, he spits it out or tries to be sick,[2] so I don't try to do that. (No pressure at all?) I say "Come along, Charles! You can surely finish this!", and sometimes, if he hasn't had sufficient, he will. But other times I think he really is full, and then nothing I could do would put it in. I'm afraid this is partly my own attitude to food. I think it should be a *pleasant* activity to eat, and I haven't had any success with being fierce in this matter. In fact, it seems to me to go in the reverse. And although, for economy and all sorts of other reasons, I would *like* to be able to, I can't do it; so I tend to give smallish helpings, and if it can't be finished then it's left.

### Policeman's wife:

I think it's a bit silly to make the child sit there and eat it if she doesn't want it. I mean, she upsets her Daddy *and* my mother *and* me; you can't enjoy your dinner when someone's being like that, so I say "All right, then, the birdies will eat it", and that's it, and we don't go on about it.

### Platelayer's wife:

The food they leave on their plates looks after the dog and the cat.

Finally, we give some examples of the mother for whom it is paramount that the child should eat; for this reason, even though she may have cooked the meal in the expectation that he will like it, his refusal is met with conciliatory accommodation

---

[1] This need involve no more than boiling an egg.
[2] This little boy suffers from cyclical vomiting.

to his wishes, and she will go to some trouble, perhaps leaving her own dinner, to find him something that he prefers. The mothers who denied doing this tended to feel that it was very over-indulgent behaviour: 'I'm not running a hotel!', as a doctor's wife declared indignantly. The shocked amusement with which the majority of mothers greeted this question perhaps underestimated the substantial size of the minority who *are* indulgent to this extent: 31%.

### Miner's wife:

I ask her what she does want. I don't like her to go without food altogether, I never have done. They say it wouldn't harm her, because she's bonny: it does, you know. *I* reckon it does, when her stomach is used to food, and all of a sudden she stops.

### Plasterer's labourer's wife:

One week she'll eat every meal you put before her. But another week, all she wants to eat is sandwiches, and fruit in between. So we just get them for her.

### Chemical worker's wife:

I'm afraid I would. I know it's not right. I give her a choice for tea, as well.

### Plasterer's wife:

Well, I have to; I have done many a time.

*'It's when you're out anywhere and they let you down. . .'*

One reason, which we have no more than touched upon, for mothers' emotional reaction to their children's refusal of food is that it is almost impossible to separate food faddiness from bad table manners. If a child cannot be bothered to come and sit up at the table when he is called, if he grumbles and grizzles at the sight of the food, if he dawdles so long over his first course that a good meal congeals into an unsightly mess and the rest of the family have to choose between eating their sweet course in this unappetizing company or waiting for him to finish: then his mother may be upset for reasons which have nothing to do with his calorie intake. By such behaviour, the child offends against the courtesy and thoughtfulness which are expected to be shown on social occasions. This is not to suggest that his mealtimes, or even the major ones, are invariably regarded as formal social occasions; but it is undoubtedly true that mothers in general feel constrained to teach their children to behave in an acceptable way when they are in public eating-places or on formal visits, and that they therefore tend to regard mealtimes as an appropriate opportunity for such social training.

Possibly an emphasis upon good table manners in children of pre-school age is a peculiarly European preoccupation. Certainly American visitors tend to be surprised by the degree of control exercised over their children's mealtime behaviour by middle-class parents in this country. However, this does not apply to middle-class parents alone; at every social level the theme is reiterated: children must learn to behave well at table from an early age, otherwise they might 'let you down' or 'show you up' in public. Home manners don't so much matter, but....

*In general, would you say you* mind *very much whether a child has good table manners or not at this age?*

Turner's wife:

Well, I mind when we're out and she lets me down! I don't mind at home at the moment; but of course, if she doesn't learn to have good manners at home, she *will* let me down when we're out.

Technical representative's wife:

Well, yes, I think you *should* mind, you've got to watch them; I mean if you take them anywhere and they're *not* good, well it does show you up, doesn't it? I think you've got to watch them and correct them if they do things wrong at table.

Milkman's wife:

We've always been a little bit keen there; we do like them to eat nicely. Some people I know let kiddies eat just ad lib, but I don't believe in it. I think if you train them while they're young, then they'll never be so much bother later on; because if I took a kiddy out to tea somewhere, and it started putting its fingers in the jam or anything, I should feel *terrible!*—which they *do* do, because they've come here and done the same thing.

Most mothers seem to have at the back of their minds the practical possibility of taking the child out to eat; and all, of course, know that the child will be starting school within a year and will then, if he 'stays dinners', be liable to 'show them up' in a manner to which they are very sensitive—before the teacher. The mother who said 'I do want to make sure she's got good table manners before she goes to school' spoke for everyone, and echoed a feeling which we have already noted with regard to general self-help. Very occasionally, a mother would look farther ahead still, to the time when uncouth manners might be a handicap to an upwardly-mobile careerist: 'He probably won't live in a house like this always when he gets older', said a driver's mate's wife; 'If he goes to college or university when he gets older, he gets a different life, and he wants to be ready for going *anywhere*'. Some mothers, on the other hand, saw little prospect of having meals in town or at other people's houses, and for them the problem was correspondingly less urgent: 'Well, I *shall* do (take trouble over table manners), specially when he gets to school age. I think they *ought* to have good manners—if they go out anywhere, you know. But I never seem to be *able* to go out anywhere, so that's why I haven't bothered yet'.

It is clear enough that table manners are a live issue at this age, and we thought it worth while to investigate the behaviour and opinions of the mothers in some detail. In order to do this, we asked a number of questions about the mother's attitude in specific situations in which good or bad manners might be thought to be involved. Answers were coded on a 3-point scale[1] according to whether the behaviour was allowed, merely discouraged or positively forbidden. The form of these questions follows:

38. Do you mind what order he eats things in? For instance, does he have to eat bread and butter before he has any cake, and that sort of thing?
39. Do you let him use a spoon instead of a knife and fork if he wants to?
40. Do you let him use his fingers?
41. Do you let him get up from the table during a meal?
42. Is he allowed to bring toys or a book to the table?
43. Do you have any other rules about mealtimes—not talking, or anything like that?

[1] See Appendix I for details.

Total attitudes on table manners were finally elicited by asking:

44. Do you take a lot of trouble to get him to eat nicely and have good table manners, or are you leaving it for the moment?
45. In general, would you say you *mind* very much whether a child has good table manners or not at this age?

An analysis by class of the replies given to the questions involving specific behaviour is presented in Table XXI.

TABLE XXI

*The enforcement of specific rules at mealtimes*

| Rule | Social Class | | | | | All classes |
|---|---|---|---|---|---|---|
| | I and II | IIIwc | IIIman | IV | V | (randomized) |
| | % | % | % | % | % | % |
| Do you let him bring toys or book to table? —M does *not* | 69 | 75 | 71 | 76 | 76 | 73 |
| Do you let him get up from table during a meal?—M says *No* | 26 | 35 | 21 | 31 | 21 | 25 |
| Do you let him use a spoon instead of a knife and fork? *No* | 12 | 12 | 9 | 11 | 2 | 10 |
| Do you let him use his fingers? M says *No* | 80 | 83 | 79 | 74 | 76 | 79 |
| Do you mind about the order he eats in? M says *Yes* | 81 | 80 | 62 | 59 | 42 | 65 |
| Other special rules *enforced* | 60 | 67 | 66 | 68 | 78 | 67 |

Some briefly illustrated comments on these individual questions may be of interest.

We have seen that food is not necessarily uppermost in the mind of the child at mealtimes. Even if he normally has a good appetite, he may easily become absorbed in some activity which he is reluctant to leave just because dinner is ready. None the less, the majority of mothers expect him to come to the table when called, though they may be prepared to give him due

H*

warning that he must shortly stop playing. With younger children still, parting the child from a favourite toy at mealtimes may cause so much fuss that the mother will prefer to let him bring the toy to the table in order to induce him to sit quietly. The snag—that this secondary interest can also slow the child up by distracting him—is not particularly important while he is still being spoon-fed, since the mother still has control over his general rate of progress; indeed, distraction in these circumstances can become an advantage in reducing whatever negativistic feelings the child may have. Once he is expected to feed himself, however, a toy on the table may prove altogether too seductive; hence the fact that, by the time the child is four, three out of four mothers have definite rules prohibiting toys at the table. The desire of the four-year-old to retain contact with a loved toy was accepted as a real one, and many mothers had a regular place, usually in sight but out of reach, where the current favourite was habitually put during meals. The objects most often mentioned as coming regularly to the table were comics at breakfast and tea (it being difficult to exclude these when the head of the household had his newspaper), and such dollies[1] or animals as were the objects of a devotion which it would clearly have been cruel to break: 'Of course, she always has her little rag doll, that goes everywhere with her'.

Related to this, in that it is another means by which the child is distracted, is the habit of getting up from the table during the meal, often between courses. Children of this age do not like sitting still for very long at a time, and there is an obvious temptation for them to relieve the monotony by wandering about or even trying to return to their play. Since the child is no longer immobilized in a high chair, this may be difficult to prevent except by being very fierce—especially as the attention of the mother herself is often directed elsewhere, bringing in the next course or feeding the baby. A university teacher's wife saw both points of view:

He's a naughty little boy in that when he's had enough he just hops down, and this is a great problem and a great menace, and

---

[1] Some dolls, of course, come to table in their own high chairs. We do not count these as toys; they are closer to the fantasy visitors whom we have already discussed.

this again is one of the things I have trouble with the children. Midday meals, particularly, I'm on my own with them, and it appears to them, I can see, that *Mummy* has liberty of movement; and this irks them very much if they have to remain seated and there's nothing actually to consume, and they hop down. And I'm cross about this—not furious, but sort of cross-*ish*—but it doesn't have much effect!

The four-year-old soon learns also that in his bladder he has a powerful excuse for leaving the table on a small excursion: 'I'm afraid Nature seems to call, and for that he *has* to get up!' Perhaps the difficulty of enforcement of this rule is the reason why —despite the fact that this sort of behaviour disrupts the meal quite considerably—only about one mother in four is strict about this. It must also be remembered that many working-class households do not sit up to meals as a family group, especially if there are too many in the family to fit the table comfortably, so that some children may habitually ease the pressure by eating elsewhere in the room; between the university teacher's wife, with two little boys, and a labourer's wife with nine children and rather fewer chairs, there is a total difference in context: 'She does do that; in fact, she *stands* at the table sometimes. Or I put a piece of paper down, and she'll have her dinner on the rug'.

Children of this age can usually handle a knife and fork fairly adequately, and were mostly doing so, but the majority of mothers were quite prepared to allow them to revert to a spoon if they wished. Some children normally were provided with all three, in the expectation that, as the meal wore on, the child would tire of the more difficult manipulations. A few children were not allowed knives and forks, either because they were thought to be dangerous or because the mother simply did not consider them suitable for so young a child.

Labourer's wife:

> He couldn't manage a knife yet; and I don't like him to use it, because I think it's an instrument that can do him harm.

Technical lecturer's wife:

> Can you imagine a little boy this age really eating properly with a knife and fork? It's silly to expect it.

But this is not a common attitude. Another middle-class mother, one of the one-in-ten who would firmly resist the child's wish to use a spoon for his dinner, said 'Oh, I don't think so at this stage; I think it would be . . . well . . . *retrograde*', and this was the general feeling among the majority whose children were using knives and forks, even if in the event they would have allowed regression.

In contrast, the use of fingers was strongly discouraged, even though the question referred specifically to relatively dry morsels of food. Again, the feeling was that this would very definitely be considered a regression, and obviously there are much more practical reasons for being intolerant of fingers than of spoons. For most of the more tolerant, 'chips, chops and chicken-bones only' was the rule, though peas were sometimes admitted because of their elusiveness to the unskilled fork. The child's persisting impulse to abandon his implements and use an older method was recognised by most parents, but by this time they felt they were beginning to master it and that laxity at this stage would be a mistake.

Metal polisher's wife:

> He does tend to use his fingers, but we try to break him of that habit, you know. It is a delicate situation at the moment as regards that, because he would *like* to use his fingers; but we keep pushing the fork in his hand. He knows about it—once I've spoken about it, he won't usually use his fingers for the rest of the meal. But every meal he *starts* to use them.

The question on the order in which different components of the meal should be eaten is of interest because it is the only one which elicits a steady and significant class trend throughout the social scale, from a substantial majority (81%) who uphold this rule in the professional class, echoed in the white-collar group, to a majority who do not mind if it is broken (58%) in Class V. Significant breaks come between middle-class and working-class mothers, and again between Class V and the more skilled manual workers. A good deal of this difference must be attributable to the greater formality of mealtimes as one ascends the class scale. Where a meal is a family gathering at which everyone sits down together and the day's news is exchanged, a deviation from a set order of eating may be considered a disruption of a social occasion; conversely, if the family eats in turn, as each

member arrives on the scene, inevitably some will be eating a
savoury course while others eat pudding, and the formal pattern
of the meal is disrupted from the outset. Even more obviously,
for children who eat mainly on demand, taking a slice of bread
and jam as they become hungry, like the little boy described on
page 222, there is no issue of a 'right' or 'wrong' order. In view
of the wide class differences, it is interesting that middle-class
mothers supported this rule more strongly than any other single
rule; and the words they used conveyed the feeling that the order
in which meals are eaten seemed a natural law, not to be lightly
tampered with: 'the accepted thing is . . .'; 'she just *knows* that
cakes come last. . . '. A salesman's wife, considering her assumptions for the first time, found the exercise amusing:

> Well, we all *do* eat bread and butter first, so I think it's a habit
> that she should do the same. I think I *would* say she must, yes,
> because I do think that's the right way to eat—and yet I don't
> know why, because it all goes the same way, doesn't it? But I
> suppose it's just how you are.

The factor of formality—mealtime as a conscious social ritual
—comes up again in the results of the question asking for 'other
rules'. Not surprisingly, since this was the example prompted,
the rule of 'no talking' was the one most frequently mentioned.
Other rules were mostly formal verbal expressions of courtesy:
'Please may I leave the table' and 'Thank you for my good
dinner' were the most frequent, with minor variations of wording. Some families said grace, but this was not counted as a rule,
since it seemed more of a family habit, observed by adults and
children together. The quotation below shows an extreme of
verbal (and postural) formality.

Professional engineer's wife:
> I like to hear them say Please and Thank you. Now my husband
> makes them say 'Please Daddy dear', and 'Please Mummy dear':
> they have to sit up and fold their arms like this, and—'Please,
> Daddy dear!'—'Please, Mummy dear!' (Don't you agree with
> that?—you sound as if this was your husband's idea?) Well,
> he started it, and I carry on with it; he suggested it, it was how
> he was brought up, you see, and he likes them to do the same
> . . . oh, and they always have to ask to leave the table when
> they've finished.

'Not talking' was a prompt brought in during the piloting, when it was several times spontaneously mentioned; if we had realised how important it was, we might have given it a question to itself. The quotations below give some idea of the attitudes surrounding this rule. The first mother (Mrs Cullinan once again) is the most persuasive; the last is perhaps more typical.

Labourer's wife:

> I have taught them all, all along, as well as Patrick, that I don't like a lot of talking at the table. I expect them all to pass whatever is needed to one another. I don't like them to get into a big conversation about something that went on in the daytime, like. I like to keep the meals nice and quiet, and have it more enjoyed that way, and respect it. The table is a place of peace and quiet for eating at.

Cook's wife:

> We're trying to get them not to talk. They *do* talk at the moment, but we're trying each mealtime, when they start talking—we make it a game—"Let's see who's the one that can keep quiet the longest"—we try not to let them talk at the table.

Porter's wife:

> Their father doesn't like them to talk while they're eating, he says they can eat their food and there's plenty of time to talk afterwards.

Metal polisher's wife:

> We try to—I keep saying to him, you know, "less talking at the table". But at the moment it—shall I say—falls on waste land! (Would you like him not to talk at all?) Oh, yes.

Nylon winder's wife:

> *I* let them chat among themselves; but when their Dad's here, especially on Sunday mornings when they're all sitting round the table here, he says "Be quiet", he says, "Shut it—that's not what you have your breakfast for. Eat it".

Miner's wife:

> I always do try to stop them from talking. If they do start to talk, I tell them to get on with their dinner, it's rude to talk at the table.

### Lorry driver's wife:

Well, you don't like them rattling on, do you? I say "Oh, shurrup and gerrit down yer!"

In contrast, the opposite attitude is expressed below:

### University teacher's wife:

Not *singing*, perhaps! But talking I *like* at mealtimes, that's one of the times we talk *most*. It's a nice sort of meeting-time, when we all find out what the others have been doing during the morning. That's what mealtimes are *for*.

### Foreman's wife:

Well, we like her to be quiet at the table, because we go in cafes pretty regularly, you know; we don't like her just to chip in and say something of no value, but we ask her what she's been doing during the day. Try and make it useful, that is.

### Miner's wife:

No—because when it's a big family, they do talk more than anything else then, don't they? I think really teatime is the time when they do have the most fun; because they're laughing and joking with one another all the time, you see.

What is most interesting about this question is the class differences which it reveals. It will be seen from Table XXI that, while class differences in these individual items are not very marked except on the issue of the order in which food is taken, they all, *with the exception of* this question of '*other rules*', show a trend in the same direction: supporting the view that middle-class mothers are stricter than working-class mothers about table manners. It is only when we come to a rule *prohibiting free verbal interaction*[1] that a change is found: not great enough to give significance in the reverse direction, but it still seems of some interest that it is on this question that the prevailing trend is both halted and turned. Briefly, the working-class feeling tends to be that eating is a serious business, calling for the undivided

1 The trend is barely altered by taking the 'no talking' rule separately from the rules on the use of formal phrases of thanks or excuse; these are not very numerous, nor systematically class-linked.

attention of parents and children alike: 'there's plenty of time to talk afterwards': while the middle-class attitude is that meal-times are social reunions, opportunities for an interchange of family news and views: so that, if talking *is* discouraged, this is only because, in the sad reality, the noise sometimes exceeds that level above which polite conversation becomes impossible. Taken in conjunction with other class differences in behaviour which involves verbalization, this divergence becomes particu-larly meaningful, as we shall see in Chapter 14.

Concern over table-manners, particularly in public, is felt by mothers at all social levels; but some groups are more actively concerned than others. While the class trends shown in Table XXI, although rather consistent, were not very striking, they can be demonstrated a good deal more convincingly by com-bining the answers to these separate questions, and also by analysing mothers' answers to the two more general questions (44 and 45) which wound up, and attempted to sum up, this section. The results for each of these three measures show class trends which are consistent and statistically significant. The combined scores for behaviour in specific situations were obtained by the use of an arbitrary but objective points system which rated each mother both as to the number of rules which she attempted to apply and as to the firmness with which they were enforced; individual scores ranged from 0 to 13. These results are presented in Table XXII.

Presumably the same factors which we have already suggested to account for individual class differences hold true for these more general trends. The formal social occasion calls for a greater ability for self-control, and therefore a need for earlier training, than does the mere consumption of food for the food's sake. It is probably also true that middle-class mothers may expect more frequently to entertain and to be entertained by people who are not relatives of the family, so that they may be for this reason more conscious of an urgent necessity to prepare their children so that they can be relied upon to do the family credit and not to 'let Mother down' or 'show her up'. In each of the measures given in Table XXII, among working-class mothers a particularly large difference is noticeable between unskilled and other manual workers, and much of this is probably accounted for by larger families in more cramped housing, combined with more haphazard eating arrangements generally.

TABLE XXII

*Social class differences in attitudes towards table manners*

| Item | Social class | | | | | |
| | I and II | IIIwc | IIIman | IV | V | All classes (randomized) |
| --- | --- | --- | --- | --- | --- | --- |
| Total points score combining no. of rules and firmness of enforcement (group averages) | 7·4 | 7·4 | 6·7 | 6·7 | 6·4 | 6·9 |
| | % | % | % | % | % | % |
| 'Do you take a lot of trouble to get him to eat nicely and have good table manners, or are you leaving it for the moment?' (3-point coding: extremes given) | | | | | | |
| % coded 'much trouble' | 31 | 21 | 21 | 21 | 12 | 22 |
| % coded 'leaving it' | 8 | 11 | 21 | 25 | 36 | 20 |
| 'In general, would you say you mind very much whether a child has good table manners or not at this age?' | | | | | | |
| % coded YES | 77 | 81 | 65 | 65 | 57 | 69 |

It must be added, finally, that we have tried to assess the *will* towards training children in good table manners, but we have no quantitative assessment of the way; nor can we judge with any exactness how successful mothers are in this task. We certainly met with a good deal of frustration among women who were finding the going very hard indeed. Three last illustrations may give heart to mothers who imagine that other people's children are all perfectly mannered, while the uphill struggle is theirs alone: these laments are many times repeated.

Company director's wife:

Well, I *try*, but it doesn't have much effect. It really is very bad—you know, it worries me rather. I like to *see* good table manners; and I admire anyone who can get a child of this age to *have* good table manners; but I'm not very successful. *Louise* (11) used to have good manners, I know she did; but I think boys must be different.

Clerical officer's wife:

I sort of . . . bring them up to date, you know! I say "Sit up properly, eat properly" and all that. Then for p'raps a week or so after I've nagged at them, they'll keep it up. Then I'll forget all about it. Then suddenly I realize how awfully they're behaving at the table, and I have to start all over again, you know. . . .

University teacher's wife:

I must say, I find the whole business unutterably boring and tedious. At the same time, it does seem to get under my skin when they eat messily—which they do, and I get very cross, *too* cross, with very little effect as yet. I just don't seem to be much good at it, so it drags on and on . . .

'Her feelings of inadequacy are matched only by her undying efforts':[1] so Johnson and Medinnus describe the modern mother. Perhaps that is a suitable note on which to end this chapter.

[1] Johnson, R. C., and Medinnus, G. R.: *Child Psychology: Behavior and Development*, Wiley, New York, 1965, p. 271.

CHAPTER 9

# MUST WE TO BED INDEED?

---

*Must we to bed indeed? Well then,*
*Let us arise and go like men,*
*And face with an undaunted tread*
*The long black passage up to bed.*

ROBERT LOUIS STEVENSON, *A Child's Garden of Verses*

Four-year-old children can seldom tell the time by the clock; but if they live in a modern urban environment their day will usually be ordered to a clock-bound schedule determined by the regular comings and goings of other members of the family. The time at which they get dressed and have breakfast is often geared to the mother's activities in getting her husband off to work and the older children to school. Meals throughout the day tend to be served at set times, often linked to school or work breaks; and the mother herself usually establishes within this frame certain habitual sequences of housework and shopping.

For the child, therefore, the normal weekday will be punctuated by a series of familiar events recurring predictably at well-defined intervals. Different periods of the day have each their characteristic feel and flavour. Breakfast-time may pass in a hectic flurry, succeeded by a short interlude of calm as the door finally slams and the stay-at-homes settle luxuriously to their second cups. The serious work of the household may be done during the morning, and the child will know that at this time he must play mainly on his own and avoid trying his mother's patience too far. By contrast, the afternoon may be a more leisurely period, a time for shopping excursions, informal visiting or a walk round the park. For most families, late afternoon and early evening are marked by the return home of the older children followed by their father. This is a time when the family, once more reunited, turns in upon itself and prepares for rest and relaxation. Typically the evening begins with a sit-down meal, during and after which the events of the day will be recounted and discussed. The television set will be turned on when the children's programmes start, and will probably be left on for the news, comedy and serial programmes that follow. For the young child, all these activities eventually culminate in his being undressed, washed and taken off to bed; but this final sequence of the day tends to be embedded in a period of social interaction between parents and their children which often expresses all that is most characteristic of the close emotional ties which bind the family together. In particular this is true because the children's bedtime is an intimate and private occasion; it is not usual for visitors to be present during this part of the evening, and to watch the family ritual which surrounds their preparation for bed is a privilege normally only accorded to relatives or very close friends. What happens during the bedtime sequence of behaviour is thus of more than incidental importance to our understanding of individual parent/child relationships and of family life generally.

In this chapter, we shall be primarily concerned with the practical workings of bedtime: how parents cope with the business of getting an active and energetic child into a frame of mind conducive to sleep, how firmly they adhere to a rigid time-schedule, how they react to the child who remains wakeful or whose sleep is disturbed, and how far they are prepared to respond to social demands, as opposed to emergency needs, in the middle of the night. There is, however, a range of childhood behaviour which, because of its nature and because of the significance with which the child invests bedtime, tends to become a part of the pattern of bedtime and sleep in particular: we refer to the child's insistence upon ritual acts and phrases, his attachment to special objects, and his persistent retention of infantile comfort habits mainly connected with sucking. Ritualistic and habitual comfort behaviour is of so much importance at this age that it demands a chapter to itself, and is discussed in Chapter X. The reader is asked to bear in mind during the present chapter, therefore, that the merely allusive reference which will be made here to such behaviour does not give proper weight to this very significant part of bedtime.

The four-year-old on his way to bed is at his most dependent, and therefore, for the parent in nurturing mood, at his most appealing. It is at this time that he reverts from the tough self-willed independence that he may have shown during the day to become a warm pink body in need of soaping, rinsing and towelling and the physical handling which these attentions involve. Most parents do not expect to do much feeding or carrying-about of their four-year-olds, but they do accept that a good deal of physical care will be concentrated into the bedtime period. For this reason, participating in the bedtime routine will tend to be the most direct way in which the father can help in looking after a child of this age. In fact, 30% of a randomized sample of all fathers are said 'often' to take the entire responsibility for getting their four-year-old to bed, and some of these fathers *always* take over this job, particularly if the wife is working on the 'twilight shift' which some factories arrange for married women. A further 37% often or always help the mother with the children at bedtime, so that only a minority of 33% of all mothers need expect normally to do the whole job themselves, and some of these will be helped by older children.

As one might expect, there is a good deal of variation in the actual times at which children are put to bed, and, beyond this, in the extent to which parents think it important to keep to any regular time. The hour at which children go to bed is a subject on which many people have strong and rather rigid views, and those who have not tend to be affected by this in that they know that their own flexibility is likely to incur criticism. We therefore adopted our usual strategy for obtaining this sort of information by asking, not for *typical* times, but for a sample time, going on to make some assessment as to how typical this was, and modifying the coded time only if the sample time had been affected by outside cause, such as visiting at a distance, or by emergency, such as illness.

50. Now, what about bedtime? Can you tell me what time he got into bed last night?
51. Is that the time he usually goes to bed, or does it vary a lot?
52. Does he have to be in bed by any special time?
53. (If YES) If he didn't seem tired and wanted to stay up a bit longer, would you let him?

On the basis of the mother's answers to these questions, her attitude and behaviour were rated on a 4-point scale: 'strict', 'flexibly strict', 'flexible' and 'no rules'. These categories are defined, and their incidence shown, in Table XXIII.

TABLE XXIII

*Categories and incidence of strictness on hour of bedtime*

| Category | Incidence (randomized) | Illustration |
|---|---|---|
| | % | |
| Strict: M insists on keeping to exact time | 29 | '6 o'clock, every night the same—regular as clockwork'; 'We're strict to time. If we've been to Grandma's, we never stop, we're always back by bedtime.' |
| Flexibly strict: strict in principle, but flexible within half an hour. | 43 | 'Usually 7.0, but 7.30 if there's a special programme on'; '7.30's bedtime, but 8.0 o'clock's my absolute deadline.' |
| Flexible: bedtime exists in theory, but varies a good deal in practice. | 19 | 'It varies; well, I *try* to get her upstairs, but she'll come down again'; 'Sevenish, but if we want to go out, we take him. We don't stay in just because he's got to go to bed—nothing like that.' |
| No rules: no pressure for any particular bedtime. | 9 | 'If he wants to go to bed, he goes'; 'I couldn't say any set time, like'; 'I let him kip down here.' |

Additional questions, which were not taken into account in this rating but which do have a bearing on the general atmosphere of strictness or flexibility at bedtime, were asked about the period of time after the child had retired to bed but before he actually fell asleep:

61. Once N gets into bed, is he allowed to get out again and play around the bedroom?
63. Is he allowed to play with toys or books in bed (with the light on)?
65. What happens if he gets up and tries to come back into the room where you are? Do you ever let him stay if he doesn't seem sleepy?

Class differences in parents' attitudes on bedtime are of some interest, and the main findings on strictness at bedtime, analysed by social class, are set out in Table XXIV. For comparison, figures for bedtimes at the age of one year are included.

TABLE XXIV

*Bedtime and parental strictness*

|  | I & II | IIIwc | IIIman | IV | V | All (randomized) |
|---|---|---|---|---|---|---|
|  | % | % | % | % | % | % |
| Bedtime normally before 6.30 p.m.: |  |  |  |  |  |  |
| Four-year-olds | 22 | 9 | 7 | 7 | 12 | 10 |
| One-year-olds | 47 | 31 | 29 | 24 | 31 | 31 |
| Bedtime normally after 8.0 p.m.: |  |  |  |  |  |  |
| Four-year-olds | 6 | 16 | 24 | 26 | 25 | 21 |
| One-year-olds | 7 | 12 | 20 | 23 | 26 | 18 |
| Parents rated strict or flexibly strict: | 87 | 79 | 69 | 62 | 66 | 72 |
| Parents rated as having 'no rules' | 1 | 4 | 11 | 13 | 14 | 9 |
| Child allowed to re-join family if not sleepy (includes those who never leave it) | 6 | 14 | 19 | 18 | 18 | 16 |
| Child *not* allowed to play in bed | 51 | 48 | 46 | 40 | 41 | 46 |

The majority of parents (69%) get their four-year-olds to bed between 6.30 and 8.0 p.m. One in ten of the random sample go before 6.30, and one in five after eight o'clock. It is not surprising that more one-year-olds than four-year-olds go to bed before 6.30, but it is interesting that the proportions going to bed after eight are very similar, despite the age difference. The class composition of these late-bedtime groups is also essentially the same. The difference between Class I and II mothers and the rest, which reaches statistical significance in the four-year-old 'late' group, is matched by a still more clearly defined divergence at this same point in the class scale among the 'early' group. More than one in five of the professional and managerial class favour bed before 6.30 at four years, compared with less than one in ten of the working-class mothers. Conversely, very few

(6%) Class I and II mothers allow a late bedtime, whereas the table shows that among working-class four-year-olds about one in four regularly goes to bed after eight o'clock. The shop and clerical workers' wives take a middle course, but on the whole range themselves with working-class mothers on this issue. In our previous study we suggested various explanations of these trends; these are confirmed by present data, and we see no reason to amend what we said at that time.[1]

On a purely practical level, strictness in enforcing a definite bedtime is somewhat complicated at this age, not only by the fact that the child can now talk and is therefore more adept at presenting his mother with excuses for staying up, but also by his greater activity in every way, which makes it possible for him to run away on being summoned or to jump out of bed again once he has been put in. The equation of the amount of sleep taken with the amount of sleep required, which seemed reasonable at twelve months, is no longer so straightforward, since the motivation for staying awake is at four more compelling and more complex; nor are parents quite so ready to ensure, by active soothing, that the child takes the maximum amount of sleep of which he is capable. Nevertheless, it would appear that sleep requirements resemble food requirements in the wide individual variations which are shown from one child to another. Most parents, however, do appear to have a defined attitude towards bedtime which is only marginally influenced by these considerations: that is to say, they believe in at least having some deadline in mind as an objective, and in trying to achieve this rather than simply allowing the child to sleep when he feels ready. Among the parents in the strict or flexibly strict groups, there was a general feeling that some routine was necessary in the management of children, and that any great relaxation of bedtime routine in particular would be inviting trouble in the future: 'give them an inch, and they'll take an ell'.

Hospital porter's wife:

We're strict to time. I mean, bedtime is bedtime, isn't it? We don't allow on that score at all. I mean, we just say "It's bedtime —let's have you undressed". No trouble. Because I think once you start giving in to them, you only do it once, and then they expect it. Children are very knowing; once you start to do a thing,

1 Newson, John & Elizabeth, 1963, *op. cit.*, pp. 182–5.

you've got a devil of a job to change it. He'll *expect* it. Well, say if we've been to Grandma's, we never stop, we're always back by bedtime; no matter what's going off, we'll get back for them children to get to bed. I mean, round here, a lot of people, their kids are running the street all hours of the night; well, in my opinion, I don't know how the mothers cope with it, because I mean I'm tired out, I'm ready for a break from them when it's bedtime.

The need for parents to have a breathing-space without the children, a time which they can really call their own and expect to keep free from interruptions, is of course a very valid one. A mother, as much as any other worker, benefits from a period of recuperation, however much she may enjoy her daytime role.

Policeman's wife:
> I like them in bed early because, well, I'm one of these persons that likes to sit down at night. I make it a rule that I don't do any work once these are in bed—only knitting, that's all, and p'raps read the paper, and I make that my evening. So I like them all in bed for a certain time.

Coal merchant's wife:
> I don't like it to be much after a quarter past six, because I like to get my hobbies done then. You don't get any time if you don't get them to bed, do you?

This need is felt among all classes, but for professional-class women it is perhaps especially emphasized in the feeling that the evening is a time when adult conversation and adult pursuits once more take over. If the wife is herself either working in or trying to keep up with her own profession, this consideration is still more compelling, and may decide the mother to be strict about bedtime where she would otherwise have been rather lax.

Social worker's wife:
> In theory, I'd let him stay up. In practice it can't happen in this house, because my husband studies in the evening and very often I have to be out. Our lives are such at the moment that during the week it just can't happen, it doesn't happen to be possible.

University teacher's wife:

> Theoretically, I would leave it to them what time they went to bed; we did with the first. In practice, I find that with three of them, in pure self-defence and because we both have to be able to concentrate in the evenings, I have to stick to a bedtime. The compromise is that bedtime means that they go to their rooms in their dressing-gowns, and they can play or go to bed as they like—the rooms are heated—but they are not supposed to come and disturb us. And I think that's fair enough.

Social class differences do not reach significance among those mothers classed as 'strict', but when these are taken together with the 'flexibly strict', as in Table XXIV, the class trend is clear and statistically significant; and this finding receives further support from the trend within the 'no rules' group, which in the opposite direction is also significant. To summarize, middle-class mothers are more often strict about bedtime than working-class mothers (and tend to choose an earlier time in the first place), while the mothers in Class I and II are most strict of all.

The group of mothers who have 'no rules', very predominantly working-class, is often (though not always) rather poorly housed and over-crowded, and the rather haphazard bedtime arrangements are sometimes an evident response to the difficulties of organising too many children in too little space. Some of these four-year-olds (though not all) sleep in the parents' bed, and there are no rules because parents and child eventually retire together. Often (but again not always) 'no rules' is associated with what we shall later in this chapter call an 'indulgent bedtime', in which the mother actively soothes the child to sleep.

Presser's wife:

> (Interviewer's report) The pattern of Jimmy's bedtime emerged gradually and piecemeal during the questions in this section. Mrs M. was a little shamefaced about it. Jimmy will not go up alone, so waits for the 10- and 12-year-olds. If he is not sleepy, he stays up later still, as he wishes. He normally goes up with the others about 9.0, gets in Nancy's bed (aged 12) and she reads or sings to him and then cuddles him to sleep. He stays with her, unless he wakes, which he does nine times out of ten between midnight and 1 a.m. He then sleeps in his parents' bed. He apparently has no bed of his own, or at least none was mentioned. The accommodation is overcrowded, only two bedrooms, and

Nancy shares a room with her 10-year-old brother. If Jimmy comes downstairs again, he is put to sleep on the sofa until the parents' bedtime, when they carry him up to their bed.

#### Unemployed labourer's wife:

He sleeps with me. He's Mammy's boy, aren't you? When he's sleepy, he'll pick my purse up and my fags and matches and say "Ta-ta", and that's it. (You mean he takes your purse with him?) *And* my fags and matches—so's I'll go to bed with him, you see.

*'I do try to work it so we don't need any fuss. . .'*

Before considering parents' strictness once the child is in bed, it is worth taking a look at some fairly typical bedtime scenes. We asked: 'Can you tell me exactly what happens from the time you start getting him ready for bed to the time he goes to sleep? Tell me about a typical bedtime'; and we were rewarded by a series of most detailed and lively pictures which formed a vivid background for our more specific and factual questions.

Most parents know from experience that if a child becomes upset and overwrought at bedtime it will probably take even longer than usual to settle him for the night; moreover, family harmony will in general be disrupted by bedtime conflict, and the whole evening may be spoiled for everyone. Mothers and fathers thus have a vested interest in being gentle and diplomatic in the handling of their children at bedtime. Expediency is not the only motive, however, and most mothers are concerned in a very positive way that their children should settle down to sleep in a calm and contented frame of mind. The clean, sweet-smelling child, naked or dressed in a minimum of clothing, provokes feelings of tenderness which at other times may be inhibited by the stresses of the day—'I look at her in her nightie and I think, Oh, I am a cruel mother to you!'—and bedtime seems to provide an opportunity for resolving in 'five minutes' love' all the little quarrels and disagreements which arise when a mother is solely responsible for dealing with an active and inquisitive child for most of his waking hours.

For a variety of reasons, then, mothers usually try to order the bedtime routine in such a way that the pace is deliberately unhurried and the occasion a pleasant one for the child: on the whole, children are coaxed rather than driven to bed, or at least this is the intention, somewhat frustrated by the child himself. It is also usually a family occasion, involving brothers and sisters together rather than separately, and the father as well if he is at home. Typically the ingredients are a warm bath, a soothing drink, a lap to sit on for a chat or a story, culminating with a good tuck-in under the blankets, snug and secure, and predisposed, it is hoped, to fall asleep quickly and happily.

To ensure that the child goes to bed with a good grace and of his own volition, parents do their best to exercise tact and patience at bedtime and are usually prepared to turn the routine into a game in order to make it acceptable to the child. An early snag often comes at the very beginning of bedtime when the child objects to coming in at all, and the mother does her best to convert this initial conflict into a game which might well be called 'first catch your child'.

Jigger's wife:

(What's the first thing you do?) Lock those doors! She's inclined to hide from you. I start on her, get her stripped undressed, and while that's happening *he's* hiding, then as soon as I've finished doing her, *she* goes and hides, and I collect him . . . .

Depot manager's wife:

Well, a typical bedtime is usually chasing him round, because he's so lively! He does it in fun, you know. He'll hide behind a chair. You'll take one sock off, and he'll hide, and you'll chase round to get the other one off.

Coal merchant's wife:

I say "Let's see who's first up to the bathroom"; and if she doesn't take any notice, I usually make out I've gone upstairs, and hide round the corner; and then she'll go upstairs and I'll dash up after her.

Now begins the main sequence of the bedtime routine, and we can hardly do better than give some examples as they were described to us. Mrs Davidson, whose very detailed description we give first, lives in a small terraced house in a poor area. She has no bathroom or inside lavatory. Philip is the younger of two children, and she herself is in her early forties. This quotation is of especial interest in that it brings together many things which are very commonly mentioned in connection with bedtime: play in front of the fire, the father's role, the childish fads which tend to become prominent at bedtime, ritual behaviour, boisterous play in the bedroom, the dummy, and the final active soothing by the mother which categorizes this particular bedtime as an 'indulgent' one.

Cycle worker's wife:

> Well, when it gets to about half-past-six, I say "Wash down, Philip," I say, "try and get your trousers off for me, and your shoes and socks, while I get your water ready". Then I go in the back place and get his soap and flannel and that, and if he hasn't took his clothes off I help him; and I carry him in and sit him on the washer, you see, and I wash him in there—strip wash him, to his vest, I just leave his vest on and give him a good going-over. And then he comes in here and has his five minutes' play with his Daddy; we let him play in here a bit, because he's undressed —he doesn't have his 'jamas on—that is a little fad he's got, I meant to tell you about that, he won't let me put his 'jama legs on till he's ready for going to bed; and as soon as he's *got* those 'jama legs on he wants to *go* to bed—he'll not walk about with long trousers on.   And his 'jama coat—I have to wait till he's actually in his *crib* before I put that on! He's aways been like that. Well, he'll say to his Dad, "I've got a little job for you, Daddy"; and his Daddy'll see to his little needs; and then I'll look at the clock between seven and half-past, and I'll say, "Well, I'm going up to put the light on now"—because we black the window out, you see, to make the room a bit darker these light nights; and I take him a little drink of water, only enough to cover the bottom of the cup; oh, and I take him his little pot and say "Come and have your tiddle before you get into bed"; and he does so. And then he has a fad about touching roofs and tops of doors and that. His Dad stands on the arm of the settee, and I toss Philip up, and he lets him touch the roof, just to, er . . . you know, his Dad likes to know he's happy before he goes to sleep, you see. "Touch the roof, Daddy, before I go to bed!" And then I go up first, and his Dad brings him up, like; because he'll not wear bedroom slippers—*that's* a fad he's got, I think it's with them being soft inside—mind you, I like him to run about with no shoes on for a bit. Well, then I switch the light off before he actually comes upstairs, because he likes to pull it on himself, you see, it's a long switch; and then his Dad larks about with pillows, you know, and when I think he's had enough, I say "Come on, now, Philip"—and he's as good as gold that way, he

doesn't say "I don't want to", he knows I mean it. Then he says "I want my dummy", and I give it him, and he's asleep in five minutes. I stop with him until he's gone to sleep—he likes just to hold my finger—but, as I say, in five minutes he's fast on.

### Cost accountant's wife:

I warn him, and then eventually I get him ready for bed. Then he comes downstairs and has a cup of milk, and then after that Daddy takes him to bed. I go up as well, you see—we both have to go, but Daddy always carries him piggy-back, and things like that. Then we talk to him for a few minutes in bed—I do, and Daddy kisses him night-night. Then we have various coloured kisses, and things like that, you know, for a few minutes. And we try to tell him his prayers—but I'm afraid he doesn't quite understand what I'm talking about at the moment. So I don't make an issue of it. And then I pull the door to, and that's it.

### Sales representative's wife:

Well, I get her ready and then she dances round a bit; if there are any nice tunes on the telly, she dances and does; she'll take something off and then dance around, she dances around in her vest—and yet if anybody came in, she'd have a fit, to think she'd got no pants on.

### Teacher's wife:

She undresses, and they both get in the bath together. She plays at the adverts on T.V., Palmolive and all the rest of it. Neither of them will let me wash them, they like to wash themselves; but of course they have to be inspected. They usually like to sing a bit and act a bit. Then they get out, and they like to play about with nothing on for a bit. It takes me ages! We have a little dance, and they like to be powdered, and we have little curlers they put in their hair at the top, and then they get into bed. They get a story, then we say prayers, and then they are *supposed* to go to sleep.

The chief difference which housing makes in the pattern of bedtime obviously lies in whether or not the household possesses a bathroom. In middle-class and council-house families, bathtime is often the focal point of the whole process, a high peak in boisterous play before the calming-down which is intended to end in sleep. Almost two-thirds of all fathers bath their children themselves at least sometimes, and more than half of these do it often. It is accepted that bathtime is a time for play, to such an extent that a middle-class mother can actually worry if her child does not conform: 'He doesn't play a great deal in the bath. I don't know if that's partially my fault—it may be. I've had a bit of a conscience about it lately'. Washing in fact often seems a subsidiary function to simply having the sort of splashy fun that is not easily come by at other times, and this seems recognized both by mothers and by the manufacturers of various child-washing detergents which are said to '*bubble* your children clean as they play in the bath'. The drying that follows is also an excellent opportunity for a pleasant regression to babyhood.

Research chemist's wife:

> I put them in the bath and leave them for a while, while I tidy up the bedroom. I *tell* them to wash. They don't usually bother! I suppose they're in the bath for about a quarter of an hour. (Child: Sometimes we wash.) Yes, *sometimes* you wash!

Policeman's wife:

> She always wants a swim, whether it's her turn to come out first or not . . . sometimes when she gets out she wants to be a baby, she plays babies, you know, when she's wrapped in the towel, and we have a little ritual, "Oh, it's not a baby after all—it's Siriol!"

Actor's wife:

> She gets a little stool and she climbs into the bath on her own, and then she'll say "Can I stay and play in the bath, while you dry Rupert?"—they're in together—and they have a splash round, and she plays all sorts of imaginary games; and then I put him to bed while she puts the toys in the bath-rack, and then I get her out, and she'll either say "Can I dry myself?" or "Will you dry me?", and very often when she wants me to dry her, she wants me to dry her like Rupert—like a baby—which I do. I dry her and pretend she's a baby.

Office manager's wife:

> He's normally undressed down here and wrapped in a towel, and either Daddy or I bath him—it's, sort of, whoever's available. With three, it's usually sort of like a conveyor belt—one bathed and one dried. He comes downstairs, and whoever didn't bath him dries him. He's dried downstairs, always, in front of the fire—he loves that!

In many families, television has a prominent place in the bedtime routine. Our questions were not designed directly to investigate television as an influence, but in the mothers' descriptions of a 'typical bedtime' it was frequently mentioned. In not a few households, the time at which the child went to bed on certain days was tied to the favourite programme he was allowed to stay up to watch, and for some children, as we noted earlier, bedtime was exactly determined by the family's viewing habits, and thus varied according to the day of the week.

British Rail fireman's wife:

> It does vary from about 7.0. You see, we've got sort of a system. Monday he goes 7.30, Tuesday 7.0, Wednesday they stay up until about 9.0. Then Thursday they go to bed at 7.0, Friday about 8.30, and Saturday and Sunday it's 7.0 again. It varies with programmes on TV that I let them stop up and see, you see. But they go to bed the *early* nights, so that they can, sort of, have that extra stay on the nights when they *do* stay up.

Not many families have a 'sort of system' quite like this, but in most families the television is on at this time of day, and it naturally follows that watching TV becomes an accepted part of the bedtime routine. At four, not many children are capable of the sustained attention necessary to appreciate a full half-hour programme which has been primarily designed for an adult audience; but, where there are older brothers and sisters particularly, the four-year-old will not be slow to recognize and demand the privilege of staying up 'just till the end of this programme'; and in this sense television regulates bedtime in a very large number of households. On the whole it is accepted by mothers as part of the natural order of things, and it appears to be fairly common for the child to be washed and got into his nightclothes rather early for the express purpose of watching TV as part of his sociable winding-down period on his mother's or father's knee. For these children, television perhaps takes the place of the traditional bedtime story; and, as happens with stories also, the four-year-old quickly picks up the habit of sitting quietly and paying intermittent attention to the screen, long before he is able fully to comprehend all that he sees and hears. In particular, these younger children seem to derive especial pleasure from the advertising breaks, perhaps because they are often pitched at about the right mental age for them. Advertisements on television are characteristically lively and attention-demanding; they frequently employ both rhythm and rhyme, often involve cartoon creatures which soon become familiar figures, and use words which are set to catchy tunes. The same plugs and jingles recur at short intervals, so that even the youngest children soon know them by heart. It may well be that advertising ditties have supplanted the old-fashioned nursery rhyme in the experience of the average pre-school child; certainly this seemed true in the household where Granny, fondly jigging the baby on her knee, punctuated the interview with a medley consisting exclusively of television jingles. Advertising breaks were often mentioned as the 'programme' which the child specifically watched at bedtime.

Clerk's wife:
> We have the telly on. We've got to see telly. It's mostly the adverts that she watches; she always likes that little bit on my knee.

Self-employed craftsman's wife:
> We sit on the chair, because the TV's usually on by then, and we have to watch the adverts. Then he drinks his milk and cleans his teeth and plays a few minutes, and by that time the adverts are usually on again. So we have to sit down and watch the adverts through. But as soon as they're through, by that time he's all ready.

Depot manager's wife:
> I tell Kim to get undressed, and sometimes she don't do it straight away. They're usually watching TV. If she don't get undressed, I turn the telly off.

Kim is somewhat distracted by the television from the more serious business of getting undressed, and some mothers do seem to find it more of a curse than a blessing. The child usually watches television on the understanding that he will go to bed once a particular programme is finished; not unnaturally, however, many find it a useful excuse for procrastination at bedtime, and some mothers apparently find it difficult to be firm over this, especially when father or an older child is un-

I

willing to have the set switched off. The first mother below resorts to ruses to beat the TV attraction; the second, with several teenage children, has completely capitulated, and allows the youngest child to stay downstairs for an 'indulgent bedtime'.

### Representative's wife:

He'll say "Can I stay up a bit longer, Mummy?", and I say "Yes", because I always get him ready that much *earlier*, because I know he always wants to stay up that little bit *longer*, you see! *That's* the biggest bind—the square box! You know, I don't like to have it on when it's near bedtime, but—you know—it's just a thing my husband and I differ with, he'll say have it on, he just doesn't bother about the children; and then Dennis'll say, "Oh, this is my *favourite* programme, I want to see it, Mummy!"

### Tyre fitter's wife:

Oh, now that *is* it—you've come to it now—bedtime! You can't *get* her to bed now, not since we've had that television, you see. The lads and Father has got it on, and it's "I want to just watch this", you know. So it's more or less *any* time—as soon as I can get her. I couldn't say any set time, like. But I think that's been the trouble, you know, because I didn't have any trouble at all, not with the others. That's what I put it down to. (So she watches it, does she?—and then what happens?) Well, then she drops off to sleep on the settee, and then I more or less take her up.

What we have said about television should not be taken to imply that there is any hard evidence for a falling-off in the telling of bedtime stories or the singing of bedtime songs. It is not in fact possible to discover in retrospect how many children in a comparable sample from the pre-television era would regularly have had either of these. For this reason, it is not very profitable to speculate further on the changes in parent/child interaction brought about by television. Perhaps one point should be made, however: that there are certainly a few homes in which personalities are such that communication between parent and child is at a minimum; the child is neither played with nor talked to, beyond the brief giving of orders, and in such homes the television set is probably his only means of escaping total cultural deprivation during the pre-school years.

In the present sample, we estimated the incidence of bedtime stories simply by noting whether these were mentioned spon-

taneously, either during the mother's account of a typical bedtime, or in the course of her replies to subsequent questions.
The singing of songs and the saying of prayers was also noted
on the same basis, and the figures which we present for all three
in Table XXV are thus fairly conservative estimates, and indicate those children for whom these activities are a normal rather
than intermittent occurrence.

TABLE XXV

*Stories, songs and prayers as part of the regular
bedtime routine*

| | I & II | IIIwc | IIIman | IV | V | All (random) |
|---|---|---|---|---|---|---|
| | % | % | % | % | % | % |
| Bedtime stories | 56 | 34 | 20 | 22 | 14 | 27 |
| Songs at bedtime | 9 | 17 | 6 | 7 | 9 | 8 |
| Prayers | 29 | 17 | 7 | 12 | 10 | 12 |

Just over one in four four-year-olds regularly have a story
told or read to them (often by their father) at bedtime. However,
the table shows a massive class difference: whereas only one in
seven of unskilled workers' wives mentioned the telling of
stories, Class I and II mothers included this rather more often
than not. From the way parents talk about bedtime stories, it is
clear that middle-class parents have a much stronger tendency
than working-class parents to think of story-telling as a part of
their educational duty towards their children—something which
the good parent provides—whereas on the whole (with exceptions) working-class parents are inclined to think of stories
merely as a diversion, a childish indulgence, one among many
ways of humouring children, but of no particular significance;
'His daddy always takes him to bed, and he says "Can I have a
story?" ', said an engineer's wife, 'but he's been told now that
he's getting a bit too old for stories'. 'Ooh, no, I don't believe in
stories', said a miner's wife; 'If you start *that* game, you have to
keep it on—you could be there for hours'. A university teacher's
wife, discussing her own and her husband's roles at bedtime,
said about story-telling: '*I* usually deal with that sort of thing.
We sort of share out the evening chores, and he tends to deal

with the physical and I with the intellectual—I think we both find that easier'; and this is of interest, not because of the division of labour described, which is idiosyncratic, but because of her assumption that intellectual pursuits form an integral part of the 'evening chores'. This attitude includes, usually, a belief that story-reading from an early age lays a foundation for intellectual tastes in later years; and the younger children, in particular, of the professional-class families will often have benefited from story-time in an imitative way from babyhood onwards: 'Then I read her a story', said an actor's wife, 'and Rupert listens, and then I show Rupert his little book'—Rupert being sixteen months old.

Social class trends in the singing of songs and the saying of prayers at bedtime are not so clear cut. For 8% of children, songs are a normal part of bedtime, but it is not at all easy to account for the significantly higher proportion (17%) in the white collar group, and we must confess ourselves baffled by this result; although it perhaps makes some sense if one thinks of stories and songs as similar but usually alternative activities, in which professional-class parents show a much stronger preference than white-collar parents for stories. However, white-collar parents also spontaneously mention kissing and cuddling as a part of bedtime significantly more often than other groups (39% as opposed to 27%), so the explanation is not quite so simple as that.[1] The class trend in the encouragement of prayers is more comprehensible in the light of what is known about class differences in church attendance,[2] although the differences which we find are particularly substantial: more than a quarter of children in the professional and managerial class are taught to say their prayers, but the figure drops to a mere 7% among the children of the skilled manual group which constitutes the bulk of the working class. The slight increase in the incidence of prayers towards the lower end of the social scale is undoubtedly due to the fact that these less skilled manual workers include a higher proportion of Roman Catholics than do other classes. Catholic parents appear to take family religious observance as a matter of course—'We always make them kneel down and bless themselves to God'—where Anglican parents often have doubts

[1] More baffling still, the use of an implement for smacking also occurs most often in the white-collar group: see p. 415.

[2] See Argyle, Michael: *Religious Behaviour*, Routledge and Kegan Paul, London, 1958.

as to whether four is not rather early for formal prayers—
'I think he's a little bit too young really; we don't believe really
that prayers are necessary at a *particular* time of the day; that's
a thing that you learn as you grow older'. Anglican parents
are also often easily discouraged if the child himself dislikes
saying prayers, and perhaps suffer sometimes from a lack of
guidance compared with Catholic parents: 'I always say "Goodnight, God bless", because he doesn't say any prayers yet, I
don't know how to go about introducing prayers really, I'd
*like* to; he knows that—er—you know—he's got to be a good
boy else Jesus won't love him; you know, I'm sure that's the
wrong way, but I sometimes say it' (miner's wife).

If we consider the class trends for stories, songs and prayers as
a whole, it is clear that there is a broad difference, which is highly
significant statistically, between middle-class and working-class
mothers in this respect. What these three things have in common
is that they all involve mother and child in close verbal
communication; and here we have one more example of class
differences in the effective use of language between parents and
children which has been discussed by other research workers,[1]
and which we ourselves specifically explore in Chapter 14.

A common ingredient of bedtime which must not be over-
looked is the private, intimate conversation which many
parents contrive to have with the child before he goes to sleep.
Sometimes this is a deliberate attempt to make the child who is
normally dealt with as one of a group of siblings feel that he is
still an individual in the eyes of his mother, with his own confidences to be listened to and respected away from the hurly-
burly of family life. It is also part of the general purpose of
composing the child's mind happily for a peaceful night. Unfortunately, we have no figures on the incidence of private
conversations; we would suppose, on incidental evidence, that
they are at least as frequent as bedtime stories and similarly,
though less emphatically, class linked.

Cabinet-maker's wife (social work trained):

If it's late, I'll let him talk a little bit; if it's early he goes to bed,
I'll let him talk a *lot;* he'll tell me what's happened in the day,

[1] Notably Basil Bernstein; see, for instance, his article 'A Socio-Linguistic
Approach to Social Learning', in Gould, Julius: *Penguin Survey of the Social
Sciences, 1965*, Penguin Books, Harmondsworth, Middlesex, 1965.

you know, and different things. But I find it's interesting to listen to them at that time of the day, you know—you can give your time to them; it's nice to listen to them, they've got a lot to tell you then, when they're lying down in bed. I find Janie (6) always talks better then, as well—whether it's because they're more relaxed and perhaps you are too, I don't know, but it is a time when they want to talk.

### Actor's wife:

I lie on the bed with her, for between five and fifteen minutes, depending on how much time I've got, and she talks about everyday things.

### Joiner's wife:

I cover him over and tuck him right under, and if we're going to the park tomorrow I say, "Oh, we're going to the park tomorrow" and "P'raps tomorrow we'll buy you a comic"—or some sweets, or something. And then he usually starts asking me about Super-car, on TV, and he reminds me a bit about it, and I have to tell him a bit about it, or he tells *me* a bit about it. Or Yogi Bear, we have a little talk on that, because they're his favourites. Then he settles down for the night and says "Night-night. See you later, in the morning"—he always says that.

### Printer's manager's wife:

He usually sits on my knee and I read him a little story or a little bit out of his book. Then we have his 'love', as he calls it, and, you know, we talk about what he's been doing during the day, and how he's going to be a good boy tomorrow, and all that sort of thing, five or ten minutes I should think we do that, and then pop him into bed and tuck him up and "Goodnight", and that's it.

### Window cleaner's wife:

I sit and nurse him a bit. I don't sing to him—I don't know, I seem a bit shy with my own children. I was always a bit reserved right back to being a girl, I can't quite do that sort of thing with them. Well, then I take him upstairs and sit and talk to him for a bit. I like to talk to them before they go to sleep. I don't just bundle them off. If you have a little talk to them, it makes them happy to go to sleep. I do that with my big boys, too (8 and 9). I like to talk to them and put their minds at ease for them.

*'He's up and down these stairs like a yo-yo'*

Parents are willing enough to make bedtime a pleasant routine; but they tend to be less tolerant when the child presumes upon their good nature and continues to call them back for renewed attention, to play noisily as if this were not bedtime at all, or to come downstairs with the hopeful idea of rejoining the family circle. The feeling is that the child has claimed a heavy share of their consideration for the past hour or so on the understanding that the sequence would culminate in sleep; when it culminates in wakefulness, and demanding wakefulness at that, patience begins to wear thin: 'I really get cross then, 'cause I explain to her that she's *been* played with, she's *had* her fun, and it's settling-down time now'.

From the child's point of view, there can be real difficulties in the way of his going to sleep which the most understanding care at bedtime may not altogether alleviate. Separation from his mother and the rest of the family, at an age when the physical presence of the mother is still very highly valued, may leave him feeling insecure and unable to sleep. He may be physiologically incapable of taking the amount of sleep which his mother deems suitable for him. He may be disturbed by older or more restless siblings, or by the noise of traffic, other children and teenagers in a busy street outside, especially in summer. Or he may simply be bored or lonely, and decide that it is worth while making a bid for a small extension of his parents' company,[1] even if he knows it will now be angry rather than friendly company.

Some of the situations that arise are described in the quotations below.

Shoe repairer's wife:

Oh, now you're asking! Well, up until the light nights, no trouble at all. But *now*, he's up and down these stairs like a yo-yo. Last Tuesday I went out, and my husband was doing his motor-bike in the back, and—"All of a sudden" my husband says, "I felt someone beside me"—and it was Robert. He'd come all the way down through the living-room, through the back and out into the back garden. He's a terror at night-time since the light nights.

[1] Our own children evolved a family word, 'comforty', which means the comfort of company. It is used almost exclusively during this period between bedtime and sleep: 'I've got to go to the bathroom, come and give me some comforty'.

He can hear the children playing, you know. We did try putting a blanket up at the window, but I think that frightened him, and we couldn't get any proper air in the bedroom that way; so we left it.

### Shop assistant's wife:

She *goes* at about eight, but she'll shout down for an hour. Well, of course, she wants a drink, she's thirsty, and she's hungry; and she gets up there and she wants to wee-wee, so you bring her down and *take* her to the toilet—and she won't *go*! Various things—anything to stay awake! Mainly it's a drink she wants, or "Oh, I've got an awful headache, Mummy!", you know, and she puts on all sorts of things, "I don't feel very well", you know, that sort of thing, just to get out of going to sleep.

### Greengrocer's wife:

After about ten minutes we hear him out of bed, running along the passage, and he calls out "I'm going to the toilet"; so I say, "All right, you go to the toilet, and go and get straight back in bed". But he generally will go three times before he'll settle down for the night. It varies from half-an-hour to an hour, generally, from going to bed and settling down. But in that time he'll have called out about three times, "I'm going to the toilet". It's really only for somewhere to walk to!

### Packer's wife:

I don't go up and see, unless they're making *too* much noise. I usually shout from the bottom of the stairs. But he's usually running from one room to the other room. But actually what he *does* I don't know—just running about. Of course, if I *do* go up, and they *hear* me going up, they're all in bed, all neat and tidy of course. They think I've gone up to give them all a good hiding. I couldn't really go up and *catch* them, unless I creep up very, *very* quiet; and I *have* done that on one occasion, and they was standing on the chest of drawers, bouncing into the middle of Ian's bed—diving, all three of them. I don't think they do that now, because they *did* get a good hiding that night. Usually I *can* creep up; but there's one stair here and there that *do* creak, and then they just—I think they must be listening. You wouldn't think anyone had *been* out of bed if you saw them, all neat and tidy and all tucked down. It's no use going up and saying who's doing so-and-so and who's doing the other, because they all say "Not me".

Manager's wife:

One night he was sick in bed; and of course we got him out of bed and brought him down; and of course a few nights later he wanted to come down and we wouldn't let him. So he's a dab hand now, if we refuse, at *making* himself sick. Oh yes—he's champion at that! Mind you, we're breaking him of it now, because the last time he did it—and you can hear him, actually making himself sick—I spanked him, I'm afraid. Because they can do that too often, can't they? But you see it's difficult these chilly nights, you have to bring him down; but if he does it in the summertime, I make him stay in his room and change him there.

On the whole, the feeling that enough is enough where coping with children in the evening is concerned results in a fairly general effort to be especially firm about this. To return to Table XXIV, p.247, only 16% of all four-year-olds are normally allowed to rejoin the family if they are not sleepy; and professional and managerial parents are significantly more strict than the rest on this point, with a proportion of only 6%. Emergencies—illness in particular—will of course usually reverse this rule, which is why some children, like those of the shop assistant and the manager above, will deliberately try to create such a situation. To allow a child to come back into the family circle after he has been 'settled' is very definitely seen as being in the 'give him an inch . . .' category, perhaps more generally than any other single item of behaviour. 'If she wasn't tired', said a doctor's wife, 'I'd probably read to her for another while until she *was* tired. But I think once you've let them down you've had it, because they'll want to come down again; I'd read with her in the bedroom, rather than let her come down'; and a supermarket manager's wife echoed her: 'Oh no, no—once you start that, I think you've had it, you know'. The child is regarded as being on the alert for signs of weakness in the mother: 'Carolyn's very crafty, you know', explained a machine operator's wife, 'I mean that would mean her doing it all the time'; and a hosiery worker's wife agreed: 'Once you did it, they'd try it on again, you see'. A few mothers back up their firmness (or rather, avoid the need for it) by making it physically impossible for the child to return: 'I lock the bedroom door once they're all in bed, or you'd have them round you all evening' said a porter's wife with four children aged one to seven sleeping

I*

in the one bedroom, and this was sometimes done in order to control what the mother felt was especially mischievous behaviour.

Salesman's wife:

> We found her in the bathroom, running the water-tap merrily and playing with the sponges and the flannels, and the floor was covered with talcum-powder and Ajax. So we decided we'd put, like, a little latch on the outside of her bedroom door, so that she *can't* get out.

Soap processor's wife:

> Well, they don't, because we've had a little lock put on the bedroom door so that they can't get out at night, you see, because the boy used to come down and have a feast in the pantry at night-time; so we had little locks on the doors, and I always put them on when we come down at night-time and take them off when we go to bed.

The 16% who allow the child to return are typically unworried by apprehensions of his taking advantage of them; they are able simply to accept the child's behaviour at its face value, without involving themselves or him in any moral issue. 'If he wants to, he just does', said a newsagent's wife; 'I love him a bit, and if he's tired, he goes to sleep in my arms, and I just lie him down again'; and this seemed to denote an attitude of mind rather than treatment reserved for babies and toddlers only: 'Like most nights', added a decorator's wife, 'Christine (7) usually comes down about ten o'clock—well, she stops up a bit, and then, when her Dad knows that she's tired, he sends her back up'. Some mothers were also flexible about this because more important considerations were involved than whether the child was being allowed to get away with something he shouldn't: 'He says, "I want five minutes with Daddy"', said a depot manager's wife, 'and Daddy lets him stay down because he doesn't see him very often'; and a labourer's wife also accepted the validity of this plea: 'If he hasn't seen his Daddy I think it must prey on his mind; he does come down to see him'. Fathers who come in late from work are also sometimes the reason for a child's regularly late bedtime.

It is worth quoting here also the opinion of Mrs West, wife of a self-employed craftsman: a quotation typical of her own thoughtful approach to any practical problem rather than of any special group of mothers, it nevertheless puts into words the feeling behind flexible attitudes among middle-class mothers in particular, a feeling which often becomes submerged in the stresses of the moment. It must be noted that Mrs West has not in fact had to deal with the situation which she discusses; in her case, however, it is likely that her behaviour would in the event reflect her principles.

> I'd let him stay for about half-an-hour, just to let him sort of think that he'd gained his point, and when he felt happy that he'd achieved it, he would go back to bed. But as I say, he never does come down. (It's very interesting you should say that, because *most* people would say that they'd send him straight back to bed so that he *wouldn't* gain his point.) Well, perhaps they would. But, somehow, you're frustrating the child; he must have come down because he was disturbed about something. You put him straight back to bed, and that disturbance is still there; so, he never gets rid of it. If you let him sit quite happily . . . (And if he wasn't disturbed, you'd still let him gain his point?) Well, I think it pays dividends, because, as I say, Simon is a really evenly-balanced child, and I think it is your *generosity* to a child, from being young, that makes them what they are at four years old. I feel that with Simon and the other two, the way I went about it seemed to be agreeable.

Among the 84% of children who are not allowed to rejoin the family circle, 9% are allowed the next best thing (from their point of view), being free to play out of bed in their room with the light on. 29% may play or look at books with the light on, provided they stay in bed. The biggest group, however (46%) are not supposed to do any of these things, with or without a light, and are expected simply to lie quietly in bed until sleep overtakes them. Class differences are not very great (see Table XXIV), but the trend towards greater strictness in the middle-class remains. However, the relinquishment of the professional class's extreme position on children returning downstairs, in favour of a 49% approval of sitting up in bed, is interesting in that it involves a greater shift than that made by other classes; and this almost certainly reflects the value set by this class upon looking at books, which in this case conflicts with the stricter course.

*'She likes cuddling, she does! . . . I like it, an' all!'*

The reader may have noticed that in Table XXIV the proportions given for children allowed to rejoin the family after bedtime include some who have never left it.[1] It became clear as the
interviewing progressed that there was a quite considerable
group of children for whom bedtime did not, as for the majority,
involve a separation from the mother, but who, on the contrary,
tended to be in particularly close physical contact with her
during the period immediately preceding sleep. We named the
bedtime sequence of this group the 'indulgent bedtime', for want
of a better phrase, and we found 60 individual cases of this,
which as a randomized proportion is expressed as 8% over all
social classes, increasing to 12% in the semi-skilled and unskilled groups and dropping to only 3% in Class I and II (see
Table XXVI p. 273). The indulgent bedtime as we are defining it
has nothing to do with the hour at which the child goes to bed,
for it can happen either early or late; its criterion is that the
mother stays with the child until he has fallen asleep. Almost
always she is touching him in some way: she holds him on her
lap and rocks him, sits beside him or lies down under the blanket
with him; occasionally she will merely busy herself about the
room (usually the living-room) until she sees that he is asleep.
In fact, what she gives him during these last minutes of his
conscious day is exactly expressed in our family word 'comforty'—the comfort of her company.[2]

**Lorry driver's wife:**

> I sit and nurse her till she's asleep—sit her on my knee and
> watch TV—she likes a lot of soft soap!

**Lorry driver's wife:**

> I put her in the zinc bath on the hearth, give her a good bath,
> powder her—she's still my baby!—then I either sit and love her,
> and she looks at telly and goes to sleep, or she lays on the settee;
> but she likes cuddling, she does! And then she goes to sleep
> and we take her up, and that's the end of it. (And that's a nice
> comfy bedtime, isn't it!) Yes, it is—*I* like it, an' all! . . . I know
> it's wrong, you know, but what can you do? *I* believe in them

[1] Not *all* children who have indulgent bedtimes come into this category: only
those who are soothed to sleep downstairs.
[2] See footnote on page 263.

going to bed, but—Elaine doesn't! But once she goes to sleep we never hear no more of her. Better than having a crying match!

**Stoker's wife:**

He gets himself to sleep—just gets on the settee and goes off himself. He's afraid of going up to bed on his own—they both are. When one's asleep we take him up, and then we get the other one to sleep and take *him* up.

**Newsagent's wife:**

He's an atrocious bedtime child! He likes me to lie beside him and hold his hand, and I do, and in a very few minutes he goes to sleep.

**Stoker's wife:**

He likes to hold my hand till he's asleep; he's got to know that I'm there before he'll go to sleep. He's got to *feel* me there—he'll get hold of my ear—*any* time when he's going to sleep.

**Setter operator's wife:**

I take her up and we get into bed and cuddle up to keep warm, and after ten to twenty minutes she's asleep.

**Teacher's wife:**

. . . And then I turn the main light off and—here it comes!—I *sit* on Gilly's bed until she goes to sleep. And that is the best, quickest, easiest-for-everybody way of starting everybody (four children aged 4 to 8) to go to sleep. Everybody else is thoroughly trained to go to sleep on their own, and do so quite happily. But somehow this dreadful habit of sitting with her has caught and stayed, and I'm trapped with it. Varying with how tired she is and how cross I've been during the past hour: if I've been quite reasonable and in my right mind, she'll drop off fairly quickly; if I've been a bit irritable, it all has to be worked off—I'd say ten minutes, a quarter of an hour—it's worth it.

It is clear that mothers have very ambivalent feelings about this behaviour—'I know it's wrong'; 'an atrocious bedtime child'; 'this dreadful habit'; 'I'm trapped with it'—even when they are also able to justify it— 'She likes cuddling—*I* like it an' all!'; 'the best, quickest, easiest-for-everybody way'; 'it's worth it'. Soothing a one-year-old baby to sleep may be accepted as normal enough;[1] but the same treatment of a four-year-old would, they know, be criticized by many mothers as a deliberate, and inexcusably indulgent, prolongation of babyhood. Class differences, though not very great, show again a significantly stronger reaction by Class I and II against a practice which they feel to be lax and perhaps feckless. Without in any way making judgments as to rights or wrongs, we ourselves felt that the main issue was not merely strictness versus laxity, but that a prolongation of babyhood, whether conscious or not, was the central feature of the indulgent bedtime. This supposition was confirmed by the number of mothers who spontaneously said that it had not happened with their elder children: that it happened *now*, they often attributed to the child's being afraid to go to bed alone, even though one might expect later children in a family to have more confidence (through the example and companionship of their elder siblings) rather than less; there thus seemed to be some other contributing factor on the mother's part. An additional confirmation came in the frequent tender remarks—such as 'She's still my baby!'—which accompanied these descriptions.

We therefore analysed the family position of children given indulgent bedtimes, and the results were closely consistent with the interpretation that they were still regarded as the baby of the family. Of the sixty children, 12 were singletons, and (including these twelve) 44 children (73%) were the latest-born in the family. A finding of still greater suggestiveness was that there was a tendency for a particular pattern of family structure to emerge: a pattern in which the child in question was the youngest and was *preceded by a gap of five years or more* between himself and the child next in age. Eighteen of these children had this rather unusual family position, and for seven of them their next sibling had already reached the teens.[2] In addition, as one might expect, given the results described, there was a highly significant tendency for the mother to be older than average.

[1] At a year, the picture is confused by the fact that most babies have the solace of bottles and/or dummies, so that the mother is not the only soothing agent normally available. Nevertheless, *in addition* to the 43% who took bottle or dummy to bed with them at that age, about a third were soothed with a bottle on the mother's lap immediately before being tucked up in bed.

[2] All the results given in this paragraph differ significantly from family structures found among children who do not have indulgent bedtimes, taking into account the class differences which appear both in family structure and in the incidence of indulgent bedtimes.

Almost three-quarters of the children having indulgent
bedtimes, then, are not in competition with any younger child
for their mother's attention. They have enjoyed the position of
being the littlest and most helpless member of the family group
for four uninterrupted years, and well over a third of these
latest-born children may expect to be mothered by brothers and
sisters in addition. From the mother's point of view, a four-year
gap since the birth of this child is likely to mean either that she
intends to have no more children or that she is having difficulty
in conceiving and therefore is beginning to regard this child as
her last. In the specific family structure described above, the fact
that the four-year-old was itself preceded by a gap of at least
five years (usually more) distinguishes the child as either an
afterthought or a late accident, and in either case gives it a
special place in the mother's affection. The result of any of these
factors is a natural tendency to prolong babyhood, to wring the
last drops of pleasure from a relationship which the mother feels
may never recur. 'You feel you've been given one more chance',
said a middle-class mother who had originally been appalled
at finding herself pregnant at this late stage, 'and you want to
make the most of it'. To be cherishing and protective towards
small helpless creatures is, after all, an emotionally rewarding
role for any adult, and the mother who knows, or suspects, or
even hopes, that this may be her last child will naturally want to
make it last for as long as she can; nor is she prevented from
doing so by the demands of children close in age to her 'baby'.

These considerations, together with the linked factor of the
mother's age, may have wider implications. Gordon Trasler, in
his study of success and failure in fostering,[1] found a most
interesting connection between the foster-mother's age and her
success, this last being judged by very rigorous criteria. He
found a peak for successful fostering between the ages of forty
and forty-five, with a considerable falling-off on either side of
this age range. When we examine the same age-group in our
own sample in relation to their bedtime practices, we find the
very striking result that more than one in four of them conform
to the 'indulgent bedtime' pattern, compared with only one in
sixteen of younger and older women, a difference which is highly
significant statistically. It may well be that this should be seen

[1] Trasler, Gordon: *In Place of Parents*, Routledge and Kegan Paul, London,
1960.

as a critical period in the mother's ability to give unstintingly the affection which Trasler emphasizes as being of primary importance in fostering: at the end of her child-bearing years, but not yet finally adjusted to being without a baby to cosset, a mother of this age perhaps offers a reservoir of undemanding tenderness which may be the first need of potential foster-children.

We do not present the mother's desire to prolong the child's babyhood as the full explanation for indulgent bedtimes; it does not necessarily account for the over-representation of singletons among these children. However, one may expect 'only' children to be slower in relinquishing the pleasures of babyhood, and mothers to be less pressing for them to do so, simply because there are no younger siblings to nudge them out of the baby role. The mere presence of a smaller child in the same house as the four-year-old will tend to have this effect, because younger children almost inevitably come to be used as negative models: 'That's only baby food, it's not for a big boy like you'; 'You used to do that when you were little, but you don't now, do you?'; 'Don't be rough, remember you're much bigger than she is'; 'Don't suck your thumb, you're not a baby now'; and so on. Whether or not such remarks are deliberately intended to push the four-year-old to more mature forms of behaviour, this is likely to be their cumulative effect. In addition, when a mother has two or more children under five years to care for, the comparison between brothers and sisters of different ages constantly reminds her that her expectations of the child's behaviour ought to change as his age increases; whereas if she has only one child, she may not know, or may easily forget, that most four-year-olds are more independent than this. As we have noted in Chapter 4, the forces of habit and inertia almost always operate in the direction of slower rather than faster social development. Finally, the arrival of a new baby can hardly fail to attract the mother's physical attentions away from the erstwhile youngest child. However conscious she may be of the need to prevent jealousy in the displaced child, the fact remains that her time and energy now have to be divided between them, so that what is feasible treatment for a single child may become excessively difficult to achieve when there are two to be coped with. It is possible for two children in the same household to enjoy indulgent bedtimes, like those of the stoker's wife quoted on page 269, but it is extremely rare.

TABLE XXVI

*Means by which the child avoids separation from the
mother at bedtime and during the night*

Social class

| | I & II | IIIwc | IIIman | IV | V | All (randomized) |
|---|---|---|---|---|---|---|
| | % | % | % | % | % | % |
| 'Indulgent bedtime' (defined on page 268) | 3 | 7 | 8 | 13 | 11 | 8 |
| Sleeps in parents' room | 7 | 7 | 15 | 15 | 19 | 13 |
| Mother willing to chat during night | 26 | 32 | 24 | 26 | 33 | 26 |
| Mother willing to take child into her bed during night | 55 | 69 | 70 | 61 | 64 | 66 |

*'Her bed's ever so comfortable, I don't know why she can't stay
in it'*

By the age of four, most children seem to sleep undisturbed
through the night. However, for one child in five it is not at all
uncommon to wake during the night, and this proportion is
made up of 13% of all children who wake once or twice in an
average week and 7% whose sleep is broken more often than
not. The remaining 80% are said to wake 'seldom or never', but
the occurrence was hardly ever so rare that the mother was
unable to answer questions about how her child would typically
behave if he did wake, and such questions were therefore included for all mothers.

How, then, do children of four behave when they wake in the
night? A small proportion—6%—are said to remain quietly in
bed talking or singing to themselves until the return of sleep.
The most normal course, however, is to try to attract someone
else's attention, most often the parents', but sometimes specifically a brother's or sister's, and this is done in three ways:
37% call or shout, without appearing upset; 34% habitually
cry or otherwise show distress if they wake in the night; and
10% get out of bed to seek their parents, half of these immediately climbing into their parents' bed as a matter of course. The
remaining 13% include 5% who *never* wake as far as the mother

knows, and a miscellaneous group who (mostly) turn to a bed-fellow for comfort, or who have more idiosyncratic reactions, such as 'Bangs his head against the head of the bed, rocks himself and mumbles' or 'Every night at about 3.30 bounces on mattress, sings, plays cowboys and trains, drives car, changes gear, imitates brakes, and "occasionally if he remembers to be very quiet not to wake anyone else up, he will call me to *tell* me he has been very good not to wake anyone up!"' One would not expect social class to affect children's behaviour on waking, and it does not.

Of the children who wake in distress, just over a quarter behave in a way which their mothers interpret as the result of disturbing dreams or nightmares, and a few show signs of having true night terrors.[1] It would be misleading, however, to discuss the incidence of night terrors in terms of percentages, since they tend to occur to individual children in temporary phases, and we would be dependent for our information upon such a phase coinciding in time with the interview. Perhaps unfortunately, we did not frame a question to investigate nightmares and night terrors as such.

Clerk's wife:

> She has this nightmare, and she's screaming "Don't, don't!" But she doesn't really wake up, you see. She's screaming and talking. She sits there, and you think she's awake, but she's not, and you really have to wake her up. (And is it difficult to wake her up?) Oh yes, awful!

Salesman's wife:

> It's a *terrible* job to wake her up—she's awake but she isn't, you know. Sometimes, you know, it seems an eternity—crying and sort of . . . but if she wakes up from an *ordinary* dream she seems a bit apprehensive, but not frightened.

The terrors of both these children, incidentally, are more successfully penetrated by their fathers than by their mothers. The first has a generally stormy relationship with her mother; the source of the second child's terrors is more mysterious, but she

---

[1] For a discussion of the distinction between nightmares and night terrors, the reader is referred to Kanner, Leo: 1957, op. cit., p. 500.

is in other ways a highly imaginative little girl.[1] Other children's sleep disturbances are less acutely distressing either to themselves or to their parents. One little boy has cried out in his sleep since his father deserted the family; another shouts 'Put my clothes on me!' or 'I'm falling out of bed!', but does not seem more than momentarily upset. A company director's wife connects her daughter's agitation with emotional stress during the day:

> She can never say what's wrong; she dreams, I think. Sometimes she wakes up crying—if they've been fighting during the day; she's re-living it, probably. I just say "It's all right now—it's all gone now", and I ask her, "Were you thinking about something?" and she'll say "Yes", and I say "What was it? Tell Mummy", and she'll mumble something, but you can't tell what she's saying, because I mean she's really asleep. I sit and hold her hand for about two minutes, then I turn her over, wipe her eyes if she's been crying, say "You're all right now, aren't you?" and she'll say "Yes". I say "Goodnight and God bless you"—"Goodnight and God bless"—and she's off mostly.

Some children's bladder tension is translated into an emotional tension which, combined with their semi-conscious state, makes it impossible for them to relieve themselves physically: a situation not uncommon in younger children also, and highly distressing while it lasts.

Dancing instructor's wife:

> If he wants to go to the toilet, he's really very . . . I don't know *what's* the matter with him or *why* he's like that. But he stamps on the floor and kicks and fights. Actually, I don't think he's quite awake, and it's an awful job with him. He just fights and cries and gets quite hysterical. Once or twice, I've just *had* to smack him, to, you know, sort himself out. He goes all stiff and rigid.

We asked every mother what she would do if the child seemed frightened in the night, and the gist of almost all the replies was that she would attempt to give the child reassurance. This was to be expected, but we were particularly interested in the ways

---

[1] 'Veronica', whose imaginary friends, Noddy, Billa and Gunny, are mentioned on page 182.

in which reassurance would be given, since we believed (and had evidence from the one-year-old study to show) that certain measures (taking the child into the parents' bed in particular) had negative *moral* attitudes attached to them. Our questions were accordingly asked in the form shown below, in order, firstly, to investigate the mother's attitude to taking the child into her bed, given what she might reasonably consider an acceptable excuse —his fear; secondly, to find out whether she would respond in the middle of the night to a purely social need—his wish to have a conversation with her. Situations of illness, an emergency rather more acute than the child's fear, and introducing perhaps the need for constant physical supervision, were discounted.

70. What would you do
     if he seemed frightened?
     if he was just feeling chatty?
     if he wanted to come into your bed?
     (If the following remedies have not been mentioned):
     Would you *ever*
     let him come into your bed?
     get into bed with him?
     sit with him?
     get him something to eat in the night?

What most children want if they wake in the night is reassurance and company, not necessarily that of their parents, and many will not need to look far, in that they already sleep in their parents' room or with a sibling. As can be seen from Table XXVI, 13% of four-year-olds sleep in their parents' room (some in their parents' bed); the steady class trend is certainly due mainly to differences in size of the family and the amount of accommodation available to house it. As one might suppose, youngest and only children are the most likely to be sleeping in the same room as their parents. In terms of the amount of comforting which he may expect, the significance to the child of sleeping in the same room as a sibling must depend heavily upon their age and protectiveness, so that percentages in this connection do not mean very much. It would be more useful to know how many children sleep in the same bed with another person, whether parent (rare), sibling (common) or grandparent (very rare); the presence of a warm body in the same bed, especially if it belongs to someone concerned to keep the child asleep, might well prevent his ever fully waking during the night, and would often forestall the need for the mother to accept or refuse the child's wish to come in with her: as a lorry-driver's wife pointed out, 'If they've got their big sister, they don't usually want to, do they?' However, we felt that to ask in such detail about sleeping arrangements was an unwarrantable intrusion, and our information on this is therefore no more than incidental.

There are obviously certain practical inconveniences in allowing the child to join the parents in bed. The bed itself may be uncomfortably small for three (one mother complained that she was 'getting fed up' with sleeping *four* in a bed); the child may be a natural fidget; or his regular time of visitation may begin to interfere with his parents' sexual life. From the manner in which the 34% who would firmly refuse to take the child into bed discuss it, however, it is clear that they have more than inconvenience in mind, and regard this as the first step on the slippery path to total indulgence: 'Once you start letting them in, they think they ought to go in *every* time they wake up', said a depot manager's wife; and a scientific research worker's wife (who had accepted her child's wish to play noisily for an hour every night at around 3.30 a.m.—page 274) said with emphatic decision, 'I've never started that, and I *never shall*. They don't know what it is to come into Mummy's bed'. A technical representative's wife was equally definite: 'It's a thing I've never done, *never*; only in the morning when we're all awake, but *never* in the night, no, I don't think it's right'; and an insurance inspector's wife, who agreed that she would *never* let her little boy come in her bed at night, felt she also had to apologize for his coming in at 6 o'clock in the morning: 'He *has* been into our bed, it's very bad, I *know;* we normally make him go back in his own; but, you know, we were past caring, and he *did* creep in'.

From the point of view of expedience, to take a wakeful child into one's own bed may in fact be the most comfortable and convenient course possible: it avoids at a stroke both the child's lonely unhappiness (and consequent disturbance for the rest of the family) and what may be the only alternative, a chilly and sleepless hour spent by his mother at his side. If the child is *not* a fidget, it also has the pleasant attraction, for mother as well as child, of additional time for the cuddling which all too soon will be taboo. Fathers, too, seem to appreciate this point: in fact, this may be an opportunity for them to cuddle their sons when

such behaviour in the daytime is already not unreservedly acceptable: 'I'll say, "No, go back in your own bed"; but he'll go
round to his Daddy, and *he'll* say, "Ah, come on, then!" ' Many
of the mothers who accept taking the child into bed as the only
really practicable course, and often give extremely persuasive
reasons for doing so, still feel extremely guilty about it; and,
since they tend to expect (sometimes from experience) that their
guilt will be confirmed by the comments of others, this is one of
those areas in which parents' communication with other parents
behaving in the same way is reduced to a minimum, with the
result that they are unaware of the normality of what they are
doing.[1] The 66% of parents who are willing to take their
children into bed with them if need be may or may not be right,
but they cannot, by definition, be abnormal.

### Lorry driver's wife:

She jumps straight in our bed and goes to sleep again. In fact,
sometimes you never know she's come till you turn over and
there she is, you know. "Ooh—are you here again?" I say—but
she's fast asleep. I've given it up as a bad job—I've tried and tried
(getting up to her), and it hasn't worked, so I thought, "I'm not
going to sit here all night, I'm losing *my* sleep, I might as well be
in bed with you". Well, so I don't bother now. If she comes in
and I see her or hear her, I say "Oh, *Sharon*, go back to your
own bed, there's no room in here"; and she'll say "Oh, no,
oh-h-h . . ."—and I say "Oh, come on, then". And she just
climbs over her father and climbs on the pillow and slides down.
I think it's company, that's what I think it is. But her bed's ever
so comfortable, I don't know why she can't stay in it, I'm sure. . . .

---

[1] An anthropological perspective is of interest here, even though the following
passage refers mainly to younger children (whose acceptance into the parental
bed is also in our culture, as we have seen, a source of guilt): 'We discovered
that only five societies out of the total number (a sample of 56 societies chosen
to be representative of all types of civilization) had sleeping arrangements
similar to our own, that is, where the father and mother share a bed and the
baby sleeps alone. In only three societies did the mother, the father, and the
baby each have his or her own bed. In the remaining 48, the baby slept with
his mother until he was at least a year old and generally until he was weaned.
In 24 of the latter, however, the father also shared the bed, the baby generally
sleeping between the mother and father. The remaining 24 societies had sleeping
arrangements . . . in which the mother and child sleep in one bed and the father
in another'. Whiting, J. W. M., Kluckhohn, R. and Anthony, A.: 'The Function
of Male Initiation Ceremonies at Puberty', in Maccoby, E., Newcomb, T. M.
and Hartley, E. L.: *Readings in Social Psychology*, 3rd edn., Holt, Rinehart &
Winston, New York, 1958.

I mentioned it to my doctor, and to the doctor at the clinic. *My* doctor said "Give her a damn good hiding". The clinic doctor put it down to me going to work and leaving her—he said that she missed me, and her only way of seeing me was at night-time, therefore she was doing this to get in with me. *He* said don't bother, don't stop her at all—leave her, and she'll gradually get over it. But *my* doctor said "If it continues, you give her a damn good hiding!"—he did! I thought, *no*, it'll never do anything, that won't! I said to him, "I don't think *that*'ll do much good, Dr. G.".

Some of the mothers who are able to accept the child into their bed without self-consciousness or disquiet, but merely as a natural response to the child's expression of a natural need, are quoted below.

### Miner's wife:

I'd let him come in five minutes, because I'd think he needed cuddling. You know yourself, if you're not feeling right, a little bit of fuss does you the world of good.

### Window cleaner's wife:

A few nights after baby was born, he woke up and was sobbing —I think he was a little pushed out. So I took him in my bed and comforted him, and he's never woken since.

### Miner's wife:

She creeps in. I don't send her back. She goes to sleep straight away, whereas if I sent her back she would only upset the whole house, really. It's when she's had a dream; I think you can't just shut the door on her—you should have her in bed, or she would be more frightened than ever.

### Boot repairer's wife:

She goes back after about a quarter of an hour; I think she's lonely, sort of thing—wakes up and feels a bit lonely, so she comes in to us, and it just gives her fresh confidence and she goes back again.

The picture may be brought into closer focus by a brief examination of some additional factors. Table XXVI shows that on this topic Class I and II mothers remain consistent with their

general position of being significantly more strict about bedtime
rules than are mothers of other social classes. When we look for
a relationship between taking into bed and the child's normal
sleeping place, we find an interesting link in that children who
are already sleeping in the parents' room are significantly more
likely to be allowed into their bed: interesting, because one
might think that parents could reasonably say 'You've got the
company you want, there's no need for you to come into my bed
as well'; but no doubt the insistent demand of a child who
cannot be banished from the room in practice prevails over cool
reason. We have already seen that youngest and only children
are more likely than others to be sharing the parents' room; this
is not an adequate reason for the finding just described, for it is
youngest and *intermediate* children who are most likely to be
allowed into the parents' bed, 'onlies' being treated on this issue
like eldests, with significantly greater strictness. We wondered
how far the father's absence from home might influence the
mother's attitude. Just over 1 in 10 fathers are away from home
one or more nights in the week, and in these families 73% of
mothers would take the child into their bed, compared with 66%
for the sample as a whole; this difference is in the direction
which one would expect, but does not reach statistical significance, and we may conclude that the father's presence or
absence is not an important factor here. Finally, since we knew
that a fair proportion of these mothers were answering somewhat hypothetically because their children were in fact suffering
few disturbed nights, we thought it important to know whether
the mothers who were in fact having to cope with the problem
had a greater or lesser tendency to say that they would accept the
child in their bed. The former turned out to be the case; 77% of
the mothers whose children wake at least once in a week are prepared to take them into bed, compared with 63% of those whose
children rarely wake, a difference significant at the ·02 level.
Presumably the hard facts of children's demands, as in other
areas of upbringing, succeed in beating down some mothers'
cherished principles. There are, it should be added, no class
differences in the *incidence* of waking to account for the
differences we have shown in mothers' attitudes.

Chatting with the child during the night to most parents seems
less necessary and less reasonable; while real distress should be
attended to, by taking the child into bed if this seems best, a

wish to talk is not an urgent need and can be put off till morning
—if the child wants to chat at such a crazy hour, the feeling is,
let him chat to himself! Three out of four mothers clearly felt
that this would be the last straw in the series of hypothetical
demands which we had suggested. 'I should just about tan him,
I think!' said a moulder's wife, and she was echoed by others:
'I'd about club him!'—'I'd murder her!' Class differences were
not significant.

It was noticeable, however, that chatting to the child at night
did not have the moral overtones that coloured the discussion
on taking the child into bed—it was merely a matter of '*I* need
my sleep!' Similarly, the 26% who were prepared to meet the
child's sociability did not feel it necessary to apologize or to
over-rationalize their action.

### Lorry driver's wife:

(Parents separated, child normally sleeps with mother.) She just
wakes me up and starts talking. (What do you do?) Well, just
lie and talk till I get fed up. P'raps for about a quarter of an
hour she talks—every night.

### British Rail fireman's wife:

I'd probably curse him! But I'd have to, sort of, listen to him.
He's the sort of child, you see, if he decides he wants to tell you
something, you may as well listen to start with, because he just
goes on and on and on, you know, until he's heard. He's very
persistent, if he once wants to tell you something! (So you'd stay
with him?) Yes, and hope it's a *short* story!

### Bricklayer's wife:

Oh, it often happens. I say, "Roy, go to sleep!" and he'll say
"Well, let me tell you another little story"—he often wants to tell
me a little story, he doesn't mind if it's three o'clock in the
morning! And I'll say "You can tell me in the morning"; but
he'll not be satisfied until he tells me the little story and I laugh.
Then, once he's seen that I'm amused, he'll be all right: but I've
got to laugh, you see!

### Miner's wife:

I suppose I would chat a bit with him and then try to get him
back to sleep. Get his steam off a bit. Because sometimes they
*do* want to talk in the night.

We have no figures on the incidence of children wanting to chat in the night, but from the content of these more permissive mothers' statements (and those above are very typical) it became clear that the majority were in fact speaking from experience: they showed a general recognition of the situation as a real one, as opposed to the 'Good heavens, what an idea!' attitude of those who said that they would not tolerate chatting. Once again, one must suppose that practice may well be modified by the actuality of the child's demands.

The other measures for soothing a wakeful child which we hypothesized—sitting with him, getting into his bed and getting him something to eat—proved of less interest. Sitting with the child tended to be regarded as definitely more virtuous than taking him into one's bed, but so very much more uncomfortable for the mother that the latter course would usually be preferred in practice; it must be remembered that most children's bedrooms are unheated. Getting into the child's bed was fraught with complications: so many children slept with siblings, and so many others still used cots, that for a high proportion of families this was simply not practicable. Getting him something to eat was a suggestion which also became hedged about with qualifications: the general consensus was No—with all sorts of emergency exceptions which boiled down to the degree of the child's desperation. The lorry driver's wife who gave an unqualified Yes may be considered extraordinary in her indulgence: 'I've got up at five o'clock in the morning to take her bread and jam to bed—if a child's hungry, she wants it where she is, doesn't she? Ooh aye, I'd give her something if she wanted it'.

The picture of the four-year-old's bedtime is one of pleasant family interaction, of daytime tensions deliberately relaxed, followed in most families by a rapid tightening-up of parental control once the child has been 'settled' to the mother's satisfaction. At this point conflict may become sharp, as the child attempts to prolong the pleasures of the social period in opposition to his parents' well-defined conception of its limits. In most of the aspects of bedtime, professional and managerial class mothers are significantly stricter than other mothers and less inclined to allow a relaxation of routine. However, they are also significantly more likely to provide bedtime amusements such as story-telling, which they regard as educational but which working-class parents often see as only one among several kinds of indulgence. In addition, where a relaxation of routine involves books or other verbalization, as is true of allowing the child to sit up in bed with the light on or chatting to him during the night, their usual separate position of greater strictness is relinquished or at least modified, and class differences smoothed out.

This discussion has been somewhat attenuated by the omission of the rituals and comfort habits which reach their peak at this period of the day, and which for many children seem the most important feature of bedtime; these we turn to in the next chapter.

# CHAPTER 10

# RITUALS AND COMFORT HABITS

In the last chapter we tried to show that bedtime for the small child is not merely an incidental episode among the many which punctuate his day, but that it has a special significance as a microcosm of family life, often directly involving every member of the family group and serving the child as a definitive statement of family roles. The image which the family thus presents of and to itself at bedtime is given greater weight by the fact that it tends, for the children at least, to be the terminal one of the day, unblurred by succeeding distractions: the picture with which the child is left as he drowses off to sleep, which he takes with him into this final unavoidable separation—and which, presumably, therefore achieves maximum retention. It is evident, from their attempts to make the bedtime experience pleasurable, that mothers recognize its significance to the child: as one woman put it, 'a child should *never* go to sleep crying and *never* go to school crying'.

It is meaningful, then, to view preparation for bed as a recurrent ceremonial rite in which each participant has his own role; from the child's standpoint, in particular, bedtime has the characteristics of a dramatic sequence, played impromptu and with certain permissible variations and developments, but rehearsed each night, and night after night, in the same traditional form. And this stylization, idiosyncratic to each individual family yet very generalized in its essential elements, seems to come about because of the characteristic tendency in children of this age to create a ritual game out of any familiar pattern of events in which they are regularly caught up. Thus the game of going to bed comes to be played out according to certain fixed rules which parents know and follow meticulously, but which are in fact dictated to them by the children themselves.

The most direct way in which this happens is that, while the whole pattern of any individual child's bedtime tends to adhere loosely to one particular scheme, some small part of the sequence begins to take on the inflexible and compulsive quality of a ritual act. Typically, and surely significantly, the event or set of events which the child invests with ritual meaning will occur very close in time to the moment of separation, and often that moment will be embedded in a series of ritualized actions and sayings which are maintained beyond the withdrawal of the mother from the child's sight. The child demands, often with some vehemence, that the things around him should always be arranged in a given way, that certain apparently trivial and non-functional events should invariably occur or that the routine should follow some prescribed order without deviation. Elaborate patterns of behaviour are not necessarily involved; it may be simply that the final kiss is given in an exact and special manner: the mother is obliged to 'kiss me first, then Teddy, then me on my *nose*' or to 'give a kiss for each finger and a great big hug'. Usually the parents are content to play along with these demands, but if on occasion they happen to forget, or if in impatience they refuse to comply, the child will become angry and upset: and it is in fact the intensity of children's emotional reaction to any neglect of the ritual which betrays the importance which they attach to it. It is noticeable that in mothers' accounts of their children's bedtime certain set phrases occur and recur: 'Of course, he *has* to . . .'; 'Then we *must* remember to . . .'; 'She always *insists* . . .'; 'We have that *every* night'; and the word 'ritual' is itself frequently used, although not specifically prompted in our questions.

At this point it seems useful to clarify the discussion by presenting a few out of the very many examples we have of this behaviour. The group that follow have in common that the ritual involves a whole series of small acts, each of which has to be carried out with rigid exactness.

60. *Is there anything special that you always have to do at bedtime —any little game you always have, or something like that?*

Engineer's wife:

Yes—half an hour's love, then we have to jump her up every stair, then she sits on the toilet and Teddy sits on the shelf, and we have to wind him up and he sings to her, you see, while she's on the toilet; then we have to hop her into the bedroom on one foot, then she says her prayers, then she jumps into bed. Then we have to give her three kisses and one squeeze, then "God bless you", and she's off to sleep. That's what she does *every* night, it's always the same.

### Packer's wife:

Oh yes—*every* night. Well, first we have to tuck her pyjamas into her trousers, it must be just so because "it hurts" if you don't. And then you mustn't pull the clothes up too far, they have to be pulled up but not too much, you see. And then we have to pull the bottom of the bed out so that the door is just open just *that* much. Then we have to kiss Teddy goodnight, and we have to say goodnight all the way down the stairs, and at the bottom "Goodnight, Teddy, God bless!" Oh, and her dressing-gown must be hung up just right behind the door, and her slippers on the chair with her books; and you have to put them straight, you don't have to put one on its side, that wouldn't be right at all—you'd have to come back and move it—and you'd *have* to go, or you wouldn't get any peace!

### Self-employed craftsman's wife:

We put Teddy on one side and Bunny on the other, and then we have to sing "Pussycat, pussycat, where have you been?" *every* night. Then Mummy always kisses him on two cheeks and his forehead. Then my husband comes in and says Goodnight, then I have to come back and kiss him again, and then that's it for the night.

### Salesman's wife:

He has lots of rituals. He goes in the bathroom and cleans his teeth, and it has to be done in a certain way—and certain things to do—and he has to face the mirror to do it—all these little things that have to be done *every* night exactly the same. Then his father takes him to bed and he has to have a story every night—it's not read, his father has to make one up. He's got Noddy wallpaper on the wall, and his father has to weave imaginary tales of what these characters have been doing each day—I mean, he's got set tales and he likes certain stories: "Now tell me about Noddy and his car"—"Tell me about Mr Plod stopping the traffic".

### School caretaker's wife:

I have to tuck them both in and kiss them both, and then I have to stand at the door and *blow* them a kiss. And if I forget . . .!

And "See you in the morning" I have to shout at the top of the stairs, and then they count me downstairs, and a few minutes after, they'll shout "Are you sitting down, Mummy?"—and then they'll go off to sleep.

## University teacher's wife:

A whole lot of things we say and things we do; the most important thing is that she asks for the sun and the moon, which means two pieces of apple, one circle-shaped and one crescent-shaped. I'm not sure how that started, but it's stuck; and when we were staying at my parents' last year, I came downstairs and said to my husband, "Clare wants the sun and the moon"—hoping *he'd* get them, you see! And he said, "Well, *give* her the sun and the moon"—which caused great amusement, because my parents thought it just about summed up the way we bring up our children!

## Company director's wife:

He has a story in bed; then he says his prayers; then he goes through a series of things he always says, and if we don't say them, there's trouble about that. He'll say: "Night-night, sleep tight, mind the bugs don't bite; if they do, squeeze them tight". Then he says, "See you later, alligator"—"In a while, crocodile". And then he always says, "Don't be long downstairs, and when you come up don't forget to light the lamp"—we have a lamp for his asthma—"and *don't* be *long*". Every night we say the same things. Then we say "Night-night, God bless", and that's that. But you have to say it, because if you forget you have to come back and go through it all over again.

Several of these sequences include a form of words which is invariably used, either by mother or child, alone or in dialogue, and we have many examples of phrases which seem to have an almost magical significance for the child. In fact, the verbal ritual is the most frequent one of all; in particular, it tends to be the words of parting which take the form of a recognized incantation, and the child is liable to object strongly if the traditional formula is varied, and will typically refuse to settle down at all until the phrases have been correctly recited. Sometimes their original use or meaning has been quite forgotten; sometimes they were introduced by the mother for no especial reason and have acquired ritual meaning through constant repetition at this time; sometimes a once-used phrase has seized the imagination of the child, who thereafter insists upon its continued reiteration.

Shoe repairer's wife:

> When I've got him out and dried him and got his pyjamas on and that, I don't know why, but he's done it for a long time, you have to clap your hands and say *"The Roaring Twenties!"*— and he takes a dive into the air and you have to catch him. And you have to do that *every* night—I don't know why!

Foreman's wife:

> As I come down the stairs, I always say "Night-night, God bless, see you in the morning"—and you know, if I don't, if I just say "Night-night", Barry will shout down, "Mummy, you didn't say it properly", and cry and cry.

Packer's wife:

> Well, he's saying, and I'm always answering, "Good night, see you in the morning, and a Happy New Year!" So I always have to say it back. It's been ever since New Year he's said it. He must insist on a Happy New Year *every* night. So of course I have to say it back, or you wouldn't get no peace until you said it.

Miner's wife:

> Oh yes—we've *always* got to say "Goodnight, me old flower", *every* night, and if I forget, she always shouts down: "Why didn't you say 'Goodnight, me old flower'?"

Some of these phrases clearly have protective meaning for the child: the words 'God bless you, see you in the morning' are obviously reassuring. Others, particularly those evolved by the child himself, are not quite so well defined. One little boy, in answer to his father's 'Goodnight, God bless', invariably says 'Don't forget!' Does he mean 'Don't forget *me*'?—it is a tempting interpretation, and his mother cannot supply a better one. Another little boy, Craig, insists on being called Richard at night-time, for no reason that his mother can understand. There is not much doubt about the reassurance value of Christine's ritual.

Builder's labourer's wife:

> She always asks you to kiss her—she'll say "I do love you, see you in the morning", and you can't come out the room unless

you kiss her goodnight and say that you love her and you'll see
her in the morning. You've got to tuck her in and let her say "I
love you million *million*"—we get that every night; you've got
to sort of wait for that—she'll say all that before she lets you
come out of the room: "I love you a million *million*", and then
she'll squeeze you and give you a kiss. Well, I say it back to her,
"I love *you*", and then she'll say "I love you a *million*" and I say
"I love *you* a million", and so it goes on, every night—I don't
think she'd go to sleep, really, without it. Everything the same,
every night—nothing different, always the same thing.

In many cases, the ritual is not merely tolerated by the mother,
but deliberately encouraged, and occasionally invented, by her
in order to help on the child's acceptance of bedtime; in these
circumstances, we would not count it unless it was evident that
the child itself had now taken over the ritual and made it fully
his own, to the extent of demanding it if the mother forgot. 'She
has this big teddy', explained a miner's wife, 'and there's always
a race to see which of them gets up to bed first—she runs up the
stairs and Teddy has to come bumping up, and see which is in
bed first'. A departmental manager and his wife are both involved in leaving their daughter in a happy mood: 'We all go upstairs, and Daddy bounces her on the bed, and then we have to
do a little dance as far as the door and *then* say goodnight. But
we *have* to do the little dance *every* night'. The mother's imaginative provision for a contented bedtime is seen in both the
following quotations, each describing a routine which has been
adopted by the child as his own special ritual.

Machinist's wife:
We collect the cat, who always takes her upstairs and watches
while she says her prayers, and then there's a scrabble while we
get the cat off the bed and we tuck in all the toys—she's got
numerous furry toys which I make a point of having in the bed,
so that she's got something to go to bed *to*; and we turn out all
the lights and come downstairs saying "See you in the morning,
goodnight" on every step, you know. . . . If pussy's asleep, we
don't *have* to take her up; but we *always* tuck in all the toys.

Fitter's wife:
If Daddy's not here when he goes to bed, Andrew blows him a
kiss, and then his Daddy has to give it back to him in a bag in

K

the morning. When his Daddy first went on shift work, you know, I found he did use to cry to kiss his Daddy. So I used to say, "You blow a kiss, and it'll go out the door and down the stairs and out, and it'll jump on Daddy's face, and then in the morning he'll give it you back". So then I had to warn my husband, and then he had to give it him back in the morning in a bag. So now it's the usual thing when his Daddy's working.

This last child, incidentally, has an additional ritual which is of interest because it shows how such actions can be valued by the child for their repetitive character, even when they are not intrinsically pleasant; his mother, with some insight, explained: 'I have a few tears from him when he goes to bed, but that is another thing that's actually more habit than anything else. One night, I said to him, "Now what did you cry for *last* night?" and he said "Oh, I've *got* to cry". I think it's just something that he's always done, you know; it's only for a couple of minutes, but he *always* cries when I shut the bedroom door, and it's not that he wants it open'. Another little boy has made into a ritual what appears to be an overt introjection of his mother's wishes: 'He says to himself "*Don't* get out of bed and *don't* open the curtains", because he knows I always say that to him, you see— so he says that to himself! And I don't say it any more, *he* just says it now!'

One final example, which again shows the child's characteristic insistence upon adult co-operation together with the frequent element of dependence, links these childish rituals with the bedtime rites more usual among adults; we are not suggesting that this child is at all typical of his age-group in the *form* which his ritual takes.

Porter's wife:

Before he goes up, it's always "Where's the tablet bottle?"—it's just Aspro, a Junior Aspro—"Where's my tablet, Mummy, or I can't sleep". (Does he always have that?) Oh yes, he can't sleep without it—well, he could, but he *thinks* he can't, he always asks for it—"My tablet, Mummy, I won't sleep". (Did the doctor prescribe it, or do you just . . . ?) Oh no—I used to give it him when he was teething, you see, and he's got that used to it, you see, he won't go to bed without it now. (And suppose you'd run out of tablets, would he . . . ?) I'd have to go out and buy another bottle at bedtime, oh yes. But I don't think it does him any harm, do you, just one Junior Aspro every night.

We estimated the general incidence of bedtime rituals by adopting the rule that such an occurrence would only be counted if the child clearly insisted on some definite mode of behaviour or form of words, and if he would be obviously upset, or would vigorously object, when for any reason this was omitted from bedtime routine: in other words, we only included those instances in which the habit had acquired some force of compulsiveness for the child. Prayers and stories were occasionally included as rituals if, and only if, they had acquired this special significance. We did not include the *fact* of insistence upon the use of dummies, bottles, or love-objects such as teddy-bears or cuddlies, although they show a close connection with ritual behaviour: these we shall look at separately in a moment. It may, of course, happen that a love-object has a place in a more general ritual, as we have seen; such rituals were not excluded.

Using these criteria, we found that one child in three (33% in a random sample) was reported as having a defined bedtime ritual. Bearing in mind that bedtime is not the only context in which ritualistic behaviour may occur (though it is almost certainly the major opportunity for this), we may conclude that such behaviour is sufficiently commonplace to be regarded as a normal manifestation at this stage of development. There was no indication of any class trend in its incidence, except that rituals were significantly less often reported of children from Class V families (21%). Since, as we saw in the last chapter, there is a tendency for Class V parents to be somewhat more casual than the rest with regard to bedtime, it seemed possible that the creation of a bedtime ritual might be related to the strictness with which the child was put to bed. In fact, however, there is no increase in the incidence of rituals either among those children who go to bed relatively early or among those whose parents strongly believe in the importance of a fixed regular bedtime; nor is there any increase among the children who are not allowed to play in bed. The sex of the child is also unrelated to the use of ritual.

It can be shown, however, that bedtime rituals are significantly more often found among those children who are also reported to have fantasy creatures or talk about fantasy happenings. We suggested in Chapter 7 that Class V mothers may be less inclined to encourage their children in communicating their fantasies, and this may well be true also in the case of rituals, particularly as in practice these tend to involve a considerable amount of patience and indeed co-operation on the part of the mother. In other ways, too, ritual and fantasy have much in common. In both there is an element of magical or autistic thinking, in which the child asserts the power of his own wishes, and in both this power is worked out in a context of social relationships, whether imaginary or real. In our discussion of fantasy play, we surmised that children may find it easier to practise human relationships in situations in which they have the power to control the other individual's behaviour, and that, for this reason, an imaginary playmate may have obvious advantages for the child in comparison with a real person. With the establishment of a ritual, the child once more places himself in a position from which he can control and direct the behaviour of other people—real people, this time—in a way which he alone decides. It is of some significance that, while the behaviour itself by definition now conforms to a stereotyped and predictable pattern, the direction of the operation, and its development if any, usually remains firmly in the hands of the child. There may also be detected a kind of *quid pro quo* basis underlying bedtime rituals, in that the child tacitly agrees to submit to the arbitrary indignity of being made to go to bed at the time chosen by his parents *on the condition*, also tacit, that the whole process shall be conducted in a way that he himself ordains. The compulsive obstinacy which the child shows if he is not allowed to carry the ritual to a satisfactory conclusion may thus be explained as symptomatic of his need to maintain at least token command, in order to save face, in a situation in which he would otherwise have to admit that his real power to control everyday events is still strictly limited. What we are witnessing in bedtime ritual is thus, in part, the means by which the child gradually and reluctantly adjusts himself to the inevitable truth that the world is not, after all, directed by his desires.[1]

To understand the attraction to the child of behaviour which conforms to a fixed and stereotyped pattern, it is necessary to recollect that children of this age, despite their social sophistication, lack the experience and reasoning ability which would

[1] It is not possible here to include a fuller discussion of the crisis of ego devaluation when the child is forced to relinquish infantile delusions of omnipotence. The reader is referred to Ausubel, David P.: *Ego Development and the Personality Disorders: a developmental approach to psychopathology*, Grune and Stratton, New York, 1952.

enable them to comprehend and predict the course of everyday events on the basis of rational deduction. Children of this age are frequently taken by surprise as one occurrence follows another, partly because the adults around them are too familiar with the common sequences of life to recognize any necessity to make them explicit to the child, partly because to give each child adequate warning of the changing minutiae of family plans would require more time and thought than most mothers can manage. On the whole small children accept, because they have to, a state of affairs which most adults in our society would find intolerably uncertain; but it requires only a small act of imagination to realize that grownups' power to anticipate and expect events must often appear to the child a magical gift of prophecy, sometimes with a distinct element of ill-wishing to it: 'You'll bump your head if you do that', cries the mother, '*There*! I *told* you you would!' Does the child take notice of his mother next time because he recognizes her ability to see retribution coming or to make retribution happen?

Be this as it may, cause and sequence retain many mysteries for the four-year-old. The average child of this age therefore tends to cling to what is familiar and repetitive. He likes best to play the games he already knows, to hear stories of which he already has every word by heart, and to listen again to the songs he has heard a hundred times before. Indeed, one of the secrets of entertaining children of this age is to exploit their love for the recurrent and the predictable. If he is removed from his accustomed environment—from the people he knows and the situations in which he feels at home—the pre-school child easily becomes bewildered and confused; and this is understandable, because he has only a narrow background of experience to help him to interpret what is new: outside his known frame of reference, the unusual can appear arbitrary, inconsequential and terrifying.[1] The constantly repeated pattern of ordinary, everyday events thus provides the young child with a sense of security: within it he knows what to expect, despite his limited powers of intellectual reasoning.

[1] The situation of the child in hospital is perhaps the most obvious example of this; like the adult in a half-understood situation, but to a far greater extent, he becomes highly vulnerable to a misinterpretation of the signs available to him in a way which tends to confirm his alarm. A little boy leaving hospital told his mother 'Well, at least they didn't do the *very worst* thing of all!' 'What was that?' 'Well, they kept saying I should have to have my bowels opened!'

It is important to emphasize that the child is not a passive participant in life: he *searches* for security, he seeks with determination to gain control over his environment. When he insists that certain things only happen when he allows them to happen, or that they happen only in the form which he has himself invented, he attempts to impose his own individual pattern upon everyday events, and so mark out an area of life, be it never so limited, over which he has undisputed dominion. Perhaps, too, this area will naturally tend to fall within some situationally determined, and therefore already moderately predictable, sequence of behaviour, such as the routine for going to bed.

At the psychological level, then, it is plausible to explain ritual behaviour in terms of the need for security which exists in every child and which is particularly urgent in the pre-school child. But the fact that this sort of behaviour is so commonplace—that is, that so many rituals ever become established—reflects something more: that the parents of these children are, on the whole, extremely tolerant of such demands, and are in general prepared to involve themselves rather deeply in what might be considered mere childish whims and fancies. No doubt there is some element of expediency in their indulgence—most parents know from experience that it can take a very long while for an angry and frustrated child to fall asleep—but, over and above this, parents seem to believe, and to behave as if, their children have a right to be humoured in this way; they will take on trust the child's own evaluation of his behaviour as necessary and justifiable. Here, as elsewhere, the degree of psychological insight shown by the ordinary parent is rather impressive.

*'She has a woolly that is second to her Mum and Dad—if not first. . .'*

Closely akin to children's rituals, and perhaps the most interesting of the 'comfort habits'—certainly the most varied and individual—are the attachments which many small children form to a particular object which comes to be uniquely valued as the one absolute necessity among all their possessions: 'You can give anything to anybody—her scooter, her pram, anything', said a miner's wife, 'so long as you don't part with the dog. It ought to be in the dustbin—here it is, look! But she wouldn't part with it'. The 'dog' in question was only just recognizable as such: battered, discoloured and ragged, it indeed looked ready for the dustbin; but in terms of the use and the love it received, it was the most valuable thing in the house.

The object in which the child invests so much emotional dependence is often, but not necessarily, a soft toy—a teddy bear, plush panda, nylon lamb or some such creature. Frequently, however, it is a much less conventional 'cuddly'—an old blanket or shawl, a towelling bib or nappy, a woolly or silky piece of clothing, a pillow or cushion. Typically, but not always, it is soft in texture; typically, but again not invariably, it has been a part of the child's experience for as long as he can remember, and the mother is unable to say at what point it acquired its special significance for him. The blanket or shawl usually was used during the child's earliest months, and often has some special characteristic—a cellular texture or a silk-bound edge—which distinguishes it from other blankets in the house and to which the child clearly attaches great importance. Not unusually, the sense of smell is as much involved as that of touch; one child's cuddly was his mother's pillow, which he would hold against him as he went to sleep—all the pillows were used as playthings by the children, and at the end of the day he would pick out his mother's by sniffing at each in turn. Several children take some article of clothing to bed with them, typically a piece that has been worn so that it has the human smell upon it: 'He always has a pyjama top, which he puts on for a day or two and then he cuddles it to go to sleep with; but it must have been on him for one night or two nights, otherwise, as he says, "It doesn't taste nice". He puts the edge of the sleeve to his nose, he's never had it in his mouth, and goes to sleep like that'. One or two children, however, love the smell left by the hot iron, and sleep with a freshly-ironed cloth over their noses. In either case, it is a positive smell rather than an absence of smell which is demanded, and this to some extent explains the apprehension of many children if the mother insists on washing the greying fabric; a photograph sent in by a mother to *PARENTS* magazine showed a small girl standing patiently beneath the washing-line, sucking her thumb and clutching the flapping corner of her beloved cuddly blanket.[1]

It is common for the cuddly to be manipulated in a fairly positive way, rather than merely cuddled, especially if it is not a conventional soft toy. Sometimes it is sucked or chewed; one

[1] *PARENTS*, Vol. 21, No. 1, 1966, p. 13.

little boy always sucks the corner of his pillow-case, now indi-
vidualized by the name of 'my Chewer', and our notes on him
record that he was already doing so, at that time together with
his fingers, at the age of twelve moths. He has matured to the
extent of discarding finger-sucking; other children have altered
their behaviour in relation to the cuddly itself—a little girl, who
at twelve months sucked whatever silky material was available
to her, now 'just holds it to her mouth—the silk ribbon on the
blanket'. Some children stroke their faces with the material or,
as we have seen, hold it over their noses; one little boy pokes
the corner of a cushion into his eye, and his mother says that
'he's always had these funny little things that he does—even
when he was nine or ten months old, he'd get the collar of my
coat and put it in his eye'. One mother was able to trace back
her son's behaviour—stroking the satin edge of his old cot-
blanket between finger and thumb, as if testing the quality of the
material—to the age of about six months, when he fingered her
nylon nightdress during late breast-feeds with precisely the
same gesture. Occasionally the manipulation involves the
gradual destruction of the cuddly:

Foreman bricklayer's wife:

> She pulls wool out of a jumper to twist it round her finger. She
> has a woolly that is second to her Mum and Dad—if not first—
> that she *must* go to bed with. It's a comfort to her—she holds
> it close in bed. (Father:) This old cardigan is called an 'Ayah';
> and my wife has now laid down the rule that it is forbidden
> during the daytime; it's strictly a bedtime comfort. It used to be
> *all* day, *any* day—she used to carry it about.

Very frequently indeed, the cloth cuddly is manipulated in
conjunction with thumb- or finger-sucking: the child falls asleep
in a bemused state induced by a complex pattern of rhythmic
activity centred upon hands, face and mouth. This particular
use of the cuddly is perhaps closest to the ritualistic acts described earlier, and, as one might expect, tends to persist unchanged
for the longest periods.[1]

[1] The Child Rearing Study at the Western Reserve University Medical
School found that half the children in their sample who had such cuddlies used
them in conjunction with thumb-sucking. Spock, Benjamin: 'The striving for
autonomy and regressive object relationship'; in *The Psychoanalytic Study of
the Child*, Vol. XVIII, 1963.

Shop manager's wife:

> He's got a shawl, and he puts that in his hand and sucks his
> thumb at the same time. He's got two shawls, actually, and one's
> got a hole, and I had to *make* a hole in the other one so that
> they're identical: he has to find this hole and hold it, and the
> other hand he sucks his thumb.

Some children integrate the two habits more closely still by
sucking their thumbs *through* a hole in the cuddly; and it seems
no accident that the cloth is thereby brought very close to the
nose, thus providing a perfect cocoon of blended taste and smell
into which to withdraw from the waking world. Helen's mother
described her daughter's behaviour, which may be taken as a
classic example:

Clerk's wife:

> She's got one habit which we're trying our best to get rid of—
> look! (She took from the sideboard drawer a piece of grey thread-
> bare wool blanket, about 6 inches square.) She cuddles it and
> sucks her thumb (Mother wound blanket round her hand and
> demonstrated thumb-sucking). Now we've had that teddy-bear
> there right from her being a year old, and we bought it with the
> *intention* of it taking this's place, but . . .! She used to do it as a
> baby through her shawl; and of course it got down to two or
> three little bits of woolly rag, and it finally got down to this.
> And I'm determined I'm *not* washing it now, because I was
> hoping that during the next two or three months I can persuade
> her . . . well, I should like *her* to throw it away, if I can. This is
> the last bit, you see; and I'm determined we're not going to find
> anything to take its place. But of course she doesn't ask for it
> *very* much during the day—though she knows where it is if she
> *does* want it, I must admit. But it's when she's got her thumb in
> her mouth, she instantly thinks of it. It'd have been easier to
> have got rid of a dummy. But she's done it ever since she was a
> baby, and of course it's just a habit. She does it whenever she
> wants five minutes, she gets it and puts her thumb in her mouth.
> The other day she had it in her coat pocket and produced it on
> the bus—I think that was the rocking of the bus did that, Helen
> suddenly thought about it, and there she sat, rocking off to sleep!

One further characteristic of the cuddly is that its use is often
extended beyond the soothing to sleep which is its primary
function: the child treats it as a comfort and a refuge at any time

K*

when his peace of mind is threatened. We are all familiar with the notion of the beloved soft toy as confidante and consoler when things go wrong: Christopher Robin's Pooh Bear is the epitome of such uncritical companions of childhood.[1] Among our sample, there are many children of whom one could say that their best friend is their favourite plush animal, usually by now much the worse for wear, from which they are never separated: 'She left Teddy next door once, and we had to turn the house upside down to find him'; 'His teddy-bear's never left his side since he was nine months old—he dropped it in his bath once, and we couldn't get it dry, and for two nights we had to nurse him to sleep, he was in such a state'. Perhaps more striking still, however, is the dependence upon their cloth cuddlies shown by those children who have them: often the first sign that the child is upset or anxious is that he collects the loved object and starts to manipulate it in his usual bedtime manner. Valerie, the child who showed the most marked eating difficulties, twists the corner of her pillow-case and makes sure that the pillow is always to hand: 'It's here, look, now', said her mother; 'she carries it around with her. When she gets up in the morning, she brings it down with her. My husband shouts, he says it looks a mess lying around here, take it back up, but if you take it back up, she fetches it down again. It's when she's tired; or when I've smacked her—then she always flies to her pillow'. The little boy who cuddles his pyjama jacket came into the room at a late stage in the interview, and after listening for a few minutes went to his bedroom and fetched the jacket, which he held to his face as he sat with his mother's arm round him.

Filing clerk's wife:

He had a nylon eiderdown bought him the day he was born, and right from when he could talk, he called it his Foofer, and he clung to it, and now there's no filling in it or anything, it's just a piece of cloth. But that must always be under his head, and if he wakes up in the night he sits up and feels for it—he must always have his Foofer. He keeps it in his crib; but if he's upstairs he'll go for it, and if he's tired he'll fetch it down and put it on

---

[1] It would be interesting to know how many of these creatures continue to have a functional existence into their patron's adult life. A few certainly come up to university; and Nottingham University is not the only one in which a student cult of Pooh ensures a steady sale of A. A. Milne's children's books in the University bookshop.

the settee, and if I've smacked him for being naughty he'll want his Foofer—he comforts himself with it.

For the purpose of analysis, we defined 'cuddlies' as meaning those objects, whether conventional soft toys or adopted cloths, etc., to which the child had a special attachment inasmuch as he would *insist* that this particular thing accompanied him to bed. The child's insistence is important to our definition, since teddy-bears are attractive to parents as well as to children, and many mothers encourage the child to take a soft toy to bed even though he is not particularly interested in it. The question 'Would he make a fuss if you couldn't find it one night?' readily established the distinction between the special objects—what D. W. Winnicott calls 'transitional' objects—and those cuddly toys which were merely passengers, so to speak, in the child's bed. Dummies and bottles are excluded from the table that follows, for the sake of clarity; there is evidence that they serve a very similar purpose in the child's development, and we shall examine this presently.

TABLE XXVII

*Child's insistence upon bedtime cuddly: bottles and dummies excluded*

|  | Social class | | | | | |
|  | I & II | IIIwc | IIIman | IV | V | All classes (*randomized*) |
|---|---|---|---|---|---|---|
|  | % | % | % | % | % | % |
| Cuddly insisted on | 43 | 34 | 29 | 26 | 21 | 31 |
| Type: |  |  |  |  |  |  |
| Cloth | 11 | 9 | 4 | 3 | 3 | 5 |
| Soft toy | 32 | 25 | 25 | 23 | 18 | 26 |

As the table shows, just under a third of all four-year-olds have an attachment to one particular bedtime cuddly, leaving aside addictions to bottle or dummy; as in the case of bedtime rituals, these objects may be considered a normal part of the child's emotional development. Rituals show, in fact, a close association with special attachments: of the children who have cuddlies, 42% also have rituals, while of those who have no cuddly, only 26% have a ritual—a significant difference. The class differences found are of considerable interest, but cannot be discussed without reference to class differences in the use of dummies, which they partly complement; we shall therefore return to them very shortly.

At a surface level of interpretation, the role of the cuddly in the child's life is made explicit in his behaviour: periodically he has a need of comfort, and the cuddly satisfies that need. One might wonder what comfort the cuddly can give him, which his mother cannot; but it tends to be in precisely those circumstances in which his mother has withdrawn from him that the cuddly is most used. We must remember that the extra maternal attention which is given to the young child as he prepares for sleep also signals his exclusion from the warmth and friendliness of family companionship, and at an hour when evening is drawing in and night beginning to fall: fears of darkness and isolation are commonplace at all ages, and it is hardly surprising that small children seek additional reassurance at such a time. On those other occasions when the child is said to resort most eagerly to his cuddly, the mother is equally unavailable to him, having temporarily abandoned her comforting and protective role: 'If I've smacked him for being naughty, he'll want his Foofer'.[1] The cuddly thus serves very well as a substitute mother, a fair imitation of the warm, stuffy, cloth-covered bosom in which the child as a baby would bury his face in drowsiness; if he sucks his thumb at the same time, the parallel is even clearer. But sucking is unnecessary to the argument; work by the Harlows and others has pointed the significance to the baby of the *feel* of his mother, over and above the milk which she provides and which has traditionally been supposed to forge the closest emotional link between mother and child. In the Harlows' now famous experiment in which infant monkeys were given two substitute dummy 'mothers', the wire 'mother' which provided the baby's milk was approached for feeding only: it was the cloth-covered 'mother', milkless though she was, to which the infant clung in times of anxiety or stress.[2]

[1] One little girl who was not alone in using her dummy in exactly the same way may be thought to have given it a nickname of some significance: 'She kept it under her pillow for bedtime; but if I was cross with her or she got upset, she'd run upstairs, and if you went to look, there she'd be, having a good go at her mum-mum'.

[2] Harlow, Harry F.: 'Development of Affectional Patterns in Infant Monkeys'; in Foss, B. M.: *Determinants of Infant Behaviour*, Vol. I, Methuen, London, 1961.

A development of this view of the cuddly as a stand-in for the mother is D. W. Winnicott's interpretation of its deeper role in helping the child through the early years of emotional adjustment. The name he gives it—the transitional object—is descriptive of its function. Through the use of the beloved object, the child achieves a gentler transition than would otherwise be possible from the passionate concentration of the feeding relationship to the more controlled warmth expected of later relationships: in short, he is weaned emotionally by degrees only. 'Its *not* being the breast (or the mother) . . . is as important as the fact that it *stands for* the breast (or mother)' (italics ours; parentheses his).[1] Winnicott draws attention to a most important characteristic of the cuddly (though not an invariable one): namely, that the child himself seldom remembers the origin of the object, so that, in contrast with later toys, which come to him as gifts from his environment, the cuddly is in effect something which he himself has created and for which he is beholden to no-one. While the breast (or bottle) is seen as the first 'not-me' object, the cuddly is the first 'not-me' *possession*. To this extent, the transitional object may form a bridge between the totally egocentric period of the child's development, when he *is* the world, and the period of what Ausubel calls 'satellization', when he is forced to acknowledge his debt to it and to the powerful adults who represent it. Once again, as in the case of ritual acts, the child is cushioned by such behaviour against the harsher shocks of reality. Once again, also, his parents are usually content to be guided by the need which he thus expresses. In Winnicott's words: 'In respect of these transitional objects the parents, as it were, conspire not to challenge the origin. They easily see that the thumb is part of the child and that the next toy or teddy bear or doll is a gift, but with regard to the object in question they undertake to refrain from challenging the infant as to its origin. There is a madness here which is permissible because it belongs to this stage of the infant's emotional development'.[2]

Winnicott is here referring to children a good deal younger than four years; and the reader must, of course, bear in mind that at this age we see the child nearing the end of a number of phases of emotional and intellectual change which were set in train at a much earlier period. Winnicott points out that an originally constructive behaviour pattern may eventually become a defence against anxiety in a regressive rather than progressive sense. None the less, the indulgence of parents towards such behaviour persists, even though many of them are beginning to find it an embarrassment and to feel that the child is old enough now to put aside such childish things.

Looking at some of these cuddlies, one can see why the parents often feel them to be a social liability. Karen's dog that 'ought to be in the dustbin'; Valerie's crumpled pillow left about in her mother's immaculately cared-for sitting room; Helen's grey and tattered 'thumb-rag'; Gilbert's dilapidated eiderdown, 'Foofer': none of these is the accessory one would choose for the well-turned-out child. The reluctance of some children to have the cuddly washed does not help: 'It's ever so difficult to get it off him to wash it', said a works manager's wife of her son's once-white shawl, 'and every time you *do* wash it, a little bit falls off. I tried giving him a white woollen stole I had; but it wasn't the same, so we had to bring the dirty piece out again'. It is characteristic that she uses this phrase 'we *had* to'. There is nothing to stop parents throwing the disreputable object on the fire and being rid of it for good; yet even when they 'think it's a silly habit'—even when, like Helen's mother, they say that they are 'trying our best to get rid of it'—they jib at doing anything more positive than discouraging the child by shaming or laughing at him, or making rules to limit the cuddly's use to the privacy of the bedroom. Helen's mother typifies the attitude when she says 'I should like *her* to throw it away': it is considered fair to persuade, but the final act of renunciation must be voluntary. Her explanation describes the strongest pressure put on any of these children to abandon their cuddlies:

(When you say you're trying to finish with it—do you in fact try to stop her?) We do *try* and stop her, but we never actually take it away from her. I do *hope* that it'll be *her* that'll turn it in. (What have you done?) Well, we tell her to put it away, Teddy's laughing at her, that sort of thing, you know. I say, "Fancy playing with all your sister's big friends, and you've got a thumb-rag"—and she'll put it away herself then, instantly. But it's only when she drops off to sleep that you can get it away from her at night. Grandpa joins in now: "Let's throw that dirty thing away!" And of course that's the reason I won't wash it; I *was* going to the other day, but I thought No, while we can say it *is* dirty and not hygienic and all that, perhaps one of us, *in* talking to her, we might get her to throw it away. Because I did think, if she does it herself she won't cry after it.

It must be added that even when things go according to plan, and the child yields to pressure and throws the object away, this is often not the end of the story. The woolly cardigan that was 'second to her Mum and Dad—if not first' was in fact a substitute for the original which had been ceremonially thrown on the fire by the child, whose subsequent distress compelled her parents to hunt for an acceptable replacement. Parents' acknowledgement of the validity of the child's need can be gauged by the trouble to which they will go in order to provide him with a substitute if the original disintegrates before his dependence is outgrown: one mother, whose daughter's towelling bib had become a shapeless ravelling, scoured the drapers' shops of the district, waiting at each with embarrassment while the child tested for texture, and rejected, one perfectly good bib after another, and at the end of a wearing afternoon finally accepted one as adequate for her adoption.

Before turning to the oral comfort habits, we should also note that a few children have other manipulative habits which are rather more difficult to classify. They tend to fall between rituals and transitional objects, having characteristic features of each yet not quite fulfilling the criteria of either. One little girl, her mother says, 'fluffs—she's done it since she was about six months old—anything that's near, a little bit of cardigan or anything like that, she'll pull it off, and she just tickles the end of her nose with it, and as soon as she's done it she's asleep'.[1] Another child 'puts on the nosebag': 'We always know when she's really tired, because she'll pick her underskirt up or go in the kitchen and get the tea-towel, and she'll put it just over her nose—like this—and sit there with it just over her nose'. Both

---

[1] Winnicott (1953, *op. cit.*, p. 90) would indeed class this behaviour as a transitional *phenomenon*, which might have, but in this case has not, become concentrated upon a single object.

these habits seem to serve much the same function as manipulation of a cuddly, yet no permanent cuddly is involved. Other
children, mainly among those who have indulgent bedtimes, use
their mothers' hands as not-quite-transitional objects: 'She
holds your thumb on her nose, like this, you know, for five or
ten minutes before she goes to sleep'; 'She likes to hold your
hand to her nose—it's ever so queer, and it gets on my nerves
sometimes; but if you do it for her straight away, she goes
straight to sleep. Ever since she was a baby she's done it—I don't
know what made her start in the first place'. A few individualists
scratch their heads, pull at their eyelashes or rub their big toes
together as they await sleep. A number of children derive
pleasure and comfort from fingering their navels, usually in
conjunction with thumb-sucking: 'If you went in there now,
you'd see—she's got one thumb in her mouth and the other in
her umbilicus, up under her skirt; it's a scream, I just sit and
laugh at her, you know'; 'She still does what she did last time
you came (at 12 months)—she tickles her umbilicus—sucks her
thumb and tickles her umbilicus with her other hand, just while
she's getting off to sleep'.[1] Obviously, with navel-tickling we
begin to move away from those habits which are soothing and
comfort-giving, and towards the stimulating and exciting,
involving the arousal of sensations which are no longer completely within the child's control: in particular, of course,
towards genital play. Parents' attitudes regarding genital play,
however, are very different from their feelings about the erotic
stimulation of other parts of the body, and will be examined
separately in Chapter 12.

'*She wants her dummy pinned on her wedding-dress. . .*'
Sucking of thumbs, of dummies, and of bottles have in common
that they are all survivals of the primary infant drive; by the age
of four, however, they differ from the infant's behaviour in that
they rarely show that fierce single-minded passion characteristic
of the sucking baby, but have mellowed into a gentler, more
contemplative act, sedative by being soothing rather than
exhausting. They also differ from each other in their significance
to the child. Thumbs are so clearly a part of the child that they

[1] Both these children, and others with the same habit, were persistently
tickling their navels at 7 years.

could hardly be called a 'transitional' object;[1] and this difference from the dummy is operationally underlined by the fact that both mother and child are conscious that, while the dummy can be thrown away or hidden, the thumb cannot.[2] Bottles stand apart from the others in providing a reward beyond the mere pleasure of sucking; they are usually filled with sweet milk or fruit juice.[3] A few, however, are retained for cuddling only, and here their function seems to be very much that of the transitional object, except in so far as they also carry memories of an earlier, more basic role: 'Like a love-toy, you know, her bottle has been', said a mine worker's wife; 'she's taken it with nothing in, like a dummy—only she didn't really suck it, she just loved it'. Dummies, in our view, are very close indeed in function to the transitional object; Olive Stevenson, in her study of 'the first treasured possession' which followed Winnicott's earlier paper,[4] was doubtful whether they should be considered relevant, but children's attitudes to them and to cuddlies seem so very similar that the only distinction appears to be that dummies are specifically oral comforters, whereas cuddlies are only sometimes, or by association, orally satisfying. Some dummies even acquire ritual manipulations in conjunction with sucking, like any cloth comforter: 'It's got to have a piece of elastic with a loop on. He puts his finger in it and twiddles it round—he won't have it

[1] Winnicott suggests (1953, op. cit., p. 89) that oral stimulation with thumb and fingers precedes and *develops into* the use of a transitional object. This is not to say that a thumb-sucking *habit* is a necessary precursor of the transitional object, nor that it always develops in this way.

[2] It is of course open to the mother to use the child's uncertainty of what is feasible to pretend that this difference does not exist: 'We say "If you don't stop, you'll have to go to the doctor and he'll chop it off" ' (Polish mother); but this is quite exceptional in our sample as far as thumbs are concerned.

[3] —disastrous to the child's teeth. A study of dental caries in pre-school children has shown a significant association between carious teeth and the use of *sweetened* comforters (either bottles of sweetened drinks or 'dipped' dummies): Winter, G. B., Hamilton, M. C. and James, P. M. C.: 'Role of the Comforter as an Aetiological Factor in Rampant Caries of the Deciduous Dentition', Arch. Dis. Childh., Vol. 41, 1966. Comforters of this sort are therefore very much out of favour with the dental profession. However, it seems a pity to blame the mere vehicle of the eroding agent along with the agent itself, particularly as recent dental opinion is disinclined to condemn sucking as harmful *per se*: a bottle of unadulterated water would presumably be positively beneficial to the teeth, sucked slowly last thing at night. No doubt a fortune awaits the first enterprising manufacturer to market a prophylactic bottle-filler with a pleasant taste. By the age of four, however, dummies are not normally 'dipped', so that only the bottle-suckers are still having their teeth damaged by their comfort habits.          [4] Stevenson, Olive: 1954, op. cit.

without the elastic'. The only major difference in practice between dummies and other sorts of cuddlies is the degree to which parents are prepared to tolerate them; but to some extent this difference can already be seen between the conventional soft toys and their less respectable rag cousins which both Winnicott and Olive Stevenson accept as functionally equivalent.[1]

Table XXVIII shows the incidence of oral comfort habits. For convenience of comparison, the figures for cuddlies are again given.

The use of the bottle can be left aside from any discussion of class differences: the numbers are rather small, and differences are not significant. Allowing the child a bottle involves active co-operation from the mother, as opposed to mere complaisance, and for this reason alone one would expect only the most persistent demands to be fulfilled at this age: this in itself would tend to reduce group differences.

TABLE XXVIII

*Incidence of bedtime comfort habits*

| Comfort habit | I & II | IIIwc | IIIman | IV | V | All classes (randomized) |
|---|---|---|---|---|---|---|
| | % | % | % | % | % | % |
| Bottle | 4 | 6 | 3 | 5 | 5 | 4 |
| Dummy | 7 | 9 | 16 | 15 | 13 | 14 |
| Sucks thumb regularly | 32 | 19 | 12 | 11 | 11 | 16 |
| Attachment to cloth object | 11 | 9 | 4 | 5 | 3 | 5 |
| Attachment to soft toy | 32 | 25 | 25 | 23 | 18 | 26 |
| Child has at least one regular bedtime comfort habit | 66 | 52 | 51 | 49 | 46 | 53 |

(These percentages do not total the column above, since some children have more than one habit.)

[1] Spock suggests that the bottle, filled or not, has a transitional function from the age of about six months. He makes the interesting point that 'It is reminiscent of pleasurable aspects of mother, it is a substitute for mother, but it is also a defense against re-envelopment by mother. It invites regression but also limits it'. Spock, Benjamin, 1963, *op. cit.*

Class trends in the incidence of other comfort habits, however, are of considerable interest. The two groups of children sucking dummies and thumbs (very few suck both) are practically equal (14% and 16%) if taken over all classes; but these proportions are exactly halved for dummy-suckers and doubled for thumb-suckers in the professional and managerial group. The difference between the working-class and middle-class figures for dummy-sucking would not be very striking on its own (it is significant at the ·05 level), but taken in conjunction with the extraordinary predilection of Class I and II children for thumb-sucking, these figures are remarkable. Among working-class children, dummies are a little more often used than thumbs; among white-collar children, thumbs are twice as often used as dummies, and among professional-class children there are more than four times as many thumb-suckers as dummy-suckers.

The first conclusion to be drawn is that children prefer dummies if they can get them, but that they will tend to turn to their thumbs if dummies are disallowed, as they are to a greater extent by middle-class mothers. We can take it as reasonably clear that thumbs and dummies serve equivalent functions as oral comfort habits, but it would appear that dummies are not so much a substitute for thumbs as thumbs for dummies. A second conclusion is that our earlier suggestion, that dummies may be classed as transitional objects, is supported by a comparison of the incidence of cloth objects and dummies: it seems fair to surmise that the children who are allowed dummies find these adequate transitional objects in themselves, while those who are not are more likely to become attached to cloth objects or cuddly toys, or to become habituated to what was only incipient thumb- or finger-sucking.

On the other hand, the final group of percentages, which draws all these comfort habits together, shows that the situation is not a simple one of a given proportion of children requiring a comfort habit and choosing whichever is most readily available. Some explanation is needed for the steady decrease in comfort habits reported as we descend the social scale, and in particular for the significant difference between Class I and II and the rest. It is obvious that the heaviest contribution to this difference is made by the thumb-sucking category, and that this is not entirely accounted for by the small proportion of Class I and II dummy suckers at this age. To understand the situation, we must look at the attitudes of mothers towards both thumbs and dummies, and how they differ in practice.

Neither dummy- nor thumb-sucking is deliberately encouraged in the four-year-old. This implies a change in the mother's attitude with the development of the individual child, at least as far as the dummy is concerned, since at one time, perhaps nearly four years ago, she herself provided him with this means of comfort; and thumb-sucking, too, is usually regarded as a rather pretty sight in babyhood. By the time children reach four, however, the feelings about these habits which the mothers communicate to them range from the merely accepting to the positively discouraging. The following quotations represent the most enthusiastic views at this age:

Social worker's wife:

> I know a lot of people do get worried about thumbs; but I don't really see why he *shouldn't*, you know. It's obviously a comfort. It sort of helps him to go to sleep, you know, relax.

Antique dealer's wife:

> Really, I don't like it (thumb-sucking), but I never stop him because I know he's resting—it's his *way* of resting, and I let him do it.

Lorry driver's wife:

> If she does wake she's usually lost her dummy, and she just shouts to Joan, and Joan has to wake up and find her dummy for her, and then she's back to sleep again straight away.

There is no lack of quotations deploring either dummies or thumb-sucking. Most mothers, in fact, by this time are wondering when the habit is going to stop and whether they can themselves do anything about it. Some find it an acute social embarrassment.

Jointer's wife:

> I'm not trying to stop her having it at the moment, although I think it's *dreadful*, that's one thing I'm really ashamed of. But so long as she doesn't suck it *outside*, you see . . . Coming back from our holidays, oh, it was awful, we were in the crowded train, and she kept on saying, really loud, "I want my dummy"—

oh, I was really embarrassed, I didn't know where to look. Well,
her dummy was locked in the case, you see, and in the end she
went all along the corridor to get the key from her Daddy, and
*he* went and *gave* it her! And she was standing there, trying to
unlock the case, and telling everyone she had to have her dummy,
and I finally had to let her have it. I could have sunk through the
floor. They do show you up, kiddies, don't they?

### Coal merchant's wife:

I have tried—I did once put sticking-plaster on her fingers, but
she sucked that and it got filthy, and it was worse than sucking
her fingers. I try now just to take her mind off it—because it
looks *awful* . . .

### Porter's wife:

No, I don't like him sucking his thumb—it makes me mad, in
fact, to see him, thumb in all the time, out on the street even.
('Him sucking his thumb' was answered to the later question,
'What kinds of things make you get on each other's nerves?')

### Grocer's wife:

She has just one bad habit. She still has a dummy when she goes
to bed, and if she's tired, and if I've got cross with her. I don't
quite know what to do about that. I've tried to break her of it;
but the third night I'd sat up there with her, well it wore *me*
out more than her, so I finally gave in and let her have it. And
Elspeth (elder sister) tried to bribe her out of it. But that's the
only habit she's got. (It seems a very common one.) Really?
I thought she was the only one! (Of course, people do tend to
hide it—I mean, I don't suppose your friends know she has it?)
No—but she likes shocking people; so I put it on a high shelf,
because I know that's what she'd go to! She says she's probably
having it when she gets married—she wants her dummy pinned
on her wedding-dress! It's a delicate subject.

However, despite the fact that the children's mothers almost
unanimously wish they would stop, they are seldom prepared to
take very drastic action. This is especially true, oddly enough,
in the case of dummy-sucking, where drastic action is so much
more feasible. The same attitude prevails as that towards cloth
comforters: pressure is put upon the child to give up the dummy
*of his own accord*; the mother who 'threw it on the fire-back and
told him he was a big boy now' (child aged 3:10) was very much
an exception. This applies also in retrospect: the children who

gave up their dummies between one and four years almost all did so voluntarily, if sometimes under persuasion. Various kinds of pressure are exerted. The mother may appeal to the child's sense of shame: 'Since we've had the workmen in, I've been saying to him, "Now, you don't want that workman to see you with that dummy"'. She may try to induce in him a disgust for the dummy—'Oh, you don't want that, it's dirty'—and occasional mothers are prepared to stretch the truth a little: 'I tell her it's dropped on the dog's mess and things like that', said a plasterer's wife, 'and I told her it's had a big fly on it'.[1] She may use various means of reducing the intensity or frequency of the habit: 'We do encourage her now to *hold* it, and she won't put it in unless I say so'; 'I'm trying to break him off it—I hide it all over the place'. Or she may make an occasion of the final relinquishment, setting a deadline weeks or months in advance, or making some exciting new privilege partly conditional on abandoning this mark of babyhood.

### Lathe engineer's wife:

When she had her new bed, she threw her dummy away—we told her you didn't have to have dummies when you had a big bed.

### Insurance agent's wife:

She has a dummy—until Saturday. Saturday's the day, you know!—her birthday, yes. Oh, she promised me, she's been promising me for months now, since it's her birthday she's not going to have it any more.

### Garage owner's wife:

Her cousin was born, and when we went to see him I said to her "Well now, Gail, I think Maurice had better have that mummum, he's the baby now". She said "All right", and next time she wrapped it up in paper and took it down to him. To tell you the truth, I never thought it would be so easy stopping it! She never had it again.

[1] See also the statement of a miner's wife, page 473. Behaviour of this sort must be seen in anthropological perspective. Many peoples traditionally invoke the child's disgust or distaste in order to hasten the weaning process. The Kwoma mother puts a slug on her breast and paints her nipples blood-colour; the Tarongan child is told 'The breast is swollen (diseased)', or manure is applied to the nipple in his presence. It is a common practice to smear the nipple with bitter or peppery substances. See Whiting, J. M. W., Kluckhohn, R. and Anthony, A., 1958, *op. cit.*; Whiting, Beatrice (ed.): *Six Cultures*, Wiley, New York, 1963.

'I'm trying my *hardest* to break him of that', said a cycle assembler's wife: 'Before he was four years old—before his birthday came up, you see—I said, "Now, when you're four, you've got to throw your dummy away; you're a big boy now, you see". Well, when his birthday came along, in the morning I said, "Now here's your dummy, look, are we going to put it in the bin?" But no—I could see it was going to upset him; I thought, well, I'll try and *gradually* keep it off him'. It is typical that, even when the mother is 'trying her hardest', this means no more than that she is hiding the dummy, 'losing' it temporarily, or at most ridiculing or shaming the child, rather than actually destroying it: the child only has to put on the pressure in return, and she relents. It must, of course, be remembered that the child at four is quite autonomous enough to have other possibilities than simply showing distress; the little girl who 'showed up' her mother in the train, by fetching the key of the suitcase to get out her dummy for herself, impressed her mother rather successfully by this determination: 'I'm not stopping it now, because she seems to want it so much—in fact, I had to get her a new one only the other day, this pink one, because I couldn't find the blue one, and then I found it, so now she has the two in her pocket'—which the child sucked alternately throughout the interview. Another mother said that she had tried hiding the dummy several times—'but he's just gone to the shop and got another one!'

Although these rather half-hearted measures often fail over a period of time, they may be expected to be successful sooner or later, and indeed in a good many cases they had already been effective: 50% of our sample were still using dummies at twelve months,[1] whereas only 14% were still doing so at four years. A much higher rate of failure must be expected, however, where thumb-sucking is concerned, since, as we have already said, it is obvious to both mother and child that the thumb can be neither hidden nor lost, let alone destroyed. The middle-class mother is thus painfully rewarded for her earlier squeamishness about dummies by finding that, in encouraging an alternative that was more aesthetically pleasing, she has saddled herself with a problem which is very much more difficult to solve. In fact, while $8\frac{1}{2}\%$ of our sample were thumb-sucking at a year, most of them middle-class, 16% were doing so at four; and the extremely

[1] Newson, John and Elizabeth, 1963, *op. cit*, pages 65–68 and 178–181.

312 FOUR YEARS OLD IN AN URBAN COMMUNITY

sharp proportional rise in Class I and II suggests that this is due to a high percentage of these babies having been weaned from their earlier guilty dummies so soon after a year that they were unable to tolerate the situation and therefore *transferred* their attention to their thumbs.

One factor which also seems relevant is an attitude of many middle-class mothers towards thumb-sucking which is not altogether shared by working-class mothers. Middle-class mothers, perhaps because they are more likely to be in touch with the literature on child-rearing, tend to have a suspicion that thumb-sucking is a symptom of insecurity in the child, especially if it persists until four, and to feel that it must therefore be treated with caution. This attitude, combined with the assumption that, even at this age, thumbs are at least preferable to dummies, makes them unwilling to do much about thumb-sucking other than occasionally offering distractions or rewards. Working-class mothers, on the other hand, do not seem to have this special feeling about the significance of thumb-sucking as distinct from dummy-sucking: most of them are lenient anyway, but some react to the more intractable nature of thumb-sucking *by stepping up the pressure*. It is thus among working-class thumb-suckers that sanctions against comfort habits reach their most unpleasant: 'I put bitter aloes on'; 'We've put salt on his thumb, and pepper and mustard'; 'I told her her thumb wouldn't grow and the wart on her finger would grow bigger'; 'I shout at him, I've told him there's maggots under his nails'. This last warning raises another factor which is also class-loaded—the use of lies to control children's behaviour; and we discuss this aspect specifically in Chapter 14.

Since the comfort habits which have been discussed in this chapter are especially associated with bedtime, we wondered whether any relationship could be found between the type of bedtime usual for the child and the incidence of such habits.[1] There appeared to be no connection between the mother's adherence to regular routine and the existence in the child of one or more comfort habits. However, a significant association did emerge between early bedtime and the establishment of a comfort habit, and this held good even when social class, a component of early bedtime, was eliminated as a factor. This

[1] The statistical associations described in this and the following paragraph refer only to those forms of comfort habit included in Table XXVIII.

suggests that, while the mother's strictness over bedtime does not in itself influence the acquisition of comfort habits, the child who spends extra time in bed, and who, perhaps, is more often bored by periods of inactivity as he awaits sleep, is particularly likely to resort to sucking something or to the use of a transitional object in order to ease his ennui. The fact that professional-class mothers are more likely to put their children to bed early presumably contributes to the heavy incidence of comfort habits in this class.

No significant differences emerge between boys and girls in this respect. However, like indulgent bedtimes, comfort habits are more common among youngest and only children. This favours the interpretation that such habits flourish in a more permissive atmosphere where time, patience and indulgence are freely granted; they are more likely to decrease than to increase in incidence if parents are very unfavourably disposed towards them or if they show intolerance or impatience. This is chiefly of interest because, while we have discussed these habits throughout as means by which the child comforts himself, we are aware of a possible implication: that, if he is in need of comfort, he is, *ipso facto*, under stress. One might on this assumption expect that comfort habits would be especially common in the *less* permissive family atmospheres; but they are not.

In summing up, we must return to what we said at the beginning of the last chapter: that bedtime allows family relationships to be played out in a very intimate and private way which few observers outside the immediate family circle are ever privileged to watch. It is perhaps the parents' awareness of the essential privacy of this time which allows them to defer to their children's fancies and compulsions, freed as they are from the censure of outsiders. We have seen how the mother, in dealing with her child's ability or otherwise to do things for himself, thinks ahead to the public testing-place of school, and wonders 'will he let me down?' We have seen how, in trying to inculcate acceptable table-manners, she asks herself 'can I take him out anywhere, or will he show me up?' Bedtime is different. Behind closed doors, with no expectation that the ritual will ever have to take place in the public eye, parents can and do meet their children a good deal more than halfway.

# CHAPTER 11

# CODA TO TOILET TRAINING

Discussion of the process of toilet training presents two major difficulties. In the first place, as we pointed out in our earlier study,[1] the development of reliable continence in a child does not occur on a precise date (as is true, for instance, of the first step, the first word or the sighting of the first tooth): for most children, the first occasion of urination into the proper receptacle, which the mother greets with such delight, will be followed by a prolonged period of rather haphazard performance, sometimes proceeding by definite stages of improvement, but often including phases of inertia or real negativism. An understanding of what is meant by saying that a child is 'reliable'[2] is itself rather difficult to arrive at in practice. A child may be so described, but enquiry reveals that this is only true *provided that* he is reminded from time to time that a visit to the lavatory is due: without these reminders, which do indeed keep his pants dry and his mother content, he may be quite undependable. Another child may use his potty for urination as a matter of course, but may absolutely refuse to sit on it in order to defaecate. A third child reverses this: willing to sit on his potty once or twice a day, his bladder's urgency habitually takes him by surprise. Other children may be entirely dependable so long as they may use the potty, but terrified of the lavatory seat; or they may be 'trained' while they remain in their own home surroundings, but afraid to use the lavatory in other people's homes. Toilet training thus tends to be achieved gradually by the attainment of a number of distinct sub-goals: it is similar to weaning in this respect, that a series of recognizable stages or transitions occur, which at the same time do not make up an invariable sequence for all children, and which for particular children may be in part omitted.

---

[1] Newson, John and Elizabeth, 1963, *op. cit.*, Chapter 7.
[2] Where the word *reliable* is used, *with respect to toilet training* should be understood throughout this chapter.

In practical terms of communication, this means that the mother may be unsure what stage we are going to count as 'trained'; and, even if we are able to make this clear to her, the long-drawn-out complexity of the process will make it difficult for her to pinpoint any particular stage in relation to the child's age.

The second difficulty is related to the first, and is the outcome of the method of investigation: that, where a continuous process is studied by means of checks at arbitrary stages, much may have happened during the interval which is no longer available in accurate form. Thus, if a child's toilet training was complete by his third birthday, any information which we may now be given about its achievement will be more than a year in retrospect. One reason why retrospective information is especially untrustworthy where it relates to toilet training is that to the natural ambiguity of the data is added an emotional involvement on the part of the mother which will, however honest she may be, tend to operate in the direction of giving herself and the child the benefit of the doubt and offering a rather earlier date for completion of toilet training than is quite accurate.[1] With these various considerations in mind, we have not attempted to date the successful termination of training where this was said to have occurred before the fourth birthday. We have assumed, however, that retrospective reports of *methods* used in training are more meaningful, especially where specific behaviour involving punishment or reward is concerned. This chapter takes such reports into account but concentrates in the main upon attitudes towards children whose training is still uncompleted at four, and upon the training background of these children now and earlier, so far as this can be assessed.

Until a child is fully reliable—in the sense that an adult is reliable—success in training will obviously be measured in relative terms, depending upon expectations linked to the child's age. In our first study, when the children were twelve months old, it was appropriate to ask 'At what age do you think a child should be dry in the daytime? At what age do you think a child should regularly ask for his potty for bowel movements?'

[1] This can sometimes be seen quite dramatically in following-up at seven years a child who was considered to be some problem at four. 'What?' almost shouted one mother, 'Hadn't I got Richard out of that by *four*? Well! *Four*, was he? We were just talking about that last week, but I thought it was younger than *four*! He was *four*, was he, really? Oh *dear*—yes, it all comes back to me, oh *dear*!'

and to accept an answer which assumed a fair amount of active support, in the form of reminders and help, from the mother. During the first year, the mother feels she is being successful if she manages to time her offering of the potty to coincide with the child's eliminative urge; and towards the first birthday she begins to hope for signs (hardly 'asking for' in a verbal sense) by which the child will inform her, not that he is now in process of elimination, but that he *will be* so in a few minutes' time: it is the development of the child's ability to foresee his need, and to postpone it for a minute or two, which is the basis of toilet training. During the second year, the emphasis is towards both lengthening the period of control and persuading the child of the necessity to ask for help at a very early stage: upon training, in effect, his awareness of minimal bladder tension, so that neither he nor his mother will be caught unprepared. Most mothers hope that this stage of training will be completed before the second birthday. By the age of four, the situation is rather different. Both bowel and bladder eliminations are now expected to be under the child's control—that is, both foreseeable and briefly postponable—at least while he is awake: at the same time, new problems arise in that the child is both more mobile and more independent than he was earlier. If he is playing in the street or garden, or at someone else's house, and no longer accessible to routine reminders, he must now take full responsibility for reminding himself, and indeed for allowing himself plenty of time to get home or to an unfamiliar lavatory. Most of the daytime wetting that occurs at four (soiling is a rather different problem) appears to come under the heading of 'accidents' which happen to an otherwise trained child who, because he is playing too far from home, or because he is absorbed in a sociable game with other children, 'leaves it a bit too long'.

Boot repairer's wife:

> When she's playing a long way, such as down the Green, she'll leave it a bit late and come running up quick—just a little wet, probably, but not much—she'll go to the toilet properly, but you can see that she's just started, you know. But she's *tried*—she knows she was doing wrong—they don't know really, at that age, do they, how far they've to go; I think it's all right, because she *knows* she should go somewhere, and she's *made an effort* to get there.

University teacher's wife:

> If you'd come a fortnight ago, I'd have said she was *completely* dry; but this last week she's been playing a lot at her cousin's house, and three times in a row she's had wet pants; and I'm pretty sure it's because at home she lives in a bungalow, she's got used to getting to the lavatory in about five seconds, whereas *there* she's got all the business of going upstairs to cope with, and she just doesn't leave herself enough time.

A few children also have intermittent 'accidents' if they have a cold, or if the weather is chilly. Although mothers are on the whole sympathetic about the child's difficulties in all of these circumstances, the fact remains that older children and adults are expected to attain a control which is immune to such things, and that to this extent children who still have 'accidents' cannot be said to have successfully completed their daytime toilet training. Getting a child dry at night is a different matter again, and must be examined quite separately.

At the age of four, questions about toilet training are not altogether easy to ask, because the general expectation seems to be that by this time all normal children should be thoroughly dependable; and those mothers whose children conform to this 'ideal' norm will tend to undermine the self-confidence of the others, both by discussing their success in 'of course' terms, as if lack of success were very abnormal, and by emphasizing the part played by their own method of training, as if (inconsistently) the credit for their child's 'normality' were theirs alone. The result is that mothers of children who still wet their pants or their beds at four tend to feel threatened in their role of 'good mother'; and, in consequence, they may prefer not to advertise their problems in casual conversation, as they might if the child were only a year old. This conspiracy of silence, incidentally, becomes a vicious spiral in that it prevents the mother from learning just how common her problem is, and therefore tends to increase her anxiety. In the interview, therefore, we treated this as a sensitive area, and accordingly provided support for the mother in whatever answer she was to give by making an explicit assumption in the question that residual difficulties of toilet training were to be expected at this age. The topic had already been anticipated by one of the questions about bedtime and sleep, 'Do you lift him for a potty at all?'; and this gave the interviewer a natural and useful lead-in later on[1] to a general discussion of both child's and mother's behaviour in this area:

71. You said that you lift/you don't lift N for a potty at night. I expect he still wets the bed sometimes, doesn't he?[2]
   *if YES:* About how often does it happen?
72. (*If ANY wetting*): What do you do if you find he's wetted his bed? What do you say to him?
   (*If NO wetting*): Did you have any problem over getting him dry at night? Did you have any special method?
73. What about in the daytime? Does he still have accidents sometimes?
   *if YES:* Is it mainly wetting his pants, or does he dirty them?
74. What do you do?
   *if punishment not mentioned:* Do you ever punish him for wetting (or dirtying) his pants?

An analysis of the incidence of residual toilet training problems at four years is given in Table XXIX. It should be pointed out that our use of the word 'problem' does not necessarily imply that serious difficulties are involved, though obviously they may be: it is simply intended to reflect the mothers' own general view that further effort is necessary on their part as well as the child's.

The fact that only a small percentage (7%) have problems both at night and during the day means also, of course, that the percentages given involve a relatively large number of children. In a random sample, 46% of four-year-olds have *some* residual problem, whether of wetting or soiling, and 54% may be regarded as completely toilet-trained.

[1] It is an interesting point of interview technique that the discussion of 'sensitive' topics will be less threatening to the subject, and therefore more productive, if it can be introduced by reference back to information which has already been given. It is necessary, of course, to have some advance insight as to what areas are likely to be sensitive. Some sensitivities are irrational, but occur nevertheless in the majority of mothers: this is one reason why we think it important that investigators of parenthood should have had practical experience of being parents themselves, for they will usually find that, however sophisticated in psychological knowledge, they themselves are by no means immune to irrational sensitivities. The no-nonsense approach, which can occasionally be effective in an advisory setting, has no place in this sort of investigation.

[2] No mother will say that her child wets his bed if he does not. Thus a leading question which leads in the direction of the socially unacceptable response has the double function of making such a response permissible to the mother who feels guilty about it, while at the same time affording added satisfaction to the mother who is able to refute the interviewer's expectation in the case of her own child.

TABLE XXIX

*Incidence of residual problems of toilet training*
*(all percentages relate to a randomized sample)*

| Bedwetting | | | | Daytime problems | | Problems both day and night |
|---|---|---|---|---|---|---|
| most nights | 1–3 nts. p.w. | occasional | never or almost never | wetting accidents | persistent soiling | |
| % 11 | % 8 | % 8 | % 73 | % 22 | % 2 | % 7 |

'*If he comes out brazen, then I get really mad . . .* '
Wetting in the daytime, although it occurs in more than one in five children of this age, is not seen by mothers as a major problem. This is partly because (as opposed to bedwetting) it is clearly residual, in that the child most of the time controls his daytime micturition satisfactorily and only sometimes has these 'accidents'; partly because (also in contrast to bedwetting) they feel that, since the child is basically in control, the completion of his training is only a matter of making him a little more *thoughtful*; and partly because (as opposed to soiling) for the great majority of children there appears to be no persistent underlying emotional element in their behaviour.[1] None the less, its occurrence cannot be ignored by the mother, if only because it necessitates a practical response on her part, in the way of changing of pants and wiping of floors; and more than half (57%) of those whose children do have accidents say that they express their disapproval in some way. There are no class differences in the proportions who show disapproval. In the *way* in which disapproval is shown—whether by punishment or merely by reproach—there is a slight difference between middle- and working-class mothers in a direction consistent with our

[1] Mothers may recognize temporary stress as an immediately precipitating cause of an 'accident'—the child wets his pants in the context of his mother's anger, or in unfamiliar surroundings, or after climbing on to a high structure, or on being frightened by a barking dog. But emotion of this sort does not threaten the whole course or training, being only momentary. More disabling is the child's insecurity after such an experience as a stay in hospital or the father's desertion, which some mothers report as resulting in an increase in 'accidents'. At least the mother can understand and accept such emotional upsets, however; whereas the emotional component of soiling tends to be seen as specifically directed against herself.

other findings on punishment, that working-class mothers tend to use smacking more often as a matter of course: but, with the smaller numbers involved here (total N $=$ 191), this difference does not quite reach the level of statistical significance. Over all classes, just over half are reproachful only, and nearly half are at least sometimes punitive. Punishment almost always takes the form of smacking, and reflects the irritability aroused in the mother at having to deal with wet pants at this stage: obviously it will usually be accompanied by verbal reproach as well.

Departmental manager's wife:

> We often don't get there quite in time, but we don't sort of have puddles here, there and everywhere. He gets a jolly good smack if he doesn't get there in time.

Miner's wife:

> Sometimes I smack him, yes. For instance, the other day I'd put him on a clean pair of underpants and clean trousers, and he'd come in and said he'd wet his trousers—smiling all over his face! So I told him off and put him fresh clothes on. He came in a few minutes later—same thing had happened! So I smacked him, you see. I mean, he's got to *realize*, you see. He's not wet them since.

Cook's wife:

> First time, "Naughty boy!", and threaten to smack; second time, smacked; third time, sent to bed for about ten minutes.

Miner's wife:

> If I thought it was idleness—that she'd been playing and hadn't bothered to come in—then I might punish her. Not so long as I know it's genuine.

Fairground worker's wife:

> ( (She had mentioned threatening with the belt) And has she ever had the belt?) About once, that's all. I used it on her one day when she'd wet herself and we were all ready to go down to the Market—I think that's about the only time. She wet herself every day about three months back, that was when this film was on TV, and her Dad used to tell her that if she didn't stop wetting herself, Tobar would come out of the TV and get her. . . . This wetting is about the only trouble—I usually say "You only wet

yourself because you don't love me, you *like* to give me washing all the time". (Family lives in a small caravan: there are four children under six.)

Reproach is used with greater or lesser degrees of severity; it often includes a deliberate attempt to shame the child out of his behaviour. Here again distinctions are made, both between 'idleness' and 'real accidents', and between the child's own postures of indifference or penitence.

Foreman's wife:

> He's got long trousers on top, and I don't think he can quite manage to get them all down in time. Usually if he's in the toilet and I'm in here, he comes out with them in his hands and he says "I've wet me pants"—well, I get a bit mad sometimes. It all depends on the circumstances. If he comes out brazen, well, then I get *really* mad. But if he comes out and I can see he's genuinely sorry, well, I don't say a lot then, I try and *ask* him not to do it. If he comes out brazen, I *tell* him—just shout at him.

Greengrocer's wife:

> I don't punish him—I just say "You're dirty and you smell—and people don't like little boys that smell, do you?"

Managing director's wife:

> I usually shout at her a little bit—if she's left it too late because she was playing, you know.

We had included in our coding arrangements a category for rewards offered in return for pants remaining dry, but we did not in fact find any instances of this still operating at four. In the American literature on child-rearing, star charts are sometimes mentioned (the idea is that the child earns a star for every dry day or night), but we found only one example, used for a bedwetting child.[1] Other bribes were occasionally offered to persistent bedwetters and to soilers, and we did find a few cases

[1] We might have found different results in the neighbouring county; Leicester Education Committee runs a twice-weekly enuresis clinic, in which part of the treatment is the keeping of a star chart: a red star is awarded for one dry night, a blue star for three dry nights running, and a yellow star (which is also 'substantially rewarded') for a dry week. City of Leicester Education Committee, 1965, *op. cit.*

L

in which bribery (or, alternatively, deprivation) had in the past been used, and were believed to have been successful. The following two examples both apply to children whose toilet-training was now apparently completed.

### Driver's wife:

We used to say "If you'll sit on the potty and have a wee-wee, we'll give you a sweetie", you see; and if she did the *other* on the potty, she'd have two sweeties. I don't know whether that's the correct or what way.

### Stoker's wife:

There was one time I thought I'd never get him out of wetting himself. I'll bet he must have been over two, and if you ever used to take him up the Forest, he'd come back and he'd be wet through, and I used to say to him, "If you wet yourself, *or* wet the bed, there'll be no more milk in your bottle"—and that's all I ever said to that boy. He goes at once either to the grating or to the toilet if he wants to go.

It is possible that rewards and deprivations are no longer considered appropriate once the fault being corrected is only intermittent; but they are not very common anyway. Some mothers, however, did point out that the way they would behave in response to occasional 'accidents' was rather different from their more intensive efforts when training was at its height. The first of the following group of mothers who were now adopting a neutral or sympathetic attitude (43% of those whose children were still wetting their pants) is an example of such a change.

### Bricklayer's wife:

*Now* I wouldn't make anything of it; but when I was learning him the potty, I'd say "Oh, you *are* a naughty boy—big boys don't wee their trousers!" So when he did it in the potty, he'd say "I'm a big boy now, aren't I, Mummy!", and I'd say "Oh yes, you *are* a big boy!"—and he'd think that was great, you know, if you'd praise him. But *now* I just say, "Well, don't do it again, you couldn't help it".

### Technical representative's wife:

If she does it, she does it—I just say she must be quicker.

**Garage manager's wife:**

I say, "Oh darling, that isn't very nice, is it? If I was you, I'd try to get to the toilet a bit sooner than that. It's much better to get to the toilet in time than make your knickers all wet"— you know, and explain to her how uncomfortable it is; and of course she agrees.

**Miner's wife:**

Maybe she'll play and she'll be holding herself, and I'll say "Now the toilet's just over there—get away". And she's just that second too late, and she just wets her pants lately. She'll come in and say "You don't know what I've got up me jumper, do you?" I'll say, "I do. You've got your knickers, haven't you?" She'll say, "Oh, I've wee'd them such a little bit!" Mind you, at one time I used to wash them straight away and hang them out—not now. If I try and do that she doesn't like it. I give her a little drop of water and she'll do them herself for you; and I say "Well, that's lovely, that is!" and she'll hang them on the clothes horse; and I've got to wait till she goes out before I re-do them, properly you know, and I always have to put them back the way she's done them.

*'. . . a great strain on the relationship . . .'*

By the age of four it seems safe to say that bowel control is no longer an important issue for the great majority of children. In our total sample of 700, only 31 were reported as having soiling problems of any kind at all, and of these only 18 could be rated as serious and persistent cases: the rest involved merely the staining of the pants with faecal matter, not the actual passing of faeces. Involuntary passing of loose stools during episodes of diarrhoea was discounted.

There is some disagreement in the literature as to the use of terms. Kanner,[1] for instance, uses the term *encopresis* to denote 'involuntary defecation not directly attributable to physical illness', and goes on to note, under the heading *partial encopresis*, the existence of some children who stain their underclothes without in fact passing stools. Apley and MacKeith,[2] however, prefer to use the term *soiling* for 'the involuntary passage of mucus and liquid faeces', and to restrict the word *encopresis* to 'the passage of stools at inappropriate occasions'.

[1] Kanner, Leo, 1957, *op. cit.*
[2] Apley, J. and MacKeith, R., 1962, *op. cit.*

We ourselves in this short discussion will retain the simpler word *soiling*, and, having excluded cases of mere staining, will use the term to refer to the passage of stools *in inappropriate places*. The voluntary or involuntary nature of the act is a moot point, which might lead one into philosophical discussion: certainly it is not involuntary in the sense that the explosive passing of diarrhoeic faeces is involuntary. Often, indeed, it seems to involve a high degree of control as the faeces are retained with the apparent *intention* of depositing them later in an inappropriate place—the place not only referring to the underclothes but also to the child's surroundings, which sometimes appear to have some ritual significance.

Loader's wife:

*Now* if she wants to do it in her pants I let her. She goes behind that chair. I know what she's going for. Just so long as she does it—because if she thinks that anybody's looking, she won't do it. (History of retention of faeces, which has now stopped with the aid of medication together with total permissiveness as to where the stools are passed.)

This child was earlier prescribed suppositories, which the mother felt had exacerbated the problem, as well they might. Retention of faeces for days at a time was in many of these cases associated with the soiling, and was often currently being prescribed for; sometimes retention had become an additional problem in response to parental pressure. 'We had a little period when I used to smack her for it', said an engineer's wife, 'and she got so she used to hold it back. So we had to stop that, and my husband's not a man that believes in hitting children anyway—he says you can sort it out another way. Another thing, it gets her all emotional—she starts crying and gets upset—so I don't do an awful lot of hitting'.

The whole situation is, in fact, fraught with emotion. Because the mother knows that the child is in some sense *choosing* to dirty his pants, rather than merely forgetting to come in quickly enough or losing control during sleep, she tends to see the child's behaviour as a deliberate defiance of her wishes. At the same time, it is a defiance which recurs regularly without a precipitating disagreement—in contrast with the temper tantrum following frustration of wishes, for instance—and is therefore bewildering as well as threatening. The mother last quoted added: 'It's a very big problem; a very, *very* big problem. I just don't know what's the matter. There's nothing the matter *with* her—it's just something that they do it *for*'. Not least among the upsetting factors in soiling, from the mother's point of view, is the physical disgust she feels at repeatedly having to clear up malodorous messes which, for a child of this age, is not a pleasant task even if she could think it justifiable. Between bewilderment, humiliation and disgust, it is hardly surprising that she often finds it difficult not to react violently, even against advice and her better judgment. The mother quoted in the footnote on page 315, who by the time Richard reached seven had forgotten how long this problem had lasted, was at four obsessed by it, bringing the topic up long before any direct question was asked.

Baker's wife:

> Well, this is really the sore point—and I don't know the reason for it, it just baffles me. He *will not* sit on the toilet. He'll use it for weeing, he's perfectly good about that, or if we're out he'll wee in a men's urinal; but, if he has to sit down, he has to have his own potty—he won't do it anywhere else. Why do you think that is?—he seems afraid to, somehow. And it's awful—it's getting so I daren't take him out—because he'll do it in his pants, rather than on a toilet. He'll say 'I want to go home', and then I always know what he wants to do. And we'll *make* him go to toilet, but he won't do that, and then he'll do it in his pants right after. That makes me really mad; I smack him for that, oh yes, I can't help myself, I get so angry. But I will *not* take a potty around wherever we go. And I wonder if it's something *we've* done, you see, I just can't understand it. I mean, what can you do? He'll be at school in a year, and *that* worries me—I mean, I suppose he'll come round *some* time, but I just can't see the end to it.[1]

Richard's mother later added (answering the question 'Do you sometimes find yourself doing things that you don't really approve of?'):

[1] The end came some time during Richard's fifth year when a repetition of the behaviour inside the home culminated in a violent showdown. He had sat on the lavatory seat for half-an-hour without result, after which he proceeded to defaecate 'all the way downstairs'. Richard was smacked very hard, in an atmosphere of some drama; the soiling was never repeated. He is an attractive, 'high-strung' child, with a number of temperamental difficulties.

Well, I *do;* and sometimes with the things *they* do, like over the
toilet, I wonder where I've gone wrong; though I suppose I'd
need a psychiatrist to tell me that. But there again—you see,
with bringing up children, you don't know if you're doing right
or doing wrong until you *have* brought them up do you? You
have to wait and see how they turn out, and then it might be too
late.

Although clearly not serious in a statistical sense, soiling
obviously poses a very serious problem from the mother's point
of view, and one which she is likely to aggravate through her
own highly-charged reaction; often this single habit can be
enough to distort, at least for the time being, the whole relationship between mother and child.

University teacher's wife:

Well, I have enjoyed her very much, but this bowel trouble
made it—er—it hasn't actually come *between* us, but it's been a
great strain on the relationship at times. Because when you have
to deal with perhaps sometimes as many as eight pairs of dirty
pants during the day, it becomes rather wearing, specially after
so long. But we have kept friends over it, but it's been rather
hard work. . . . It really has spoilt all the pleasure in her over the
last year or so, because I think the age of three is such a nice age.

'He says "Yes, well, somebody's got to wet the bed!" '
The most common problem is in fact bedwetting, with 27% of
these children wetting their beds at least sometimes. 19% of all
four-year-olds are enuretic at night frequently enough to cause
their mothers some concern—once a week or more—and 11%
are chronically enuretic in that they have more wet nights than
dry ones. Even the mothers who take pains to make as little fuss
as possible *to the child* are beginning by this time to feel that
some problem exists.

Furniture dealer's wife:

He's still wearing nappies at night: he still wets both before and
after I get him up, *every* night. I don't make any comment at all
about it; actually, he *wants* to stop wearing a nappy, he keeps
asking me if he can; but he's obviously not ready to go through
the night yet. But I'm not worrying him about it, because I think
he will eventually . . . (So it's not really the subject of any bother
at all?) No . . . no—I think *inwardly* I'm beginning to think it *is*
rather long, you know, but I wouldn't let *him* see that.

Company director's wife:

I'm having great trouble over that, I'm glad you mentioned it, because he still wets the bed *every* night, it's dreadful. I don't know what to do about it. It's awful, you know. During the day he's all right, he'll go for ages during the day—in fact, you have to say "For goodness' sake, go and spend a penny"; but I can put him in bed, and he spends a penny the very last minute, and then he'll be wet again in about a quarter of an hour. I don't know *what* to do; but I don't emphasize it too much, because I think if I keep on about it it'll make him nervy . . . I thought, if I worry him *too* much, he'll perhaps start doing it during the day. So I still put a towelling nappy on; my mother says perhaps it'd be better if I *didn't* put a nappy on, but then he'd be so sopping. It's difficult . . . but if I wake him up for a potty, you see, he's one of those people who if you wake him up he's awake for hours, so I don't; but if he *does* wake up, when I go to bed or something, well then I have the whole contraption to change—he's *always* wet by then. But I don't know what one does to stop it . . . (What do you say to him?) I've said to him, "Well, Giles, I do think it's time you finished with wetting your bed, you're four after all". He says, "Yes, well, *somebody's* got to wet the bed!" It doesn't worry him in the least. He says "I can't help it, Mummy"; so then I sort of leave it. (You don't say anything stronger than that?) Well, I have said "Well, I do think it's too bad". But I don't hit him, I don't do anything like that. I've tried rewards; but he says he can't help it—he'd very much like the reward, but he can't help it. But I think the more you worry about it, you probably transmit the worry to them. (But all the worry is really in you, rather than between you and him?) Oh yes. (There's no tension between you?) Oh no—I particularly *don't*, because I think it's a bad thing.

Only a few mothers of bedwetters do not appear to be worrying at all; and they tend to be those whose four-year-old manages at least a few dry nights a week and who have already experienced much more persistent enuresis with an older child. Philip, for instance, wets his bed as often as not, but his mother's expectations have been shaped by his elder brother's behaviour, and she is thus able to react to Philip on the whole with positive approval.

Cycle worker's wife:

Well, when I take his bedclothes off him in the morning, I just run my hand over him and I say "Are you dry?" He'll say "Yes", and I say "Oh, you good boy!" But if he's wet I stand him up and just—(demonstrated token pat)—like that, not to hurt him at all, and I say "That's for tiddling the bed!" And he's got that little look in his eye. But it's just (demonstrated again) a little love-tap. And then, when his Dad gets back from work, I say, "You know our Philip? He wet the bed last night!" His Daddy'll say "I thought you was getting a big boy now!" But I'm not cross with him—I'm just a bit disappointed he hasn't kept dry. But I've had a lot of trouble with his elder brother (10)—in fact he still does it, George does; his Daddy's going to take him in to the doctor's, I mean, he's ten, and it's time he stopped it, you see. That's why I'm quite pleased with Philip.

Bedwetting tends to be regarded as a much more serious problem than daytime 'accidents', for the obvious reason that it seems so little amenable to the child's own will, and therefore the mother is at a loss to know where to direct her efforts. It also puts her to a good deal of personal inconvenience, since the child, because he is asleep, tends to void his bladder completely and is thus not merely damp but soaking. A four-year-old's urine output is usually more than the most efficient plastic pants over the nappy can contain, which means that the mother has both nappy and sheet to wash, sometimes two sets in a night. If the four-year-old's cot is needed for another baby, and he is intended to sleep in the same bed as a sister or brother, this presents further difficulties. In addition there is, once again, some social stigma attached to having a child still bedwetting past the toddler stage. Shortly after a baby is born, the appearance of a pristine string of bright new nappies blowing in the breeze proudly advertises the happy event to the whole neighbourhood; four years later, the same line of nappies—now somewhat discoloured and fraying at the edges—is more likely to be interpreted as a signal of distress. Mothers are likely to be sensitive to the implication that for some reason they have failed over a task in which the majority appear to be successful earlier, and, while they do not know *what* to do, they feel they should be doing *something* to improve matters.

Auto-electrician's wife:

Well, at first I used to be very kind and understanding, and then I started to scold her in the mornings; but I thought "Well, I think I've done the wrong thing", because it sort of preyed on her mind, and when it got to bedtime she said "Oh, I do hope I won't wet the bed tonight", you know, three or four times, and I thought I'd better not scold her any more, so we haven't done too well. I say "Call Mummy if you want to go"; but it doesn't seem to work—nothing does. She's gone to bed without any milk or anything, but she's *still* wet. I've gone in to her, "Do you want to go to the toilet?"—but she struggles so much, she's only half awake; so I'm afraid I've just about given up! I know I shouldn't do, but I have!

### Miner's wife:

I shout at him. I know you shouldn't do, but it's just the thought of washing sheets every day that does me.

### Builder's wife:

Just say she's naughty and change her. I did think she was slow on that, and I did take her water down to the doctor's to have it examined. . . . I made quite a few promises at first, if she didn't wee the bed, but it didn't seem to do much good.

### Greengrocer's wife:

Well, actually he's very proud of his tie, and I say "When you don't wet the bed, you'll be a big boy and you'll be able to have another tie, so that, like Daddy, you'll be able to have one hanging in the wardrobe and one to wear". So he's really, now, starting to think of this tie!

### Steel erector's wife:

He's soaking in the morning. I just smack his bottom and tell him that's naughty. But he still does it again. I can't understand it. He doesn't have anything to drink before he goes to bed. I thought that were it at first.

### Window cleaner's wife:

I used to tell him, "You must try and not wet the bed". I used to smack him for it sometimes—I know you didn't really ought to do that, but I *have* done it a few times, when it got on top of me a bit, you know.

### Labourer's wife:

Tell her she's a dirty little madam. I slap her if she's awake, but if she's asleep there's nothing I *can* do.

L*

Labourer's wife:

> I shout at him, and I *threaten* to hit him; but I never do. When I take him to bed, I say "Do you want to use a pot?" He says "No", and I say "You wet that bed! Let me find that bed wet in the morning, and see what you'll get!" And he don't seem to do it if you threaten him. I think he's just a bit lazy.

Miner's wife:

> We don't tell him off, because we had the same trouble with the two girls, so I thought it might be in the family, one side or the other, so it's not much good scolding him if it's really our fault. When he's *not* wet, he's ever so excited, and we're ever so pleased with him when he's not wet. I get excited *with* him, and we all jump about—"He hasn't wetted the bed!"—and everybody hears that he hasn't. When his sister comes: "He hasn't wetted the bed tonight!"

Cook's wife:

> That is quite a problem, I've tried everything . . . well, I've tried all sorts of things. I've promised him different things if he's dry next morning, and I threaten to smack him, but it doesn't seem to make any difference, so I suppose he'll grow out of it in time. At present I promise him a shilling every day to spend on ice-cream and sweets—it'd really be worth it.

Shoe repairer's wife:

> I never say anything to him now. I used to shout at him. It was when I used to hear people whose children were the same age as Robert, and sometimes even younger, where they never wet the bed, and I used to shout at him for it, you see—"Well you're old enough now", you see. But I found it wasn't making any difference. So I just ignore it now.

These quotations are fairly representative. An underlying thread of anxiety is clearly discernible, together with the feeling that there must be some way of dealing with the situation more effectively. The expedients mentioned are among many which are tried, either simultaneously or one after another, and it seems very difficult for mothers to sit back patiently and do nothing while waiting for the problem to solve itself in the fullness of time. Table XXX gives some indication of the variety of methods employed: we do not attempt to quantify at this stage, because so many of these devices are tried a few times and discarded.

Not all these techniques are used with equal frequency, and some tend to be tried for a much shorter period than others, or with less consistency. For instance, bribes tend to be changed or dropped altogether when they prove unsuccessful and therefore

TABLE XXX

*Expedients adopted by mothers in attempting to deal with bedwetting*

| Technique | Example |
|---|---|
| Punishes | 'Smack his bottom'; 'Slap her legs'. |
| Threatens | 'Threaten to take him to the doctor'; 'Tell him he'll have to sleep on the floor'; 'See what you'll get!' |
| Shows anger | 'Shout at her'; 'Get very cross'; 'Lose my temper'. |
| Attempts to shame child | 'Oh, you dirty lad!'; 'Oh, you lazy madam!'; 'Say big boys don't do that'; 'You're four years old, it's not necessary to wet the bed'. |
| Adopts changes in routine | 'Not let him drink after tea'; 'Nothing after 4 o'clock'; 'Lift her for a potty when I go to bed'. |
| Uses bribery | 'Money for sweets'; 'A new dolls' house'; 'Another tie'; 'Buy you a treat'; 'Real pants, like Daddy'. |
| Praises success | 'Praise her up to the hilt'; 'We all jump about'; 'Make a fuss of him'; 'Say she's a clever girl'. |
| Shows kindness and understanding | 'Well, you're at it again, never mind'; 'Never mind, love, when you get bigger you won't'; 'Never mind, we'll see if we can do better tomorrow'; 'I just change it and say "Don't say nowt to your Dad" '. |
| The grand gesture | Dramatically leaves off nappies and rubber sheet. Buys new pyjamas. Gives child a new bed. Redecorates child's room. Lets him sleep with Grandma! |
| Deliberately plays the whole thing down | 'Just be resigned and put up with it'; 'Just hoping he'll grow out of it'; 'The more you draw his attention to it, the more he'll do it'. |

lose reality to the child; anger, shaming and praise tend to recur over longer periods, since they reflect the mother's emotions. Kindness and understanding are often the result of the mother's 'good resolution', which may or may not be kept up. 'Playing the whole thing down', since it is so often born of resignation, tends to come at the end of a period of more active efforts. Some expedients are not really considered appropriate for the situation: bribery, for instance, tends to be the resort of desperation rather than of reason, and recognized as such. Punishment is also considered both inappropriate and ineffective by the great majority of mothers, and only 5% of those whose children still wet their beds admit to smacking them for it. This percentage is in fact the same as the one obtained when mothers whose children no longer bed-wet are asked about their methods earlier on. Mothers who seek advice about bed-wetting are invariably told, it seems, that neither scolding nor punishing will be of any use; and many know from experience that getting angry does more harm than good.

However, it must be stated that each and every one of the methods quoted has been known to work with individual children, in the sense that the child became dry shortly after the method was adopted; and this includes smacking and threatening. On the other hand, it is easy to find numbers of mothers who have used any of these tactics to no avail.

Perhaps the main point of agreement is that a *change* of tactics can help to produce the desired result. Of particular interest in this connection is what we have called the 'grand gesture'. The essential ingredient here, apparently, is drama; the mother makes an offer to the child, which is not a bribe for it does not depend upon his *first* becoming dry, but which rather presents the child with a dramatic demonstration of the mother's faith in his power to change. With a great show of confidence (though inwardly trembling) she tells the child: 'Here's your new bed: now you're big, you won't need this rubber sheet any more'; or, 'I've bought you proper striped pyjamas like Daddy, so we'll put your nappies away for the new baby'. If this method is to be successful, it is no doubt important for the mother to choose her moment carefully—there must be some evidence that the child basically has control and is ready to make the change—for a dramatic build-up followed by failure can be damaging to the confidence of both mother and child.

One mother spoke sympathetically of her child who had 'let herself down in her own estimation, I think' by such a failure; in this case, the mother was able to repeat her gesture successfully some weeks later. What is interesting about such cases is that, despite the general belief that a change of behaviour is not entirely within the compass of the child's conscious will, nevertheless this final step to success appears to be achieved by somehow motivating the child to rise to an occasion. It may well be, of course, that a significant factor in this is a sudden strengthening of his security by his mother's display of confidence in him: a welcome relief from the implicit lack of confidence shown by her former nagging and pleading.

One other aspect of change of tactics as a successful means of motivating the child is that the child may simply be bored by the whole situation, and needs some alteration in it to catch his interest. This is nicely illustrated in the following story.

Miner's wife:

> She used to wet the bed *every* night. In the morning she'd be *soaking*. But—I hadn't been too well, and I had to drink a lot of fluid, I had a terrible sore throat—well, having to lie all the way upstairs in bed, I couldn't keep nipping down to the toilet sort of every half-hour, so I had a bucket up there; so I got out of bed one night, and she said "Where you going?"—I said "I'm just going for a wee, shan't be a moment"; and *went*, ever so crafty, so she wouldn't see. But she *heard*, you see. So she said "Are you going to wee in that bucket?"—I said "Yes, just a little one". Well, she automatically got out of the cot herself, and *she* had one; and after that, I never had a wet bed with her. No, if she wanted to wee, she got straight out of the cot, and go and wee in the bucket. I only had the bucket up just for me when I was ill; but anyway, I keep it up there now.

There is a very general feeling that it is unwise to bring a great deal of pressure to bear on the child, and often treatment seems to alternate between pressure and relaxation according to whether training the child or reducing his resultant tension seems most urgent at the time. It is also clear, however, that most mothers think it important not to show so little concern that the whole matter is allowed to go by default. What the majority would *like* to be able to do is to take the heat out of the situation while at the same time keeping the child aware of the necessity for eventual change: as a boot repairer's wife put it, 'Let it take its course, you know, just mention it to her, not *grumble* at her; just so she knows it's something *different* that she wets the bed, her brothers don't wet the bed—let her know she's doing something different and she shouldn't, like, but never grumble at her'. Even though it is said that the child cannot really help himself, because he is asleep at the time, the mother has the (apparently justified) suspicion that the child's will does contribute *something* to the situation, so that it seems necessary at least to keep him aimed, so to speak, towards change. If advice is sought, the practical methods most often suggested are to cut down the child's fluid intake at bedtime and to lift him at more frequent intervals.[1] While some advisors believe that these expedients will at least reduce the frequency of wet beds, it is not at all clear that they do anything to ensure that the child will wake up when the need arises, which is to say before the accident occurs. The conditioning method, which is directed to this end, is not normally prescribed for children of this age, and none of our sample had used it, though a few mothers were beginning to make enquiries about it.[2]

Implicit in much of the advisory literature on toilet training is the suggestion that in normal children control is achieved entirely through maturation; but where bedwetting at four is concerned, this is probably an over-simplification. Some children, it is true, seem to train themselves spontaneously at a comparatively early age, and with no exertion on the mother's

[1] It must be added that many advisors reject these methods as useless, and some think they increase or prolong enuretic behaviour. Cutting down on drinks is rejected on the grounds that this makes the thirsty child go to sleep thinking about water, and therefore more likely to wet the bed; lifting the child when half asleep is said to encourage the child to pass water while asleep, rather than teaching him to wake up first.

[2] In the conditioning (or 'bell and pad') method of curing enuresis, the child sleeps on a pad lined with metal foil and so constructed that the first trickle of urine completes an electrical circuit and causes a bell to ring. (It is sometimes thought that this method conditions the child by giving him an electric shock, but in fact no electric shock is involved in any way.) The bell wakes the child, who has been told that when he wakes he must get out of bed and go to the lavatory. The theory is that bladder tension quickly becomes associated with being waked, and that the child soon learns to wake up in response to the bladder tension which regularly precedes the bell. Obviously the child must be maturationally ready for such learning; once he is, such a device can be valuable in removing behaviour which is in itself anxiety-provoking. The 'bell and pad' can be bought privately, but is also available on loan from child welfare clinics: there is usually a waiting-list.

part; and for them it seems reasonable to suppose that they acquire control by a process of maturation rather than learning. Probably a fair proportion of these fortunate children never initially fall into the habit of urinating during sleep, so that all they have to be taught is not to wet the bed after they have awakened. For the child who has developed a persistent habit of wetting while asleep, on the other hand, learning of some sort, whether amenable to the will or not, must eventually take place, and mothers suspect, perhaps rightly, that if they ignore the habit altogether it may continue almost indefinitely. Because their own motivation is overcharged, however, they may at this point induce in the child an anxiety which itself inhibits the learning process and so creates a vicious spiral of pressurization and failure. As usual in child-rearing, the balance that is struck depends to a large extent upon the child's own reaction, which is partly temperamental. The first two children whose mothers were quoted in this section (pp. 326–7) are good examples of individual differences between children. Giles, the company director's child, blithely comments 'Yes, well, *somebody's* got to wet the bed!' The furniture dealer's son, whose mother is both less anxious and less communicative of anxiety, is much more sensitive to criticism: 'Actually someone mentioned it to him, a few months ago, they were saying to him "Oh, it's time you didn't wear these nappies now"; and that night when he went to bed he started to cry, it really had upset him, you know'. Many other examples could be given of the child's temperament colouring the issue more or less independently of the mother's attitude: two will suffice.

Dyer's wife:
> She worries more than I do. I have *never* shouted at her. "Never mind", I say; but, as I say, she *always* worries about it.

Policeman's wife:
> It doesn't seem to affect *him* at all. He just wakes up in the morning and slips his pyjama trousers off and gets out of bed and larks around.

Any attempt to explain why children wet the bed must obviously take into account the age of the child. For infants under a year, incontinence is the accepted norm; it is generally assumed that babies of this age cannot be taught to hold their urine because the necessary neural inhibitory mechanisms are not yet developed. By the age of seven or eight, on the other hand, it is usually agreed that control should be possible for all normal children. Most authorities would, in fact, put the age a good deal lower than this: Kanner, for instance, defines enuresis as 'the involuntary passage of urine by persons more than three years old'.[1] Once the age of 'normal control' is reached, at whatever point this may be set, bedwetting is usually explained either in terms of parental mishandling (including inadequate training) or as a reaction by the child to some particular emotional stress. If there has been a continuous history of bedwetting, the former explanation will seem plausible, while a period of fairly complete control followed by a lapse into bedwetting, especially if the child is known to have suffered stress, will favour a reactive explanation. At the age of four, however, it is not so easy to draw confident conclusions on these lines, particularly when we find so large a proportion of children wetting their beds. Most of the bedwetters are in fact perfectly reliable during the day: 27% are at least occasionally enuretic at night, but only 7% wet both bed and pants. This suggests that their training has not been particularly neglected. On the other hand, only a handful of cases present a convincing picture of reaction to stress: a few children had been dry at night until, variously, the birth of a new baby, the father's desertion, moving to a new house, or the death of a smaller sister. For the majority of bed-wetters, night-time control had never been established and it would have been difficult to single out any special focus of emotional distress. There remains, of course, the possibility that less dramatic emotional difficulties, arising from more subtle disturbance between parent and child, could be an important factor in the child's enuresis. The most obvious conflict, as we have seen, was tending to arise out of the situation itself; so that, if it is true that enuresis results from emotional upset, it follows that enuresis is self-perpetuating: and this is, of course, the major justification for the use of appliances such as the 'bell and pad', which cure 'symptoms' without reference to their aetiology. It seemed worth while, however, to look beyond the circular stresses of the situation, and to ask whether particular styles of child rearing, or particular practices within

[1] Kanner, L., 1957, *op. cit.*

these, were associated with success or failure in toilet training. A number of comparisons were therefore made between the group of children who were completely dry at night and those who were still having difficulty at the age of four.

The suggestion that the mother's child-rearing practices are not irrelevant receives some initial support from the fact that there is a significant social class difference in the proportions of children who have any sort of bedwetting problem. Table XXXI shows that middle-class mothers are rather more successful in this area than working-class mothers. This class trend corroborates a similar one found at twelve months, when it was shown, not only that more middle-class mothers had started training by that age, but also that, of all the mothers who had started training, more middle-class women had been rewarded by some preliminary success for their efforts.

TABLE XXXI

*Proportions of children bedwetting at least occasionally at four years, by social class*

| I & II | IIIwc | | IIIman | IV | V | | All |
|--------|-------|---|--------|-----|-----|---|-----|
| % | % | | % | % | % | | % |
| 14 | 22 | | 31 | 27 | 30 | | 27 |
| 18% | | | 30% | | | | |
| middle class | | | working class | | | | |

The fact that a class difference exists suggests that the answer may lie in parental handling and may be found by means of cross-correlating bedwetters and non-bedwetters with various practices already known to show class differences. It might be, for instance, that bedwetting is associated with more frequent use of physical punishment and successful toilet training with a preference for verbal means of control. It might be that greater emphasis on physical modesty and punishment for genital play in some way encourages bedwetting. The mother's pressure for neatness and tidiness might be associated with the child's ability or inability to become dry at night. Each of these hypotheses was tested: for none of them could we find even a suggestion of a difference between the bedwetting and the non-bedwetting groups. We then wondered whether the deciding factor lay in the convenience of toilet facilities: obviously training a child should be easier where he only has to run across the landing to the lavatory, compared with the arrangements in the old terraced houses, which involve keeping potty or bucket upstairs or else a trip downstairs and across the yard. To test this hypothesis, we used the working-class sample only to compare those living in older housing with those living in council houses. Again, however, no significant difference could be found. We can thus suggest no single important reason to account for the class difference, and can only guess at variables (perhaps of maternal persistence?) which are much less amenable to identification.

TABLE XXXII

*Mothers' response to bedwetting compared with their success in training*

| | Predominant response | | | |
| | Punitive | Reproachful only | Rewarding of dryness | No pressure (neutral or sympathetic) |
|---|---|---|---|---|
| | % | % | % | % |
| Successful (no bedwetting now) | 3 | 7 | 2 | 88 |
| Not yet successful | 5 | 42 | 5 | 48 |

The most direct means of comparing mothers who have and have not been successful in toilet training is simply to ask them about their method of dealing with the child's failures of control, now or earlier. This we had done, and had been able to rate both groups on a four-point scale (the same as that used for daytime 'accidents'), according to whether their predominating response to the child's problem was punitive, reproachful, rewarding of control or without pressure (neutral or sympathetic). Table XXXII compares the 'successful' and the 'unsuccessful' mothers in terms of this scale.

Obviously it would be very misleading to interpret these results in a simple causative way: the two groups are not fully comparable, in that the first is talking about behaviour in the past, in relation to a child both younger and less likely to be considered a problem as yet, while the second group is talking about on-going behaviour towards an older child. The difference between present and past behaviour in itself is probably almost enough to account for the large group of mothers saying that they *now* take a reproachful line: if only this morning they were telling the child that he is a 'mucky little ha'porth', they will remember this as their reaction; whereas over the months of triumphant dryness mere reproach becomes blurred into 'I never did anything, it just seemed to come to him', which would be classified as 'no pressure'. Add to this that the mother *feels* more reproachful to a four-year-old than to a younger child, and the difference is fully explained; we have no grounds at all for concluding *on the basis of the final column* that sympathetic behaviour pays off in terms of results. These figures are not in fact very helpful in providing a rule of thumb for toilet training. They are mainly of interest, in a rather negative way, for their indication that the use of formal rewards and of punishments (so far as these are admitted, at least) is confined to a small minority of mothers, even at an age when the bedwetter is beginning to be considered a problem.

It is often said that boys are more difficult to train than girls, partly because (it is sometimes averred) they need to micturate more frequently.[1] Perhaps we should note in passing that our data does not clearly support this belief. 11% of our four-year-old boys were wetting the bed most nights, compared with 9% of the girls; 72% of the boys, compared with 77% of the girls, were entirely reliable at night. These differences are in the usually accepted direction, but are certainly not large enough to reach statistical significance, and individual mothers might well find more difficulty with their daughters than with their sons.

*'They've been on the potty since they were four hours old. . .'*

Since we do not expect to return to toilet training in much detail in later reports, we include here a short section relating our findings at the four-year level with data collected when the

[1] Kanner (1957, *op. cit.*) states that, *of the child patients referred to his psychiatric clinic*, 26% were enuretic, of whom 62% were boys and 38% girls: 78% of his enuretic patients had never been 'dry'. Douglas and Blomfield find only 3·68% (boys) and 3·21% (girls) persistently enuretic at 4:3 years; Macfarlane *et al.*, however, found 18% (boys) and 31% (girls) enuretic at 3 years. Blomfield, J. B. and Douglas, J. W. B.: 'Bedwetting Prevalence among Children aged 4–7 years'; *Lancet*, 1, 1956. Macfarlane, Jean, *et al: Behaviour Problems of Normal Children*, Univ. of California, 1962.

children were twelve months old. The discussion that follows refers to the sample of 275 children whose mothers were interviewed at both the first and the fourth birthdays.

At the four-year level we may divide all children into two groups: those apparently completely reliable both by day and by night, and those who still have residual problems of toilet training in that they at least sometimes wet the bed, have daytime 'accidents', or soil their pants. Taking the follow-up sample only, 60% were found to be apparently fully trained, against 40% who still were unreliable. In Table XXXIII the two groups are presented in relation to the age at which potty-training was started.

TABLE XXXIII

*Age at which toilet training was started compared with behaviour at four years (N = 275)*

| | Training started at: | | | |
| | 0–2 mos. (n = 75) | 3–8 mos. (n = 93) | 9–12 mos. (n = 61) | After 12 mos. (n = 46) |
| --- | --- | --- | --- | --- |
| | % | % | % | % |
| Reliable at 4 years | 65 | 63 | 54 | 54 |
| Residual toilet problem | 35 | 37 | 46 | 46 |
| | *(differences not significant)* | | | |

It is frequently suggested by contemporary writers on baby care that it may be a mistake to begin toilet training too early, on the grounds that, because the baby is not capable of sphincter *control* but only of an automatic reaction to the touch of the potty on the buttocks, the mother may be led to expect too much, and will be disappointed later on, when automatic responses cease without learning having taken place. It is also said that early training is often followed by negativistic reactions on the part of the baby, leading to emotional conflict between them.[1] The mother who can say 'They've been on the

[1] For instance: 'Although some children do learn to become toilet-trained at an early age, much to their parents' pride, these same children show a marked tendency to lapse, usually with a great aversion towards the article of training, at a later date.' Audrey Kelly: *The Physical Health of Children*, Penguin Books, Harmondsworth, 1960.

potty since they were four hours old—ever since the first feed—
—and when they got to about a year old, I put them into pants
and every hour put them on the potty' will find herself more at
home with the baby-books of the Truby King era than with
Spock or the Glaxo Baby Book;[1] though she is not entirely out
of fashion among other mothers (more than one in five of our
original sample had started training before the baby was 2
months old, usually as soon as they got up after their confine-
ment). In terms of results at four years, there is nothing in our
data to suggest that mothers who begin training early are more
likely to have difficulties which persist: in fact, the results given
in Table XXXIII suggest that the reverse may be the case, with
the late-trainers having slightly more trouble at four. The differences shown in this table are not great enough to reach statistical significance, however, since the sample is a good deal smaller
than that on which our tables are normally based. Probably a
more meaningful, if rather negative, way of putting this finding
is that successful completion of toilet training by the age of four
cannot be guaranteed whatever age is chosen for its beginning,
if 35% of those starting before two months and 46% of those
leaving it until after twelve months still, at four, have some way to
go. This is perhaps of particular interest in the case of the former
group, since the mother who is determined enough to have
started training so very early probably also has that persistence

---

[1] (i) 'Early training is of great importance; from the third day the nurse
should have a small chamber, soap dish, or small pudding basin with a rounded
edge on her knee, and the baby should be held with the back against the nurse's
chest, the cold rim should just be allowed to touch the child at the back of the
anus, and very soon a good habit is established. Many nurses train their babies
so that they have no soiled napkins after the first week or so, and very few wet
ones.' Liddiard, Mabel: *The Mothercraft Manual*, Churchill, London, 1928
edition: stated to be 'an outline of the principles taught by Sir Truby King'.

(ii) 'Generally speaking, babies gradually gain control of their bowels and
bladders as they grow. The most that a mother needs to do is to watch her child
—to see what stage of readiness he is in—and give him some positive encouragement.' Spock, Benjamin: *Baby and Child Care*, revised edition; Duell, Sloan
and Pearce, New York, 1967.

(iii) 'Holding out a small baby on a pot, waiting and hoping for him to perform
only to find that he wets his napkin immediately you take him off, wastes a lot
of time and, moreover, makes it very difficult to preserve the detachment
necessary for success. The better method, therefore, is not to introduce the baby
to the pot at all until he is able to sit on it unaided, say at about ten or eleven
months old, and some authorities think it is wise to leave the whole matter
until the age of fifteen months.' *Glaxo Mother and Baby Book*, published by
Glaxo Laboratories in the 1960's and enjoying a wide circulation via chemists'
shops.

which we have suggested may be the vital factor: as one of the few mothers already successful at twelve months said, 'I spent hours, but it was worth it in the end ... I have a lot of patience, you've got to'. Presumably it would also be the early starters who would be the more dismayed if they could foresee the prospect before them; on re-reading some of their confident intentions, one cannot help speculating upon their comments if only the interviewer could have let them listen in advance to what they would be saying three years later.

All mothers who had started training by the time their babies were twelve months old were asked at that time what success they had had so far, measured not by reliability, of course, but by whether their babies did in fact ever use the pot or not. In Table XXXIV this measure of success at twelve months is compared with success in terms of reliability at four years; the children who had not started training by the first interview are omitted. Again, however, it cannot be shown that progress in toilet training at an early age is indicative of the situation at four.

TABLE XXXIV

*Progress in toilet training at twelve months compared with reliability at four years (n = 228)*

|  | Often successful at 12 months (n = 48) | Occasionally successful at 12 months (n = 119) | Never successful at 12 months (n = 61) |
|---|---|---|---|
|  | % | % | % |
| Reliable at four years | 58 | 61 | 64 |
| Residual toilet problem | 42 | 39 | 36 |
|  | | *(differences not significant)* | |

In achieving success in toilet training, it may be more important that the mother have a relaxed attitude than that she should start at any particular age; certainly most contemporary baby books would seem to convey this message. Two attitudinal measures were available from the first interview: the first an assessment of the mothers' concern over toilet training at that time, the second a measure of her aspirations in terms of the age at which she then thought that a child 'should' be clean and dry. Table XXXV compares mothers' attitudes towards toilet training at twelve months with their children's reliability at four years. Once more, no consistent significant association with success at four can be found for either of the attitudes measured, and we must conclude that there is no evidence for the mother's attitude early in toilet training having any effect upon her success or otherwise as assessed at this rather late stage. If these proportions were maintained in a larger sample, however, they would indicate that higher aspirations and greater concern are both reflected in the child's reliability at the age of four.

TABLE XXXV

*Earlier attitudes and aspirations towards toilet training compared with later success (n = 275)*

| | Mother's attitude/aspiration at 12 months | | |
| --- | --- | --- | --- |
| | Very concerned (n = 20) | Mildly concerned (n = 100) | Unconcerned (n = 155) |
| | % | % | % |
| Reliable at four years | 75 | 58 | 60 |
| Residual toilet problem | 25 | 42 | 40 |

| | "Before 18 months" (N = 41) | "18 months— 2 years" (N = 115) | "Later" (N = 82) | "Depends on the child" (N = 37) |
| --- | --- | --- | --- | --- |
| | % | % | % | % |
| Reliable at four years | 71 | 56 | 68 | 54 |
| Residual toilet problem | 29 | 44 | 37 | 46 |
| | *(differences not significant)* | | | |

It must be reiterated that, by not returning to these children at, say, six-monthly intervals throughout toilet training, we have lost the chance of a much more detailed and perhaps more positive picture of the causal factors involved in this process;

data for even one intermediate age might have made it possible to make more definite statements. We could also have drawn conclusions from mothers' retrospective reports of the ages at which different stages of progress were reached, but, for the reasons discussed earlier, we have been unwilling to make possibly misleading inferences from data which we could not trust.

In terms of individual cases, the baby-book prognostications of negativistic phases in the earlier-trained baby are upheld: we found many examples of this even at twelve months, and more still when asking at four about the course of toilet training. Again, it cannot be said that a late start *guarantees* freedom from negativism, but it does seem to help; at the same time, the mother who is relaxed enough not to be rushed into toilet training will tend also to be more ready to postpone it still further if the baby shows signs of negativism, and for these mothers such phases are likely never to reach the stage of conflict. For this reason, late-starting babies' negativistic reactions may be under-reported. An interesting sidelight was thrown by one mother upon the recurrent optimism of those who gamble on an early start. In our last report, we quoted her as saying:

> I made the same mistake over Stephanie, they told me that start a child off early, they usually do finish up where they won't use the potty. Well, I found that with Stephanie, and I've also found that with Adrian.

When we went to talk to her about four-year-old Adrian, we found that she now had another baby, Yvette, aged 14 months.

> (What have you done about Yvette and her toilet training? I remember you saying you thought you'd made a mistake with both the first two, starting them early.) And yet I *still* didn't learn from it! At first—well, for the first few weeks she was born, I didn't know what it was to have a dirty nappy. But you see she lacked later on, she rebelled against the pot, and still is doing. . . . But I've found each one, as I've started them with the potty, they've rebelled later on, and they *still* haven't, er . . . (Do you think you'd do the same thing again?) I suppose I would, and I think, really, you're that proud at such a young baby sitting on a pot, I think that's one of the reasons you do it.

The findings of this section have been mainly negative ones. Nevertheless, perhaps they can be combined in order to draw one positive conclusion: that toilet training is one area where the mother can do what suits her in the short term, without worrying whether she is endlessly extending the long-term process by her choice of an earlier or later start. Some mothers think it worth while taking a good deal of trouble over potting during the first year, simply in order to have fewer nappies to wash *at that time*; others find the recurrent ritual and its pre-occupations so uncongenial that they prefer to leave the whole business of training until as late as friends and relatives will tolerate, and put up with the heavy wash-load meanwhile. So long as they realize that they are choosing between here-and-now emphases on potting or on washing, without any built-in guarantees for the future, they may as well please themselves. The mother whose child learns quickly will doubtless continue to attribute her success to the method she used, whatever it was; the mother whose child is tardy will still fail to understand what went wrong. Meanwhile, it must be remembered that there may yet be conclusions to be drawn, which would be premature at this stage, about the effect of toilet training methods upon the mature personality.

# CHAPTER 12

## WHO TOLD THEE THAT THOU WAST NAKED?

*And the eyes of them both were opened, and they knew
that they were naked; and they sewed fig-leaves
together, and made themselves aprons. . . . And the
Lord God called unto Adam, and said unto him . . .
'Who told thee that thou wast naked?'*

GENESIS III. 7–11.

Almost every aspect of human bodily behaviour is brought
under the regulation of social control: codes and customs
govern even the simplest of our natural physical actions. For
example, human beings all over the world cough, yawn, sniff,
spit, belch and pass wind; but even such automatic and apparently trivial habits tend to be controlled in both the manner and
the incidence of their expression by strict rules of what is considered proper to time and place. Culture patterns differ from
one another in the approbation or disapproval with which they
endow individual functions: they have in common that the
value judgment is made. Similarly, the universal activities of
personal grooming are influenced by powerful social conventions, so that everyday acts such as combing the hair, cleaning the
fingernails, clearing the nostrils and picking the teeth all tend
to be restricted according to the occasion, and modified or
inhibited by the presence of certain other individuals. The socio-
cultural controls exerted over the natural processes of elimination are even more obvious. It is only during early infancy, in
most societies, that a child may empty bowel or bladder as the
urge takes him; sooner or later, often sooner than the infant can
possibly conceptualize what is being asked of him, pressures will
be brought to bear directed towards ensuring that these activities take place only in a socially appropriate context.

Pressures towards cultural conformity are particularly evident where the behaviour concerned involves the display or exposure of the naked body. The adult, and even the older child, is expected to know that within the individual culture, and making due allowance for the minor revolutions of fashion, certain styles of dress are generally taken to be sexually provocative and certain states of undress regarded as indecent. Children learn early that some of the postures and movements which their bodies adopt naturally in the course of active play are considered impolite, and that a few individual gestures are especially 'rude'; their learning may well be reinforced by the practical usefulness for peer-group conflict of signs so generally recognizable as insulting, but they will be left in no doubt of the views of adult society. Convention thus directs and circumscribes both the ways in which we arrange or handle our own bodies and the situations in which it is permissible to make physical contact with other people's bodies, and to what extent. In all group behaviour—which is to say, in all public behaviour—such codes will tend to be adhered to and socially enforced; while private behaviour, either by single persons or between pairs of persons, will tend to be privately assessed in terms of the prevailing codes. The reason for human subservience to these restrictions is clear enough: conventions of this sort serve to buttress more important sanctions and prohibitions regulating the expression of sexual and aggressive feelings, and such powerful forces need to be kept under some degree of social control if a society is to be strengthened and motivated rather than destroyed by them. All known societies have rules, more or less restrictive than our own, governing who may make sexual advances to whom, and in what circumstances; often such rules, or some of them, will be formalized in explicit legal codes, and their contravention will attract severe penalties.

Paradoxically, however, evidence from anthropological sources also demonstrates that the social conventions which decide how physical modesty shall be expressed are neither universal nor static.[1] In other words, we must accept as a fact

---

[1] The terms *modesty* and *modesty training* perhaps ring oddly in English ears; the Concise Oxford Dictionary gives '*modest* . . . (of women) decorous in manner and conduct, scrupulously chaste', and comes no nearer to physical prudery (a word which it also confines to women!) These terms are commonly used in anthropological literature, however, and we retain them here, to denote decorum in relation to physical nakedness and to sexual or eliminative behaviour, whether applied to boys or to girls.

that the degree to which it is considered socially permissible to expose the body, and the specific parts which may properly be exposed, vary not only from one society to another but also within any given society from one point in time to another. More complex societies, particularly those whose communication facilities are sophisticated, will tend to change especially rapidly: in our own culture, for instance, dramatic changes in physical modesty take place within decades. A simple example is provided by a woman in the act of sitting down. At the end of the forties, considerations of modesty as she sits down do not worry her, because her skirt is so long and full that it will naturally cover her knees and part of her calves without effort on her part; as the fifties wear on, skirts rise and narrow, but it is still immodest to uncover the (stockinged) knees completely— women are reduced to constant tweaking of skirt hems as they seat themselves, lest their skirts 'ride up' beyond the bounds of decency; but by 1966-67, era of the mini-skirt, the only worry is that the long sleek line of thigh might be spoiled by the glimpse of a too-low stocking-suspender. Still more strikingly, whereas it is now commonplace to see women exposing their navels on the beach, it is exceptionally rare to see a woman baring her breasts in a public place, even for what was once considered the quite legitimate purpose of feeding a hungry baby. Comparison between different culture patterns makes the same point even more forcefully. In our own society, even parents who believe themselves to be 'emancipated' will show signs of disturbance if their children play in overtly sexual ways, and it is rare for parents to witness and allow play that has sexual overtones, particularly if this involves children handling each others' genitals: yet there are societies where such activities excite neither comment nor action, where children are recognized to imitate copulation in play, or where the handling of children's genitals, by adults or others, has its own place within accepted social behaviour.[1] Cross-cultural studies emphasize very clearly

[1] See, for instance, Romney, K., and Romney, R.: 'The Mixtecans of Juxtlahuaca, Mexico'; in Beatrice Whiting: 1963, *op. cit.* 'The Balinese', writes Margaret Mead, 'place very early emphasis on the genitalia. A little boy's penis is being continually teased, pulled, flipped, flicked, by his mother, his child-nurse, and those around him. With the slight titillation go the repeated words, "Handsome, handsome, handsome", an adjective applied only to males. The little girl's vulva is patted gently, with the accompanying feminine adjective "Pretty, pretty, pretty".' (Mead, M.: *Male and Female*, Gollancz, London, 1950). In the Tarongan community of the Philippines, touching of little girls'

that our own social conventions of modesty, powerful and binding though they may appear to us, are by no means fixed or absolute. The customs and taboos which we take for granted, and which enter into all aspects of our social lives, are no part of our biological inheritance: they result from a process of learning, and each generation of children has to acquire them anew.

If the concept of 'modesty training' seems alien or odd, this is probably because children are expected to learn many rules of behaviour, including those of modesty and decorum, without the formal and explicit instruction which we tend to associate with the idea of training. What happens in practice is that the child's actions are continually subjected to parental evaluation which has the intention, and usually the effect, of modifying and shaping his future behaviour to conform with social expectation. The process is constant and indirect; the child is not told on what principles he should act, but nevertheless learning is accomplished, because at every point his actual behaviour is measured against the unstated convention: 'Don't do that, dear, it isn't very nice'; 'We wouldn't like Mrs Brown to see us doing that, would we?'; 'That's enough!'; 'Jimmy is a very rude little boy, and I don't want you to play with him if he does that sort of thing'—or merely the raised eyebrow, or the warning look.

This sort of learning appears to take place in many different areas of child development, and is by no means confined to the acquisition of modesty. It must certainly be the basis for the complex process whereby cultural norms in general are transmitted from parent to child. The child during his daily life behaves in a very great variety of ways, and is normally highly sensitized to the responses which his activities evoke. Some of his doings will be approved, some will be disapproved, others will be merely ignored: from the pattern of reaction which they attract, the child will gradually learn to piece together the rules according to which his parents and other adults seem to operate; in some cases, he will have to extrapolate different sets of rules for use in his dealings with different people. Just how such learning happens is not altogether clear. It does not seem to be

genitals is absorbed into a strict modesty training: 'it is a prerogative of young boys to lightly pinch girls' genitals if they are exposed. This privilege is exercised with hilarity and enthusiasm and is a most effective training method'. Nydegger, W. F. and Corinne: 'Tarong: an Ilocos Barrio in the Philippines'; in Beatrice Whiting, 1963, *op. cit.*

necessary for the parents to spell out the behavioural codes in any verbally explicit form, nor does the child need to make the rule system explicit even to himself in order to come to abide by it. Rather, merely through being exposed to *examples* of the rules in operation—especially as they are applied to his own conduct—the child somehow begins to incorporate the code into his behaviour. In other words, because the child's actions are evaluated and moulded in accordance with certain unstated rules, he begins to behave *as if* the rules themselves had been intuitively understood. There are a number of reasons for believing that learning of this kind is not at all uncommon in young children, even in the acquisition of concepts usually thought of as more intellectually mediated than cultural learning: for instance, the achievement of language seems to take place by similar means.[1] Language is in fact a particularly interesting example of the process, in that its rules *can* be stated (though perhaps not by the majority of parents), and indeed it is traditionally considered appropriate to state them when teaching a second language later on; yet most children learn to use it very adequately without becoming fully aware of the rules which they are obeying. One is tempted to describe such learning as 'intuitive' or 'unconscious', partly because no formal tuition is involved: more important, perhaps, is the fact that it is efficiently completed at an age when the child is still too young to understand, let alone to put into words, the underlying principles of what he has learned.

In modesty training, however, there is a further factor to be considered. It may be assumed that, were it possible to explain the rules of language to a small child, parents would be prepared to do so in order to aid his learning. Where modesty is concerned, however, it is not merely the youth of the child but the unwillingness of the parents which prevents full explanations being given. This is true even of those parents who believe themselves to be very frank with their small children and who are fully prepared to answer children's questions about reproduction. The reason is that the roots of physical modesty lie not in the *facts* of sexual reproduction but in the feelings, emotions

---

[1] This is now explicitly recognized by students of verbal learning. A useful review of work in this field will be found in George Mandler's 'Verbal learning': in Mandler, G. and Mussen, P.: *New Directions in Psychology III*, Holt, Rinehart and Winston, New York, 1967.

and desires that surround sex: and these, parents do not wish to discuss with their children. Thus the little girl who lies naked on the hearthrug with her legs spread wide open is likely to be diverted from that position, even in a household which allows nakedness, and certainly if visitors are present; but if she asks *why* she can't lie like that, she is unlikely to be told that she is in a conventional posture of sexual receptivity, though this is the real reason. Similarly, the small boy may be allowed to dance about bare after his bath; but if he has an erection while so doing, his mother will probably put his pyjamas on with some speed, though she will be unwilling to acknowledge to him her reason for cutting short his dancing-time. A five-year-old girl confided to her mother: "You know what me and Sarah do? Sometimes we *lick tongues*!—and then we say *Ugh*!—but actually I think it's rather nice." This mother laughed sympathetically, remembering her own childhood; others might murmur deprecatingly something about germs; but how many would enlighten the child to the extent of explaining that this is in fact how Daddies and Mummies kiss?

It appears, then, that even parents who pride themselves on their emancipation from prudish attitudes will in practice tend to draw the line at some point in the information which they will allow young children; and the reasoning on which this is based, if one traces it to its conclusion, seems to be as follows: 'Children are interested in sex only out of intellectual curiosity, which we will satisfy; they can't understand sexual feelings, let alone experience them, so it would be ridiculous to discuss them; but *just in case they can*, we had *better not* discuss them, lest we put ideas into their heads'. Thus we find the double view, which will be illustrated thoughout this chapter, that children's sex interest is 'only innocent' *and* that it is important to keep it so: the implication being that it might *not* be 'only innocent'. The practical outcome in terms of the training process is that parents expect children to obey the principles of modesty while at the same time they object to making those principles explicit. Over and above this, for large numbers of parents in our culture, failure to communicate goes much deeper, in that they feel a positive embarrassment about discussing with their children *any* aspect of sex, and, indeed, may avoid doing so at any greater length than the sharp suppression of 'rudeness'.

Perhaps enough has been said to indicate that the whole

process of the transmission of cultural norms, particularly with reference to attitudes on physical modesty, is extremely subtle and complex. We have suggested that the learning involved is 'implicit' rather than explicit, but at the same time it would be absurd to suppose that it takes place without any kind of verbal communication between parents and children, even in the most inhibited families. It is in fact the *quality* of the communication which takes place—its awkwardness, its use of polite euphemism and its significant omissions—which forms the subject matter of this chapter. Fortunately for the research worker, there are also social conventions which make it possible for mothers to discuss *with another wife and mother* their feelings about sex in so far as they are related to child upbringing: so that a woman may 'get all hot under the collar' at the thought of discussing with her children where babies come from ('It's the sort of thing I'm frightened of having at this stage', said the mother of three little girls, 'when they all come and ask me. I've always got a terrible fear about explaining')—yet she is quite able to discuss with the interviewer the *fact* that she cannot discuss it. Indeed, conversation on child-rearing provides a context for learning about an individual's attitudes towards sex which might otherwise be rather difficult to achieve.

The basic questions through which this area was investigated follow. It should be noted that the questions do not all appear as a single group; the way they fit into the interview can be seen in Appendix I.

47. Does he play with his private parts at all?
    (If NO) What would you do if he did—would you mind him doing that at this age?
    (If YES)
49. Do you try and stop him, or don't you really mind?
75. Of course, most children go through a stage when they think anything to do with the toilet is terribly funny. Has N got to that stage yet?
76. How do you feel about children giggling together over that sort of thing? Would you discourage it, or just take no notice?
77. What about children wanting to go to the toilet together, or wanting to look at each other when they're undressed? Would you mind them doing that?
78. Does N ever see you or his Daddy undressed?
    *prompt:* How do you feel about that?

79. Does he know where babies come from yet?
(If NO) Would you tell him if he wanted to know, or do you think he's too young?
(If *too young*) What would you say if he asked you?

'*He sits fiddling where he ought not to do—then I do shout at him*'
The questions which we asked about genital play are substantially the same as those we originally used in our study of one-year-olds; and, in terms of maternal attitudes, our conclusions are not at variance with those we arrived at then.[1] At that stage, however, only mothers whose children did in fact sometimes play with their genitals were asked about their attitudes, which meant that discussion was confined to a minority sample; at four, we introduced a methodological difference in that every mother was questioned about her attitude, whether or not the behaviour was said to occur. In 1963, we wrote: '. . . we suspect that the cultural pressures are such that very few mothers would go to the extent of ignoring masturbation altogether, once their children had passed the toddler stage'; and this suspicion is borne out by results at four. At this age, the great majority of mothers (90%) admit that they would be disturbed by the occurrence of genital play at least to the extent that they would discourage it in one way or another; and, although the response of the remaining 10% was finally classified as 'ignore or permit' (see Table XXXVI), some mothers ignore such behaviour in practice not because they are unconcerned, but rather because they feel or have been told that this is the best way of bringing it to an end, and that drawing attention to it may cause it to be intensified. The quotations below give an idea of the attitudes behind permissive responses.

Technical lecturer's wife:

He does it at bath-times and things like that. At the moment he thinks it's really wonderful, you know, he really has a great interest—especially when we had our little girl, you know, and he knew that she hadn't got the same as what he'd got; he feels he's one over her at the moment, and he takes a delight in showing her—yes, he delights in showing that he's got something that she hasn't got. It's only playful, like. We're quite open with him on those sort of things—it's no good hiding those sorts of things.

[1] Newson, John and Elizabeth, 1963, *op. cit.*, pp. 127–132, 190–192.

M

**Cabinet maker's wife (social work trained):**

Well, I don't mind a little, you know—because they all do it, don't they? Janie (6) does. And as long as I feel they're not doing it *too* much, I let them do it.

**Unemployed labourer's wife:**

All little boys play with themselves when they're babies. I mean, as soon as you take their nappy off, ever since they were tiny, their hand goes straight down for it. There's nothing you can do about it.

**Sub-editor's wife:**

I don't like her to really—I try to take her mind off it without drawing her attention to it too much.

**Decorator's wife (herself a teacher):**

I had suspicions at one time—when I went into her room she looked guilty, so I started giving her things to go to bed with—a book. I read in a book that this was what you should do.

**Laboratory technician's wife:**

I'd try and divert his attention. I mean, it's pretty natural, isn't it, that they do. I think the more you make of it, the worse it's likely to become, isn't it?

However, while many mothers preface their remarks with words like 'natural', 'normal' or 'just innocent', only a small proportion are prepared to regard genital play as both natural and *acceptable*. For the majority, the issue is not whether the child should be discouraged or not, but rather of *how* he should be discouraged: a matter of selecting the most appropriate strategy to check behaviour which is assumed to be undesirable. Thus the 90% of mothers who discourage genital play most clearly divide on the question of whether or not punishment is resorted to. Table XXXVI gives an analysis of mothers' responses to genital play, actual or hypothetical, broken down by occupational class. Punishment consists almost entirely of smacking, and makes up the bulk of the 'Punishment or threat' category; it seemed more appropriate to include threats (mainly of the 'it'll fall off' variety) in this category rather than the previous one, but the numbers involved are negligible.

TABLE XXXVI

*Maternal attitudes towards four-year-olds' genital play, analysed by social class*

|  | I & II | IIIwc | IIIman | IV | V | All (random) |
|---|---|---|---|---|---|---|
|  | % | % | % | % | % | % |
| Ignored/permitted | 17 | 11 | 10 | 5 | 10 | 10 |
| Discouraged without punishment | 78 | 71 | 54 | 54 | 42 | 59 |
| Punishment or threat | 5 | 18 | 36 | 41 | 48 | 31 |
| Genital play discouraged at one year (actual cases only) | 25 | 50 | 57 | 69 | 93 |  |

It is clear that, as the child grows older, the mother becomes much more likely to take action against genital play; and the change seems to occur for three distinct but related reasons. In the first place, at four the child may be considered a more active participant in this sort of play and therefore more emotionally disturbing to the onlooker: as a baby, he engages in exploration of all parts of his body, so that the mother is more easily able to think of this particular exploration as 'just innocent', whereas the four-year-old, it is felt, 'knows what he's doing'. Secondly, with the child's increase in age the mother becomes more concerned lest both she and the child come under social censure for this behaviour—visitors will be embarrassed, and the mothers of younger children with whom her child plays may take an intolerant view—and this will weigh with her, even if she has no strong personal feelings about it herself. Thirdly, once she has decided that the behaviour should be checked, she now has a wider range of methods of dissuasion open to her than was available when he was a baby: he is more sensitive to subtle tones of voice, he may be controlled by reasoning or by threats, or she may now feel that smacking is justifiable whereas she 'wouldn't have believed in it' at a year.

The social class trend, now based on the total sample of 700 cases, still broadly corroborates that found earlier. It can be shown that significantly more mothers in Class I and II fall into the category 'Ignored/permitted' ($p < 0.02$). In particular, however, the class trend in the punishment of genital play is exceptionally striking, showing a consistent increase through the classes from only 5% in the professional and managerial group to 48% in the unskilled group. Initially, however, it must be interpreted with caution, since two possible explanations might be suggested for its occurrence. While it may be an indication of an increase in prudery as one moves down the social scale, it could simply reflect a class-linked preference for punishment rather than verbal discouragement when dealing with mis- demeanours of any kind. It is not possible, on the statistical evidence alone, to assess the relative importance of each of these factors in contributing to the observed overall trend, although one may safely suppose that the two factors reinforce each other. Fortunately, attitudes to other aspects of sexual modesty, discussed later in this chapter, are not contaminated by the punishment issue, and provide a forceful indication of the link between prudery and social class. The question of punishment will be dealt with separately in the next chapter, and need not be pursued here.

Some of the attitudes of the nine-out-of-ten mothers who would take action against genital play may now be illustrated. The first three are typical of the uncertainty which exists among some mothers who tend on the whole to be rather permissive generally, but find that this behaviour offers unexpected perplexities.

Machine operator's wife:

He's quite *interested*, but I wouldn't say he *played* with it. When he's undressed, he's quite aware of himself, but he's too occupied in other things—I think it's usually when a child is bored. I'd tell him it's rude, but I don't know whether I'm saying the right thing—there's a lot of thoughts on this matter in these kind of things, isn't there?

Salesman's wife:

I think he mostly does it in bed. I usually say, you know, "What are you doing?" But I try not to say very much—I more or less

pull his hands away without saying anything. I don't *speak* to
him about it. (Long pause.) He's very interested in that, because
his little sister hasn't got one, and he's always asking me about it,
about three or four times a week—who has a tail and who has
not. He seems to be *too* interested in the subject. Most children
never notice that their sisters are different. But he noticed she
was different as soon as she was born.

Tailor's presser's wife:

> Yes, he has a bit, just lately. . . . I haven't quite worked it out yet,
> what to do. I shall have to see. I might see the doctor about it,
> to be on the safe side.

Although genital play clearly is potentially emotionally
disturbing for the mother, this should not lead us to overlook
the simple fact that it is also mildly unaesthetic, in the same way
that eating with the mouth open or picking the nose may be
considered unaesthetic. This in itself might be enough reason
for parents to try to prevent it, and a few otherwise permissive
mothers do discourage it on social occasions only. It must also
be borne in mind, however, that a mother might *feel* disturbed
but choose to present the issue to the child as a matter of ordinary politeness. The mothers in the next group of quotations
manage to keep the heat out of the situation by using this
rationale.

University teacher's wife:

> Well, I discourage it a little, especially at meal times, because it
> offends me, but I try not to make too much of it, I know it's
> wrong to do so; so I try to discourage it at *inconvenient* times,
> although I know he must do it at night.

Advertising manager's wife:

> I think *mind* is the wrong word; I think I'd expect him to under-
> stand at this age that it wasn't the done thing in society; I wouldn't
> tell him it was a dirty habit or anything.

Publisher's wife:

> I think at this age I probably would say to him, "I don't think
> you should do that"; I don't think I should make a *fuss* about
> it, not to draw a lot of attention to it. (If you said "I don't think
> you should do that", and he said "Why not?"—what *sort* of

358 FOUR YEARS OLD IN AN URBAN COMMUNITY

reason would you give him?) Well . . . I should say . . . well, for one thing, those sort of things, as you're growing older, *aren't done; other people* don't like to see it. I wouldn't sort of make an issue that you shouldn't because . . . I mean, I certainly wouldn't say it was *rude*, or anything like that; but I should try and find a logical explanation, that you shouldn't do these things because . . . well, people think they just aren't quite the thing to do. I should probably say some people are silly, try and . . . but I wouldn't make a real *fuss* about it.

Clerk's wife:
I'd probably try to explain to her that it's not a very nice thing to do, not the sort of thing that *ladies* do. . . .

Traveller's wife:
I'd just say, "Well, you don't see your Daddy doing things like that", and hope . . .

The rest of the verbally discouraging category are more definite in their attitude and leave the child in little doubt.

Miner's wife:
Oh yes, I would mind, I'd be very upset; I wouldn't like him to. I'd tell him it's rude, it's naughty, he mustn't do that, he'll be poorly if he does it.

Rigger's mate's wife:
I tell him that's naughty—those sort of things are not to play with.

Chauffeur's wife:
I'd just say, "You'll hurt yourself doing that, and not only that, the other children'll laugh at you"—try and pass it off like that.

Hospital porter's wife:
I think it's because he's got to the age when he knows he's got something and wants to show it off. I just say "Put your trousers down and don't be a dirty boy—who wants to see your bingo?"

Warnings of being 'poorly', or of hurting the place or making it sore, approach the borderline of threats; however, we have only included the more drastic threats in the category that is mainly taken up with actual punishment. Some of these follow:

it must be reiterated that there is only a handful of such cases. Occasionally a warning will be implied rather than directly stated: such a one was the remark of a hosiery trimmer's wife, 'I used to say "That's got to last you a lifetime!"', which was not, however, counted as a threat.

Builder's wife:
> He used to sit and watch television, you know, and put his hand there over his trousers; and one day his Dad said to him, "Come here", he said; "If you keep doing that, it'll drop off and you'll have to go to the hospital!" He never did it again.

Insurance agent's wife:
> Yes, I'd try and do something about it—probably what might happen, you know, your fingers might drop off or something like that. . . .

Electrician's wife:
> I just tell him it'll drop off if he's not careful. I don't shout at him, I don't think you ought to, do you?

Clerk's wife:
> I tell him it'll drop off and all sorts, but it don't make any difference.

Finally, some quotations from the mothers who physically punish for genital play: one in twenty in the professional and managerial class; almost one in two, and the majority group, in the unskilled manual class.

Departmental manager's wife:
> (Laughed) You asked me that last time, and I said no, and I was thinking, I'd have to say Yes if you asked me now. (He does do that?) Well, it's at the table when he refuses to eat, funnily enough—that's the only time. (Do you try and stop him, or don't you really mind?) Oh, definitely, yes. I give him a sharp rap across the knuckles. (And does this happen most mealtimes?) Yes.

Miner's wife:
> I'd smack his hand or leg and make him know it would do more harm than good—"Tommy, that's a very wrong thing to do, love".

Machine operator's wife:

> Once or twice I have caught him, but it's not a habit. I smack him hard. I don't believe in anything like that. I tell him it's dirty.

Miner's wife:

> I think it's bad—if I did see her, I'd smack her for it. She used to do it when she was a small baby, and I used to smack her for it, and now if I did see her she'd get smacked.

Twist hand's wife:

> Smack him—I would definitely—I think it's awful. Give his hand a good smack and tell him it's rude.

Labourer's wife:

> Oh, I *should* stop him—I should slap him. I don't like smacking them, but I should do for that.

Window cleaner's wife:

> Yes, I *would* mind—I'd go up the wall! Yes, I should smack and point out how naughty it was, and if it did continue I should go to the doctor.

We were in fact more interested in attitudes towards genital play than in the behaviour itself and its incidence: for the record, 17% of the children were known to behave in this way at four, and no class differences were found. The absence of class differences is in itself interesting, in view of the massive divergence in attitude: one might expect less genital play to be reported further down the social scale, both because it had been suppressed and because these mothers might be more unwilling to admit its occurrence. One can only assume both honesty of report and that punitive measures are no more efficient than either verbal discouragement or *laissez-faire* tactics.

### 'a little family vulgarity . . .'

Most children of this age have only recently learned to manage alone in the lavatory—indeed, as we have seen, 41% still like to have at least some help from their mothers. They may still have difficulty in doing up their clothes or in pulling the chain, and it is rather a lot to expect that they should lock themselves away in complete privacy to cope entirely on their own. Often, then, an older child will be asked to go with a younger brother or sister to provide companionship and assistance. Again, when a small child has a friend in to play, the two children will often want to visit the lavatory together, either because one must show the other the way or because the urge to 'go' is contagious. At the same time, the child of this age is becoming increasingly aware that uncovering the genital area is not socially acceptable, that his mother prefers him to be discreet if he needs to ask for the lavatory in public, that it is usual for the sexes to be segregated in public conveniences, and that it is considered 'rude' to show an obvious interest in the details of another person's private anatomy or to be curious about the way acts of elimination are performed by other people.

The child will also soon sense that lack of privacy can cause grownups or older children considerable embarrassment, and that to be surprised while using the lavatory may be thought of as simultaneously shocking and funny. Once at school, probably most children will be exposed to the time-honoured little-boys' competitive games of shocking little girls or 'peeing-up-the-wall', so that the majority of four-year-olds will have learned from older siblings that bare bottoms are laughable, even if their own peer-group has not yet caught on. The whole situation thus provides an introduction to a further small group of questions on attitudes to sex interest in the child, via the issue of whether ribaldry should be tolerated. An analysis of mothers' responses to this question is given in Table XXXVII.

### TABLE XXXVII

*Mothers' attitudes towards 'giggling over the toilet'*

|  | I & II | IIIwc | IIIman | IV | V | All (random) |
|---|---|---|---|---|---|---|
|  | % | % | % | % | % | % |
| Giggling ignored | 60 | 45 | 45 | 44 | 54 | 48 |
| Mildly discouraged (scorn, 'silly') | 32 | 46 | 34 | 29 | 21 | 33 |
| Strongly discouraged, punished | 8 | 9 | 21 | 27 | 25 | 19 |

M*

It is fairly clear from these results that the majority of parents do not regard 'giggling over the toilet' as a particularly serious offence; nearly half ignore it altogether, and a further third do no more than mildly deprecate it as 'silly'. Just under one in five takes a firm line and would react with anger or punishment.

**Cabinet maker's wife (social work trained):**

Well—I let them do it up to a certain point, you know; because, as you say, they all come to that stage. Janie (6) has, you know; and she, er, likes to show her bottom and things like that; or if they make a rude noise, they joke about it; things like that, you know. But, as I say, it is just a phase they get to, and I let them joke about it and do what they like, as long as they don't go too far with it, you know.

**Labourer's wife:**

I'm always amused at them. A few of their jokes are quite funny; I'm tickled at them.

**Publisher's wife:**

We did have one stage where Martin (6) came home and someone had taught him "Three old ladies locked in the lavatory", and I did find that they thought that was very funny, both of them; but I pointed out to Martin that that wasn't a very nice song . . . it just died a natural death. I think it's just a stage they go through, just a form of schoolboy humour. I try not to . . . after all, I think a little *family* vulgarity is something that . . . I mean, it's going to take *some* form, and I think if it's in the home you know where it is . . . I don't want to drive anything underground.

**University teacher's wife:**

I would say rather scathingly that it was rather babyish, not very polite or something like that, but I wouldn't harp on it.

**Mine worker's wife:**

Tracey started that, she was saying "I'll smack your bum" and "Noddy's bum" and everybody's bottom was "bum"; and she came to me for a bit of love, and I said "I don't want to love you". She said "Why?"—"Well, you're a rude little girl, and I don't like rude little girls".

**Miner's wife:**

I don't like him talking like that to other children; I should give him a good smack, because I think it leads to him being—you know—I think they get dirty-minded, and I don't like dirty minds, do you?

As far as class differences are concerned, there is some similarity between these results and those in the previous table. An interesting change is that Class V mothers this time join with Class I and II mothers in being significantly more likely than the rest to ignore ribald behaviour altogether; those who do discourage it, however, are as likely as other working-class mothers to do so very firmly, which is rare for middle-class mothers generally. Once again, the two factors of prudery and punishment are confounded.

### 'They come to be inquisitive soon enough'

The next question, on children 'wanting to look at each other when they're undressed', followed on naturally enough. Here, as elsewhere, the coding categories which were eventually chosen arose out of the spontaneous qualifications which the mothers themselves made in elaborating their answers. Fortunately this time there was no tendency to confuse feelings about modesty with attitudes towards punishment: the essential distinction which emerged was that between *seeing* and *looking*. Some mothers emphasize that it is permissible for children to be naked together just for so long as no interest is shown in each other's bodies: rather in the same way as it was occasionally suggested, in our first study, that a baby must be weaned from the breast 'once he got to know', i.e. started looking. For a larger group of mothers, it does not seem to occur to them to make this sort of reservation; though this does not imply, of course, that they would allow unlimited sexual exploration: most mothers will draw the line at some point, but some mothers are distinctly more permissive than others, in the sense of ignoring a certain amount of mutual interest and examination. A further distinction seemed to be called for to allow for special restrictions which some mothers made against children of the opposite sex. Finally, a three-way classification of attitudes was arrived at as follows:

1. *Sex interest allowed.* 'With her little friend Garry, when he goes to the toilet, she looks at him as if to say "Oh, he's different", but we don't take any notice.' 'She's queried her

brothers (7 and 11)—she's had a good look around them and wanted to know why they were different and I've explained that.' 'Derek often wants to go in the toilet while Heather's there, and I don't discourage it because I think the more they get to know about each other the better—I think that's one of the blessings of having a mixed family.'

2. *'See' either sex; 'look' only at same sex.* 'When we've been at the sea and that, she's seen little boys, but as for *individuals*, no, I wouldn't encourage that.' 'They don't pay heed to one another. (If they did seem interested, would you mind?) Oh yes, I would, I'd put a stop to that, I'd tell them that's very naughty, that's not nice at all.' 'I was helping getting Billy (baby cousin) undressed one day, and on his pot, you know; she came up and had a look and she says "Oh, *look*, Mummy!" Well, I just took him off and said to her "Don't be cheeky".'

3. *'See' same sex only; no 'looking' allowed.* 'That I *don't* like. She knows now, she'll always, when she's undressing, take off her knickers behind the chair if the boys are around.' 'Oh, I don't believe in anything like that. I'd make them go separate. I don't let them look at each other. I make them turn their head away. I say to him, "Turn your head while Terry gets undressed".' 'I wouldn't let them have a bath together, they're always separate there (3 girls, ages 4–11).'

In coding mothers' responses, cases were only assigned to the extreme categories (1 and 3) if the attitude was unambiguously specified; doubtful cases were placed in the middle category. Despite this, it can be seen from the overall results in Table XXXVIII that the middle category was in fact used less frequently than the other two; this indicates a fairly sharp polarization of attitudes on this question.

That this polarization of attitudes is a function of social class is demonstrated very clearly in the table: once again, it is the Class I and II mothers who stand out as exceptionally permissive, although there is a well-defined and substantial class trend throughout the whole table. Exactly half of the Class V mothers allow the child to show no interest in other children's bodies at all, while well over half the professional and managerial class mothers permit an active interest in the anatomy of children of the opposite sex. If we remember that a difference of 10% between any two adjacent categories is normally enough to prove a statistically significant difference between them, it can be seen that the overall pattern of differences is very striking indeed.

It should be borne in mind that the attitudes assessed in this table sometimes apply to hypothetical cases: not all children had the opportunity to observe nakedness in children of the opposite sex, perhaps because they were singletons or had only like-sexed siblings. Mothers of such families sometimes realized

TABLE XXXVIII

*Mothers' attitudes to children seeing each other naked, analysed by social class*

|  | I & II | IIIwc | IIIman | IV | V | All (random) |
|---|---|---|---|---|---|---|
|  | % | % | % | % | % | % |
| 1. Sex interest allowed | 62 | 45 | 35 | 39 | 25 | 40 |
| 2. 'See' either sex; 'look' only at same sex | 21 | 30 | 30 | 21 | 25 | 27 |
| 3. 'See' same sex only; no 'looking' allowed | 17 | 25 | 35 | 40 | 50 | 33 |

that their own attitude might be changed by practical experience of a mixed family: 'When you've not experienced it, you can't really say, can you?' A number of parents felt that it was a great advantage to have both boys and girls in a family, and that this afforded the most 'natural' way for children to learn about sex differences; a few who 'didn't believe in it' thought that having a mixed family simply made it rather difficult to achieve necessary decorum, but some were equally careful with a single-sexed group.

Driver-salesman's wife:

I *don't* let them. With being a big family, they do have to get undressed together, but it's done *proper*, you know what I mean? If they were naughty about that, I should have to find words to alter that (8 mixed children, aged 4–16).

Window cleaner's wife:

> Well, they don't really have much chance to look at each other, because I'm here when they're undressing and I make sure they keep covered up and get changed as quickly as they can—I don't like them to look (4 boys, aged 4–9 years).

One aspect of children's sex interest, which we did not directly investigate, but which was quite often mentioned spontaneously, is the games which children play in which the primary aim is sexual exploration. It appears that there are certain games at the mention of which the mother is immediately suspicious of the motives involved: 'mothers and fathers' alerts her to possibilities of unseemly behaviour, while 'doctors' or 'hospitals' are often banned altogether for a whole street. Here again, however, mothers vary a good deal as to how far they wish to restrict their children; some are aware of the nature of the game, yet feel that it should be allowed so long as no child becomes upset or frightened (and so long as much older children are not involved). However, because these are essentially group games, and because curiosity tends to take this form between friends rather than siblings, a social situation of some delicacy can develop between mothers, especially where they differ in attitude or where one child is considered to have 'led the others on'. Some examples of mothers' comments on this topic are given, not in illustration of any quantitative analysis, which we cannot make, but simply to show the sort of feelings which are aroused; it is perhaps of interest that the subject was often raised early in the interview, triggered by the question 'Is there any sort of play you don't allow'—which had not been intended to refer to sex play!

Stonecaster's wife:

> We had some trouble about that last summer round here—with the little boys and little girls shutting themselves in the outhouses and that sort of thing, and I used to watch wherever they was, and if they shut themselves into these little tents they make, and that sort of thing, I used to go and fetch him out. He used to make a lot of fuss about it, but "Out!—come on, out! Let's have you play out here!" But there was all of us stopping them, all round here. Eight of them always used to be messing about in the outhouses and taking their clothes off. And with him being the only boy!—it used to be a proper exhibition for them, I think. I think they've probably outgrown it now.

Departmental manager's wife:

There's been one or two occasions recently when she's been with a little girl together and they've been playing doctors and nurses and looking at each other . . . you know, I think it depends on the other parents in that case. They've been together, looking at their tummies, and *her* mother doesn't like it, and smacks her and takes her in, you see. Well, I feel a bit awful about it, because I think really she's making too much of it.

Lorry driver's wife:

Well . . . in fact we've had a bit of a . . . there's a child she plays with, a little boy, and then there's a little girl and this one: and we've found them in the passage-way with their clothes up—showing their bottoms. And I've been to all their parents and told them. And we've tried to tell them that it's wrong and they mustn't do that—it's rude—try to put it the best possible way we can, because we know they're innocent and they don't realize what they *are* doing. But I've been this morning, as a matter of fact, to the boy's mother, and she said she'd see his father and he'd give him a good talking-to.

Research chemist's wife:

Her little friend introduced 'hospitals', where that seemed to be the main examination, and the other child's mother disapproved strongly of that. I'm not sure where I stand on this, really, because Eleanor wasn't guilty about it; but I think she is now, and I think it would be difficult if they went on playing hospitals in that way. They *do* play hospitals—but not always in that way. I have a feeling actually that they shouldn't play it, because I think it *worries* the other one. I *think* I don't mind; but I'm not sure.

Plasterer's wife:

They play shops, but I don't believe in children playing mothers and fathers, because that may be very *bad;* and I had to give them a slap when they was playing in the yard, because some of the children was going a bit too far with it, you know, so I stopped them playing that game.

One difficulty which makes the repressive line a little more understandable is that, as we pointed out in Chapter 5, the mother in the older working-class areas may have no power to control the composition of the neighbourhood play-group except by the rather drastic and impracticable measure of keeping her child indoors. Since she cannot exclude 'undesirable' playmates, she thus has the anxiety that children with 'unhealthy' attitudes towards sex, particularly older children, may exploit and corrupt her own child. The difference between professional-class and lower working-class wives, however, lies in which attitudes they take to be unhealthy. The professional class mother tends to feel that guilt is unhealthy, and that these games are acceptable so long as the child appears guilt-free; the research chemist's wife quoted above added later: 'I don't mind if it's just curiosity; I don't mind if they don't *look* guilty about it. But if they look guilty about it, I think there's usually something wrong'; and an advertising manager's wife said: 'I think if you tell them not to, it gets a bit unhealthy—they start doing it behind your back'. At the other end of the social scale, however, the main aim seems to be to instil a sense of guilt into the child, and morally-toned words such as 'bad', 'naughty' or 'rude' are used to the child, even though he is also described as 'innocent'.

*'When I dress me down here, I say "Turn your heads!"—and they do'*

For the child to be allowed to see his parents unclothed may be considered a stage further on in permissiveness. Once again, three categories were found to be adequate for coding the replies given to this question, and these can be defined quite straightforwardly as follows:

1. Child permitted to see both parents undressed.
2. Child only permitted to see parent of same sex as himself undressed.
3. Child not permitted to see either parent undressed.

It should perhaps be mentioned that the earlier distinction between 'seeing' and 'looking' came up again here: some parents were careful to explain that, while they would not mind the child seeing them briefly or 'inadvertently', 'in the natural course of events', they would not approve of 'parading around' in front of the children (one father expressed this view rather oddly by apparently taking the Lord Chamberlain's view, that the parents' nakedness would be permissible provided they didn't actually move). Clearly the parents' own embarrassment

WHO TOLD THEE THAT THOU WAST NAKED? 369

at having their bodies scrutinized by the child was often a factor
—'I can't say I'm actually *pleased* when I see his beady eyes
looking!' said a hosiery mechanic's wife—and some conflict was
felt between what was felt to be the rational approach and a
certain underlying personal squeamishness. 'We wouldn't like a
constant regular audience', said a shop manager's wife, 'because
he will come in and have a really good look—I have to try not
to laugh'; and a social worker's wife explained: 'I don't particularly *like* it, but I think it's part of living in a family, I mean it's
bound to happen. You must just not appear to object. There's
no *rational* reason why one should object, I think'.

Apart from the washing and dressing period in the morning
(and it must be remembered that 13% of these four-year-olds
sleep in the parents' room), the issue normally arises when the
parents want to change their clothes during the day, when the
children are up and about and may come wandering into the
bedroom; or, for mothers in particular, when they want to take
a bath during the day. Children of this age are still likely to
make frequent checks that their parents are accessible, and to
be distressed if they are directly excluded from the room. Difficulties are especially likely to occur, of course, in houses which
have no bathroom: the mother may well choose the daytime,
when the older members of the family are out, as the only time in
which she can secure enough privacy to wash all over; and if she
feels that modesty is necessary before her pre-school children,
this will certainly curtail her freedom of activity. 'If he comes in,
I don't stand myself out for show', said a foreman's wife, 'I'd
use a bit more discretion, kind of thing; I don't believe in
shutting him out'; not many mothers could be so firm as the
bricklayer's wife who said that, because her little boy had
laughed about 'Mummy standing in her petticoat', she would
now 'always send them out in the yard and always bolt the door
and have a wash down, and never let them see a thing—*never*'.

Before illustrating parents' attitudes further, an analysis of
the incidence of the three categories described above will show
how closely these feelings are linked to social class: indeed, the
correlation is still more striking than that presented in the last
table.

Both at a subjective level and in terms of the way in which
mothers' opinions were expressed, there seems to be a greater
behavioural distance between allowing the child to see both

parents and restricting him to his like-sexed parent than between the minor and the major restrictions. Thus, if one chose to make a single distinction between the more and the less permissive parents in this area, category 1 would most naturally separate off from categories 2 and 3 taken together. In these terms, it can be said that more than two-thirds of all these mothers fall into the less permissive category: this means that the attitude which is *most characteristic* of mothers in Class I and II is in fact a minority attitude for the population as a whole. Perhaps it is also worth noting that, while the greatest divergence is between working-class and middle-class, sharp changes in attitude also occur both between the two middle-class groups and (especially in category 3) between the skilled or semi-skilled and the unskilled groups. This last difference was also noticeable in the table on attitudes towards children seeing each other naked.

TABLE XXXIX

*Mothers' attitudes towards child seeing parents unclothed*

|  | I & II | IIIwc | IIIman | IV | V | All (random) |
|---|---|---|---|---|---|---|
|  | % | % | % | % | % | % |
| 1. Child may see both parents | 59 | 45 | 27 | 24 | 15 | 32 |
| 2. May see only like-sexed parent | 22 | 23 | 22 | 22 | 17 | 22 |
| 3. Child may see neither parent | 19 | 32 | 51 | 54 | 68 | 46 |

With the quantitative data in mind, the picture may be filled out by the mothers themselves. Among those who did not allow the child to see either parent, there were some who had undressed in his presence when he was a good deal younger, but now felt that he was becoming 'too knowing' or 'too conscious'; an opposite view, not altogether contradictory, was that older children, being more discreet in their interest, could be allowed but not a young child, whose 'innocence' needed to be preserved: 'they come to be inquisitive soon enough, without you making them inquisitive', as a miner's wife said ruefully. Among these parents there was a feeling that this sort of knowledge could be dangerous in the sense of worrying the child unduly. A machine operator's wife said she thought it was 'wrong', and her husband backed her up with 'I think it's frightening to a child, you know'; while a storekeeper's wife agreed that 'at this age it's not right —he's too young—at this age they brood about these things. He thinks a lot—I think it would trouble his mind.'

Opinion was very much divided as to whether children were in fact interested in what they saw, and, if they were, whether it mattered. For the child to regard the body as 'natural' was the aim of the permissive mothers, though not all of them could say 'it doesn't bother me in the least': some were learning from the child to be relaxed over this. 'They're so unconcerned and undisturbed by it that it just sets you completely at rest, and you *can't* feel embarrassed really', said a teacher's wife; and a production manager's wife thought it was 'silly to make a big mystery of it: if they see you undress, they just take it in their stride and treat it as a natural thing'. As usual, however, there could be more than one view on what was natural or normal.

Plant engineer's wife:

> Well, we don't let it worry us, we just ignore it, he just thinks "Oh, Daddy is bigger than me", and that's it. Oh yes, I think the more you try to hide it, the more you make them want to come and have a look; so we just ignore it and act normal.

Newsagent's wife:

> I don't think it's necessary. It's like the business of wandering in and out of each other's bathrooms—if you are normally happily married, you *don't*; sex isn't the beginning and end of everything. And I don't see any point in allowing a child of mine to ever see his mother and father undressed—we don't walk about undressed anyway.

Some mothers were in no doubt that the child *was* interested, having already been the recipients of comments and questions; a few had thereupon decided that the time had come to call a halt to permissiveness. Ability to tolerate and to respond to the child's interest varied considerably, partly according to whether the mother's chief emotion was amusement or embarrassment.

Miner's wife:

> Not now—he did use to see me when he was smaller, but he asked me what *those* were, and I said "cherries", just in the moment;

and you know he's never forgot it; and he does sometimes now ask if his cherries are going to get big like Mummy's. I got quite embarrassed about that; so I don't do it now. I don't *mind* him knowing, if he knows it in a nice way; I don't mind him knowing where he came from, even (she does not in fact intend to tell him until he is 7 or 8, even if asked); but I want him to know it nicely, not dirty. I'm terrified of him growing up to have a dirty mind (same miner's wife as quoted on page 362).

Laboratory assistant's wife:
She always comes into the bath with me. I don't mind, except that the last couple of times she keeps saying "Why are you so big, Mummy?" or "Why are you so fat?" So I told her she can't come in any more, if she's going to be rude.

Cycle worker's wife:
Well, I dress me in the morning, and Philip's awake, so he sees me through the bars of his crib, you see. If he asks me any questions, I try to answer them as best I can, like. In fact, the other morning he wanted to know why I'd got three bellies! I said to him, "Well, that's because I'm your Mummy, all mummies have three". But they catch you unawares, you see, you don't know how to answer them for the best, do you?

Publisher's wife:
He does make remarks sometimes, I mean about a year ago he remarked on the fact that I'd got two big fat tummies that Daddy hadn't got, you see; and of course I just said that was Mummy's bosom—I think I said bosom, or breast or something; and he said "What's bosom?" and I just said ladies are made that way.

Lorry driver's wife:
She doesn't see her Dad undressed, but she sees me. Oh, she goes in the bath with me sometimes, it doesn't worry me. And if she asks questions, I say "Oh, shurrup, you'll get them when you're big!"

If a child asks awkward questions or makes embarrassing comments (for either of these adjectives, the word *frank* may be substituted), the mother may feel that it is only a short step from her ears to those of the neighbours; and to some mothers this is a deterrent, or at least produces one or two qualms. The publisher's wife quoted above spoke for many permissive mothers when she added:

> I think a little frank curiosity doesn't hurt them. I should expect curiosity; but on the other hand I should expect questions; and once I'd answered those frankly, I should hope that it would just sort of pass. If it didn't, I suppose I should have to start talking in terms of, you know, what other people think. But, as I say, they've got to grow up in a framework; and, while I don't want to drive it underground, I don't want a child going round saying things that are going to put *him* in a bad light with other people; it's a very difficult thing, I feel.

A labourer's wife said 'I don't like her to see me, I don't think it's right, not the age what she is now, because I think she'd giggle and tell folks, kind of thing'; the retort 'What is there to tell?' would not have been enough to reassure Mrs Windsor, who, like her husband, a cook, had been brought up with 'everything hidden from you', and who was now breaking away from her upbringing with some trepidation:

> Not often her Daddy, but she *has* seen him. She goes in the bathroom with me, and wants to wash my back and that; well, I never discourage that at all. Her Daddy tries to—he gets upstairs before she does! (Your husband's a bit shy?) Yes, well, he is; because I mean, the things she comes out with!—"Oh, Daddy's got a bigger one than Harry!" and things like that, I mean . . . well, *we* don't mind that so much, but other people would think, "Well, what do they *do*?" Well, I mean, we do *nothing*; but at the same time, if a child comes out with talk like that, well, if anyone else heard, they'd say, "Well, what do people like that *do*?" We're not flaunting it, but at the same time she's a child that soon picks things up. The same as this about the chest—"Daddy's little here, and Mummy isn't—you're bigger, aren't you?" She doesn't miss much, and if she wants to say something, I mean, she'll say it. (So it's other people you're bothered about, rather than within the family?) Well, really, yes; 'cause that's my way of bringing them up, and it isn't everyone else's.

Mrs Windsor was right in her belief that people with different ideas from herself would be shocked and critical.

Hosiery worker's wife:

> Well, we both feel very strong about it. You see, I've got a sister-in-law, and—my husband and I think it's disgraceful!—the things they do in front of the children. My husband says they can't have any pride. Her boys are five and eight, and she even has a bath in front of them, and my husband thinks it's *awful*. And if *he* only wants to change his trousers, he won't allow Victor in that room, and I don't allow him either.

Lorry driver's wife:

> I don't think it's really a bad thing—not if it's the same sex. (You wouldn't like her to see her Daddy?) No, I wouldn't, no; because that's entirely different, isn't it? I mean, mother and daughter is one thing. Now, the lady across the road, I know for a *fact*—now she's got two children—and she herself has told me that her children get in the bath with their father! Now that's a boy and a girl—entirely different sex, you see! Now I don't agree with *that*—I mean, the boy and his father is one thing, that's the same sex, but not a little girl of five with a man of *his* age; I do think that's really . . . a bit beyond *my* taste in things!

Among both mothers and fathers there were some who were prevented by personal 'shyness' from being relaxed in this situation, even though they might think a less prudish attitude more sensible. 'I'm very funny', said a bulldozer driver's wife, 'I don't get out of bed until the door's shut—it's silly in a way. I don't even undress in front of my husband; I don't know where it's come from—I've been the same always'. Sometimes there was a clash of attitude:

Decorator's wife (herself a primary teacher):

> Her Daddy always tries to dress by himself, and she's started to ask questions about it, because I've always dressed in front of her; and he's not quite sure what ought to be done about this, he seems to think there should be some sort of modesty. I think he *should* dress in front of her, otherwise it's going to be difficult for her later on. You see, they always *did* in my family, but *his* family were different, you see—they're Yorkshire people, and I think Yorkshire people seem to be like that, don't you?

A problem of a slightly different kind was voiced by a professional engineer's wife:

I think . . . had we *thought* about it a bit more, when Lisanne (eldest, age 6½) was a baby, we might have done differently. I don't *mind* them seeing me at all, and they see me washing, from the waist up; but they never see us in the bath or anything. But you see we just didn't think of it when they were babies, and now it's difficult. I think probably it's better if they *are* brought up to take it as natural, and if we'd thought about it then we'd have brought them up to see us in the nude, or anyhow we would have discussed it. I often wish we'd thought about it a bit more.

We should not leave the topic of parents' attitudes towards nudity without mentioning that a few parents were more prudish than our question allowed for, in that they did not permit little girls to be seen naked by their own fathers. We had in fact encountered this earlier, when one or two fathers had been said not to change baby girls' nappies for this reason; but we had not thought to include a direct question on it at four. Information was volunteered in a handful of cases when the things which fathers do for their children were being discussed: 'Well, I undress her *to a point*, you know' explained a miner, and his wife hastened to add, 'He don't undress her any further'; while a fitter's wife said firmly 'We don't believe in the father bathing or dressing or undressing the girls'. Obviously it is not practicable for the mother to take the same line with her boys; nevertheless, in one or two cases there were already signs that the seed had taken root. An Irish labourer's wife said of her four-year-old son: 'As a matter of fact, he's embarrassed at me stripping him round there, when he has a pair of pants on that he can't manage too well. He comes to me to put it on, but all the time I know he's entirely embarrassed lest I might see him even'.

'*Mummy's going to buy a new baby when she's got enough pennies*'
The attitude which we have described as 'see, not look' seems to be based upon the principle that it is all right for children to know about sex differences provided they are not actively aware that they know. The final question of this group, however, asked about knowledge which could not be acquired by the child at a subliminal level—certainly not in our culture, where children are only through unpremeditated crisis present at the birth of their siblings. As usual, we asked the most factual

question first: Does the child actually know where babies come from?—and for this purpose he was defined as 'knowing' if he had at least been told that babies grow in their mummies' tummies. In a sense this definition is arbitrary—we could have included the knowledge of how the baby gets out of mummy's tummy, or how he got in there in the first place—but, having in mind the age of the child, it seemed most important at this stage to distinguish those mothers who are prepared to take what is normally the first step in explaining human reproduction to the child from those who prefer to be evasive or tell a direct lie; and to leave aside the question of whether these more informative mothers would be prepared to follow up the basic information with further details.

Whether the child already has this amount of knowledge is a fair indication of the mother's attitude if one assumes that what he knows is by her consent: and this is a fair assumption at this age, though of course it would not be true of the school-age child. In practice, the mother is the usual source of information during these early years; there are just one or two cases in our sample in which the child learned from someone outside the family, and these were coded in accordance with the mother's attitude towards his having this knowledge. The second coding category, which is in fact fairly close to the first in the attitude it describes, consists of those mothers who were prepared to tell the child the truth as soon as he asked them, allocated on the basis of their answers to the question: 'Would you tell him if he wanted to know, or do you think he's too young?' Some of the mothers in this category might have told the child a good deal earlier if the question had arisen. The third category includes mothers who definitely felt that the child was too young and would not tell him even if he asked the direct question. A necessary check was provided for this group by the supplementary 'What would you say if he asked you?'—occasionally a mother would express her opinion that the child was too young to know, but, faced with the hypothetical situation of actually being asked, and forced to state her response to that situation, would decide that in fact she would then *have* to tell him: 'I just hope it doesn't arise for a while yet.' To the extent that many mothers in category 2 hope to postpone telling the child for a year or two, even though they would feel in duty bound to meet his questions truthfully, this category does in fact reflect a meaningful difference in attitude from that of the mothers in the first category, though the boundary between them is not clear-cut. The third category is very well-defined indeed, however; and within this a further distinction can be made, to which we shall return presently, between the mothers who evade the child's questions and those who answer them with deliberate falsehoods. The three basic categories are presented in Table XL in terms of social class; here again, fortunately, punishment is not an issue.

TABLE XL

*Attitudes towards telling child the basic fact of reproduction,*
*i.e. that 'a baby comes from its mummy's tummy':*
*by social class*

|  | I & II | IIIwc | IIIman | IV | V | All (random) |
|---|---|---|---|---|---|---|
|  | % | % | % | % | % | % |
| 1. Child already knows at four | 44 | 26 | 15 | 14 | 15 | 20 |
| 2. Mother would tell now if asked | 44 | 47 | 30 | 39 | 10 | 34 |
| 3. Mother would not tell yet | 12 | 27 | 55 | 47 | 75 | 46 |

The large class differences shown in this table in the first place confirm the assumption which we made earlier that the fact of the child knowing is an indication of his mother's attitude, since the working-class child might otherwise be expected to have more opportunity for picking up information from his peers because he enjoys more unsupervised street play than the middle-class child. There is, of course, the possibility of the child having knowledge which he is keeping from his mother, but this is not very great at this age, when frankness is a characteristic of the child: he is more likely to blurt out his knowledge, and *then* find that it is unacceptable.

One in five children, then, know where babies come from at the age of four; but this figure increases to one in four of white-collar children and to nearly one in two of professional and managerial class children. Significant differences are found both between the two middle-class groups and between middle and

working classes as to the number of children who have this knowledge; but whereas unskilled workers' wives are no different from other working-class wives on the question of whether they have already told their children, they differ as to whether they would do so now if the issue arose: three-quarters of all Class V mothers intend to evade or prevaricate in such a situation, compared with about half of the skilled or semi-skilled group. Here, too, significant differences appear both above and below the white-collar group, in the proportions of mothers stating this intention. It is in this last category that social class differences are in fact most striking, with a class trend running from 12% in Class I and II up to 75% in Class V. Two quotations for each of the three categories will be enough to illustrate the general flavour of these differences in attitude.

Chrome polisher's wife:

> Every one of them's known where they are; they used to feel at my tummy, to feel it kick!

Administrative assistant's wife:

> I don't think he's terribly interested, I wish he was. The lady down the road where we used to live was having a baby, and she was sitting on a high stool playing with him and he pushed her against the tummy; and I said "You mustn't do that hard, because you'll hurt the little baby that's inside her tummy". Well, that was that—even when the baby came, he didn't show the slightest interest in where it had come from, although I did sort of say "That's the baby that's come out of Auntie Kate's tummy".

Publican's wife:

> I'd say "They sleep in their Mummy's tummy, ready to come into light". If she's old enough to ask questions, she's old enough to be told the truth.

Cook's wife:

> Well, I think she *is* a bit young, but on the other hand, I think if she asks me I will just tell her a *small* version—just tell her they were in Mummy's tummy and leave it at that.

Stoker's wife:

> He's too young yet; I wouldn't tell him. I've never had to face that yet—the *big* lad (15) hasn't asked me yet. I shouldn't tell

him the truth—anything but the truth—the first thing that come in my mind—tell him I should buy one. I should never tell him the truth.

## Fitter's wife:

I think if she *did* ask me, I'd be really shocked, a child of that age, thinking she'd been mixing in the wrong company while she's been out playing. I should go round wanting to know where she'd got that kind of talk from. I mean, at four years old, I don't think they ought to have anything like that. I'd tell her, from the hospital.

In our earlier study, we found that one of the salient ways in which parents felt that child upbringing had changed since their own childhood was in an increasing frankness on both sides between parents and children;[1] and 'the changing times' were often mentioned by mothers who felt that this particular kind of frankness was a part of the modern mother's role. 'I wouldn't tell her all that silly rot they told me, about being found under a gooseberry bush', said a driver's wife, 'with children today, it wouldn't wash with them'; and a miner's wife, who had been brought up on the same story, agreed: 'Ooh no—we're in modern times now! Some kiddies know more than what *we* know!' Another driver's wife, who had waited until her eldest daughter was eleven to tell her, and who herself had been ignorant until the age of seventeen, felt that the times were changing so fast that Denise would have to be told much earlier: 'Nowadays they do want to know, don't they? She's enquiring, she wants to know things that even Pam's amazed at—you can't put Denise off so easily! I mean, I say "Well, I'll think about it"; and she waits while I think! She won't be put off with that sort of thing'. On the other hand, the very fact that children nowadays expect to be heard as well as seen, and to be answered as well, put off a few mothers altogether: Mrs Griffiths, a British Rail fireman's wife, was for the moment sticking to her story of the hospital in the hope that it would stimulate fewer questions.

I think at four, knowing Larry, I don't want to sort of *face* the task of saying anything to him, because he's the type that, if you tell him one thing, the questions just come tumbling out.

[1] Newson, John and Elizabeth, 1963, *op. cit.*, pp. 226–9.

You get yourself into the state where he's asking questions you can't possibly answer, because they're just questions he's thought of out of his own head, and you get yourself terribly involved if you start trying to explain anything.

Where the mother is quite happy to tell the child where the baby comes from, this does not necessarily mean that she will elaborate further than the fact that we have used as our basic criterion. We had expected that many mothers would be less inclined to explain about the father's role in reproduction at this age; but we had not anticipated the number of those who would be reluctant to explain how the baby emerged.[1] This was considerable, and indeed we wished afterwards that we had deliberately asked for mothers' attitudes towards imparting this particular information. The quotations below illustrate various points at which the mother decides to stop short; the first was in fact classified as 'would not tell'.

### Wireman's wife:

I think I should make a little tale up, you know—it's a seed planted, and it grows and grows, and eventually it's *brought about*. I don't think I should actually tell him. I wouldn't say *where* it grew, or anything like that.

### Lorry driver's wife:

The little girl (then 5) asked me when I had the last one, "How do they get out?" I can't think of anything to tell her. I said "I'll tell you when you get a little bit older"—but, I mean, how can you explain that to a kiddy of six? You can't really, can you? (You think she wouldn't be able to understand?) Well, it isn't that. But I should imagine it would frighten a little kid of six.

### Labourer's wife:

Well, he knew the baby was *there*, and he kept saying "How does it come? How does it come?"—and of course I just ignored him.

---

[1] This same reluctance is expressed by a Russian children's writer, introduced in an English edition as 'the most loved author of books for children in the Soviet Union': he favours the explanation for a 4-year-old that 'the tummy is cut open and the child is lifted from it'. Chukovsky, K.: *From Two to Five*, Cambridge University Press, 1963.

Clerical officer's wife:

> He knows they're in Mummy's tummy, you know. But I haven't told him Brian's (husband's) part in it. I've just told him there's a seed. But I haven't told him Brian's part, because he's the type that would want to practise, I'm sure! He so wants to get down to the bottom of everything.

The mother who wants to tell the truth but at the same time does not want to tell the *whole* truth often snatches gratefully at fortuitous circumstances that let her out of her dilemma; thus we had several instances of mothers who had had Caesarian operations who were glad to be able to say that they had 'had an operation', which was apparently a more palatable admission than the baby's more normal means of exit.

Cabinet maker's wife (social work trained):

> He's not quite sure how they come out, he keeps asking me how they do; and I say, "Well, the doctor and the nurses take them out for Mummy", you know, and try and pass it off like that. (You don't want to explain that yet?) No, not just yet, where they actually come from; out of the tummy, yes. But he thinks they've got to cut open your tummy to get them out—which they did with Janie, so it was all right, I could say "Yes, they did with Janie".

Other mothers were similarly relieved to escape from having to tell the child at all; 'He did once ask', said a surveyor's wife, 'My friend had just had a baby, and before I could think of an answer, he said "Did he come from the hospital?" and I said "Yes". So I let it slide. It was true, she *had* had him in the hospital, so I thought, well, I'll let that go for now'. Another child had been told (by no less an authority than the midwife's little girl who lived up the road) that when enough pennies had been saved up, the midwife would bring a box with the baby in it; '—so neither of them's asked any more—they think you save pennies, which you *do* really, don't you?'

The fact that the mother chooses not to tell the child the truth of where the baby is before birth does not necessarily imply that she will tell him a direct lie. She may simply ignore the child's questioning or make it plain that the subject is taboo— 'Don't be rude!'—or she may honestly postpone the convers-

ation—'I can't tell you that now, when you're as big as Michael
I'll tell you all about it'. Another ploy is to say that it costs a lot
of money to have babies, thus *implying* that they are bought,
without actually spelling out the lie. Other mothers fall back on
Heaven: 'He thinks he comes from Jesus, and I let him accept
that'; 'I'd say that Almighty God sent them'; 'I'd say "It's up to
God", that's what I should say'. A bricklayer's wife had substituted Heaven for her husband's less vague explanation:

> I always tell him they're from Heaven, God, you know. They
> kept asking their Dad, and their Dad was at work one day, and
> Andy said "Miss Evans has got babies, hasn't she, Mum, why
> don't you get one?"—that's the baby-shop (*sic*) on the corner!
> I said, "Oh no, love, she doesn't have babies". He said "Well,
> me Dad said so". Well, I didn't know *what* to say then, without
> contradicting my husband, so I said "Well, God makes little
> babies". And now Andy keeps asking God for another little baby
> —now he knows where they are!

A child's questions may be ignored for a time; but four-year-
olds tend to be persistent where their interest is aroused, and
can seldom be put off with no answer at all. At this point, the
mother who 'gets all hot under the collar' may, as Mrs Cullinan
put it, 'make up some past fairy-tale that's been told about
babies'. Table XLI presents an analysis of the mothers who
would not tell their children where babies come from, according
to whether they merely avoid telling the truth or give a definitely
false explanation. It should be added that 'from Heaven' is not
counted as a false explanation; nor is 'saving up pennies' unless
buying the baby is actually specified.

Once again, the class trend is dramatic: while just over a
third of all mothers will deliberately mislead the child on this
topic, this proportion rises to two-thirds in Class V and dwindles
to one in twelve in Class I and II. The relationship of social
class with attitudes towards verbal truthfulness or distortion
in other areas besides this one is a theme to which we attach
some importance, and to which we shall return in Chapter 14.

The 'little tales' which mothers told their children varied a
good deal both in originality and in plausibility. Traditional
'past fairy-tales' are certainly not extinct: 'I say the same as

TABLE XLI

*Means by which mothers avoid telling their children
where babies come from: by social class*

(*percentages of total class groups*)

| | I & II | IIIwc | IIIman | IV | V | All (*random*) |
|---|---|---|---|---|---|---|
| | % | % | % | % | % | % |
| Mother would not tell yet | 12 | 27 | 55 | 47 | 75 | 46 |
| Avoids telling without falsehood | 4 | 8 | 14 | 7 | 9 | 11 |
| Gives false explanation | 8 | 19 | 41 | 40 | 66 | 35 |

everybody else tells them—the stork!' said a dustman's wife, and a miner's wife who had answered our query as to whether Gwen knew with an astonished 'No!—I hope not!', assured us: 'They come by Santa Claus or the stork'. A labourer's wife, like several other mothers, had 'bought Edna from Woolworth's—she's always thought that, and I don't think she'd take it into her head that we got her from anywhere else'. All of a nylon winder's children had been 'born under a goosegog bush', a lace machinist's wife found her two sons in the back garden, and a metal polisher's wife specified that she had found Una's baby sister 'under a cabbage patch': 'She said "They don't though, Mummy, they come out of your tummy", and I said "Who told you?" and she said "The little boy next door"'. As is appropriate in a Welfare State, however, most of these babies seem to come on the National Health: 'The Clinic nurse brings them'; 'You have to order them from the hospital'; 'The midwife brought it in her little black bag'. Those who lament the decline in traditional folklore may be heartened to learn that new myths can be generated in a modern social context. A number of Nottingham children know perfectly well that a baby arrives in the form of a large egg, packed in a brown cardboard box and delivered by the nurse or handed out at the clinic; eventually, after a period of incubation, the midwife comes to the house in order to break the seal and take out the newly-hatched baby. This story has precipitated at least one premature opening by an impatient four-year-old of the surgical dressings pack that is normally provided in advance for home confinements.

It remains true, then, that a considerable proportion of parents are reluctant even to begin to tell their children about human reproduction at this age. Their reasons include prudery on the child's behalf, an emotional aversion of their own which makes it impossible to approach the subject without manifest embarrassment, a fear of getting involved in complex explanations, and a foreboding, as we saw in the case of nudity, lest the child 'might start telling things, say, when there might be other people there that are a bit narrow-minded'. None the less, many of them realize that they are fighting a losing battle against a social trend towards more open discussion of sexual matters generally. While some parents are clearly disturbed by the fact that the child may be exposed to sex information without warning via the television screen ('farming programmes and that, you know—I tell them to go in the kitchen, I don't let them look'), others are reassured by the knowledge that the responsibility is taken out of their hands eventually: 'I tell her I bought her from the doctor's', said a labourer's wife, 'but I think they learn a lot at school now. I'd tell her, if she asked me, when she's about ten; but I mean, if she learned from school, I mean, she'd *know*—she wouldn't ask *me* about it then, would she?'

The material which has been presented in this chapter shows that, on every issue of physical or sexual modesty as it affects the four-year-old, differences can be demonstrated between social classes which are both consistent and sizeable: indeed, these differences are so striking that it has been suggested to us that attitudes towards sexual modesty might be a better index of social class affiliation than the more conventional 'occupation of father'!—though perhaps not the most practicable measure. At opposite ends of the class scale, these attitudes tend to be sharply polarized and to indicate two quite separate philosophies of behaviour. At the upper end of the scale, parents subscribe to the view that it is natural, and therefore right and proper, for children to be curious about their own bodies, to be interested in the anatomical differences which distinguish the sexes, and to want to know the source of new life. In order to engender 'natural', 'healthy' attitudes to sex in adult life, they believe that a child's curiosity should be satisfied frankly and openly, and as early as his own questioning dictates. While they usually are conscious that the child must be taught some social discretion, he must also learn that nakedness as such is nothing to be ashamed of, and that the naked human body, whether as a subject for the visual arts or in the context of a group of small children splashing water in summer on a secluded middle-class lawn, is something which adults accept as aesthetically pleasing. Because the mother expects to know a good deal about the company kept by the child, she can afford to be permissive about his curiosities; because she expects to have a high degree of communication with him, she can also allow 'family vulgarity' on an open level, which 'if it goes too far' she reckons to be able to perceive and control.

At the other end of the scale, the contrasting philosophy is that sexual curiosity is suspect, sexual information dangerous and perhaps frightening for the young child, and both must be controlled by being suppressed. Parents are proud if they manage to prevent their children from 'seeing anything'—the ideal is, indeed, that they should not be interested—and it is thought proper to punish the child for 'being rude', and to divert him with 'any little tale' from acquiring the most elementary knowledge of reproduction. There is, in fact, a deliberate attempt to keep the child in a state of complete sexual ignorance for as long as possible, and, linked with this, an assumption that the child cannot be trusted to be discreet enough not to disgrace his parents.

On one thing, however, these two philosophies are agreed: that the child's sexual 'innocence', better termed sexual naïveté, should be preserved. Few professional-class mothers would remain undisturbed if the young child showed an intense or sustained sexual interest and pleasure such as is considered appropriate to grownups. For both groups of parents there exists an underlying concept of what is childlike, and it has very little to do with adult sexual behaviour, even after sixty years and more of psychoanalysis. Professional-class mothers seek to *neutralize* sex interest by 'bringing it into the open' and making it a part of their own relationship with the child, in an atmosphere of indirect but effective control and supervision; the

N

unskilled-manual class mother seeks to *suppress* it by outlawing it from the outset and by keeping it outlawed by whatever means will serve in the short term, including punishment and prevarication. It is in the strategies chosen for the protection of the child's sexual naïveté that the social classes differ so profoundly.

# CHAPTER 13[1]

# PATTERNS OF PERSUASION
# AND COMPULSION

---

*'If she wasn't so naughty, she'd be quite a good child'*

In any discussion of child upbringing, the question of discipline must be at once the central and the most controversial issue. It is central because it arises in some form at every turn of the child's daily life; it is controversial because human beings, whether parents or not, tend to have views on how parents ought to behave towards their children.

We suggested earlier that most people regard criticizing other people's child upbringing methods as a rather pleasurable right. The fact that the majority of adults are prepared to commit themselves for or against specific practices in child-rearing derives in part from their status as parents, forced to take their own decisions, for good or ill, in practical situations with their own children, and to justify them in comparison with what they see of the decisions of others. People without parental experience, however, are equally ready to make critical judgments of how children are handled in the home, and there seems little doubt that the root of our ego-involvement in child upbringing goes right back to the experiences of our own childhood and to the lessons which we all learned the hard way—at the receiving end, as it were, of parental discipline. For every man and woman, the control of children is a part of real experience: for all of us, the basic stuff of our memories; for some of us, an immediate practical issue in our relationship with our own growing families; for most of us, something which we also watch and assess in other people.

The word 'discipline' may itself be controversial, or so we

---

1 Part of the material in this chapter has been published in Newson, John and Elizabeth: 'Patterns of Discipline: the four-year-old and his mother', in New Barnett Papers No. 1: *The Family in Modern Society*, Department of Social and Administrative Studies, Oxford University, 1965.

have found in our conversations with parents.[1] Occasionally it is objected to by the more soft-hearted mother on the grounds that to her it implies harshness, or perhaps a formality, which is alien to her own relationship with her children, at least with her four-year-old. Perhaps we need to say at this point, therefore, that to us 'parental discipline' is a neutral term: in using it, we imply no more than that *all* parents attempt, by *some* means, to exercise *some* control over their children. The degree of control which they hope for may vary; their purposes may differ; the methods by which control is gained and maintained are certainly very diverse indeed: but common to all parents is this feeling that they are in charge of their children's behaviour, and that they have some need or responsibility to guide that behaviour, whether with subtlety or by brute force, along the way which they believe to be right.

To the reader who has stayed with us thus far, it will be very clear that control or guidance of the child's actions enters into every area of his relationship with his parents, and particularly with his mother. Whatever the child is doing, at whatever point in his daily routine, he has *a continuous choice* of behaving either in a way which is acceptable to his mother or in a way which she will not tolerate. In earlier chapters, we have seen example after example of the way in which the child's behaviour is reflected back to him by his mother in terms of her evaluation of it. Let us consider a sequence of ordinary events in a four-year-old's morning. He wakes to find his pyjamas are wet; waits for his mother to put his clothes on him; refuses his breakfast; makes a 'train' out of chairs and shouts as he drives it; quarrels with the little boy next door, hits him and runs in to his mother; grizzles round her skirts because he wants a cuddle; sits sucking his thumb and playing with his penis; and tells her a long story about a polar bear he saw in the yard. All of these everyday actions are forms of behaviour which may or may not be tolerated, according to the attitudes of the individual mother; and the individual child has to learn which carry the label 'naughty' and which are approved. So throughout his day: conflict with his mother may arise over dinnertime, bedtime,

---

[1] The word does not in fact appear in the schedule until the first of the three 'summing-up' questions: 104. *On the whole, are you happy about the way you deal with discipline in general, or do you sometimes find yourself doing things that you don't really approve of?*

competition with siblings, comfort habits, attention demands, or his own expressions of independence as shown in fighting, tantrums or 'answering back'. Thus, as we have seen, in the course of discussing the child's ordinary daily life we encounter many points of conflict and control, many potentially explosive situations, long before we actually start asking the mother what she does in cases of disobedience, whether she believes in smacking, and so forth.

This gradual approach is in fact very useful to the interviewer, since parents' emotional involvement in the control of the child, coupled with the feelings of anger, humiliation and violence which can arise on both sides during conflict, are apt to invest any direct discussion of discipline with a certain amount of guilt, even where the mother believes she is doing the best she can. Some mothers approach the whole question with a wariness which seems to seek reassurance and approval before they can fully commit themselves; and the first, less threatening, half of the interview serves to create an accepting atmosphere for whatever they need to say in the second. For the majority of parents there is, to some degree at least, a gap between principle and practice; as parents ourselves, we are all too painfully aware of the discrepancy between the way one knows one ought to behave (or the way one would advise others to behave) and the behaviour into which one is driven by circumstance and the heat of the moment. For these various reasons, we have regarded discipline as a sensitive area; and we tried in the interview not to harp more than was necessary upon these rather negative aspects of the child's relationship with his mother. The main discussion was prefaced by a number of questions on the more positive aspects of their relationship: what she especially enjoyed about him, and whether they were reserved or demonstrative in showing their affection towards one another; we felt it important to give the mother an opportunity to express her warmth towards the child and to say pleasant things about him before being asked to talk about him in a way which might involve criticism of his behaviour. The subject of discipline was introduced by a question which by its wording accepted conflict as normal:

82. What about disagreements? What sort of things make you get on each other's nerves (you and N)?

At first sight, the answers given to this question appear to defy classification by their diversity. Sources of annoyance to the mother range from general whining and babyishness, very frequently mentioned, to idiosyncratic habits—'banging her porridgy spoon into the hair of one of the others'; 'always putting my shoes on'—which become bones of contention in individual families. However, an overall review of these replies discloses an interesting common denominator: what 'gets on the mother's nerves' more than anything else is a tenacious and obstinate *persistence* of behaviour which seems to be highly characteristic of children of this age. It can take both positive and negative forms. We saw in Chapter 3 how an endless stream of chatter or a non-stop series of questions can drive the mother to distraction even though she may also value the child's talent for 'conversation'; similarly, his insistent clamour for her to do something *there and then*, despite her obvious busyness, or his dogged determination to continue in a course of action in spite of her polite and reasoned requests for him to stop, can very effectively undermine her own intentions to remain calm and pleasant in her dealings with the child. On the negative side, he may give repeated excuses for procrastination when asked to do some simple thing, or, most maddening of all, may feign total deafness to his mother's courteous but urgent requests. 'Children aren't happy with nothing to ignore', wrote Ogden Nash, 'And that's what parents were created for';[1] certainly the four-year-old already exploits his parents in this small trial of strength.

Lorry driver's wife:

He's got a terrible habit that he'll just talk and talk and talk and talk, until in the end you can hear his voice going through you, you know. I usually tell him to be quiet then. He'll say "All right"—and he just keeps right on! He doesn't take a bit of notice. He just keeps on, and on, and on, and on; and perhaps there's something I'm a bit interested in on the TV, and he just keeps on and on and on, and in the end I don't know whether I'm listening to him or listening to that.

Electrician's wife:

Questions! I get a bit annoyed with him. You know, when he keeps on and on and on, it aggravates me. Then afterwards I

[1] Nash, Ogden: 'The Parent'; in *Family Reunion*, Dent, London, 1951.

think, "Well, he's only asking me. He really wants to know things". I try to answer him, but . . . .

## Optician's wife:

Well, sometimes when I'm doing something she will keep *on*—if she wants something doing and I'm not just doing it *then*, you know, for her—then I do get annoyed with her. She'll never let a thing drop. You know—you say to her "I'll get you that bathwater when I've done this"; and she'll say "*You're* a long time getting that bathwater!"—"*Are* we going to get this bathwater, then?"—on and on!

## Railwayman's wife:

It's her ordering me about. She'll want some water for her paint: I say "Wait a minute, will you, please?"—"I want it *right away*, Mummy!" And she's on and on all the time until I go to get it her. (That gets on your nerves a bit?) Ooh, it does an' all! I mean, when we was kiddies, we had to do as we was told, didn't we?

## Administrative assistant's wife:

He's beginning to go through the stage when I must admit he's disobedient; when he constantly does a thing, and I say "Don't do that"—sometimes I give a reason and sometimes I don't—and he does it again, and I say "Don't *do* that!" And he still goes on and does it; and that really does it, he annoys me. If I stopped to think about it, and didn't get a bit mad at him, I'd probably decide he was just asserting himself—trying it on, beginning to feel his own feet. But that's the main thing.

## Milkman's wife:

When he makes excuses—he's always got an answer! Although he does *do* the things; but he's always got to have his little word *first*, and that makes me real cross. I know he's *going* to do it, but as I say, he always has to have this little argument, he'll say "I don't want to do it" or "I'm just doing so-and-so".

## Clerk's wife:

When she doesn't listen—she just shuts her ears, and that annoys me; I could hit her—well, I *do* hit her. It annoys me to think that she's ruling me. I smack her—*ooh*, she annoys me! I have to tell her about half-a-dozen times. She doesn't seem to be listening, whether she is or not. She doesn't seem as if she *wants* to hear you, she just shuts her ears off. She's so contrary—she can hear what I'm saying, but she doesn't want to do it, so she just shuts her ears.

**Office worker's wife:**

When she starts being naughty and not doing as she's told, and I get mad with her and start yelling at her, and she just ignores me if I start that, you know—as though I'd not spoken—and that gets me *really* worked up! And she'll start talking about something else, entirely different to what you've been telling her about; and it really gets me mad, that does. She seems to shut her ears and not listen.

**Cycle worker's wife:**

If you ask him to do a certain thing, he'll see you in hell before he'll do it! I never thought I'd let go at my child as much as I do.

**Miner's wife:**

Well, you look a fool if they just ignore you.

Many workers have attempted to trace the development of specific personality patterns to the means and principles through which parents control their children; and the process of discipline too often tends to be discussed as if parents adopt certain modes of behaviour to which the children duly respond. It must not be forgotten, however, that young children are not merely creatures of response; they are, on the contrary, instigators and innovators. Normal children do not wait to react simply and passively to parental efforts to guide their behaviour: they are by nature active explorers and experimentalists, and this means that often they are as strongly motivated to direct their parents' actions as their parents are to dominate them. Typically it is the child who will, in practice, force the pace: making the reluctant father pay attention, coercing or blackmailing adults into co-operating with him in his doings, or goading and hustling his elders into activity on his behalf. The healthy child is concerned to induce change and to make things happen: given the chance, he would like to bend the whole world to his will. In the nature of things, children inevitably discover that their own powers are limited, and learn traumatically or otherwise to resign themselves to their impotence; but at the same time they also come to realize that an effective way to control events is to persuade and influence those who are more powerful than themselves. The characteristic persistence of the four-year-old can thus be seen as a manifestation of a healthy determination to master his own environment, instead of being mastered by it, and it indicates that the child is taking an important step towards becoming an autonomous personality with a valid identity of his own. It is of survival value to the child, so to speak, to be able to manipulate the human beings who surround him, because in them lies his best, often his only, chance of manipulating his environment: and he is in practice a rather sophisticated operator of human relationships, but, as we have seen before, much less skilled in the abilities needed directly to change material circumstances.[1] As time goes on, of course, the exertion of power over people can become a reward in itself; certainly some of these four-year-olds are already betraying a satisfaction in the use of such power for its own sake—James and Vicky (page 59) and Valerie (page 215) are perhaps instances of this, and so probably are some of the children who rile their mothers by 'turning a deaf ear'. Other examples are provided by the children who occasionally make remarks to the interviewer deliberately calculated to embarrass their mother (rather than innocently intended): the most successful of which was 'my mam's got tits!' dropped artlessly into a pause in the conversation by a little girl who, according to her mother, was well practised in 'showing her parents up'.

While mothers almost inevitably are drawn into conflicts with their children, and equally inevitably feel that they have to impose limits upon the child's defiance of their wishes, many of them express an understanding, implicit if not explicit, of the child's need to make a bid for power; and some recognize the role of 'contrariness' in the development of his sense of identity, and can feel some pleasure in this sign of his growing up, even while they are irritated by the way in which he shows it: as Mrs Ellis said, 'If I *stopped to think about it*, and didn't get a bit mad at him, I'd probably decide he was just asserting himself —trying it on, *beginning to feel his own feet*'. They will often show a good deal of tolerance, therefore, in the face of what to an outsider might appear to be obstinate and unreasonable demands. The mother's anger or annoyance with the child, while it is real enough, can also be ambiguous in the sense that it is

---

[1] See pp. 292–3.

N*

tinged with secret pleasure and amusement to see an adult determination (often mirroring her own or a close relative's besetting faults) in a child who is still little more than a baby in other ways. 'He is very stubborn, and so am I', said a scientific research worker's wife; 'sometimes I can take it as a joke; but, depending which mood I am in, I can't take it at all'; and, in answer to the question 'What sort of things do you specially enjoy in him?' she said: 'It's rather funny—he has very much the same temperament as my father, and I can see in him the things I have always objected to in my father; and this amuses me now'. Edwina's mother (page 60) provides another example of the parents' rueful recognition of imitative adult postures.

*'If he's in one of his dream moods, I can speak to myself'*

This same ambivalence recurs in the answers given to a subsequent question:

> 84. Suppose you asked him to do something for you, and he said "No, I can't do it now, I'm busy". What would you do? (If necessary, exclude things that might have to be done at a certain time, such as mealtimes or going out. If the mother says it never happens, insist: 'But what would you do if he *did* say that?')

The question deliberately suggested a situation in which the child seeks a right of autonomy which in an adult would normally be respected: moreover, it is a situation which in almost every home occurs the other way round at least occasionally, often daily, when the mother puts off the child's demands in these same words. What this question is testing, then, is the mother's recognition of a principle of reciprocity in her dealings with the child: her willingness to allow the issue of fairness and democratic rights to prevail over her wish to maintain authority. One aspect of this reciprocity which is directly probed by the question is the kind of child-centredness on the part of the mother which allows her subjectively to evaluate the child's activities—his 'busyness'—as worth while in their own right, to the extent that they constitute sufficient excuse for her own demands to take second place.

Table XLII presents a four-way classification of the answers given to this question. In terms of reciprocity and child-centred-

TABLE XLII

*Mothers' responses to the child's excuse 'I can't do it now, I'm busy'*

| Category | Illustration |
|---|---|
| **A. Mother accepts this excuse as valid**<br><br>30% in a random sample | 'I'd do it myself, because that'd be me—that's what I say to her.'<br>'I like *him* to wait until *I've* finished doing something. So I think it's only fair for *me* to wait until *he's* finished.'<br>'I probably wouldn't have asked him to, in that case, because I'd look to see if he was busy first.'<br>'He's just as much right to think he's busy as I have.' |
| **B. Mother allows time but finally insists**<br><br>26% in a random sample | 'I'd say "Well now, will you say that when you've done that thing you'll come and do it?" '<br>'I'd have to laugh if he said it that way! I'd say, "Well, do it when you've finished".'<br>'If it was a reasonable thing, I'd leave her and get her to do it later.'<br>'I'd think to myself, "*He's* waited while *I've* been busy, so it won't hurt me to wait just five minutes".' |
| **C. Mother accepts, but shows disapproval**<br><br>13% in a random sample | 'I wouldn't make her, but I'd tell her she was naughty if she wouldn't help me, I'd say that Holy God would not love her.'<br>'That often happens—I'll p'raps say "Oh, you're an old meanie—all right, if you don't love your Mummy you needn't bother, I'll do it myself", and he'll do it straight away then.'<br>'Well, I should point out that it was very unkind.'<br>'I often say "It's a different tale, isn't it, when you want *me* to do something!" ' |
| **D. Mother insists on immediate obedience**<br><br>31% in a random sample | 'Well, then I should say "Now *get* up and *do* it"; because I think that's the age when they start to tell *you* what to do, I mean Carolyn would.'<br>'Tell him off. I say I won't cook him any dinner.'<br>'Tell him his toys are going on the fire unless he does it for Mummy.'<br>'Well, if I've promised her a thing, I usually hit back at her like that: "Well, if you don't do it for me, I won't buy you that bike for Christmas".'<br>'I should say "Next time you want me to do something for you, I shan't do it"—and I should remember and *not* do it.' |

ness, the first category includes those mothers who allow full validity to the child's activities and try to act on democratic principles. In the second category, where time is given, the attitude is much the same, but over and above this the mother is concerned to make the child aware that he has obligations to her which must eventually be fulfilled: her role as the final authority is here made fairly explicit. In the third category, the mother's acceptance *with disapproval* of his excuse is hardly an acceptance at all: while she does not overtly press the point (as, eventually, the Category B mother does), in a more subtle way she exerts pressure towards his compliance, and concedes no *rights* to the child. Reciprocity may be appealed to, but in the negative form of 'What about when you want *me* to do something?' This acceptance is actually a pseudo-acceptance, more for a quiet life than for fairness, and often she does in fact get her way where the child is unable to withstand her disapproval. Finally, the mothers in the fourth category work on a clear principle that orders are orders, and that the child has no rights in the matter, only privileges by grace and favour: in this situation, the maintenance of authority is preferred to the granting of favours. The distinction can be seen where the mother tolerates the child's 'busyness' once or twice, but very definitely draws the line at the establishment of a precedent: 'That's a phase they all go through', said a labourer's wife, 'and I usually let it go on two or three days, and then my hand comes down pretty sharp'. Once again, the principle of reciprocity may be referred to, but this time in terms of a definite threat: 'Right, you wait till *you* want something . . .!' Where reciprocity is made an issue in the 'I'm busy' situation, the difference between the first and the last categories in the way it is presented is in fact the difference between Kingsley's Mrs Doasyouwouldbedoneby and Mrs Bedonebyasyoudid[1]—between mutual help and retribution.

The quotations given in the table serve to illustrate rather briefly the four main trends taken by the generality of mothers; but it is necessary to quote a little more extensively in order to illumine the feelings and attitudes that accompany them. Inevitably, there were some replies of the 'it depends' kind: usually these involved an assessment by the mother of what *kind* of busyness the child was occupied with, and whether it deserved her consideration. 'If she's doing something *instructive*, in

[1] Kingsley, Charles: *The Water Babies*, 1863.

educational form, then let her carry on', said a foreman's wife, 'but if she's just watching television, then I should say she had to come'; it is perhaps of interest that this is the child whose conversation at table had to be 'useful' (page 239). Mrs Cullinan, Irish labourer's wife, also brought the child's activity under scrutiny: one felt that Patrick would find it hard to satisfy her that his need was greater than hers.

> The first thing I would ask him would be what had him busy, or what should he be busy *at*, that he can't do something for me. I'd demand an explanation of what the busy thing was, that I was kept waiting, and why I should have to wait; because I think the thing I would be after asking to be done would be more particular than the business they were at. I've never asked them to do beyond their means or asked them to do something they couldn't do. So when I ask them to do some little thing, I'd expect that child to do it, because they surely know by now all I've done for them, in their own little way of course, so I'd ask them to be obedient at least.

Mrs Cullinan emphasizes her children's general duty of obedience to her, in return for her care of them; Mrs Jepson also insists on immediate obedience, but (unusually) out of a principle of specific reciprocity that arises from her own child-centredness in responding to June's demands:

Lorry driver's wife:

> Well, first of all I'd say "Come on, pet, do it for Mummy", and then "Now, June, come along"; and if that wasn't enough, I'd say "Well DO IT!" And by the time I've got to that, she's usually done it. (You like her to do it at once?) I do, yes, I think she should. I try to do *their* things, I try to do them as soon as I can, there and then, and in that case I think she should do the same.

In contrast to the mothers who demand special standards of activity before it, as it were, 'counts', mothers in Categories A and B are often very explicit in stating their acceptance of the child's busyness entirely on his own terms.

Shop manager's wife:

> If he says he's busy, he must be. A child might invent fairy tales, but I don't think he would invent *inconveniences* like that. I think

that really if he is busy, in his mind he is doing something just as important as what I want him to do, and he hasn't got the time. He is quite genuine in what he thinks, he quite honestly has *not* got the time.

### Bus conductor's wife:

Well, I think if he thinks he's busy, then that's it. I mean, it's the same if *I'm* busy, I couldn't be bothered to stop for him. Well, I mean, if he thinks he's busy, he's just as much right to think he's busy as I have, really.

### Lorry driver's wife:

Well, I should leave it, because I think it's a sign of her growing up—a bit of *me* coming back out of her, because that's what I say—"You'll have to wait until I've got time". I mean, she *very* often turns round and tells me the same thing. Well, I can't tell her one thing and expect her to obey, and then her say it to me and complete reverse, because that's silly. I'd say, "Well, don't be too long then, and do it in a bit", and she would.

A few children had themselves put into words the principle of fairness and reciprocity, and were sometimes successful in converting their mothers, at least for the time being, if only by their own surprise tactics.

### Aircraftsman's wife:

Well, that did happen—she said "I can't, Mummy, I'm busy"—so I said "Well, all right, then", and left it at that, because it wasn't very important at the time; and then it happened again, and I thought, well, I'm not going to let her just get away with it, like, so I said "Now, you must do what Mummy tells you *straight away*". And she said "Well, when *you're* busy you always *tell* me when you're busy!"—and she'd just got me overbowled, and I didn't quite know what to do; but by that time it was too late to enforce the law, sort of thing.

Some mothers, while not really accepting the child's behaviour, are prepared to tolerate what they see as a phase of development, if not quite a positive 'sign of growing up'; they may find it irksome, but presume it will pass without an issue being made of it.

Company director's wife:

These are awkward questions, aren't they? Well, I think—er—I say "Well, I do a lot of things for you when *I'm* busy"—but it never works. So I think I'd let her get away with it. As a matter of fact, Katy is usually most unwilling to do anything for me. But I think that's age, because Rosalind used to be, and now she's very willing, so, you know, I think it comes.

Examples have been given in Table XLII of direct threats— no dinner, toys on the fire and so on—and other children were threatened with loss of sweets or spending-money; but it was noticeable in the answers to this question that a large proportion of the threats were veiled or implied, rather than deliberately stated: 'Oh, all right then, we'll remember that when the ice-cream man comes round'; 'What was it you wanted me to buy you on Friday?' Threats of smacking, and smacking itself, were rare, presumably because the situation presented was one of attempted evasion rather than downright refusal. In general, threats of any kind in this context should be regarded as merely incidental to the basic attitude that the child's wish may justifiably be over-ridden by the mother's will: 'I'd say "Never mind busy, go on, get it done!" '

In summary, nearly a third of all mothers can be said to regard the child's claim to be busy in the face of their demands as a disciplinary issue, an affront to their parental authority which necessitates a firm stand if the child is not to 'start to tell *you* what to do'. A further 13% make it plain to the child that they disapprove of his behaviour, even though they may not think it worth while making an issue of it. The majority (56%) accept the child's excuse at least to the extent of giving him time. It must be remembered in evaluating these figures that activities which have to be performed by the child to a certain time were deliberately excluded from the question; so that the mother is here considering her behaviour with regard to requests to the child which do not matter except from the subjective point of view that she has made the request and he is trying to evade it.

The principle of reciprocity and its role in mothers' dealings with their children can be usefully pursued a little further by bringing together the two questions which we have so far considered in this chapter. The question 'What sort of things make you get on each other's nerves?' was worded on purpose to give the mother an opportunity not only of mentioning the ways in which the child annoyed her, but also of considering her own behaviour from the child's point of view and saying how she irritated him. The quotations we have given earlier all give the mother's angle; and this reflects the bulk of the responses, in that only 12% spontaneously accepted this invitation to take the child's-eye-view of themselves. The interviewers were instructed *not* to prompt 'What about the way *you* get on *his* nerves?' once the question had been asked; and we make the assumption that, while failure to mention the child's annoyance is not necessarily of any significance, a positive consideration of it is a positive sign of child-centredness in the mother, at least in the sense that it is practical evidence of her willingness to look at herself through his critical eyes.

*What sort of things make you get on each other's nerves?*

Fitter's wife:
> Following me about—hanging on to my skirts. I don't think there's anything else really. *He* can probably think of one or two things that I annoy *him* over, but I don't know: you should ask *him*; you'd probably get an answer, as well!

Publisher's wife:
> Oh, I *frequently* get on his nerves when I say no; and he gets on mine when he refuses to take any notice. He doesn't like to be told.

Greengrocer's wife:
> Well, I don't think we do really—we always seem very happy together. Probably like just now, he can't come into the lounge, so he's quite cross with me at the moment; but we get along very well, really.

Maintenance worker's wife:
> He annoys me asking questions over and over again; and if I can't answer them, *he* gets annoyed then—he thinks I'm doing it on purpose.

Laboratory assistant's wife:
> She tells me that I'm too fussy; I think I *have* been, because we've had a lot of trouble with her tonsils, and I was always on

to her, "Is your throat sore?" She used to say "Stop fussing—I'm perfectly all right". That probably irritated her. Since she's come out of hospital—at the beginning I automatically cut her crusts off, and she says "You keep forgetting that I'm better".

## Lathe engineer's wife:

I don't know really whether I get on her nerves—I suppose I do many a time.

## Machine operator's wife:

Sometimes, you know, when I have to *keep* telling him, sometimes he'll say "Oh, you're getting on me nerves, Mummy—let's go and see me Nana". He does come out with some sayings—like the other week I was on to him, and he said "Mummy, you'll send me grey!"

Table XLIII combines mothers' awareness of the possibility of their getting on the child's nerves and their acceptance or semi-acceptance of the child's 'busy' excuse, both of which are taken to be indications of reciprocity; and it adds another possible indication, the mother's willingness to play with the child on his own level, which was discussed in Chapter 7.

All three social class trends in Table XLIII are in the same broad general direction: reciprocity as shown by these three

TABLE XLIII

*Indications of reciprocity; by social class*

|  | I & II | IIIwc | IIIman | IV | V | All (random) |
|---|---|---|---|---|---|---|
|  | % | % | % | % | % | % |
| Mother mentions possibility that she may get on child's nerves as well as vice versa | 18 | 10 | 12 | 12 | 4 | 12 |
| (overall class differences significant at ·05 level) | | | | | | |
| Mother does not insist on instant obedience if child says he's busy | 77 | 77 | 65 | 73 | 63 | 69 |
| (overall class differences significant at ·02 level) | | | | | | |
| Mother wholeheartedly participates in child's play | 71 | 74 | 63 | 74 | 45 | 66 |
| (overall class differences significant at ·01 level) | | | | | | |

indices tends to decrease at the lower end of the social scale. It would perhaps be misleading to make too much of the greater proportion of Class I and II mothers mentioning the child's annoyance with them: this may in part reflect a greater *verbal* facility among better educated women which made them more sensitive to the fact that the question called for a double answer. The second line of the table is less ambiguous: even with the half-expected anomalous result in Class IV (see p. 538), significantly more middle-class than working-class mothers are tolerant or semi-tolerant of the child's excuse of 'busyness'. The same is true of the final line, with the addition of a dramatic difference between Class V and the rest. A fourth example of some interest is the case of reciprocal apologies between parent and child: this is discussed on pages 441–5.

*'Somebody's got to be gaffer—well, that's the situation, isn't it?'*
We have stressed that children of four are fairly sophisticated social manipulators, capable of consciously exerting social pressure on other people, because the situations of conflict which arise between parents and children in our contemporary culture pattern derive from two basic facts: not only is the child a fully active protagonist, concerned to fight for his own interests (including his own self-esteem), but parents are on the whole *willing to concede this autonomous role* to him, and indeed to protect to some extent his illusions of independence and free will, even though they thereby create a more vigorous opposition to their own authority. Strict training in unquestioning obedience to an autocratic mother and father is no longer a normal or acceptable way of bringing up children in the climate of opinion which prevails in the English-speaking world today. Child-rearing of the nineteenth and early twentieth centuries was dominated by authoritarianism, first in the guise of the religious morality of the Evangelical movement, later by its natural heirs, the medical moralists of the Truby King era: while these doctrines afforded to parents the comfortable certainty that they were invariably in the right in their conflicts with the child, they were too uncomfortable in their frustration of ordinary parental tenderness to have lasted, even if they could have survived the introspective doubts of the post-Freud world.[1] Four

[1] An analysis and discussion of the successively prevailing moralities of child upbringing will be found in Newson, John and Elizabeth: 'Cultural Aspects

representative quotations—from Susanna Wesley's influential letter to John, from Mabel Liddiard, the voice of the Truby King doctrine in Great Britain, from Sir Truby King himself, and from John Watson, father of Behaviourism, who added his intellectual cachet to the authoritarian medical advice—will serve to underline the contrast with the more democratic mood of the present time.

'I cannot but earnestly repeat,—Break their wills betimes; begin this great work before they can run alone, before they can speak plain, or perhaps speak at all. Whatever pains it cost, conquer their stubbornness; break the will, if you would not damn the child. I conjure you not to neglect, not to delay this! Therefore (1) Let a child, from a year old, be taught to fear the rod and to cry softly. In order to this, (2) Let him have nothing he cries for; absolutely nothing, great or small; else you undo your own work. (3) At all events, from that age, make him do as he is bid, if you whip him ten times running to effect it. Let none persuade you it is cruel to do this; it is cruel not to do it. Break his will now, and his soul will live, and he will probably bless you to all eternity.'[1]

'Self-control, obedience, the recognition of authority, and, later, respect for elders are all the outcome of the first year's training . . . the infant who is fed regularly, put to sleep, and played with at definite times soon finds that appeals bring no response, and so learns that most useful of all lessons, self-control, and the recognition of an authority other than his own wishes. . . . To train an infant for the first year is comparatively easy, but after that the child begins to resent authority, and the conscientious mother has to be prepared to fight and win all along the line, in matters small and great.'[2]

'The leading authorities of the day—English, foreign and American —all agree that the first thing to establish in life is *regularity of habits*. . . . The establishment of perfect regularity of habits, initiated by "feeding and sleeping by the clock", is the ultimate foundation of all-round obedience.'[3]

'There is a sensible way of treating children. Treat them as though

of Child Rearing in the English-Speaking World'; in Rivoire, J. L. and Kidd, A. H.: *Handbook of Infant Development*, Aldine, Chicago, 1967; a shorter version also appears in *Public Health*, Vol. LXXXI, May 1967.

1 *The Works of John Wesley*, Wesleyan Conference Office, 1872.

2 Liddiard, Mabel: *The Mothercraft Manual*, 6th Edn.; Churchill, London, 1928.

3 King, Sir F. Truby: *Feeding and Care of Baby*; revised and enlarged edn., Oxford University Press, 1937.

they were young adults. . . . Let your behaviour always be objective and kindly firm. Never hug and kiss them, never let them sit in your lap. If you must, kiss them once on the forehead when they say good night. Shake hands with them in the morning. Give them a pat on the head if they have made an extraordinarily good job of a difficult task. Try it out; in a week's time you will find how easy it is to be perfectly objective with your child and at the same time kindly. You will be utterly ashamed of the mawkish, sentimental way you have been handling it.'[1]

It is a salutary thought that the parental behaviour so confidently recommended in this last paragraph would, in the context of contemporary attitudes, probably be considered pathological.

If the tone and content of these strictures are nowadays rejected, this is not to say that parents do not want their children to respect their authority and to comply with their wishes: but it does mean that they hope for voluntary and rational co-operation, as opposed to automatic obedience and servile docility. In other words, they want their children to comply willingly and spontaneously, out of a sense of reciprocal obligation and general goodwill, and not primarily out of fear or in response to the threat of loss of privileges. In a sense, a parallel can be drawn with the Christian doctrine that, because God wished man to love Him freely, He had to permit him the choice of turning away from righteousness, and thus allowed sin to enter the world. Parents like to feel, almost as a matter of self-respect, that the co-operation which they receive from their children is freely and lovingly given, not extorted by coercive means. The difficulty of producing children who are willingly amenable, while consciously rejecting the might-is-right philosophy, lies at the heart of the parental dilemma which is explored in the final chapter of this book.

Since both children and parents live in a world of social involvement, a totally democratic relationship between parent and child is impossible to maintain. However sincere are the parents' intentions of allowing the child full autonomy and equal rights in decision-making, the fact that children's socialization proceeds originally from a state of complete egocentricity inevitably means that some of their desires will be incom-

---

[1] Watson, John B.: *Psychological Care of Infant and Child*, Allen & Unwin, London, 1928.

patible with the needs and rights of other people or with their own safety, even leaving aside the lesser considerations of everyday family expediency. Parents, especially highly-educated parents, often enter parenthood with the idea that coping with children is merely a matter of applying an intellectual understanding of child development to specific practical situations. This can lead to a rather painful and guilt-provoking confrontation with reality, when the professional-class mother, having committed herself heavily to the theory that friendly verbal explanations will produce rational co-operation in a toddler, finds that he is rationally *un*co-operative, and that in practice her careful explanation tends to degenerate into an exasperated and undemocratic screech of 'GET on and DO it!' 'I shall never prevent him doing anything he really wants to do' said a teacher's wife, with fond determination, of her twelve months old first baby, 'and I shall never force him to do anything that he *doesn't* want to do'; one year later, she had the grace to blush at the memory of her words. With the best will in the world, parents are bound to find themselves in situations in which real necessity dictates that they impose certain behaviour on the child against his wish, or restrict or forbid his chosen activities; and this is true even before one begins to consider the intense social pressures which impel parents to make their children's behaviour conform with social expectations that are alien to their own attitudes.[1]

Conflict and the clash of wills will thus necessarily arise at least in some degree during the process of child-rearing, and parents will be forced to demonstrate that the relationship between adult and child is not truly egalitarian after all, but that there are issues in which parents decide and children perforce submit. How far the parents' authority is made fully obvious will depend upon their ability to hide iron hands in velvet gloves: but the authority will finally be there, whether they like to admit it or not. Obviously some parents are quite content that the demonstration should be unambiguous: the mother who says 'They've got to know who's boss' believes in a

[1] Modesty is a case in point. Parents who positively approve of their children running around naked will tend to restrict them according to the company, and will usually feel that it is unnecessarily aggressive to force their tolerance on visitors known to be shockable. In this and other situations, possible damage to the child's own social relationships has to be considered. As the publisher's wife (page 373) pointed out, 'they've got to grow up in a framework'.

benevolent but open autocracy. Others may agree with this view, but in practice find it expedient to act *as if* democratically, because the child's independent temperament demands it: a comparatively authoritarian professional-class mother said 'He'll obey me provided I don't give him straight orders. If I say "do this" or "don't do this", then he's like a mule. You have to wrap it in tissue paper!' Those who really believe that they never resort to authority, however, are simply extremely subtle not only in disguising it to their children but in deluding themselves. One remembers a couple who continually congratulated themselves upon bringing up their children in almost complete freedom. The mother related the way she coped with bedtime when leaving the children with a baby-sitter: *some* parents, she told her children, would say 'You are not to watch television after eight o'clock'; *she* was not going to say that, but she knew they were going to be sensible and *not* watch television after eight o'clock. This sort of pressure, which implies an obligation on the part of the child to uphold the honour of families Brought Up In Freedom, seems no further removed from authoritarianism than the injunction used in some schools, 'Girls, I put you on your honour not to talk': in both cases, honour is substituted for naughtiness (a word that was taboo in that household), but the child's real autonomy is hardly enhanced; in fact, it is more likely to be eroded because subtle pressures are more difficult to withstand.

*'There seems to come a point where words just won't do . . .'*
The fact that conflict does arise between mother and child, and has to be resolved by some relinquishment of the democratic posture, does not necessarily mean, of course, that compulsion has to be carried out by resorting to physical punishment; but it must be understood that the more intimate, spontaneous and committed the relationship between human beings, the greater will be the emotional involvement when conflict does arise. In a clash of wills between two people who love each other, each will be vulnerable to the other's anger; and where self-esteem is also threatened on each side by the course of action proposed by the other, feelings are likely to run high, tempers rise, and aggressive acts of one sort or another all too easily follow.

We have already seen how the factor of self-esteem enters in a very practical way into the relationship between mother and child. Perhaps the need for social approval is especially strong among women: most mothers seem to be permanently sensitized to indications of their rating as 'good' or (intolerable thought) 'bad' mothers. The refusal of food, for instance, we saw to be a potent source of distress because the child, by rejecting the meal which his mother has prepared for him, directly challenges her performance in her most clearly nurturant role. Dummies are discouraged far more because they represent a risk of incurring social disapproval than because of any intrinsic harmfulness: 'So long as she doesn't suck it *outside*, you see . . . they do show you up, kiddies, don't they?' Good table manners and independence in dressing are pressed for chiefly because the mother has an eye on future social situations: 'I don't mind at home at the moment, but of course if she doesn't learn to have good manners at home, she *will* let me down when we're out'; 'I don't want her teacher to think I've made her quite helpless'. Tolerance of 'cheekiness' depends very much upon whether anyone else hears it going on: 'If they show me up inside, then I would talk to them and explain to them, but if they showed me up outside, then I would smack them most definitely'; 'Sometimes if I tell her to do anything, and her friend is there, she will try to be *bigger*, you know; well, that *does* annoy me, because perhaps children think "Well, her mother's a bit of a fool, she can do what she likes with her". I don't like that, naturally'. Temper tantrums, too, tend to be dealt with in direct accordance with how shaming they are in their context.

Textile worker's wife:

> I told him he couldn't have it, and the lady told him he couldn't have it; so he decided he was going to have a screaming tantrum, and he *wouldn't* shut up. So I *did* smack him that day. I was really annoyed. It wasn't just the fact that he'd been naughty; but it made *other people* . . . looked as though I'd got no control at all.

Metal polisher's wife:

> Yesterday we were at Goose Fair, and the roundabout he was on was just slowing down, and he shouted "I want to go on that one!" So I said "Just take your turn"—so he starts *stamping*. So right then and there I walloped his backside, and he was

crying, he still wanted to go on; but I wouldn't let him go on it, on principle, you know, for showing me up in front of others.

'They make you feel silly'; 'you look such a fool'; 'there I was, *shrivelling*'; 'I could have sunk through the floor'; 'I had to pretend not to hear her': the effect of an audience in heightening the stress of conflict situations is constantly reiterated. We quoted earlier the professional-class mother whose *au pair* girl's departure was 'a tremendous relief' because at last she could 'be natural with them again'; whether the presence of onlookers inhibits or stimulates overt aggression, it inevitably has some effect in distorting the interchange between mother and child.[1] Often a minor disagreement, which would normally be resolved quickly and easily, escalates into a confrontation of exaggerated magnitude because the mother feels that her authority has been publicly defied and that her loss of face must be avenged in some over-emphatic way if she is to retrieve any part of her self-esteem.

Builder's wife:

One day last week I took him up Alfreton Road, and we were in a shop, you see, and I told him not to touch the glasses; and he put his hand to them, and I said "Oh, you *are* a naughty boy" —and he lifted his hand to me! Well, I felt *stupid*. You know, you try to bring them up well, and then he'd lifted his hand and hit me! Well, I felt really *furious*, you know—you feel embarrassed, and made little of. Well, I don't like slapping children in the street, but I did, I slapped his hand—which I was sorry for afterwards, I mean I could have waited till I got him in the house and then checked him. But it just got me roused up, you know, the shop full and then him lifting his hand. Well, what I was worried about was what all the people thought, you know, what way I was bringing him up; I was really mad at him.

The effect of an audience upon the child works in two ways: either he reacts in the same way as his mother, feeling the situation as a blow to his own self-esteem, or, if he is not yet so personally vulnerable to other people's opinion, he may use his

---

[1] For this reason, we prefer to develop and refine methods of observing relationships at second-hand, rather than trying to use first-hand observation to study a situation which is immediately thereby invalidated. A more detailed exploration of individual episodes of conflict is in preparation.

mother's sensitivity as a weapon against her. Another child who is sometimes slapped in shops shows his humiliation quite clearly: 'He usually cries and hides in my coat—hides his face, because he's ashamed of being slapped in front of everybody else'. For the little girl who told the interviewer 'My Mam's got tits', on the other hand, the power which she is conscious of wielding over her mother's feelings outweighs any qualms about what people might think of her. Her mother's distress is evident, her dilemma not easily resolved:

> Hey! You've let me down, you have. That's another thing she's always saying. She's said that on the *street*. (Child repeats: Got tits.) Don't be rude! That's rude! I've told you before about that! You're a very naughty girl! (Child laughs.) You know, there's a crowd of youths come along this street, and you ought to just hear the things that some of them say. These pick it up from them, you know; then they get a good hiding for it. You just don't know what to do. You try and keep them away, but what *can* you do? But she always lets me down. Wherever I take her, she always lets *something* out that she shouldn't. That's the only big disappointment that I've had with her.

While the exacerbating effect of the onlooker is clear, this does not mean that conflict in private is always on a low emotional level. The factor of self-esteem or loss of face still operates, if not quite so obviously; both child and mother have a notion of certain limits to their own compliance, beyond which they will feel themselves to be the losers. The mother is conscious that she *commits herself to an attitude* by her actions, which therefore need to be consistent with her purpose. In practice, this means that more authoritarian mothers justify smacking (even though they may not like it) by appealing to the necessity to make the child sharply aware of their attitude: 'If you don't smack them now and again, they soon try to rule you, they think they can get away with it'; whereas more democratic mothers (even if they smack quite a lot) do not justify it, because it is inconsistent with their intentions, but merely try to explain it: 'I usually do it in the heat of the moment—I think it relieves your own feelings, rather than does any good to the child'.

Thus the giving and receiving of a smack has to be understood as happening on two levels and in two contexts. In the first place, it happens as one part of a more or less complex *sequence of events.* The mother begins to override her child's wishes; the child resents her attempts to interfere with his freedom of choice and retaliates by being obstinate and unco-operative; the mother feels that her authority is challenged, and, after some small or lengthy discussion of the issue, smacks him to settle the point. Emotion of various sorts is generated, usually on both sides, and the episode eventually subsides. In the second place, smacking happens as one element in a *pattern of understanding* between the mother and the child. The mother has a fairly consistent set of principles, roughly corresponding to her authoritarian or democratic attitude, which she hopes in time to communicate to the child by her words and actions, and through which she expects to socialize him into the sort of person she values; and, within this framework of principle, she not only smacks but tries to evaluate for the child the meaning of her smack. It is probably true to say that the precise form of an aggressive act is less important than the fact that it has occurred; and it is certainly true that the objective force of a smack is less significant to the child than the spirit in which it is delivered. The mother of the child who hid his face in her coat after a public smack said: 'I'm sure it's not that it hurts; because I often in playing with him give him a slap on his bottom which is probably much stronger than the one I give when I am annoyed; and he doesn't object to that; it's not the pain.' Mothers expect, however, to convey to their children much subtler shades of meaning than the difference between a play-smack and a punishment-smack: they hope to transmit their own feelings about it, to make the child aware of its role in their relationship, to make it in fact a meaningful symbol rather than a mindless act of violence. Often they will actually interpret the smack in words: 'Mummy has to smack you when you're naughty'; 'You've got to learn to do as you're told'; 'I'm sorry I smacked you, but you've gone too far'; 'I don't believe in smacking, but you're driving me up the wall'; 'This is wrong, not just naughty'; 'Now you know what it feels like to be hit'; 'Stop ignoring me!'; 'DO it, I say!' At other times they rely on the child's familiarity with their basic attitude, as presented to him by the whole pattern of their relationship, to enable him to construe the smack in the spirit of their intentions. Perhaps a spectrum of opinions on smacking will illustrate the range and interplay of these contexts. The questions were: 'How do you feel about smacking? Do you think it's necessary to smack children?'

Social worker's wife:

Necessary from whose point of view? I don't think it *gets* you anywhere. I smack purely to relieve my own feelings. There seems to come a point where words just won't do. You just can't find the right ones, and you're being pushed by all sorts of people, and you just find you've got to get certain things done, and you just smack and that's all there is to it. But I never fail to feel guilty, and I *always* feel myself to be the loser.

Research chemist's wife:

It's necessary for *me*, and it's soon over. I'd rather smack and get it over with, than have a nagging battle and recriminations and threats. I don't really like doing it; I find it's probably the best thing in the situation. It's like a thunderbolt—crash, bang, wallop, and then it's over and you're happy again!

University teacher's wife:

I think it's a waste of time really. It's a great relief to the feelings, but it just sets you back in dealing with the child.

Greengrocer's wife:

It isn't very often they need to be smacked. I say "Now, if I have to tell you again, it'll be with my hand next time". They know that I do mean it. I don't just give him a sharp slap in temper, sort of thing. I don't smack to relieve my own feelings, but for something he really must understand was very wrong, you see.

Scientific research worker's wife:

I think it is sometimes; I think it releases something in the child and in the mother—releases the tension sometimes. As far as I'm concerned, I think this is so, because I only slap him if I get very annoyed: I get very annoyed and he gets more and more stubborn; and I find when I've given him a slap on his bottom, all my anger is gone *with* the slap, and somehow *he* seems to be much softer.

Setter operator's wife:

That's the first thing I do if she really annoys me. I just land out and give her one. Quite honestly she does get some awful smacks sometimes. I feel as if I'll feel better when I smack her, but I don't, not when I think about it.

### Bleacher's wife:

If it's delivered at the proper time. I don't believe in this do it now, pay later. I know you shouldn't hit children in a temper, but I couldn't hit them afterwards.

### Local government inspector's wife:

I don't think it's necessary a lot, to smack. I find when I've smacked, it's me—I've been in the wrong. I've been tired or irritable, and I've given them a hit, you see. I can't be bothered to sort it out properly, and then I'm sorry. It's a mistake then, you see. You feel sorry for your child, and you're trying to make things right, and it's dreadful . . .

### Clerk's wife:

I just want to be able to speak to them and they're going to listen and do as they're told; but they don't, and I can't cope. I don't know what to do, and so I smack. I haven't got the patience to keep off—I can't help myself, you know—I'm like a child myself, I suspect. I just haven't got the patience. I know I'm wrong—*I* think I am—I don't *want* to be like that. I don't want to keep begging and praying them to do something; I think they should do as they're told straight away. But I have to smack before they'll take notice. They always get smacked in the end.

### Building foreman's wife:

Well, it helps; because children seem to overpower you, and you've *got* to smack them.

### College teacher's wife:

Well, I think it's a very poor argument. I do, really. I feel as if I've lost, as soon as I've done it. I don't think it does any good. (Father): I don't feel so guilty about smacking as my wife does. I don't go around beating them!—but I sometimes think that just a gentle one is often the quickest way. (Mother): *I* think it's the *quickest* way. But I don't know that it's the *right* way. (Father): I don't think it leaves such a mental mark, either, as a long lecture or a fit of temper. I think it's clean and quick and soon forgot. I *think*—but I don't *know*.

### Doctor's wife:

I think it's very necessary. I think you're undoing everything you've done if you're, sort of, petting them up afterwards. I think if you smack them you must stick to it, and not go back again and say you're sorry for smacking them, and that sort of thing. I know very often I smack her and feel sorry, but she doesn't know it.

### Insurance inspector's wife:

Well, I don't believe in child psychology, if that's what you mean! All these jargons about you should do this, you should do that. I believe in the old-fashioned way: you try reasoning with them first; if that doesn't do any good, you smack them. I don't think it does any harm at all. I've found that if I say to him "Now look —if you don't do it, I shall smack you", he usually gets on with it.

### Electrician's wife:

Oh, I think so, yes, because a child's mind is very funny, I think; if *they* get a hold over *you*, then that's it! I believe you've got to be the master of your children, and I *do* believe in smacking them.

### Toolmaker's wife:

Yes, I do at times. If she's done something I don't like, I smack her, it's just a matter of course. She gets a bit full of her own importance; I think it just puts them in their place a bit. I have a stick, if everything else fails; which I show her. I've never used it yet—usually if I reach my hand up to the cupboard where it's kept, that's enough.

### Packer's wife:

Well, I think, the children nowadays, it is; because I don't think talking seems to do much at all. I mean, my neighbour, she keeps saying to hers, "I'll give you the stick, I'll give you the stick!" But they go off and turn round and laugh at her. Well, mine'll *get* the stick. I couldn't stand that. I do keep a little cane; and he does take more notice of the stick than my hand. (He has had it, has he?) Oh yes. He usually gets it on his bottom. But they know then—if they see me looking at them and go quickly to that door, they all finish up in a corner, terrified. They're not really; but anyone that walked in would *think* they were, you know, seeing them. . . . Even from being babies, mine have been smacked from about 4, 5, 6 months, you know, for grabbing and things like that . . . I've had my own way, you know, and they've done as I've said, right from being small. . . . If they've cried for no reason at all in the pram—when you've picked them up, they've laughed, when you've put them down they've cried—well, I've smacked their behinds: I've put them down and said "Now you've got something to cry for", from about 6 months. They've known that I've meant it, and they have done right from being small.

The reader who will imagine being in the child's place during conflict with each of these mothers will understand that the experience of smacking would vary very much from one family to another, even if the actual weight of the smack could be kept constant—which, of course, it is not. At this point it seems appropriate to set against this background of the subjective meaning of smacking an attempt to put in objective terms the degree to which it actually happens. It is obviously very difficult indeed to assess just how hard are the slaps given by different mothers, and indeed most mothers will vary from one occasion to another; we therefore rejected any attempt to make such an assessment, and have concentrated upon frequency of smacking, the 'naughtinesses' for which smacking is used, and the mood in which smacks tend to be given. It proved possible to rate average frequency on a 4-point scale: *Never*; *Low* (less than once a week); *Moderate* (once a week–once a day), and *High* (more than once a day). It must be borne in mind that these are conservative estimates: mothers are more likely to under-estimate than to overestimate the frequency with which they smack. Because frequency also varies from one week to another, we did not feel justified in making any more detailed division within the 'moderate' category, though many will no doubt object that 'once per day' is in fact high; comparatively speaking, however, it did not seem unduly different from the rest of the category. While an assessment of the force of the smack seems both impracticable and not very meaningful, the use of an implement does seem to imply a further dimension in the smacking situation: the blow becomes potentially more painful and actually more formal and deliberate. Perhaps naïvely, we had not originally included direct questions as to the use of an implement, considering it inappropriate at this age; and it was not for some time that we realized the need for such a question. For most of the sample, therefore, our knowledge of the existence of an implement depends upon the mother's spontaneous mention of it. For this reason, we have simply included mothers who use or actively threaten[1] with an implement in the category of *high frequency*, whether or not they in fact smack more than once a day. The total number involved is 19 out of the 700; 7 of them are in the shop and clerical class.

TABLE XLIV

*Frequency of smacking*

|  | I & II | IIIwc | IIIman | IV | V | All (random) |
|---|---|---|---|---|---|---|
|  | % | % | % | % | % | % |
| Never | 2 | 2 | 3 | 3 | 3 | 3 |
| Low (less than once per week average) | 33 | 23 | 20 | 24 | 11 | 22 |
| Moderate (between once per week and once per day, inclusive) | 61 | 68 | 70 | 66 | 79 | 68 |
| High (more than once per day: or implement used or actively threatened)[1] | 4 | 7 | 7 | 7 | 7 | 7 |

Some examples follow in illustration of these four categories:

*Never*

Tailor's presser's wife:

I *don't* think it's necessary. I never smack either of them. I don't like it at all. I think before—five, say—they're too young; and after five they're too old!

*Low*

Accountant's wife:

I try to reason; I try to put myself in the child's place. I'll try everything before I will get really cross. As a last resort I will smack him—but it *is* a last resort, because it upsets me just as much as it upsets him, I think. It's weeks and weeks since I last did.

[1] By using the phrase *actively threatened*, we imply exclusion of those children who belong to families in which an implement is used for the older children but has not yet been directly appealed to in connection with themselves. Obviously the knowledge that it exists and *could* be used affects their view of the situation, however.

*Moderate*

Machine operator's wife:

> I don't hit them all *that* often; because I always feel guilty after, I always wonder, well, was it me being not in a very good mood, was she really as bad as I made out? (About how often *does* she get a smack?) Well, she hasn't had one this week yet! (Laughed—it was Tuesday.) She had one or two last week. It's something like two a week.

*High*

Manager's wife:

> (About how often does he in fact get smacked?) Well, he's had two really good hidings today; and if it wasn't for the fact that we went out, he'd have had another one. (And is that about average?) That's about average, I'm afraid! (And you mentioned a wooden spoon just now—do you use that?) Yes, it's quite serious; I use that on Eric (8), and I have used it on Peter, *once*. It's usually just a threat for him. I keep it by the gas stove. I find that if they know that you can use it and you *will* use it, it does have its effect. (And when you say 'a good hiding'—just how hard is it, and where?) On his bottom usually, or on his legs if I can't take his pants down then and there. If he knows his trousers are coming down and he's going to get a really good one —oh, on his bare bottom, yes. (And this happens two or three times a day?) Yes.

Packer's wife:

> (How often do you in fact smack him?) Well, it's just one of those things—he has more one week than he does the next week. On average, he gets the stick about three times a week—on average; sometimes more. (And you sort of smack him with your hand in between?) Yes—oh, very often; every time he passes me, I'm helping him on his way!

*'These women that say they've never had to raise a hand to their kiddies—they must either have perfect kiddies or very loud voices!'*

Throughout this exploration of the various areas of child upbringing, we have met with examples of children being smacked for behaviour which their mothers do not approve. They may be smacked for bad manners or refusal of food, for running home instead of fighting out their battles, for bed-

wetting or genital play. Wherever the mother evaluates behaviour as 'naughty' and tends to meet naughtiness with
punishment, or wherever her anger is roused and demands the
relief of violence, smacking is liable to take place, whatever the
specific precipitating behaviour. However, there are certain
actions on the part of the child which seem to invite smacking
more often than others; and these may be looked at in quantitative terms.

The most common misdemeanour to which smacking is the
response comes under the very general heading of 'disobedience'
or 'defiance'; one cannot separate the two, since for most
mothers disobedience *involves* defiance. The child's specific
action is immaterial: the common element is that he has left
undone those things which his mother said he must do, or has
done those things which she said he must not do, and either way
her wishes have been defied. The questions with which we
probed such situations follow; they precede the first mention of
smacking (which comes at 88), and include (at 84) the 'I'm busy'
situation.

83. Of course, this is an age when children often don't want to
do as they are told. What do you do when that happens?
85. Does he usually obey you fairly quickly, or do you have to
keep on at him to get him to do things?
86. If he refuses to do something that he really *must* do, what
happens? (If M says 'I make him', prompt:) How?

In question 86, we are in fact hypothesizing the moment of
truth which we have suggested comes to every mother/child
relationship, however democratic, egalitarian or permissive,
when something *has* to be done whether the child likes it or not
and the mother *has* to impose the necessary behaviour. Thus
the mother is here no longer allowed the opportunity of saying
'I just leave it'; she must commit herself as to *how*, in fact, she
will enforce her will. Whether she is angry or not, however, does
not necessarily come into it. In practice, the answers to this
question polarize quite simply into two groups: those who at
this point expect to smack, and who do at least threaten
smacking, and those who would normally use other methods.
The other methods are various: most common are raising the
voice, assuming a stern expression, continuing to repeat the

O

demand, and taking the child bodily to the scene of action and standing over him (or removing him, as the case may be); often these tactics are used in combination, so they may fairly be grouped together.[1] 'When my voice rises above a certain pitch', said a social worker's wife, 'he knows that the situation is crucial. If he refuses, I just reply by looking very fierce'; and a miner's wife agreed that this was effective: 'I haven't really smacked him, never for anything like that—he just reads my face and thinks "I'd better do it"!' A fireman's wife, who was in fact often involved in prolonged conflicts with her very determined little boy, said 'Usually, if I can stick it out long enough—it's a battle of wills, who can stick it out longer—when it gets to that sort of thing, I know I've just *got* to win. I just keep on at him. I don't take any notice of time and that, I mean I *spend* the time on doing it'; and a teacher's wife, who on the question of minor issues had said 'If it comes to a head-on clash, well, Gilly sometimes wins, I sometimes win', replied: 'I can generally talk her into it, given the time and the patience; if I can't, I pick her up and put her where she has to be'. One longer quotation vividly illustrates such a situation between an intelligent, high-strung and strong-minded little boy and his mother who prefers not to smack.

University lecturer's wife:

> For instance—we had infectious diseases and had to be isolated, and Charles got *out* of his social behaviour; and it was time for him to go to his play-group, and he wouldn't go. I dressed him, and got the car out, and when I came back he'd taken all his clothes off and hidden, and he said "I'm in Africa. You can't come in, it's against the rule. I'm not going"; and I went in and picked him up and put him in the car, and I tried to distract him on the way there, because he said "I'm not going—that's the rule"; and I talked about things I thought would distract him, and *occasionally* I thought of something so interesting that he would answer. But then he'd say "But don't ask me any more, because I'm not going and I'm not going to talk about that". Then when we arrived, he cried and he screamed and he clutched on to the car, and said "I'm not going, I'm not going"; and I managed to *de*-clutch him and deliver him, and I left him, and that was the end. Once I'd gone, it all packed up, everything

---

[1] Sundry non-smacking threats may also be used; these are discussed in the next chapter.

was all right. Now that I could do, because I was physically stronger, and I just went ahead. I decided this *should be done*, and I wouldn't give way, because once I gave way then that's his victory, and this is something I consider he should do.

More specific examples of generally disapproved behaviour include telling lies in response to an accusation, temper tantrums, and displays of violence directed against the mother herself. Each of these situations was proposed separately (Questions 97, 100 and 102) and the mother asked what she would do in each case. Table XLV gives an analysis by social class of mothers' use of smacking in these various instances.

TABLE XLV

*Use of smacking in specific situations*

|  | I & II | IIIwc | IIIman | IV | V | All (random) |
|---|---|---|---|---|---|---|
|  | % | % | % | % | % | % |
| Obedience, if refused, enforced by smack or threat of smack (Q.86) | 56 | 63 | 70 | 63 | 79 | 67 |
| Child smacked for lies (Q. 97) | 27 | 37 | 38 | 44 | 42 | 38 |
| Child smacked for trying to smack his mother (Q. 100) | 43 | 50 | 63 | 60 | 64 | 58 |
| Child smacked for temper tantrums (actual cases only) (Q. 103) | 20 | 33 | 36 | 38 | 25 | 33 |

Before going on to discuss the data presented in this and the preceding table, we can complete the statistical picture with one more table which may help us to understand the mother's mood when she smacks and how this ties up with her actual use of physical punishment. The questions which elicited this information follow; usually they were adequate for an assessment of the mother's approval or disapproval of smacking in principle, but if necessary this was directly prompted by asking 'Would you say you believe in smacking on the whole?' Mothers' principles on smacking were thus rated independently of their actions.

88. How do you feel about smacking? Do you think it's necessary to smack children?
89. Do you have to be angry when you smack N, or do you smack him simply as a punishment?
90. Do you think smacking does him any good? (Prompt:) In what way?

TABLE XLVI

*Mothers' mood when smacking and belief in smacking*

|  | I & II | IIIwc | IIIman | IV | V | All (random) |
|---|---|---|---|---|---|---|
|  | % | % | % | % | % | % |
| Smacks only when angry | 48 | 46 | 57 | 44 | 45 | 51 |
| Smacks only when calm | 20 | 17 | 21 | 24 | 26 | 21 |
| Might be calm or angry | 30 | 35 | 19 | 29 | 26 | 25 |
| Believes in smacking | 80 | 86 | 84 | 84 | 78 | 83 |
| Disapproves in principle | 20 | 14 | 16 | 16 | 22 | 17 |

Mothers' belief in or disapproval of smacking has already been sufficiently illustrated; some examples of what they say about the mood in which smacking takes place are given below. Shaw's dictum—'If you strike a child, take care that you strike it in anger, even at the risk of maiming it for life. A blow in cold blood neither can nor should be forgiven'[1]—was often echoed, and the minority group (17%) who disapproved of smacking in principle tended to fall into this category of smacking only in anger. Those who only smacked when calm usually believed in smacking, and felt that punishment needed to be demonstrably deliberate in order to be taken seriously; a few working-class women in this category consciously refrained from smacking in anger for fear that they should indeed maim the child. The mothers who might smack in either mood tended to be believers in smacking, who neither required anger to bring them to that

[1] Shaw, George Bernard: Preface to *Man and Superman*: 'Maxims for Revolutionists'.

point nor invested it with enough significance to make an effort at calmness. These links between mood and principle were also consistent with practice: of those who restrict their *mood* of smacking to only calm or only angry, the percentage who actually smack once a week or more drops slightly to 75% and 73% respectively, from an overall 77% (mothers who never smack excluded from consideration in each case); whereas, of those who might smack in either mood, 88% smack once a week or more: and this difference is significant.

*Smacks only when angry:*

Lorry driver's wife:

> I start off speaking kindly to them; but I end up shouting like a maniac! I've got to be a bit het up over something; then I will land one at him. I feel sorry straight away; I always regret it afterwards. I don't really believe in smacking; I don't like it; but I think everybody gets to that pitch sometimes when they've just *got* to smack them.

Painter's wife:

> I think I have to be cross. I don't think I could, sort of, meditate about it.

*Smacks only when calm:*

Miner's wife:

> Oh no, I never smack her when I'm angry; or how would she know that I really mean it, if I'm in a temper? I don't believe in that, you must let them see you're doing it for a reason.

Presser's wife:

> Sometimes if I'm *really* cross I think to myself "If I do start to smack him, I'll really hurt him"; so instead of that I send him upstairs out of the way, I say "You must go to bed until I've calmed down a bit", and then I know I won't hurt him; because I'm afraid I *have* got a bit of a temper.

*Might be either calm or angry:*

Insurance agent's wife:

> He doesn't make me angry very often. If I smack, I smack because I mean to smack.

Milkman's wife:

> I smack him when I think he needs it, irrespective of whether
> I'm really angry; if he's really naughty, obviously it *does* make
> me angry, though.

We can now briefly discuss the evidence presented in the last
three tables. The first general finding is that smacking is in
practice used in dealing with four-year-olds to a very considerable extent: three-quarters of all mothers smacking on average
at least once a week, many of them a good deal more often, adds
up to a very large number of aggressive acts, whether or not the
smacks themselves are objectively painful. We have, as we have
said, no way of judging this last dimension; however, on the
basis of the verbatim transcripts, we would tentatively suggest
that those mothers who smack most frequently are also likely
to smack hardest. Not only do the frequent smackers talk as if
their smacks hurt more (see, for instance, those quoted on page
416), but further evidence from some mothers who *used* to
smack often, and no longer do so, supports this hypothesis. The
reason for this is easy to understand. Once a mother accepts
smacking as a means of discipline suitable for many occasions,
and begins to use it often, she thereby debases her own currency
of methods of control: that is to say, if smacking is the response
to everyday 'naughtiness', she has nothing in reserve for more
serious misdemeanours. Because, every now and then, the child
will do something which the mother feels needs a special mark
of her disapproval, she will therefore tend gradually to increase
the severity of her blows, either by hitting harder, or by moving
to a more vulnerable part of the body—from legs and bottom
to the face, for instance. Most mothers have certain taboos
about where they will 'draw the line' in smacking: most suppose
that they would never use an implement or slap the child's face,
others restrict themselves firmly to the leg or the bottom or the
hand; but once the current taboo has been broken, and smacking
has escalated to a new level, even for one occasion, that new
level has a much better chance than before of becoming the
mother's normal practice. This is why frequent smackers are
also likely to be objectively hurtful smackers. The process of
escalation does not usually continue indefinitely, of course; and
the reason why much of this evidence comes from *erstwhile*
frequent smackers is that there comes a point when the mother is

brought up short by a sudden traumatic realization of what she is doing to her relationship with the child. We have a number of these special cases: two quotations will adequately illustrate the point.

I'm trying to stop smacking. I did have a time—I don't know how I got into it, every time he used to do something I used to smack him, and it used to be across his cheek; and I *know* it was wrong. He used to cry after; and for a bit, every time I went to him, he went like *this* (guarding cheek)—flinch, as though I'd been cruel to him. I *knew* I didn't ought to, but I did. So I'm trying to stop now, and he's forgotten it, he doesn't do that.

I will admit—I used to smack him and smack him, and I realized it wasn't doing any good. One day, I'd smacked him, and he looked really terrified, and he just—"Oh, not again, Mum—don't!" He was really terrified of me—I told my husband about it at night—well, *he* didn't know I *did* smack him. He doesn't believe in smacking. So I said, "Well, I don't care how cheeky he gets, I'll never do it again". And I don't think I *have* ever smacked him so hard since. I said, "Well, I was terrified of my mother, and I don't want him to be terrified of me", and I think that did it. He *is* getting more cheeky, I think, because I've stopped it—I try and talk to him. I don't care *how* cheeky he gets, though: I wouldn't like him to be frightened of me, same as I was my Mum. But I just remember when I was walking round the yard, and he walked backwards away from me, and he was *terrified*, and I came in and had a good cry. And I made my mind up; and afterwards worked it out.

Perhaps the most interesting finding on frequency of smacking is that, while the overall class differences are significant, they occur with reference to low frequency of smacking rather than high frequency, and are restricted to the top and bottom ends of the class scale. There is no significant class difference within the relatively small groups who smack either more than once a day or not at all; but significantly more Class I and II mothers and fewer Class V mothers are found in the group who smack occasionally but less than once a week. It looks as if smacking very frequently and eschewing it altogether both have more to do with the mother's individual personality than with class-correlated attitudes.[1]

[1] We reached the same conclusion about mothers who spontaneously expressed disapproval of smacking in the first survey (Newson, John and Elizabeth, 1963, *op. cit.*, p. 195); at the age of one we did not have a category for high-frequency smacking.

Two other variables can be mentioned here: housing and the child's sex. One might assume that smacking is more likely to happen when mother and child are thrown together in closer proximity than they might wish. Once again, to test this, we took the working-class sample only and compared mothers living on estates with those in the more over-crowded central areas. A significant difference is found in that *frequent* punishment is more likely in the more overcrowded districts; no difference can be shown with regard to frequencies below once a day. Between treatment of girls and boys, the opposite is true: there is a slight tendency ($p < \cdot03$) for more of the girls to be smacked *seldom* (less than once a week), but no difference can be shown in the other categories.

The findings for smacking in specific given situations, presented in Table XLV, reflects for the most part the figures for smacking frequency as a whole: Class I and II mothers are on the whole less prepared to smack, and Class V mothers are more inclined to do so. On the issue of enforcement of obedience by smacking or by other means there is a significant overall class difference, rising to a peak between middle-class and working-class mothers; Class IV mothers, as so often happens, show an anomalous result. Children's lies in response to an accusation are not so often met with smacks as is ordinary disobedience and this applies to all classes; but Class I and II mothers are rather more likely than others ($p < \cdot02$) to deal with the situation in other ways, usually verbally: we will return to this in the next chapter. Violence on the part of the child towards his mother is more likely than not to be met with retaliation, in the sample as a whole; but again there is a significant overall class difference whereby middle-class mothers in general, and Class I and II mothers in particular, are less likely to take the child's smacking of them seriously (see pages 486–90). The final line of this table refers only to the children who do in fact have temper tantrums (68%), since it seemed difficult to hypothesize realistically a situation as emotionally charged as this to mothers who were not currently experiencing it; Class I and II mothers smack in this situation less often than other mothers ($p < \cdot02$), but it is of some interest that on this issue the trend is turned at the bottom of the class scale, showing Class V mothers to be rather more tolerant of temper tantrums than other working-class mothers.

The general import of Table XLV is that professional and managerial class mothers consistently differ from the other class groups in the degree to which they use smacking as a response either to general 'naughtiness' or to specific offences; at the other end of the scale, unskilled workers' wives are more inclined to smack but their consistency in holding this attitude is liable to break down in particular instances.

The main interest of Table XLVI, which examines both the mood of smacking and the principle behind it, is the lack of disagreement between classes. No significant differences can be found here. Half the sample smack only when they are angry with the child; nevertheless, there is a certain resignation towards the use of smacking, not to say a complacency about it, and more than four out of five say that they 'believe in it'. The difficulty about this finding is that belief in smacking may denote different attitudes: the great majority of mothers think that 'you can't manage without it', 'you'd have to be a saint or else your children would', 'you just can't help it'; but, over and above this general acceptance of smacking's *inevitability*, some mothers 'believe in it' in the sense of finding it *justifiable*, others because they think it *effective*, and it is very difficult in practice to draw a firm line between these two emphases. Nevertheless they are important, because the quotations suggest that different emphases are linked with different social classes: professional-class mothers tending to say that smacking is not really justifiable but that it does work and therefore they believe in it, working-class mothers taking the view that it works and that is justification in itself. This rather subtle difference is probably responsible for the apparent rapprochement between the top and bottom classes as to their belief in smacking. The slightly larger-than-average groups in these classes who do *not* believe in smacking seem to give this answer for different reasons: Class I and II mothers have qualms about its moral standing, Class V mothers begin to lose faith in its effectiveness. (Whether smacking is in fact effective as a long-term socializing measure is a judgment which we cannot make at this stage.)

We may now ask how belief in smacking ties up with the degree to which mothers actually do smack their children. On rational grounds one should, of course, expect a correlation between belief and practice: if life were wholly rational, the correlation would be 100%. It is only the mothers who succeed

o*

in never smacking at all, however, who show a perfect correspondence between what they believe and what they do. We
have seen that 83% of the total randomized sample believe in
smacking and 17% think it wrong in principle: of those who do
believe in it, 83% smack their children once or more per week;
of those who disapprove of it, 40% smack their children as
often as this. There is thus a strong association between belief
and actual smacking, in statistical terms: in commonsense
terms, however, the most interesting thing about this result is
not the correlation, but the fact that 40% of the mothers who
think smacking a mistake *in practice do smack* not rarely but at
least once in an average week.

*'By the time they get to nine and ten, they should be all right'*
Why, then, are children of four smacked? The majority,
because their mothers think it a useful and reasonable thing to
do, although half of them would not do it at all if they did not
become angry with the child. The emotional component is thus
a very real one. The question remains, however, as to what the
mother thinks she is doing when she gives the child a smack.
Those who think it wholly regrettable are clear enough about
what is happening: human nature is violent, they feel, and they
smack because they willy-nilly find themselves doing so, and do
not try to give any rationale for their actions. Most, however, as
is clear from the high proportion who 'believe in it', admit that
in practice they are usually driven to smacking by their own
emotions, but at the same time think that it has a positive
function in teaching the child something about how to behave.
At the least hopeful level, this function is seen to be an immediate one: 'It makes him realize that he can go just so far';
'It shows him that I mean what I say'; 'It's pure drama': in
these cases, smacking is simply a means of emphasizing a
message which the mother would have preferred to convey by
other means—'I think word of mouth *should* be enough for
them', as a railwayman's wife said. Others expect the smack to
exert an effect lasting into the immediate future: that the child
will, in a similar situation, remember that he was smacked, and
that this memory will obviate the need for smacking next time. 'I
think it does do them good', said a chemical worker's wife,
'because if she gets a good smack for something, she doesn't
do it again. She remembers—she'll go for it again, and then

she'll say "You'll smack my bottom"—you see—she remembers what she's had a smack for'. If the child fails to remember spontaneously, the original smack can be used as reference-point for a warning: 'Now mind—you'll get what you got!' The mothers who think in these terms form a large group; at the same time many of them are conscious of holding this opinion against all practical evidence in the case of their own child. A jointer's wife admitted that, when you came down to it, smacking was not really for the child's good, though she felt it *ought* to work out that way: 'Sometimes they do the same thing all over again next day; so really it's more for me than them, I mean you don't get it out of *yourself* when you don't smack them. But sometimes it *must* do them some good—don't you think—I mean, they don't *like* it, do they?' 'Well, I *do* believe in smacking', said a metal polisher's wife who was now changing her tactics from physical punishment to isolation, 'but I can smack Derek until my hand tings: you just can't get through to him that way'. Finally, a small group of mothers, most of them smacking more than once a day, seemed to be using smacking as a sort of insurance policy; they could not see results at the moment, but they were hoping that the child would over the years come to respond to their efforts.

Foreman's wife:

(Do you think smacking does him any good?) Sometimes I begin to wonder. I think it does *later on*, if you know what I mean. At this age I don't think it's doing a lot of good. But I think that you're kind of moulding them now, and it's sinking in, so that a bit later on . . . I mean, if I thought that when he was about seven or eight he were going to back-chat me like he does now, and I thought smacking would stop that, I'd half-kill him *now*, you know what I mean?

Plant driver's wife:[1]

They'll get the belt if they really need it, and I won't think twice about it—I don't care what *anybody* says. To a certain extent, if you see what I mean, if they *want* it then it's better to give it to them, right there and then, than to have to give it to them later in life. Well, they're put away in homes or put away in institutions for not behaving themselves and being naughty. Well, I think

[1] As this book goes to press, the eight children in this family have been temporarily taken into care and their parents convicted of neglect.

*that*'s where the trouble starts, when they're young—I think so myself.

Labourer's wife:

If I'm going to hit them, I might as well hit them now, while they're little, rather than thrash them like I was thrashed when I was older. If I can knock good manners and common sense into them now, by the time they get to nine and ten they should be all right.

It is perhaps a point of some interest, in the light of theories on the relationship of punishment to learning, that those mothers who think that smacking has any functional role in learning invariably talk about the results it will have in the *future*, whether immediate, short-term or long-term; whereas the act of smacking invariably occurs as the culminating point of a sequence of events, and therefore has its roots in the immediate past. This in effect means that punishment in the context of mother/child conflict differs in two very basic ways from the experimental learning situation of the laboratory from which evidence is sometimes adduced to explain socialization. Not only does punishment in the family context involve social inter-action of a very intimate and emotive kind; it also comes about after a series of behavioural events in which the child is an equal participant, and during which he is given the opportunity of becoming aware of his own role as provoker of punishment and of his mother's intention to punish if he continues in it. It is in fact only in the situation of sudden danger, where the child approaches the busy road and is without warning snatched on to the pavement and smacked, that the punishment of a child of this age in any way approximates to the laboratory analogue of aversive stimulation: and this situation is surely of negligible importance in the process of socialization. To regard smacking as an ordinary example of avoidance conditioning, rather than as one part of a complicated communicational pattern between mother and child, is to simplify it out of all recognition: not least because, while a laboratory experiment can continue the process until learning occurs, the mother in practice is restricted in her behaviour, both by the individual reaction of the child—'You just can't get through to him that way'—and by her own conscience—'I came in and had a good cry, and I made my mind up'.

In this chapter we have concentrated for the most part upon mothers' use or threat of physical force in their efforts to secure 'good' behaviour from their children. Obviously there are other means than smacking, however, by which parents attempt to control and to guide their children: some of them clearly punishing, such as deprivation of sweets or privileges, others more subtle attempts to persuade or compel the child by verbal means. The four-year-old's ability to respond to language, to communicate with his mother in a more exact and particular fashion than ever before, gives her, for good or ill, a marvellously flexible socializing tool. It is to her use of this tool that we now turn our attention.

# CHAPTER 14[1]

# VERBALIZATION AND THE
# QUESTION OF TRUTH

Several times in the course of this book we have had occasion to emphasize that at four we are dealing with a child whose ability to talk and to respond to talk is enjoying its first flowering. At the height of his fantasy life, no longer held back by an inadequate grasp of words and syntax, and not yet inhibited by preoccupations with realism or considerations of propriety, his restless mind urges him to continual enquiry and comment; and this flood of communication will, because she is the most available audience, be directed chiefly towards his mother. Most mothers seem to appreciate their role of conversationalist, even if they sometimes find it wearing; and for many, the child offers a *quid pro quo* in his readiness to listen to them, which for the housebound woman can answer a real need: 'I forget she's only four, and I go rambling on, you know, as if she's a grown-up, sometimes'. 'I couldn't do without him—I love him talking to me', said a clerk's wife; a teacher's wife said 'She's such good company and chatters away—she's good at conversation'; and a miner's wife, who was going through a period of ill health and finding the children a physical strain, said: 'Well, me and Tom get on well together, you know: he's an attractive little fellow, you know, he'll jabber to you; he'll come in and say something—something to make you laugh and give you courage—or something loving, so that you could squeeze him'.

Because the four-year-old is so manifestly a verbal animal, socialization at this age takes on a new dimension. To the baby and the young toddler, 'naughtiness' is identified by means of bodily gesture, facial expression and a sharpened tone of voice:

[1] Part of the material in this chapter is published in Newson, John and Elizabeth, 'Some social differences in the process of child rearing': in Gould, J.: *Penguin Survey of the Social Sciences II*, Penguin Books, Harmondsworth, 1968.

the mother stretches a warning hand, frowns or grimaces and utters a brisk 'No!', or, if she is a Nottingham working-class mother, 'Baba!' If she verbalizes to any greater extent, it is not because she seriously expects her words to have any effect upon the baby: words here are merely a vehicle for the special intonation which carries that part of her meaning which is not conveyed in mime. Thus, if she says to him 'Oh darling, use your spoon, Mummy doesn't want baby's dress to get all messy', or 'Let nice Mary have a little play with your car', or 'That policeman's coming for you!', these words will be accompanied by explanatory gestures, and expressed in remonstrative, persuasive or warning tones, which are sufficient in themselves to make her intention clear; indeed, it would be equally effective so far as the child is concerned for her to say 'Bla bla oogle bla' with the same intonation. The main immediate function of the words she uses at this stage is in fact to clothe her intonation conveniently, and perhaps also to elucidate the interchange *for her own benefit* and for the benefit of onlookers.

At four, however, not only simple commands or warnings but highly complicated and subtle verbal explanations become possible. The mother if she wishes is now able to take advantage of her child's interest in explanations of the world in general and to bring to his attention notions of fairness and democracy, respect and authority, or whatever principles she wishes to instil in him as a guide in his dealing with human relationships. From the practical event she can draw a moral to explain her reason for approving or condemning, and thence can look forward to some hypothetical situation and discuss what *should* be done in such a case. Or she can in words reverse a situation for the child in order to make him understand mutual social obligations and to convey a principle of reciprocity: 'You've knocked over my flowers: now what would I say to *you* if I knocked down your bricks by accident?'—'If I let you play with my button-box, it's only fair for you to put it back tidily'—'I know you don't want Mary to play with your cars, but what about when you go to *her* house next week?' Four-year-olds are positively attracted by ideas of this sort which allow scope to the exploratory bent of their thoughts; one little girl was intrigued by the new angle offered by her mother, who asked her 'What do *you* do when your dolly makes such a fuss about having her hair done?' In the first of the quotations that follow,

Lance, whose mother does not readily volunteer explanations, is searching for his own principle.

Machinist's wife:

> Well, when I smack him, he'll have a good cry—"What did you smack me for?"—so I sort of tell him. So he'll sit and think, and then say, "Well, if I did so-and-so, you wouldn't smack me *then*, would you?" Then he keeps saying, "You know if I . . . if I spilt that tea, would you smack me then?"—"No"—"Why?" —"Well, if you did it on purpose I might"—working out *why*, you see.

Teacher's wife:

> Well, recently we've got to the stage of people's feelings. If he goes down to play past my mother's, and my mother's in the garden, he didn't use to sort of acknowledge she was there, you know, and I explained how this hurt my mother's feelings. And I explained how if you do something for someone and they don't expect it, you get a nice sort of feeling inside, and he's rather keen on this at the moment. I think a mother has to teach a child to be affectionate, to some extent. My mother used to wait for a child to give affection—she did with me—she didn't say to me "You must kiss me", and I think this is important, to a degree, because my father has always been very demonstrative: I think there's been p'raps too much of a tie between my father and I—my mother was left out—and I think she should have said "I *want* you to love me—I want you to cuddle me". And I found that Bruce would go off to school on his own, you see, until I started saying "I'd love to have a kiss and cuddle before you go"—and now he wants it. I think you have to teach them sometimes to show affection.

Dancing instructor's wife:

> Yesterday he couldn't have a lollipop when the other children went to get one. He stamped and jumped. I just said, "Now *look*, dear: you've already had sweets today. I just can't *afford* to buy you sweets just any time you want them". I had to explain *why*, you see. So he said, "It's all right Mummy. I don't mind"— with the tears streaming down his face!

Clergyman's wife:

> If it's a *bad* squabble . . . I separate them, and they have one corner each until everyone's quietened down; and when we've said we're sorry, we go into it and work out what it was all about.

Diesel engineer's wife:

> What I've done is, I've talked it over. It doesn't matter how young they are, I think you can still try and make them understand. It doesn't matter what the age is. I think if they're intelligent children, they get to understand . . . I think the only way to sort that sort of thing (quarrels) out is to talk it over between them, you see.

Sales manager's wife:

> I'm not happy when I have to smack her, ever, and I'm not happy about having to shout, and those are the two things I'm not happy about. But if I can reason with her and deal with it properly, I'm happy then.

Teacher's wife:

> I prefer to *talk round* things that have been done wrong, so that she puts them right *herself*.

It may be noticed that five out of these last six mothers who consciously reason with the child are middle-class;[1] the quotations were chosen for their content, and only later checked for the class of the speaker, but the class affiliation found is in fact no accident: and the argument which we shall try to justify and illustrate in this chapter is that perhaps the most salient way in which total patterns of upbringing differ from one class to another can be seen in the *kind* of control which mothers attempt to exert over their children. One aspect of this difference appears in the characteristic attitude of middle-class mothers which runs as a theme through the quotations above: a preference for managing children as far as possible through the use of reasoning. Whether the matter at issue is one of persuading or of preventing behaviour, the mother will try to give the child an explanation rather than a bald command, and will be (theoretically at least) prepared to countenance argument and to meet it with calmness and further explanation: 'I think a certain amount of obedience is necessary', said one white-collar mother, 'but I don't demand *unquestioning* obedience'. Tantrums and displays of violence against the mother are treated similarly, as the middle-class mother tries to get through to the child with a determinedly cool voice of reason, and makes a deliberate effort not to be in-

---

[1] The exception is in fact an upwardly mobile family, which had reached Class II living standards by this child's seventh birthday.

fected by his own emotionality. Anyone who has experience of children of this age will know that appeals to the reason of a furious four-year-old are often rather poorly rewarded; but it is typical of middle-class mothers—and, in particular, of the professional-class mother—to treat their children from a very early age (long before their language skills are adequate for understanding, in fact) *as if* they were capable of being persuaded by rational argument; and, because this line of action is rooted in attitudes and ideals about life to which they are deeply committed, they tend to persist in their pursuit of rationality, even when the initial success rate of this strategy is clearly very low. Working-class mothers, on the other hand, are less likely to embark upon any course which looks like involving them in lengthy verbal explanations of the whys and wherefores of their actions; on the whole, they show a preference for short-cut methods which get results quickly for the minimum of outlay in time and thought.

Driver's mate's wife:

I don't believe in all these books which tell you "Don't smack". If you're going to *talk* the child out of it, you're going to spend half your day standing there *talking* to them. I think it does them good to have a smack if they've done something wrong, you know, I think it lasts longer than simply talking to them.

Other workers in the field of child-rearing have looked for dimensions of greater or lesser permissiveness or of maternal warmth, and we ourselves, in our study of one-year-olds and their mothers, suggested that a permissive/restrictive continuum was meaningful in that context. We should make it clear at this point that, in discussing qualitative class differences in maternal control, both these issues seem largely irrelevant so far as four-year-olds are concerned. We did attempt to make a rating for maternal warmth, on the basis of the entire interview; but, using a four-point dimension of *very warm and demonstrative, warm, rather cool* and *negative*, we were unable to rate more than a handful of mothers as anything less than *warm* towards their four-year-olds: and the *negative* rating was used only twice. The actual proportions were 16%, 78%, 6% and 0%. This may be partly due to the niceness of our interviewers, who were commendably loth to rate mothers as *cool;* at the same time,

we seldom disagreed with their assessments, and can only conclude that mothers do have an extensive reservoir of warmth for
children of this age, which might, of course, be dissipated later
on. While the dimension of maternal warmth may have a
useful application in the field of child guidance, then, it seems
to be merely misleading in the present context.

Similarly, but for rather different reasons, the dimension of
permissiveness/restrictiveness at this stage seems to us confusing
and inadequate. As a simple measure of whether the mother
regards baby care as a potential battlefield, the concept is
useful:[1] there are not so many things to be restrictive *about*,
where infants are concerned. The four-year-old, however, is a
much more complicated creature, leading a much more complicated life; and the social classes tend to part company, not so
much on the issue of whether to be permissive or restrictive, as
upon which issues demand restrictiveness and which permissiveness. Mrs A, for instance, is a professional-class wife: she keeps
a close supervisory eye on Edmund, vets his friends discreetly,
makes him stay in the garden if he fights with neighbouring
children, insists that he obeys her for reasons which she carefully explains to him, and puts him to bed at seven o'clock;
however, he may jump on his bed and use finger-paints, is
ignored if he plays with his penis, and has been told where babies
come from. Mrs B is a labourer's wife: she lets Ronnie play in
the street with whoever he finds there, shouts at him if he
refuses to fight his own battles, insists that he obeys her because
if he doesn't he'll get a slap, and cuddles him to sleep with a
dummy (which Mrs A would never dream of doing) when he
comes in at nine; jumping on his bed and genital play both merit
a smack, and his mother insists in the face of his questioning that
babies come from the sweet-shop. Which of these mothers is the
more restrictive?

Although we shall in our final chapter return to the permis-
sive/restrictive continuum in terms of the subjective view which
individual mothers take of their own strict or easy-going position
in comparison with others, for the moment we propose to
explore differences in kind or quality of control by bringing
together from earlier chapters certain specific findings which
shed light upon the verbal communication that takes place
between mother and child; and, by knitting them into a cohesive

[1] See Newson, John and Elizabeth, 1963, *op. cit.*, Chapters 6 and 7.

pattern, we hope to show how such communication is linked, both as cause and as effect, with the basic attitudes to child-rearing which inform each parent/child relationship.

### 'I do try to make a point of being fair . . .'

As an example of a class difference in the use of verbal control, let us take the question of whether or not parents should inter-vene in children's quarrels (Chapter 5). Mothers' attitudes towards this issue are classified into two main types (Table X): the view which accepts the role of arbitrator, as a result of which the mother typically intervenes, tries to discover the ins and outs of the case, and 'helps them to see reason'; and that which prefers to remain aloof from children's conflicts, refuses to listen to complaints, and believes that they must learn to 'stick up for themselves'. In analysing individual mothers' positions, it was found necessary to assign 45% to an indeter-minate middle category, either because their attitudes seemed ambiguous or depended upon the specific details of the situation, or because the mother said that in normal circumstances she found her preferred attitude impracticable. However, a class breakdown of the very clear cases that were finally allocated to one group or another (Table XI) showed a significant class trend in which mothers higher up the social scale were more likely to intervene and arbitrate, while mothers further down the scale preferred children to settle their own differences; the biggest divergence occurred between the professional and mana-gerial class and the rest. This result is confirmed by a further class difference in the extent to which mothers are prepared directly to encourage children to hit back (Tables XII and XIII) once more, and very strikingly, separating Class I and II mothers from the rest: 65% of 'the rest' subscribe unequivocally to the principle of retributive tit-for-tat, while 64% of Class I and II at least have reservations and more than one in three would *never* tell their children to hit back. Twice as many pro-fessional and managerial class women as other white-collar wives can think of no circumstances in which they would say such a thing.

Now what is the immediate consequence of subscribing to the principle of arbitration? In the first place, the mother is brought into closer touch with the child; the mother who tells her child to work things out for himself deliberately brushes him off:

'Don't come tittle-tattling, go back and hit him', whereas arbitration involves the mother's presence and active attention. In the second place, the arbitrator at once commits herself to a higher valuation of the child's own verbalization: if one is going to arbitrate fairly between children, one must be prepared to listen with patience to their various accounts of the dispute. This means that middle-class mothers, and Class I and II mothers especially, pay more serious attention to the verbal complaints and excuses offered by their children; and it follows that middle-class children will have both greater incentive and more practice in learning the techniques of elaborate verbal self-justification, and are generally likely to become more adept at explaining themselves in a way which is acceptable to adults. In the third place, arbitration involves the following-up of the children's explanations by summary, homily and judgment from the mother: this, too, not only has its intended function of making the child understand the principles involved, but also heightens his awareness of the sort of verbal appeals which are likely in the future to be effective.

The middle-class mother's belief in arbitration comes into operation again in certain situations in which she herself is in conflict with the child; once more, she shows a willingness to listen to the child's own views in order to make sure that she is not acting unfairly towards him. An example is the question with which we were concerned in the last chapter: 'Suppose you asked him to do something for you, and he said "No, I can't do it now, I'm busy". What would you do?' In this case, a standard verbal excuse is proposed by the question, and the mother may or may not accept it, to her own inconvenience. We saw that significantly more middle-class than working-class mothers are tolerant of the child's subjective 'busyness', at least to the extent of giving him time before he has to accede to their demands. While the difference is not very large, and the majority of mothers are rather indulgent anyway to what they tend to see as an amusing spirit of independence in so young a child, the words in which they answer underline the statistical difference in the divergence of attitude which they convey: the 'Never mind busy, get it done!' of authority, as against the democratic reciprocity shown in 'I like *him* to wait . . . so it's only fair for *me* to wait'.

Here again, the working-class child is significantly less often rewarded for making verbal excuses, while the middle-class child finds this a rather potent means of getting his own way. Given experiences such as these, it follows that, for the working-class child, protests are more likely to become increasingly a matter of form only, the expression of rebelliousness against an authority which he has little hope of converting to his own view by the time-honoured democratic process of discussion and compromise, and which, because it is inflexible, invites eventual rejection rather than offering a possibility of coming to terms. For the middle-class child, on the other hand, there is every incentive for refining the ingenuity with which he states his case, encouraged as he is by the knowledge that it will be duly weighed and taken into consideration in deciding the outcome of a situation; and this will help him to co-operate with authority, and eventually to internalize its values, rather than turning his back on it altogether.

It must be understood that, while middle-class mothers are prepared to listen to the child's point of view, they are no more prepared than other mothers to tolerate what might be construed as 'answering back' or 'cheek'. 'Answering back' implies defiance rather than rational objection for most mothers, and in addition there is the complication of rudeness as shown by 'deliberate mocking—repeating everything I say back to me' and 'calling me every name under the sun', actions which are calculated to provoke and which often have that effect. Our questions on 'cheek' invited the mother to specify for herself the kind of behaviour she would and would not tolerate; and this was not altogether successful, as many mothers found it difficult to be specific. Prompted examples were provided for mothers who 'dried up' completely, but we were not very happy about putting words into their mouths in this way. The result showed no significant class difference in the tolerance of cheek (only 5% of mothers were completely permissive, and one in five were 'very strict'); but the transcripts suggest a difference between classes (which we cannot numerically prove) in the emphasis which is given to different *kinds* of 'cheek'. Working-class mothers tend to specify a deliberately defiant attitude as the main ingredient of the sort of cheek which they would condemn: the recurrent phrases which they quoted were 'I'm *not!*' (i.e. 'I'm not going to do it') and '*You!*' (which in Nottingham gains added vituperative force, in the mothers' own opinion, by being pronounced '*Yo!*'). Middle-class mothers, on the other hand, most often mention the sort of conscious rudeness which they feel is out of place in any social interchange: the principle of reciprocity is frequently invoked by the phrase 'I wouldn't speak to *you* like that, don't do so to me'. Thus for middle-class mothers cheek seems to be mainly an issue of courtesy; for working-class mothers, the basic question of 'who's gaffer'.

Chemical worker's wife:

> Well, I don't tolerate a lot of cheek; I do draw the line, when she answers me back, I say "That's enough!" She will say "Well I'm *going* to" or "I'm *not* going to", "I'm *not*"; and I say "You *are* going to. Don't answer me back". She'll ask me why not, why she shouldn't, and I just say "Children do not answer people back when they're as young as you".

Bleacher's wife:

> Well, as I say, she tries to hand it out to Stuart;[1] and of course she tries it with Mother as well!—"*I'm* not doing that", you know, and all this little *nodding* at the end. "Well, we'll see about that, then; you've got a long way to go yet, madam, before you start telling Mummy what you're going to do—get on with it!" And get on with it she does. I should let her see I was the boss, you know—for a while yet, anyway!

Labourer's wife:

> Well, I don't mind, like, when I tell him to do something and he turns round and says something comical like "Big ears!"—I don't mind that. But when he's really cheeky—you know, when you tell him to do something and he'll say "Oh, do it yourself", "I'm not going to do it"—oh, I *don't* like it when they're like that.

Lorry driver's wife:

> If she said "shut up", or something like that, then I'd say "Don't talk to me in that tone of voice". But if she was to be in the *right* about it—"old fat mum" and things like that, well then of course you don't mind, *that* don't matter.

University teacher's wife:

> This is a little bit emotional, I suppose: I can't bear being called a "fat nit". This annoys me disproportionately, and I say firmly "I'm *not* a fat nit, and you're not to call me one". If a seven-

[1] A longer description of this child's 'cheek' will be found on page 44.

year-old said "Shan't" very impertinently to me, that would get me. (Would you mind that from Charles?) No, he would just be showing off, and I would take a very humorous line with this, and he would pack it in.

Greengrocer's wife:

They mustn't shout at their mummy and daddy, ever: that's a very firm rule.

Publisher's wife:

Well, he's said to me, "That's the sort of thing you get your bottom smacked for!"—but, I mean, you can't grumble at it, because it's what you've said to him. But he might say "You're a big beast"—or worse; he's picked that up in the street; and then I do put my foot down.

Teacher's wife:

I think so very often children are justified in being cheeky, in so far as not showing what is considered normal respect for adults, because many things that adults do don't *need* respect. . . . If *we* shouted at her and upset her, *we* shouted and she shouted *back*, well, in many ways she has a fair *right* to shout. (Suppose she said "I'm *not* sorry"?) Well, then again, that is a kind of defiant remark that is usually dragged out from a situation in which somebody's trying to pressurize, and I don't like the idea of pressurizing anyway. There's something degrading in one human being, by sheer adult brute force, imposing their will upon a small child—I don't like it at all, grinding a small child down because the adult is bigger and stronger.

It may well be that middle-class mothers' high valuation of verbal interaction in general is one factor in their concern to encourage every aspect of social good manners, whether between child and adult or between the child and other children with whom he plays and disagrees. In our culture, of course, all parents will say that they want their children to be polite and well-mannered: the fear of being 'let down' or 'shown up' is, as we have seen, very real, and one which is shared by all parents. On the whole, however, middle-class mothers emphasize polite-ness rather more than others, and put more effort into its incul-cation, even with children of this age. The reader may recall that, when we investigated mothers' attitudes towards children's table manners, we found consistent and significant class trends on each of the three measures obtained from a points score for number and enforcement of rules at table, an 'extremes' rating of mothers said to be 'taking a lot of trouble' or 'leaving it for the moment', and an affirmative response to the question 'Would you say you mind very much whether a child has good table manners or not at this age?' In each case, the further up the class scale, the more emphasis was placed upon the importance of good table manners. However, in one single item only, a contrary trend was found: a greater proportion of working-class mothers specified 'no talking at the table'. While the difference here does not reach significance in the opposite direction, it seems to us of no little interest that it is *on the question involving verbalization* that the generally consistent trend is both halted and reversed. The difference in the mothers' behaviour reflects in fact a difference in attitude to the importance of conversation: those who forbid talking take the view that a child should 'shurrup and gerrit down'—'you can do your talking afterwards'—whereas the middle-class woman likes to think of mealtimes as social events and the dining-table as a focus for intelligent discussion of the day's happenings, and only discourages talking if in practice it deteriorates to mere noise.

*'I would try and make the child aware that he should have feelings of remorse . . .'*
In the last chapter, we tried to show that it is inappropriate to study socialization in terms of a disjointed series of short-term behaviour events, each being met on the part of the parent by some *ad hoc* response of punishment or reward. Parents are not solely, or even mainly, exercised with the checking of snippets of unacceptable behaviour in the here-and-now: they are in fact very self-consciously aware of a responsibility to achieve some sort of long-term moral training which will have a lasting effect upon the character of the child. To some extent this is true of all class groups, in that all mothers expect the discipline which they exert on specific occasions to have repercussions upon the child's total mode of behaviour: 'If I can knock good manners and common sense into them now, by the time they get to nine and ten they should be all right'. However, middle-class mothers do seem more concerned to point the *generality* of the principles which they try to instil; and they do this mainly by emphasizing their democratic application. We come back once more to the

mother's appeal to reciprocity: the adult's duty towards the child is continually drawn attention to, as a parallel to the child's duty towards the adult—'I wouldn't treat *you* like that, don't you do it to me'. The working-class mother, on the other hand, tends to lean more heavily upon appeals to a natural authority vested in adults in general, and parents in particular, and seems less often aware of any need to justify this in terms of 'fairness': 'I'm gaffer in this house, not you, milady!'

Thus in teaching politeness and good manners mothers are not merely trying to ensure that their children learn to observe certain arbitrary conventions of social behaviour: they are equally concerned to lay down general ethical principles about how people behave towards one another, which will later form the basis of some consistent moral philosophy; and the middle-class mother continually makes this explicit in verbal terms, not simply relying on the child to generalize from event to principle, but interpreting her attitude for him in terms of social laws.

An example of this can be drawn from those situations between mother and child in which an apology might be thought necessary. To the question 'Do you think it is important for him to say he's sorry when he's done something wrong?', nearly all mothers answer 'Yes'; and from their replies to the complementary question, 'Do you ever *make* him do that, even if he doesn't want to?', we learn that two out of three mothers would enforce an apology: there is no indication of any class difference.

Insurance inspector's wife:

Oh yes, we do, we make him say sorry. Sometimes it takes quite a time for the words to come out, but we insist until he does, you know—probably say, "Well, you just stay there until you do", and then he does. Although sometimes he *whispers* them so we can't hear it, and says he's said it; and then we make him say it louder!

Coal delivery man's wife:

Well, I've often said to him "You'll sit there till you say you're sorry", and even if he was sitting there all day, I'd make him say it in the end.

University teacher's wife:

If he *is* sorry, I don't think there's any virtue in making this be uttered as a formula, and I think very often, with children, they don't want to *say* that. You can tell whether they are sorry or not. I would try and make the child aware that he should have feelings of remorse! But I'm not bothered about the uttering of the *words*—at his age, anyway.

### Labourer's wife:

No. What's the point of saying you're sorry if you've been *forced* to say it?

### Export packer's wife:

I've never known her to say she's sorry. She's always got a perfectly sound reason *why* she's done anything—whatever she's done, it's perfectly logical, it's always *you* that's wrong!

Suppose, however, we approach apology from another angle: the circumstances in which a mother might herself feel an obligation to apologize to the child. We have such a situation proposed in a question from the group that explored mothers' attitudes towards children's property rights: 'If you've broken something of his by accident, and it can't be mended, what do you do about it?' We saw in Chapter 6 that the majority of mothers feel that something positive should be done about this: only 15% blame the child for 'leaving his things where I'll trip over them' and 6% try to avoid trouble ('hide it and say nowt'). 60% of working-class mothers, compared with 50% of middle-class mothers, emphasize that they would feel a duty to replace the broken toy: working-class mothers tend to be conscious of material obligations towards their children, and take pleasure in 'giving them just that little bit more than what we had'. However, although they implicitly acknowledge their fault by accepting the duty of restitution, they are not so ready as middle-class mothers to make an explicit statement in the form of an apology to the child: only 18% of working-class women emphasize the importance of apology in this situation, compared with 31% of middle-class mothers. This divergence in attitude can also be found in the responses given to the question 'Do you sometimes find yourself doing things you don't really approve of?', although, because we did not specifically ask about apologies in this context, we have no quantitative data here. None the less, one can clearly detect a predominantly working-class feeling that for the adult to apologize to the child for her behaviour to him would in some way diminish her authority over him in the future: quite prepared to be self-critical in her discussion with the interviewer, she draws the line at admitting any doubts to the child: 'Afterwards you reflect about it, and you realize you were in the wrong, but there again, you don't go apologizing to the *child* if you're in the wrong'.

### Driver's wife:

Sometimes I've said no to things instinctively, when with a little bit of thought I could have said yes; but I don't go back on it. In a case like that, I'm sorry to *myself*. I'll say no, and then on second thoughts I'll think to myself, "Well, she wouldn't have been doing any harm"; but I still leave it at that, I don't change my mind; I don't think you *should*.

### Machine operator's wife:

I sometimes feel sorry when I've smacked her, because when I *do* smack them, I *smack* them, you see; as I say, I marked her this morning, and I feel sorry after. But I wouldn't tell *her* so.

### Wirer's wife:

Once I ripped a book that one of them treasured—I don't know, something made me so mad I just tore this book up; and I thought at the time, I don't think I ought to have done that. (And did you say you were sorry to them?) No, I didn't say anything. I *was* sorry, though, actually.

### Teacher's wife:

I'm frequently sorry for snarling at them. I usually try to apologize to them if I've been unfair—or *extra* unfair!

### Garage manager's wife:

Well, sometimes I smack him (for tantrum provoked by mother's irritability), and sometimes I've cuddled him afterwards, and told him it's not really his fault, it's mine, with being nasty[1] to him. *Very* often, when I've let fly at him, I've consoled him afterwards.

Middle-class wives are not only readier to acknowledge themselves in the wrong, but also often make very explicit the principle which they are trying to follow by doing so. 'I'd discuss it

[1] *Nasty = bad-tempered* in Nottingham usage.

with her', says a teacher's wife in answer to the question about breaking the child's possessions—'an example of what ought to happen the other way round, if she breaks something of mine, what should *she* do?'; and an insurance clerk's wife, discussing whether the child should apologize, says 'He very often doesn't want to. But I put it to him: "If *I'd* done it, I'd say sorry to *you*, and you'd want somebody else to", and usually, reluctantly, he does'. By both apologizing and explaining to the child in this way, these mothers are deliberately and self-consciously providing their children with a model of 'correct' social behaviour with moral overtones; and this seems to be especially characteristic of the pattern of control which middle-class mothers exercise over their children.

Findings on a related topic—the question of confession of misdeeds—are of some interest. While parents of four-year-olds look mainly to the future for the fruits of their various methods of discipline, and do not usually expect very impressive rewards at this age, a difference can in fact already be seen in the actual behaviour of middle-class and working-class children in the situation proposed by the question 'Does he ever come and tell you he's been naughty before you actually find out?' Mere guilty expressions ('You can always read his face') or acts which indirectly convey guilt to the mother ('I know straight away, because he'll come in and say "I didn't do it"') were discounted as confession, and answers were simply rated on a YES/NO basis. 60% of middle-class children confess voluntarily at least sometimes, as against 48% of working-class children, and the overall trend is significant at the ·001 level. The difference in attitude is nicely highlighted by the answers of two mothers in Class II and Class III: the wife of a teacher says, with quiet assurance, 'Oh yes; certainly'; a lorry driver's wife gives a short laugh, and answers 'No—well, she'd be a fool if she did, wouldn't she?'

The reverse of this question is also worth looking at in this connection. The mother is asked: 'Suppose he says he *hasn't* done something naughty, when you know quite well that he has. What do you do then?' In this situation, the mother has effectively three choices: she can ignore the fact that he has told a lie, she can punish him for the lie, or she can, without punishing, simply ensure that the child understands that she has recognized his statement as a lie. One in ten mothers ignore the incident altogether, and this group shows no class difference: for them, the child is still too young for an issue to exist.

Coal merchant's wife:

> Well, I don't think I'd persist too much with it; because I think the more you persist, the more they think about it. You know, if you don't bother, they forget, and then they're not so likely to do it again.

Metallurgist's wife:

> Nothing. I don't think Roland knows the difference between lies and the truth.

On the question of punishment, however, there is a significant difference (at the ·02 level) between Class I and II mothers and the rest: as we saw in the last chapter, they are rather less likely than others to smack their children for telling lies. This is not because they consider the issue less important than other mothers; all mothers think it important that their children should eventually learn to tell the truth. Working-class mothers, however, regard lies as one among many possible crimes which, if they consider the child old enough, must be met at once by effective checks: 'That's the time when I usually *do* smack her, because I don't want her to grow up and go through life telling fibs—if you don't prompt them when they do little things, as they get older, I mean, it can only grow into bigger things'. The professional or managerial class mother is less inclined to regard this as a crime to be punished, but rather as something which the child has to learn to *understand:* in a sense, she takes the line that lying is *too* important a concept for punishment to be appropriate. An administrative assistant's wife, who in other situations believes quite strongly in the dramatic value of smacking, expresses this point of view very clearly when she says 'I'm not angry, because it's one of those things that a child has to *learn*'. It is worth quoting her at length.

> I'd deal severely with that. Truth is a very important thing. At this age you can tell them and they'll recognize; later on they can become proficient at *hiding* that they're telling lies, and therefore it's one of those things that you *have* to learn early in life. I'm not angry, because it's one of those things that a child has to

*learn*. For example, Jeffrey and the neighbour's boy went over the wall at the bottom of the garden and stole some blackberries. His mouth was covered with juice, and the first thing that struck me was that he'd been eating berries that were poisonous. So I, urgently, if you like, got the information out *what* they'd been eating, and then told him he wasn't to go over the wall again, because he was stealing, because that was another thing that people don't *do* in modern society. He must have sneaked off and gone over again. Now I wasn't angry with him, but when he came back I said "Have you eaten them again?" and he said "No". So he was brought in and it was *explained* to him: on two counts, you see: he'd *stolen*—and he'd *lied*.

A clergyman's wife, following up the general question of lies and broken promises, came back once again to the principle of reciprocity:

I think this whole business of deceit . . . if you show that you don't like it at all, and you try and point out that you never let *her* down—I mean, you never tell her that you're going to do something and don't do it. She must never do the same to you. But it is a difficult point to get across, I think . . .

—*too* difficult, in fact, to get across by the more clumsy method of smacking and punishment.

*'She's got a bitch of a temper, she has—like her Grandad!'*
A further example of class differences in the actual behaviour of the child occurs in the incidence of temper tantrums, and this also appears to have something to do with the rather different patterns of control which middle- and working-class mothers exert over their children. The temper tantrum is the child's response to extreme subjective frustration: that is to say, the child appears to think that he is being severely frustrated, but children differ considerably as to what objective event triggers off this behaviour. Exaggerated aggression is shown, though not necessarily against the mother unless she gets in the way of it: indeed, it is characteristic of the temper tantrum that aggression is rather generalized in its expression, directed against the environment as a whole, and sometimes also against the child himself. It is also typical that the tantrum is an emphatic state-ment to the world at large of the child's anger, rather than

having any effective function in putting right what has frustrated him. The descriptions below are representative.

### Packer's wife:

He *has* got a temper—do you mean sort of writhes and kicks? (That sort of thing, yes—and banging doors and shouting.) Yes, he'll go upstairs and slam the door, or in the front and slam that door. And he'll run his head into the wall. (On purpose?) Yes, or he'll run in that corner and bump his head. He thinks he's hurting *you*. I say "You aren't hurting my head, Ian, you're hurting your own". More often, he'll lie and kick on the floor. I see him getting mad—"What's the matter, Ian?"—"I can't *do* the damn thing!" he says. He gets so aggravated, he'll just throw himself on the floor, and then he starts.

### Office worker's wife:

If she can't have her own way she'll scream and yell and carry on, then she gets a wallop, then she screams and yells a bit longer, then she shuts up.

### Miner's wife:

Not very often—but when it comes it's a smasher! It's a wonder that door's never come off its hinges. She bangs it, and she stamps, and she has them chairs over. Then the rug comes up— *that* goes through it—*that* gets kicked to bits.

### Plasterer's wife:

Not very often—but once he went wild. It was cold, and I'd got a load of shopping in the pram, and the baby, so I made him walk from the shops. And when he got home, he went mad! He kicked the furniture, kicked everything upside-down—he really went mad. Then he slept all afternoon.

Table XLVII shows the incidence of temper tantrums in relation to social class: *often* means that the child has tantrums on average once a week or more frequently. The last line of the table repeats, for convenience, the proportions of mothers who smack their children for tantrums, and the percentages in this line refer only to children who actually have tantrums: as we noted in the last chapter, hypothetical questions were avoided in this case.

TABLE XLVII

*Incidence of and response to temper tantrums*

|  | I & II | IIIwc | IIIman | IV | V | All (random) |
|---|---|---|---|---|---|---|
|  | % | % | % | % | % | % |
| Tantrums often | 25 | 28 | 38 | 39 | 49 | 36 |
| Tantrums sometimes | 36 | 42 | 31 | 33 | 18 | 32 |
| Tantrums never | 39 | 30 | 31 | 28 | 33 | 32 |
| Child smacked for tantrums (actual cases only) | 20 | 33 | 36 | 38 | 25 | 33 |

Behaviourally speaking, we may assume that the three groups of children shown in the first part of the table are meaningfully distinguished from each other: if a child has tantrums at least once a week, this may be considered normal behaviour for him, in that his mother may be upset by it but she is not particularly *surprised* when it occurs; while children who occasionally have these displays of rage, even if rarely, seem to be distinguishable in a rather important way from those for whom tantrums are quite outside their behavioural repertoire. This being so, the findings in this table are of considerable interest. Significant class differences can be seen among the group of children who have tantrums 'often': there is a steady and consistent class trend towards more frequent tantrums as one descends the class scale, with two main breaks, between middle-class and working-class, and between unskilled and skilled or semi-skilled.

Before we can interpret these data in terms of cause and effect, we need to look briefly at the means by which temper tantrums are dealt with. The easiest response to distinguish is, of course, smacking: this either does or does not happen, and mothers who do smack for tantrums seem to do so fairly consistently. 'Usually we have to end up giving him a darn good hiding, when he's like that' says a joiner's wife; and the farmer's wife whose daughter inherited her temper from Grandad agreed: 'It does just drive you up the wall. She stamps and screams and carries on. Of course, she gets a smack then, across the legs'. Smacking must be seen not just as an act of punishment, but also as an attempt to get through to a frantic child—'I usually break her

P

out of it with a sharp smack'—and is often used in the hope of reaching the usual aftermath of submissive exhaustion rather more quickly, though it does not always have that effect.

Other ways of coping with tantrums include isolation, soothing and ignoring: but since these often happen in sequence, it is not practicable to separate these groups. Isolation, especially, is seldom total, and tends to happen in conjunction with soothing; and ignoring usually has a soothing culmination.

### Self-employed craftsman's wife:

I bring him in the house and he just sits there until it wears off; and usually within about ten minutes the tears dry, and he says "Can you wipe my tears now?"

### Architect's wife:

If she raises a tantrum at mealtime—no question of punishment—we just say "There are too many people in this room for us to have this noise—you can either stop crying and stay here, or you can be carried out, whichever you like"; and quite frequently she will stop crying and be reasonable. But if she won't be, there's no question about it—usually her Daddy just picks her up bodily and takes her out. It's not a punishment in any way.

### Nylon worker's wife:

I tell her she can't have it and take no notice of her. She has her bout out, and she's all right after that.

### Miner's wife (same as page 448):

I leave her alone. I just leave her alone. She finishes, and then I'll say "Oh, what's the matter, me old flower, then?"—and she'll come and maybe sit on my knee, or she'll lean here, and I'll just stroke her head and talk to her. She's all right then.

We may now try to answer the question why children further down the social scale have more tantrums. It has sometimes been suggested that the use of smacking in response to tantrums has a reactive effect of making further tantrums more likely: of creating a tantrum-prone child, so to speak, by storing up aggression in him. While this is a plausible enough hypothesis, it is not supported by our findings: if it were true, one would expect Class V mothers, whose children have the most tantrums, to be smacking for tantrums more than anybody else. While Class V mothers do do a good deal of smacking, however, where tantrums are concerned they smack less than any other group except professional and managerial mothers. We must thus look for another explanation; and we believe the answer lies in the pattern of verbal control which we have been looking at in this chapter, which includes a greater willingness on the part of middle-class mothers to spend time on lengthy explanations; and which also, as we found in our study of babies as well, involves what we then called 'a greater consciousness of the total sequential pattern of their actions'. At that time, we wrote that 'this *taking thought* about the methods they use, typical of white-collar wives, is probably as important as any other factor in reducing the frequency of temper tantrums'. Our present findings give us no reason to modify this view: indeed, they fully confirm it. In practical terms, what seems to happen is that middle-class mothers are more able to divert the child from his tantrum before it comes to a head: the heat is taken out of the situation partly by *taking thought* at an early stage in the process and partly by using mainly verbal means to reduce the child's frustration, offer him active attention, and thus make it unnecessary for him to demonstrate his anger so fiercely. A coal merchant's wife illustrates the point: eight months pregnant, she was sometimes finding her patience lagging behind her good intentions.

> It all depends how *I* am, at the moment. You see, you get a situation and if you're feeling right you deal with it in a good frame of mind, whereas another day you perhaps aren't, and then they *have* a tantrum; but if you dealt with it gently, well, they wouldn't bother, they wouldn't have one at all.

The greater toleration of tantrums in Class V, together with their more frequent occurrence, can also be interpreted in terms of special class attitudes. In our earlier study, we suggested that Class V babies are often teased and exploited for their elders' amusement, and that this sort of treatment is likely to produce temper tantrums.[1] This impression is maintained and confirmed in the present study: we found a rather widespread feeling in this class that it is justifiable to provoke and bait children in small ways, short of actually being cruel, in order to enjoy their

[1] Newson, John and Elizabeth: 1963, *op. cit.*, pp. 199–200.

reaction. The greater unwillingness to punish for temper tantrums found in the top and bottom classes thus reflects two rather different attitudes: in Class I and II, a solicitous desire to reduce the child's emotion as quickly and gently as possible; in Class V, an amused tolerance of a display which is worth a laugh to the onlookers, and which will therefore be met either with equanimity or with ridicule, the latter course often only adding fuel to fire. Sometimes, in fact, this seems to be its intention: the following quotation is an extreme case of the general attitude which we have described.

Unemployed labourer's wife:

> Ooh, definitely; that's what she does more than owt, temper. She gets into a temper two or three times a day, 'cause we torment her, 'cause we like to see her in a temper, you see. She flies at you when she's in a temper, she claws at your face. Usually it's her Daddy torments her, or me; we all have to laugh at her. (And how do you torment her, to make her get in a temper?) Oh, usually we pretend she's not going to do something she wants to do—we say we're taking someone else's little girl out, taking the little girl next door into town, and all like that, you know. (And when she flies into a temper, what do you do?) Oh, just laugh at her. I mean, it's really amusing, really laughable.

There is no significant class difference among the group of children who never have temper tantrums; and we would suggest that constitutional factors probably come into play here, in that some children are, from a very early age indeed, more equable and amenable, with a greater frustration tolerance than others. Most mothers can point to one of their children who is 'the easy one', and it is often quite impossible to explain this on environmental grounds alone.

Perhaps one further point should be made about temper tantrums in general. If 36% of children have them often and 32% sometimes, they may certainly be considered a normal manifestation in the four-year-old. At the same time, the mother finds that their occurrence in public is particularly shaming, because for a short time at least it is all too clear that she has lost control over the child. She will therefore do all she can to avert such a scene in a public place, and to escape from observation if one overtakes her. It is also true that a child's tantrums, though not overtly directed against the parents, usually take place only when they are there, and seldom when he is in the charge of other people less intimately connected with him: perhaps this extreme expression of emotionality, this breakdown of social control, needs as a sounding-board the on-going and permanent relationship which the parent represents. The practical result is, however, that those whose relationships with children are mainly more formal ones—teachers, doctors, nurses and so on—may be relatively inexperienced in this normal flashpoint of the socialization process, and may interpret it when they do see it as evidence of the parent's ineffectuality: still more so when they are able to pride themselves on the fact that the child who throws a tantrum in its mother's presence becomes amenable as soon as she leaves him in their care. No-one is more conscious of this interpretation than the mother herself: as the primary school teacher who was having trouble with her little boy's obstinacy over meals said, 'I mean, it is the sort of generally accepted idea that it's the parents who are to blame, isn't it?—the parents are too soft with them. The *doctor* would say that to *you*. I'd have said it myself'. Temper tantrums thus provide an exceptionally 'showing-up' situation (as we have already seen—page 407), and the mother who is caught in such an incident is likely to be badly flustered by embarrassment, and hence to respond abnormally. It must also be remembered that one of the lessons of socialization is that scenes of extreme emotion should be kept privately in the bosom of the family: so that for most children there comes an intermediate stage in which they have learned not to throw tantrums in the presence of an outsider, but still do so with more than adult frequency within the intimate family circle. For these various reasons, tantrums and parents' response to them are not at all available to direct scientific observation, but necessarily have to be studied at secondhand, particularly as the child grows older.

*'A good sharp slap, it shows a sense of authority'*
*'I'd rather have an understanding between the two of us'*
At this stage, it seems necessary to draw together the threads of our argument before carrying it one stage further. While almost all parents agree that some guidance is necessary during the early years in order that a child should develop into an acceptable, i.e. socialized, member of society, and while they all

accept responsibility for providing this guidance, they differ, not so much in their basic aims, as in the stress they lay upon certain aspects of behaviour. The middle-class style of parental control puts greater emphasis upon reasoning, adjudication of quarrels, fairness in the sense of 'do as you would be done by' and general good manners: values are transmitted by means of a pattern of reciprocal rights and obligations which the mother continually brings to her child's attention in words and by the example of her own actions. The working-class style of control emphasizes authority, self-reliance in quarrels, fairness in the sense of 'be done by as you did' and respect for adults. A central feature of this class difference is the premium which middle-class parents put upon explicit verbal communication with their children, not only for the purpose of checking unwanted behaviour, but in order to sow the seeds of ideas, including moral ideas, to make them think about and evaluate their own actions and those of other people, and to make them aware of what other people might think of them. By the age of four years, the problem is no longer to teach the child in terms of simple avoidance conditioning (as one speaks sharply to a baby when he approaches a hot stove), nor to drill him in specific motor habits. Parents, of whatever class, are now primarily concerned to educate the child by passing on broad general principles: 'It's not fair to hit someone smaller than you are'; 'Don't take people's things without asking first'; 'Be kind to pets'; 'It's greedy to snatch'; 'People will never believe you if you sometimes tell lies'; and because general principles are better learned for being better comprehended, and better comprehended if stated verbally in a variety of ways according to the needs of the occasion, it may be expected that parents who both verbalize themselves and value verbal response will be the most successful in imparting their ideas to the child. In the process of socialization as a whole, the importance of verbal communication as both supportive and interpretive of parental example can hardly be over-rated.

This is not to say that verbal and explanatory means of control are necessarily pleasanter for the child. The picture of a kindly explaining mother as opposed to an unkindly smacking mother is not an impression which we wish to convey; it would be quite false. Different degrees of kindness or unkindness can flourish in either of the settings which we have described: and probably most mothers are occasionally unkind. Mothers sometimes express the view that the child *prefers* a quick smack to a 'talking-to', and this is also an argument which is often used to support the retention of corporal punishment in schools. However, we are not in fact concerned here with what the child prefers in the short term, so much as with what is in the long term effective in achieving socialization; the question which we are ultimately asking is: by what means is conscience evolved in the child, and what kinds of conscience emerge from what kinds of disciplinary experience? One can see how a child might very well prefer the short sharp slap to the verbal explanation of why he must do as he is told: the slap compels him only to momentary obedience in the present situation, whereas the explanation of principle involves him in a lasting commitment over many similar incidents to come. What is more, the slap provides him with an enemy and therefore an excuse for rebellion: 'she's hurt me, she's horrid, I hate her'; whereas the mother who is always patient and reasonable, always ready to listen, and always prepared to explain at a little more length if necessary, is plainly an inappropriate candidate for the role of enemy and can only be hated at the expense of an uncomfortable amount of guilt: she is thus a much more potent threat to the barbarian in the child. Taking this to extremes, probably the most difficult mother for a child to cope with is the one who *never* makes it possible for him to hate her; fortunately most mothers lose their tempers occasionally and give the child that opportunity. Short of this unnatural ideal (for which mothers strive in the reassuring knowledge that they will never attain it), the most effective conscience, which is comfortable neither to acquire nor to possess, is likely to be achieved by the process of cumulative verbal reasoning which we have described.

Quite apart from an emphasis upon discipline through the use of words, there are numerous indications in this, as in other studies, that middle-class mothers tend to interact generally with their children more often and in a more verbally articulate way. We have already seen how their closer supervision and the fact that they tend to draw their children into the house away from conflict, rather than send them out to meet it, means greater opportunity for interaction. Many other situations of everyday life confirm the highly verbal nature of the association. For instance, verbal fantasy as a part of their children's play-life was described by 28% of our total sample of mothers: but this is quite clearly linked to social class, with a trend ranging from 45% of the professional and managerial class to only 14% of unskilled-class mothers. As we pointed out in Chapter 7, the fact that mothers do not know about fantasies does not necessarily mean that the children do not have them privately; but the essential fact for our present purpose is that *verbal communication* of fantasy differs between the top and bottom of the class scale to the degree shown. The extent to which the singing of songs, telling of stories and saying of prayers forms a regular part of the child's bedtime pattern is another example of class differences in children's verbal experience at this age: for 48% of middle-class mothers (rising to 60% in the professional and managerial class), songs and stories are normal at bedtime, but this is true for only 24% of working-class households (dropping to 20% in Class V). Taking prayers separately, even the fairly high Irish Catholic population in the unskilled class cannot bring the working-class proportion of bedtime prayers (9%) anywhere near the middle-class proportion, which is 23%. A further finding which may be of interest is on the question of the father's participation. When the children were twelve months old, fathers were found to be highly participant in their care generally, with a class trend towards greater participation higher up the social scale: an exception to this trend was that shop and clerical workers were more participant than any other group. By the time the child is four, the father is still more active in caring for him; but this time the class trend shows a straight run, with the professional and managerial fathers in the lead. Internal evidence from mothers' comments suggests that the reason for this is that fathers of four-year-olds are beginning to warm to what is now an educative rather than a purely nurturant role: and that professional fathers therefore move ahead of others because of the special attractions to them of a child who is now responsive to verbal communication (see page 549).

In these various ways, our findings complement and support those of Bernstein,[1] Douglas[2] and other workers on the social differences that exist in the use of language. At this point,

[1] Bernstein, Basil: 'Language and Social Class', *British Journal of Sociology* xi, 1960; and 'A Socio-Linguistic Approach to Social Learning', in Gould, Julius: *Penguin Survey of the Social Sciences, 1965*.

[2] Douglas, J. W. B.: *The Home and the School*, MacGibbon & Kee, London, 1964.

however, we would enter a caveat. It is sometimes suggested that children at the lower end of the social scale have a more attenuated verbal experience mainly because their mothers' impoverished linguistic abilities make it difficult for them to communicate with their children adequately. Our own experience of talking to mothers at all social levels would lead us to reject lack of skill as the *major* factor, if only because they are so clearly able to communicate their thoughts and feelings about their children to the interviewer. We would not question, of course, that people at the lower social levels do have greater communication difficulties: but we would suggest that, in almost every case, it will be found that other factors—of attitude, emotion, situation, or even simple decision, are of equal or greater consideration than the factor of pure verbal facility. This contention is well illustrated in some of the tape records we have from mothers of handicapped children, in which mothers and fathers describe in vivid detail, and with humour or pathos, their own failures to communicate:[1] those mainly in which the situation of being a working-class person in the alien professional-class context of hospital or school set up barriers which words could not be found to penetrate. It must also be remembered that failure to communicate in an advisory setting may be a form of passive resistance: we saw in our first study how many mothers (not only in the working class) give up breast-feeding as soon as the midwife is out of the way, rather than join issue with her earlier; another example is provided by one of our most talkative and interesting mothers, who will gladly 'let her hair down' for two or three hours on end to the uncritical interviewer, but whose schedule was originally returned by her first Health Visitor interviewer marked 'very low mentality—impossible to interview'.

Communication with one's own children is hardly a matter of situation, however, and it is here that other factors come into play. The comments which we quoted in Chapter 12, for instance, make it clear that it is the prudish attitudes and emotions with which working-class people tend to surround sex function and nakedness which are mainly responsible for their reluctance to discuss such topics with their children: they are usually able to discuss with the interviewer the *fact* of their reluctance. The Class IV mother below can be relied on to talk through two

[1] Report by Sheila Hewett: in preparation.

P*

2-hour interviews at each age-stage; her inability to talk to her children about reproduction is essentially emotional.

> Ooh no—because I've not even said anything to William yet, and he's ten. It's so difficult, isn't it? I wouldn't *want* to tell him . . . When I was carrying Jimmy, William and Nancy started to notice, you know, and one day William passed a remark, he said "Our Mum's getting fat, isn't she?" Well, it made me feel *ever* so badly; and I said to them, straight away, "Now that's *naughty*"—oh, I did feel badly about it. Well, when the midwife came, I told her about it, I said they'd been passing remarks. "Well", she said, "you'd better sit them down and tell them about it". I said, "Now you're asking me to do summat I *can't*".

The father's comment which follows (Class III) was made during the discussion of cheekiness; again, he does not have particular difficulty in expressing himself, but he does not intend to do so on this topic to his children.

> Well, I don't know whether it could be termed as cheekiness, but there's a sort of *inquisitiveness*. If it's something she's heard, and that she wants an explanation for, well I do draw the line at that. (What sort of inquisitiveness do you mean?) Well, at her age and Kenneth's age (6), you do find that they ask all sorts of things bordering on sex, even at their age. It's nothing *absolutely* . . . but it could lead . . . it's just bordering on it, you see.

We do not wish to deny that there *are* some mothers who find the linguistic difficulty the main problem: but they are rare, compared with the constantly repeated examples of embarrassment and panic. The clearest statement we have of language inadequacy is given below; even here, however, there seems to be some strong emotional factor which prevents a mother ever having mentioned the topic *at all* to daughters who have now reached sexual adulthood.

> Well, I don't really know—I don't know *what* I should say to her; as a matter of fact, I've never told any of them (girls aged 22, 16, 6 and 4, boys aged 12 and 10). To tell you the truth, I don't know how I should put it in the best way; I've never been out and mixed a lot, you see, with people; I've been on me own such a lot; and I don't think I'd be very good at explaining that, I don't think I would myself. If somebody could, you know,

*tell* me how to explain it to them, I would do, but I don't think I'd be capable of explaining it to them properly.

*'I shouldn't tell him the truth—anything but the truth . . .'*

We saw in Chapter 12 how mothers who are pressed by their four-year-olds to explain where babies come from may take refuge in 'any little tale'—'the first thing that come in my mind' —rather than admit even the abridged truth that a baby grows in its mummy's tummy. While 46% of the total sample would withhold all information (rising to 75% of unskilled workers' wives, falling to 12% of professional and managerial workers' wives), 35% would give a definitely false explanation (rising to 66%, falling to 8%); Table XLI gives the full class figures. It should be borne in mind that 'from Heaven' is not counted as false, nor is 'we have to save up our pennies' unless *buying* a baby is specifically mentioned: so these figures are conservative.

More lies are told to children of four in this situation than in any other, fraught as it is with deep-seated taboos and uncertainties; but the very striking class divergence here reflects not only different feelings towards sex but also *different attitudes towards truth*; and further evidence to support this can be found when we turn our attention to the sort of threats which parents use towards their children. In our discussion of sanctions and other means of control thus far, we have concentrated mainly upon explanation, smacking and 'fierceness' of expression or voice. This does not by any means exhaust the mother's repertoire, however: other sanctions which she may use include deprivation (of sweets, ice-cream or television), isolation (sent out of the room or to bed), threats of punishments which cannot be carried out, and the ultimate threat of withdrawal of her love.

The use of isolation and deprivation is not of very great interest, although both are much threatened. Isolation when it happens does not usually seem to last very long, and is more of a gesture than a punishment; it is normally immediately ended as soon as the child becomes submissive, i.e. when his tantrum subsides or when a demanded apology is forthcoming. 36% of all mothers resort to isolation or the threat of it occasionally, and class differences are not significant. Sweets and ice-cream are the most usual things of which the child may be deprived, but the threat is a good deal more common than its carrying-out, not so much because the mother fails to carry through an earned punishment, but because the threat usually seems to be effective in itself. 69% of all mothers use this sanction, with a slight reduction of this figure in Class I and II (60%—significantly different from the rest at the ·02 level). Most interesting in the present context, perhaps, is that it is working-class mothers almost exclusively who use the bluff of a deprivation so severe that it is unlikely to be carried out: 'Santa Claus won't come', 'no birthday presents', 'no Easter eggs at Easter', 'throw her toys in the dustbin' or 'not let her go to Goose Fair with the others'.

Threats of punishments which are beyond the parents' ability to carry out are a not uncommon technique of control which capitalizes on the four-year-old's limited knowledge and understanding: the child is told or warned of various supposed results of his misbehaviour which, were he older and more experienced, he would at once recognize as being far-fetched, ridiculous or untrue. Probably all parents occasionally stretch the truth a little, if only with the intention of gently teasing the child; however, it is clear that some parents are prepared to go very much further than this, and that, for some, considerations of truth or falsehood are less of an issue than those of immediate expedience and the chance of bluffing the child into compliance with their wishes. We were particularly interested in assessing the extent to which parents were prepared to compromise their veracity by using the distortion of truth as a deliberate technique: the relevant questions follow:

95. Do you ever say that you'll send him away, or that you'll have to go away from him, if he's naughty?
96. Do you ever try and frighten him with somebody else—his Daddy, or a policeman, or a teacher or doctor—someone like that?

These results are presented in Table XLVIII. It must be mentioned that the figures for threats of being sent away or of the mother leaving the child are not based on the whole sample; this question was omitted if the child was present and there was any chance of his overhearing, since we did not wish to put this possibility into his mind if it was not there already. 37% of all mothers were not asked the question for this reason: the percentages given in the table are thus proportions of a reduced sample

TABLE XLVIII

*Threats of authority figures, fear figures, and*
*abandonment by mother*

|  | I & II | IIIwc | IIIman | IV | V | All (random) |
|---|---|---|---|---|---|---|
|  | % | % | % | % | % | % |
| Threatens with authority figure | 10 | 23 | 29 | 29 | 46 | 27 |
| Threatens with fear figure | 1 | 1 | 2 | 1 | 1 | 1 |
| Threatens to send child away (reduced sample) | 8 | 18 | 18 | 19 | 26 | 17 |
| Threatens to leave child (reduced sample) | 4 | 18 | 14 | 17 | 9 | 13 |

comprising 442 cases, which we have no reason to suppose to be different from the total sample.

Threatening with an external authority is very significantly related to social class (at the ·001 level); it is used much less and much more by Class I and II and Class V respectively. Fathers are not the most widely used authority figure: often, it seems, because they themselves strongly object to being presented in this way. A British Rail fireman's wife said: 'Oh no, his Daddy would be very annoyed if I tried to frighten him like that—in fact that's one of the things he's very insistent on. He's known other people do it, and he sort of feels that he's away from them all day, and if he's going to be held up as something to be feared when he comes home . . . well, it'd upset him if I did that'. Some mothers reckon that such a threat would be quite ineffective anyway: 'Oh, his Dad don't frighten him', said a dry cleaner's wife, 'If I said "Here's your Dad coming, do as you're told", he'd just think "Well, my Dad don't hit me, I'll do as I like!"' Doctors and teachers are used very rarely indeed; the teacher is not, of course, a very real figure yet to most four-year-olds. One father, a railway worker, told his daughter 'The teacher will give you a taste of the cane, the teacher will give you the strap', deliberately in order to put the child off the idea of school: this was to spite his wife, who wanted to get her into school early in order to go out to work; and a miner's wife said 'I did use to say "You're going to school if you're not a good boy", but I found that turned him away from school [*sic*], so I can't use that any more'. Doctors are almost exclusively invoked to make children take medicine or to discourage genital play: 'If you won't take it for me, I'll have to get Dr J. and see if *he* can make you'; 'If I see you doing that again, I'll have to take you to the doctor'.

The chief authority figure is the policeman, and he accounts for most of the threats in the category '*Idle* threat of authority figure' (Table XLIX), from which fathers as sole threat have been removed. Sometimes he involves also the threat of sending the child away. 'If he throws stones', said a labourer's wife, 'I say "A policemen will come and take you away and you'll have no Mummy and no Daddy" '; and a fitter's mate's wife echoed her: 'I always say that the policeman will come if you're not very, very good, and he'll have no mummy and daddy, you know, if he's a naughty boy—that they'll take him away. He says "I'm going to be good" and everything, you know—he says "You won't send me away, will you?" and I say "Not if you're a good boy", and he's all right after that'. Quite often the interviewer witnessed, or even became involved in, the threat; a miner's wife answered the question on 'cheek' by turning to the child: 'I won't allow you to say naughty words, will I?— because that's when the bobby comes, isn't it?'—and a machine operator's wife checked her little girl's attempt to play with the tape recorder by warning her 'This lady's a policewoman— she'll take your name down if you do that!' Some mothers demurred at the word 'frighten'; we rather wished we had not used it, for their objection to the idea of 'frightening' did not seem to make much difference to the essential situation of appeal to a more awesome authority, as can be seen in the first three of the quotations that follow.

Presser's wife:

> Sometimes we tell her we're going to take her down to the police station and see what the policeman *says*. She isn't *frightened* of them—I don't want her to be frightened of policemen, you see.

Cook's wife:

> We never *frighten* them with policemen—if they're naughty, and we threaten them with a policeman, they're not *frightened* of

him. They know that if they're naughty we tell them a policeman will come, but at the same time when they're good they know that they're all right. I say "That policeman will come and take you away" or "We'll fetch the policeman"—same as, on the other hand, if they've done something good or *been* exceptionally good, their Daddy always says "I'll tell the policeman, when I see him tomorrow, that you've been good". Therefore they've got it both ways, so they're not frightened of policemen—if they see a policeman, they go out of their way to say Hello to them. They're frightened *at the time* we say we're going to fetch one, they don't *want* us to fetch one, but at the same time it doesn't scare them *off* of policemen.

### Labourer's wife (Mrs Cullinan once more):

I don't really terrify him. You see, I myself am terrified of the streets round here, and there's more fear in me than I could put into Patrick, that he might stray away there. So I told him that there's always a policeman standing on the corner to watch him—now he's not *terrified* of him, but he's always watching to see him, and by good luck a policeman sometimes passes up and down here; so Patrick thinks that that's the policeman that I have plotted out to *be* at that corner so he can't go past it, and I know he has the vision of the policeman in his mind that he mustn't pass.

### Lorry driver's wife:

If you mention a policeman, that quietens her down. She says "No, no! Don't say a policeman!"—"All right, you be a good girl, then", I say, "Come on, make haste—a policeman!" and she says "No, don't mention that", and she'll come.[1]

Mothers who do *not* use policemen to back up their own authority tend to be very strongly against the practice, always on the grounds that policemen should be built up as protective figures. 'I don't do any of that at all', said a local government inspector's wife, with some heat; 'It's false and wrong, to me. I try to teach them that if you're lost you must go to a policeman,

[1] Compare the methods of Balinese mothers: '. . . the mother of the straying child gives a histrionic fear-laden cry, "*Aroh!*" followed by the mention of any one of a dozen scare symbols, chosen at random and without any concern for their relevance—"Fire!" "Snake!" "Feces!" "Scorpion!" "Witch!" "Elf spirits!" "White man!" "Chinaman!" "Policeman!" "Tiger!"' Mead, M. and Bateson, G.: *Balinese Character: a photographic analysis*; Special Publications of the New York Academy of Sciences, Vol. II, New York, 1942.

they'll help you—I feel this approach, a bogey or something, is absolutely wrong'. A knitter's wife agreed: 'I don't like to, because they might need them people some day'; and another hosiery worker said 'No, never—I always tell him a policeman's his friend'. Several mothers said that they had been admonished by policemen when they had threatened their children within earshot; a labourer's wife who lived next door to a policeman said:

> Sometimes when he wasn't a good lad, you know, we used to tell him "We'll get the policeman to you, next door"; but he used to like him, he used to say "I'm not frightened of the bobby next door, he talks to me, I like him". Anyhow, he told me off about it. He were quite nasty about it. He said "You should *never* frighten a child with a policeman"; so I've not done it since he told me about it.

Figures of fear—by which we mean bogey-men and the like—are extremely rarely used by mothers, as can be seen from the table. One mother took up her child's suggestion of witches (see page 474); another warned of 'Sister Maggie', an imaginary lady with whom she herself had been threatened as a child. 'A man with a bag' was going to come and take one child away; and the reader may remember the little girl who was told that 'if she didn't stop wetting herself, Tobar would come out of the TV and get her'.

Threats to leave the child or to send him away from home are very similar to each other in that they both involve abandonment of child by mother; we have separated them in Table XLVIII for interest, but they are combined in Table XLIX and show a significant overall class difference, mainly due to the large gap between the professional/managerial group and the rest; the combined figures cannot be obtained by simple addition, as some mothers threaten both kinds of abandonment. The most notable features of these findings are that the shop and clerical group firmly align themselves with the working class and that the unskilled group are much more likely to threaten sending the child away than going themselves: possibly this is a question of credibility. Such threats range from joking expressions of despair—'I'll end up in Mapperley (mental hospital)'—'It'll be Borstal for you, m'lad, at this rate!'—to threats which are backed up by an elaborate act by the parents, such as the last three quotations below describe. We have not counted threats which are quite clearly both intended and accepted as a joke. Here again, the interviewer is sometimes, to her embarrassment, caught up in the situation: one interviewer was introduced to the child by his salesman father with the words: 'This lady's come to take you away with her, Alan—she's going to take you away in her car'. This was another instance of plain teasing, unconnected with the child's behaviour in any way; the first quotation below describes an incident which started as a tease but ended with a moral twist.

Nylon winder's wife:
After I got your letter, mester asked what it was for; so my girl, naturally enough (sic), she said to Freddie, "Oh, it's to take you away, a lady's coming to take you away". He said "I don't want to go away"; so I said "Well, you'd better be a good lad, then—or else she will". (Do you often say that sort of thing?) Yes. (And do you ever say you'll go away from him?) Yes. I did the other week—I said "One of these days I'm going to put on my coat and I'm walking out and leaving you all".

Labourer's wife:
I often say "If I have to keep shouting at you, I'm going to the doctor's, and if I don't get any better, I'll have to go away". I've been saying that often this week, because I've been getting a bit worked up myself, you know—I haven't felt too good, and things have got on top of me a bit this week.

Office worker's wife:
I threaten I'll send her away into a home for naughty children; and she sort of *looks* at me, but I don't think she believes me.

Miner's wife:
I have said that if he makes me poorly when he's naughty I shall have to go away, and then he'll have no Mummy to look after him, and he'll have to live with someone else. I know that's all wrong, but I do. His Daddy'll say to him, "Pack his bags—get that bag out, and get his toys, he's going!" And he has one time put some of his clothes and toys *in* the bag; and it made him nearly demented—it upset me, but I didn't like to interfere, you see. And I asked him after, I said "*Don't* do that again, I don't

like it, it'll make him feel unsafe, and he belongs here as much as we do. Find another way to punish him, I don't like him to think that". I thought it was going *too* far.

### Packer's wife:

I used to threaten him with the Hartley Road Boys' Home, which isn't a Home any more; and since then, I haven't been able to do it; but I can always say I shall go down town and see about it, you know. And Ian says "Well, if I'm going with Stuart (7), it won't matter"; so I say "Well, you'll go to different ones— you'll go to one Home, and *you'll* go to another". But it really got him worried, you know, and I really got him ready one day, and I thought "I'll take him a walk round, *as if* I was going", you know, and he really *was* worried. In fact, I had to bring him home, he started to cry. He saw I was in earnest about it—he *thought* I was, anyway. And now I've only got to threaten him, I say "It won't take me long to get you ready".

### Miner's wife:

No—oh, I tell a lie, I once did—and upset her that much that I've never said it any more. (What did you say?) Well, she was having an argument with me, and she says to me "You don't live here! Hop it!" So I says, "Oh, well, I can do that! Where's my coat? I'm moving!" So I got my coat from the back, and I was gone. I just stood outside the door; and she cried *so* bitter, she did. As soon as I came in, she got hold of my leg and wouldn't let go, sort of thing. I'll *never* say it no more.

Mothers' comments make it very clear that threats of this kind (like threats to withdraw love, as we shall see presently) distress the child, on a quite different level from his emotions on being smacked: 'You won't go, will you, Mummy, you *won't* have to go—I'm good now!' On some mothers, the child's response has the effect described by the two miners' wives above: they had not meant to cause this amount of unhappiness, and they immediately draw back, deciding that they are 'going *too* far'. This reaction is very similar to that described in mothers who find with a shock that the frequency and violence of their smacking has escalated beyond their intentions; the woman whose husband made their little boy 'pack his bags' is in fact also the first speaker on page 423, who has found to her own dismay and shame that her dealings with her child seem to proceed in periods of escalation followed by periods of guilty retraction. For most of the mothers who employ this technique, however, its use is entirely dependent upon its effectiveness; so far from dropping it because it distresses the child, they use it for this very reason, that it 'hurts her more than a smack does'. 'That works on her more than what a smack would', said a painter's wife, 'she doesn't like it; she says "Don't leave me, Mummy, I won't do it again", and she doesn't'. This same mother, in common with others, has given up using it with her older children, not because she thinks it wrong, but because they have now called her bluff. Similarly, some mothers say they use it with one child and not with another because of differing temperaments which decide its effectiveness; a lorry driver's wife said:

> I've said it to Michelle (6), but not to him. She's very highly strung. You've only got to speak to her and she'll start. But Julian—I don't think he'd take any notice, to tell you the truth; but I've never had cause to, because you've just got to give him a tap and he shuts up. But if I smack Michelle, she just screams all the more, you see; but if I say something like that, she'll keep quiet.

This chief concern with the technique's effectiveness is, of course, the reason for the play-acting, where the mother finds that her words no longer convince the child that she is in earnest, and so resorts to staging the preliminaries of her abandonment by putting on her coat, 'packing his bags' or 'taking him a walk round', in order to postpone the inevitable moment when her bluff is finally called. In the same way, the mother may elaborate the lie if she finds it losing weight, as we saw when the packer's wife changed the threat to 'two *different* Homes' since her little boy was unmoved at the prospect of going with his brother.

Although we have mentioned mothers who stop using this kind of threat because they find it too upsetting to the child, most of those who do not use it have refrained on principle: there is a very strong feeling against it among the majority of women, and some of them were extremely vehement. 'That's *wrong* altogether', said a lorry driver's wife, 'I mean, your *mother* to turn round and say that to you—it's awful!'—and a commercial traveller's wife agreed: 'Oh no, that's another thing I don't believe in, because I always think if anything *does* happen to you and that's in a child's mind, it'll think that really is the cause of your going away'. 'It takes the child's security away', said a publican's wife: 'You are the whole of their security, and you mustn't take that away'. A few were sure it was wrong, but had used the threat under stress: 'I *have* said it—it's no use saying I haven't'; 'I think I said it once, and that was just after my little girl had died—I felt very awful about it afterwards'.

*'I do think there has got to be a feeling of trust between you'*

We are now in a position to bring together from various parts of the interview schedule a series of items which we can call 'evasion or distortion of truth', which have in common that they in some way break or injure complete trust between parent and child, either by deliberate lying to the child or by neglecting to tell him the truth in such a way that a lie is implied. The scale is made up of the following items, for each of which the mother is given a YES/NO score.

1. Gives a false explanation of where babies come from.
2. Uses idle threats of an authority figure (threatening with the father does not count, as this may be no idle threat; Jesus and God also excluded).
3. Threatens to leave the child or send him away (score of 2 possible if threatened both ways).
4. Leaves the child with a minder surreptitiously (slips off without telling him).
5. Frequent use of unfulfilled punishment threats other than in (2).
6. Any other definite instance mentioned or shown.

We did not include the threat 'Mummy won't love you if you're naughty', although this could well be thought to come under our heading, since we have no means of knowing to what extent mothers might indeed stop loving naughty children; this topic is left until our final chapter. The last three categories above need brief explanation.

'Leaving a child with a minder surreptitiously' implies the lie of 'Mummy isn't going out'; it is thus an evasion of the truth, almost invariably to avoid the fuss which the child will make if he is told that his mother is going. If the child is asleep, the mother risks his waking and finding without warning that she is no longer there; if he is awake, the greater risk is taken that he will discover her disappearance, again without having been warned. In either case, she takes away from him the possibility of being certain of her presence unless he can actually see her, even during periods when she has no intention of leaving him. Some mothers find the child's protests so insupportable that they feel the risk is worth taking; others think that coping with this sort of fuss is one of the ways in which they teach the child to come to terms with reality and the needs of other people, and in any case would bear any amount of fuss for the sake of keeping their own dependability intact. Class V differs from the rest on this issue (significance at the ·05 level).

'Frequent use of unfulfilled punishment threats' was judged on the basis of mothers' general discussion of the way in which they dealt with discipline, and was usually scored on the mother's own admission of this; it was also sometimes scored on the basis of observation, but this had to be confirmed by what the mother said, to avoid possible distortion of behaviour owing to the interview situation. Differences here did not reach significance level. The following account is an example of unfulfilled punishment threats in action: in this case the police-man also makes an appearance, and the threat of the father *is* an idle one.

Builder's wife:
(Raymond dropped coat on settee) Take your coat upstairs. (R. argued) Take your coat upstairs and do as you're told. (R. argued) Here's your Dad, quick! Get that up the stairs! Go on! (Dad didn't arrive—he was at work; child made to leave room without coat) Pick that coat up! *Will* you put it upstairs? (R. ignored) Well, you'll get no threepence at lunchtime! I won't get Auntie's sewing machine out for you! (R. took out coat reluctantly, then brought in a flexible bottle of water, threatened to squirt walls, floor, mother. There was a lengthy, half-joking interchange, i.e. R: "I know what I'm going to give you!"—M: "I know what I'm going to give you, an' all!" This warmed up.) Go in the yard with that! Raymond, if you put that on the floor, I mean it, I'm going to fetch the belt now, it's in the cellar. (To interviewer): I've got a carpet-beater, too, you know, I just frighten him with it and that's enough. (To Raymond): I'm going to use it on your bottom. Hey, don't be silly! Hey, I'm

going to tell that policeman that you threw snow against Margaret's door! (R. went on threatening to squirt) You dare! Just you dare!

'Any other definite instance' might be either reported by the mother or observed by the interviewer; though we do not necessarily trust as normal the way child and mother interact before a third person, the instances mentioned are not such as would be said only *because* they were observed: they involve a willingness on the mother's part to distort truth in this way. Examples of such instances are: 'God will do something to her hand' (for smacking mother); 'You might have your fingers drop off' (for genital play); 'It'll cut your finger off—there's a little man in there and he'll bite you!' (for playing with tape recorder); 'I've told him there's maggots under his nails' (for nail-biting); 'I tell her the nails'll all collect in her tummy and all sorts' (for nail-biting); 'I tell her it's dirty and her nose will fall off' (for nose picking); 'I tell her little girls don't grow if they sleep with their mummy and daddy'. Again, class differences on this criterion alone do not reach significance.

Table XLIX presents the items involving 'evasion or distortion of truth' separately, analysed by social class; the last line gives percentages of 'more evasive' mothers (scoring two or more YES answers), as opposed to 'less evasive' (scoring one or zero YES answers). The overall class trend reaches a significance level of ·001. It is of some interest, perhaps, that on this general issue the shop and clerical group remains closer to the skilled working class than to its more usual middle-class partners.

This final summary of class differences in the degree to which mothers evade or distort the truth, underestimated though it may be because of the reduced sample in the third line of the table, enables us to understand much more clearly the way in which the language factor in socialization is linked with social class. The major divergences separate Class I and II at the top end and Class V at the lower end from the three central class groups. Although it is true that Class I and II mothers lean heavily upon the use of reasoned verbal explanation in order to make their children behave acceptably, while those in Class V are less concerned with verbal communication of any sort, the salient difference between the classes appears not so much in parents' ability or lack of it to make themselves understood in words, as in *the valuation which they place upon words as the agents of truth.* For the professional-class mother, in particular, the putting of an idea into words invests it with a *permanence* which cannot be ignored; she will therefore take great care not to say anything to the child which might be considered untruthful, and if the child accuses her of deceiving him in any way she will be at pains to explain to him how his own misunderstanding was the cause. Sometimes this attitude towards verbal truth appears

TABLE XLIX

*Evasion or distortion of truth*

|  | I & II | IIIwc | IIIman | IV | V | All (random) |
|---|---|---|---|---|---|---|
|  | % | % | % | % | % | % |
| False account of where babies come from | 8 | 19 | 41 | 40 | 66 | 35 |
| Idle threats of authority figure | 6 | 17 | 23 | 26 | 39 | 22 |
| Threats to leave child or send him away (reduced sample) | 10 | 34 | 29 | 27 | 30 | 27 |
| Leaves child surreptitiously | 20 | 21 | 25 | 15 | 32 | 23 |
| Frequent unfulfilled punishment threats | 9 | 13 | 17 | 15 | 18 | 15 |
| Any other definite instance | 4 | 12 | 11 | 15 | 10 | 11 |
| 'More evasive' i.e. scores 2+ on above scale | 12 | 29 | 42 | 37 | 62 | 37 |

almost as a squeamishness or superstition about the significance of language, particularly where the mother finds herself impelled to adopt a course of action of which she disapproves: a good example occurs on pages 118-9, epitomized by the phrase 'encourage him to stand up for himself, but not *use the word* "hit" '. She may carefully use a form of words which implies a threat while not actually stating it: a professional-class woman (let us be honest: one of the authors), going away for the week-end with a car-load of quarrelsome children, stops the car with the words 'We don't *have* to go away, you know, and I'd rather *not* if you're going to quarrel all the time', thus satisfying her own verbal sensibilities. In the same way, this group may be prepared to *act* a lie so long as they are not forced to verbalize it: it is of some significance that the only one of our categories of 'distortion' in which Class I and II mothers appear in double figures is the negative, non-verbal one of leaving the child without telling him beforehand; one of our assistants found it extremely unpalatable to have to code this as 'evasion of truth'!

As one descends the social scale, however, the general attitude towards what is or is not permissible to say to the child becomes far more a matter of experience and quick results. If the truth cannot (in the mother's opinion) be told, as in the case of sex questions, then 'making up some little fairy story' is considered a perfectly feasible alternative, and the one which they would in fact choose, by almost half of all working-class mothers, and by two-thirds of those in Class V; if it is found that threats of unenforceable sanctions such as abandonment or policemen have a quelling effect upon the child's behaviour, then a considerable proportion will willingly use such threats, so long as they continue to be practically useful. And, to anticipate, more than twice as many working-class (42%) as middle-class (17%) mothers are prepared to tell the child that they won't love him any more if he's naughty: a statement which, though we have not counted it as distortion of truth for scoring purposes, seems at least to be very close to it. In these cases, discipline is in fact maintained by verbal means, in which the mother, so far from being at a loss for words, deliberately uses the more subtle power of words to suggest more dramatic sanctions than the simple slap, in order to attain her immediate ends. The difference in attitude is summed up by the contrast between the labourer's wife, who met the last of these questions with 'I do—ooh aye, the lot!' and the shop manager's wife who said 'No, no!—I think they're *terrible, all* of those questions, those last three'; still more significant is the acceptance of such methods implied in a presser's wife's reflective 'Um . . . you say so many things, you can't really remember, can you?' One aspect of this use of what is simply expedient at the time is that the mother will often seize on some misunderstanding of the child's, and deliberately prolong it for her own convenience; the nylon winder's wife on page 465 takes up her elder daughter's tease and turns it into a homily, the first mother quoted below used the child's sickness to draw a false conclusion, and the second nurtured a purely chance misunderstanding because it suited her to do so:

## Miner's wife:

He wouldn't leave his dummy off, he had it until he was three; and he was sick one day, and it fell in it: and I picked it up and gave it to him, it was an awful thing to do, and he *shuddered*; and I told him that it had *made* him poorly. And it's a thing with him now, anything I say'll make him poorly, he thinks it will, you see: so that's my usual fall-back, he'll be poorly, if he does things I don't want him to do.

## Chemical worker's wife:

I tell her I'll put the light on in the hall if she's naughty—that works wonders. (How did you find out she didn't like it?) Well, we were coming back from my mother's one Saturday night, and there was a little boy crying, and the hall light was on; and she said "Look at that light", and I said "Yes, that's on because that little boy's crying". I meant that his mummy had gone upstairs and put the light on, but *she* thought it was on to *let everybody know* that he was crying. So now you only have to say you'll put the hall light on!

It must be emphasized once more that these differences have nothing to do with kindness and warmth. The professional-class reader who finds the distortions of truth which we have described alien and horrifying must not leap to the conclusion that the mothers who use them are unkind or have unhappy relationships with their children: they may be, they may have, but not in any systematic connection with this factor. Let us quote one more example of truth distortion, by a Class III wife:

(Do you ever tell him you won't love him if he behaves like that?) Often, yes. (What sort of thing would you say that for?) Oh, when he's being cheeky—he tries to cheek me back; and often I threaten to leave him and go back to Ireland, and he doesn't like that, it worries him, you know. And I say "Well, be a good boy and I'll not leave you". I often put on my coat to leave them, I often do. And they'll be quite quiet for a bit, you know. (Do you ever say that you'll send *him* away if he's naughty?) I did; and it worried him. And he kept saying "When will you send me away?" And I said "I'm going to get another little baby to look after, a *good* little baby"—well, *that* was inclined to worry them, and me and my husband had a talk about it, and we decided not to say that any more to them. Because it *did* worry them, they kept on and on talking about it, you know.

(Did you say *where* you'd send them?) Yes—a Home. And Andrew (5) said "Are there witches in the Home?"—I said, "Yes, there are". He said, "Would they hit you?"—I said "Yes, you'd have ever such a bad time there if you're going to be naughty to Mummy".

This mother has in fact an exceptionally warm and happy relationship with her two little boys; we mentioned her much earlier as having, when they were younger, kept all her housework for the evening so that she could play with them during the day, and no-one could possibly doubt, on watching them together and listening to the children's conversation with her, that she is a delightful companion to them. She is rated as 'very warm and demonstrative', and the love in that household is almost tangible. Other mothers whom we have quoted for their 'evasions and distortions' also stand out for the obvious warmth in their relationship with their children: notably the chemical worker's wife whose quotation precedes the last one, and the lorry driver's wife on page 467. We are clearly dealing with subcultural mores which have rather little to do with the mother's personality and her ability to reach her children through her own love for them.

*'I think they're beginning to know now that it's just an idle threat'*
The very high score on the use of truth distortion which characterizes unskilled labourers' wives as a group must nevertheless lead one to speculate upon the results of such methods upon their children, not now, but in the future. Here, it must be understood, we move from what we know to what we can surmise. The suggestion which we want to put forward is this: whether there might not be some link between treatment of this sort now and attitudes showing total distrust of authority which emerge in the child's later life.

   The mother is, in normal circumstances, the child's first experience not only of a loving protector but of someone in authority over him; and it is she who must *set the pattern* for his feelings towards others in such a position. The mother who upholds her authority by resorting to deceit cannot hope to succeed in this for longer than the limited period of the child's gullibility; sooner or later, the child must inevitably come to realize that she never does in fact put him in a Home, call the policeman, send him to hospital to have his genitals cut off, nor (for most children) pack her bags and leave him; nor, indeed, are babies dug up in the garden or bought from Woolworth's. He therefore learns at an early age that authority in the person of his mother, *despite her pretensions to having his own welfare at heart*, is yet not averse to using trickery whenever this suits her purpose of controlling him.

It seems feasible to suppose that what the child finds to be true of this first 'pattern' authority will be generalized to colour his feelings and attitudes towards the manifestations of authority with which he later comes in contact: school, police, social agencies, employers and so on. It is just such an attitude which contemporary working-class spokesmen for the delinquent express in their descriptions of the unbridgable gulf between Them—the people who try to do the controlling—and Us, who attempt to keep out of their control as far as possible: the two camps of society, whom Alan Sillitoe, through the voice of his 'long-distance runner', names as the In-laws and the Out-laws. Like the deceiving mother, the In-laws assert that they only seek control for the good of the controlled: but the child whose earliest experience of verbal communication may have been 'Bobby p'liceman's coming!' knows, as he grows up, just how much value to set on the sayings of authority, whether in the home or out of it. 'Oh yes, they'll help you', said Robert Allerton, with nine convictions totalling 18 years in sentences by the time he reached 33—'on condition you let them do all the deciding about what's good for you, and let them tell you how you should do it'.[1] 'Whether I ever pinch another thing in my life again or not', says Sillitoe's adolescent delinquent, 'I know who my enemies are and what war is'.[2] From this point of view, it is perhaps significant that, apart from the stories about where

[1] Allerton, Robert, and Parker, Tony: *The Courage of his Convictions*, Hutchinson, London, 1962.

[2] Sillitoe, Alan: *The Loneliness of the Long-Distance Runner*, W. H. Allen, London, 1959. Alan Sillitoe was brought up in Radford, Nottingham. Robert Allerton says of this study of the relationship between Them and Us: 'That's a marvellous book. I suppose at one time or another I must have read most things written on the subject of crime and criminals, because I've got an interest in it and I consider I know a bit about it. This book isn't merely the best I've read, it's so far ahead of all the others it's in a class of its own. Sillitoe has got a terrific grasp of the workings of a criminal mind. I can't imagine how, unless he's been inside himself. To me, he sounds as though he must have done a lot of bird, and I mean that as a compliment. He gets over the relationship exactly in that book'.

babies come from, the most widely used deception in Class V is the idle threat of authorities outside the home—the policeman, or, less often, the teacher or doctor: so that many children must initially meet these personages as allies of an angry mother, whose own falseness they must soon discover.

Is it too far-fetched to suppose that attitudes of mistrust may have their roots in the child's earliest struggles against such a mother's authority? At this stage in our own study, while the data is very suggestive, questions of this sort can be only a matter for conjecture. Eventually, however, as our children reach adolescence, such speculations may be given form and substance by the long perspective which we have of their childhood and infancy.

CHAPTER 15

# SATISFACTION AND DOUBT IN
# THE PARENTAL ROLE

———————

If we have succeeded in fulfilling our intentions adequately, we have presented a picture of the four-year-old, not as a lay figure passively waiting for Child Upbringing to be practised upon him, but as an active personality in his own right, a creature of variable personal needs and temperaments, whose determination to make his mark on his parents' awareness is nearly as great as theirs to socialize him. There is little doubt that this very individuality, despite the fact that it inevitably increases the likelihood of clashes of will between mother and child, is something which most mothers find attractive, and which they value rather highly.

We have mentioned in passing the question which opened that section of the interview mainly concerned with conflicts between mother and child: 'I wonder if you could tell me now about how you and N get on together? What sort of things do you specially enjoy in him?' This question we came to regard as something of a 'blockbuster': it tended to have the effect of making the mother take a new breath, as it were, in her account of the child and her relationship with him, and of helping her to focus for a while upon the pleasures and special joys of that relationship. Sometimes the mother was startled by the question, and dithered mentally before being able to express her thoughts on it: one felt (and this was quite often put into words by mothers) that in the day-to-day bustle of family life the conscious contemplation of one child's qualities can all to easily become a casualty. For most mothers, answering this question was a pleasurable experience, a welcome chance to dwell upon the niceness of their own children: it offered an invitation to praise the child without diffidence, which many would hesitate to do in ordinary conversation. For a few, however, focusing upon the pleasant aspects of the child seemed a task of such unfamiliarity that they could not succeed in finding an answer, even after some thought. A railway worker's wife was completely baffled for some moments, and finally said 'Well—really—I never worry; I take him for granted just as he comes'; a packer's wife commented, 'I don't know. It's a very funny question to ask, really. Oh, I can't answer that one'; and a lorry driver's wife also said she didn't know—because 'he's hardly in'.

Although the question's chief function was to allow the mother to praise her child before discussing conflicts, with the incidental intention of filling out the picture of the child's personality, we thought it worth while to classify the mothers' answers on the basis of what aspect of the child they especially emphasized in their valuation of him. It proved possible to categorize almost every answer under one of three headings: the child might be valued mainly for his good behaviour, for his affectionate behaviour, or for himself alone. The principle which underlies these headings is that the first two—good or affectionate behaviour—both relate the child to the mother in that the aspect which she chooses to emphasize is seen primarily as satisfying her own needs or demands; while valuation 'for himself' emphasizes some personality trait or behaviour which is not immediately relevant to her, except in so far as her pleasure in it will obviously tend to improve the relationship. In the event, we also had to add an extra heading to accommodate a few mothers of little girls who appreciated most the doll-like opportunities they afforded for dressing-up: 'valued for appearance' was clearly a mother-centred rather than a child-centred answer.

Class differences in type of valuation were not significant. The difference in attitude expressed can best be shown by giving some representative quotations.

*Child valued for good behaviour* (7%):

Window cleaner's wife:

> He's a good boy, very good; he plays nicely; he asks for things nicely—"Please, Mummy, can I have that?" or "Can I do that?" —very nicely. He's very good all round, he does as he's told. I can't grumble at all.

Sales manager's wife:

> His company—because he is so *good*. I mean, it's quite a pleasure to take him to town, because he doesn't give me any trouble.

With the girl, she was always wanting to run away and finger everything, you know, but he doesn't; he'll hold my hand and take an interest and—er—he'll *fit in*, you know, he doesn't want to be awkward or difficult.

*Child valued for affectionate behaviour* (12%):

Shop owner's wife:

He's a great source of joy to me; I don't think there's anything, really, that we don't get on about. (What do you specially like about him as a person?) He's a very loving child—a very affectionate child—and at the moment tremendously helpful; he sort of has a wonderful knack of knowing just what you want just when you want it, you know; if you say "I want so-and-so", he's gone to fetch it almost before you've thought about it. He's got some very affectionate little ways.

Clerk's wife:

Well, I think it's because she's so lovable.[1] Sheila (8) never was a very lovable child, Sheila doesn't see any sense in this kissing business on the TV; she'll hide her face in a cushion, she's not very demonstrative at all. Now Helen *is*—that's the main difference between them. Of course, you enjoy it when you haven't had it with the other one.

*Child valued for appearance* (1%):

Mine worker's wife:

Well, I like—to be honest, I like taking her out when she's all dressed up, and people saying "Hasn't she got lovely blond hair!" She does look nice when she's dressed up, you know, people say "Hasn't she got lovely hair!", and I feel ever so proud of her, you know. (It's the way she looks that gives you most pleasure?) Yes, I like to see her looking nice.

Clerk's wife:

Don't know—I really don't know what you mean. Do you mean why do I like her? (Yes) I like her because I can dress her up and do her hair and that kind of thing.

[1] 'Lovable' is used synonymously with 'affectionate': an extremely common misusage.

The category 'valued for himself alone' is much less homogeneous than these, as one might expect from the fact that its basic characteristic is that it centres upon the child and is therefore as varied as children's personalities. Comments range from the very general to the very specific; of the more specific, the child's value as friend, companion and conversationalist, of which we have given a number of examples earlier (pp. 53-6, 430), and his 'comical' or 'funny' ways, were emphasized most frequently.

*Child valued for himself* (80%):

Storeman's wife:

> Every moment of her—*every single moment*—even when she's naughty. She's the most precious . . . both of them . . . I had them late in life (now 38). My goodness, I wish I'd had them young, when I got married, though I was late getting married, because there's so much happiness they can give you. Ooh, every moment's precious with them.

Accountant's wife:

> I enjoy our good relationship. We go for walks, and I enjoy everything. I'm in tune with this one.

Electrical engineer's wife (this is Valerie, who gives her parents such anxiety over her food refusal—see page 215):

> Everything she does, everything; she's marvellous. I wouldn't be without her for the world. She's ever so entertaining; of course, she can talk as well as anyone I know, for her age—endless conversations. She'll bring her babies, and then she'll come and ask do I want any shopping fetching today, and what would I like, and could she have the money, and here's the change, and all like that. This is going on while I'm washing pots and making beds and all that sort of thing. She's real good company.

Research chemist's wife:

> I enjoy the development of speech—I always have done, from the beginning. I enjoy talking with her and I enjoy watching her play—the physical aspect of it. I like seeing her swing. She's *very* sweet with the baby. She's a nice companion.

Miner's wife:

When he's grinning. He's ever such a jolly child! He's not really a child that anybody can dislike—in fact, I don't think there *is* anyone that dislikes him. He's ever such a friendly child. He's a really good mixer.

Representative's wife:

Oh, watching his face!—you know, all the kind of different expressions; and listening to him sing, and that sort of thing.

Scaffolder's wife:

I like the way he's rough. He's a proper lad.

Lorry driver's wife:

Well, he's so clumsy! (That's what you like best about him, is it?) Well, that's about the thing I remember best. He'll be walking along and there'll be nothing there at all, and he'll fall over. Yet if the room's absolutely cluttered up, he'll step over it! And he puts two shoes on one foot, and then he says to me "My shoe won't go on"—and it's on top of his other one! He's very absent-minded. He lives in a dream world.

Chemical worker's wife:

Her comical ways. She's very comical at times, Hazel is. And she can win herself out of trouble with being comical. She can give you just a little sly smile; or if she's been naughty and you smack her, she'll come and put her arms round you and say "Mum, I still love you!" She's very comical, she's got a nice little way.

Caretaker's wife:

I think I enjoy practically everything about him. I like little boys very much. We're good pals, you know. We go shopping together. I don't know whether it's me or what, but he's very sensible when we go shopping, you know, he'll talk about going to one shop because it's a bit cheaper and that sort of thing. I like the little ways that he's got, you know; and he's a *boy*—he's not a sissy-type child, you know.

Lorry driver's wife:

Oh, I enjoy all of her. We're pals, you know. My *eldest* girl and me was—we still are—I mean, she's 24 now and courting, but

Q

she's still my girl; and *she's* the same. She's one of them *carefree* sort of kids, you know. Oh, we enjoy each other, Elaine and me.

For the interviewer, the pleasure of this question lay in the rush of warm feeling towards the child which it stimulated, sometimes in mothers who until this moment in the interview had adopted a comparatively detached attitude. Clearly there is a deep reservoir of tenderness towards children of this age; we wished to know, however, how far this was made obvious to the child himself. Ordinary observation shows that the cuddlings and endearments, which are naturally expressed by most mothers towards small babies, at some point during childhood become gradually inhibited so that physical tenderness between mother and ten-year-old, for instance, becomes far less commonplace; for how many mothers is this process already advanced by the time the child reaches four? The question through which this was explored was:

81. Do you show your affection towards each other quite a lot, or are you fairly reserved with one another?
(Prompt if necessary): Do you think kissing and cuddling should be discouraged at this age?

The great majority of mothers (95%) enjoy and encourage cuddling so far as their four-year-olds are concerned: 'giving him his little five minutes' (of lap-cuddling) is an institution which few are in a hurry to give up.

Newsagent's wife:

Oh yes—when he comes to me for love, he gets it. I don't ever push him away or say he is a big boy or that sort of nonsense, because he *wants* loving, and I love him because I *do* love him.[1]

Publican's wife:

It's bad for a child to be reserved—you need to show your affection. Every child wants to be shown that it's loved. We are often what I call sloppy with one another—kissing, putting our arms round one another.

[1] A nice example of the two ways in which the word 'love' is commonly used: 'I love him because I *do* love him' = 'I (physically) *show* love for him because I *feel* love for him'.

**Publisher's wife:**

Oh, we all cuddle each other and, sort of, "darling" and "sweetheart"—it's quite a natural thing with us.

Among the 5% who definitely discourage displays of affection, numbers are too small to show a significant class difference; it is rather noticeable how Irish names recur, however. The first three mothers whose comments follow are Irish.

**Labourer's wife:**

Well, I tell you honestly, I was brought up the hard way myself, and I suppose it's not only the kissing and the cuddling but it was very strict too. I just tell her she's a good girl, you know. She's a great wee girl for kissing you. *She* does—I don't know where she's got it—*and* her brother. But *we* don't.

**Labourer's wife:**

We don't make a lot of all that. I've never bothered. Well, I can't see anything in it, really. I mean, my husband's never really been like that—*he* says he can't understand what kissing's supposed to be *for*, you know.

**Car-body worker's wife:**

I don't make ever such a lot of fuss, because I think it makes them mardy. (Do you think kissing and cuddling should be discouraged at this age?) Well, it should be really, yes. We kiss them goodnight, that's all—or if they fall over, we kiss them better.

**Office manager's wife:**

Oh, isn't that a *difficult* question! I don't sort of keep calling him "darling" all the time, like some people do, but you never know whether that's really for affection or not, or just, sort of, a thing to say. I don't really know. Other people see it more than you do yourself. When he requires it, I do it back, but I wouldn't say I do it of my own accord. . . . He doesn't need an awful lot of affection, I don't think.

**Press operator's wife:**

Well, we are fairly reserved, aren't we, all of us? We don't mollycoddle them. Do you mean are we all over them all day?

(FATHER:) Well, there's different ways. You can, sort of, "Mamma's darling", or you can show it in different ways. Buy her an ice-cream, and she thinks the world of you!

Railway worker's wife:

I don't believe in showing affection, no. (Do you think kissing and cuddling should be discouraged at this age?) Yes, I do. I don't like that at all. Not even from being tiny—I don't believe in it.

The withholding of affection from one child in favour of another is very generally regarded as deplorable; no doubt it happens more often than it is admitted. The lack of concern in the comment that follows was most unusual:

Labourer's wife:

Well, she's really had her nose shoved out, you know, we've not had an awful lot to do with each other since Bobby (3) came along; she was only a year old, you see, and with him being a *boy*, you know—the only boy! She's more or less the outcast, you know—*he's* had it all. It's changing a *little* bit now, since I've noticed she's jealous, she's been crying a lot; but she really has been the odd one out, the outcast of the family.

Some mothers are clearly reserved as a personal trait rather than on principle: 'No, I don't think it should be discouraged' said a clergyman's wife, 'It's just that I'm rather a reserved person, and it just doesn't come very *easily* to me'. Most mothers who feel in this way do, however, discourage open affection: 'I think it *should* be discouraged', said a setter operator's wife, 'I can't bear it. I feel for people, but I don't like to show it; though I love her'. An engineer's wife seemed to have passed on her inhibition to her little girl: 'I don't know how to explain it. She can't show her affection, not a lot, like; but *I'm* one of them—*I* can't. It's . . . it's all of it *inside* me. It's the same, like, if anyone gets to give me anything—I can just say "thank you", and they think I don't think anything of it—I can't *show* my feelings a lot, sort of thing, you know; I can't *express* my feelings. I can write about my feelings, whereas I can't *say* anything. But I mean, the feeling, it's *there*—but I can't show it'. Once again, however, the fact that the relationship is two-way makes a difference to how far personal reserve is reflected in actual behaviour. A company director's wife illustrates how the child can to some extent influence events for itself: 'Well, *I'm* reserved; but not so much with her as with Frances (11), because Frances is more like me. Ellen takes more notice of me, really—she puts her arms round me and gives me a love and says "You're nice"—but Frances wouldn't'.

Not many mothers could resist the child who takes the initiative in such a way. 'She's a bit naughty, but she's lovely', said a milkman's wife; 'We just went to the shops this morning, and she said "Mummy", and I said "What?" and she said "I love you"—she just *said* it, you see; yes, she's lovely!' The spontaneous sweetness of the young child is felt as both touching and infinitely rewarding. The second wife on page 423, who had shocked herself out of smacking, said later: 'He says he's got the bestest Mummy in the world—and tears run down my face!'

Actor's wife:

> Yesterday, for instance, I was in a state. They were all yelling and screaming and everything, and I hadn't washed, and she suddenly looked round and said "Oh Mummy, you *do* look lovely!" And I said, "Oh, Juliet, I wish I did!" and she said "You look lovely to me"—and this was very thrilling, that she said this.

Among the 95% who would like to encourage cuddling, however, there are a number who are prevented from this by their own child's reserve; and, here again, we have an example of the way in which intended parental behaviour is influenced and modified by the child's own temperament. There are certainly some children who at four do not welcome their mothers' loving advances, and the mothers will tend in such a situation not to press the child, though, as a fitter's wife put it, they may manage to 'get in a crafty cuddle now and again'. 'I make quite a lot of fuss of him', said a university teacher's wife, 'but he's not terribly fond of me. He makes a fuss of his father. I wouldn't mean that he *dislikes* me—but he's definitely more fond of his father, and he'll say "There are the two of you; I like one better than the other, and it isn't *you*!" '

Greengrocer's wife:

> I show my affection, but she doesn't much to me; I mean, she doesn't ever kiss me, I have to say "Well, kiss your Mummy, then", and she will do then. No, she's not demonstrative that way.

Miner's wife:

> She's not very affectionate, not with me—with the girls more, she'll kiss them, and with her Daddy, but not with me. (Do you think kissing and cuddling should be discouraged at this age?) No, no—oh, it's her choice, and I don't force my affection on to her.

Metallurgist's wife:

> No, we don't—she's not one of these loving, cuddly children. I wouldn't discourage it if she wanted it; if she wanted it, I should give it to her. She doesn't bother.

The clerk's wife quoted on page 479, who valued her four-year-old for her affectionate behaviour in comparison with the elder daughter, and who said 'Of course, you enjoy it when you haven't had it with the other one', gives point to the fact that the mother is indeed limited in her expression of warmth and affection by the child's willingness to accept it; similar examples arose in discussing mothers' responses to clinging behaviour, where some felt that this afforded a pleasant opportunity for protectiveness which they themselves were missing through their child's independence (page 99). We have already noted the common vernacular use of the words 'love' and 'lovable' to mean, respectively, 'cuddle' and 'affectionate'; and it is perhaps of interest here to find that these two misusages hang together very logically in terms of behaviour: the child who is not *lovable*, in the sense of showing affectionate response, cannot in fact easily be *loved* in the sense of cuddled.

*'I'd just say "We do not smack our mothers"' . . .*

Mothers appear to accept their children's relative coolness towards them, even if they feel somewhat wistful for the 'little bits of lovey-dovey' that they see going on in other families, and they are also usually reconciled to a child's preference for the father, in which they find it possible to take pleasure: 'When his Daddy comes home, that's me finished!' said a miner's wife with some pride; 'He don't know me any more then!—he's all his Daddy'. This equanimity about the child's preferences is, of course, dependent upon a happy relationship between husband and wife: 'She's all her Daddy—that's really upsets me at times' said a mother whose contact with her daughter seemed chiefly harshly disciplinarian and for whom the child had become one of several bones of contention between herself and her milder husband. On the whole, however, in this area of behaviour the child makes the running; though this is not to say that children's affectional attitudes now are not probably determined in most cases by much earlier love experiences.

The child's more momentary and more violent expressions of temporary dislike, on the other hand, are by no means acceptable to most mothers. Question 100 asked: 'Does N ever try to smack *you*, or hurt you in any way? What do you do if he does? (What would you do if he did?)' Clearly, no mother will actually *like* being smacked by her child; however, attitudes may differ as to whether she regards this as a moral issue, in the sense that children must not be allowed to strike those in authority over them, or simply as a matter of antisocial behaviour ('It's not nice to smack people'). The difference in approach can be seen in the following quotations.

*Moral issue:*

Milkman's wife:

> I should tell him he *mustn't* smack his Mummy. I should try and explain that when Mummy smacks *him* it's because she has to, not because she wants to, that it's for his *good*, sort of thing, and that he *must not* smack back again.

Cook's wife:

> Smack her on her bottom and tell her to go upstairs. (Are you smacking her because you don't like her smacking other people, or because you don't like little girls smacking their Mummies—is it the disrespect you don't like, or . . . ?) It probably is smacking someone *bigger* . . . well, I don't really know . . . why do I smack her?—Well, I think she just shouldn't smack her *Mummy*, that's the whole thing, I think. I think it's awful to see little kiddies going for their mothers—and yet you do often see it. (So you're trying to teach her that you have the right to smack her, but she hasn't the right to smack you?) That's right (laughed)—yes!

Teacher's wife:

> Oh, I wouldn't allow it, because I *hate* to see a child raise its hand to its parents! I think it's *awful*—I see red when I see a

child do that. I could hit the child—it's one of those things with me.

*No moral issue:*

Publisher's wife:

Yes, he smacks me back. It's usually in the middle of a battle. I tell him not to, but I feel I can't do much about it, because it *is* in a battle: I just say "Don't do that".

Driver's mate's wife:

I don't know. I suppose I'd love him. A child must be pretty upset if he does that, I think, if it tries to turn round and smack you back.

University teacher's wife:

I don't know. His brother used to bite me a lot, and I put up with that, because I thought "He feels like doing it, and he'll stop it sometime"—and he did. I'm not sure *now* whether that was the right thing to do. I think I would check another child who did this. But usually it's very instinctive, and I think you've got to sort of find out *why* it is that he's choosing to do this rather unreasonable thing. (Would you check him in the same way as you would for biting another child?) No. I'd be *much* more fierce with him for biting another child.

Within the group who regard the situation as a moral issue, we can also distinguish between those who punish the child for smacking them (by smacking him themselves) and those who merely reprimand him and call his attention to their feelings about such behaviour.

*Punishment:*

Packer's wife:

If he hits me, I hit him back, and if he does it again I hit him harder, and I let him carry on. But he doesn't carry on *too* long, because my smacks get harder and harder and his don't. He finishes up crying after two usually. (Are you smacking him because you don't believe in children smacking their parents? Or simply because it's hurt you?) No, not because it's hurt me, because it's *wrong*.

Lorry driver's wife:

Oh, I wouldn't have it—if Elaine lifted her hand to me, I should immediately turn round and clout her one. I wouldn't tolerate that for a minute, and she knows it.

*Reprimand:*

Foreman's wife:

. . . I just turned on her and said "Well, that *was* a naughty thing", and I let her see that I was angry, you see; I said "Mummy has to smack you, but you mustn't smack Mummy back". It's difficult, you see, when you *tell* them to smack the other children back; when she's smacked me, she's said "Well, you told me to smack Robert back"; and I say "Well, that's different—that's another *child*—that's a different matter, because if I smack *you* I'm smacking you because you are naughty, but you don't have to smack Mummy, or Daddy, or any grownup back, you see— you never answer grownups back or cheek grownups, either".

Teacher's wife:

I think I'd just say "We do not smack our mothers", and leave it at that.

76% of all mothers take a moral stand on this question. There is a difference in the treatment of boys and of girls (significant at the 0·03 level) in that the mother is rather more likely to take such a stand where the child is male. Analysed by social class, the trend is towards a more moral attitude as one descends the social scale (in accord with the authoritarian bias at the lower end of the scale), but this does not reach overall statistical significance; the chief divergence is found in the professional and managerial class, of whom 68% regard the situation as presenting a moral issue. Of the 'moral issue' group (randomized), 77% would punish the child for smacking his mother, and here a significant class trend is found towards an increase in verbal reprimands as opposed to smacking at the top end of the scale; even in Class I and II, however, the majority of those who feel a stand needs to be taken show it in a punitive way. The detailed findings are given in Table L.

*'Oh, I'm always telling him I won't love him—aren't I, Trevor?'*

If 95% of mothers still encourage an active display of love and affection between themselves and their four-year-old children,

Q*

TABLE L

*Mothers' response to their children smacking them*

|  | I & II | IIIwc | IIIman | IV | V | All (random) |
|---|---|---|---|---|---|---|
|  | % | % | % | % | % | % |
| Regards as moral issue | 68 | 72 | 76 | 82 | 77 | 76 |
| No moral issue | 32 | 28 | 24 | 18 | 23 | 24 |
|  | (n = 88) | (n = 78) | (n = 172) | (n = 112) | (n = 78) | |
| Moral issue, punitive | 64 | 69 | 83 | 73 | 83 | 77 |
| Moral issue, verbal reprimand | 36 | 31 | 17 | 27 | 17 | 23 |

it may be expected that the child will be particularly vulnerable to any threat that this love will be withdrawn. Obviously withdrawal of love may be expressed in a number of different ways; a mother might refuse to speak to or smile at the child, for instance, so conveying that the loving relationship was no longer intact. However, our main interest was to discover how far mothers used this threat, openly and verbally expressed, as a deliberate technique for controlling the child. The question, part of the group asking about other 'idle' threats, was: 'Do you ever tell him you won't love him if he behaves like that?' As we found when asking the other questions from this group, those mothers who did *not* use such a threat tended to be extremely vehement in their replies, and to show some disapproval of the interviewer for thinking such a question appropriate. A lorry driver's wife was indignant: 'No, why should you? People shouldn't *do* that. You can't stop loving them because they're naughty, can you?'—and responded to the interviewer's deliberately provocative 'The last lady I went to said that a lot' with a round 'Well, she's a fool, then!' The child's security was felt to be at stake: 'That's a thing I'm *dead* against', said a builder's wife, 'It's just playing with fire to say you don't love them, I think'. A shop manager's wife said 'I don't think that would be fair to him. You *do* love them, whether they're naughty or not—that's the child's *life*'; and a machine operator's wife echoed the feeling of a large number of mothers when she said 'If you tell a child that you don't love it, it sticks—it sticks in the mind'. Once again, some had threatened the child in this way once, but had resolved not to again because of its effect; the comment of a lorry driver's wife seemed to confirm the truth of the belief that such a threat 'sticks in the mind'.

> Well, I did once; but I don't think that's a good thing myself, because they never forget. I once said it to her, quite a long while ago; and for days afterwards, every time we got together on our own, she said to me "Do you love me?"—and I thought to myself, well, I must have given her the impression that I *don't*, because of saying it that once: so I don't say that now. Because children, I mean, they rely on you for everything, you're everything they've got.

'I shouldn't like to put that idea into his head, that he's only loved *on good behaviour terms*', said a British Rail fireman's wife; but this was exactly the intention of more than a third (36%) of all mothers. 'I do say that', said the wife of a railway-man, 'and, you know, when I smack her and she's crying, she'll say "You don't love me any more, do you?"—I say, "Yes, *when you're a good girl* Mummy loves you, but *not without*"'. There is a strong class difference in this attitude, however: all three working-class groups closely agree, 42% of them using this threat; in the middle-class, this percentage drops to 21% for the shop and clerical group and only 12% in the professional and managerial class (significant at the ·001 level). Here again, as we saw where the 'sending away' threat was concerned, the threatening mother's chief consideration seemed to be that her words were effective in their context: they caused the child to capitulate; and his evident distress, which once more seemed to be on a quite different level from his reaction to ordinary punishment, was thus seen by this group as a sign that the right means of controlling the child had been found, rather than suggesting doubts as to its wisdom.

Labourer's wife:

> Yes, I have done. (What sort of thing would she have done when you say that?) Well, if she goes and touches her Dad's flowers, I say "Now, I don't love you now, you've been naughty". Or if she's gone into the kitchen and she's touched, p'raps, some food or something, I'll say "No, I don't love you—that was naughty of you". And she comes and says "I'm sorry. I love you—love me". And I'll say "I'll love you when you're a good girl", you see. (Does it upset her more than other things?) Yes,

if you say you don't love her it hurts her very much—more than cancelling her sweets or anything. I only say that if it's something really bad that she's done—what I don't want her to do again, sort of thing.

**Painter's wife:**

Once or twice; and that more or less upsets her, and she seems *quiet* if you tell her you don't love her. She sits there and sulks; and then a bit later she'll come round you and love you, and say "I'll not do it again, you do love me, don't you?"—and then, come another day, she'll start again! But she's *different* altogether when you say that.

**Diesel engineer's wife:**

Often. "Mummy doesn't love *naughty* girls—I won't love you any more". I've often said that, if she's been very naughty or playing me up.

**Jigger's wife:**

(On lying) I've found if I tell her I don't love her I can get the truth out of her; otherwise I can't. Then I just tell her I love her because she's told me the truth. She'll do anything if you tell her you don't love her.

**Service layer's wife:**

Oh yes, I have done several times. (What would she have done when you say that?) Well, it really depends where I am more than what she's done. If we're out—if we're in a shop and I can't smack her, then I might say that to her.

**Hospital porter's wife:**

Once you get him in bed, he'll get out. But if you say to him "If you get out of bed, I won't be your friend any more", he'll say "All right, if I don't get out of bed I'll be your *bestest* friend then"; and he won't get out of bed. But say one night I *don't* say it, he *will* get out. (You do this every night?) Most nights, yes; I can do more by saying that to him than smacking him. It works wonders.

**Miner's wife:**

Yes, I often tell her I don't love her when she's doing something to annoy me: "I don't love you now. No, you're a bad girl"—something like that. (Does she mind that?) Oh, she don't like that. She don't like it at all. She'll say, "I don't love *you*, then". I say, "I don't care if you do—I don't love you now, Susan!"—"You don't love me, but you love our Shirley (baby), don't you?"—that's what she says. (What have you usually told her that *for*—I mean, what has she usually done?) Well, say I won't let her have any more toffees, and she's going on about it. I say, "Oh, I don't love you then, if you're going to keep on about it"—just to upset her, because she gets on my nerves. Or when she's done something to our baby, smacked her; or being naughty about going to bed; I say "Oh, I don't love you". I say it quite a lot to her, because I know it hurts her, and then p'raps she'll do as she's told.

Most of these quotations vividly illustrate the way in which, for this group, immediate expedience is served by means of exploiting the child's special vulnerability in a way which the majority of mothers consider quite unjustifiable and indeed morally wrong. The last comment, 'I say it quite a lot to her, *because I know it hurts her*, and then p'raps she'll do as she's told', underlines the fact that these mothers are deliberately trying to get under the child's skin in the most effective way they can: one more quotation will illustrate this attitude from a slightly different angle—that of the mother who is somewhat vexed because *in this child* she has not succeeded in finding the vulnerable point which experience of her other children had led her to hope for. In this case, withdrawal of attention backs up the statement of withdrawal of love.

Packer's wife:

Oh, I often tell him I don't; but he just turns around and says "Well, I don't love you either". He just couldn't care less, you see. I say "Don't talk to me. I don't want to talk to you—I don't like you—I don't love you no more". He'll say, "Well, Mam . . ."—"I don't want to talk to you, Ian. You're a naughty boy, and I'm *not* talking to you". "All right then—*don't* talk to me. And I don't love *you*"—and he'll walk off. He's annoyed when I won't listen to him, and I do try and do that *as* a punishment, because, one of my others, it did really upset him if you didn't talk to him. But it doesn't work so well with Ian. It does *annoy* him; but it doesn't *do the trick*, you know.

One might suppose that the threat of so cataclysmic a punishment—the destruction of the keystone of the child's emotional life implied in "Mummy won't love you any more"— would occur only as the climax of a passionate battle between the two; but it is obvious from the quotations that the emotion is almost entirely on the child's side: in fact, the acceptance of such sanctions as commonplace techniques of control, used without emotional involvement on their part, is a salient feature of this group—'You say so many things, you can't remember really, can you?' A few mothers, however, have some doubts on account of the child's distress, and for them the threat bursts out, as it were, under stress of conflict: 'I've always regretted it', says a bus conductor's wife, 'because I don't think you *should* say that to children'.

Metal polisher's wife:

> I think I've done it a couple of times—I'd forgotten about that. It's not a thing I've done regular. Until you mentioned it just now, it never entered my head. But I know I have done it a couple of times. (You're rather emphasizing that this is a thing you *don't* do regularly—is it a thing you disapprove of really?) Oh, yes; because Derek is sensitive; and the couple of times I *have* said "I don't love you", it really broke his heart. I've got to be really mad to say that.

Nevertheless, we think it still fair to classify these mothers among the group which does readily use this threat, since for the alternative group such words are so completely taboo that they are not even contemplated, however 'mad' the mother may feel with the child.

The reader may have noticed that among the quotations given there is a preponderance of girls over boys: this is not a true reflection of the actual incidence of the use of this technique with sons and daughters, however, which shows no significant difference between them—in so far as any trend can be detected, it is in fact in the opposite direction.

A variant of the "Mummy won't love you" threat (not coded as such, however) is the occasional use of accusation of the child's lack of love for the mother, as supposedly shown by his bad behaviour; we made no direct enquiry on this, but it was sometimes mentioned in response to this question. Its intention is, of course, to provoke guilt in the child; a production manager's wife used it to back up her own punitive reaction to the child's smacking of her: 'I say "You keep telling me you love me, but when you act like that, I don't think you do". Then he starts to cry'. In a context such as this, the mother immediately risks the child's reasoning: 'Mummy says I don't love her if I smack her; so when she smacks me, that means *she's* stopped loving *me*'.

Speculation about the reasoning sequences which may be sparked off in the child by verbal sanctions of this sort immediately raises a much more basic and interesting question about the development of moral concepts in the child: how far does the child assume from the outset a natural equation between 'goodness' and lovableness? Does the mother who deliberately threatens that 'When you're a good girl Mummy loves you, but not without' merely put into words and openly confirm a belief which the child already possesses?

If this is so, part of the child's misconception may stem from a confusion between *liking* and *loving*, and also from an identification between himself and his behaviour. The mother makes it plain that she does not always like the child's behaviour; and this very obvious fact may be speedily developed into the notion that she does not *love* the *child*. The distinction was frequently made during the interview by the mothers themselves: 'I always say that I don't *like* naughty boys, but never that I won't *love* him', said a civil engineer's wife; and a clerk's wife agreed: 'I tell her I won't *like* her, but I don't tell her I won't *love* her, because I think she should believe that her parents *always* love her, whatever she does'. Middle-class mothers in particular often try to make the distinction explicit in words, and seem very conscious of the conceptual difficulty for the child.

Company director's wife:

> If he's naughty, sometimes *he* says "You're naughty, Mummy, I don't love you"; and I say, "Robin, *I* know you don't mean it and *you* know you don't mean it". Then of course I explain to him that *love* doesn't come into it at all; because I don't want him to use this expression saying you don't *love* me if you do something wrong—I don't believe in that, and I always like to give him a reason for everything.

University teacher's wife:

> For instance: she wet her pants several times running—no puddles, just enough for her to have to have both her pants *and*

her tights changed—and apparently simply because she couldn't
be bothered to leave her play till it was just too late. So I was
cross, and I explained what a nuisance it was because of the
tights, and that she was old enough to be more sensible. So that
evening I was cuddling her at bedtime, and I said "Oh, I do love
you"; and she said "You don't love me when I wet my pants".
That was rather a shock, actually. So I explained that of course
I did, I *always* loved her, I wouldn't stop loving her just because
she'd wet her pants or anything else she did. She said "You get
cross, though". We had quite a talk about it, I had to explain
that I might not always like the things that she *did*, but that
made no difference to how I felt about *her*; she *seemed* to understand, but whether she did . . .

A clergyman's wife said 'Oh no! *No*! No, I've occasionally
said "I don't like you very much at the moment", but it's well
understood that loving and liking are two very different things'.
The wife of a scientific research worker, however, was less sure
that her child really comprehended this subtle distinction.

I don't tell him I won't love him, I tell him he won't be a good
boy if he does that—which really amounts to the same, doesn't
it? (Well, I don't know—do you think being a good boy is linked
up with your love?) I think it *is;* because you say you don't
like bad boys, I think it's an accepted fact that good boys are
liked and bad boys are not liked. (How much is it a matter of
*liking* and *loving*—do you think your children distinguish between
these two things?) I don't think they do; because—without
telling him that I don't love him if he's naughty—if he has got
one of these fits of being stubborn, and runs to his room and
slams the door, I don't call him or go upstairs, but eventually
he will come down, not crying, but pulling a sad face, and saying
"I'm nice now—I'm good now", and wanting a kiss, which he
then gets: so *something* must connect the two.

Perhaps a little further light is thrown on the child's eye view
of the link between love and merit by a short note on an ex-
change with one of our own children, then aged four.

*Carey*, 4:1
Her goldfish had died, and I told her so. She said mournfully
"Oh . . ."; then, visibly becoming practical, "Well, you'd better
give it to the cat, because she's been wanting it for ages". Slightly

taken aback by this apparent callousness, but wanting to follow up her thoughts, I asked "Which do you love most, the cat or the fish?" I expected her to say "The cat"—because, behaviourally speaking, she did seem to love it better: she fondled it, played with it, fed it, and talked to it and about it a great deal, whereas she took little notice of the goldfish. She said "The fish". "The fish?"—"Yes, of course, because the cat would eat the fish if she could, but the fish would never *dream* of eating the cat!" Clearly in this case she was assuming that love is given to the good.

To sum up, it would seem that the majority of mothers are concerned that the child should understand a concept of maternal love as something which persists under all circumstances, and that some mothers, especially in Class I and II, deliberately try to define and elaborate this concept verbally, rather than merely leaving the child to attain a tacit understanding of it from their warmth towards him; however, a very considerable minority group of 36% intentionally exploit the child's conceptual uncertainty for their own immediate convenience of securing his compliance. This technique, although we did not include it in the group of idle threats for the purpose of scoring 'distortion of truth', seems to have much in common with them: not least in the class difference which it shows between an overall incidence in the middle-class of 15% and in the working-class of 42%.

'*I do it for him at once, believe it or not. I mean, you may think it's nothing much and he can wait, but in a kiddy's mind it's important, just as much as your things are to you. . . . We don't get on each other's nerves—I don't get on his nerves, and he doesn't get on mine. . . . You've got to take some notice of their likes and dislikes—if he doesn't want to do something I can usually persuade him, but then I usually start off by making it sound a nice thing to do, I don't just tell him . . . (If he says 'I'm busy' . . . ?) I probably wouldn't have asked him to in that case, because I'd look to see if he was busy first.*'

The mother whom we quote above, a tailor's presser's wife, is perhaps the most consistently 'child-centred' of all our 700, both from one situation to another, and from one year to another as her child grows from one to seven. In every encounter with the child, she is aware of his point of view, and takes it into account as readily as, if not more readily than, her own. Other workers in the field of child rearing have proposed the dimension of child-centredness as a measure of some importance in assessing methods of upbringing, and we would agree that, while it has much in common with the authoritarian/democratic dimension, it adds something to it in terms of warmth and a willingness to take trouble for the attainment of aims in which the parent has no immediate interest. At the beginning of this chapter, we suggested that valuation of the child 'for himself' might be some indication of child-centredness: not a very discriminating one, however, if 80% of mothers come into this category. However, it is possible to bring together a number of items from the interview schedule, chosen for their face validity as positive indications of child-centredness in the mother, and thus to devise a composite index with much greater discriminatory possibilities.

The following six items were chosen for this scale: the page numbers given refer to the main discussion in the text of each item.

1. Mother is 'invariably' or 'mostly' responsive to the child's demands (pages 87–97).
2. Mother participates 'wholeheartedly' in the child's play (pages 166–73).
3. Mother is willing to 'chat' during the night at child's request (pages 280–2).
4. Mother unreservedly accepts child's 'I'm busy' excuse (pages 394–402).
5. Mother values child 'for himself' (pages 477–482).
6. Mother chooses not to make a moral issue of the child smacking her (pages 486–9).

Table LI presents an analysis by social class of mothers' positions on the child-centredness dimension. For simplicity, scores have been allotted on a scale 0—6 (i.e. a score of 1 for each item in which the mother is positively rated), and the table shows low scorers (0, 1 or 2) against high scorers (4, 5 or 6). It should be noted that, although we believe that child-centredness inevitably contains some component of 'warmth', we have deliberately excluded this rather subjectively estimated factor from our list of items.[1] Class differences over the whole table

---

[1] There is no overall class difference found in our not very discriminating estimates of warmth (see pages 434–5), but significantly fewer class V mothers can be rated as 'very warm and demonstrative'.

are significant, showing a trend towards child-centredness higher up the social scale and away from it as the scale is descended: the main difference lies between middle- and working-classes, and these results are shown in combined form in order to show this. The difference is not a very emphatic one; nevertheless, it is interesting in its confirmation of our findings on authoritarianism and reciprocity.

TABLE LI

*Class differences in child-centredness*

| Child-centredness scale | I & II | IIIwc | IIIman | IV | V | All (random) |
|---|---|---|---|---|---|---|
| | % | % | % | % | % | % |
| Low scorers (0, 1 or 2) | 27 | 23 | 39 | 31 | 39 | 34 |
| | | 25 | | 38 | | |
| High scorers (4, 5 or 6) | 45 | 42 | 34 | 30 | 30 | 36 |
| | | 43 | | 32 | | |

'*I just wish I could be a little more civilized with them at times . . .*'
We come finally to the group of questions with which the interview was drawn together, which attempted to look at the mother's behaviour with her child as a total pattern, and invited her to comment upon it and to introspect on her feeling towards the relationship which she and the child had created. Evaluation of her own behaviour was intentionally encouraged, and she was also asked to compare her role with that of her husband in the discipline situation. The basic questions were asked in the following words:

104. On the whole, are you happy about the way you deal with discipline in general, or do you sometimes find yourself doing things that you don't really approve of?
105. Compared with other people, do you think of yourself as being very strict, or rather strict, or rather easy-going, or very easy-going?
106. Do you agree with your husband about discipline, or is he a lot more strict or less strict than you are?

117. Would you say that you have changed in your ideas about bringing up children, since you started? I mean, you've had . . . years' experience now since . . . (eldest child) was born—do you think your ideas have altered during that time?

54% of all mothers are self-critical in reply to Question 104; but there is a significant difference between middle-class and working-class mothers, showing a greater tendency among middle-class women to examine their own methods critically, *and to find themselves wanting*. The percentage of mothers who criticize themselves rises to 64% in the white-collar and professional groups (who agree closely in this respect) and drops to 51% in the skilled and semi-skilled groups and to only 39% in the unskilled group. Those who are entirely happy about their methods naturally tend to have less to say on the question than those who are not: the self-critical give specific examples of where things go wrong, and often go on to worry at the problem from a number of angles, while the less critical will let it go with a brief 'Yes, yes; I think I'm doing all right'. 'Normally I feel confident that I am doing the right thing in whatever I *do* do', said a teacher's wife. Some examples of mothers who are content with the discipline situation follow.

Bleacher's wife:

Well, I'm satisfied for myself. You know, I think, as well as I'm able, I do it for the best—for them as well as for myself. As I say, the times when I *would* have had a doubt, something's always seemed to say "don't do that" or "leave it alone"—I rely on instinct, you know, to tell you whether it was better to leave things alone or not.

Teacher's wife:

No, we're quite happy; we do *occasionally* wonder whether we're a bit too strict. Of course, my husband being a teacher, he's very much inclined to say a thing and expect the same response he'd get in the classroom, and I do occasionally say that he expects them to be too much . . . but it's very difficult to know where to draw the dividing line, we often feel that. And yet I don't think so, looking back; because you do find that your children are better behaved than anyone else's, and yet they're still very happy with it.

Optician's wife:

> I don't know. I'd say—I've got to think!—I'd say I get on all right. I mean, the neighbours tell me, and my friends tell me, that they're well-behaved children—I don't know what they're like behind my back! Mind you, especially with the older ones, I rule them with a rod of iron, and people have said to me "You're too strict"; but when I've been to friends, you know, I look at myself and think I'm lucky, you know, especially with the teenage one. Mine don't back-answer, you know, they never cheek me.

Some mothers were now happy with the way things were going, but only because they had in the past been self-critical and changed their tactics. 'Oh yes, I think I'm quite happy now', said the mother who had resolved to stop smacking after the traumatic experience of seeing her child back away from her in the yard, 'I think he's brought up the way I always wanted him to be'. Another had revised her methods between one child and the next: 'He's been very good—he's just more or less fell in to what he should do. The other one would bang on the floor with his heels and see you anywhere before he'd do as he was told. And I don't somehow think . . . I felt that I wasn't handling him right, and I tried to handle this one differently, and I think we've got past that showing-off stage—we seem to get *round* it *without* that showing off'. A few mothers distinguished between feeling sorry for their actions out of emotion and out of reasonable doubt; they felt that what they did was right, but that the pathos of the child could easily beguile them into sentimental and unjustified regret.

Driver's mate's wife:

> Well, I don't find myself doing things that I don't *approve* of. But afterwards I feel sorry for what I've done, especially if I've really lost my temper and yelled and cursed and given them a smack. Then they get ready for bed and look like three little eggs, all nice, and I get a lump in my throat and feel sorry then.

The group of mothers who criticize their own behaviour do not, of course, all do so in the same way. They can be divided into three sub-groups: those who think they are too strict, those who think they are too easy-going, and those whose criticism is rather more complex and less easy to classify in such terms. The total 54% who 'find themselves doing things they don't really

approve of' break down into 26% who behave more strictly
than they would feel necessary, 12% who feel they should be
more strict than they are and 16% who give more complicated
answers. We have noted a class difference in general self-
criticism, middle-class mothers having more regrets than others;
class analysis of the *kind* of criticism involved shows that this
difference is wholly due to middle-class mothers who think they
should be less strict: that is to say, if working-class mothers were
as much inclined as middle-class mothers to deplore their own
strictness, class differences in self-criticism would disappear.

Among the mothers who think themselves too strict, some are
unhappy about the total pattern of their behaviour to the child,
while others regret single aspects of it, usually smacking or
shouting. 'I sometimes feel I'm a bit too hard on him', said a
policeman's wife, 'but with the two of them, I feel I've *got* to be,
or they'd get on top of me, you know—I do shout at them
rather a lot sometimes, you know, and I don't really like to do
it'. A packer's wife, who by any assessment would have been
rated at the extreme end of a scale of strictness, was unhappy
about her relationship with her children; in search of a well-
behaved and united family, she had not succeeded in finding it,
and was beginning to wonder whether her efforts were mis-
directed.

> Well, you do what you think is right, don't you, and that's all
> you *can* do. I think we *are* very strict; and yet, somehow, they
> don't seem to show the . . . results, shall I say. I often wonder . . .
> I've said many a time to my husband, I'm sure *one* of them will
> grow up to be a delinquent. We shall have trouble somewhere.
> And I wonder if perhaps we're not *too* strict—we've often dis-
> cussed that, sitting here. Perhaps we push them into it, *by* being so
> strict. I mean, they know they'll get a good hiding for the least
> little thing—and I think perhaps, *knowing* that, they think "Well,
> I might as well do a *big* thing", you know.[1]

'Say you smack them', said a hospital porter's wife, 'and then
you think to yourself, "Well, was it really necessary?" And then
you start to think—"Well, come to that, what they *done*?"' Two
more mothers who were brought up short by the patently vul-

[1] The reader may be interested to look again at other quotations from this
mother's interview in the light of this comment; they will be found on pages
413, 416, 448, 466, 488 and 493.

nerable look of the child asleep thought their methods unjusti-
fiably harsh: the second uses a great many idle threats.

Shop assistant's wife:

> I find I'm sometimes a little bit harder than is necessary. I think
> sometimes I shout at her for nothing, and then when she's fast
> asleep in bed and looking as if butter wouldn't melt in her mouth,
> you know, I stop and think . . . I think "Oh dear, poor little devil,
> I *have* been cruel today to you, and punished you far too much!"
> I stop and think then—if I've slapped her in anger.

Jointer's wife:

> Sometimes I do feel really remorseful: usually if I've said some-
> thing to them to frighten them, like I'll leave them; and then I
> look at them lying in bed, all peaceful, like, and I say to my
> husband, "Oh, dear, I'm a wicked woman, it's really wicked to
> talk like that to them". But then the next day they're on again,
> and I get nasty all over again! I got *really* nasty-tempered one
> time—I couldn't stay, I was afraid of myself, I just had to go
> and walk round the houses for a bit.

Bad temper is regretted very frequently indeed, not only on
the grounds that it so often results in unkind treatment of the
child, but also by mothers who succeed in controlling actual
hitting out of temper, but who find that their anger leads to
unreasonable demands on him, and to guilt and self-reproach in
themselves. The mother quoted below, who said 'I didn't know
I'd *got* a temper until I had Laurence, actually', puts her finger on
a potent source of distress. In our culture, the physical chastising
of children for moral purposes is condoned; violence as a result
of anger (the actual situation in which smacking usually in fact
takes place) is not. Crimes of violence against children, whether
premeditated or not, naturally incur universal horror and
revulsion; the newspaper story of a father who has inflicted
injury upon his baby because it would not stop crying is discussed in buses and shops with total condemnation: 'How could
anyone hurt a poor little mite like that?' The truth is, however,
that violence lies beneath the surface in all too many of us; a
discussion with mothers which begins by openly recognizing
that parents can feel an unreasoning violence against their own
children will often stimulate many admissions of such taboo
emotions, frequently accompanied by a sense of relief that

others, too, have experienced such disturbing impulses. Anger against a small child is doubly disturbing for the mother, both because its force is so often an utterly new and unlooked-for experience, and because its direction against so pitiful and helpless an object is clearly indefensible. The situations of anger to which young adults are accustomed before they have children tend either to be resolved by the use of well-defined social codes of behaviour or to be unresolvable and therefore to be abandoned. The mother who is faced with a screaming, colicky baby, however, can neither talk her way politely through the situation nor abandon her part in it; she can only continue to do her best to pacify the child, in an atmosphere of growing physical tension exacerbated by the frustrating knowledge that she is failing in her role of comforting mother; small wonder that, in their heart of hearts, many mothers know that the difference between themselves and the parent whose anger erupts into physical violence is only one of degree and of rather more effective controls. The four-year-old is less guilt-provoking as an enemy, because he is clearly better able than the baby to take responsibility for the anger which he stimulates in his mother; it is not for nothing that the mother is so often stricken with pangs of conscience when she looks at him all defenceless in sleep. Violence of emotion remains, however, to shock the parent with its own force, simply because the parent/child relationship is probably more totally involving of the ego than any which the adult has hitherto experienced.

Surveyor's wife:

> The only thing I *don't* approve of—and it *is* a weakness—I have a temper; and I didn't know I'd *got* a temper until I had Laurence, actually. I must admit that if he tries me and tries me—this isn't very often—there are just the odd times when he will persist in trying me beyond . . . and if you feel a bit off, or something—then my temper does sometimes get the better of me. I'm ashamed of that; I mean, I wish I hadn't . . . if I lose my temper, I perhaps smack him harder than I mean to.

Administrative assistant's wife:

> The main thing is knowing my failing of losing my temper very easily. I think I could possibly deal with the situations that arise easier if I didn't lose my temper. It's a bad failing of mine, I know, but I can't do much about it: I keep trying, but I don't

seem to get anywhere. If I didn't lose my temper so easily—I'm *quick*-tempered, rather than *bad*-tempered—I think I'd make a better job of it. I keep trying, as I say.

Teacher's wife:

I wish . . . I *really do wish* that I wasn't so quick-tempered with him. Because I find that with *being* quick-tempered, sometimes I *will* smack him, and then I think about it afterwards . . . it's often depending on my mood, you see. I am *very* sorry at times about that, I really am—I'm awful.

The two mothers whose comments follow are similar to these in the sense that they feel that their emotions involve them more deeply than they wish in conflicts with the child; the second quotation came at the end of a long sequence of answers describing specific examples of situations of this mother's conflict with her rather high-strung little boy, with whom she has a particularly warm if stormy relationship.

Publisher's wife:

I'm afraid I do sometimes. I find myself getting angry, and then there's a battle, and instead of being detached I get *embroiled* in it: which isn't the right thing to do, of course.

British Rail fireman's wife:

Oh yes! I mean, one has an idea in one's mind of how a mother should be, and you very often don't come anywhere near the picture of what you'd like to be. (Is it mostly the smacking?) Yes—and, you know, I sort of wish I could get him to do more of the things he was told *when* he was told—at the moment, I mean, we have to have an *argument* about it. (Do you mean you wish *he* was just a little bit different?) Well . . . I think perhaps it's the fact that I *do* argue back and smack him, that could probably *stop* him from being obedient. The fact that I would be willing to *have* an argument with him sort of puts him on a level with me. We're really as bad as one another. If I got less worked up about it, I might achieve more. I do think a lot of it is *from* me. I can see how he's feeling, you know; I can remember my own childhood very clearly, and how I felt and that. And of course, being handicapped by a terribly quick temper myself, I can always sympathize with anyone else with the same.

Mothers who think they are too easy with the child usually speak in terms of letting him 'get away with things' rather than

taking a firm stand. 'I give way to them sometimes, when I
know very well that I didn't ought to do', said a chemical
worker's wife, and the wife of a policeman agreed with her:
'Mind you, it's easier to say yes than to say no, isn't it, and
sometimes if I've had a tiring day, I say "Oh yes, go on then"—
and really, at the back of my mind, I think I really ought not
to have given in like that'.

Cycle assembler's wife:

I think I ought to be sterner; I give way a lot, you know. I love
the kid really—and I think you *do* give way, you can't help it.
But it's a silly mistake, to give way, it is really—I mean, it's the
same with George (10), I can see no end of mistakes I've made
with George, and really I could kick myself about it.

Metallurgist's wife:

Well, I sometimes think, you give in for peace and quiet when
you should have stuck it out. My husband points that out to
me *very* often. He says, "When you say a thing, you should
stick to it". But it's very hard when you've got three children
squabbling round you—your standards and what you know is
right goes a bit beside the board, doesn't it?

A jointer's wife who also found herself giving in too easily
provided a practical illustration during the interview:

Interviewer's report:

The ice-cream man's chimes were heard outside. Both children
asked for ices; mother said very firmly, "*No*, not on a wet day
like this"—"Oh Mum!", "Oh please!"—"No, you can't, you've
already had all that Skeggy rock"—"Oh Mum, let us!", "I *want*
one!", "He's only just outside, quick!"—"I said NO, you heard
me!" The children jumped about, panicking that the van would
go before they had worn her down. Finally: "Oh, where's my
purse? You see (to me), I give way, and the trouble is they *know*
I do. But what can you do? If you didn't give way, you'd just
about explode sometimes, when they go on and on at you. Tessa's
supposed to be on a diet, too". Tessa (8) is obese; during the
interview she asked for, and was given *after argument*, rock,
ice-cream and sweet tea.

'If you're feeling a bit tired, it's much easier to turn a blind
eye', said a representative's wife; and a number of mothers

emphasized the fact that housewives are not invariably either in perfect health or well rested, and that this in practice makes a good deal of difference, in either direction, to their behaviour. 'If I'm tired myself', said an insurance agent's wife, 'I'll p'raps bribe her, just to save her from crying; and I don't like myself when I do that'; and the wife of a chartered accountant explained: 'Sometimes when my nerves are a bit on edge I shout at him, and I think that's wrong; but you can't help yourself some days, can you?' A clergyman's wife said: 'Generally speaking, I don't get very easily rattled; but just sometimes I get extremely sort of irate—you know, obviously sometimes pre-menstrual tension or something like that—and then I might be more irritable than I would otherwise be'. Force of circumstance also sometimes made mothers behave otherwise than they really approved of: two children prone to attacks of, respectively, asthma and eczema were given in to far more often than their mothers thought right, for fear of upsetting them and provoking a new bout; difficult neighbours or in-laws sometimes made mothers stricter than they wished to be; and two mothers bringing up their children without fathers found that this affected their attitude to discipline.

Separated wife (Class IV):

Well, I think I ought to be harder with them, really. I think I make the mistake, with being parted from my husband, I think I try to *make it up to them* that way, you know, letting them have a bit more freedom. It might be wrong, but . . .

Widow (Class III manual):

Yes I do—I sometimes think that I'm very soft with them. As I say, I don't smack much, they very rarely get a smack; and some of my friends think I let them get away with an awful lot. But you see, if I'm cross with them, they've got no-one else to turn to . . . you know how it is, when Mummy's cross you run to Daddy—well, they can't do that. So that sometimes I give way when I think perhaps I should have been sterner.

Perhaps the most interesting forms of self-criticism came from those who committed themselves to regrets neither of over-permissiveness nor of over-strictness, but who were dissatisfied to a greater or lesser degree with some rather vaguer lack in themselves. Although we began by thinking that this third category was something of a ragbag, most of the comments boiled down to one of two things: failure to be consistent and failure to achieve results.

Inconsistency may be simply over-permissiveness and over-strictness occurring in sequence: 'Sometimes I smack him a bit too quick; other times I let things slide, which is just as bad really'. 'I do wonder sometimes if I've done right or wrong, and wish I were more consistent', said a nylon knitter's wife. Circumstances and mood tend to come into it.

University teacher's wife:

> On the whole we're happy enough. Sometimes if I'm tired, or in an awful rush, I think I'm a bit inconsistent; things that I would allow, I just pounce on; and I don't think they've meant any more harm on that occasion than on any other occasion when I've let it pass.

The factor of consistency or lack of it is often given a good deal of importance in theoretical papers on child rearing in relation to personality, and parents' handbooks have laid down consistency as a precept with greater consistency through the years than any other piece of advice! Nevertheless, we would doubt whether the majority of parents succeed in even approaching perfect consistency in their behaviour towards their children. We might also suggest that this may be fortunate: total lack of consistency may be disturbing and disorienting, but total consistency is likely to be extremely inhibiting to the child's development of social flexibility and understanding. Sympathy and tolerance in meeting the immediate needs of associates are qualities which are valued in the adult; but the child may not be helped to learn a flexible social response if he never has to learn to consider and adjust to the changing moods of his parents.

We quoted in an earlier chapter the mother who pointed out that 'you don't know if you're doing right or doing wrong until you *have* brought them up—you have to wait and see how they turn out, and then it might be too late'. Others made the same point, that methods can only be judged by results; and more than half of our third category of mothers were self-critical because they were already not happy about their results and felt that they themselves must be to blame in some way, though they were at a loss to know how. Some began to feel themselves caught up in a desperate escalation of disciplinary measures which they did not approve of; and there was a central thread of bewilderment, combining both resentment against the child and feelings of personal inadequacy, because their pre-conceived ideas of child-rearing as a *reasoned* relationship were being frustrated by the harassing reality. The lorry-driver's wife whose comment heads this section—'I just wish I could be a little more *civilized* with them at times'—also provided an earlier quotation: 'I start off speaking kindly to them; but I end up shouting like a maniac'; she would have liked not to smack at all, but found that she could not get her children to listen to her.

Miner's wife:

> I don't seem to be very successful. Other people's seem to be more polite and less cheeky—it sometimes makes you wonder what they do that I don't do. I've often felt like crying, you know—say I've smacked them a bit harder than usual; it's very upsetting, because I love kiddies . . .

Aircraft fitter's wife:

> I find myself shouting more than I think is necessary; because, I don't know whether this is what other people find, but I just wish they'd do what they're told without having to *shout* at them. . . . My mother was the kind of person you'd do things for without having to be spoken to many times—without having to be punished, you know what I mean?—she'd got that *firmness* with her. I can never remember my mother smacking me. I don't think I've got that same firmness—I have to get mad with them before they'll do as they're told.

Fairground worker's wife:

> I sometimes wonder if I do it the right way—you know, whether you should have more control over them; they don't seem to take any notice of what you say. But I think it's a bit too late to start trying now—how do you start on a different way of trying to learn them *now*? As I say to my husband, there should *be* some other way, you shouldn't have to keep giving these little smacks out all the time, should you? I do sometimes wonder if there's a book you could get that'd tell you—I suppose it's child psychology. I'm all right with babies, but if I get mad with these, I say "Ooh, I'd swop you all for ten babies!"

Clerk's wife (continuation of quotation on page 412):

> What I think—why *should* I have to keep on and on at them? I mean, they should do as they're told straight away, shouldn't they? But they just don't listen. (Why do you think it is?) Well, they're not frightened of me, are they? I don't know—I've *never* been strict enough—I haven't *started* to be strict, have I? If I had have done, they'd have been fri . . . well, not frightened, but know that when I spoke they'd *got* to do what they were told. (Have you done a lot of threatening without carrying it out?) Yes; and I've blamed other people for doing it, but I do it myself, I can't help it, I don't know why . . . I suppose really, it's because I don't *want* to do the things to them that I'm threatening them with: you know, I'll say "I'll put you to bed in a minute", and really and truly I don't *want* them to go to bed, but I have to punish them, you see; so rather than do that, I smack them. (So they've really got into a sort of habit of waiting until you do smack them before they . . . ?) Yes—my husband says it's my fault, I should smack them first instead of keep talking. *I* don't know—it's an awkward thing . . .

*'It's very difficult to detach yourself and see yourself as others do'*

We pointed out in Chapter 14 that it can be extremely misleading to talk about one group being more strict or restrictive than another group, simply because different classes tend to be restrictive in different areas; nevertheless, it seemed worth while to ask mothers for a subjective view of their own behaviour and to discover something about their own private image of themselves in terms of how they stood on the strictness continuum in relation to what they saw of other people's methods. They were asked to rate themselves on a 4-point scale—*very strict, rather strict, rather easy-going* and *very easy-going*—which deliberately prevented them (as it was often necessary to point out) from choosing a 'just about average' position, but forced some decision to be made towards one side or the other.

A class analysis of self-ratings on this scale is given in Table LII. A significant class trend may be shown, whereby mothers further up the social scale tend to regard themselves as strict compared with other mothers, while mothers further down the scale are more likely to rate themselves as easy-going. In the extreme ratings, Class I and II mothers are significantly more likely to rate themselves as 'very strict' and less likely to say they are 'very easy-going' than mothers in other classes.

TABLE LII

*Mothers' self-ratings, strict/easy-going*

|  | I & II | IIIwc | IIIman | IV | V | All (random) |
|---|---|---|---|---|---|---|
|  | % | % | % | % | % | % |
| Very strict | 7 | 1 | 3 | 1 | 1 | 3 |
| Rather strict | 53 | 50 | 32 | 27 | 28 | 36 |
| Rather easy-going | 36 | 43 | 54 | 59 | 54 | 51 |
| Very easy-going | 4 | 6 | 11 | 13 | 17 | 10 |

Not all mothers found this an easy rating to make, and the interviewer was instructed not to help them or lead them in any way, since we wished to have a clear indication of the mother's subjective feeling rather than of an outsider's judgment; it should perhaps be borne in mind that an individual mother will tend to rate herself in comparison with other mothers of similar class, whereas an interviewer would see her as related to the total pattern. The interviewers' success in keeping aloof from the rating task can be judged from the class differences obtained, which by no means reflect actual behaviour except in the sense of closeness of supervision, which on its own is not what most mothers mean by strictness. Some mothers mentioned the two difficulties to which we have called attention elsewhere: that people can be strict in one way and lenient in other ways, and that it is not at all easy to judge the private behaviour of others from what one sees in public places. 'That's a *very* difficult question', said a cost accountant's wife: 'I won't allow mine the *freedom*, probably, that some children get—but there again, other mothers I know do smack their children and shout at them more than I do'; and the wife of a craftsman in his own business said, 'I don't really *know* how other people treat their children; I see how they treat them in front of other people, but I don't know what they do when there's nobody looking, so I can't really say'. Brief illustrations of the four categories of Table LII appear below.

Engineer's wife:

> *Very* strict compared with the people round here—well, some of them; I tell Mandy she can't do something, but then she'll come

in and say "Bernadette's mother doesn't smack her for that". Some of the mothers round here let them get away with anything.

Accountant's wife:

Rather strict, I'd say. It sounds a bit stronger than what I really am. But it's better than the easy-going bit!

Lorry driver's wife:

Oh, I'm easy-going; but I like manners, so you'd better make it "*rather* easy-going"; you've got to make them behave themselves to a *certain* extent.

Window cleaner's wife:

Easy-going—*very* easy-going, I think I am. I've p'raps done a lot of things I didn't ought to have—I mean, I'm no model for bringing up kiddies and that, I've brought mine up the way *I* thought; I've been silly over my kiddies, I think, most of the time, but they've not turned out bad. I mean, when they open the gate and come in at dinnertime and find me here, well, you can tell they appreciate you.

*'I can make porridge, but I can never quite make it for her the same as Daddy can!'*

For the child, of course, the mother's strictness or lack of it is only one half, if the salient half, of his relationship with his parents. With 51% of fathers taking a highly participant role, and 40% fairly participant (see Table LIII), the child is seldom dealing with a single authority, but rather with an association of two personalities, with all the complications that come from their own satisfactions or conflicts within the web of social relationships which makes up the family. Thus the father may invariably present a united front with the mother, so that the child knows that his participation in any argument will only confirm her demands; he may represent a possible court of appeal, so that negotiation and compromise at least seem feasible when he is around; or he may assume the role of dependable refuge from maternal demands, always to be relied on to (from the mother's point of view) undermine her authority. In general, the father provides an *alternative* authority to the mother; he at least affords some variation in discipline and general treatment, and may offer special leniencies, as well as special intolerances, when he is in control. He may even actively conspire with the child to subvert the mother's jurisdiction.

### Labourer's wife:

Well, she had gone and torn her frock the other night and she was scared, because she thought she was going to get smacked when I got home. So Daddy said "We'll say Baby tore it", you know. I came in the door and "Oh, Mummy", she said, "I've had my frock torn"; and I said "Oh, did you? How did you do that, then?" So she looked at her Daddy and he made the sign for her to say that the baby done it. But then she told me. Of course I didn't say nothing about it.

### Plasterer's wife:

He's pretty strict in some things, you know; if they wanted to stop up, *I* might say they could, but *he'd* say "No, it's school tomorrow—it's late enough".

### Garage manager's wife:

Sometimes he has those little plastic figures, and he likes to put them at the side of his plate while he eats. Well, *I* don't mind; but my husband does. So if I'm at the meal alone he has them, but if my husband's at the table he doesn't.

### Foreman's wife:

No, I don't let her jump on her bed. (Father): Well, I do, and I take her up to bed every night and she has a good session bouncing, and in fact I encourage her—I give her somersaults and that. I always jumped on *my* bed, and always enjoyed it so.

### Bleacher's wife:

If Daddy's on days, he'll go up and just read them a story in bed for ten minutes; but if he's on nights, they don't expect that from me, I don't know why. With me, I think they realize that, once they're in bed, mother's finished, and I expect them to go to sleep; whereas their Daddy's just that little bit of a *luxury*, if you know what I mean!

### Clerk's wife:

He's got more patience than I have—a lot more patience. I mean, Helen at the moment has a scab on her knee, through falling on the garden path; now I'd sort of just sit her on the draining-

R

board and pour Dettol and clean it and put a plaster on. Well, her Daddy'll do all that *and* love her better. He'll put the extra finishing touch to it.

TABLE LIII

*Fathers' participation in children's care*

| | I & II | IIIwc | IIIman | IV | V | All (random) |
|---|---|---|---|---|---|---|
| | % | % | % | % | % | % |
| High participation | 64 | 59 | 48 | 44 | 49 | 51 |
| Fair participation | 32 | 36 | 42 | 42 | 41 | 40 |
| Little or none | 4 | 5 | 10 | 14 | 10 | 9 |

The father's authority is, however, likely to be more intermittent in character, simply because in the majority of cases he will be out of the house for most of the day; and this inevitably makes his role rather different from that of the mother, who is the permanent authority. However participant he may be, the final responsibility for bringing up a small child rests in our culture pattern with the mother: even if the father is in the unusual situation of taking an equal part in the children's care, the pressures of society are such that the mother still knows that it is she who is 'shown up' by the child's bad behaviour or untended appearance; she who has to negotiate for free time, while the father may take it of right. Mothers themselves are extremely conscious of the basic difference in their situation *vis-à-vis* the child: 'It's all right for *him*, you know', said a technical lecturer's wife—'He only wants Rory *if* he wants him, and if he doesn't it's "Take him and go away". It's different for the mother, isn't it?—you've got to have him whether you want to or not!' and a fairground worker's wife neatly summed up the position: 'I often say to him, "You get your coat and you're off on your own, but if I get *my* coat there's five of us going!"' A very frequent result of the father's less complete involvement with the child is that, while familiarity breeds contempt as far as the mother's disciplinary efforts are concerned, the father often finds it easier to achieve quick results—to the mother's disgust: '*He* never has to raise his voice or smack them, never *ever*; they'll do it quicker for him than they will for me', said a clerk's wife; and the bleacher's wife who said that Daddy was a 'little bit of a *luxury*' described their daughter's reaction to his occasional crossness: 'She cries very quickly then, straight away—"You don't have to *shout*", she says, in a *sobbing* little voice. She's so used to him *not* shouting at her that when he does it makes her really jump, you know, and of course the tears come straight away; but only with *him*, like—with me . . . well, she just *looks* at me, sort of "there she goes, on again!" '

Miner's wife:

> Their Daddy never smacks them, or almost never; he only has to say a word, though, and they take notice—oh, there's no questions then! "Sit down!" he'll say: and they'll sit down *right* away. And yet he doesn't hit them. Except when they've been telling lies or something like that—then they do really *know* they've got a father! (Four of the eight children were listening, and corroborated the whole of this; father is a man of considerable warmth, who as a principle always makes the currently displaced child his special responsibility.)

Engineer's wife:

> Well, they do more for their father than me; and that annoys me sometimes. I sometimes think, well, is it me?—am I too strict, or not strict enough? Because, you know, if their father walked in and said something to them, they'd do it straight away; whereas I've got to get mad or keep on at them. That's the thing that does make me wonder: do I smack them too much, or don't I do it often enough? Because he's only got to *talk* to them—*I* have to shout.

Some mothers felt that the rather simplified view which the father thus had of everyday dealings with the child led to misunderstanding on his part, both of the mother's own difficulties and of the standard of behaviour which might be reasonably expected of children. Another technical teacher's wife said that her husband complained that the children could wind her round their little finger, but justified herself: 'You can't be strict with them all the time. You're with them a long time, I mean a woman is; and *he* can be strict with them the short time he's with them, and get away with it—but if I was as strict as he is *all the day*, the poor kids wouldn't have any life'. A chemical worker's wife made the same point: 'While you can be strict on certain things that you've *got* to be strict on, you've got to let certain other things go; otherwise I should be at them all the time, I should never finish, it'd be a fulltime job sitting here saying don't do this, don't do that, do the other'; her husband, who was present, had agreed to abide by her decisions: 'I think she ought to be stricter, but then I'm not here, so I can't do anything about it; I usually accept what she says if she contradicts me, or if I've said something to them that she thinks is wrong.'

TABLE LIV

*Comparative strictness of husband and wife in relation to social class and father participation*

| | I & II | IIIwc | IIIman | IV | V | All (random) | Highly participant (random) | Moderate or low participation (random) |
|---|---|---|---|---|---|---|---|---|
| | % | % | % | % | % | % | % | % |
| Husband stricter | 22 | 31 | 46 | 35 | 52 | 39 | 32 | 47 |
| Wife stricter | 23 | 22 | 22 | 27 | 28 | 24 | 25 | 22 |
| Agree on strictness | 55 | 47 | 32 | 38 | 20 | 37 | 43 | 31 |

In asking mothers to say whether they thought their husbands to be stricter or less strict than themselves, then, we were looking as much for a measure of the degree to which the mother felt herself to be fully backed in the methods which she used, as for an assessment of direct paternal behaviour towards the child; for the mother who disagrees with her husband on this question does not always come to the amicable arrangement of the chemical worker and his wife quoted above, but may find her self-confidence constantly sapped or her energies diverted into continual arguments with her husband, as will be obvious in one or two of the illustrations which follow. The table itself shows two interesting and significant class trends. On the simple question of which spouse is stricter, mothers further up the social scale are much less likely to think that their husbands are stricter than they are: and this is not because their husbands are more easy-going, but because they *agree* on strictness (p < ·001). Further down the social scale, mothers are more likely to disagree with their husbands (80% in Class V, against 45% in Class I and II), most often because they consider their husbands to be too strict. In the second place, an analysis of the relationship between parents' agreement or disagreement on strictness and the degree to which the father participates in the child's care shows a significant link, in that fathers rated as 'highly participant' in the objective terms of the schedule tend to be considered by their wives as closely in agreement with themselves on discipline, whereas less participant fathers are more likely than others to be regarded as 'stricter'.

*Husband stricter:*
Unemployed cleaner's wife:

> If he had his way, I think he is *very* strict. He has a temper as well, and I know he'd hit them to really hurt them, he'd hit them *too* hard. That's one reason why I do everything for them, he hasn't got the patience. He doesn't do any of those things you said—he doesn't do a *lot* of things that he should do. He loves them in his own way, like, but he thinks I should do everything for them. He goes out *several* nights a week, and in the daytime too, but I haven't been out for years and years.

Greengrocer's wife:

> He's much more strict than I am—he believes in the cane. Well, I never give them the cane—I threaten them with it at times—but he says, if you're going to hit them, you've got to hurt them or they don't know they've had it. And clearing up—he can make them do it, I can't. I have to get on to them, and they *still* don't do it.

*Wife stricter:*
Window-cleaner's wife:

> Stricter than me? No, he's a nit! He's never raised his hand to them, and they know jolly well he wouldn't do a thing.

Coal merchant's wife:

> Ooh, he's less strict—he makes me mad. What I need from him is co-operation. He's sloppy.

Engineer's wife:

> I don't agree with his discipline one little bit. In fact, where he's concerned there *is* no discipline—he just lets them go and do as they like. In other words, they're the gaffer—he's not.

Miner's wife:

> He's *not* strict. It causes a lot of trouble. I feel as if I've got a lot on my shoulders—and also, you see, when their father's there they'll not take notice of me. It upsets me—it grieves me—if they're confused between the father and the mother, you see, they're in the middle and they're not learning much. . . . He's *good* with them—he can sit and talk to them and tell them stories far better than what I can—I can't sit and talk to them like he can, and I feel grieved at *that*: I'd like to, but . . . I've got to keep that *strictness* there, you know, or else . . . I'm trying to bring it home to him that it is *his place* to be firm, more so than mine. As I say, he's just that type that's soft-hearted, and there you are, you see.

*Parents agree on strictness:*
Teacher's wife:

> It works out the same. He has the odd little thing that gets under his skin, I have mine; but broadly speaking we're very similar in our general outlook.

Shop manager's wife:

> Pretty generally we both feel the same as regards discipline. We talk the children over such a lot that we know what we should do in any crisis, with the result that we stick to these methods, so we're always sure ourselves, you see.

*'If I had my time again, I should know how to cope better'*

It is a widely-held belief among mothers that the eldest child tends to be the most difficult and temperamental, or at least that parents tend to have more trouble with the first than with later children. If this is true, it might conceivably be explained in terms of minimal brain damage,[1] but it is much more plausibly attributable to parents' own tensions in bringing up their first child. Possibly a conjunction of the two factors is the answer:

---

[1] Average length of labour for first children is 14 hours, average for later children 8 hours (Montagu, A., *Life Before Birth*, Longmans, London, 1964). This implies a correlated possibility of minimal brain damage as a result of oxygen deficiency.

children who are already congenitally more temperamental are likely to exacerbate the anxiety of inexperienced parents. Our question on changes in mothers' child-rearing ideas which might have occurred over the years of parenthood were rather inconclusive, however. The main change which seemed to occur was not so much from strictness to leniency, as from rigidity to flexibility; mothers seemed on the whole to become less inclined to think that specific details of upbringing mattered, and more confidently reliant upon a *generally* happy relationship with the child. Experience was valued in two ways: it helped the mother to cope easily and flexibly with individual situations, and it showed her that she could depart from approved practice and get away with it. '*Fundamentally* I think it's about the same', said a self-employed craftsman's wife, 'but more *subtle*, I think that would be the word, rather than easy-going: where you sort of upset them a bit and things don't run so smoothly, I think if you'd known with the first what you know with the third, you would have got over problems with them perhaps easier'. A newsagent's wife whose elder child was now 21 said: 'We don't disagree much—I'm not being smug about it, I just put up with things from him: he's little, and I'm not a baby, I'm 45. I've had one child, and I have the great advantage of knowing that he grew up to be a man all right, and eventually this one will—I don't ever worry as much as a young mother would worry'.

University teacher's wife:

> I think the main thing is that you acquire a sense of proportion, you see things in their proper perspective. For instance—Becky, as I said, still gets rocked to sleep on my lap every night of her life. Now I like that, and she likes it—partly, I suppose, because I expect her to be my last, but also because she's a nice cuddly dumpling and she likes the songs I sing to her then, and I like singing them. But now suppose it had been Ben, my eldest—and with Ben there was something similar, the bedtime bottle in his case—my mother or someone would have said to me "But when is it going to *end*?" and I would have thought "My goodness, she's right, when *is* it going to end?"—and then I would have tried in a half-hearted sort of way to stop it, and we should all have been upset. But now I can see it in the perspective of growing-up, and I know perfectly well, from experience of three children, that eventually she won't *want* to be rocked to sleep, because

she'll prefer to have a little bedtime play in her nursery, or to read in bed for a while. There's a *natural progression* of things, which with your first child you're just not really aware of, and that's where most of the worry comes from, in my experience.

We have given examples in earlier chapters of mothers who had radically revised their behaviour, usually by resolving not to smack so much after finding that their violence towards the child had escalated enough to shock them out of it; but our general impression is that mothers do not as a rule alter their total attitude towards child upbringing. They may through 'good resolutions' become kinder or more strict or more consistent, but they do not change from being democratically oriented to authoritarianism, or vice versa: as a window cleaner's wife said with some insight, 'You learn by your mistakes, but you never alter *yourself*'.

#### '*I wasn't allowed to have a mind of my own; I want mine to be different*'

In this final chapter, we have included many quotations from mothers in a highly introspective mood, as they examine their feelings about the child himself and question their own ways of dealing with his behaviour. It is perhaps the most characteristic feature of the present generation of parents that they are no longer prepared to accept either expert advice or their own authority on trust, but continually submit both to the test of their own doubts and uncertainties. We have explored elsewhere the historical and sociological background of the trend away from authoritarianism and towards individualism in child-rearing;[1] and this trend is reflected in the post-Spock baby books, especially those of American origin, which recognize as a fundamental need the wish of parents to be happy in parenthood. The old bullying manner of Truby King and his contemporaries gives place to a persuasive, chatty, essentially *democratic* approach, and the stern warnings against disobeying the rules are metamorphosed into mere gentle suggestion, perfectly represented by Spock's 'Here's what happens once in a while when the needs of the child aren't recognized'.[2] A further and

---

[1] Newson, John and Elizabeth, 1967, *op. cit.* Part of the material of this paper forms the basis for the final section of the present chapter.

[2] Spock, Benjamin, 1955, *op. cit.*, chapter on 'The Two Year Old'.

highly significant change appears in the content of the advice given. Where formerly it was extremely specific, more recent books tend to emphasize not so much the details of child care as the principles that parents should follow in deciding the details for themselves: no longer are they told what methods to adopt, but rather the *frame of mind* in which to adopt the method which suits them best. Flexibility is the keynote of modern advice to parents: indeed, this very word 'advice' is thoroughly out of fashion, and modern trainees for what are (equally significantly) known as the 'helping professions' now learn that their role is 'supportive' rather than 'advisory'. A major aim of flexibility is, of course, to allow parents to enjoy their families; and no-one would wish to decry it. The trouble arises when the injunction to 'have fun with your children' itself begins to acquire the pressurizing character of earlier, more authoritarian and less subtly moralistic demands upon parents, as Martha Wolfenstein has pointed out in her study of changes in government-sponsored advice published over the years for American parents. In her rather sinister phrase, 'Fun has become not only permissible but *required*'; the fun morality implies that the mother's self-evaluation 'can no longer be based entirely on whether she is doing the right and necessary things but becomes involved with nuances of feeling which are not under voluntary control'.[1]

We do not have the impression that mothers in Britain are strongly expert-oriented so far as child-rearing is concerned; nevertheless, the majority expect to be able to find fun in parenthood, if necessary rejecting more authoritarian advice in order to do so. The active participation of fathers in the family unit is one aspect of the fun morality which is heavily underwritten by our popular culture, and which has partly been made possible by improvement in housing conditions: where the family home is an attractive and comfortable place to be, and particularly where husband and wife have both been responsible for achieving this, to be houseproud becomes acceptable in father as well as in mother, and there is little motivation for him to look for leisuretime activities outside the family. Indeed, as can be seen in any television commercial, the well-turned-out family and the

[1] Wolfenstein, Martha: 'Fun Morality: an analyis of recent American child-training literature'; in Mead, M. and Wolfenstein, M.: *Childhood in Contemporary Cultures*, University of Chicago Press, 1955.

R*

sprucely decorated home are perfect foils one for the other; and advertising interests give full support to the advisory literature in holding out 'having fun as a family' as the ideal situation for any well-adjusted parent. The broadening image of education also helps to make the father feel that he can and should be contributing to his young children's developing personalities in other ways than the traditional disciplining role: in fact the one way in which the father seems to be retreating from contact with his children is in this matter of discipline, which, as we have seen, many prefer to leave mainly to the mother.

Beyond all else, the salient feature of the fun morality is the desire of both mothers and fathers to be the *friends* of their children. Many parents remember with regret the psychological distance which separated them from their own more authoritarian parents, and hope to achieve a closer relationship with their own children: a relationship which allows not only fun to be had but confidences to be exchanged and differences of opinion to be accepted between parent and child. 'They're real good pals', says the mother, fondly, of her husband and children: 'He's as much of a kid as they are'. We have quoted in this and other chapters numerous mothers who chose their children's companionship and conversation as the aspect of the child which they especially valued; and it was not unusual for hopes to be expressed for the future: 'I'm trying to *keep* them as friends' said an engineer's wife, 'so that when they're grown-up we can have a good natter together!'

This climbing-down from the parental pedestal of a generation ago was something which we noted in our first study, in which we discussed present-day mothers' comments on differences between their own and their children's upbringing; the change in parental attitude continued to be emphasized in these later interviews. One mother deplored the fact that she found herself swearing in front of her child, who then copied her: 'She says "Well, bugger me, it's started to rain—bloody weather, isn't it, Mum!" But she knows it's naughty, and I let her know that *I'm* naughty—not that I'm different to her'; another explained the difference between her attitude and her own father's: '*He* wants to be a friend, but a *bossy* friend—as long as you do what I say, that's all right!—my sister and I were brought up to *have to* respect our parents'. A driver's wife said 'My mother was one of the best you could ever wish for, *in a sense*; but I mean you weren't *consulted* in those days at all, were you?—we certainly weren't; if it was mother's and father's wish, well, that was it! They're a different sort of generation now, aren't they?' A manager's wife agreed: 'I've gone out of my way to try and give him the idea that he's got a mind of his own; we don't sort of practise this heavy hand business—we like *him* to make decisions, within what a child can'.

In throwing out the pedestal and becoming the 'good pals' of their children, however, many parents are finding that they have got something more than they bargained for. Rejecting rigid authoritarianism, and choosing because it is pleasanter a more permissive approach, it is not always so easy to accept the more spirited, disrepectful child which is the result. In very many mothers (and fathers), from every social class, can be detected an uneasiness, a confusion, as to what they are achieving and what they are trying to achieve.

It is in this confusion that we can discern the major dilemma of contemporary parents, particularly those further up the social scale. On the one hand, they have embraced an egalitarian relationship with their children, and genuinely enjoy and value the friendship that goes with it; as a matter of principle, they reject plain coercion as a method of dealing with children. An outstanding feature in the care of the very young child in particular, as we have seen, is that the mother will worry and complain, sometimes for years, over some habit which could easily be suppressed *if she were prepared to do so*—the dummy or the sordid cuddly, for instance, could simply be destroyed—and yet she will go on worrying, and devising endless persuasive methods of changing the child's behaviour, rather than exert the sort of repressive authority which was the approved method of the twenties and thirties. On the other hand, parents cannot entirely divorce themselves from their historical antecedents: no longer believing that children should be seen and not heard, nevertheless they still retain, at the back of the mind as it were, an image of the 'good' child who, while obviously bright and alert, at the same time defers to parental wishes and in general makes a pleasant public impression unmarred by displays of egotism, rowdiness or greed. The attainment of this fleeting vision of 'goodness' by methods more suited to producing an independent spirit, full of Kingsley's 'divine discontent', is the impossible task which parents half-unconsciously set themselves; inevitably, compromise in aims, means, or both has to be accepted somewhere along the way. In the democratic context, too, anti-social behaviour on the part of the child can be doubly disturbing to the parent: 'naughtiness' under an authoritarian regime can be viewed with equanimity as natural rebellion against what the child does not like, to be met with an extension of repressive measures; but 'naughtiness' under an egalitarian system involves *a rejection by the child of the parent's proffered friendship*, which he *is* supposed to like—and, so far as the mother can see, eventually has to be met by a change in policy away from the rational permissiveness to which she is idealogically committed and towards the authoritarianism which she had put behind her. Working-class parents lag always a few years behind their middle-class counterparts as trends in child-rearing change: will they meet them one day on the way back?

So we continue to watch 'our children' as their personalities unfold; watch their parents as they bring them up; watch as the children bring up their parents. Next time we meet them, they will be seven years old.

# THE INTERVIEW SCHEDULE

Note: It has not been possible to discuss in the text every item of information available from our interviewing records; such information is, however, available on request.

UNIVERSITY OF NOTTINGHAM
CHILD DEVELOPMENT RESEARCH UNIT

District ...................

Interviewer .................

Date ......................

GUIDED INTERVIEW SCHEDULE
(*For mothers of children aged 4:0*)

## A. BACKGROUND

*Child's full name* ......................................

*Address* ...............................................

...............................................

*Date of birth* .............. *Sex:* Boy/Girl

*Family size and position* (for each child in family, indicate sex and age; include foster children, marked F)

| sex | | | | | | | | |
|-----|--|--|--|--|--|--|--|--|
| age | | | | | | | | |

1. You haven't had any miscarriages or stillbirths . . .?
   (*Give dates, and include deaths, with cause if mentioned.*)

   ..................................................

   *MOTHER: Age.... Not working/working part-time/full-time*
   *Occupation if at work* ..............
   *If working, who looks after N/the children?*.................

2. Did you have a job before you had children?
   (*details*) ...............................................

   *FATHER: Age.... Precise occupation*................

3. Does he have to be away from home at all, except just during the day?
   *Home every night/up to 2 nights away p.w./3 nights + p.w./*
   *normally away/separation or divorce/dead/other*..............
   *Shift work?* YES/NO *What shifts?*......................

4. Does any other adult live here, apart from your husband and yourself?

    YES......................./NO

5. Has N ever been separated from you for more than a day or two—has he ever been in hospital, for instance, or have you been in hospital since he was born? (*Details: age at separation, how long, etc.*)

## B. *INDEPENDENCE*

6. First of all, we'd like to know something about what sort of things N can do for himself. Does he usually dress himself in the morning? Do you give him any help with that usually?

    *Mother helps a lot/some help/no help given*

    Does he undress himself at night?

    *Mother helps a lot/some help/no help given*

    Does he tidy up his clothes when he's taken them off?

    *Mother helps a lot/some help/no help given*

    When he goes to the toilet, does he look after himself or do you help him? (*prompt*) Does he wipe himself, or do you do that for him?

    *Mother helps a lot/some help/no help given*

    What about clearing up things he's been playing with? Does he do that at all?

    *Mother helps a lot/some help/no help given*

7. What do you feel about making a child do things for himself at this age? Do you think he should be made to do things for himself, even if he doesn't want to?

8. *If 'no help' checked three or more times:*

    Have you taken a lot of trouble to get N to do these things for himself?

    *Otherwise:*

    Would you like N to be doing more for himself at this age? (*Prompt if necessary*): Does he do as much as you think he ought to be doing now? Do you think you should be stricter than you are over this, or are you quite happy to leave it for the moment?

## C. *INDEPENDENCE IN PLAY*

9. How much do you like him to do other things on his own? For instance, does he ever go into a shop or to an ice-cream van on his own? (*If 'danger' or 'distance' response, prompt*): But does he ever go into a shop on his own while you wait outside?

    YES/NO          (*specify*)

10. Does he ever take messages for you? YES/NO
11. What about playing in the house? Does he like to play on his own?
    *Mostly/sometimes/not at all/* . . . . . . . . . . . . . . . . . . . . . . . . . . . . . . . .
12. About how long will he play by himself without wanting your attention?
    *Up to half-an-hour/31–60 minutes/longer*
13. If he keeps wanting you to do things for him when you're busy, what do you do?
14. Does he ever come clinging round your skirts and wanting to be babied a bit?
    *Often/sometimes/never*
15. What do you do? (*or*) What would you do if he did that at this age?
16. Do you think a child of this age should be able to amuse himself most of the time, or would you expect to have to spend a lot of time on keeping him happy? (*Explain if necessary:* 'when he's on his own', *i.e. without other children.*)

## D. *AGGRESSION IN PLAY*

17. Does N play with any other children at all?
    *Siblings: Often/sometimes/never*
    *Others: Often/sometimes/never*
18. What do you do if there's a disagreement or a quarrel?
19. In general, do you think children should be left to settle their own differences at this age, or would you interfere? (*Explain if necessary*: 'so long as there's no real bullying going on'.)
20. Suppose N comes running to you complaining of another child? What do you do?
21. Do you ever tell N to hit another child back? YES/NO
    *If YES:* Can you give me an example of when you might do that?
    *If NO:* Is there any situation in which you might do that? YES/NO
    *EXAMPLE in either case:*
22. *If child plays with his own sibling(s):*
    There seem to be two sorts of quarrelling he might get into—quarrelling with his brother/sister, and quarrelling with other children. Do you find you act differently in those two situations?
    YES/NO            (*specify*)
        *Rating: encouragement of aggression in self-defence:—*
        *general encouragement/special circumstances (not age difference)/never*

23. *If any siblings:* Does N ever seem jealous of his brother/his sister/the other children?
24. *If YES:* What does he do (when he's feeling jealous)?
25. How do you deal with it?

## E. *AUTONOMY IN PLAY*

26. Does N make a fuss if you give away something of his to another child?   YES/NO   Does it often happen that you do this?
    *Mother wouldn't do this/might do this*
27. Suppose you were having a good turn-out, and you wanted to throw away some broken bits of toys, but he wanted to keep them: what would happen then?
    *Mother wins/he wins/compromise*
28. If you've broken something of his by accident and it can't be mended, what do you do about it?
    *Restitution/apology/concealment/nothing*
29. Is there any sort of play you don't allow? For instance, Do you let him make a lot of noise in the house if he wants to? YES/NO
    Do you let him jump on his bed and use furniture for his play—like making a train out of chairs?
    *Bed:* YES/NO   *Chairs:* YES/NO   *Other:*
    Do you let him make a mess playing with water or paint or earth or flour?   YES/NO
    Does it bother you if he gets really dirty while he's playing? YES/NO
    *If YES:* What do you do to make him keep clean?
30. When he's playing at something, do you ever join in? (*i.e. games of mothers and fathers, going for train-rides, shops etc.*) YES/NO
    *EXAMPLE:*
31. Has he any imaginary people or animals or places that he brings into his play? (*Explain if necessary: things that he often talks about or talks to, but which don't exist even in the form of dolls.*)
    YES/NO   (*details*)
32. How do you react if he talks about them to you?
    *sympathetic/unsympathetic*
33. Does he sometimes tell you about some happening as if it were true, when you know it's not? (*Exclude lying to avoid punishment*)
    YES/NO   (*details*)
    What do you do when this happens?

34. Is there anything special that he is afraid of?—the way some children are afraid of tiny insects, or the plug-hole, or things at the bottom of the bed?
    YES/NO   (*details*)
    *If YES:* Do you know *why* he is afraid of that? do you know how it started?

35. Does he make a fuss when he has to stop playing?   YES/NO/ SOMETIMES.   What do you do when he does?
    (*If necessary, prompt*): If it's time for a meal and he wants to finish something he's started, what do you do then?

## F. *MEALS*

36. We'd like to know something about N's mealtimes now. Is he a good eater, or do you have any trouble about that?
    *Good/varies/finicky*

37. Do you have any rules about eating up food?
    *PROMPT as necessary:*
    Are there any foods that he never has just because he dislikes them?   YES/NO
    Do you let him leave food on his plate?   YES/NO
    Do you let *him* decide how much he will have of a food that he dislikes?   YES/NO
    If he really refused to eat something, what would you do?
    *Prompt ALL mothers:* If he didn't like a meal after you'd cooked it, would you make him something else?   YES/NO
    *Rating: Unlimited pressure to finish/child normally* has *to eat M's amount/has to eat amount he takes himself/may leave a little/no pressure/alternative provided* after *refusal/other*.......
    ..................................................

38. Do you mind what order he eats things in? For instance, does he have to eat bread and butter before he has any cake, and that sort of thing?
    *Strict on order/some attempt but flexible/doesn't mind*

39. Do you let him use a spoon instead of a knife and fork if he wants to? (*Prompt if necessary*): Would you let him if he did want to?
    *No/discourages/allows*

40. Do you let him use his fingers? (*Explain if necessary: for things like pieces of meat, cut-up vegetables and so on.*)
    *Never/discourages/allows*

41. Do you let him get up from the table during a meal?
    *Often/sometimes/never/special circumstances only*........

42. Is he allowed to bring toys or a book to the table?
    *Never/discourages/allows*

43. Do you have any other rules about mealtimes—not talking, or anything like that? YES (*specify*)/NO
44. Do you take a lot of trouble to get him to eat nicely and have good table-manners, or are you leaving it for the moment?
    *Much trouble/some training/leaving it*
45. In general, would you say you *mind* very much whether a child has good table-manners or not at this age? YES/NO

## G. *PERSONAL HABITS*

46. Going on from table-manners now, what about other sorts of habits? Has N any little habits that you've noticed? Does he twist his hair (*demonstrate*) or anything like that?
    *CHECK each: hair twisting or pulling* .....................
                     *thumb sucking* ...........................
                     *nail biting* ...............................
                     *rock himself* ..............................
                     *dummy if mentioned only* ...................
47. Does he play with his private parts at all? YES/NO
    *If NO:* What would you do if he did?—would you mind him doing that at this age? (*verbatim answer*)
48. Is there anything else you can think of that he does as a habit? Anything he does when he's overtired or worried, perhaps?
49. Do you try and stop him (doing any of these things) (*prompt back for each one mentioned*) or don't you really mind?
    *If YES:* How do you stop him?
    (*Prompt if necessary*): What do you say to him? (*verbatim*)

## H. *BEDTIME*

50. Now what about bedtime? Can you tell me what time he got into bed last night? ......................................
51. Is that the time he usually goes to bed, or does it vary a lot?
52. Does he have to be in bed by any special time? YES..../NO
53. *If YES:* If he didn't seem tired and wanted to stay up a bit longer, would you let him?
    *Rating: Rigid/flexibly rigid/flexible/no rules*
54. Does N sleep in a room on his own, or is he with somebody else?
    *Alone/with*...... *Same bed?* (*do not prompt*)...........
55. Can you tell me exactly what happens from the time you start getting him ready for bed to the time he goes to sleep? Tell me about a typical bedtime.
    (*Prompt if necessary*): What's the first thing you do?

56. Does your husband (or anyone else) help with getting him to bed?
....... *often takes full responsibility*/................*often helps*/*M alone*

57. Is there anything that he takes into bed with him, like a teddy, or a piece of cloth, or a bottle or dummy, or anything like that? (*PROMPT ALL*)
Soft toy/cloth/bottle/dummy/other (*specify*) ................
Would he make a fuss if you couldn't find it one night? YES/NO
(*If toy*) Does it have to be that particular toy? YES/NO

58. (*ONLY IF STARRED*) When N was a year old, you told us that he was still using a bottle, and we found that most babies do at that age. We've got a feeling that a lot of children go on having bottles much longer than most people think. Does N *ever* have a bottle now? (*give details*)
*If NO:* Can you tell me when he gave it up for good?

59. (*IF STARRED and not already mentioned*) Does he ever suck his dummy nowadays? YES/NO

60. Is there anything special that you always have to do at bedtime—any little game you always have, or something like that? (*specify*)

61. Once N gets into bed, is he allowed to get out again and play around the bedroom? YES/NO

62. Does he have the light on in his room for a while?
*No light*/*night light*/*indirect*/*full light for short time*/...........
............................................................

63. (*If full light*): Is he allowed to play with toys or books in bed?
(*If not full light*): Would you allow him to have the light on and play with toys or books in bed if he wanted to?
YES/NO

64. Does he have anything to eat in bed? ................/NO
or to drink? ................/NO
What about sweets in bed? ................/NO

65. What happens if he gets up and tries to come back into the room where you are? Do you ever let him stay if he doesn't seem sleepy?
*Often*/*occasionally*/*only in emergency*/*never*

66. Suppose he was hungry about an hour after he'd gone to bed? Would you let him eat at that time? YES/NO/*only*..........
*DO NOT PROMPT, but record if mentioned spontaneously:*
........*Stories told or read*       ........*Songs*
........*Prayers with child*       ........*Cuddling, kissing etc*

67. Does N usually sleep right through the night? (*Exclude illness throughout, if mentioned.*)
*Wakes often*/*sometimes*/*seldom or never*

68. Do you lift him for a potty at all? YES/*sometimes*/NO
69. If he does wake, apart from needing the toilet, what does he do? Does he cry?

    > *Lies awake quietly/talks quietly/calls parents/cries/very distressed/seems frightened/seems angry/other (specify)*

    ...............................................................

    (*If at all distressed*): What seems to be the matter?
70. What do you do about it? (*Note any different responses to different sorts of behaviour.*)

    (*If the following have not been mentioned, ask*): What would you do

    —if he seemed frightened? ...........................
    —if he was just feeling chatty? ......................
    —if he wanted to come into your bed? .................

    (*If the following remedies have not been mentioned*): Would you *ever*

    —let him come into your bed?     YES/NO
    —get into bed with him (if he slept alone)?     YES/NO
    —sit with him?     YES/NO
    —get him something to eat in the night?     YES/NO

## J. *TOILET TRAINING*

71. You said that you lift/you don't lift N for a potty at night. I expect he still wets the bed sometimes, doesn't he? YES/NO
    *If YES:* About how often does it happen?

    > *Most nights/1–3 nights p.w./less than once p.w./almost never*
72. (*If ANY wetting*): What do you do if you find he's wetted his bed? (*Prompt if necessary*): What do you say to him?
    A. *Very concerned/mildly concerned/unconcerned*
    B. *Punitive/reproachful/rewarding/neutral or sympathetic*
    (*If NO wetting*): Did you have any problem over getting him dry at night? Did you have any special method?

    > *Punishment/reproach/rewards/no pressure*
73. What about in the daytime? Does he still have accidents sometimes? YES/NO
    *If YES:* Is it mainly wetting his pants, or does he dirty them?

    > *Wet/dirty/both/neither*
74. What do you do?
    (*If punishment not mentioned*): Do you ever punish him for wetting or dirtying his pants? YES/NO
    A. *Very concerned/mildly concerned/unconcerned*
    B. *Punitive/reproachful/rewarding/neutral or sympathetic*

75. Of course, most children go through a stage when they think anything to do with the toilet is terribly funny. Has N got to that stage yet? YES/NO

76. How do you feel about children giggling together over that sort of thing? Would you discourage it, or just take no notice?

77. What about children wanting to go to the toilet together, or wanting to look at each other when they're undressed? Would you mind them doing that?

78. Does N ever see you or his Daddy undressed?

    *Sees father*    YES/NO

    *Sees mother*   YES/NO

(*Prompt*): How do you feel about that?

79. Does he know where babies come from yet? (*i.e. from mummy's tummy*)

*If NO:* Would you tell him if he wanted to know, or do you think he's too young? YES, *would tell*/NO

*If NO:* What would you say if he asked you?

## K. *GENERAL DISCIPLINE*

80. I wonder if you could tell me now about how you and N get on together? What sort of things do you specially enjoy in him?

81. Do you *show* your affection towards each other quite a lot, or are you fairly reserved with one another? (*Prompt if necessary*):

Do you think kissing and cuddling should be discouraged at this age?

    *Child caressed during interview?*......................

    *Rating: Very warm, demonstrative/warm/rather cool/ negative*

82. What about disagreements? What sort of things make you get on each other's nerves?

83. Of course, this is an age when children often don't want to do as they are told. What do you do when that happens?

(*Dangerous situations discounted*)

84. Suppose you asked him to do something for you, and he said 'No, I can't do it now, I'm busy'. What would you do?

(*If necessary, exclude things that might have to be done at a certain time such as mealtimes and going out. If mother says it never happens, insist:* 'But what *would* you do if he *did* say that?'

*Accepts/accepts with disapproval/gives time/enforces immediate obedience.*

85. Does he usually obey you fairly quickly, or do you have to keep on at him to get him to do things?

86. If he refuses to do something that he really *must* do, what happens then? (*If M says 'I make him', prompt:* How?)

87. Do you ever promise him something (in advance) as a reward for being good? YES/NO

88. How do you feel about smacking? Do you think it's necessary to smack children? YES/NO

89. Do you have to be angry when you smack N, or do you smack him simply as a punishment?

90. Do you think smacking does him any good? (*Prompt*): In what way? YES/NO
    Rating
    A. *Smacks only when calm/only in anger/both/almost never*
    B. *Mother believes in smacking/disapproves in principle*

91. Is there anything else you do when he's naughty?

92. Do you ever say he can't have something he likes—sweets or television, or something like that? YES/NO

93. Do you ever send him to bed? YES/NO

94. Do you ever tell him you won't love him if he behaves like that? YES/NO

95. *OMIT IF CHILD IS ATTENDING*
    Do you ever say that you'll send him away, or that you'll have to go away from him, if he's naughty? OMITTED/YES/NO

96. Do you ever try and frighten him with somebody else—his Daddy, or a policeman, or a teacher or doctor—something like that? (*Prompt ALL.*)

97. Suppose he says he hasn't done something naughty, when you know quite well that he has. What do you do then? (*Example if necessary: if he's broken something.*)

98. Does he ever come and tell you he's been naughty, before you actually find out? YES/NO

99. Do you think it's important for him to say he's sorry when he's done something wrong? Do you ever make him do that, even though he doesn't want to? *Makes*/NO

100. Does N ever try to smack *you*, or to hurt you in any way? What do you do? (What would you do if he did?) YES/NO

101. What about answering you back, and being cheeky, and that sort of thing? Do you allow that?
    Could you give me an example of the kind of cheekiness you would allow, and what you'd draw the line at?
    (*Prompt only if unavoidable; prompt ALL*)
    *Saying 'you're silly'; saying 'shut up'; shouting at M; running away laughing at M; saying 'I'm not sorry'; mimicking; calling*

*names (M should give examples).*
*Allowed.............. Not allowed................*

102. Does N ever have a real temper tantrum? About how often does it happen?
*Most days/twice a week + /once a week/rarely/never*
What sort of thing seems to start it off?

103. How do you deal with it?

104. On the whole, are you happy about the way you deal with discipline in general, or do you sometimes find yourself doing things that you don't really approve of?

105. Compared with other people, do you think of yourself as being very strict, or rather strict, or rather easy-going, or very easy-going?
*Very strict/rather strict/rather easy-going/very easy-going*

106. Do you agree with your husband about discipline, or is he a lot more strict or less strict than you are?
*Husband stricter/wife stricter/about the same*

## L. *FATHER PARTICIPATION*

107. How much does your husband have to do with N? Does he play with him a lot? YES/NO
*often*      Does he: Bath him? O/S/N Dress or undress him?
*sometimes*   O/S/N Read to him or tell him stories? O/S/N
*never*      Take him out without you? O/S/N Look after him while you're out? O/S/N

108. Is there anything else your husband does for N?............
........O/S/N Is there anything he won't do—that he draws the line at?

109. Is there anything else that they regularly do together?
(*Examples as suitable—gardening, van or doctor's round, carpentry etc.*)

110. Does your husband look after (the other children) a lot?
*Rating:* (*Father*) *Highly/fairly/non-participant*

## M. *BABY-SITTING*

111. Do you and your husband ever manage to leave N/the children so that you can both go out together?
*1 p.w. + /1 per month + /seldom/1 or less p.a.*

112. What happens when you do that? (*Prompt*): Does somebody come in? Do you pay her?
*Paid babysitter/unpaid (specify)................/neighbour listens/other children responsible/nobody responsible/.........*

113. Do you ever leave N at someone else's house for a while?
*Almost daily/2+ p.w./1–2 per fortnt./occasionally/never*
*Nursery school?..............per wk.*

114. How does he seem if you leave him with somebody else?
Does he mind you leaving him?   YES/NO

116. *If YES:* What do you do about that?
*If NO:* Was there ever a time when he minded? (*age*)........
What did you do?

116. Do you always tell N when you're leaving him, or do you
find it easiest to slip off without him knowing?

## N. *CHANGES IN UPBRINGING*

117. Would you say that you have changed in your ideas about
bringing up children, since you started? I mean, you've
had......years' experience now since..............(*eldest
child*) was born—do you think your ideas have altered during
that time?

*Space for additional comments:*

*HOUSING: Modern detached/modern semi/Victorian detached/
Victorian semi/terraced with bays/terraced without bays/self-
contd. flat/rooms/council house on estate/council (not estate)/
flat/other* ........................................................
*Dirty?*   YES/NO

# APPENDIX II

## SAMPLING AND STATISTICAL PROCEDURES

### Sampling

The sample of 700 children comprised 275 follow-up cases whose mothers were first interviewed when the child was one year old, and 425 new cases whose mothers were seen for the first time as the child reached four years. All mothers were approached within one month of the child's fourth birthday. Both the original sample and the newly drawn sample were class-stratified but statistically random: that is to say, a fully random sample was drawn from the birth records in order to establish the class composition in Nottingham of the families of four-year-olds (which in fact approximates to that in the country as a whole), and additional numbers were added in the upper and lower social classes (still chosen randomly apart from the class variable) in order to make class comparisons possible. The 275 follow-up cases included as many as possible of those previously interviewed by the University interviewer (Elizabeth Newson), together with additional cases first interviewed by Health Visitors and retained on the basis that their earlier schedules contained particularly detailed information on the child. Our aim in this was to provide at least a viable sample of children for whom adequate data at the one-year level was available. No attempt was made to follow up the total sample of one-year-olds because, in view of the slight distortion of information in the direction of known health visitor attitudes which was found in the earlier study,[1] we wished to sever as far as possible any link which our interviewers might be thought to have with a local authority advisory service.

The social class distribution of the sample is shown in Table LV.

*Definition of social class.* A discussion of the class factor will be found in our previous study (Chapter 9); we can only briefly repeat here a note on the classification which has been adopted for the whole of this longitudinal survey.

Our use of the father's occupation to determine social class was based upon the Registrar General's Classification of Occupations,[2]

[1] Newson, John and Elizabeth, 1963, *op. cit.*, pp. 24–5, 27–9.
[2] General Register Office: *Classification of Occupations 1960*; H.M.S.O., London.

modified somewhat to meet the special requirements of our subject. Thus the R.G. Classes I and II have been combined into one class for the purpose of our analysis, while Class III has been divided into two classes (III white collar and III manual), separating the white collar and *supervisory* manual occupations from the skilled manual. Where occupations have been re-graded in the most recent edition of the Registrar General's Classification, we have followed this re-grading. Class IV remains an ambiguous class, including both workers in heavy manual jobs, such as stokers and quarry surface workers, and those in semi-clerical jobs, such as bus conductors, hall porters and mail sorters: this ambiguity is reflected in our results throughout the survey. As before, we have used our discretion to upgrade the family status on the basis of the mother's occupation (or occupational qualifications) if she has a higher grading than the father. Income has not been taken into account.

TABLE LV

*Composition of sample of 700 4-year-old children*

|  | I & II | IIIwc | IIIman | IV | V | All |
|---|---|---|---|---|---|---|
| Follow-up sample | 65 | 57 | 70 | 50 | 33 | 275 |
| New sample | 64 | 51 | 156 | 86 | 68 | 425 |
| Totals | 129 | 108 | 226 | 136 | 101 | 700 |
|  | % | % | % | % | % | % |
| Class composition of a simple random sample | 14 | 13 | 50 | 15 | 8 | 100 |

Spot checks on a variety of items in the data show that the follow-up sample and the newly-drawn sample yield similar results when corrected for their different class compositions, and we have therefore felt justified in treating the total sample of 700 cases in a unitary fashion. It should be noted that in this total sample no social class group includes less than 100 cases, and that Class III manual, which would be the most heavily represented in a straight random sample (see last line of Table LV) is also the group most heavily represented here.

*Exclusions and losses.* As before, children were excluded from the sample on four bases:

1. Illegitimate, and not legitimized by the date of the first birthday.
2. Immigrant families, unless in England for ten years or more.

# Appendix II 539

3. Children having gross mental or physical handicaps, diagnosed during the first year.
4. Children not in the care of their mother.

The first exclusion was made because we wished to include paternal roles in our study; the second, because Nottingham is host to enough immigrant families, maintaining their own national upbringing customs, materially to distort some of our findings (such as those on mothers at work, for instance) if they were included 'blind' in the sample. The third exclusion recognized that much of a mother's behaviour to her child is likely to be altered by the fact of his handicap;[1] and the reason for the fourth is obvious. A few of our follow-up children have turned out to have major or minor handicaps, mental or physical, diagnosed since the first birthday, and they have been retained in the sample; similarly, a very few have lost their mothers, but remained in the family: here the father or grandmother now in charge of the child has been interviewed where possible. In making the above exclusions, we do not by any means suggest that these groups are of no interest; on the contrary, we hope eventually to make separate studies of the upbringing of immigrant, illegitimate and institutionalized children, and a research project on bringing up handicapped children is already nearing its conclusion.[2]

Losses in the sample (after attempted contact) remain low for

TABLE LVI

*Classification by father's occupation*

| | Class | Description |
|---|---|---|
| 'Middle-class' | I and II | *Professional and managerial:* Doctors, solicitors clergymen, teachers, nurses, company directors shopkeepers (own business), police officers etc |
| | III wc | *White collar:* Clerical workers, shop assistants etc,; policemen; foremen and supervisors in industry. |
| 'Working-class' | III man | *Skilled manual:* Skilled tradesmen in industry, drivers etc. |
| | IV | *Semi-skilled:* Machine operators, bus conductors, stokers, storemen, caretakers etc. |
| | V | *Unskilled:* Labourers, cleaners, messengers etc.; persistently unemployed. |

[1] See Newson, John and Elizabeth: 'Child Rearing in Socio-Cultural Perspective'; in Loring, J. and Mason, A., Ed.: *The Spastic School Child and the Outside World*, Heinemann/Spastics Society, London, 1966.
[2] Report by Sheila Hewett for the Spastics Society: in preparation.

this type of work: the rate was 3% refusal and 5% non-contact after at least three visits.

*Proportions given in tables.* The use of a class-stratified sample, together with knowledge of the class composition of a random sample of 4-year-olds in Nottingham (given the exclusions noted), allows us both to give reliable percentages for each individual social class and to convert the data into estimated proportions for a straight random sample of this population. Thus all tables presenting class analyses have a final column headed *All* (*random*), which shows percentages derived from the class data and referring to the proportions which would be expected had we selected a simple random sample without class stratification. These estimates can be assumed to have a probable error which is not greater than plus or minus 2%.

## Tests of statistical significance

For simplicity, a uniform method of statistical testing has been adopted throughout. The results have been presented as percentages; in order to test for the significance of a difference between two or more percentages, it is necessary to prepare a contingency table showing actual numerical frequencies before calculating chi-squared. If the value of chi-squared is sufficiently large, the null hypothesis may be rejected. The usual convention, which we have followed, is to reject the null hypothesis without reservation only if the observed result would have occurred by chance with a probability of 0·01 or less. Thus wherever, in the body of the text, we simply state that a difference is significant, without giving a probability level, the reader should assume that the test has been applied and the null hypothesis rejected with a probability of 0·01 or less. Significance levels are therefore normally included only when the probability level falls a little short of this: as, for example, when the null hypothesis is tentatively rejected with probability less than 0·02 or 0·05.

Many of the findings presented refer to differences between the five occupational class groups, and our standard procedure has been to look for evidence for an overall class difference before combining the results in any way. The procedure adopted can best be explained by using a specific example. For instance, social class differences in thumb sucking are given in Table XXVIII, page 306, as follows:

| I & II | IIIwc | IIIman | IV | V | All (random) |
|--------|-------|--------|-----|-----|--------------|
| % | % | % | % | % | % |
| 32 | 19 | 12 | 11 | 11 | 16 |

The contingency table showing the exact frequencies is first constructed, and an overall test of significance applied:

|                   | I & II | IIIwc | IIIman | IV  | V   | Totals |
|-------------------|--------|-------|--------|-----|-----|--------|
| Thumb-suckers     | 41     | 21    | 28     | 15  | 11  | 116    |
| Non-thumb-suckers | 88     | 87    | 198    | 121 | 90  | 584    |
| Totals            | 129    | 108   | 226    | 136 | 101 | 700    |

Chi-squared $= 30 \cdot 4$   Degrees of freedom $= 4$
$p$ is less than $0 \cdot 001$   — null hypothesis rejected.

This result indicates that there is good evidence for a non-chance difference overall; but we may wish to test the hypothesis that Class I and II children differ significantly from a group which comprises a random sample excluding Class I and II. To do this, it is first necessary to derive a weighted average percentage for Classes III white collar, III manual, IV and V, which in this case works out to 13%. To test this difference between 13% and 32%, however, it is necessary to construct a contingency table showing actual frequencies: and this poses a problem. In order to decide the number of cases upon which the value of 13% should be based, we make the clearly conservative assumption that our stratified random sample of 700 cases is equivalent to a simple random sample of 500 cases. Of these 500, however, 70 cases would be in Class I and II, leaving a sample of 430 cases. This leads us to a contingency table and test of significance as follows:

|                   | Class I and II | All other classes combined | Totals |
|-------------------|----------------|----------------------------|--------|
| Thumb-suckers     | 41 (32%)       | 56 (13%)                   | 97     |
| Non-thumb-suckers | 88             | 374                        | 462    |
| Totals            | 129            | 430                        | 559    |

Chi-squared (corrected for continuity) $= 23 \cdot 0$   Degrees of freedom $= 1$
$p$ is less than $0 \cdot 001$   — null hypothesis rejected.

We are thus entitled to conclude that significantly more of the children in Class I and II are thumb-suckers, as compared with a random sample of all other children. Except where notice is given to the contrary, the assumption of an equivalent random sample of 500 cases has been used consistently when combining proportions for different social class groups. As noted above, it is an undoubtedly conservative assumption, and this means that the differences which we present are probably somewhat more significant than the quoted probability levels would indicate.

There is a further reason why the statistical levels of significance which appear in the following pages may be regarded as conservative estimates: that the chi-squared test, when applied to contingency tables, takes no account of consistency in overall directional trends. For example, the proportions of children allowed to rejoin the family after having been put to bed (page 247) are given as follows:

| I and II | IIIwc | IIIman | IV | V |
|---|---|---|---|---|
| % | % | % | % | % |
| 6 | 14 | 19 | 18 | 18 |

and the result is stated to be significant at the 0·05 level only. This, however, takes no account of the fact that the rising class trend is quite consistent in direction except where the differences between adjacent class groups are obviously very small. Had the result been:

| I and II | IIIwc | IIIman | IV | V |
|---|---|---|---|---|
| % | % | % | % | % |
| 18 | 14 | 19 | 6 | 18 |

the resulting test would still have yielded significance at the 0·05 level, but interpretation in terms of an overall class trend would have been a good deal less convincing.

Some statistical technique more sophisticated than the general one we have adopted might have been used to test for the consistency of trends; but we have deliberately preferred to keep to the simpler, though cruder, conventional use of the chi-squared test with which more of our readers will probably be familiar. It is in fact doubtful whether any of our conclusions would have been materially affected by the use of more refined statistical procedures.

*A guide to interpreting differences in percentages.* Having conducted a very large number of similar tests of significance upon this particular sample, we now know that a difference of the order of about 10% between any two percentages will usually prove to be significant statistically. It may help the reader in interpreting our tables to know that whenever there is a consistent pattern of differences, with a discrepancy as large as 10% between adjacent classes, testing will almost certainly lead to a rejection of the null hypothesis at the 0·01 level.

A summary of statistical differences (social class and other) follows.

# A SUMMARY OF SOCIAL CLASS DIFFERENCES REFERRED TO IN THE TEXT

Significance level conventions: * * * * 0·001; * * * 0·01; * * 0·02; * 0·05

| Topic | Table | Page | I & II % | IIIwc % | IIIman % | IV % | V % | All (random) % | Chi-squared | Degrees of freedom | Significance |
|---|---|---|---|---|---|---|---|---|---|---|---|
| House rated 'dirty' | II | 36 | (⎯⎯⎯ 5 ⎯⎯⎯) | | | | 25 | 7 | 39·2 | 1 | * * * * |
| 4 or more children | III | 41 | 15 | 12 | 23 | 33 | 57 | 30 | 68·8 | 4 | * * * * |
| *Mother working:* | | | | | | | | | | | |
| Full time | — | 42–3 | 5 | 6 | 4 | 4 | 3 | 5 | not significant | | |
| Part time | — | 42–3 | 18 | 22 | 25 | 24 | 17 | 23 | not significant | | |
| Other adult in house | — | 47 | 7 | 10 | 12 | 8 | 9 | 10 | not significant | | |
| *Independence:* | | | | | | | | | | | |
| Shopping alone | — | 74 | (⎯ 72 ⎯) | | (⎯⎯⎯ 81 ⎯⎯⎯) | | | 79 | 4·5 | 1 | * |
| Messages | — | 70 | 66 | 62 | 61 | 65 | 60 | 62 | not significant | | |
| Dresses without help | — | 75 | 18 | 16 | 16 | 18 | 19 | 17 | not significant | | |
| Tidies up clothes, no help | — | 75 | 18 | 22 | 28 | 27 | 28 | 26 | not significant | | |
| Toilet, no help | — | 75–7 | 47 | 52 | 63 | 56 | 65 | 59 | 13·7 | 4 | * * * |
| Clears up toys, no help | — | 75–6 | 29 | 33 | 35 | 35 | 28 | 34 | not significant | | |
| Children rated 'more independent' | — | 76–7 | 54 | 54 | 60 | 66 | 61 | 59 | not significant | | |
| Dislikes playing alone | — | 88 | 10 | 4 | 23 | 19 | 32 | 19 | 37·1 | 4 | * * * * |
| Dislikes playing alone | — | 88 | (⎯ 7 ⎯) | | (⎯⎯⎯ 23 ⎯⎯⎯) | | | 19 | | 1 | * * * * |
| *Attention demands:* | | | | | | | | | | | |
| Demands 'often' | — | 98 | 14 | 18 | 18 | 11 | 16 | 16 | not significant | | |
| M invariably or mostly responsive | — | 96–7 | 76 | 78 | 71 | 69 | 69 | 72 | not significant | | |

A Summary of Social Class Differences referred to in the Text—continued

| Topic | Table | Page | I & II | IIIwc | IIIman | IV | V | All (random) | Chi-squared | Degrees of freedom | Significance |
|---|---|---|---|---|---|---|---|---|---|---|---|
| | | | % | % | % | % | % | % | | | |
| *Children's quarrels:* | | | | | | | | | | | |
| Mother arbitrates | XI | 114 | 37 | 25 | 21 | 18 | 20 | 23 | 15·3 | 4 | *** |
| Mother lets children settle own differences | XI | 114 | 19 | 25 | 33 | 38 | 43 | 32 | 20·1 | 4 | **** |
| *M encourages hitting back:* | | | | | | | | | | | |
| YES (unambiguous) | XIII | 120 | {36 | (——— | 65 | ———) | | 61} | 38·9 | 2 | **** |
| NO, never | XIII | 120 | {35 | (——— | 15 | ———) | | 18} | | | |
| *Property rights:* | | | | | | | | | | | |
| High respect | — | 153 | 37 | 27 | 36 | 32 | 36 | 34 | not significant | | |
| Little or no respect | — | 153 | 13 | 10 | 11 | 14 | 16 | 12 | not significant | | |
| *Mother breaks toys:* | | | | | | | | | | | |
| Restitution | — | 150 | 52 | 48 | 58 | 69 | 51 | 57 | not significant | | |
| Apology | — | 150 | 30 | 32 | 20 | 12 | 20 | 22 | 20·5 | 4 | **** |
| No action | — | 150 | 13 | 15 | 15 | 15 | 24 | 15 | not significant | | |
| *Neatness and tidiness:* | | | | | | | | | | | |
| Much restriction | XVI | 155 | {3 | (——— | 14 | ———) | | 12} | 12·5 | 2 | *** |
| Almost no restriction | XVI | 155 | {21 | (——— | 15 | ———) | | 16} | | | |
| Play participation, wholehearted | XVII | 172 | 71 | 74 | 63 | 74 | 45 | 66 | 29·5 | 4 | **** |
| Play participation, wholehearted | XVII | 172 | (—— | 73 | ——) | (——63——) | | 66 | 3·8 | 1 | ** |
| *Fantasy:* | | | | | | | | | | | |
| Communications generally | XVIII | 185 | 45 | 30 | 26 | 24 | 14 | 28 | 30·1 | 4 | *** |
| Imaginary companions | — | 186 | 22 | 25 | 23 | 21 | 8 | 22 | 12·4 | 4 | ** |
| Imaginary companions | — | 186 | (—— | 23 | ——) | | 8 | 22 | 10·6 | 1 | *** |

| Item | s | N | | | | | | | stat | df | sig |
|---|---|---|---|---|---|---|---|---|---|---|---|
| *Eating:* | | | | | | | | | | | |
| Child rated 'finicky' | XIX | 209 | 15 | 11 | 14 | 21 | 6 | 14 | 11·3 | 4 | * |
| Child rated 'finicky' | XIX | 209 | (——— 15 ———) | | | | 6 | 14 | 6·1 | 1 | ** |
| M 'very concerned' | XIX | 209 | 12 | 9 | 6 | 7 | 5 | 7 | not significant | | |
| C must leave clean plate | XX | 224 | 16 | 10 | 9 | 9 | 8 | 10 | not significant | | |
| M provides alternative | XX | 224 | 18 | 26 | 35 | 28 | 44 | 31 | 21·3 | 4 | **** |
| *Mealtime rules:* | | | | | | | | | | | |
| No toys at table | XXI | 233 | 69 | 75 | 71 | 76 | 76 | 73 | not significant | | |
| No getting up | XXI | 233 | 26 | 35 | 21 | 31 | 21 | 25 | not significant | | |
| No spoon | XXI | 233 | 12 | 12 | 9 | 11 | 2 | 10 | 9·1 | 4 | **** |
| No spoon | XXI | 233 | (——— 10 ———) | | | | 2 | 10 | 7·3 | 1 | p<0·06 |
| No fingers | XXI | 233 | 80 | 83 | 79 | 74 | 76 | 79 | not significant | | |
| M minds about order | XXI | 233 | 81 | 80 | 62 | 59 | 42 | 65 | 23·9 | 4 | *** |
| Other special rules | XXI | 233 | (——— 24 ———) | | (——— 66 ———) | | 78 | 67 | 5·7 | 1 | ** |
| No talking | — | 239 | (——— 26 ———) | | | | | 25 | not significant | | |
| Overall points score averages, tested by analysis of variance | XXII | 241 | 7·4 | 7·4 | 6·7 | 6·7 | 6·4 | 6·9 | F = 3·8 | 4/695 | *** |
| *Mealtime manners:* | | | | | | | | | | | |
| M takes much trouble | XXII | 241 | 31 | 21 | 21 | 21 | 12 | 22 | 12·6 | 5 | *** |
| M 'leaving it' | XXII | 241 | 8 | 11 | 21 | 25 | 36 | 20 | 35·2 | 4 | **** |
| M 'minds about manners' | XXII | 241 | 77 | 81 | 65 | 65 | 57 | 69 | 18·0 | 4 | **** |
| *Bedtime:* | | | | | | | | | | | |
| Before 6.30 p.m. | XXIV | 247 | 22 | 9 | 7 | 7 | 12 | 10 | 22·1 | 4 | **** |
| After 8.0 p.m. | XXIV | 247 | 6 | 16 | 24 | 26 | 25 | 21 | 23·4 | 4 | **** |
| Strict/flexibly strict | XXIV | 247 | 87 | 79 | 69 | 62 | 66 | 72 | 25·2 | 4 | *** |
| 'No rules' | XXIV | 247 | 1 | 4 | 11 | 13 | 14 | 9 | 21·9 | 4 | **** |
| C may rejoin family | XXIV | 247 | 6 | 14 | 19 | 18 | 18 | 16 | 11·3 | 4 | * |
| No playing in bed | XXIV | 247 | 51 | 48 | 46 | 40 | 41 | 46 | not significant | | |

A Summary of Social Class Differences referred to in the Text—continued

| Topic | Table | Page | I & II % | IIIwc % | IIIman % | IV % | V % | All (random) % | Chi-squared | Degrees of freedom | Significance |
|---|---|---|---|---|---|---|---|---|---|---|---|
| **Bedtime—continued** | | | | | | | | | | | |
| Stories | XXV | 259 | 56 | 34 | 20 | 22 | 14 | 27 | 69·2 | 4 | * * * * |
| Songs | XXV | 259 | (——13——) | | 7 | (——6——) | | 8 | 4·4 | 1 | * |
| Prayers | XXV | 259 | 29 | 17 | 27 | 12 | 10 | 12 | 36·7 | 4 | * * * * |
| Kissing, cuddling, at bedtime | — | 260 | 29 | 39 | 27 | 24 | 24 | 28 | almost sig, overall at p = 0·05 | | |
| 'Indulgent bedtime' | XXVI | 273 | (——5——) | | (——10——) | | | 11 | not significant | | |
| Sleeps in parents' room | XXVI | 273 | (——7——) | | (——15——) | | | 13 | 5·4 | 1 | * * |
| M will chat in night | XXVI | 273 | (——29——) | | (——25——) | | | 26 | not significant | | |
| M takes C in own bed | XXVI | 273 | 55 | (——68——) | | | | 66 | 7·3 | 1 | * * * |
| **Rituals and comfort habits:** | | | | | | | | | | | |
| Bedtime ritual | — | 291 | (——34——) | | | | | 33 | 6·0 | 1 | * * |
| Insists on 'cuddly' | XXVII | 299 | 43 | 34 | 29 | 26 | 21 | 31 | 15·3 | 4 | * * * |
| Cloth cuddly | XXVII | 299 | (——10——) | | (——4——) | | | 5 | 6·7 | 1 | * * * |
| Soft toy cuddly | XXVII | 299 | 32 | 25 | 29 | 23 | 18 | 26 | not significant | | |
| Bottle still | XXVIII | 306 | 4 | 6 | 3 | 5 | 5 | 4 | not significant | | |
| Dummy still | XXVIII | 306 | 7 | 9 | 16 | 15 | 13 | 14 | not significant | | |
| Dummy still | XXVIII | 306 | (——8——) | | (——16——) | | | 14 | 4·1 | 1 | * |
| Thumb sucking | XXVIII | 306 | 32 | 19 | 12 | 11 | 11 | 16 | 30·4 | 4 | * * * * |
| 1-plus comfort habits | XXVIII | 306 | 66 | 52 | 51 | 49 | 46 | 53 | 11·9 | 4 | * * |
| **Toilet training** | | | | | | | | | | | |
| Daytime wetting | XXIX | 319 | 24 | 16 | 23 | 24 | 23 | 22 | not significant | | |
| Soiling (all cases) | XXIX | 319 | 5 | 6 | 4 | 4 | 3 | 4 | not significant | | |
| Bedwetting | XXXI | 337 | 14 | 22 | 31 | 27 | 30 | 27 | 14·7 | 4 | * * |
| Bedwetting | XXXI | 337 | (——18——) | | (——30——) | | | 27 | 7·7 | 1 | * * |

*Modesty:*

| | | | | | | | | | χ² | df | |
|---|---|---|---|---|---|---|---|---|---|---|---|
| Genital play ignored or permitted | XXXVI | 355 | 17 | (———9———) | | | | 10 | 5·7 | 1 | * |
| Punished | XXXVI | 355 | 5 | 18 | 36 | 41 | 48 | 31 | 71·5 | 4 | * * * * |
| Giggling ignored | XXXVII | 361 | 60 | 45 | 44 | 44 | 54 | 48 | 11·5 | 4 | * * |
| Punished | XXXVII | 361 | 8 | 9 | 21 | 27 | 25 | 19 | 26·5 | 4 | * * * * |
| Seeing other children naked: allowed | XXXVIII | 365 | 62 | 45 | 35 | 39 | 25 | 40 | 50·1 | 8 | * * * * |
| Not allowed | XXXVIII | 365 | 17 | 25 | 35 | 40 | 50 | 33 | | | |
| Seeing parents naked: allowed both | XXXIX | 370 | 59 | 45 | 27 | 24 | 15 | 32 | 86·8 | 8 | * * * * |
| Neither allowed | XXXIX | 370 | 19 | 32 | 52 | 54 | 68 | 46 | | | |
| Where babies come from: C already knows | XL | 377 | 44 | 26 | 15 | 14 | 15 | 20 | 134·1 | 8 | * * * * |
| M would not tell | XL | 377 | 12 | 27 | 55 | 47 | 75 | 46 | | | |
| False explanation | XLI | 383 | 8 | 19 | 41 | 40 | 66 | 35 | 101·2 | 4 | * * * * |

*Discipline:*

| | | | | | | | | | χ² | df | |
|---|---|---|---|---|---|---|---|---|---|---|---|
| Reciprocity: M on child's nerves | XLIII | 401 | 18 | 10 | 12 | 12 | 4 | 12 | 10·4 | 4 | * |
| Instant obedience not insisted on | XLIII | 401 | 77 | 77 | 65 | 73 | 63 | 69 | 11·8 | 4 | * * |
| Instant obedience not insisted on | XLIII | 401 | (———77———) | | (———66———) | | | 69 | 5·0 | 1 | * |
| Smacking: none | XLIV | 415 | 2 | 2 | 3 | 3 | 3 | 3 | not significant | | |
| less than 1 p.w. or none | XLIV | 415 | 35 | 25 | 23 | 27 | 14 | 25 | 14·5 | 4 | * * * |
| 1-plus per day | XLIV | 415 | 4 | 7 | 7 | 7 | 7 | 7 | not significant | | |
| Obedience enforced by smacking | XLV | 419 | 56 | 63 | 70 | 63 | 79 | 67 | 14·0 | 4 | * * * |
| Smacking for lies | XLV | 419 | 27 | 37 | 38 | 44 | 42 | 38 | 9·3 | 4 | p<0·06 |
| Smacking for lies | XLV | 419 | 27 | (———39———) | | | | 38 | 5·9 | 1 | * * |
| Smacking for smacking M | XLV | 419 | 43 | 50 | 63 | 60 | 64 | 58 | 17·9 | 4 | * * * |

A Summary of Social Class Differences referred to in the Text—continued

| Topic | Table | Page | I & II (%) | IIIwc (%) | IIIman (%) | IV (%) | V (%) | All (random) (%) | Chi-squared | Degrees of freedom | Significance |
|---|---|---|---|---|---|---|---|---|---|---|---|
| *Discipline—continued* | | | | | | | | | | | |
| Smacking for tantrums (restricted sample) | XLV | 419 | 20 | 33 | 36 | 38 | 25 | 33 | 9·8 | 4 | * |
| Smacking for tantrums (restricted sample) | XLV | 419 | 20 | | 35 | | | 33 | 6·2 | 1 | ** |
| M smacks only in anger | XLVI | 420 | 48 | 46 | 57 | 44 | 45 | 51 | not significant | | |
| Smacks only when calm | XLVI | 420 | 20 | 17 | 21 | 24 | 26 | 21 | not significant | | |
| Both calm and in anger | XLVI | 420 | 33 | | 24 | | | 25 | 3·8 | 1 | * |
| M disapproves of smacking | XLVI | 420 | 20 | 14 | 16 | 16 | 22 | 17 | not significant | | |
| Child confesses voluntarily | — | 445 | 65 | 54 | 52 | 44 | 31 | 51 | 29·7 | 4 | **** |
| Child confesses voluntarily | — | 445 | 60 | | 48 | | | 51 | 4·8 | 1 | * |
| Tantrums: often | XLVII | 449 | 25 | 28 | 38 | 39 | 49 | 36 | 18·4 | 4 | **** |
| Tantrums: never | XLVII | 449 | 39 | 30 | 31 | 28 | 33 | 32 | not significant | | |
| Deprivation (sweets etc.) | — | 460 | 60 | 77 | 69 | 72 | 67 | 69 | 9·1 | 4 | p<0·06 |
| Deprivation (sweets etc.) | — | 460 | 60 | | 71 | | | 69 | 5·6 | 1 | ** |
| Threat of authority fig. | XLVIII | 461 | 10 | 23 | 29 | 29 | 46 | 27 | 37·8 | 4 | **** |
| *Evasion or distortion of truth:* | | | | | | | | | | | |
| Idle threat of authority figure | XLIX | 471 | 6 | 17 | 23 | 26 | 39 | 22 | 39·2 | 4 | **** |
| Send away/leave (threat) | XLIX | 471 | 10 | 34 | 29 | 27 | 30 | 27 | 13·5 | 4 | **** |
| Send away/leave (threat) | XLIX | 471 | 20 | | 29 | | | 27 | 10·8 | 1 | **** |
| Leaves surreptitiously | XLIX | 471 | 10 | | 22 | | | 23 | 3·9 | 1 | * |
| Unfulfilled punishment threats (many) | XLIX | 471 | 9 | 17 | 13 | 15 | 18 | 15 | not significant | | |
| Any other definite instance | XLIX | 471 | 4 | 12 | 11 | 15 | 10 | 11 | 8·4 | 4 | p<0·06 |
| Total points score 2+ | XLIX | 471 | 12 | 29 | 42 | 37 | 62 | 37 | 40·3 | 4 | **** |

| | | N | | | | | | | χ² | df | |
|---|---|---|---|---|---|---|---|---|---|---|---|
| *M's valuation of child:* | | | | | | | | | | | |
| For good behaviour | — | 478 | 5 | 5 | 8 | 5 | 12 | 7 | | | not significant |
| For himself | — | 478 | 88 | 81 | 80 | 83 | 77 | 81 | | | not significant |
| Kissing and cuddling discouraged | — | 483 | 5 | 3 | 4 | 8 | 5 | 5 | | | not significant |
| *Child smacks mother:* | | | | | | | | | | | |
| Seen as moral issue | L | 490 | 68 | 72 | 76 | 82 | 77 | 76 | | | not significant |
| *Of these,* punished | L | 490 | 64 | 69 | 83 | 73 | 83 | 77 | 15·8 | 4 | ** |
| M says 'I won't love you' | — | 491 | 12 | 21 | 42 | 43 | 42 | 36 | 44·4 | 4 | **** |
| M says 'I won't love you' | — | 491 | (——17——) | | (——42——) | | | 36 | 27·7 | 1 | *** |
| *Child-centredness:* | | | | | | | | | | | |
| Low scorers | LI | 499 | (——25——) | | (——38——) | | | 34 | 9·0 | 2 | ** |
| High scorers | LI | 499 | (——43——) | | (——32——) | | | 53 | | | |
| Mother criticizes self | — | 500 | 63 | | 51 | 52 | | 54 | 19·7 | 4 | **** |
| Mother criticizes self | — | 500 | (——64——) | | (——50——) | | 39 | 54 | 7·0 | 1 | *** |
| *M's self-rating:* | | | | | | | | | | | |
| 'Very strict' | LII | 511 | 7 | | (——2——) | | | 3 | 12·3 | 2 | *** |
| 'Very easy-going' | LII | 511 | 4 | | (——11——) | | | 10 | | | |
| *Father's participation:* | | | | | | | | | | | |
| High | LIII | 514 | 64 | 59 | 48 | 44 | 49 | 51 | 15·6 | 4 | *** |
| Little or none | LIII | 514 | 4 | 5 | 10 | 14 | 10 | 9 | 11·3 | 4 | * |
| Little or none | LIII | 514 | (——4——) | | (——11——) | | | 9 | 4·0 | 1 | ** |
| F tells stories to child | — | 456 | 91 | 81 | 72 | 70 | 67 | 75 | 25·6 | 4 | **** |
| Husband rated 'stricter' than self by M | LIII | 514 | 22 | 31 | 46 | 35 | 52 | 39 | 31·7 | 4 | **** |

*Results of other tests of significance referred to in the text*

(All these relationships are calculated on the basis of an equivalent random sample n = 500)

*Page*

76 More girls than boys are self-reliant in dressing themselves.
Chi-squared = 19·8, degrees of freedom = 1, $p < 0·001$.

77 Children who take messages and/or go shopping by themselves are more often rated 'independent' on other criteria also.
Chi-squared = 12·5, d. of f. = 1, $p < 0·001$.

95 Mothers who exert pressure for independence are more likely to have children who objectively behave with greater independence.
Chi-squared = 54·6, d. of f. = 1, $p < 0·001$.

171 Mothers of children in small families are more likely to be 'whole-heartedly participant' in playing with their children than those of larger families.
Chi-squared = 18·4, d. of f. = 1, $p < 0·001$.

185 Mothers of children in small families more often report that their children have an active fantasy life (social class held constant).
Chi-squared = 13·6, d. of f. = 5, $p < 0·02$.

209 Mothers of finicky eaters are more likely to be concerned over the eating behaviour of their children.
Chi-squared = 49·6, d. of f. = 1, $p < 0·001$.

280 Mothers whose children have a waking problem at night say more frequently than other mothers that they would be prepared to take the child into their own bed.
Chi-squared = 6·4, d. of f. = 1, $p < 0·02$.

291 Children said to have an active fantasy life are more likely than other children to have a regular bedtime ritual.
Chi-squared = 7·2, d. of f. = 1, $p < 0·01$.

299 Children who have a regular bedtime ritual are more likely than other children to insist on having a "cuddly' in their bed.
Chi-squared = 8·7, d. of f. = 1, $p < 0·01$.

312 Children who are put to bed comparatively early are more likely than other children to exhibit some recognizable comfort habit.
Chi-squared = 9·3, d. of f. = 2, $p < 0·01$.

313 Comfort habits are more frequently found among *youngest* and *only* children than among *eldest* or *middle* children.
Chi-squared = 11·0, d. of f. = 1, $p < 0·001$.

*Page*

421 Mothers who smack both when calm and when angry tend to smack more often than mothers who restrict themselves to one mood (non-smackers excluded).
Chi-squared $= 11\cdot4$, d. of f. $= 2$, $p < 0\cdot01$.

425 Mothers' belief in smacking is positively correlated with the degree to which they use smacking in practice.
Chi-squared $= 42\cdot1$, d. of f. $= 3$, $p < 0\cdot001$.

517 Less participant husbands are more often rated by their wives as 'stricter than I am'.
Chi-squared $= 11\cdot5$, d. of f. $= 2$, $p < 0\cdot01$.

# APPENDIX III

## *INTERVIEW WITH A FOUR-YEAR-OLD*
### (*see page 177*)

———————

Note: Carey was interviewed at age 4:6 about her doll, Susanna Mary-Dick, supposedly aged 4 years. Carey herself had been a very 'easy' baby and toddler: at 3 her parents realized that they had never refused her anything because she had never yet made an unreasonable demand. By four she was becoming more self-assertive and temperamental; she was now the middle one of three. Her interest in dolls and her pleasure in fantasy both appeared very early indeed, and both have persisted; among a very large family of dolls, a small *élite* were and are always spoken of as if alive, Susanna and her brother Tim being the founder members of this *élite*. The background of the Mary-Dick family, as described to the interviewer, is professional: the father teaches writing at the University of Pasjill, India, and is therefore frequently away from home, but 'a lady called Judy' lives with the family: 'We found her for a friend when we got married, so we took her to our wedding and she came to live with us after that'.

The authors are conscious that interpretations damaging to themselves as parents may well be made from this material, but they are prepared to run that risk in the interests of science; they themselves have found the document a salutary warning against too-enthusiastic interpretation of children's fantasies. The interview is abridged, but only to the exclusion of short answers of little interest.

12. (About how long will she play by herself . . .?) Seven minutes. (If she keeps wanting you to do things . . .?) Well, I say she's not to, and give her a slap, because I don't want to do things for her; because it has to be done by 20 minutes, you see. (What has to?) The thing I'm doing. (Does she ever come clinging . . .?) Sometimes she does. (What do you do?) I just give her a hard slap on her bottom. (Do you think a child of this age should be able to amuse herself . . .?) Quite a lot of time keeping her happy; because I don't like all the noise in the house, you see, if she's doing those things; because some other children are playing as well, and they don't want to be disturbed.

18. (. . . disagreement or a quarrel?) I slap them *all*. (. . . settle their own differences . . .?) Well, I should let them settle their

own—I wouldn't come and interfere. (Suppose Susanna comes running to you complaining of another child?) If she said it had done something naughty, and she hadn't done something to *it*, I would go and slap it. (Would you slap it if it wasn't your child, or would you slap it only if it *was* your child?) Only if it was *another* child. (Not if it was yours?) No, because I would like my children more, a tiny bit. But I *sometimes* slap my children. (. . . if she's quarrelling with her brother . . .?) Well, I still slap them—I only slap one—I only slap the one which was quarrelling about something.

23. (Does Susanna ever seem jealous of her brother?) Only a bit. (What does she do?) I hear her being jealous and crying because Tim hit her. (How do you deal with it?) If she does, I say to her brother that she *must* do the thing, that she *can*. Because she's got a blue dress on, and blue's nice and lovely, and he's got a cardigan which is red, you see, and I like the blue colour best, you see. But I just whisper in her ear: "*Say* it's right, but it's not really"—that's a good thing to say, isn't it? Or I pick her up, and if she wants to go to bed I just put her to bed and give her a bottle.

26. (Does Susanna make a fuss if you give away something of hers . . .?) Not very much, because I get it back. (Do you ever give something right away and not get it back?) No, no. (Suppose you were having a good turn-out . . .?) I should say they were broken. (But if she said "I want them, I like them"?) I should say I should find them from the place where I had thrown them away, and I should put them tidied up in a lovely place on her bed. (If you've broken something of hers . . .?) I put a wire all the way round and stick things all over with Bostik all over it. (But if you can't possibly mend it because it's in tiny pieces—suppose you stood on her dolly's cup, or something like that?) Well—she just says she wants it, and I say it's broken. So I buy a new whole teaset, and throw the *rest* away, and give her another teaset just the same colour.

29. (. . . Do you let her make a lot of noise in the house . . .?) No—I slap her if she does, and send her to bed. (. . . use furniture for her play . . .?) I let her make a train out of chairs, but I don't let her jump on her bed, because it untidies it, because in the morning when she gets up she comes into our bed, and we try and get up, and then she gets up and we make her bed, and you see she starts jumping on it, and I tell her not to, and I have to make it again. (But suppose she jumps on it *before* you make it, is that allowed?) No, because I'll

S*

be making it in two minutes. (Do you let her make a mess . . .?) Yes. (Does it bother you if she gets really dirty . . .?) No, I just tell her to go and wash her face and hands; and she doesn't, you see, so I *make* her wash her face and hands, I do it myself. (When she's playing at something, do you ever join in?) Only when I'm not busy. (What sort of things?) Only when I'm in bed; I just put the light on and play a lovely game, she just chooses it and says "Play Ludo", and I try and play Ludo with her. (Do you ever play shops or mothers and fathers with her?) Yes, but only when we're in bed, because when she doesn't go in bed with me I get busy.

31. (Has she any imaginary people . . .?) Yes. She talks about *your* family, and tells things that aren't true, like "Roger does hit me and Joanna does slap me". (Does she ever talk about a *person* who isn't true?) Yes—she says "Goggy plays with me", and she doesn't mean Goggy at all. (Who's Goggy?) Nobody. (What do you say when she says things like that?) I say that's not true, someone'll think it's a *real* name. (Does she sometimes tell you about some happening . . .?) She says "A wolf tried to eat me up". (What do you do?) I say "Don't tell not-the-truth, it's silly". (Is there anything special she's afraid of . . .?) The plug-hole—she had a bath, and she bringed in some tiny weeny weeny dolls-house people, and she said "I'm frightened, I'm frightened, they'll go down the drain!" (Anything else she's afraid of?) Er—yes—when she's in bed, she says "I'm frightened of a lion coming in the night!"—and that's not true. It won't, will it? She puts her head under the blanket so the lion can't get her; and I say "It's not true, there isn't a lion". And she really *knows* there aren't a lion, truly, and she's making a joke and *thinking* it is. So I try to tell her, there's *no* wolf and there's *no* animals, and they're not *anywhere*, and I know there perfectly *aren't*, I know very well, don't I?

36. (. . . Susanna's mealtimes now. Is she a good eater . . .?) Well, she's not *very* good; she sometimes puts cereals all over the pussy-cat, so that the pussy-cat can lick them off when she starts washing herself. (. . . Do you let her leave food on her plate?) Well, yes, I do, but I don't let her put it on the pussy-cat. It's *horrible*, isn't it? Because she puts it on the pussycat's face, and on her eyes. If she does that, I just take it off the pussy-cat, and take the pussy-cat outside to lick herself and shake herself. (If she didn't like a meal . . . would you make her something else?) No (laughed)—I'd just not let her have dinner. (Do you mind what order . . .?) No, she can have

toast or whatever she likes. (. . . use a spoon . . . ?) Yes. (. . . use
her fingers . . . ?) No, only to eat her tea. (. . . get up from the
table . . . ?) Oh no. (. . . bring toys or a book to the table?)
No—I say leave them on the kitchen floor, and nobody'll
touch them at all if she's very quick eating dinner. (Any other
rules . . . not talking . . . ?) She *shouldn't* talk, but she *does*
talk; she says "Do you know, there's not such a thing as a
wolf"—and there are, aren't there?

46. (. . . any little habits . . . twist her hair . . . ?) Yes she does.
(. . . bite her nails?) Yes. (. . . suck her thumb?) Yes, but I
don't like her doing it, I always get afraid she might pull it
off (*Carey had no experience of thumbsucking in the family*).
(Does she play with her botty at all, touch it, that sort of
thing?) No. (Would you mind her doing that . . . ?) No I
wouldn't; only if she had an itchy botty, or if she went out
shopping and wanted to do a wee-wee or a jobby. (Do you
try and stop her sucking her thumb?) I say "You're not to",
and she doesn't. (. . . twisting her hair?) I say stop it. (. . .biting
her nails?) Oh no—that's how she cuts them, she bites them.

50. (. . . bedtime . . . what time . . . ?) Four o'clock. She usually
goes then. She has a little bit of supper every day, she can have
soup if she likes, and even she can have all the supper that me
and Mary-Dick have. (Does she *have* to be in bed by that
time?) I don't really mind, I let her play, and if she wanted to
not go to bed until *daytime*, I'd let her. I just put her to bed
when she wants to. (Does your husband help . . . ?) Oh no,
he never does it, she doesn't like it. (. . . anything that she
takes into bed with her . . . ?) She takes a bottle and she takes
a dummy and she takes a piece of cloth. (. . . if you couldn't
find it . . . ?) I would just try and find where it can be, you see,
and when I found it I would give it to her, I wouldn't just
leave her crying without any piece of cloth. (. . . anything
special that you always have to do at bedtime . . . ?) Well,
something that I always have to do, you see, I always have to
put her blanket up, and then I have to go and find a shop
which is open, which is an ice-cream one, and get her an
ice-cream to eat in bed. (. . . anything to drink in bed?) Yes:
a drink of milk and some water; and some orange juice; and
a dummy and a bottle. It's a lot, isn't it? It's quite good!
(What about sweets in bed?) Yes—a 'currant-juice sweet, and
all sorts of sweets—every sweet she wants. (. . . if she wakes . . .
what seems to be the matter?) She wants a potty, or an apple.
(What would you do if she seemed frightened?) I would say
"Put your head underneath the blankets", or "It's not true".

(. . . if she was just feeling chatty?) Let her get up. (. . . if she wanted to come in your bed?) Just let her (*totally permissive at night*).

72. (*No bedwetting:* . . . any special method?) I said "Always sit on the potty". (*Daytime accidents: both wetting and soiling*) Well, I take her things and give her some new pants, but first wipe her botty and put water on it. (. . . giggling over the lavatory . . .?) I just take no notice. Susanna says she'll go down that lavatory, and I say "You won't, silly". (. . . looking at each other when they're undressed—would you mind them doing that?) No, I should let them. (Does Susanna ever see you or her Daddy undressed?) Yes, she does, and she says "Why don't you come to breakfast?" (Does she know where babies come from?) Yes—she knows where *she's* come from, you see.

80. (What . . . do you specially enjoy . . .?) I specially enjoy with her doing all these letters that I give her that I say she must do. (. . . show your affection . . .?) Yes—kissing and hugging. (. . . get on each other's nerves?) When she jogs me when I'm writing. (What makes her cross about *you*?) Things that are so tiny that I can't see them and I've broken them. (. . . children often don't want to do as they're told—what do you do . . .?) Well—what she doesn't do when she's told—I say "Please: you're to go and pick all your toys up and put them in the right place—or I'll come and throw them away!" (And she doesn't do it?) No. (What do you do?) I say "I'll throw them away . . ." (*warningly*): and she goes and picks them up. (Suppose . . . "I'm busy" . . .?) I would do it myself. (If she refuses . . . what she really must do . . .?) Well, you see—I just give her things to put in her cupboard. (You mean when it's picking up toys?) Yes. (Suppose she's playing outside, and she's *got* to come in and have her dinner quickly, she really has *got* to—then what happens?) Oh—well, I put her things away *in*side, and then she cries and comes in, and she just comes in. (Do you ever promise . . . a reward . . .?) Yes—sometimes she picks me some flowers when I tell her to, so I give her some chocolate, *and* ice-cream. (. . . necessary to smack children . . .?) Not very much. (. . . does her any good?) No, not very much. (Why do you do it, then?) Just for fun—so that she gets a bit good; she's *trying* to get very good, so I'm not smacking her, you see, now. (*On hearing play-back, Carey at this point commented "I jolly well are, aren't I?"*) I'm saving it. (Saving what?) Saving my smacking for a little bit. (Until when?) Until Thursday.

91. (Is there anything else you do when she's naughty?) Yes—well, sometimes, when she's very very very very very very *very* naughty, I think of something which is really really hard to do to her. (What?) Well—I pick up a stone and plop it on her head. (Do you ever send her to bed for being naughty?) Yes, sometimes. (... tell her you won't love her ...?) No. (... say you'll send her away ...?) Ah, *no*! (... frighten her with somebody else ...?) Yes—a policeman I do. (Suppose she says she hasn't done something naughty when you know ... she has ...?) I say "You have"; and she just stops, she does, because she knows herself that I know she has really done something naughty. (Does she ever come and tell you ... before you actually find out?) Oh *no*, she wouldn't *dare* tell me! (... important for her to say she's sorry ...?) Yes. (Do you make her ...?) She says "No no no no!" But I see a dot on her hand, and I say "Look at that dot on your hand, it means you must"; and she does. (What do you mean?) I *pretend* it does, to make her do it.

100. (Does Susanna ever try to smack you ...?) No, she never does. (What would you do if she did?) I would say "You mustn't do that, it's naughty". (But you smack *her*?) If I smack her, *she'll* say "You mustn't do that, it's naughty". (And what do you say?) I say "I am now if you're naughty, I know you're perfectly well naughty, so I'm smacking you". (What about answering you back ... being cheeky ...?) I don't know what that means. (Being rude—saying something rude.) She sometimes says "Put my hand in my bottom". (And is that rude?) Yes, it's quite rude. (Suppose she said "You're a silly old mummy"?) I should say "I'm not a silly old mummy, I'm a *big* old mummy". (Does she ever have a real temper tantrum?) Yes, she does; she just *lies* on the floor, and says "I want to go shopping", and we say "You can't, it's too late, we've just got to get in the car and go on holiday". So I take her away and put her in the car, and she just lies in the car, and we just go off in the car.

104. (On the whole, are you happy about the way you deal with discipline in general ...?) What does that mean? (When you're doing things with Susanna, do you think you do all the right things, or do you think sometimes you do things you *shouldn't* do?) I think sometimes there are things she shouldn't do in general. (But do you think *you* do things that *you* shouldn't do—I mean, things like smacking her and so on—do you think you should smack her?) Oh *yes*—all the people *there* say I *should* smack her. (Which people?) The people at General.

*(Question was abandoned at this point, nor could any understanding be reached on the following two.)*

107. (How much does your husband have to do with Susanna?
. . . play with her?) No. (. . . bath her?) No, he's not allowed
to. (. . . dress, read to, tell stories, look after while you're out?)
No. (. . . take her out?) Oh no, he wouldn't; he says "You're
going across that road to buy sweets without me"—and she
can quite well get run over on that road, you know! (. . . anything he draws the line at?) Well, looking after her. (. . . look
after Tim a lot?) No—well, he sometimes takes Tim a little
way down the road. (. . . Does she mind you leaving her?)
No, she doesn't—she just plays with those other children,
because I find a place where there *are* children. (Do you
always tell her when you're leaving her . . .?) I tell her. She
says "Oh do, do—I like those other people".

117. (Alternative last question, see 1-year schedule) (Would you say
you are bringing up Susanna the same way you yourself were
brought up, or differently?) A bit different. (In what way?)
I take her out shopping and buy her chocolate for when she
goes boating. (Doesn't your mummy do that for you?) No—
it's not very kind of her, is it? (Is there anything else you do
differently?) I say "Eat your crusts and have curly hair".

# LIST OF REFERENCES

ABEL-SMITH, BRIAN, and TOWNSEND, PETER. *The Poor and the Poorest:* Occasional papers on Social Administration, no. 17. Bell, London, 1965.

APLEY, JOHN, and MACKEITH, RONALD. *The Child and his Symptoms.* Blackwell Scientific Publications, Oxford, 1962.

ARGYLE, MICHAEL. *Religious Behaviour.* Routledge and Kegan Paul, London, 1958.

AUSUBEL, DAVID P. *Ego Development and the Personality Disorders: a developmental approach to psychopathology.* Grune and Stratton, New York, 1952.

BERNSTEIN, BASIL. 'Language and Social Class', *British Journal of Sociology*, xi, 1960.
'A Socio-Linguistic Approach to Social Learning', in Gould, J. *Penguin Survey of the Social Sciences, 1965.*

BOSSARD, JAMES, and BOLL, ELEANOR. *The Sociology of Child Development*, 3rd ed., Harper Bros., New York, 1960.

BRITISH FEDERATION OF UNIVERSITY WOMEN (ed. C. ARREGGER). *Graduate Women at Work.* Oriel Press, Newcastle-upon-Tyne, 1966.

CATTELL, PSYCHE. *The Measurement of Intelligence of Infants and Young Children*, 1960 revision. Psychological Corporation, New York.

CHRISTIANSON, H. M., ROGERS, M. M., and LUDLUM, B. A. *The Nursery School: adventure in living and learning.* Houghton Mifflin Co., Boston, 1961.

CHUKOVSKY, K. *From Two to Five.* Cambridge University Press, 1963.

City of Glasgow. *Annual Report of the Medical Officer of Health*, 1964.

City of Leicester. *Annual Report of the Principal School Medical Officer*, 1962 and 1965.

Commissioners on the Employment of Women and Children in Agriculture. *Report*, XII, 1843.

DOLL, E. A. *The Measurement of Social Competence.* Educational Test Bureau, Minneapolis, 1953.

DOUGLAS, J. W. B. *The Home and the School.* MacGibbon and Kee, London, 1964.

DOUGLAS, J. W. B., and BLOMFIELD, J. B. 'Bedwetting Prevalence among Children aged 4–7 years', *Lancet*, I, 1956.

DUNLOP, O. J. *English Apprenticeship and Child Labour*, Macmillan Co., New York, 1912.

EDGE, PATRICIA. *Child Care and Management from Birth to Adolescence.* Faber, London, 1953.

FREUD, ANNA, with DANN, SOPHIE. 'An Experiment in Group Up-bringing', in *Psychoanalytic Study of the Child*, Vol. VI. Imago, London, 1951.

FREUD, S. *Beyond the Pleasure Principle*. Hogarth Press, London, 1950.

GALE, STANLEY. *Modern Housing Estates*. Batsford, London, 1949.

GAVRON, HANNAH. *The Captive Wife*. Routledge and Kegan Paul, London, 1966.

General Register Office. *Classification of Occupations 1960*. H.M.S.O., London.

GESELL, A. *The First Five Years of Life*. Methuen, London, 1954.

Glaxo Laboratories. *Glaxo Mother and Baby Book*. London, 1960's.

GROOS, KARL. *The Play of Animals* and *The Play of Man*. Originally published 1896 and 1899.

HALL, G. STANLEY. *Adolescence*. Appleton, New York, 1920.

HARLOW, HARRY F. 'Development of Affectional Patterns in Infant Monkeys', in Foss, B. *Determinants of Infant Behaviour*, Vol. I. Methuen, London, 1961.

HEBB, D. O. *A Textbook of Psychology*. W. B. Saunders Co., Philadelphia and London, 1958.

H.M.S.O., *Britain: an official handbook*. London, 1967.

HOGGART, RICHARD. *The Uses of Literacy*. Chatto and Windus, London, 1957.

HURLOCK, E. B., and BURSTEIN, W. 'The Imaginary Playmate', Journal of Genetic Psychology, 41, 1932.

JACKSON, BRIAN, and MARSDEN, DENNIS. *Education and the Working Class*. Routledge and Kegan Paul, London, 1962.

JACKSON, SHIRLEY. *Life among the Savages*. Michael Joseph, London, 1954.
    *Raising Demons*. Michael Joseph, London, 1957.

JEPHCOTT, P., SEEAR, N., and SMITH, J. H. *Married Women Working*. Allen and Unwin, London, 1962.

JOHNSON, R. C., and MEDINNUS, G. R. *Child Psychology: Behavior and Development*. Wiley, New York, 1965.

KANNER, L. *Child Psychiatry*, 3rd ed., Blackwell, Oxford, 1957.

KELLY, AUDREY. *The Physical Health of Children*. Penguin Books, Harmondsworth, 1960.

KERR, MADELINE. *The People of Ship Street*. Routledge and Kegan Paul, London, 1958.

KING, SIR F. TRUBY. *Feeding and Care of Baby*. Revised ed., Oxford University Press, 1937.

KINGSLEY, CHARLES. *The Water Babies*. 1863.

KLEIN, MELANIE. *Contribution to Psychoanalysis, 1921–1945*. Hogarth Press, London, 1948.

KLEIN, VIOLA. *Britain's Married Women Workers*. Routledge and Kegan Paul, London, 1965.

LIDDIARD, MABEL. *The Mothercraft Manual*. Churchill, London, 1928 and 1954 editions.

LOWENFELD, MARGARET. *Play in Childhood*. Gollancz, London, 1935.

MACFARLANE, J. W., ALLEN, L., and HONZIK, M. P. *A Developmental Study of the Behavior Problems of Normal Children between twenty-one months and fourteen years*. University of California Press, Berkeley, 1954.

MANDLER, GEORGE, and MUSSEN, P. *New Directions in Psychology III*. Holt, Rinehart and Winston, New York, 1967.

MEAD, MARGARET. *Male and Female*. Gollancz, London, 1950.

MEAD, MARGARET, and BATESON, GREGORY. *Balinese Character: a photographic analysis*. Special Publications of the New York Academy of Sciences, Vol. II, New York, 1942.

MONTAGU, A. *Life Before Birth*. Longmans, London, 1964.

NASH, OGDEN. *Family Reunion*. Dent, London, 1951.

NEWSON, JOHN and ELIZABETH. *Infant Care in an Urban Community*. Allen and Unwin, London, 1963.

'Patterns of Discipline: the four-year-old and his mother', in *New Barnett Papers No. 1: The Family in Modern Society*. Dept. of Social and Administrative Studies, Oxford University, 1965.

'Child-Rearing in Socio-Cultural Perspective', in Loring, J., and Mason, A., ed., *The Spastic School Child and the Outside World*, Heinemann/Spastics Society, London, 1966.

'Cultural Aspects of Child Rearing in the English-Speaking World', in Rivoire, J. L., and Kidd, A., *Handbook of Infant Development*. Aldine, Chicago, 1968.

'Some Social Differences in the Process of Child Rearing', in Gould, J., *Penguin Survey of the Social Sciences II*, Penguin Books, Harmondsworth, 1968.

NEWSON, ELIZABETH. 'Provision for the Pre-School Child', in British Federation of University Women (ed. C. Arregger), *Graduate Women at Work*. Oriel Press, Newcastle-upon-Tyne, 1966.

NYDEGGER, W. F., and CORINNE. 'Tarong: an Ilocos Barrio in the Philippines', in Whiting, Beatrice. ed., *Six Cultures*. Wiley, New York, 1963.

OPIE, IONA, and PETER. *Lore and Language of Schoolchildren*. Oxford University Press, 1959.

PACKARD, VANCE. *The Hidden Persuaders*. Longmans Green, London, 1957.

PAKENHAM, ELIZABETH (now Elizabeth Longford). *Points for Parents*. Weidenfeld and Nicolson, London, 1954.

*PARENTS* magazine, Vol. 21, no. 1. Haymarket Publishing Group, London, 1966.

PARKER, TONY, and ALLERTON, ROBERT. *The Courage of his Convictions.* Hutchinson, London, 1962.

PARKINSON, C. NORTHCOTE. *Parkinson's Law.* John Murray, 1958.

PINCHBECK, I. *Women Workers and the Industrial Revolution, 1750–1850.* Routledge, London, 1930.

RAVERAT, GWEN. *Period Piece: a Cambridge childhood.* Faber and Faber, London, 1952.

ROMNEY, K. and R. 'The Mixtecans of Juxtlahuaca, Mexico', in Beatrice Whiting, 1963, *op. cit.*

SANGSTER, PAUL. *Pity my Simplicity.* Epworth Press, London, 1963.

SHAW, GEORGE BERNARD. Preface to *Man and Superman:* 'Maxims for Revolutionists'. 1905.

SILLITOE, ALAN. *Saturday Night and Sunday Morning.* W. H. Allen, London, 1958.

*The Loneliness of the Long-Distance Runner.* W. H. Allen, London, 1959.

*Key to the Door.* W. H. Allen, London, 1961.

SPENCER, H. *Principles of Psychology*, Vol. II. Williams and Norgate, London, 1855.

SPOCK, BENJAMIN. *Baby and Child Care.* Bodley Head, London, 1955; also revised edition: Duell, Sloan and Pearce, New York, 1967.

'The striving for autonomy and regressive object relationship', in *The Psychoanalytic Study of the Child*, Vol. XVIII. Imago, London, 1963.

SPROTT, W. J. H. *Social Psychology.* Methuen, London, 1952.

STEVENSON, OLIVE. 'The First Treasured Possession', in *The Psychoanalytic Study of the Child*, Vol. IX. Imago, London, 1954.

STOTT, D. H. *Bristol Social Adjustment Guide.* University of London Press, 1958.

SVENDSEN, M. 'Children's Imaginary Companions'. Arch. Neurol. and Psychiat., 32, 1934.

TERMAN, L. M., and MERRILL, M. A. *Stanford-Binet Intelligence Scale, 3rd revision.* Harrap, London, 1961.

TRASLER, GORDON. *In Place of Parents.* Routledge and Kegan Paul, London, 1960.

WATSON, J. B. *Psychological Care of Infant and Child.* Allen and Unwin, London, 1928.

WESLEY, JOHN. *Works.* Wesleyan Conference Office, 1872.

WHITING, BEATRICE, ed. *Six Cultures.* Wiley, New York, 1963.

WHITING, J. W. M., KLUCKHOHN, R., and ANTHONY, A. 'The Function of Male Initiation Ceremonies at Puberty', in Maccoby, E., Newcomb, T. M., and Hartley, E. L. *Readings in Social*

*Psychology*, 3rd ed., Holt, Rinehart and Winston, New York, 1958.

WIDDOWSON, E. M. *A Study of Individual Children's Diets*. Medical Research Council Special Report No. 257, H.M.S.O., London, 1947.

WINNICOTT, D. W. 'Transitional Objects and Transitional Phenomena'. Int. J. Psychoanalysis, Vol. XXXIV, 1953.
Preface to Stevenson, Olive. 'The First Treasured Possession', 1954, *op. cit.*

WINTER, G. B., HAMILTON, M. C., and JAMES, P. M. C. 'Role of the Comforter as an Aetiological Factor in Rampant Caries of the Deciduous Dentition'. Arch. Dis. Childh., 41, 1966.

WOLFENSTEIN, MARTHA. 'Fun Morality: an analysis of recent American child-training literature', in Mead, Margaret, and Wolfenstein, Martha. *Childhood in Contemporary Cultures*. University of Chicago Press, 1955.

YOUNG, MICHAEL, and WILMOTT, PETER. *Family and Kinship in East London*. Routledge and Kegan Paul, London, 1957.

YUDKIN, SIMON, and HOLME, ANTHEA. *Working Mothers and their Children*. Michael Joseph, London, 1963.

# INDEX

## GEORGE ALLEN & UNWIN LTD
Head Office:
*London: 40 Museum Street, W.C.1*
*Trade orders and enquiries:*
*Park Lane, Hemel Hempstead, Herts*

*Auckland: P.O. Box 36013, Northcote Central, N.4*
*Barbados: P.O. Box 222, Bridgetown*
*Beirut: Deep Building, Jeanne d'Arc Street*
*Bombay: 15 Graham Road, Ballard Estate, Bombay 1*
*Buenos Aires: Escritorio 454–459, Florida 165*
*Calcutta: 17 Chittaranjan Avenue, Calcutta 13*
*Cape Town: 68 Shortmarket Street*
*Hong Kong: 105 Wing On Mansion, 26 Hancow Road, Kowloon*
*Ibadan: P.O. Box 62*
*Karachi: Karachi Chambers, McLeod Road*
*Madras: Mohan Mansions, 38c Mount Road, Madras 6*
*Mexico: Villalongin 32, Mexico 5, D.F.*
*Nairobi: P.O. Box 30583*
*New Delhi: 13–14 Asaf Ali Road, New Delhi 1*
*Philippines: P.O. Box 157, Quezon City D-502*
*Rio de Janeiro: Caixa Postal 2537–Zc–00*
*Singapore: 36c Prinsep Street, Singapore 7*
*Sydney, N.S.W.: Bradbury House, 55 York Street*
*Tokyo: P.O. Box 26, Kamata*
*Toronto: 81 Curlew Drive, Don Mills*

HILARY PAGE

# PLAYTIME IN THE FIRST FIVE YEARS

Hilary Page is the designer of the well-known Kiddicraft 'Sensible' Toys for babies and young children. He has made a life-long study of the playtime of young children and their needs in play material. For many years, he used to spend the whole of every Wednesday in a different nursery school, sitting on the floor and playing with the children, to find out exactly what type of toys would be of the greatest interest to them.

In this book, he describes every aspect of playtime and shows parents and teachers what sort of toys are going to hold the interest of children for the longest possible time and help them in their development through the various stages of childhood.

Mr. Page started the business of Kiddicraft with a capital of £100 in 1932, and today his toys are made and known all over the world, though the design and control are still in his hands. He has always encouraged mothers, nannies and school teachers to write to him and has relied on their co-operation and criticism in order to produce what they want. Many of his best ideas for toys have come from the thousands of letters he receives every year. He has developed these suggestions and put them into practical form in this book.

The chapter headings are: (1) The Power of Play. (2) The Toy-Maker and the Child. (3) Sensible Toys. (4) Early Infancy. (5) Curiosity and Will Power. (6) The Creative Impulse. (7) Toddlerdom. (8) The Three Year Old. (9) Dolls and the Doll's House. (10) Nearly Ready for School. (11) The Value of the Nursery School. (12) Quarrelling in Young Children. (13) Destructiveness. (14) Tidiness and Untidiness. (15) Discipline. (16) Childhood Fears. (17) Intelligence Tests. (18) Looking, Listening and Reading. (19) Simplicity. (20) A Plea to Potential Parents.

# SUPERVISION IN SOCIAL WORK

## DOROTHY E. PETTES

Social workers concerned with training have long looked forward to a succinct but comprehensive analysis of their responsibilities as teachers. Both student and staff supervisors will welcome this definitive discussion of the task before them. As with medical training, this task becomes more important when students and staff are learning through work with actual clients. Miss Pettes has employed her wide experience both in England and in the United States to illustrate the process by which both student supervisors and staff supervisors can increase their skill in training social workers in the field. She includes a comprehensive discussion of the supervisors' administrative functioning and how this meshes in with the training function.

The book falls into three sections: firstly, four introductory chapters addressed 'to all supervisors, but perhaps particularly to staff supervisors' on the functions of the supervisor, administration related to supervision, teaching related to social work, and casework related to supervision; secondly, six chapters on different aspects of student supervision from the beginning to the end of placement and finally, a shorter section relating staff supervision to the previous discussions.

# DECISION IN CHILD CARE

## R. A. PARKER

Responsible decisions are continually being made in social work. In particular the decision to place a child in a foster home can have far-reaching consequences for his welfare and it is vital that we make the best possible choice on his behalf. Although thousands of children are boarded out every year no systematic attempt has yet been made to summarize this experience as a guide for practice. Thus important decisions lack the help which past experience could provide.

This study has assembled the past experience of foster care in one area, analysed it and presented it in such a way that prediction can be made of the outcome of a potential placement. It offers an important contribution to the task of providing the best possible care for children separated from their own families.

MARY MILES
# LIVE AND LEARN

The idea that difficulties in growing up are always somebody's fault dies hard. Frequently, the author comments, when talking about the fears or difficult patches of behaviour, common from time to time in the lives of children, she has met many parents who blame themselves excessively for their children's problems. Others feel that they have failed badly because they have to seek help or psychological treatment for their offspring. On the other hand, there are parents who constantly blame their child for behaviour which is perfectly normal for his age, although it may seem unbalanced.

The main theme of *Live and Learn* is that no two individuals are alike, and that parents must adjust themselves to this fact of life. Temperament, rate of growth, development, both mental and physical, all are different for each child. Similarly, parents possess the whole range of human attributes, and while some are easily able to come to terms with the challenge of parenthood, others find the task more of a burden, and are more sensitive to their own shortcomings in this respect. Mrs. Miles points out that parental love is not simple. It easily becomes mixed with feelings such as domination, possessiveness, a desire to create one's child in one's own image or to be a better parent than one's own parents. On the child's side, the belief that his parents are reliable and dependable people gets him through.

Perhaps the greatest lesson to be learned from this always sensible and practical book is that parents cannot solve their children's problems for them. They have to do their own growing up, and have to sort out for themselves a balance between their personal wishes and the demands of society. If they grow up with parents whom they know and trust from birth onwards, then children will have the best chance of working out the problems of development for themselves.

## J. S. LAWES AND C. T. EDDY
# UNDERSTANDING CHILDREN

The two authors combine skill in their subject with experience of teaching it to students in Africa and elsewhere. Their aim is threefold. First and most important to emphasize to teachers in training how essential it is to regard children as individuals, each with a character and problems resulting from heredity and environment. Secondly, to give the teacher enough knowledge of psychology to help him to understand each pupil's learning process and behaviour. Thirdly, to stimulate the teacher to observation, enquiry and thought. Each chapter ends with suggested exercises, discussion points and reading references.

The book is one of a series offered to African teachers in training. The series is designed to help those who are called upon to teach the many subjects of the primary school curriculum or two or more subjects with the junior forms of secondary schools. It is dedicated to the proposition that giving a good basic education to a country's children is vital to its development programmes.


## GERALD H. J. PEARSON, M.D.
# EMOTIONAL DISORDERS OF CHILDREN

Behaviour disorders in children have almost always a psychological origin. This book outlines these disorders and shows what is likely to cause them. The author approaches his subject as a psycho-analyst and gives a psychoanalytic interpretation of emotional disorders. The treatment which he suggests is the result of many years' experience, and has been successful in many cases.

His presentation of the text is clear and interesting and will be found valuable by many parents but the book is primarily intended for child psychologists and doctors.

D. M. DYSON
# NO TWO ALIKE

The care of children deprived of normal home life is a national problem. All who pay rates or subscribe towards the work of the voluntary child care societies accept some measure of responsibility, willingly or unwillingly.

Foster parents, and those who could be foster parents but are not, those who recommend foster parents and those who could promote fostering but do not, all have their share of responsibility in helping or failing to help.

Members of local authority children's committees and councils of voluntary services employ residential staff in Homes and Child Care Officers, and they have to make decisions for individual children; they need to understand as fully as possible the problems in the Homes and the individual and time-consuming work of the Child Care Officers. Residential staff and Child Care Officers accept their share in this enthralling and responsible work.

This book will help towards deeper understanding for it is written out of the experience of one worker who has tried to see below the surface, and to be guided not too much by generalizations and by current theories, but by consideration of how each individual child can best be helped.

JILL NICHOLSON
# MOTHER AND BABY HOMES

There has recently been much discussion about the plight of the unmarried mother and her child; but very little of it has been based on fact. Mother and Baby Homes cater in fact for between 11,000 and 12,000 unmarried mothers each year, out of a total of 70,000; but there is hardly one generalisation that would be applicable to all the homes. Some are run by voluntary organisations, some by local authorities and some by religious groups. While some still retain the punitive attitude; others set themselves with much kindness to help the women— some of them mere schoolgirls, to face the difficulties of their position and to plan constructively for their own future and that of their babies. This book gives the facts but, even more, it gives the feelings and ideas of those most concerned—the mothers-to-be and those who care for them.

**LONDON: GEORGE ALLEN & UNWIN LTD**